'How would early twentieth century international criminal lawyers look upon the field which bears that name today? Would they recognise it as theirs? Would they be proud and cheer? Would they despair and distance themselves? We'll never know for sure, but no book gets us as close as this thoughtfully curated volume.'

Sarah Nouwen, Faculty of Law, University of Cambridge

'The essays in this superbly edited collection are richly entertaining and insistently intelligent acts of historical retrieval. A marvellously resonant volume!'

Gerry Simpson, Professor, London School of Economics and Political Science.

THE DAWN OF A DISCIPLINE

The history of international criminal justice is often recounted as a series of institutional innovations. But international criminal justice is also the product of intellectual developments made in its infancy. This book examines the contributions of a dozen key figures in the early phase of international criminal justice, focusing principally on the inter-war years up to Nuremberg. Where did these figures come from, what did they have in common, and what is left of their legacy? What did they leave out? How was international criminal justice framed by the concerns of their epoch and what intuitions have passed the test of time? What does it mean to reimagine international criminal justice as emanating from individual intellectual narratives? In interrogating this past in all its complexity one does not only do justice to it; one can recover a sense of the manifold trajectories that international criminal justice could have taken.

Frédéric Mégret is a Professor and Dawson Scholar at the Faculty of Law, McGill University. From 2006 to 2016 he held the Canada Research Chair on the Law of Human Rights and Legal Pluralism. His research focuses on the theory and history of international criminal justice.

Immi Tallgren is a Docent (Adjunct Professor) of International Law, University of Helsinki and a Senior Researcher at the Erik Castrén Institute. She has worked as a diplomat, legal advisor in international organisations, and researcher, e.g. at the MPI Luxembourg and LSE. She currently studies the history of international law and gender, international criminal justice, law and cinema.

THE DAWN OF A DISCIPLINE

International Criminal Justice and Its Early Exponents

FRÉDÉRIC MÉGRET
McGill University

IMMI TALLGREN
University of Helsinki

CAMBRIDGE
UNIVERSITY PRESS

University Printing House, Cambridge CB2 8BS, United Kingdom

One Liberty Plaza, 20th Floor, New York, NY 10006, USA

477 Williamstown Road, Port Melbourne, VIC 3207, Australia

314–321, 3rd Floor, Plot 3, Splendor Forum, Jasola District Centre,
New Delhi – 110025, India

79 Anson Road, #06–04/06, Singapore 079906

Cambridge University Press is part of the University of Cambridge.

It furthers the University's mission by disseminating knowledge in the pursuit of
education, learning, and research at the highest international levels of excellence.

www.cambridge.org
Information on this title: www.cambridge.org/9781108488181
DOI: 10.1017/9781108769105

© Cambridge University Press 2020

This publication is in copyright. Subject to statutory exception
and to the provisions of relevant collective licensing agreements,
no reproduction of any part may take place without the written
permission of Cambridge University Press.

First published 2020

A catalogue record for this publication is available from the British Library.

Library of Congress Cataloging-in-Publication Data
Names: Dawn of a Discipline: International Criminal Justice and Its Early Exponents (2016 :
Helsinki, Finland) | Mégret, Frédéric, editor. | Tallgren, Immi, editor.
Title: The dawn of a discipline : international criminal justice and its early exponents / edited
by Frédéric Mégret, McGill University, Montreál [and] Immi Tallgren, University of
Helsinki.
Description: Cambridge, United Kingdom ; New York, NY, USA : Cambridge University
Press, 2020. | Includes index.
Identifiers: LCCN 2020005709 | ISBN 9781108488181 (hardback) | ISBN 9781108769105
(epub)
Subjects: LCSH: International criminal law – History – Congresses. | International criminal
law – Biography – Congresses.
Classification: LCC KZ7047 .D39 2020 | DDC 345–dc23
LC record available at https://lccn.loc.gov/2020005709

ISBN 978-1-108-48818-1 Hardback

Cambridge University Press has no responsibility for the persistence or accuracy of
URLs for external or third-party internet websites referred to in this publication
and does not guarantee that any content on such websites is, or will remain,
accurate or appropriate.

CONTENTS

List of Contributors   *page* ix
Foreword   xv
MARTTI KOSKENNIEMI

1 Introduction   1
FRÉDÉRIC MÉGRET AND IMMI TALLGREN

2 Hugh H. L. Bellot: A Life in the Service of the Prevention and Punishment of War Crimes and Crimes Against Humanity   24
DANIEL MARC SEGESSER

3 Vespasian V. Pella: International Criminal Justice as a Safeguard of Peace, 1919–1952   49
ANDREI MAMOLEA

4 Emil Stanisław Rappaport: His Road from Abolition to Prosecution of Nations   93
PATRYCJA GRZEBYK

5 International Criminal Justice as Universal Social Defence: Quintiliano Saldaña (1878–1938)   118
IGNACIO DE LA RASILLA DEL MORAL

6 Henri Donnedieu de Vabres: Penal Liberal, Moderate Internationalist and Nuremberg Judge   146
FRÉDÉRIC MÉGRET

7 Not Just Pure Theory: Hans Kelsen (1881–1973) and International Criminal Law   174
MÓNICA GARCÍA-SALMONES ROVIRA

8 Principled Pragmatist?: Bert Röling and the Emergence of International Criminal Law   205
JAN KLABBERS

viii CONTENTS

9 Retelling Radha Binod Pal: The Outsider and The
Native 230
ROHINI SEN AND RASHMI RAMAN

10 Aron Trainin: The Legal Mind Behind A Soviet
International Criminal Law Project 260
GLEB BOGUSH

11 The Complex Life of Rafal Lemkin 280
VESSELIN POPOVSKI

12 Stefan Glaser: Polish Lawyer, Diplomat and
Scholar 306
KAROLINA WIERCZYŃSKA AND GRZEGORZ
WIERCZYŃSKI

13 Yokota Kisaburō: Defending International Criminal
Justice in Interwar and Early Post-War Japan 335
URS MATTHIAS ZACHMANN

14 Jean Graven: Interdisciplinary and International Criminal
Lawyer 358
ROMANE LAGUEL AND DAMIEN SCALIA

15 Absent or Invisible?: 'Women' Intellectuals and
Professionals at the Dawn of a Discipline 381
IMMI TALLGREN

Index 414

CONTRIBUTORS

GLEB BOGUSH is Associate Professor of International Law at National Research University – Higher School of Economics, Moscow, and Adjunct Lecturer at the Moscow State University and the University of Luxembourg. His research interests include international criminal law, international criminal justice, human rights law, and Russian criminal law. In 2012–2014 he was an Alexander von Humboldt Fellow at the Max Planck Institute for Foreign and International Criminal Law. He is an editorial board member at *Criminal Law Forum* and *Russian Law Journal*, and a vice-president of the Russian national group of the International Association of Penal Law.

MÓNICA GARCÍA-SALMONES ROVIRA is Research Fellow at the Erik Castrén Institute of International Law and Human Rights, Finnish Cultural Foundation Senior Research Fellow, and Adjunct Professor of International Law at the University of Helsinki, where she teaches in the area of international law and philosophy. She is the author of *The Project of Positivism in International Law*, winner of the European Society of International Law Book Prize 2015. Mónica visited the Hans Kelsen Institut at the University of Vienna in January 2017. In 2017–2018 she was Osk Huttunen Visiting Fellow at the University of Cambridge (Faculty of Law) and Clare Hall. Her recent work studies the conceptual, philosophical, and historical continuities between modern international lawyers and previous theological theories.

PATRYCJA GRZEBYK is Assistant Professor at the University of Warsaw. Her fields of research are international humanitarian law, international criminal law, human rights law, and use of force law. She is the author of numerous publications, including the monograph *Criminal Responsibility for the Crime of Aggression* (2013). She has held several scholarships at the Foundation for Polish Science, the Polish Ministry of Science and Higher Education, Winiarski Scholarship. She was visiting professor or research fellow at the universities of Cambridge, Geneva, Zagreb, Barcelona, Munich, and Madrid as well as at Peking University and Renmin University. She is a director of the Network on Humanitarian Action at the University of Warsaw.

JAN KLABBERS is Professor of International Law at the University of Helsinki. His research interests include the law of international organizations, legal theory, and global ethics. He is the author of several monographs, and has held visiting positions at, among others, New York University, the Sorbonne, and the Graduate Institute of International and Development Studies, Geneva.

MARTTI KOSKENNIEMI is Professor of International Law (University of Helsinki) and the author of *From Apology to Utopia: The Structure of International Legal Argument* (1989/2005) and *The Gentle Civilizer of Nations. The Rise and Fall of International Law 1870–1960* (2002). He is currently working on a history of international legal thought.

ROMANE LAGUEL is a doctoral student at the Université Libre de Bruxelles working on the concepts of international criminal law and criminal law as objects conveyed by NGOs in their fields of intervention. She conducts interdisciplinary research in law and social sciences through the realization of different ethnographic terrains.

ANDREI MAMOLEA is Assistant Professor of International Law and History at Boston University's Frederick S. Pardee School of Global Studies. His research has been supported by the Swiss National Science Foundation, Canada's Social Sciences and Humanities Research Council, and the Max Planck Institute for European Legal History. He is currently working on a manuscript about the US approach to the laws of war in the late nineteenth and early twentieth centuries.

FRÉDÉRIC MÉGRET is a full professor and William Dawson Scholar at the Faculty of Law, McGill University. From 2006 to 2016 he held the Canada Research Chair on the Law of Human Rights and Legal Pluralism. Before coming to McGill, he was an assistant professor at the University of Toronto, a research associate at the European University Institute, and an attaché at the International Committee of the Red Cross. His research interests are in general international law, the laws of war, human rights, and international criminal justice.

LIST OF CONTRIBUTORS

VESSELIN POPOVSKI is Vice Dean of the Law School and Executive Director of the Centre for UN Studies at O. P. Jindal Global University. In 2004–2014 he was Senior Academic Officer at United Nations University in Tokyo. Prior to that he was assistant professor at the University of Exeter (1999–2004) and co-directed the EU project 'Legal Protection of Individual Rights in Russia' (2002–2004). He holds a PhD from King's College London, MSc from the London School of Economics, and a BA/MA from Moscow State Institute of International Affairs.

RASHMI RAMAN is currently Assistant Professor and Assistant Director, Centre for International Legal Studies at the Jindal Global Law School, where she teaches courses in public international law and human rights law. She holds a BA LLB (Honors) from the National University of Juridical Sciences in Kolkata and LLM degrees in international law from both New York University School of Law and the National University of Singapore. Prior to joining academia, she worked with the International Criminal Tribunal for Rwanda in Arusha. Her past work experience includes positions with the International Law Commission, the United Nations Assistance to the Khmer Rouge Trials, the International Criminal Court, and the Supreme Court of India.

IGNACIO DE LA RASILLA DEL MORAL holds the Han Depei Chair in Public International Law and is a Thousand Talents Plan Professor at Wuhan University Institute of International Law. He was educated in Spain (LLB, 5 years – University Complutense of Madrid); Switzerland (MA and PhD, The Graduate Institute, Geneva); the United States (LLM, Harvard Law School; Fellow in Global Governance, Law and Social Thought, Brown University); and Northern Italy (Post-Doctoral Max Weber Fellow in Law, European University Institute, Florence).

DAMIEN SCALIA is Professor at the Faculty of Law and Criminology of the Université libre de Bruxelles. After writing his PhD thesis on the *nulla poena sine lege* principle in international criminal law, he conducted research on sentencing at Geneva Academy, Oxford Institute for Ethics, Law and Armed Conflict, and at Columbia Law School. He has also worked on international prison law. He is currently working on international criminal justice, considered from the experience of the acquitted and the convicted.

DANIEL MARC SEGESSER is Adjunct Professor (Privatdozent) and Director of Undergraduate Studies at the History Department of the University of Bern. He specializes in the study of international history and politics, international relations, and conflict processes and has written extensively on the punishment of war crimes in the period between 1872 and 1945.

ROHINI SEN is Assistant Professor and Assistant Dean (International Collaborations) at the Jindal Global Law School, O. P Jindal Global University, where she is also Assistant Director in the Centre for Human Rights Studies. She has obtained an LLM in International Law from the University of Leeds in 2012 and an Undergraduate Degree of BSc LLB Law from Gujarat National Law University (2006–2011). She is currently pursuing her PhD from the University of Warwick under the Chancellor's Scholarship. She teaches and researches in the areas of critical international law, pedagogy of international law, TWAIL, feminist and queer theory, international humanitarian law, and international criminal law.

IMMI TALLGREN is a Docent (Adjunct Professor) of International Law, University of Helsinki, a researcher at the Erik Castrén Institute and a visiting fellow at Centre for Women, Peace and Security, London School of Economics. She previously worked as a diplomat, legal advisor at EUROPOL and the European Space Agency and researcher, including at the MPI Luxembourg. She is currently researching gender in histories of international law, international criminal justice, and law and film. Her recent publications include *The New Histories of International Criminal Law: Retrials* (2019, ed. with Thomas Skouteris), and the special issue 'International Criminal Justice and/on Film', *London Review of International Law* (2018, ed. with Kirsten Ainley and Stephen Humphreys).

KAROLINA WIERCZYŃSKA is an associate professor at the Institute of Law Studies of the Polish Academy of Sciences in Warsaw. Her research interests focus on international criminal law and jurisprudence. Her doctoral dissertation (published in Polish in 2010) explored the notion of genocide in the context of the jurisdiction of international criminal tribunals ad hoc. Her current research relates to the problem of admissibility issues before the International Criminal Court, and the scope of individual responsibility. Karolina co-edited (with

Andrzej Jakubowski) a volume entitled *Fragmentation vs. the Constitutionalisation of International Law: A Practical Inquiry* (2016). She also serves as a deputy editor-in-chief of *The Polish Yearbook of International Law* and as a member of the ILA Committee on Complementarity in international criminal law.

GRZEGORZ WIERCZYŃSKI is an associate professor at the Faculty of Law and Administration of the University of Gdańsk, and a chief of the department of legal informatics at that university. His research interest focuses on theory of law, including legal informatics and principles of creating and publication of the law. He is the author of several monographs and articles regarding the official publication of normative acts and the principles of legislative techniques in Poland and other countries.

URS MATTHIAS ZACHMANN is Professor of History and Culture of Modern Japan at Freie Universität Berlin. He received his undergraduate and graduate training in Law and Japanese Studies at the Universities of Hannover and Heidelberg, and completed his Habilitation in Japanese Studies in 2010 at the University of Munich (LMU). Zachmann is a trained advocate in Germany (2nd State Exam 2002). From 2011–2016, he held the position of inaugural Handa Chair in Japanese-Chinese Relations at the University of Edinburgh. He is author of *Völkerrechtsdenken und Außenpolitik in Japan, 1919-1960* (The Japanese discourse on international law and foreign policy; 2013).

FOREWORD

'Always historicize!' The famous opening of Frederick Jameson's *Political Unconscious* reminds us that there can be no critical awareness of the present without an ability to see that present as the realization of some past future.[1] Dialectical – or as I would like to say, critical – awareness of the present, again, seems necessary for the development of present futures, assessing their quality and foreseeable effect, and then finding the appropriate action to implement them. 'Necessary' not in any naturalist moral sense – you 'have to' do this – but so as to make sure future action is loyal to the imagination that once brought it about. In most cases, the distance between any present and its future cannot be adequately grasped as a narrative of heroes and villains – that may seem particularly problematic if one is engaged in a project such as setting up 'international criminal law'. It is a space of truth and virtue but also of ignorance and failure of the will and the question is how to understand such human successes and failures. Jameson's focus on the 'political unconscious' reminds us (though not necessarily in the Marxian sense he was employing) that the narratives within which a legal form such as international criminal law are presented and understood constitute symbolic openings within which the struggles and conflicts of an otherwise absent reality can be seized. The wisdom of the morning and the wisdom of the evening ought to be brought to conversation with each other, for there is the next day and then the next and the next . . .

And why not just live in the present and think about the future? For men and women critical of the way the world is, eager to bring their ideas to bear on an improved future, history might seem a distraction from what is really pressing, the pastime of people waging bygone battles like old generals, instead of the many that need to be fought now. Well, well.

---

[1] Frederick Jameson, *The Political Unconscious: Narrative as a Socially Symbolic Act* (Cornell University Press, 1981).

xvi FOREWORD

Let's be clear at the outset – the point of historicization is not to uncover lessons waiting there to be dug up, dusted and taken to use in the present. The past is not an inert mass of separately identifiable pieces of information of how it 'really' was, like a photo album found on the attic as the time had come to move on. As Jameson carefully explained, historicization is not at all so much about the past as the present, the formation of the constituent parts of what now seems to us as the unthinkingly self-evident and single truth of the world we live in. We too are among those parts. Most of the time we simply embody our unproblematic subjecthood, directing our action to a world out there, doing what we do, thinking what we think. Historicization offers us that subjecthood instead as the problem, turns something about us into the proverbial fly on the wall for which we are just one of the many elements of the present, brought to relation to each other through some process, constituent particles of a structure. It 'reassert[s] the specificity of the political content of everyday life and if individual fantasy-experience' and invites us to question the immediacy of our doing and thinking[2]: What am I doing, and why? What has made me think this? Who is this 'me' anyway?

I have elsewhere tried to assure sceptics that the historicization of something does not mean that this something is dead.[3] The 'turn to history' in international law and relations and in legal and political thinking generally does not mean that those disciplines or professions, or those projects, no longer have any life in them. But it is true, and welcome, that interest in the past suggests that something is happening that will not leave these professions and projects quite as they have been. When Jameson instructed his readers to think of the texts and the understandings that were their objects historically, the point was not just to open them to a fuller or deeper insight about the world, though it is that, too, but to awaken them to a sense that their subjecthood was also agency in processes and structures that have nothing necessary about them and that the world that they took for granted was also in part 'their' doing, or the doing of people who thought like they think, and that it was up to them to decide whether to continue that thinking as in the past.

---

[2] Jameson, *Political Unconscious*, 22.

[3] "What Should International Legal History Become?", in Stefan Kadelbach, Thomas Kleinlein and David Roth-Isigkeit, *System, Order and International Law: The Early History of International Legal Thought from Machiavelli to Hegel* (Oxford University Press, 2017), 381.

But that of course requires that we remember how we thought in the past – what we believed would come of the invasion of Iraq in 2003 for example, or the NATO intervention in Kosovo in 1999 – and what we now know about their outcome. That more complex wisdom is invaluable now for thinking about action in the future. The same with the topic of this book, of course. It is impossible to debate intelligently about international criminal law without recourse to narratives about Rwanda, Vietnam, Nuremberg, Leipzig, and not just as clichés but as immensely complex, many-sided histories in which all aspects of human wisdom and stupidity were at play. But it does not stop here; the ethical and the individual do not exhaust the interest of historical understanding. In any story about the 'international' world, legal and ethical categories, narratives of individual action and imagining are important so as to access the way in which ideological and institutional structures mediate the contradictions of the political world and thus help it survive from one day to the other. It is often illuminating to examine the choices important actors made in past cases, and what became of those choices.[4] But it may be even more significant to try to understand how those actors came to those choices in the first place, or what were the narratives that formed their 'political unconscious'.[5]

It is a familiar critical insight that we can understand any present only by taking a standpoint somewhat outside it – becoming the fly on the wall. Travelling, or at least living abroad for some time, offers that position with regard to our *Heimat* and so does the past when, as the cliché has it, we enter it as a 'foreign country'. It then makes it possible to see the familiar as strange and to pose questions about it that would never occur to us as long as we are unthinkingly following its many enchantments. In particular, it creates distance to the narratives with which we justify, both formally and informally, the doings and thinkings of which the experience of the present consists. Because those justifying narratives are an important part of the way we envisage the future, taking a distance from them will finally disclose the dialectical (but I prefer 'critical') relationship persisting between the three temporal categories and makes historicization such an important imperative of political action.

---

[4] One famous example of using history in this way is Michael Walzer, *Just and Unjust Wars* (Basic Books, 1977) and especially his more recent *A Foreign Policy for the Left* (Yale University Press, 2018).

[5] For a pertinent critique, see Anne Orford, "Moral Internationalism and the Responsibility to Protect", 24 *European Journal of International Law* (2013), 103–8.

xviii   FOREWORD

And how to go about historicization? Again, it is possible to create many kinds of narratives to enlist the past in an effort to attain critical distance to the present. As I already noted, trying to find lessons used to be one way of doing this but its critical power was undermined both by an overly neat idea on how the past would be met but also by the suspicion that one never left the present in the first place. As long as we are anxiously looking for lessons for well-formulated present problems, we are unable to take critical distance to those problem-formulations. There are many ways in which the present tries to prevent us from loosening its hold on us (and thus our doing and thinking) and one of them is precisely by suggesting that we already 'know' what the most important problems are. Conversely, travelling in that foreign country with eyes open may enable us not only to relativize problems that formerly seemed pressing but also to configure as problems aspects of our world that we used to think of as natural and not problematic at all.

The rise of international criminal law with formal institutions such as the International Criminal Court and the consolidation of a professional language on international 'crimes' is a relatively recent phenomenon. Depending on what aspect of it one wants to concentrate on – the institutions, the profession, the vocabulary – its history can be told in different ways. As part of consciousness of the destructive capabilities of modernity, its rise may be linked to the atrocities of the Second World War, with some antecedents in the early part of the century and perhaps the later Victorian era. If one subsumes it under large historical categories such as 'imperialism' or 'colonialism', or 'militarism', 'racism' or 'slavery', then its past will look different from what it would be in case it is viewed as part of the vocabularies of *bellum iustum*, the professional construction of 'criminal law' or 'the law of nations'. Was Nuremberg about 'killing innocent civilians' or 'attempting to annihilate an ethnic group'? Whether the crushing of the Herero uprising in German South-West Africa in 1904 is or is not part of a story of the concentration camps also speaks to the political unconscious of the narrator. One surprising aspect of international legal histories is that they usually take their subject-matter as given: it is about 'war and peace' among 'states' and involves 'public law' aspects of 'official' behaviour. There is a definite temporal limitation: the International Criminal Tribunal for the former Yugoslavia jurisdiction covered acts committed from 1 January 1991, for example. Such words, concepts and temporal understandings are the bread and butter of international lawyers. But for a historically inclined fly on the wall, each seems immensely problematic, raising a number of further questions about the meaning of war and peace, about what is a state and why would the official quality of some action be decisive for how it is treated. Why begin treatment of the Balkan crisis on that date and not include the last stages of the Milosevic regime, or indeed extend it all the way to NATO bombing in 1999? How does something become a 'crime' – and more interestingly, how does action with comparable consequences not become a crime?

Such conceptual histories are often useful precisely owing to their critical import – the way they make meanings that seem self-evident today seem problematic and even arbitrary. But it is useful to remember that concepts and meanings do not exist by their own intrinsic force; they live as parts of systems of human thinking. One fruitful way to study them historically is to link them to such thinking to the extent that it takes place in human communities. But thinking does not appear to an outside observer as such. It appears in speech and writing, in texts that men and women compose or have composed in order to do something – to justify a decision, to make a proposal, to respond to an interlocutor or a critic, to persuade an audience. Moreover, when it is a question of thinking that is intended to prompt institutional action – as thinking in international criminal law is – then it is often useful to examine the relevant texts as 'action' produced by human beings with some authority as representatives of their collectivities, the group of international criminal lawyers, say.

'History of international law is history of men (and very few women) with projects.'[6] This book is part of the stream of recent historical writings on international law where the focus has been on interesting, influential or representative (the categories do not necessarily coincide) jurists themselves, their lives and writings, understood as part of their and their colleagues' 'projects'. International criminal law is one such project. This focus has a number of advantages. First, its gives concreteness and tangibility to its object (international criminal law) by enabling a close examination of how the meaning of important expressions such as, for example, international law, genocide, war crime, crime against humanity, have been constructed by their use in the practice of the field: each expression has prompted institutional action as a result of the project of some professional persons. What were they trying to do when employing such expressions? Who did they try to persuade and

---

[6] See my *The Gentle Civilizer of Nations: The Rise and Fall of International Law 1870–1960* (Cambridge University Press, 2001).

about what? For whom and against whom were they writing and speaking? Philippe Sands' *East West Street: On the Origins of Genocide and Crimes Against Humanity* (2017) is perhaps the most well-known recent example of what can be done with international criminal law by focusing on 'men with projects'. Many other recent studies have taken a similar perspective on more or less known internationalists and lawyers, seeking by this means to make sense of the trajectory of international law and activism in the twentieth century. By focusing on human beings, professional actors in the dramas of the century, it has been possible to make abstractions such as development of international criminal law, history of terrorism, or the rise of twentieth-century cosmopolitan legalism tangible as aspects of human thinking and acting.

A second virtue in history of the type persons with projects lies in its anti-ideological orientation. A project such as international criminal law is like a religion. It has its sacred texts, its authorities and internal hierarchies, its ethos and its mythos. It also tends to produce its own histories that, precisely because they are inspired by the faith of the believers, fail to lead to the foreign territory that the past, at its best, can be. Histories that are part of the project become ethical stories with heroes and villains, where the expansion and flourishing are a romance and setbacks merely 'challenges' to be overcome by progress. Such histories are propaganda. By contrast, describing international criminal law as a project aims at critical distance. The point is not to celebrate the handful of European or European-educated men in this collection of essays but to understand them. What has been their project? Such description may inspire sympathy or admiration, of course – but it may equally well highlight ignorance or incompetence, failure of the imagination. It brings large ideas such as peace, justice, fight against impunity down to the human scale. That is the scale at which we can learn to relate to the choices of the protagonists, and think about their freedom and the constraints they faced, the compromises they had to make. This would, it is hoped, enable the readers to see that whatever exists today as international criminal law is not the result of some historical necessity but of choices of more or less well informed men and women, made within a structure of possibilities but that could also have gone the other way.

Producing a history of international criminal law in the twentieth and early twenty-first century as a narrative of a project might enable the readers, too, to reflect on their professional activities as projects, involving uncertainty and real choices; it prompts enquiring into what they would have done in such or similar situations. The world is a terribly

FOREWORD

unjust place where many people are subordinated and suffer as a result of other peoples' choices and preferences, typically not seen as such, but instead as unavoidable necessities. Action and institutions, lawyers as well as – probably – systems of criminal punishment are needed. But improving things is really hard; we disagree not only on how to go forward, but also on what is there to aspire to in the first place. And the road to hell is still paved with good intentions. Therefore, alongside persons with projects, it is also imperative, as Jameson would be the first to stress, that we read larger meanings into history. To paraphrase Marx, men make their own projects, but they do not do this as they please; they do not make them under self-selected circumstances, but under circumstances existing already, given and transmitted from the past. The tradition of all dead generations weighs like a nightmare on the brains of the living.

The choices that have made international criminal law what it is cannot, of course, be described only from the 'inside'. Many aspects of the world that pre-exist international criminal law have constrained those choices. They reflect other projects and other priorities that have made the international world we have today. These structural conditions cannot be wished away. They delimit the ways in which something may appear as a crime and determine how resources are allocated and priorities are made for dealing with the causes of crime. Whatever the name one gives to those structural features, they do provide a rather narrow space within which technical vocabularies such as international criminal law may operate. They support themselves with ideological narratives that make them seem simply a 'natural' aspect of modern internationalism. The greatest service that historical work can provide is to break that illusion of naturalness and show that after all is said and done, injustice, too, no less than its contrary, is an effect of persons with projects.

Martti Koskenniemi

1

Introduction

FRÉDÉRIC MÉGRET AND IMMI TALLGREN

Human beings are too important to be treated as mere symptoms of the past.[1]

1.1 What is the history of international criminal justice about?

International criminal justice has by many accounts a long and chequered past. Histories of that past have tended to be dominated by narratives of the institutional development of international criminal justice.[2] The great diplomatic conferences, jurisdictional initiatives and adoption of treaties that have accompanied its existence at regular intervals are emphasized. The historical-legal narrative that dominates the scholarship is that of linear evolution from custom to conventions, noble plans to concrete institutions, from ad hoc to permanent. The undertone often is that of celebration of the progress accomplished, but also perhaps more problematically one where the past is seen to merely foreshadow the present and thus read in that light.[3] Much legal scholarship, perhaps understandably given its emphasis on legal and institutional form, errs closely to this genre.

One of the consequences of this historiography is a misplaced sense of continuity and a lack of granularity. For example, contemporary tribunals are typically seen as the heirs to the post–World War II ones, and the

---

[1] Lytton Strachey, *Eminent Victorians* (Simon and Schuster, 2012), p. 45.

[2] See M. Cherif Bassiouni, 'From Versailles to Rwanda in Seventy-Five Years: The Need to Establish a Permanent International Criminal Court' (1997) 10 *Harvard Human Rights Journal* 11; Cenap Çakmak, *A Brief History of International Criminal Law and International Criminal Court* (Springer, 2017).

[3] Tilmann Altwicker and Oliver Diggelmann, 'How Is Progress Constructed in International Legal Scholarship?' (2014) 25 *European Journal of International Law* 425; Thomas Skouteris, *The Notion of Progress in International Law Discourse* (TMC Asser Press, 2010).

latter as a reaction to what was planned and done after Versailles. However, the discontinuities in that institutional history may be as interesting as its continuities. 'International criminal tribunals' may well be that – part of a broader international phenomenon that carries over different epochs – but situated in their own respective histories they can also be seen as primarily responses to irreducible temporal circumstances. More importantly for our purposes, the emphasis on institutional and jurisdictional developments tends to obscure the extent to which the history – or rather, the pre-history – of international criminal justice was shaped at least as much by intellectual developments and notably the ideas that were developed by a number of scholars as by institutional developments. Those intellectual developments, moreover, are often much richer and iconoclastic than a tendency to see them as mere oracles for the future would suggest.

This book's ambition, part of a renewed interest in the history of international law and justice,[4] is to rediscover some of the 'intellectual origins' of international criminal justice by focusing on some of its key scholars and situating their ideas within their times. In that respect, the book can be seen as a useful complement to broader histories of early international criminal justice such as Mark Lewis's ground breaking *The Birth of the New Justice*.[5] It re-contextualizes but also re-inscribes that broader narrative within the disjointed trajectories of individuals who, each in their own way, were trying to make sense of it in the present they inhabited, and which must have seemed full of mystery and potential. The scholars surveyed have names that in some cases may be forgotten today, or only briefly mentioned to validate the idea of a certain trajectory of international criminal justice; but they are arguably worth more than these passing and obligatory references. As they reacted to the events of their time, tried to reconcile them with their training, and engaged in broad attempts to sketch the contours of an emerging discipline, they also set the basis for what it would become.

At the same time, many of them are interesting precisely for their idiosyncrasy and the way they struggled with the early dilemmas of the

---

[4] Mark Lewis, *The Birth of the New Justice: The Internationalization of Crime and Punishment, 1919–1950* (Oxford University Press, 2014); Morten Bergsmo, Klaus Rackwitz and Tianying Song, *Historical Origins of International Criminal Law* (Torkel Opsahl Academic EPublisher, 2017); Çakmak, *A Brief History of International Criminal Law*, note 2; Immi Tallgren and Thomas Skouteris (eds.), *The New Histories of International Criminal Law: Retrials* (Oxford University Press, 2019).

[5] See in particular Lewis, *The Birth of the New Justice*, n. 10.

field: what is international criminal law? Who does it apply to? Who should it be adjudicated by? And what is its purpose? That the answers they gave to these questions were strikingly different from some of the responses that have since become accepted makes them no less interesting and is a reminder both that the fate of ideas is unpredictable and that the origins of international criminal justice are much more diverse than is sometimes thought. Indeed, emphasizing the differences between what was imagined as international criminal justice then and what it is understood to be now can help us recover a sense of the openness and possibilities of the discipline.

1.2 From Versailles to the Cold War

The temporal framework of this volume is crucial to defining what we identify as the intellectual origins of international criminal law as a discipline. Although some international lawyers such as Gustave Moynier began working on the issue as early as the nineteenth century and there were many precursors to the idea of unification of penal law, for example, this book has elected to focus on what is arguably the truly foundational period intellectually for international criminal justice, namely the interwar period up to the years immediately following World War II. The intellectual ebullience of the interwar period and its unexpected aftermath in the Nuremberg and Tokyo trials set the stage for an era of thinking about international criminal justice that was extremely productive and dynamic. It also bookends this period neatly: against the devastation of World War I and the considerable early intellectual investment in international justice it triggered on the one hand, and the fossilization of the Nuremberg/Tokyo precedents with the beginning of the Cold War on the other.

Contra conventional narratives which foreground the contemporary Hague international tribunals as the historical culmination of this earlier trend, the beginning of the Cold War will not be seen here as a mere interruption but as, in a sense, the end of an era. That era was characterized by considerable optimism about the place that the criminal law could play in world affairs. The unwillingness of most states to set up a more permanent international criminal court even after the Nuremberg and Tokyo tribunals had, by some accounts at least, managed to deliver justice in difficult circumstances, belied the notion that institutionalization would be a straight path following on the heels of early success. Moreover, these early tribunals had hinted at what cost international criminal justice might come at, or under what highly peculiar circumstances it might be set up. The post-Nuremberg and Tokyo era would, perhaps paradoxically given how henceforth tantalizingly possible international criminal justice must have briefly seemed, be marked by much less creativity than had been the case in an earlier, seemingly more innocent age. Indeed, the 'tyranny of the real' ensured that these precedents simultaneously seemed hard to emulate even as they significantly reduced the scope of what could be understood to constitute international criminal justice.

The period is sufficiently large that it includes both relatively early and late figures in this broad movement. It includes, for example, individuals who had begun being active in the early twentieth century but came to prominence in relation to international criminal justice at Versailles as well as, at the opposite end, figures whose intellectual formation may have started before World War II but whose imprint on international criminal justice was mostly manifested in its wake. At its broadest, the temporal cycle we have decided to focus on can thus be described as 1900 to 1950, albeit it will be clear that the period from 1918 to 1945 is at the heart of our preoccupations. The emphasis on the first half of the twentieth century will allow us to evaluate the interwar moment both from the point of view of what international criminal justice had been imagined following the cataclysm of the First World War and what it became following the cataclysm of World War II.

What is particularly interesting to us is how the world of ideas and global events interacted: how ideas first hinted at Versailles were developed in the 1920s, sometimes abandoned in the 1930s and then selectively and strategically resurrected in the 1940s with a view to dealing with the Axis powers, even as they came under attack from new and emerging views about the international legal system that would mark the 1950s, etc. At each stage, various generations of international law and criminal law scholars debated, disagreed, reverted to earlier positions or developed new ones, in dynamic relationship to various scholarly and institutional developments but also personal hobby horses, professional rivalry and changing life circumstances. Rather than merely the beginning of a new era, Nuremberg and Tokyo were complex epilogues to these earlier debates about international criminal justice, debates that could not have foreseen the upending of the international legal order, the demise of the League of Nations, and the newfound importance of human rights.

1.3 The 'Presentist' Fallacy

The contributors to this book are, perhaps unsurprisingly, wary of reification, of intemporal monuments to the role of law in history. International criminal justice then is a poor guide to international criminal justice today and vice versa. The 'project' is often principally shaped by the prejudices and fantasies of whatever group can manage to accede to positions of authority within it. The most recent twenty-five years boom of what is today called international criminal law, starting with the creation of the ad hoc tribunals and leading to the creation of the International Criminal Court (ICC) would have been inconceivable in the early twentieth century or at least inconceivable in quite the technocratic jargon in which it has become conceivable. International crime, for example, was long understood only as crime that transcended borders. When it became the utopian project of regulating international politics through criminal law, it was often more about targeting states than individuals. In the 1920s, the emphasis was on what criminal lawyers thought possible to achieve in order to safeguard world peace, with little interest in crimes against humanity let alone genocide.

Writing a history of international criminal justice today, one is constantly at risk of falling for the 'presentist fallacy': taking a model or a concept, an institution, a feeling, or a symbol from the present and finding that it had a parallel meaning in the past. The three words – international criminal court – in Lemkin's and many others' passionate dream meant very different things than what has today become the institutional vehicle for that particular idea. Indeed, at the risk of counterfactual speculation, we may wonder whether some of the early advocates of international criminal justice would see today's 'dream come true' ICC as the fulfilment of their aspirations. For example, they might be surprised that the ICC does not prosecute states, or that aggression is not the centrepiece of the international criminal justice edifice.

Moreover, this book seeks to compensate the tendency in institutional histories to focus on the successes of efforts at international criminal justice, when the project's failures may be just as instructive. It acknowledges openly how many of the ideas propounded by the early architects of international criminal justice have remained dead letter; some would even appear largely unfamiliar to contemporary readers, oddities that are difficult to make sense of except through a conscious effort to re-situate oneself within the intellectual climate of the age. In many cases, the claim that these ideas were forerunners of contemporary international criminal justice will be a deeply anachronistic one. Despite the misleading familiarity of some of the terms used, theirs were projects steeped in their times, seeking to address questions that appeared in historically situated contexts and which, in some cases, have either long ceased to interest us, or at least interest us in very different terms. In scrutinizing their writings, the book seeks to explore both the extent to which they announced contemporary international criminal justice, but also the extent to which they were preoccupied with projects that are so at odds with what it has become that they cannot possibly be seen as its forerunners. Next to the narratives of great plans, the book introduces small coincidences, confusion, mysteries and ruptures.

1.4 'Something Old, Something New, Something Borrowed, Something Blue'?

We have chosen to focus on a dozen leading figures of international criminal justice in this era, with a view to understanding where they came from, and how their names became associated with what was not quite a movement but was at least a growing field, and exhibited increasingly strong disciplinary aspects. These figures have in common that they were interested in exploring more systematically the contribution that repressive justice might make to international peace and public order, although their take on international criminal justice varied quite significantly. Selecting key figures in an exercise such as this is always a challenge. We have sought to problematize the notion of 'key figure' by discovering and suggesting that some far less-known characters actually had a remarkable role. In choosing personalities, no doubt choices could have been made differently: all lists are both under- and over-inclusive. We were nonetheless mindful that over time certain individuals did emerge and stood out as more systematically committed to the idea of international criminal justice – the organic intellectual of the discipline as it were – or at least as more emblematic of one of its facets. They were at the heart of what it means to forge a new discipline: consolidating its conceptual backbone, highlighting what properly counted as its object and, more often than not, busily advocating for their particular vision of what it should be.

Some were clear leaders in terms of their productivity and institutional leadership; others left a deep imprint as a result of merely one major encounter with the project. Accordingly, the book includes both

1 INTRODUCTION

personalities that were central to the constitution of international criminal justice as an idea (Pella, Donnedieu de Vabres, Lemkin, Saldaña), and what might be described as key interlopers, whose connection to it was strong but also more short-lived (Bellot, Pal, Röling). The interaction between an emerging core of the discipline of international criminal law and its 'periphery', trail blazers and normalizers, those with more of a criminal law background and those whose professional associations were with international law, will be familiar to observers of what the discipline of international criminal law has become, even if the fantasies and anxieties were often quite different. The book, mindful that all lists can have exclusive undertones, also seeks to highlight some of those who remain persistently beyond the list, but whose absence is revealing, notably women and non-Europeans.

Some of the figures selected, such as Vespasian Pella, Henri Donnedieu de Vabres or Raphael Lemkin are particularly revealing because, emerging after Versailles, their careers span the entire arc of that period. Their work thus provides an opportunity to reflect on some of the contradictions that arose between the earlier era of the 1920s and their much later roles as judge at Nuremberg (in the case of Donnedieu de Vabres) or members of the Genocide Convention committee (all three). However, to use one counter-example, the meteoritic trajectory of Radhabinod Pal, the Indian judge at the Tokyo tribunal, is in a sense no less revealing. Not an international (criminal) lawyer by profession, Judge Pal wrote a scathing dissent to the judgment, one that laid the basis for and announced the future anti-colonial critiques of international criminal justice. Bert Röling, a Dutch criminal lawyer who also sat on the Tokyo bench, is another interesting transitional figure, one who contributed to prolong the legacy of the post-war tribunals into the Cold War and its own specific concerns.

Geographically, many of the key players were Europeans, although not necessarily (what would become known as) Western Europeans. The Germans and Italians were, understandably with the rise of Nazism and Fascism, remarkably absent despite their traditional centrality to criminal and criminological legal thinking. Some, such as Kelsen or Lemkin, were Jewish refugees now working in the New World. A comparable figure was Hersch Lauterpacht in Cambridge.[6] Remarkably, the first German criminal law scholars that became influential in international

---

[6] See, Martti Koskenniemi, 'Hersch Lauterpacht and the Development of International Criminal Law' (2004) 2 *Journal of International Criminal Justice*, 810–25.

criminal law discourse, such as Hans-Heinrich Jescheck, did so after our period of focus and with works critical of the Nuremberg International Military Tribunal (IMT).[7] Although Hugh Bellot appears briefly as a striking figure at Versailles, no major British international criminal lawyer emerged in the interwar period. In fact, many of the prominent figures of the time were Eastern Europeans or from the Balkans. These include Vespasian Pella, Emile Rappaport, Stefan Glaser and Raphael Lemkin. This Eastern European contingent was heavily invested in the prevention of war, and one senses that their enthusiasm for international criminal law could partly be attributed to the sense that it might provide a fragile protection of the territorial status quo, in a context where it was felt that League of Nations' guarantees badly needed to be supplemented. American scholars were relatively absent from the early years of international criminal justice with the exception of a few Nuremberg protagonists, most notably Telford Taylor, who would become famous in later years as influential commentators on their earlier experience.[8]

Beyond Europe, this book also seeks to open up the geographical and linguistic perspectives of the field of international criminal justice. The Japanese international lawyer Yokota Kisaburo, the Russian/Soviet scholar Aron Trainin and the already mentioned Indian judge and scholar Radhabinod Pal were all active and alert intellectual figures operating in complex national environments. In their own idiosyncratic and influential ways, they participated in and contributed to the discipline, even though they have often remained in the shadows of its historiography. Understanding them to have been part of the development of international criminal justice from the start is not an anachronism, but a way of conceptualizing the discipline as broader than even it conceived itself to be.

1.5 Between Field and Discipline

What is international criminal law or international criminal justice? It could be seen, of course, as merely a system of rules. In truth, however, the rules during that early phase had barely begun to emerge, and an intense investment in intellectual foundations is what characterized the

---

[7] Hans-Heinrich Jescheck, Theo Vogler and Joachim Herrmann, *Festschrift für Hans-Heinrich Jescheck zum 70. Geburtstag* (Duncker & Humblot, 1985); Ronen Steinke, *The Politics of International Criminal Justice: German Perspectives from Nuremberg to The Hague* (Bloomsbury Publishing, 2012).

[8] Telford Taylor, *The Anatomy of the Nuremberg Trials: A Personal Memoir* (Knopf Doubleday, 2012).

discipline. That investment was often quite theoretical, doctrinal and speculative because it preceded the institutionalization of the discipline and because it sought to respond to the controversies of the time. In that respect, international criminal justice is perhaps unusual in that, contrary to the domestic sphere in which penal practices typically long preceded their legal rationalization, internationally the proverbial cart was clearly put in a sense before the horse. Much energy was spent debating the conditions of possibility of a system whose realization was at the time not plausibly on the horizon. This more innocent or at least impromptu era protected the discipline from being absorbed by the study of the latest developments of actual institutions of international criminal justice. It also meant that, seen with the benefit of hindsight, some of the scholarship gained in utopian appeal at the risk of losing in apologetic credibility, albeit in ways that make it no less interesting or revealing of largely distinct and historically situated modes of thought.

Ideas about international criminal justice, however, were not merely debated as pure ideas. Debates operated against the background of a dense network of socialization and even competition. In highlighting individual figures, for example, it will also be suggested that they were more than individualities. The chapters in this book draw the connections between personalities. Not all, by any means, knew each other, although over time there definitely emerged a core of scholars who frequently interacted, notably under the banner of the various associations in the field. The International Union of Penal Law (IUPL/UIDP) had been founded in 1889 in Vienna by three important penalists: Franz Von Liszt, Gérard Van Hamel and Adolphe Prins. When this association was dissolved as a result of World War I, the Association internationale de droit pénal (AIDP), created in Paris in 1924, became a key venue for international criminal law. The International Law Association's role was less central but provided a continuous connection to committed international lawyers who were intrigued by the potential of international criminal justice as a mode of international co-operation, organization and securitization. These scholars' networking occurred at regular intervals during international conferences, but it is also clear that they read each other, engaged each other's arguments and occasionally entered into controversies. The book is also an effort to reconstruct, from the perspective of each individual, what these exchanges looked like and what their acknowledged and unacknowledged stakes were.

One tendency in the literature is to describe international criminal justice as a 'movement', advancing through history. The idea of a movement suggests both change and dynamism within continuity, but also a collective of persons. But it is unclear that the early conceptualizers of international criminal justice ever thought of themselves as part of a movement, or at least the sort of movement that in the last thirty years arguably has led to the creation of the ICC. The early movement for international criminal justice was certainly not a social movement with large support from civil society. Rather it involved a small elite of mostly criminal lawyers working on domestic criminal matters who, over time, developed an enthusiasm for the internationalization of their project. Many of them were universalists who found the expansion of criminal law to the international sphere to be a natural result in a society marked by the densification of exchanges. They were eventually joined by international lawyers who saw the potential of some sort of universal repression for ensuring the goals that they cherished, most notably peace. All were wary of appearing too idealistic even as they were cautious about some of the limitations of an exclusively state-based system of criminal law. Rather than a movement, they were at least a network of scholars who operated across borders and managed to achieve a certain degree of influence.

Perhaps more plausibly and neutrally, the participants in international criminal justice can be seen as various actors in a field within which competing visions of international criminal law and justice were articulated and tested. That field was structured by its main sites of socialization, its common sense and its habitus. It existed beyond professional and scholarly organizations to encompass a variety of actors who at any given time strongly identified their careers and trajectories with the movement, real or imagined, of international criminal justice. The field solidified over time by developing a sense of a common scholarly discipline – international criminal law – that stood at some distance from both criminal law and public international law. In fact, the discipline's relative strength – despite its limited concrete outcomes – emerged from its ability to mediate, translate and orchestrate these respective influences. The more prominent members of the international criminal law field, for example, were active both in national penal associations, the AIDP and the International Law Association.

International criminal law became a language to develop a certain knowledge about international events. Martti Koskenniemi observes that international law is more accurately viewed as an argumentative

1 INTRODUCTION

practice rather than as 'a set of theoretical or technical propositions'.[9] If that is the case, then international criminal law was the specific discourse of seeing 'crime' in international events, and developing the sort of professional vernacular that would make it possible to articulate claims about such crimes. Attention to the argumentative practices of scholarly international criminal lawyers thus opens up rich vistas for the study of what international criminal justice stood for at any one time, how it related to sister disciplines, and how the field of international criminal justice both drew on its connection to other fields and sought to distance itself from them by developing its specific intellectual know-how.

1.6 Individual Trajectories as Method

The book seeks to show how individual academics and professionals grappled with some of the early debates about international criminal justice, debates that continue to haunt the discipline: what might be the legitimacy of international criminal courts? What sort of crimes should they punish? By what means? Whose laws should they apply? What might be their contribution? How different figures approached these questions often had a lot to do with where they came from, what their education had been, their political experience and their scholarly investments. Many were marked by close personal experience of the chaos and violence of their era, particularly the two World Wars but also political upheaval, pogroms and exile. The scholars surveyed were also figures of their time in how they related to political circumstances of their era, such as colonialism, and the flagrant inequalities of sex, gender, class and 'race'. The early narratives of international criminal justice varied, but few included eventualities such as victimization of Africans by the colonial powers, even if it was amply documented in the Africa *Blue Books*, published in 1916 and 1918. Hugh Bellot, for example, the honorary secretary of the International Law Association and the Grotius Society, 'referred to the poisoning of wells by Germans in South-West Africa discussed at the end of the recently published 1916 Blue Book in some detail, but failed to mention any of the war crimes committed against Africans in the preceding 70-odd pages',[10] as Christopher Gevers writes.

---

[9] Martti Koskenniemi, 'Law, Teleology and International Relations: An Essay in Counterdisciplinarity' (2012) 26 *International Relations* 3.

[10] Christopher Gevers, 'The "Africa Blue Books" at Versailles: World War I, Narrative and Unthinkable Histories of International Criminal Law', Immi Tallgren and Thomas Skouteris

Methodologically, the book is inspired by the move to individual trajectories as a way of linking complex historical and legal developments to the ambiguous life world of certain key personalities. Biographical histories are a particular manner of representing the past. This type of historiographical work has for long been met with scepticism.[11] Today, however, there are signs that the much commented 'turn to history in international law' might be developing into a 'turn to intellectual biographies in international law'. Perhaps following the wave set in motion by Koskenniemi's *The Gentle Civilizer of Nations*,[12] a number of biographical and autobiographically flavoured studies on international law have been published.[13] Moreover, the project can be situated at the intersection of several traditions: the intellectual history or the history of ideas and thinkers (Cambridge school); the history of (political) thought; the history of law, legal institutions, legal professions, legal scholars; and biographical historiography. Further, the 'legal life-writing' paradigm, combining elements of legal history, biographical historiography and prosopography, has also served as an inspiration.[14] A range of sociological, anthropological, political science or international relations-oriented writings on international criminal justice and its professionals have also inspired this book.[15]

(eds.), *The New Histories of International Criminal Law: Retrials* (Oxford University Press, 2019).

[11] Mathew Craven, Malgosia Fitzmaurice et al (eds.), *Time, History and International Law* (Brill, 2006).

[12] Martti Koskenniemi, *The Gentle Civilizer of Nations: The Rise and Fall of International Law* (Cambridge University Press, 2002).

[13] For discussion, see Thomas Skouteris, 'The Vocabulary of Progress in Interwar International Law: An Intellectual Portrait of Stelios Seferiades' (2005) 16 *European Journal of International Law* 823; Paolo Amorosa, 'James Brown Scott's International Adjudication between Tradition and Progress in the United States' (2015) 17 *Journal of the History of International Law/Revue d'histoire du droit international* 15; Philippe Sands, *East West Street: On the Origins of 'Genocide' and 'Crimes Against Humanity'* (Vintage Books, 2017); Andrew Lang and Susan Marks, 'People with Projects: Writing the Lives of International Lawyers' (2013) 27 *Temple International and Comparative Law Journal* 437.

[14] Linda Mulcahy and David Sugarman, *Legal Life-Writing: Marginalised Subjects and Sources* (John Wiley, 2015). On life writing, see Hermione Lee, *Body Parts: Essays on Life-Writing* (Random House, 2010), p. 100 and Hans Renders, 'The Limits of Representativeness', in Hans Renders and Binne de Haan (eds.), *Theoretical Discussions of Biography: Approaches from History, Microhistory, and Life Writing* (The Edwin Mellen Press, 2013), p. 129.

[15] Kevin Jon Heller et al (eds.), *The Oxford Handbook of International Criminal Law* (Oxford University Press, 2020); Gerry J. Simpson, *Law, War and Crime: War Crimes, Trials and the Reinvention of International Law* (John Wiley, 2013); Julian Fernandez,

One of the key problems in this type of research is the question on the extent to which individuals' choices or writings can be explained by reference to their personal life experiences. In general, contemporary writings in this genre seem to be less interested in the individuals themselves than in what their life stories can teach us about international law as a discourse. And it is precisely here that biographically oriented research can offer an alternative to traditional legal scholarship. The author of an intellectual portrait has the choice to either seek to legitimize present doctrinal developments or institutional designs by reference to origins or tradition, or to use the genre of biography to shake up established positions and hierarchies. By highlighting conflicts, discontinuities, discrepancies, the ever-present choices of values and politics, and thereby the role of personal struggles in the formation of international law, biography can be used to challenge historical narratives and shake up trajectories and hierarchies that appear as natural parts of the way the world appears to us today. This has been the general focus at the beginning of this book. Yet the authors have each had the liberty to deal with these choices and dilemmas in their chosen manner.

As the start of the work, our group of contributors openly discussed the dilemma of how each author's own standing with regard to the field they were writing on mattered. In today's dominant understanding, histories are always authored, as are all stories, and there is no way for the author to neutrally transmit the past, as if untouched by their subjectivity, no matter how tightly controlled.[16] Authorship and agendas are an inseparable part of the exercise of 'writing history' – a pertinent reason to question both. In international law scholarship, active participation in the progressive strengthening and broadening of law and its institutions

---

Justice pénale internationale (CNRS Editions, 2016); Elies van Sliedregt and Sergey Vasiliev, *Pluralism in International Criminal Law* (Oxford University Press, 2014); Kjersti Lohne, *Advocates of Humanity: Human Rights NGOs in International Criminal Justice* (Oxford University Press, 2019); Ilias Bantekas and Emmanouela Mylonaki, *Criminological Approaches to International Criminal Law* (Cambridge University Press, 2014); Bruce Arrigo and Heather Bersot, *The Routledge Handbook of International Crime and Justice Studies* (Routledge, 2013); Mark J. Findlay and Ralph Henham, *Transforming International Criminal Justice* (Routledge, 2005); Mikkel Jarle Christensen and Ron Levi, *International Practices of Criminal Justice: Social and Legal Perspectives* (Routledge, 2017); David Bosco, *Rough Justice: The International Criminal Court's Battle to Fix the World, One Prosecution at a Time* (Oxford University Press, 2014).

[16] See, for example, Michel De Certeau, *The Writing of History* (Columbia University Press, 1988); Keith Jenkins, *Rethinking History* (Routledge, 2003); Hayden White, *Tropics of Discourse: Essays in Cultural Criticism* (Johns Hopkins University Press, 1985).

has traditionally been a condition of meaningful participation in that scholarly community. Many recent histories of international criminal justice have been self-portraits, in the sense that they have been written by legal experts, academics, international civil servants, practitioners and NGO activists associating and investing themselves in international criminal justice. The way they account for its past reflects the self-understanding and identity of that rapidly growing community. Writing histories of international criminal law participates, in its particular way, in the creation of a collective memory of the discipline and its actors, melding together the questions such as: 'how did this law and these institutions come about?' 'what does it mean today?' and 'who are we and who are we the inheritors of?'

Conscious of this, we have aimed at diversifying the approaches by inviting contributions by professional historians, experienced international criminal lawyers and by newer voices inside the field. We have also sought to diversify the geographic diversity of contributors, compared to what often remains a Western-European centric narrative on international criminal justice. In contrast to current publications on the history of international criminal justice which openly declare their intentions to 'strengthen and expand the foundations of this relatively young discipline of public international law', or pursue its 'vertical consolidation',[17] this book also starts from a more neutral basis. We are not suggesting that research on a highly controversial field such as international criminal justice can be conducted free from moral and ethical connotations or agendas; yet nor is the objective of this book to reinforce the sense of international criminal justice's unmistakable pedigree and establish its promise for the future. The turn to the individual and the biographical, in fact, inures against such a danger by emphasizing the accidental, the inchoate and the stochastic in the genesis of ideas about international criminal justice.

Choosing in what style to write biographical texts involves important choices and methodological dilemmas. Faced with the broad spectrum of psychological explanations for an individual's decisions, at risk of divulgating intimate details that are merely of anecdotal interest, or tempted to champion its object/subject, the author of biography also struggles with

---

[17] The concept outline of the seminar 'The Historical Origins of International Criminal Law' organized in Hong Kong in 2014, see Immi Tallgren, 'Searching for the Origins of International Criminal Law', Morten Bergsmo, Cheah Wui Ling and Yi Ping (eds.), *Historical Origins of International Criminal Law: Volume 1*, FICHL Publication Series No. 20 (Torkel Opsahl Academic EPublisher, 2014).

1 INTRODUCTION

questions of scope and tone. A reductive choice is to define a part of available information as private and omit it altogether, and concentrate on taking stock of official accomplishments and quoting major works. Many of the chapters in this collection, by contrast, emphasize the degree to which the personal background and life trajectories of participants influenced their scholarship. A particular aspect relates to gendered differences in how individual figures are represented. As Immi Tallgren's chapter discusses, scholars in women's history have to cope with a 'double marginalization' of women – in their life context and in the sources that remain – as well as intertwinement of the public and private in the sources one can access, and to which value judgements of legitimacy are attached.[18]

1.7 Personal Narratives, Grand Narrative?

How then did these figures broadly participate in and shape the intellectual origins of international criminal justice? What is the chronology of their involvement? Which most stand out and why? And how do their personal stories coalesce, if at all, to form a broader picture of early intellectual investment into international criminal justice? One dimension that stands out is that not many were particularly predestined to become leading voices in international criminal law; rather many seemed to burst onto that particular scene following the chance of an article, an encounter or a nomination. Some then never departed international criminal law, whilst others had more of a meteoritic trajectory in relation to it. The historiography of these various participants sometimes gives them a larger-than-life status which few of them truly had. The truth is that the degree of their impact on the discipline is not closely correlated to how strongly they invested in it or came to be identified with it. Rather, each in their own way contributed a particular professional background, an ideological bias and a personal sensitivity to an ongoing intellectual project.

The book opens with a chapter on Hugh Bellot by Daniel Segesser. Bellot provides an interesting connection with the ideas that began to

---

[18] See, for example, Rosemary Auchmuty, 'Recovering Lost Lives: Researching Women in Legal History' (2015) 42 *Journal of Law and Society* 34; Mary Jane Mossman, *The First Women Lawyers: A Comparative Study of Gender, Law and the Legal Professions* (Bloomsbury Publishing, 2006); Sue Morgan, *The Feminist History Reader* (Routledge, 2006); Phyllis Holman Weisband, Teresa A. Meade and Merry E. Wiesner-Hanks (eds.), 'A Companion to Gender History' (2004) 25 *Feminist Collections* 19.

emerge during World War I – a founding event for many of the personalities surveyed in this book – and that would go on to influence the early genesis of international criminal justice. Many of these ideas had their foundation in earlier nineteenth-century debates about the humanization of war, for example, and were not as novel as sometimes claimed. Bellot, a founding member and honorary secretary to the Grotius Society, felt that the laws of war and peace needed to be adapted in view of the new conditions that had emerged during the world conflict. He would go on to become a key member of the International Law Association and was a participant in the discussions within it about the prospects for an international criminal jurisdiction. Bellot was capable of both idealism (in suggesting that individuals be able to bring a complaint to an international criminal court) and pragmatism (in accepting that this suggestion was going nowhere as far as other ILA members were concerned).

The book then moves to four figures most keenly associated with the AIDP and its early work, particularly in the 1920s, on the possibility of international criminal law. The chapter by Andrei Mamolea on Vespasian Pella seeks to re-evaluate that leading but sometimes neglected Romanian figure at the very heart of the project. Pella emerged as probably the most active voice in favour of the creation of an international criminal court and would pursue that idea single-mindedly all the way to his contribution to the drafting the Convention on the Prevention and Punishment of the Crime of Genocide. Pella had been considerably influenced by early French ideas about the *psychologie des masses* and was above all, like many of his peers, committed to the prospect of an international criminal court in order to sanction states that engaged in crimes against peace. A master networker, he used a variety of institutional vehicles to push his ideas and seek to garner influence. Although chiefly remembered today for his calls for an ICC, the chapter shows him to have in many ways been a more complex and complete political thinker, one who did not neglect for example the problem of the economic conditions of states. In many ways, his vision for an ICC was far more ambitious than what has come to pass.

Emil Rappaport was a Polish lawyer who is an interesting reminder of how the experience of political repression and instability shaped the outlook of many of these interwar figures. Like many others, Rappaport was first and foremost a criminal lawyer, one whose skills had been honed in defence work for activists and through participation in various legislative endeavours. A classic liberal criminal lawyer heavily invested in the modernization of Polish criminal law, Patrycja Grzebyk reminds us that one of his great causes was the unification of criminal laws. As a founder of the AIDP but also a Vice-President of the International Bureau for the Unification of Criminal Law, he pleaded throughout the interwar period for the penalization of war propaganda with only limited success. His experience during World War II led him to articulate an extremely broad notion of the penal responsibility of entire nations – in his mind, first and foremost, that of the German people – and informed his participation in the Polish Supreme National Tribunal which prosecuted war crimes after the war. Marginalized by the Communists after the war, he is remembered for his ideas, international involvement and support to other colleagues such as Lemkin who are better remembered today.

Also a criminal lawyer by training, Quintiliano Saldaña was one of the earliest voices in international criminal law in Spain and Europe, having taught the first course on international criminal law at The Hague Academy of International Law in 1925. Closely associated with the creation of the AIDP, Ignacio de la Rasilla del Moral reminds us that he was also a leading proponent of legal pragmatism in European criminal law circles who had been influenced by the 'program of Marburg' and the idea that social defence should be the central idea behind criminal repression. This led him to develop an idea of universal social defence, based on the perceived failure of inter-state adjudication, which would have transcended nationalism and led to ever higher degrees of supranational integration. One of the ways in which this would be achieved was through the unification of penal laws and the codification of international criminal law, something which he contributed to by drafting one of the first international criminal codes. By the 1930s his international criminal ambitions had dampened somewhat, but he was particularly associated with efforts that led to the Conventions on the Punishment and Prevention of Terrorism, and the first proposal for the creation of an international criminal court under the auspices of the League of Nations in 1937. In the final years of his life, he was caught up by the Spanish Civil War and died in isolation.

Henri Donnedieu de Vabres was a French international criminal academic trained initially as a private international lawyer and whose ideas about international criminal law were very much influenced by his work on conflict of jurisdiction. This made him less of a cosmopolitan system builder than Pella or Quintiliano Saldaña, but also someone who, in the vein of a Rappaport, paid close attention to the problems of an international criminal law as they would inevitably arise from the multiplicity of criminal law traditions. As both an international lawyer and a criminal lawyer, moreover, he was one of the central minds who sought to merge these two in many ways incompatible modalities of thinking about the law through an attention to what we might today describe as transnationalism but that continued to treat the state as its main problem. As Frédéric Mégret notes, what makes him particularly interesting was that he was the only veteran of the moment of intellectual ebullience around the AIDP who went on to become a judge at Nuremberg. The irony is that he sat on the bench of a tribunal that was in many ways a refutation of his own scholarly ideas, and in particular his emphasis on the centrality of state rather than individual criminality.

Beyond these towering figures associated with the AIDP, a number of leading intellectual figures also thought about international criminal law. These include a number of Jewish exiles and lawyer-intellectuals such as Hersch Lauterpacht.[19] Hans Kelsen was of course a giant of international law in his own right, but less well known are his contributions to international criminal law. Although on some level not someone who came with a strong criminal law background or, for example, ever a member of the AIDP, he had served during World War I as a specialist in military law for the Austrian Ministry of War. As a European exile in the US, he was made a legal adviser to the US War Crimes Office. The question of international criminal law, Mónica García-Salmones Rovira's chapter shows, fitted well within his broader interrogations about the nature of sovereignty and its compatibility with international law. It led him to develop the notion of individual responsibility of international criminal law from the point of view of his 'pure theory' of international law, but also to test the limits of his own theory of positivism when it might clash with the need to punish truly abhorrent conduct retroactively.

A number of the personalities surveyed in this book have an association that is mostly in relation to the post–World War II tribunals, although their careers had begun much earlier. Their connection to international criminal law is more fragile than that of those who devoted their entire career to it, but it is no less significant perhaps especially because it expressed itself in dissent. Indeed, both Bert Röling and Radhabinod Pal, sitting as judges in the Tokyo tribunal, had serious misgivings about some of the directions in which the newly and precariously institutionalized international criminal justice might be going. As such, they suggest the early birth of a critical sensitivity in international criminal justice, one that probably did not emerge in the Far East by

---

[19] Koskenniemi, 'Hersch Lauterpacht', 810.

1 INTRODUCTION

chance as Röling and Pal were confronted with the complex circumstances of the war in the Pacific.

Röling, the Dutch judge at the Tokyo trial, was in many ways, as Jan Klabbers points out, an accidental figure in the Pantheon of international criminal lawyers. His early fixation with the idea of crimes against peace and aggression following his participation in the Tokyo tribunal is a reminder that relatively late in the history of international criminal justice, this idea continued to exert considerable attraction. Röling's musings about international criminal justice also suggest a particular position of ambivalence that has since been identified as quite characteristic of critical voices in the field. For example, Röling at times appeared as a stickler for rules, insisting that the category of crimes against peace was problematic unless it could be proven that it existed as such before World War II; at other times, he argued that the victorious powers had the right to create new categories to neutralize leading Japanese criminals. Röling was also troubled by the harshness of ex post international criminal justice, and his dissenting judgment denotes a willingness to understand the circumstances in which defendants operated, as well as the specificity of their cultural background. A somewhat contrarian iconoclast, he struggled with his role in what he increasingly came to see as a show trial and would go on to develop the field of polemology as well as militating in his final years for an ICC.

Radhabinod Pal is one of the most ambiguous and controversial intellectual figures the book presents. Judge at the International Military Tribunal for the Far East (IMTFE) nominated by the freshly independent state of India, submitting a massive and fiercely critical dissent, Pal was until the emergence of the Third World Approaches to International Law movement in the late 1980s celebrated by the nationalistic apologists of the Japanese imperialist aggressions only. Rohini Sen and Rashmi Raman represent Pal in a somewhat different light, as a truly idealist international lawyer from utterly modest Bengali origin, influenced by the tradition of Hindu legal philosophy and growing into 'an *ancestral* voice in the struggle of the third world to articulate its stance in international law through the prism of international criminal justice'. Since the IMTFE was, for Pal, singularly an institution representing the 'victors' justice', he chose to use his one big moment in international criminal justice for the virulent expression of his anti-colonial conviction. Pal's total rejection of the IMTFE majority judgment was, in Sen and Raman's reading, the logical consequence of the urge he felt to condemn colonialism and imperialism, crimes larger and graver than (Japanese) aggression. The Korean, Philippine, Chinese and other oppressed victims of the Japanese imperialism did not waver Pal's convictions, neither in the trial nor in his later academic work.

Including a chapter on Aron Trainin in the book serves a twofold purpose. As Gleb Bogush argues, all Soviet influence in the history of international criminal law tends to be reduced to participation in the political organization of the trials in Nuremberg and Tokyo. One purpose is to counter this excessively narrow historiographical truism of international criminal law as exclusively a Western and liberal project by bringing to light of an intellectual figure from the Soviet Union whose views were quite distinct. The other purpose is to reflect on the singular fate of Trainin, a socialist criminal law scholar of Jewish origin and never a member of the Communist party, who managed to get his book read by the legal minds in Washington at the end of World War II and thus leave his intellectual mark on the international criminal law project, notably the definition of crimes against peace. Bogush does not hide how Trainin's academic work and international collaborations remained submitted to the changing political parameters of his totalitarian home state throughout his career. Nevertheless, the history of Aron Trainin up to its bitter end as a victim of anti-Semite discrimination shows that marginalizing Soviet academics' investments in international law exclusively as a sham by diligent and obedient servants of their political leaders is reductive.

Raphael Lemkin is today perhaps the best-known name of the early intellectuals of international criminal law, at least for the general public. His solitary battle for criminalizing the crime he baptized genocide and the tragic fate his family as victims of anti-Semitism in the two World Wars have grown into powerful legends marking the international criminal law project, as Vesselin Popovski explains. Popovski navigates the rich and at times contradictory sources on Lemkin in the effort to capture the intellectual trajectory behind the Genocide Convention, and the individual human being behind the intellectual. Did Lemkin really arrive to it all so alone, both identifying the crime of genocide as an ever-present danger in human history and independently convincing delegations in New York to join his passionate quest to criminalize it? Tellingly, Lemkin has a frequent presence in several other chapters of this book where contemporary protagonists are shown to have fought many intellectual or political battles with him. Perhaps more than anywhere else, the project of international

1 INTRODUCTION

criminal law here shows its face as a battle of agendas, of egos, of prestige.

Stefan Glaser is another of the long-term figures of the international criminal law project, present in the various international collaborations from early on, as Karolina Wierczyńska and Grzegorz Wierczyński show. As a member of the Polish exile intelligentsia during World War II, he was active in the International Commission for Penal Reconstruction and Development and the United Nations War Crimes Commission. Sidelined in Communist Poland after the war, he settled as an academic in Belgium. 'An international criminal cooperation enthusiast', to quote the authors, he devoted much effort on questions of extradition and universal jurisdiction, imagining ahead of his time a criminal justice system in which national borders mattered much less. His subsequent prolific authorship of doctrinal works aimed at systematizing and advocating for international criminal law, to the point that he was ready to compromise on principles he had been adamant about in his youth and in the Nazi German context, such as the *nullum crimen sine lege*. His main accomplishments beyond the academic publications were his active participation within the framework of the AIDP, in particular the Convention on the Non-Applicability of Statutory Limitations to War Crimes and Crimes Against Humanity.

Yokota Kisaburo's role in international criminal law connects, in Matthias Zachmann's chapter, to the story of Japan's entry to the sphere of actors of international law starting at the end of the nineteenth century. Japan was, as the most advanced industrializing country amongst the non-Western states, determined to integrate but also reluctant to commit itself to the international legal order, out of fear of being forced into legal arrangements dictated by others. Yokota's stance in this delicate balance of domestic and international was committed internationalism, as an ideological and perhaps idealist inclination. Yokota started to advocate for the criminalization of war in the early 1930s. He held this position throughout the nationalistic, aggressive politics of Japan in the 1930s and early 1940s, and was rejected and threatened as a traitor in Japan. At the end of the war and the start of the occupation, however, he became 'the most credible spokesman and advocate' of the Tokyo tribunal, to quote Zachmann. He remained true to his idealism in this respect, underlining the political and pedagogical importance of international criminal law and international trials and in consequence downplaying the legalistic criticisms, not without the risk of occasionally losing the red line of his own previous theoretical underpinnings.

As Romane Laguel and Damien Scalia write, Jean Graven was a criminal lawyer with a strong humanist and interdisciplinary inclination. His life's work led him to assume the roles of a legal professional (lawyer, notary, judge) and professor of criminal law in his home state Switzerland. His was thus a peaceful and organized life, with more distance to the immediate effects of the World Wars that took hold of the fates of many other protagonists, most notably Lemkin or Kelsen, losing families or becoming refugees. Graven's role thus nicely bookends the project of international criminal law as someone who sought to draw the lessons of the post-Nuremberg moment, connecting it to an earlier moment of interwar ebullience but also imagining the future of international criminal law. He was, as Laguel and Scalia state, ardently 'a defender and a broker of international criminal law', who worked readily in collaboration with others, notably at the International Bureau for the Unification of Penal Law and the AIDP. Graven's voluminous scholarship aimed at strengthening the doctrinal basis of international criminal law, rendering it a place in the legal science. Even if less known today because authored in French and not translated, Graven's inputs had influence at his time – in particular with regard to the definition of crimes against humanity – where the project of international criminal law was not yet as unequivocally unilinguist as today.

The thirteen intellectuals mentioned so far were men. Immi Tallgren's chapter tells the story of how that happened to be the case, and tries to explain why. Aspiring to ask 'large questions in small places', Tallgren presents two microhistories starring two contrasting types of individuals: the first a professional of international law, Katherine B. Fite, the second an intellectual with no legal background, Rebecca West. The objective is to question the sense of representing individuals as 'women', as such by definition deviant from a normative understanding of an 'international criminal lawyer' – or of an 'intellectual', for that matter. The chapter discusses various ways in which an absence or marginalization by sex and/or gender in histories can be countered, reflecting on the choices that matter in representing presence – and absence. The way these two individuals have been so far represented (against the wide canvas of ignoring them) point to frequent tropes in narrating the 'first and only'. Through the microhistories of the two protagonists, selected as examples of the tacit presence in the shadows of the dominant (male) narrative, the chapter questions the roles these individuals could be claimed to have exercised, compared to other figures elevated as intellectuals worthy of inclusion in the intellectual history of international criminal law narrated

1 INTRODUCTION

in this volume. It thus examines more broadly what it means to be in the margins of what is in many ways a dominating project.

Beyond epistemological challenges and broad sociological explanations, the politics of memory and identity are at stake. Whose experiences and accomplishments are valued, rendered authoritative in curriculums and footnotes, cherished in *festschrifts* and colloquiums? What images of past actors are transmitted further to students and young professionals? The final chapter – but in a sense also the book – concludes with thoughts on why one asks the question on sex and gender of those who figure in our intellectual histories and on the moves or desires that figure behind the search for 'women'.

What did international criminal justice mean to its early exponenents and, in turn, what have they meant for international criminal justice? The answers to these questions have, no doubt, changed considerably over time; but the questions remain as remarkably relevant today as they were then. Our aim in editing this book was to throw light on how international criminal justice was also constructed through intellectual inquiry and imagination, and how what it has become and often not become can be enriched by a rediscovery of some of these neglected genealogies.

2

Hugh H. L. Bellot

A Life in the Service of the Prevention and Punishment of War Crimes and Crimes Against Humanity

DANIEL MARC SEGESSER

Figure 2.1 Hugh H. L. Bellot (d.1928), Ivon Hitchens (1893–1979), © the artist's estate. Photo credit: Trinity College, University of Oxford.

"The subject of war crimes, their prevention or punishment, is, I have always felt very strongly, one which should engage the close and earnest consideration of the general public."[1] These are the first sentences that Hugh Hale Leigh Bellot (1860–1928), a barrister and member of the Honourable Society of the Inner Temple, wrote in his article on the prevention and punishment of war crimes during World War I. Up to that time Bellot had not been a key figure in the international debate on the issue of the punishment of war-related crimes. His 1916 article, however, which he contributed at the same time to the public journal *Nineteenth Century and After* as to the *Transactions of the Grotius Society*,[2] proved to be a starting point from which he became influential on the issue. In his positions first as honorary secretary of the Grotius Society, of the Cabinet Committee on German Crimes in the War, as a secretary-general to the International Law Association and as a member of the editorial board of the *British Yearbook of International Law* he became a key figure in British efforts to promote the prospects of the punishment of war-related criminality.[3] This chapter seeks to look at Bellot as a figure in the transition between an older debate on the punishment of war-related crimes linked mainly to the activities of people like Gustave Moynier, Gustave Rolin-Jaequemyns or Louis Renault and later interwar debates related to names like Vespasian Pella, Henri Donnedieu de Vabres, Quintiliano Saldaña or Megalos Caloyanni.[4] It will try to show that Bellot played a central role in this transition, but that the ideas presented were not as novel and innovative as has recently been claimed,[5] not least when they are looked at in an international context that reaches beyond World War I back into the nineteenth century.

[1] Hugh H. L. Bellot, War Crimes, their Prevention and Punishment, *Nineteenth Century and After* 80 (1916): 636–660, here 636.

[2] Hugh H. L. Bellot, War Crimes: Their Prevention and Punishment, *Transactions of the Grotius Society* 2 (1917): 31–55.

[3] In this I agree with Matthew Garrod, The British Influence on the Development of the Laws of War and the Punishment of War Criminals: From the Grotius Society to the United Nations War Crimes Commission, in Robert McCorquodale and Jean-Pierre Gauci (eds.), *British Influences on International Law 1915–2015*, Leiden 2016: 317–366, here 320–325.

[4] For a more detailed account of the international debates cf. Daniel Marc Segesser, *Recht statt Rache oder Rache durch Recht: Kriegsverbrechen in der internationalen wissenschaftlichen Debatte 1872–1945*, Paderborn 2010 and Mark Lewis, *The Birth of New Justice: The Internationalization of Crime and Punishment, 1919–1950*, Oxford 2014. On people involved in the interwar debate cf. also the contributions of Frédéric Mégret (Chapter 6), Ignacio de la Rasilla del Moral (Chapter 5) and Andrei Mamolea (Chapter 3).

[5] Garrod, The British Influence: 323 and 331.

2.1 A World Born Into

Hugh Hale Leigh Bellot was born on 19 October 1860 into a well-off family of surgeons in Manchester. He was educated at Leamington and Trinity College in Oxford, taking the degree of Doctor of Civil Law in 1907. Already before that Bellot had been practicing as a barrister – called to the bar as a member of the Inner Temple in 1890 – and had begun to publish on several legal as well as historical issues. His major publications included *Ireland and Canada: Studies in Constitutional Law and History*, *The Inner and Middle Temple: Legal, Literary and Historic Associations*, *The Law Relating to Unconscionable Bargains with Money-Lenders*, *The Miner's Guide* and *The Law of Children and Young Persons* and *Commerce in War*. The last three were published in collaboration with judge Llewellyn Atherley-Jones, who together with Bellot later became one of the founding members of the Grotius Society in 1915.[6] According to his friends he was a man of kind and considerate nature, who had an "aversion to causing even justified pain".[7]

At the time of Bellot's birth and youth international law was a discipline in transformation. While the first half of the nineteenth century had been dominated by a consensus of (mainly) absolutist monarchs to uphold law and order (including peace) by restricting the freedoms of their subjects, many bourgeois and liberal legal professionals began to wonder, whether law would not be able to play a more positive role in building a more just and co-operative future for national societies as well as the international community. While almost nobody amongst those men challenged the right of states to go to war, they began to wonder to what extent the brutality of warfare could be confined by setting up international standards as to the methods of warfare, the treatment of the wounded and prisoners of war, the status of combatants as well as issues of the treatment of civilians and their property.[8]

Some senior military leaders such as British admiral Sir John Fisher, Prussian chief of the general staff Helmuth von Moltke or German

---

[6] Alexander Pearce Higgins, Dr. H. H. L. Bellot, *British Yearbook of International Law* 10 (1929): 204–206, here 204; Robert Arthur Humphreys, Hugh Hale Bellot, *Transactions of the Royal Historical Society* 20 (1970): 1–4, here 2; Members, *Transactions of the Grotius Society* 1 (1916): 6.

[7] Wyndham Anstis Bewes, Hugh H. L. Bellot, D.C.L., *Transactions of the Grotius Society* 14 (1929): xi–xiv, here xiv.

[8] Geoffrey Best, *Humanity in Warfare: The Modern History of the International Law of Armed Conflicts*, London 1980: 128–215; Martti Koskenniemi, *The Gentle Civilizer of Nations: The Rise and Fall of International Law 1870–1960*, Cambridge 2001: 28–47.

general Julius von Hartmann considered the humanising of warfare a nonsense and demanded that all means be used in war (not least to end it more quickly).[9] Some distinguished jurists such as Gustave Rolin-Jaequemyns, Johann Caspar Bluntschli, Gustave Moynier, Tobias Asser or John Westlake, however, believed that it was essential for their profession to agree as much and as quickly as possible on written rules, in order to alleviate the suffering of any victims in war. A common legal framework and a common ability to know right from wrong were considered to be constitutive elements of the community of civilised states and most of the men involved believed that the second half of the nineteenth century was clearly a period in which great steps had been taken to rise from "barbarity" to "civilization".[10] However, this "standard of 'civilization' tended to remain a European standard, if not a standard of European civilization" as Gerrit Gong has rightly claimed.[11]

Although most jurists in the second half of the nineteenth and at the beginning of the twentieth century shared common goals in regard to the importance of law for international relations, most of the time they disagreed when it came to details. Two examples must suffice in this context. In 1872 Gustave Moynier, president of the International Committee of the Red Cross, who just ahead of the Franco-Prussian War had been convinced that the military of all civilised nations would observe the written rules of international law,[12] presented a proposal for the creation of an international criminal court for judging violations of the Geneva Convention of 1864.[13] The jurists involved in this debate – amongst them Francis Lieber, John Westlake, Franz von Holtzendorff, Carl Lueder, Achille Morin, Gustave Rolin-Jaequemyns and Leonid Kamarowsky – agreed in principle that violations of rules of international law needed to be dealt with. They were not, however, able to agree as to

---

[9] Reginald H. Bacon, *The Life of Lord Fisher of Kilverstone*, 2 Vols., London 1929, Vol. 1: 121; Letter of Field-Marshal Helmuth von Moltke to Johann Caspar Bluntschli 11 December 1880, published in Johann Caspar Bluntschli, *Denkwürdiges aus meinem Leben*, 3 Vols., edited by Rudolf Seyerlen, Nördlingen 1884, Vol. 2: 471–472; Julius von Hartmann, Militärische Notwendigkeit und Humanität, *Deutsche Rundschau* 14 (1878): 71–91, here 89.

[10] Segesser, *Recht statt Rache*: 29–31.

[11] Gerrit W. Gong, *The Standard of "Civilization" in International Society*, Oxford 1984: 22.

[12] Gustave Moynier, *Étude sur la Convention de Genève pour l'Amélioration du Sort des Militaires Blessés dans les Armées en Campagne (1864–1868)*, Paris 1870: 303–304.

[13] Gustave Moynier, Note sur la Création d'une Institution Judicaire Internationale propre à prévenir et à réprimer les Infractions à la Convention de Genève, *Bulletin International des Sociétés de Secours aux Militaires Blessés* 11 (1872): 122–131. Cf. also Segesser, *Recht statt Rache*: 90–92.

28 DANIEL MARC SEGESSER

whether it would make sense to limit state sovereignty, whether the states would at all agree to such a court, and whether such a court made sense at all.[14] In 1899, at the First Hague Peace Conference, another group of jurists – amongst them Fjodor Fjodorovitch Martens, Heinrich Lammasch, Karl von Stengel, Philipp Zorn, Édouard Descamps and Édouard Rolin-Jaequemyns – proved as incapable of agreeing on the exact wording of rules of land warfare as their predecessors had been in the 1870s. Russian expert on international law and president of the commission dealing with the issue of the laws of war, Fjodor Fjodorovitch Martens, therefore made the following statement:

> The dominating idea of the Brussels Conference [. . .] was that it devolved upon all Governments as a sacred duty to do all in their power in an endeavor to diminish the evils and calamities of war. [. . .]
>
> It is not our province [. . .] to set limits to patriotism; our mission is simply to establish by common agreement among the States the rights of the populations and the conditions to be fulfilled by those who desire legally for their country.[15]

After an arrangement with the Belgian delegate Auguste Beernaert, he therefore suggested that committee and conference agree on the following:

> The Conference is unanimous in thinking that it is extremely desirable that the usages of war should be defined and regulated. In this spirit it has adopted a great number of provisions which have for their object the determination of the rights and duties of the belligerents and populations and for their end a softening of the evils of war so far as military necessities permit. It has not, however, been possible to agree forthwith on provisions embracing all the cases, which occur in practice.
>
> On the other hand it could not be intended by the Conference that the cases not provided for for want of a written provision, be left to the arbitrary judgment of the military commanders.

---

[14] Gustave Rolin-Jaequemyns, Note sur le Projet de M. Moynier, relatif à l'Etablissement d'une Institution Judiciaire Internationale, Protectrice de la Convention, avec lettres de MM. Lieber, Ach. Morin, de Holtzendorff et Westlake, *Revue de Droit International et de Législation Comparée* 4 (1872): 325–346; Carl Lueder, *Die Genfer Konvention: Historisch und kritisch-dogmatisch mit Vorschlägen zu ihrer Verbesserung. unter Darlegung und Prüfung der mit ihr gemachten Erfahrungen und unter Benutzung der amtlichen, theilweise ungedruckten Quellen*, Erlangen 1876: 431–433; Leonid A. Kamarowsky, *Le Tribunal International* (Bibliothèque Internationale & Diplomatique Vol. 21), Paris 1887: 402–419. Cf. Segesser, *Recht statt Rache*: 92–95.

[15] James Brown Scott (ed.), *The Proceedings of the Hague Peace Conferences: The Conference of 1899*, New York 1920: 547.

> Until a perfectly complete code of the laws of war is issued, the Conference thinks it right to declare that in cases not included in the present arrangement, populations and belligerents remain under the protection and empire of the principles of international law, as they result from the usages established between civilized nations, from the laws of humanity, and the requirements of the public conscience.[16]

The last paragraph, which since has become known as the Martens clause, is still valid international law, although it is so wide as to open up a vast scope of interpretation as to its meaning. It is hence perfectly true that the "law of war [...] entered its epoch of highest repute" in the second half of the nineteenth and at the beginning of the twentieth century, and "was more enthusiastically studied and widely talked about than ever before" to use the words of Geoffrey Best.[17] Yet it is at the same time also true that neither jurists nor politicians or any other social group had been able to agree on a clear legal framework for war before 1914. Although many jurists – in a manner similar to Moynier in 1870 – hoped that the military would make sure that the laws of war would be observed, such a hope for a "uniformity of doctrine amongst jurists"[18] proved in vain.[19] It was into this world that Hugh H. L. Bellot was born and in which he made his first steps as a jurist.

2.2 Hugh H. L. Bellot and World War I

When World War I began in August 1914 nothing seemed to point to the fact that Hugh H. L. Bellot would play a major role in the debate on violations of the laws of war. While he himself as well as his older son of the same name did not join the military, his younger son Bryson did, serving in the North Somerset Yeomanry until his death of war-related disease on 27 March 1918.[20] This was a huge loss and his work became "his chief allevation of his unconquered woes."[21] It became clear, however, early on in the war that even those jurists that did not join the forces would not remain aloof of the war. On the one hand, international organizations of jurists such as the International Law Association or

---

[16] Scott, *Proceedings of the Hague Peace Conferences*: 547–548.
[17] Best, *Humanity in Warfare*: 129.
[18] Gustave Moynier, *L'Institut de Droit International*, Paris 1890: 4.
[19] Segesser, *Recht statt Rache*: 140–142.
[20] Commonwealth War Graves Commission (www.cwgc.org/find-war-dead/casualty/78115/bellot,-bryson/, 18 February 2020); Humphreys, Hugh Hale Bellot: 2.
[21] Bewes, H. L. Bellot: xiii.

the Institut de Droit International were not able to continue their work. On the other hand, the violation of Belgium's as well as Luxemburg's neutrality and the atrocities in Belgium and Northern France pushed many legal specialists on both sides to come to the defence of their country. Their task in this context was to identify the specific rules amongst the laws and customs of war that the enemy had broken and to show herewith that while one's own side was abiding by the laws of war, the enemy was definitely not. In this perception the enemy had to be considered an unlawful and uncivilised power. With very few exceptions jurists thus became part of the different propaganda efforts of the belligerents.[22]

This was also true for Bellot, and he was therefore no exception when he began to be interested in the rules of international law. In May 1915 he was among the founding members of the Grotius Society, where he joined men like Llewellyn Atherley-Jones, Sir Thomas Barclay, then vice-president of the Institut de Droit International, Sir Graham Bower, a late Royal Navy jurist, with whom he was to have strong disagreements in the interwar period, Sir John MacDonnell, later president of the British committee of enquiry on breaches of laws of war, and John Hartman Morgan, for whom he filled in as professor of constitutional law at London University during the war. The aim of the society was to "promote an impartial discussion of the Laws of War and Peace, and on their reform in view of the new conditions arising from the present war."[23] At once Bellot became one of its honorary secretaries.[24]

Although the society officially was to "treat all international questions in an absolutely independent spirit, endeavouring to discover the truth whatever it may be, to discuss all the doctrines of international law, to examine them in the light of present war, and to suggest reforms based on

---

[22] Henry Goudy, Introduction, *Transactions of the Grotius Society* 1 (1916): 11–18, here 11; Segesser, Recht statt Rache: 143–176. On the more general issue of recruiting academics for the national war effort cf. also Marta Hanna, *The Mobilization of Intellect: French Scholars and Writers during the Great War*, Cambridge 1996; Wolfgang J. Mommsen, *Die europäischen Intellektuellen, Schriftsteller und Künstler und der Erste Weltkrieg, in: ibid. (ed), Bürgerliche Kultur und politische Ordnung: Künstler, Schriftsteller und Intellektuelle in der deutschen Geschichte 1830–1933*, Frankfurt a. M. 2000: 196–215 and Stuart Wallace, *War and the Image of Germany: British Academics 1914–1918*, Edinburgh 1988.

[23] Hugh H. L. Bellot and Malcolm Carter, Editorial Note, *Transactions of the Grotius Society* 1 (1916): 4; Members, Transactions of the Grotius Society 1 (1916): 6 for the list of the founding members of the Grotius Society.

[24] Officers of the Grotius Society, Transactions of the Grotius Society 1 (1916): 5.

humanity and justice wherever possible",[25] this was less than true. This becomes clear notably from the articles published in the first volume of its transactions for 1915 and the introduction by Vice-President Henry Goudy. Although the latter pointed to the fact that the "well-established rules of International Law have been violated by each and all of the belligerents",[26] he primarily called German acts "illegal", while for example trying to excuse the landing of British and French troops in neutral Greece by the fact that "Greece (though protesting *pro forma*), encouraged *de facto* such landing and promised her benevolent neutrality."[27] To justify violations of international law by referring to "extreme military necessity" for Goudy equalled "the negation of all International Law"[28] and he therefore finished his introduction by saying:

> There can be no glory in victory by *Schrecklichkeit*. If we are to be beaten let us fall with honour and clean hands. If we are victorious let us afterwards exact reparation from those in authority who have been responsible for brutalities. Unless this is done, International Law will be degraded, if not destroyed, and civilization itself will be in danger.[29]

In his contribution presented to the Grotius Society on 30 June 1915 on the destruction of merchantmen by a belligerent, Bellot himself followed the line of his vice-president. Although he did not mention the study he had published with judge Llewellyn Atherley-Jones in 1907,[30] it becomes clear from the detailed knowledge he presented that it was this work which got Bellot involved in issues of international law. He criticised the British government for implicitly accepting the German doctrine of military necessity during the negotiations that had led to the Declaration of London. He also called on the British government to make sure that the old rule that under no circumstances neutral vessels ought to be destroyed by belligerents on the high seas be restored at the end of the war. He finished his contribution on a clear note: "If Germany, in pursuance of her present theories of military necessity, refuses to fall into line and continues to flout the rules and usages of

---

[25] Goudy, Introduction: 12.

[26] Ibid.: 13. In this Goudy used words similar to those of Carnegie Endowment of International Peace: *Report of the International Commission to Inquire into the Causes and Conduct of the Balkan Wars*, Washington 1914: 208.

[27] Goudy, Introduction: 14–15.

[28] Ibid.: 16.

[29] Ibid.: 17–18.

[30] Llewellyn Atherley-Jones and Hugh H. L. Bellot, *Commerce in War*, New York 1907.

warfare, she must be treated as the pariah of nations. The actual perpetrators of outrages authorised by her must be treated as outlaws and war criminals."[31] With these words, which bore no reference at all to the sinking of the Lusitania on 7 May 1915 just shortly before his presentation,[32] Bellot began his work on the criminality of violations of the rules and usages of international law which he took up again one year later in more general terms.

2.3   War Crimes: Their Prevention and Punishment

On 24 March 1916 Hugh Bellot presented his more general ideas on the prevention and punishment of war crimes to the Grotius Society. His aim was to make sure that the issue of the punishment of war crimes would continue to be discussed, even though governments as well as "organised and unorganised opinion in all countries" tried to excuse or even justify such cruel and indefensible acts committed by the armed forces of the enemy against people as well as property.[33] His words came at a moment between the sinking of the Lusitania in May 1915 and the execution of Captain Charles Fryatt after a trial in a German military court in July 1916.

While there was a lively debate on the possible punishment of those responsible for violations of the laws of war in France and Germany,[34] except for investigations into crimes committed in Belgium,[35] British jurists preferred discussions on the laws of the sea. They proved to be more reluctant on violations of the laws of war, not least after the Asquith government – and especially its First Lord of the Admiralty, Winston Churchill – had to back down when the German government threatened to take reprisals after some German U-boat officers and soldiers had been

[31]   Hugh H. L. Bellot, Destruction of Merchantmen by a Belligerent, *Transactions of the Grotius Society* 1 (1916): 51–59, here 59.

[32]   On the sinking of the Lusitania and the debate in the press as well as amongst jurists on this issue cf. Paul Halpern, *A Naval History of World War I*, London 1994: 298–299; Diana Preston, *Wilful Murder: The Sinking of the Lusitania*, London 2003: 345–349 and Segesser, *Recht statt Rache*: 179–182.

[33]   Hugh H. L. Bellot, War Crimes, their Prevention and Punishment, *Nineteenth Century and After* 80 (1916): 636.

[34]   Segesser, *Recht statt Rache*: 193–198.

[35]   Committee on Alleged German Outrages, *Report of the Committee on Alleged German Outrages*, London 1915; John Hartmann Morgan, German Atrocities in France, with unpublished records, *Nineteenth Century and After* 77 (1915): 1213–1233 and Morgan. *German Atrocities: An Official Investigation*, London 1916. Cf. Segesser, Recht statt Rache: 157–170.

detained in penitentiaries instead of prisoners of war camps,[36] a fact that one of Bellot's colleagues had severely criticised in his presentation to the Grotius Society on 27 May 1915.[37]

Bellot's aim was to strengthen the hands of those men who, like Sir Robert Cecil, demanded that the British government would at least exact punishment for violations of the laws of war at the end of the war.[38] He admitted that the threat of trying war criminals would not "produce an immediate effect and induce the German government to abandon forthwith its methods of barbarism", but he was convinced that "the public opinion of the civilised world will not rest satisfied unless, upon the termination of the conflict, not only the instigators but also the actual perpetrators of the more heinous offences against the usages of war are brought to trial before some impartial tribunal".[39] Bellot did not go into details as to the exact composition of such a tribunal, but rejected proposals for a neutral and independent tribunal composed of judges nominated by neutral states. Under the existing laws, Bellot was convinced, "the Entente Powers are entitled to try and punish all offenders against the established laws and usages of war by court-martial". Bellot, however, preferred a court "composed of eminent civilian judges versed in criminal law and practice", which would make sure that there would be "as impartial a tribunal as any likely to be obtained".[40]

What was most important to Bellot was that the offenders be brought to justice, not in a spirit of revenge, but in order to maintain and strengthen the rules of international law.[41] Furthermore he made it clear that superior orders would not be accepted as an excuse to avoid trial as this would mean to indict a government, which in his eyes was

[36] James F. Willis, *Prologue to Nuremberg: The Politics and Diplomacy of Punishing War Criminals of the First World War*, Westport 1982: 17–20 and Segesser, *Recht statt Rache*: 177–179.

[37] Graham Bower, The Laws of War: Prisoners of War and Reprisals, *Transactions of the Grotius Society* 1 (1916): 23–37.

[38] *House of Commons Debates* Fifth Series, Vol. 71, 1915, cc. 651 and 1201–1207 (27 April and 5 May 1915). For further similar voices cf. Wallace, *War and the Image of Germany*: 185 and Segesser, *Recht statt Rache*: 188.

[39] Hugh H. L. Bellot, War Crimes, their Prevention and Punishment, *Nineteenth Century and After* 80 (1916): 658–659.

[40] Hugh H. L. Bellot, War Crimes, their Prevention and Punishment, *Nineteenth Century and After* 80 (1916): 659. He made his point again in Hugh H. L. Bellot, War Crimes and War Criminals, *Canadian Law Times* 37 (1917): 9–22, here 17–22, giving more details as to how such a process could be formalised at the end of the war.

[41] Hugh H. L. Bellot, War Crimes, their Prevention and Punishment, *Nineteenth Century and After* 80 (1916): 659; Hugh H. L. Bellot, War Crimes and War Criminals, *Canadian Law Times* 36 (1916): 754–768 and 876–886, here 885; Hugh H. L. Bellot, War Crimes and War Criminals, *Canadian Law Times* 37 (1917): 22.

futile.[42] In this the English jurist took a similar approach to many of his French colleagues, who following the lead of their doyen Louis Renault[43] demanded that a legal punishment be meted out only against persons who committed violations of the laws of war and that such a punishment was possible with the existing laws. Most French jurists in this context advocated trials in national either civilian or military courts.[44] Only Jacques Dumas demanded that such trials take place in an international criminal court and deplored that earlier attempts such as those of Gustave Moynier had failed in the past.[45]

2.4 Terminologies: War Crimes and Crimes Against Humanity

Bellot was not just one of the important British voices calling for the punishment of violations of the laws of war, but in his presentations and publications he also discussed the issue of terminologies. Up to the time of World War I the terms "war crime", "*crime de guerre*" or "*Kriegsverbrechen*" had not been very common in the language of jurists. Most of them had used phrases like "violations of the laws (and customs) of war", "violations of the Geneva (or Hague) Conventions" or had just named the elements of the crime such as murder, robbery, theft or rape.[46] After the Franco-German War Johann Caspar Bluntschli for the first time used the term war crime, but he did not explain why and did not use it in any other publication than his *Das moderne Völkerrecht der civilisirten Staten als Rechtsbuch dargestellt*.[47] In 1906 Lassa Oppenheim was the first jurist to define his use of the term war crime as "such hostile or other acts of soldiers or other individuals as may be punished by the enemy on capture of the offenders".[48] He distinguished between four elements of the crime, that is, (1) violations of recognised rules regarding warfare committed by members of the armed forces, (2) the same

---

[42] Hugh H. L. Bellot, War Crimes, their Prevention and Punishment, *Nineteenth Century and After* 80 (1916): 650–651, who on this point disagreed with Lassa Oppenheim, *War and Neutrality (International Law: A Treatise*, Vol. 2), London 1906: 264.

[43] Louis Renault, Dans quelle mesure le droit pénal peut-il s' appliquer à des faits de guerre contraires au droit des gens? *Revue Pénitentiaire et de Droit Pénal* 39 (1915): 406–493.

[44] Segesser, *Recht statt Rache*: 196–198.

[45] Jacques Dumas, *Les Sanctions Pénales des Crimes Allemands*, Paris 1916: 64 and 82–93.

[46] Segesser, *Recht statt Rache*: 49–50.

[47] Johann Caspar Bluntschli, *Das moderne Völkerrecht der civilisirten Staten als Rechtsbuch dargestellt*, 2nd ed., Nördlingen 1872, S. 358 (§ 643a).

[48] Oppenheim, *War and Neutrality*: 263–264.

violations committed by individuals, who were not members of the armed forces, (3) espionage and war treason and (4) all marauding acts. Oppenheim also gave a list of sixteen specific violations of the rules regarding warfare – amongst them the use of poisoned arms and ammunition, the killing of wounded or otherwise disabled soldiers, the ill-treatment of prisoners of war, assassination, unallowed destruction of enemy prizes or violations of the Geneva Convention – and clearly stated that such violations could only be punished if no order of the belligerent government existed.[49] Oppenheim's use of the term war crimes and his systematisation of the concept was novel, but his ideas on the mode of punishment of war crimes and on the fact whether such crimes could be punished at all did not differ that much from ideas put forward by others such as Moynier or Rolin-Jaequemyns, whom he failed to mention as part of the literature he had consulted.[50]

During World War I, Bellot was one of the few to use the term[51] and the only one giving a definition as "those acts of the armed forces of a belligerent against the person or property of the enemy, combatant or non-combatant, which are deemed contrary to the established usages of war".[52] While he did not explicitly refer to Oppenheim in his presentation at the Grotius Society, he made the corresponding reference in a longer article, which he published in 1916–1917 in the *Canadian Law Times*.[53] Bellot gave no reason for concentrating on the first two elements of the crime defined by Oppenheim, but over time his understanding became accepted, even if in a modified form. Up to the end of World War I, however, notable jurists such as Louis Renault or Thomas Erskine Holland would not resort to the term.[54] Although not using Oppenheim's and Bellot's term, the Commission on the Responsibility

[49] Oppenheim, *War and Neutrality*: 264–266.
[50] Ibid.: vi and 263–270. On the issue of the punishment of war crimes – or violations of the laws of war in the period between 1872 and 1907 cf. Segesser, *Recht statt Rache*: 90–140.
[51] Amongst the authors doing so were an anonymous author of the *Law Journal* – Reparation for War Crimes, *Law Journal* 50 (1915): 276–277 – as well as Fernand Engerand in his comments to Renault, Dans quelle mesure le droit pénal peut-il s' appliquer à des faits de guerre contraires au droit des gens?: 451–456.
[52] Hugh H. L. Bellot, War Crimes, their Prevention and Punishment, *Nineteenth Century and After* 80 (1916): 636.
[53] Hugh H. L. Bellot, War Crimes and War Criminals, *Canadian Law Times* 36 (1916): 754–768 and 876–886 and War Crimes and War Criminals, *Canadian Law Times* 37 (1917): 9–22.
[54] Segesser, *Recht statt Rache*: 52–53. Cf. Heiko Ahlbrecht, *Geschichte der völkerrechtlichen Strafgerichtsbarkeit im 20. Jahrhundert*, Baden-Baden 1999: 427–430 for the most recent definition of war crimes in the ICC Charter of 1998.

of the Authors of the War and the Enforcement of Penalties at the Paris Peace Conference defined violations of the laws and customs of war with an extended, but in general similar, list[55] to the one Bellot had used between 1915 and 1917.[56] While in general he was very consistent in his use of the term war crimes, at one stage he also used the term crimes against humanity, however, without giving any exact definition as to why he used it.[57] It is therefore not exactly clear what Bellot precisely meant when using the term. However, considering the fact that he referred to the principles of humanity at different stages[58] and looking at the way the term was used during World War I by others such as Simeon North or Édouard Rolin-Jaequemyns, it is fair to say that, for Bellot, crimes against humanity were all those crimes that could be summed up as war-related crimes irrespective of whether or not they could be designated as war crimes proper.[59]

2.5 A Committee on War Crimes: Hugh Bellot and Post-War Peace Treaties

Hugh Bellot's statements did not evoke a lot of feedback. An anonymous author in the *Law Quarterly Review* described Bellot's article in *Nineteenth Century and After* as "useful and well reasoned" and especially pointed to the fact "that superior orders are no excuse for manifest breach of rules that every soldier ought to know".[60] *The Times*, which in the decade before and during the war had published letters of the renowned jurist Thomas Erskine Holland on the laws of war,[61] just noted that Bellot had published

---

[55] Commission on the Responsibility of the Authors of the War and the Enforcement of Penalties, Report Presented to the Preliminary Peace Conference, *American Journal of International Law* 14 (1920): 95–154, here 112–115.

[56] Hugh H. L. Bellot, War Crimes, their Prevention and Punishment, *Nineteenth Century and After* 80 (1916): 640–642 and War Crimes and War Criminals, *Canadian Law Times* 37 (1917): 756–759.

[57] Ibid.: 659.

[58] Ibid.: 640 and 659; Hugh H. L. Bellot, War Crimes and War Criminals, *Canadian Law Times* 36 (1916): 760, 762 and 876; War Crimes and War Criminals, *Canadian Law Times* 37 (1917): 21.

[59] Daniel Marc Segesser, Die historischen Wurzeln des Begriffs "Verbrechen gegen die Menschlichkeit", *Jahrbuch der Juristischen Zeitgeschichte* 8 (2007): 75–101, here 82–87 and 89–93.

[60] Anonymous, Dr. Hugh Bellot on War Crimes, their Prevention and Punishment, *Law Quarterly Review* 32 (1916): 350.

[61] Thomas Erskine Holland, *Letters to "The Times" upon War and Neutrality*, 3rd ed., London 1921.

"an important paper on war crimes and their punishment".[62] While at the height of the public debate on the execution of Captain Charles Fryatt[63] there had been many calls for "treating criminals as criminals"[64] and British Prime Minister Henry Herbert Asquith had made it clear that "such crimes shall not [...] go unpunished" stressing the fact that the government was "determined to bring to justice the criminals, whoever they may be and whatever their station",[65] the determination of the authorities waned in 1917 and well into 1918.[66]

Attorney-General Sir Frederick E. Smith, however, still made it clear already early in 1918 that in his mind those who had broken criminal law or the law of nations had to be punished, not least in order to vindicate international law.[67] He reiterated his views in September, telling an audience in Liverpool plainly "that there is in international law abundant warrant for the punishment, both in their persons and in their purses of proved and identified criminals".[68] Calls for such a punishment of war crimes grew in France as well as in Britain and finally Prime Minister David Lloyd George, who for a long time had taken no action, gave in and accepted the establishment of a committee to collect evidence and make recommendations on the punishment of war crimes.[69] Bellot, who in the meantime had unsuccessfully tried to set up a co-operation between jurists in Britain, France and Russia,[70] was – like many other members of the Grotius Society[71] – amongst the men nominated to be part of this committee and he again became one of its secretaries.

---

[62] *The Times*, 2 September 1916: 9.

[63] During the night of 22–23 June 1916 Captain Charles Fryatt was taken prisoner by the crew of a German destroyer. He was found guilty in July in a military court of having tried to injure German military forces as an irregular civilian fighter, because he had tried to ram a German submarine in order to avoid the sinking of his merchantmen earlier in the war. He was shot on 27 July, a fact that Bellot (War Crimes, their Prevention and Punishment, *Nineteenth Century and After* 80 (1916): 660) called a judicial murder and a war crime. Cf. Halpern, *A Naval History of World War I*: 296 and Segesser, *Recht statt Rache*: 182–183.

[64] Letter of W. Boyd Carpenter to the editor, *The Times*, 3 August 1916: 7.

[65] *House of Commons Debates* Fifth Series, Vol. 84, 1916, c. 2081 (31 July 1916).

[66] Willis, *Prologue to Nuremberg*: 35–36 and 49–51.

[67] *New York Times* 12 January 1918, p. 3; Speech of Frederick E. Smith, later Lord Birkenhead, to the New York State Bar Association on January 11, 1918 and published as Law War and the Future in: *The Speeches of Lord Birkenhead*, London 1929: 93–115 here 109.

[68] *The Times*, 19 September 1918: 3.

[69] Willis, *Prologue to Nuremberg*: 51–53.

[70] Segesser, *Recht statt Rache*: 201.

[71] Garrod, The British Influence: 319.

The aim of the committee was to establish the facts as to breaches of the laws and customs of war affecting British subjects, to ascertain the degree of responsibility for these offences incurred by members of the armed forces of the Central Powers and to discuss the constitution as well as the procedure of a tribunal appropriate to try such offences.[72] Soon, however, the committee also had to deal with the issue of the punishment of the former German Kaiser Wilhelm II, which had been put on the agenda by Prime Minister David Lloyd George. In a manner similar to that in France, the British committee finally agreed that the former German Kaiser be tried for his responsibility for the invasion of Belgium in contravention to international law, for all criminal acts that took place as a consequence of this decision, for his responsibility for the crimes committed in the context of unrestricted submarine warfare and for other offences such as the illegal execution of Captain Charles Fryatt.[73]

On this point both the British committee as well as French jurists departed from earlier positions, expressed for instance by Bellot or Renault who had described such an approach as "futile", "bold" or as having "no equivalent in positive law".[74] To what extent Bellot had changed his mind by 1919 is difficult to ascertain, but he was not a member of the sub-committee that dealt with the issue of a trial of the former German Kaiser and whose deliberations were not recorded.[75] Looking at his first post-war proposals,[76] it is more likely that Bellot kept a rather low profile on this hot political issue.

What is clear, however, is that the reports of the Attorney-General's committee were more than an internal British affair, as they shaped the British position within the Commission on the Responsibility of the Authors of the War and the Enforcement of Penalties at the Paris Peace Conference. Furthermore, the committee compiled important arguments that Attorney-General Smith was able to use to convince sceptics in cabinet such as George Nathaniel Curzon and Winston Churchill. As Bellot remained in Britain, he played no role at the Paris Peace

---

[72] Anonymous, German Crimes in the War, *Law Journal* 53 (1918): 387–388.

[73] Garrod, The British Influence: 325–326; Segesser, *Recht statt Rache*: 213–215; Willis, *Prologue to Nuremberg*: 54–55.

[74] Hugh H. L. Bellot, War Crimes, their Prevention and Punishment, *Nineteenth Century and After* 80 (1916): 650; Renault, Dans quelle mesure le droit pénal peut-il s' appliquer à des faits de guerre contraires au droit des gens?: 423.

[75] Willis, *Prologue to Nuremberg*: 58.

[76] See below.

Conference. In its meetings two other members of the Attorney-General's committee, the two cousins Frederick and Ernest Pollock, were more influential than Bellot, Solicitor-General Ernest being the main British spokesman in the Paris Commission.[77]

In the resulting debates "feelings ran about as high as feelings can run", as American delegate James Brown Scott reported: "It ran especially high in the British membership and it ran extremely high in the French members. It ran so high that relations were somewhat suspended [...]."[78] Finally, however, the American and Japanese delegates had to give in and accept that the former Kaiser would be arraigned (but not necessarily indicted) "for a supreme offence against international morality and the sanctity of treaties".[79] Furthermore the defeated countries had to recognise "the right of the Allied and Associated Powers to bring before military tribunals persons accused of having committed acts in violation of the laws and customs of war".[80] Bellot and his colleagues had succeeded in getting the principle of the punishment of war related crimes accepted in the Peace Treaties, but instead of "eminent civilian judges versed in criminal law and practice", which would make sure that there would be "as impartial a tribunal as any likely to be obtained",[81] military tribunals would be in charge. Furthermore the term "war crimes", which Bellot had deliberately tried to push and which especially stressed the criminal character of

---

[77] Anonymous, German Crimes in the War: 387; Willis, *Prologue to Nuremberg*: 69. Cf. also Gary Jonathan Bass, *Stay the Hand of Vengeance: The Politics of War Crimes Tribunals*, Princeton 2000: 64–73, Garrod, The British Influence: 333–343, Lewis, *The Birth of New Justice*: 39–47 and Segesser, *Recht statt Rache*: 214–215.

[78] James Brown Scott, Stenographic Notes of Questions Asked and Answers Given after the Lectures in Philadelphia: The Trial of the Kaiser, in Edward M. House and Charles Seymour (eds), *What Really Happened at Paris*, New York 1921: 475–481, here 480.

[79] Article 227 of the Versailles Peace Treaty, printed in Willis, *Prologue to Nuremberg*: 177. None of the other peace treaties with other members of the Central Powers contained a similar clause, arraigning any of the other heads of state of the defeated countries. Cf. Willis, *Prologue to Nuremberg*: 178–181. Ernest Pollock's statement – cf. Garrod, The British Influence: 339 – that the Peace Conference representing the "whole of civilisation" had the "necessary authority and weight" to develop international law was therefore probably an excuse to find a way to put Wilhelm II on trial, in order to fulfil the promises made by the Lloyd George government in the 1919 election.

[80] Art. 228 of the Treaty of Versailles, Art. 173 of the Treaty of St. Germain, Art. 118 of the Treaty of Neuilly, Art. 157 of the Treaty of Trianon and Art. 226 of the Treaty of Sèvres, all printed in Willis, *Prologue to Nuremberg*: 177–181.

[81] Hugh H. L. Bellot, War Crimes, their Prevention and Punishment, *Nineteenth Century and After* 80 (1916): 659.

40 DANIEL MARC SEGESSER

violations of the laws and customs of war, was not included in the Paris Peace Treaties.

2.6 Hugh H. L. Bellot, Walter George Phillimore and the International Law Association

At the end of the war and in the early months of the interwar period Bellot was busy with his work as a secretary of the British committee of enquiry on breaches of laws of war and with putting together its reports. Furthermore – in his position obtained in 1915 as one of the secretaries-general – he was also involved in restarting the activities of the International Law Association after the war.[82] He also continued to be responsible for the publication of the *Transactions of the Grotius Society*[83] and – together with George Grenville Phillimore – presented a paper in 1919 on the issue of prisoners of war, which called for personal legal consequences for offenders against the laws related to the maintenance of prisoners of war.[84] Due to the fact that he was busy with other matters and not having a direct knowledge on the matters discussed at the Paris Peace Conference, Bellot decided to abstain from commenting the outcome. While other authors such as Quincy Wright and Norwood Young also pointed to the treatment of Napoleon Bonaparte in 1815, when talking about the possible punishment of the former German Kaiser,[85] Bellot did without any reference to the Paris Peace Conference or the Versailles Peace Treaty in his historical analysis of that case[86] and temporarily left the field to others.

Amongst the men taking up the issue after the end of the Paris Peace Conference was another member of the Grotius Society, Walter George Baron Phillimore of Shiplake. Son of judge Robert Phillimore, an authority in international law,[87] he himself became a renowned lawyer. In 1920

---

[82] Higgins, Dr. H. H. L. Bellot: 205. Garrod, The British Influence: 319 and 326 mentions the several reports put together, but not published by the committee of enquiry on breaches of laws of war, but does not refer to Bellot's exact contribution to the committee's work.

[83] Hugh H. L. Bellot, Editorial, *Transactions of the Grotius Society* 5 (1920): v–vi; Ibid., Editorial, *Transactions of the Grotius Society* 6 (1921): v–vi.

[84] George Grenville Phillimore and Hugh H. L. Bellot, Treatment of Prisoners of War, *Transactions of the Grotius Society* 5 (1920): 47–64, here 62.

[85] Quincy Wright, The Legal Liability of the Kaiser, *American Political Science Review* 13 (1919): 120–128; Norwood Young, Ex-Emperor William and the Napoleonic Precedent, *Nineteenth Century and After* 86 (1919): S. 575–584.

[86] Hugh H. L. Bellot, The Detention of Napoleon Buonaparte, *Law Quarterly Review* 39 (1923): 170–192.

[87] Robert Phillimore, *Commentaries upon International Law*, 3 Vols, Philadelphia 1854–1857.

he was appointed to the Advisory Committee of Jurists, which was to set up the Permanent Court of International Justice.[88] This body sat between 16 June and 24 July 1920 and not only devised a statute for the Permanent Court of International Justice, but also called for the creation of an international criminal court. Its chairman, the Belgian Baron Édouard Descamps, who as a junior delegate had already been involved in setting up the Hague Rules of Land Warfare, was well aware that to deal with international criminality was not the central task of his committee. Nevertheless, he pointed to the fact that international law recognised the existence of crimes against the law of nations and that all members could be affected by such acts. A pre-existing court would be a better solution that an ex post facto tribunal, because it could not be considered as an act of revenge. Its very existence might even have a preventative effect.[89] Phillimore did not participate in the controversial debate following Descamps' proposal and only began to comment on the issue of an international court of criminal justice in 1922.[90] At that point, however, he made it clear that he had always been critical of the attempts to punish the former German Kaiser Wilhelm II. To him an international court of criminal justice was nevertheless best suited for trials of violations of the laws of war:

> On the whole as it will nearly always happen that the complaining State, if it has to proceed before the tribunals of the other State, will not think that it gets its full measure of justice, while if it proceeds before its own tribunals it will be suspected of injustice or hardship, [... Therefore] it would be better that there should be an international high court of justice which could exercise criminal jurisdiction in such cases.[91]

---

[88] Wyndham Anstis Bewes, The Right Hon. Baron Phillimore of Shiplake, Baronet, P.C., D. C.L., LL.D, J.P, *Transactions of the Grotius Society* 14 (1929): v–ix, here v–vii.

[89] Advisory Committee of Jurists – Permanent Court of International Justice, *Procès-Verbaux of the Proceedings of the Committee, June 16th–July 24th, 1920 with Annexes*, The Hague 1920: 498.

[90] In his presentations to the Grotius Society and the Institut de Droit International, Walter George Phillimore, Scheme for the Permanent Court of International Justice, *Transactions of the Grotius Society* 6 (1921): 89–98 and Rapport sur la Cour Permanente de Justice, *Annuaire de l'Institut de Droit International* 28 (1921): 110–124 he did not make any comment on the issue of an international court of criminal justice.

[91] Walter George Phillimore, An International Criminal Court, *British Yearbook of International Law* 3 (1922–23): 79–86, here 83. He used similar words in his Spanish presentation to the 1922 meeting of the International Law Association, Las Propositiones del Comite de Jurisconsultos, *Report of the Thirty-First Conference (Buenos Aires 24th August–30th August 1922)*, London 1923: 49–62, here 57.

Although – regrettably in his eyes – the Assembly of the League of Nations had considered the proposals made by Descamps and the Advisory Committee of Jurists in regard to an international criminal court premature, Phillimore was convinced that it made sense to press ahead with this idea, not least within international bodies of jurists such as the International Law Association.[92]

It was at this point that Bellot took up the issues again that he had left to others since the Paris Peace Conference. While Phillimore's ideas were presented to the conference of the organisation in Buenos Aires in August 1922 in his absence, Bellot was able to present his ideas in person. He pointed to the pressing need for the creation of an international criminal court in view of the many crimes that had been committed during World War I. Bellot highlighted the attempts of the British Committee of Enquiry into Breaches of the Laws of War and the Commission on the Responsibility of the Authors of War and on the Enforcement of Penalties.

In doing this, he omitted earlier attempts such as those of Gustave Moynier and Gustave Rolin-Jaequemyns, probably because he – like many British authors on international law[93] – did not have any knowledge of them, as can be deduced from the fact that he quoted a lot of British and American authors to prove his point that for "centuries, indeed, offences against the laws and customs of war have been punished, and without protest, in accordance with the common law of war, by belligerents of all nationalities, [. . .]".[94] Nevertheless, Bellot continued, trials in national courts had always proved unsatisfactory, as, depending on who was in charge, one party – victors or vanquished – would always believe that such trials were unfair. Furthermore, national trials could result in conflicting decisions and varying penalties and only a trial in an international court established by the co-operation of all nations could satisfactorily enforce international law.[95]

The jurisdiction of such a court was to be as wide as possible and it was to be competent to try criminal offences against law and order during peace time, as well as war crimes during or after the conclusion of a war,

---

[92] Phillimore, An International Criminal Court: 59 and 84–85.

[93] Cf., for example, Holland, *Letters to "The Times" upon War and Neutrality* or Oppenheim, *War and Neutrality*.

[94] Hugh H. L. Bellot, A Permanent International Criminal Court, in *Report of the Thirty-First Conference (Buenos Aires 24th August–30th August 1922)*, London 1923: 63–86, here 68 for the quote and 68–73 for precedents.

[95] Ibid.: 74.

on the basis of the principles of international law "as they result from the usages established among civilised peoples, from the laws of humanity and the dictates of the public conscience".[96] In this, Bellot, who as in his presentation to the Grotius Society in 1916 excluded the excuse of superior orders,[97] was much less strict than Gustave Moynier had been in his 1872 proposal, but at the same as convinced of the urgency of his proposal as the then president of the International Committee of the Red Cross.[98]

As for Moynier in 1872, Bellot also faced opposition within the International Law Association. His colleague from the Grotius Society, Sir Graham Bower, was to become his main antagonist. While he acknowledged Bellot's special authority in the field, he disagreed with his analysis on the inabilities of national (military) courts to deliver fair trials. Bower was sure that "justice would have been done", had any case been brought before the naval courts that he had been sitting on. Furthermore, he was not ready to accept Bellot's argument on superior orders. It was unacceptable that servicemen "may be brought before an International Tribunal charged with doing his duty to his own country in obeying orders of his own superiors [...]".[99]

Finally Bellot got his way, and the meeting of the International Law Association decided to entrust him with the elaboration of a draft statute of an international criminal court, whose jurisdiction was to be limited to trying war criminals for war crimes during wars as a court of appeal and after a war as a court of first and final instance.[100] Due to the death of the president of the International Law Association at the 1923 London meeting,[101] the discussion only continued in September 1924 in Stockholm. According to Bellot's draft submitted on this occasion, the court was to be established as separate from and in addition to the existing Permanent Court of International Justice. It was to be composed of a body of independent judges regardless of their nationalities. They were to have practiced either as judges or as lawyers for at least for fifteen years and were to be elected by the assembly and the council of the

[96] Ibid.: 77, deliberately quoting the famous Martens clause of Hague Rules of Land Warfare.
[97] Ibid.: 78.
[98] Moynier, Note sur la Création d'une Institution Judicaire Internationale: 122–131; Hugh H. L. Bellot, A Permanent International Criminal Court, in *Report of the Thirty-First Conference (Buenos Aires 24th August–30th August 1922)*, London 1923: 80–81.
[99] Graham Bower in the discussion of Bellot, Ibid.: 81–83.
[100] Ibid.: 86.
[101] Segesser, *Recht statt Rache*: 240.

League of Nations for nine years. The court's jurisdiction was to be limited to violations of the laws and customs of war – the term war crimes was not used – including "all offences committed contrary to the laws of humanity and the dictates of public conscience".[102] Individual citizens were to be allowed to launch a complaint, if they were able to obtain the consent of their own state.[103]

In his introductory comment at Stockholm, Bellot showed himself very aware of possible criticism especially on the issues of the "laws of humanity" or the right of individuals to put forward a complaint. He justified his proposal by pointing to the impossibility of knowing exactly what crimes could take place in future wars and to the existing safeguards in regard to complaints by individuals.[104] Faced with renewed and strong opposition by Graham Bower, but also from American jurists Charles Henry Butler and John Hinkley, their German colleague Edwin Katz, as well as Ludwik Ehrlich from Poland and Nils Stjernberg from Sweden,[105] it was Walter George Phillimore who came to Bellot's rescue with a suggestion that his draft be referred to a committee to reconsider the general question of the expediency of such a court in general and some of the issues raised by Bellot in particular. In this Phillimore was mainly referring to the right of individuals to launch complaints and to issues of the jurisdiction of the court.[106]

The committee finally set up consisted of Phillimore himself, Bellot, William Latey, Bernhard Loder, Edwin Katz, Ludwik Ehrlich, Alexander Wood Renton, who took the chair, as well as two men who had so far not taken part in the discussions of the International Law Association, Megalos Caloyanni and Vespasian Pella. The first four men did most of the job and finally took their report to the 1926 meeting of the International Law Association in Vienna.[107] In this report, which included a revised draft, the committee proposed to abandon the

---

[102] Hugh H. Bellot, Draft Statute for the Permanent International Criminal Court, in *Report of the Thirty-Third Conference (Stockholm September 8th to 13th, 1924)*, London 1925: 75–111, here 81. At this stage Bellot again used the terminology of the Martens clause of the Hague Convention respecting the Laws and Customs of War on Land.

[103] Ibid.: 81–82.

[104] Ibid.: 89–90.

[105] Ibid.: 91–95 and 99–110.

[106] Ibid.: 95–98, 106 and 110–111.

[107] Segesser, *Recht statt Rache*: 241–242. Caloyanni and Pella were major protagonists in the debate of the same issue within the Association internationale de droit pénal and the Union interparlementaire. Cf. Segesser, *Recht statt Rache*: 248–254 and the contribution of Ignacio de la Rasilla del Moral (Chapter 5) and Frédéric Mégret (Chapter 6).

proposal that individuals would be entitled to launch a criminal procedure before the court, and slightly amplified the jurisdiction of the court to "non-military as well as to military offences, whether committed in time of peace or in time of war".[108]

Although some participants, like Graham Bower and James Leslie Brierly, still opposed the idea of an international criminal court in principle,[109] the main debate in Vienna revolved around the issue of the law to be applied by the court. Vespasian Pella, who himself was not present in Vienna, but had submitted a paper that was read by Judge Fitzgerald, together with some jurists with a continental European background, suggested a more precise wording for the articles relevant on this issue, in order to avoid criticism based on the principle of *nulla poena sine lege*.[110] Finally the meeting agreed that in addition to international treaties, conventions and declarations, international custom, general principles of Public or International Law recognised by civilised nations as well as judicial decisions and doctrines of highly qualified publicists the court was to observe the following aspect:

> Provided that no act may be tried as an offence unless it is specified as a criminal offence either in the Statute of the Court or in the municipal penal law of the defendant or, in the case of a heimatlos, in the law of his residence at the time of the commission of the crime or, failing such residence, the law of the State where the crime was committed.[111]

As German jurist Hans-Heinrich Jescheck has pointed out, this was a compromise between Anglo-Saxon and continental legal traditions. The elements of a crime were to be examined according to the standards of continental penal law, but no specific rules were included. The illegality of an act was to be decided according to international law, while the penalty was to be handed down at the discretion of the judges, as was common in Anglo-Saxon countries.[112]

---

[108] International Law Association (ILA), The Permanent International Criminal Court, in *Report of the Thirty-Fourth Conference (Vienna August 5th to August 11th, 1926)*, London 1927: 105–225 and 279–309, here 109–142 for report and draft and 111 for quote.

[109] Bower ibid.: 153–155; James Leslie Brierly, Do We Need an International Criminal Court? *British Yearbook of International Law* 8 (1927): 81–88.

[110] Pella in ILA, The Permanent International Criminal Court: 146–153. On page 148 Pella explicitly referred to the resolutions of the Association internationale de droit pénal and the Union interparlementaire. Cf. Lewis, *The Birth of New Justice*: 103–109.

[111] ILA, The Permanent International Criminal Court: 119–120 and 280.

[112] Hans-Heinrich Jescheck: *Die Verantwortlichkeit der Staatsorgane nach Völkerstrafrecht: Eine Studie zu den Nürnberger Prozessen*, Bonn 1952: 96–97.

2.7 International Co-operation: Bellot and Alternative Concepts to Combat International Macro-Criminality in the Interwar Period

The Vienna meeting of the International Law Association in 1926 concluded the debates within this organisation, but were not the end of Bellot's efforts to bring out the creation of an international criminal court. His role was, however, not a major one any more, as others took over especially within the Association internationale de droit pénal. While it had been Bellot, so far, who had largely dominated the debate on an international criminal court, others gained ascendancy.

Amongst them Greek judge Megalos Caloyanni was the person who took over Bellot's work as a synthesiser of ideas. Already in 1925 and 1926 he published several articles,[113] in which he summarised the different ideas that had so far been presented on the issue of an international criminal court and also discussed Bellot's ideas as well as the debate that had resulted from them. Caloyanni made it clear that Bellot's draft had helped to clarify many points in regard to the drafting of a statute of an international criminal court.[114] Although Bellot had himself presented the report of the committee of the International Law Association to the Association internationale de droit pénal a few weeks before the Vienna meeting of the International Law Association,[115] Caloyanni and others did not often refer to Bellot any more in their later publications.[116] Calling the idea of an international criminal court his "original pet

[113] Megalos Caloyanni, La Cour Permanente de Justice Internationale, *Revue Internationale de Droit Pénal* 2 (1925): 298–325, The Permanent International Court of Criminal Justice, *Revue Internationale de Droit Pénal* 2 (1925): 326–354, La Cour Permanente de Justice Criminelle Internationale, *Revue Internationale de Droit Pénal* 3 (1926): 469–491, Permanent Court of International Criminal Justice, *Revue Internationale de Droit Pénal* 3 (1926): 492–515.

[114] Caloyanni, The Permanent International Court of Criminal Justice, *Revue Internationale de Droit Pénal* 2 (1925): 337–340; Permanent Court of International Criminal Justice, *Revue Internationale de Droit Pénal* 3 (1926): 500–501.

[115] Hugh H. Bellot, La Cour Permanente Internationale Criminelle, *Revue Internationale de Droit Pénal* 3 (1926): 333–337. On the chronological sequence of the meetings cf. Lewis, *The Birth of New Justice*: 102.

[116] Megalos Caloyanni, La Justice Pénale Internationale, *Revue de Droit Pénal et de Criminologie et Archives Internationales de Médecine Légale* 7 (1927): 139–145; La Cour Criminelle Internationale, *Revue Internationale de Droit Pénal* 5 (1928): 261–264, La Réforme du Statut de la Cour Permanente de Justice Internationale, *Revue Internationale de Droit Pénal* 7 (1930): 151–193.

scheme",[117] Bellot had to remind Caloyanni at a meeting of the Grotius Society on 10 May 1928 of the efforts of the British committee of enquiry on breaches of laws of war.

Furthermore, Bellot pointed to the fact that his continental colleagues had "become enamoured of codes [...] that they have forgotten that there is such a thing as common law". It seemed to Bellot "that there is already sufficient common law in International Law for a Court to make a beginning and to build up law, as we have done this in this country [i.e. the United Kingdom]".[118] As to the idea of furthering the unification of penal laws[119] he had not yet been able to study the issue in depth and therefore abstained from saying anything on this issue. These comments were the last that Bellot made in regard to an international criminal court and a possible international criminal code.

2.8 Sudden Death: Warsaw 1928 and Conclusion

Soon after the meeting with Caloyanni at the Grotius Society in London, Bellot went to Warsaw for the annual meeting of the International Law Association. At this meeting, he wanted to discuss a new issue that he had become acquainted with, the laws of military occupation, which in his eyes had to be discussed again in the light of the experiences of past wars. Once more he intervened in his clear and forceful manner in a debate, in which a revision of the regulations of the Hague Rules of Land Warfare was at stake. He was clearly opposed to "giving the occupying forces a far greater jurisdiction over the persons and property of the inhabitants of the occupied regions [...]".[120]

Retiring for the night after a last talk to the chairman of the session on the laws of military occupation, Lieutenant-General George Macdonogh, he died in his room at Hotel Europa in Warzaw, in all probability of a heart attack.[121] He was remembered as a determined and vigorous man, who fought energetically for his ideas, but always remained friendly. His colleagues described him as an "uncompromising opponent of the

---

[117] Megalos Caloyanni, An International Criminal Court, *Transactions of the Grotius Society* 14 (1929): 69–85, here 79.

[118] Ibid.: 80–81.

[119] On this movement cf. Lewis, *The Birth of New Justice*: 113–117 and Segesser, *Recht statt Rache*: 259–261.

[120] *The Times*, 13 August 1928: 11; André Prudhomme, La Conférence de Varsovie de l'International Law Association, *Journal de Droit International* 56 (1929): 300–301.

[121] *The Times*, 13 August 1928: 11.

doctrine of the absolute sovereignty of the state" and as a man, who believed "that all states were subject to the Law of Nations, [...]".[122] His lasting, but nevertheless not unchallenged legacy was certainly his fight for the punishment of war criminals during and after World War I and his commitment to the idea of an international criminal court,[123] for which he was ready to sacrifice the idea that individuals might be entitled to launch a prosecution, if their home country's legal officers agreed. His ideas were not completely new, but even though for whatever reasons he ignored earlier attempts to fight violations of the laws and customs of war by means of an international criminal court, he was nevertheless an important link in the process of transition generated in international criminal law by World War I. Bellot had stood at the crossroads and a large circle of friends lamented the death of a man, who had "literally died at his work for the improvement of international relations".[124]

---

[122] Higgins, Dr. H. H. L. Bellot: 205.

[123] Alexander Pearce Higgins Notice nécrologique du Dr. Hugh H. L. Bellot, *Annuaire de l'Institut de Droit International* 34 (1928): 762–764, here 764; Bewes, H. L. Bellot: xiv.

[124] *The Times*, 13 August 1928: 17.

3

Vespasian V. Pella

International Criminal Justice as a Safeguard of Peace, 1919–1952

ANDREI MAMOLEA

Figure 3.1 Portrait of Vespasian V. Pella, permission granted by the Vespasian V. Pella Association.

Vespasian V. Pella was an early twentieth-century Romanian jurist who conceived and championed a system of international criminal justice that was designed to prevent war, punish atrocity, and vindicate humanity's political and economic rights. He argued that governments had a duty to prevent economic dislocation as well as criminal acts capable of undermining international order. To construct these safeguards, Pella promoted the unification of domestic criminal law and the incorporation of international norms into domestic law. He also argued that an assembly of nations and an international criminal tribunal should play a subsidiary role by resolving disputes, imposing sanctions, and punishing aggression and violations of the laws of war. According to Pella, these institutions were necessary safeguards against the root cause of aggressive war—a small, disciplined, and ideologically rigid cadre of men who threatened to use the power of the state to manipulate the public into war.

In this chapter we will excavate the ideas, people, and events that shaped Pella's politics—the influence of his parents, the role of republican, pacifist, and socialist ideals, his desire to understand the psychological reactions of individuals and crowds, as well his response to the atrocities of World War I. It was these atrocities that ultimately led Pella to dedicate his life to advancing what he called the "international criminal law of the future." He did so through his scholarship, his diplomacy, and above all, through his advocacy in organizations such as the Association internationale de droit pénal and the Bureau international pour l'unification du droit pénal. In a relatively short period, Pella forged a professional consensus on previously controversial questions such as universal jurisdiction and corporate criminal liability. Yet though his ideas made great strides within the legal profession, the political support that was required to bring his system to life never materialized, either before or after World War II. We will examine the obstacles that Pella encountered and the underlying values of his project. Finally, the chapter challenges and overturns the many misconceptions about Pella that have proliferated in recent years and calls for further research into his life and work. Today's international criminal justice system is a mere shadow of what Pella had conceived and yet, even in this greatly diminished state, it still bears the traces of his legal vision.

3.1 Early Life

Vespasian V. Pella was born on January 4, 1897 in Bucharest, but spent most of his childhood in Râmnicu Sărat, a town in the Carpathian foothills, and in Iaşi, Romania's second city. His mother, Cornelia Pella (née Roşcu) was considered at the time of her wedding "one of the most distinguished students in philosophy" at the University of Bucharest.[1] His father, Vespasian I. Pella, was a journalist, political activist, and lawyer. Nine months after the birth of their son, the couple moved to Brussels where they quickly earned doctorate degrees in law from the Université Nouvelle de Bruxelles, a vibrant left-wing laboratory of ideas

---

[1] *Epoca* (Feb. 3, 1896), 3.

that had split from the oppressively clerical Université libre des Bruxelles in 1894.[2] At the time it was remarkably rare for a woman to earn a doctorate in law.

After returning to Romania in 1899, Vespasian practiced law and published in various journals, including *Adevărul*, a democratic, republican, and anti-monarchist daily, famous for challenging injustice and corruption in government and championing the rights of marginalized groups, including women and the peasantry. Elected as a deputy to the Romanian parliament for the National Liberal Party, Pella later joined Take Ionescu's Democratic Conservatives, a new centrist party that promised to deliver reform faster than either the Liberals or the Conservatives. Professionals, especially lawyers, flocked to its ranks. Vespasian I. Pella took over as editor of one of its official organs, *Opinia*. Later, he was elected to the Romanian Senate. Cornelia Pella was active in social welfare organizations and, after the move to Iași, hosted a weekly literary salon.[3] In short, Vespasian V. Pella's parents were both highly educated and deeply engaged in the reformist politics of the age. Their influence on him must have been considerable and likely inspired his progressive political values.

Vespasian V. Pella did not immediately go toward law, despite having scored well in the subject during his final year of high school. Instead, during his first year at the University of Iași, he opted for multiple courses and seminars on psychology, aesthetics, and pedagogy.[4] These interests led him to publish two studies, one on the "sentiment to protect the species" and another on "ugliness in art."[5] Although not directly connected to law, the first of these two works, published in 1915, when Pella was only eighteen, already contained elements that would become central to his legal thought. The book even elicited a letter of praise from Ioan Tanoviceanu, the father of Romanian criminal law.[6]

---

[2] The diplomas and correspondence related to these studies are in Mapa 16, Fondul Vespasian V. Pella, ach. 22/2001, Biblioteca Academiei Române. This uncatalogued collection consists of 21 containers.

[3] Mircea Ștefănescu, *Un Dramaturg își Amintește* (Bucharest: Eminescu, 1980), 12. Among those who attended this salon was Mihai Ralea, future left-wing political theorist for the National Peasant Party, and a close friend and classmate of Vespasian V. Pella.

[4] The high school diploma and course selections for 1914–1915 are in Mapa 16, Fondul Vespasian V. Pella.

[5] Vespasian V. Pella, *Cercetări asupra Sentimentului de Apărare a Speciei* (Bucharest: Speranța, 1915); *Urâtul in Arta* (Iași: Goldner, 1916).

[6] Ioan Tanoviceanu to Vespasian V. Pella, Nov. 19, 1915, Mapa 1, Fondul Vespasian V. Pella.

For our purposes, the most interesting section is a chapter on the "role of the social medium." Following Gustave le Bon, the popularizer of crowd theory, Pella argued that crowds were ruled by a well-defined, though transient, collective psychology in which the sentiments of all participants were channeled in the same direction. "Within the crowd," Pella observed, "every sentiment, every idea, contrary to the objective for which it was formed melts away."[7] The individual interest was sacrificed to the common goal and reason subordinated to action. "The socialist wants war, the antimilitarist volunteers to serve, the law-abider and the law-breaker give proof of their sacrifice for the common good, and all seem to be led by a unifying spirit that endows them with the same concepts, the same ideals." "The European War," Pella added, "confirms these statements in whole."[8] Pella associated the spirit of the crowd with the ideal of solidarity. In marked contrast, he attributed fanaticism to an excess of individualism. In the penultimate chapter of his work, Pella warned that when cultivated to excess the instinct of self-preservation threatened to annihilate all other sentiments to the detriment of both the individual and the community.[9] Those who were "drunk on patriotism and valor" lacked the discipline to serve society in a time of need.[10]

The power of collective psychology, the danger of fanaticism, and the threat of the faction to general welfare—all these ideas anticipated Pella's later work on the origins of aggressive war and the means to prevent it. In certain other respects, however, this early study differed markedly from Pella's later thinking. War, for instance, is described as a natural and progressive force. "Except for religious wars, all past and present wars are nothing but the efforts of the species to grow and develop."[11] We must keep in mind when reading such passages that Pella's attitude to war must have been heavily influenced by the fact that, only two years earlier, his father had served with distinction in the Second Balkan War (1913), in which Romania joined Serbia, Montenegro, Greece, and the Ottoman Empire against Bulgaria.

That this war had a powerful effect on the sixteen-year-old is also suggested by a remarkable, likely autobiographical, "psychological self-analysis," included in Pella's first book. Distraught by reports of an

---

[7] Pella, *Cercetări asupra Sentimentului de Apărare a Speciei*, 50. Other influences included Arthur Schopenhauer, Ernest Renan, Louis Joseph Roger, and Pyotr Kropotkin.

[8] Ibid. at 51.

[9] Ibid. at 55.

[10] Ibid. at 57.

[11] Ibid. at 63.

impending war, the author of the "self-analysis," a young man, sympathetic to pacifist, socialist, and humanitarian ideas, locks himself up in a small house outside Iași. After a few days of quiet solitude, he emerges, weak and tired, and decides to seek out news. During his drive back into the city, he suddenly begins to hear a distant and mysterious sound, gradually revealed as that of church bells. He experiences "a frisson," "an earthquake," that runs through his "entire being," and is seized by "a curious dizziness." He arrives in the city feeling both delirious and strangely serene. He is transformed. Hearing the bells, now joined by trumpets, he is filled with "an insane desire, a desire for war." The streets become thronged with people and he is swept up by the crowd, forgetting the ideas he had previously professed.[12]

Cast in this light, Pella's references to the "the socialist," "the anti-militarist," and "law-abider" swept by the unifying spirit of the crowd takes on an entirely new meaning. If the anecdote is indeed autobiographical, it suggests a more personal, more introspective, motive behind Pella's interest in crowd theory: the desire to understand his seemingly inexplicable reactions that day. Pella was clearly troubled by the fact that an intelligent person, "capable of forming a personal opinion," "a pacifist" who "controlled his emotions according to his individual reason," could nevertheless react this way.[13] Initially, Pella appears to have resolved this internal conflict by concluding that emotions were largely unmasterable and that war was inevitable. Four years later he would set forth a dramatically different view.

When Pella's book was published in 1915, Romania had not yet entered World War I. A year later, it joined on the side of the Entente. The Romanian army secured several successes and a few tactical retreats before it was gradually overwhelmed by the arrival of German reinforcements over the course of 1917. After Russia withdrew from the war in October of that year, Romania was forced to sign an armistice. Pella did not serve in the war because of a serious lifelong disability to his right leg that made him unfit for service.[14] The experience of war, nevertheless, had a profound and transformative effect on the young man. Having previously described war in positive terms, Pella emerged from the chaos convinced that war was a crime.[15]

---

[12] Ibid. at 22–25.
[13] Ibid. at 25.
[14] Lt. Col. Rădulescu, Adeverință, Dec. 5, 1916, Mapa 1, Fondul Vespasian V. Pella.
[15] Much more research remains to be done into this period of Pella's life.

3.2 A System of International Criminal Justice

By 1919, much of Pella's legal thought had already taken form. Nearly all the ideas and projects to which he would devote himself for the next three decades can be found, sometimes in embryonic form, sometimes in a very mature form, in the final chapters of his doctoral dissertation, *Delicte Îngăduite (Tolerated Criminal Offenses)*.[16] Pella's initial engagement with international criminal law took place in the context a much broader survey of criminal offenses that, according to him, were essentially "tolerated" as a result of inadequacies both in the substance and application of criminal law. Although largely focused on gaps in Romania's penal code, the work culminated, surprisingly, with a profound examination of the failures of international and domestic criminal law, as well as the social responsibility of governments.[17] One finds here the three interlocking and overlapping strands of legal thought that would occupy Pella for the next thirty years. We will examine each of them in turn.

First, Pella argued that international criminal law no longer corresponded to "the moral demands of humanity." It failed to address international crimes and ordinary crimes committed in foreign jurisdictions. Pella recognized, from the outset, the political nature of the problem. Even where ordinary criminal law had been violated, "the lack of trust and cooperation among nations produced a callous indifference that reinforced the prevailing sense of impunity."[18] Where international law had been violated, the challenges proved even greater. There was "no sanction and no jurisdiction," Pella lamented, "against the perpetrators of crimes that killed thousands." Domestic criminal law had suppressed the waging of private war, but international law continued to tolerate the recourse to "barbarous force."[19]

States had tried to establish laws to govern the conduct of war but these agreements, according to Pella, "remained only on paper. Nobody took

---

[16] Vespasian V. Pella, *Delicte Îngăduite* (Bucharest: Cartea Româneasca, 1919).

[17] The long list of offenses that domestic criminal law failed to address, according to Pella included: criminal negligence; the duty to rescue; the abandonment of the sick, the infirm, children or elderly; child abuse and child neglect; the willful or negligent spread of contagion; falsehoods that produced moral or material harm; incitement; the assistance of criminals and fugitives; the concealment of evidence; unlawful arrest; euthanasia; forced abortion; dueling; the abuse of diplomatic office; counterfeiting; and many others.

[18] Pella, *Delicte Îngăduite*, 441.

[19] Ibid. at 442. Pella focused almost entirely on the shortcomings of international law rather than on the things it entailed at the time.

note of them." War was becoming more terrible, humanitarian principles had been swept aside, and humanity had reverted to more primitive times.[20] Pella reminded his readers of the killing of hostages; the deportation, internment, and forced conscription of civilians; the bombing of undefended cities; the destruction of monuments and religious buildings; the use of expanding bullets and poisonous gas; the numerous thefts and unjust confiscations; and the rape of women. "The most monstrous of massacres," had been perpetrated during the war.[21]

Preventing these atrocities was the central aim of Pella's engagement with international criminal law. He offered a psychological explanation for the extreme violence unleashed during war and an institutional solution to limit or, better yet, prevent it altogether. In accounting for these atrocities, Pella argued that there existed within humanity "a crude and primitive underlying instinct" that was "more deeply rooted" in individuals "than the tendencies formed through continuing moral evolution and perfection of the human species."[22] War unleashed these primitive instincts. It swept morality aside. Society, Pella argued, was complicit. Whenever war was declared, the very society that had previously upheld the law became the "source of the most horrible crimes."[23] International institutions, Pella suggested, were the only means with which to deter and punish those who instigated war and violated its norms. "So long as there was no international tribunal and no league of nations capable of giving primacy to justice over the interests of any individual state, international crimes will continue to be tolerated."[24]

Pella had not yet theorized the relationship between these two prospective institutions but he indicated that the tribunal would serve two functions—peacefully resolving disputes between states and prosecuting the "leaders of states that unleash bloody wars." At the time, Pella did not specify whether these leaders could be held liable individually or collectively, but he listed some of the crimes that had been committed during the war, aside from aggression, which an international tribunal would be expected to prosecute: "orders to kill women and children, the placing of hostages in the line of fire, the destruction of cities such as Louvain and Reims, and the torpedoing of neutral ships."[25] The desire to prevent war

---

[20] Ibid.
[21] Ibid. at 443.
[22] Ibid. at 445.
[23] Ibid. at 444.
[24] Ibid. at 446. Pella's argument here drew heavily on the analogy to domestic law.
[25] Ibid. at 475. On the crime of aggression: Ibid. at 491.

and its atrocities was central to Pella's commitment to international criminal law. He recognized, however, that this objective could not be obtained through international law alone.

A truly preventive approach, one capable of suppressing the ordinary criminal offenses that helped provoke war, required the incorporation of international norms into domestic law. It required the standardization and unification of all domestic criminal law. This was the second strand in Pella's approach. Obstacles to extradition, jurisdictional loopholes, and a lack of solidarity among nations had allowed dangerous fugitives to escape justice. Pella's solution was unconventional and went beyond demands for the reform of the laws governing extradition. He believed that inconsistencies in the laws of different states would be gradually resolved through the unification of all of humanity's legal practices. "Through the close connections that exist among nations, every invention, discovery, and work of art eventually comes to be used and appreciated by all humanity." So too, argued Pella, the norms of criminal law would eventually "progress, evolve, and internationalize."[26] Criminal offenses, he noted, were already more or less indistinguishable across different systems. It followed that criminal procedure and punishment should also be standardized to reflect emerging international norms.[27]

The most striking norm advocated by Pella was the recognition of an international duty to prosecute and punish criminal offenders in the interest of "international public order."[28] This responsibility appears to have covered all possible offenses but Pella paused to highlight the importance, especially for the maintenance of peace, of prosecuting acts of terrorism and counterfeiting, subjects to which he would return in subsequent years.[29] Pella did not yet invoke universal jurisdiction or coin the principle of subsidiarity, but both concepts are already evident throughout the final chapters of the dissertation. Domestic criminal law had to anticipate the demands of international order. International and domestic criminal law would complement each other in preventing and punishing injustice. Disputes related to jurisdiction, meanwhile, would be decided by an international tribunal.[30]

---

[26] Ibid. at 449. Pella supported European federation throughout his adult life.

[27] Ibid. at 452.

[28] Ibid. at 450–451.

[29] For terrorism: Ibid. at 453. For counterfeiting: Ibid. at 457, 461.

[30] Ibid. at 475. Pella argued that the tribunal should have authority to determine whether or not an individual was entitled to the immunities normally extended to political criminals.

The final and most overlooked element in Pella's approach to international justice was his understanding of the social responsibility of states, or put differently, the "tolerated" abuses committed by the governing elite. Pella's writings on the subject demonstrate a sophisticated understanding of the relationship between law, politics, and society. They also help explain the emphasis he later placed on the responsibility of governments in preventing the social dislocations that facilitated wars of aggression. Pella began by surveying contemporary society. All of the advantages and all the rights remained concentrated in the hands of a small class that placed its "own interests above the needs of the whole community."[31] Although power was no longer maintained by the privileged through violence and brutal force, it continued to be obtained by them through fraud. "Under the mask of legality, also created by them," the elite "commit the same tolerated abuses [as before]."[32] But whereas physical violence had been self-evident, fraud proved more difficult to combat, because it was less visible and because the law itself had been made to serve the interests of the privileged.

These numerous abuses, meanwhile, caused its victims to lose consciousness of their fundamental rights. They were condemned from birth to labor for the "parasitical classes that benefit unjustly from the fruits of their labors." The victims, Pella observed, were born, raised, and buried in misery, enduring the same injustice suffered by their parents and to which their own children were condemned. "For the disinherited, social justice no longer exists in its true sense," he observed. Law had been used to perpetrate "the most painful injustices and the most brazen assaults on human liberty, on equality and the right to life."[33]

Yet despite this cutting view, Pella continued to believe that law was ultimately the political instrument with which to vindicate the fundamental rights of humanity. The laws of the future, he argued, would have to defend freedom, protect truth, prevent harms to the common interest, contribute to the development of individual initiative, and, ultimately, "ensure improvements in the wellbeing of those struck by economic injustice."[34] Pella argued that "just as the actions of an individual render him accountable to society, so too must society be held accountable to

---

[31] Ibid. at 482.

[32] Ibid. Pella attributed this insight to the Italian criminologist and crowd theorist Scipio Sighele.

[33] Ibid. at 484.

[34] Pella's left-wing ideals were largely inherited from his parents but they were also likely inspired by Garabet Ibrăileanu, a sociologist, literary critic, and the editor of *Viaţa*

those who have suffered its abuses." Leaders had the duty to meet social needs, to end the capitalist exploitation of the working class, and to "remove 'the surplus value' and surplus labor that is, as the Marxists claim, the unmerited tribute sent by the working classes to the privileged few who hold capital in their hands."[35] Pella agreed with the "followers of juridical socialism" that there existed "a social claim that working classes exercise over the capitalist class."[36] He argued against trusts, cartels, and policies that enriched producers at the expense of consumers. Indeed, he later wrote extensively on the criminalization of speculation, price fixing, and fraud.[37] Criminal law, Pella argued, should also be used to prevent overwork. But he recognized the dangers of over-criminalization and consequently argued for extensive penal reform.[38]

Apart from the occasional analogy to domestic law, the argument in his dissertation was breathtakingly normative. There was no hint of formalism, no obsequious deference to precedent, and no attempt to divorce law from politics. The emphasis, from beginning to end, was on the needs of domestic and international society, the obligations of government, and the rights of humanity. Pella's politics were unquestionably democratic, republican, and internationalist. He also clearly embraced socialist thinkers and their ideas. Yet despite these sympathies, Pella drew a clear line at what he considered senseless violence. In an earlier section on extradition, Pella argued that because Bolshevism was a purely destructive and reactionary movement, its members should not be entitled to the immunities from extradition normally accorded to political prisoners.[39] He described revolutionary communism in the same language he used to characterize war. It unleashed the most primitive sentiments. Five years later, as a newly elected deputy in the Romanian parliament, he condemned the injustices and atrocities perpetrated by the Soviet Union. Pella's position serves as a useful reminder that anti-Bolshevism was not only perfectly compatible but also consistent with a commitment to socialist values.

Românească. Pella's friend Mihai Ralea was a contributor to this journal and later took over as editor.

[35] Ibid. at 486.

[36] Ibid. at 488. This was a reference to the Austrian jurist and social theorist Anton Menger.

[37] See for example, Vespasian V. Pella, *Explicațiunea Teoretică și Practică a Legii și Regulamentului pentru Infrânarea și Reprimarea Speculei Ilicite* (Bucharest: Imprimeria Statului, 1923). Pella published several other works on this subject.

[38] Pella, *Delicte Îngăduite*, 488.

[39] Ibid. at 475.

The relationship between social justice and criminal law was not elaborated as fully in the dissertation as in later works, but it was set forth sufficiently for us to pause and examine how the different moving pieces in Pella's theory fit together. Social justice was imperative both on its own merits and because it prevented the conditions that allowed leaders to unleash bloody wars. The unification and standardization of domestic criminal law was necessary to prevent and address the kinds of crimes that created tension between states and destabilized the international order. Finally, the League of Nations and an international tribunal with criminal jurisdiction would play a subsidiary role by addressing the failures to implement international norms through the domestic criminal system, as well as punishing the waging of aggressive war and violations of the laws of war.[40]

The sum of these different parts made for an incredibly novel and sophisticated approach to international criminal justice. More remarkable still, was that Pella had assembled it single-handedly. His only points of reference were the works of René Garraud and Ioan Tanoviceanu on extradition and the writings of Joseph Tissot, Charles Gide, Charles Rist, and Léon Bourgeois on social justice. A handful of jurists, including Gustave Moynier, Jacques Dumas, Hugh H. L. Bellot, Ferdinand Larnaude, and Albert Geouffre de Lapradelle, had already contemplated the need for a system of international criminal justice but none of their ideas had circulated widely and none had engaged with the problem as deeply as Pella.[41] Indeed, Pella's approach would have also remained largely unknown had he not decided to continue his studies in Paris, which at the time was the center of the international legal world and an unusually receptive environment to the ideas of foreign jurists. There, Pella began elaborating and translating his ideas into French as well as constructing the transnational academic networks that would eventually launch them into practice.

[40] Pella later christened these two categories "international criminal law" and "international interstate criminal law." In order to avoid confusion, I will continue to refer these bodies, respectively, as domestic criminal law and international criminal law.

[41] Individual criminal responsibility emerged over the course of the nineteenth century as a substitute to the practice for reprisal. Scholars have discovered several examples of international criminal tribunals prior to World War I, including the 1893 Franco-Siamese Mixed Court, the 1898 International Military Commission in Crete, and the 1900 International Military Commission for the Boxer Rebellion. One scholar has argued that the commission of inquiry for the 1905 Dogger Bank Incident functioned like an international criminal tribunal. On Bellot see Daniel Seggeser, Chapter 2.

3.3 The International Criminal Law of the Future

Pella was very productive during his one year at the University of Paris under the supervision of Alfred Le Poittevin and Émile Garçon. He published four works, the most important of which was *L'Esprit de Corps et les Problèmes de la Responsabilité Pénale*.[42] This work contains the seeds of the theory of collective criminal responsibility with which Pella is most closely associated. The book represents a shift in his interests from the collective psychology of crowds to the collective psychology of small groups, variously identified throughout the work as sects, associations, corporations, and *corps*. Pella distinguished from the outset between the two. Crowds were heterogeneous, temporary, and often spontaneous. Sects, however, were much more homogenous and characterized by uniformity in thought and action. Sects pursued and defended their autonomy, made their own rules, and disciplined members accordingly. They cultivated conformity, ideological rigidity, and a sense of superiority that manifested itself in contempt for non-members.[43] The result was fanaticism. Fanaticism was also stoked by a desire for approval and reinforced by ostentatious expressions of enthusiasm.[44] Essentially, Pella diagnosed the manifestation in civil society of certain characteristics normally associated with military culture. Although never explicitly mentioned, the menacing presence of the paramilitary is palpable throughout the work.

Pella identified religious orders as the prototypical example of the *corps*, the incubators of fanaticism, and the enemies of public authority. Here Pella shifted from organizational theory to political theory, specifically republicanism. Corporations usurped the representative function of government, invading its remit, imposing extra-parliamentary impediments, and, ultimately, thwarting the political expression of the general will. These organizations made their own rules, imposed their own justice, and often settled disputes by means outside the law, including by threats and violence.[45] This often entailed the will of the few prevailing

---

[42] Vespasian V. Pella, *L'esprit de Corps et les Problèmes de la Responsabilité Pénale* (Paris: Sagot, 1920). The other three works examined the extraterritorial effects of criminal convictions, the crime of speculation, and amnesty. See Vespasian V. Pella, *Des Incapacités Résultant des Condamnations Pénales en Droit International* (Paris: Tenin, 1920); *Le Délit de Spéculation Illicite* (Paris: Sagot, 1920); *Les Principes Généraux de l'Amnistie* (Paris: Sagot, 1920).

[43] Pella, *L'esprit de Corps*, 21–28.

[44] Ibid. at 33.

[45] Ibid. at 42–43.

over the wishes of the majority. The proliferation of factions, meanwhile, undermined a broader sense of solidarity. Each one pursued its own interests without regard for the "common good."[46]

To illustrate the problem Pella turned to history. The Papacy was an obvious example. During the middle ages it "frequently exceeded its purely religious authority" and constantly attempted to acquire "political power" over states. Feudal guilds likewise interfered with policy by imposing internal barriers to trade and by denying women and married men entry into the workforce.[47] The leaders of the French Revolution understood that these entities, "constituted a permanent danger to the sovereignty of the state."[48] They banned them and recognized within society "only the individual, the commune, and the state." All other units tended to illegitimately encroach on individual rights and the legitimate public authority. Yet despite this reform, the power of unions had grown over the course of the nineteenth century, becoming tyrannical and oppressive, violating individual liberty, and subordinating the common good to the interest of the faction. Corporatist discipline ruled imperiously to the detriment of society.

The language invoked by Pella is immediately recognizable as that of the eighteenth-century French republicanism embodied in the Le Chapelier Law of 1791 which banned corporations.[49] The law was passed to protect individuals from the tyranny of private power and to ensure the unhindered and unmediated expression of the popular will in government. But whereas earlier republican thinkers emphasized the importance of the state as the agent of this emancipation, Pella focused on the role of politics and law. Already by 1925, he worried about the role of statism in producing nationalism and militarism.[50]

Still the argument was unmistakably republican in origin, which is remarkable, considering the reactionary origins of crowd theory. Though he immersed himself in the literature, Pella rejected both the pejorative image of the crowd and the reactionary politics conjured by leading crowd theorists such as the historian Hippolyte Taine, the sociologist Gabriel Tarde, and the popularizer Gustave Le Bon.[51] In Pella's work, the

---

[46] Ibid. at 45.
[47] Ibid. at 39.
[48] Ibid. at 40.
[49] Ibid. 41. Pella explicitly invokes the law.
[50] Vespasian V. Pella, *La Criminalité Collective des États et le Droit Pénal de l'avenir* (Bucharest: Imprimerie de l'État, 1925), 28–30.
[51] The best study of this phenomenon remains Suzanna Barrows, *Distorting Mirrors: Visions of the Crowd in Late Nineteenth-Century France* (New Haven: Yale University Press, 1981). Pella was deeply indebted to Gabriel Tarde for his understanding of the crowd and

working class is cast as heroic and dignified. The crowd, meanwhile, was neither bad nor good, but merely suggestive. This insight led Pella to reflect on the negative influence that corporations can exercise over the public at large. He located the danger, not in the shortcomings of democracy and mass politics, but in the power of highly organized groups. Pella observed that sects were most dangerous when they used propaganda to incite and direct the crowd.[52] In later works he argued for the criminalization of propaganda, false news, and hate speech designed to incite a war of aggression.[53]

The profoundly republican gloss on crowd theory was also reflected in Pella's legal proposals. He distinguished between crimes committed by organized groups and those committed by unorganized crowds. The latter were almost always spontaneous and unpremeditated, the result of a force that could sweep up even "the most peaceful individual" and for which each member of the crowd was only partly responsible. Crimes committed by organized groups, on the other hand, were usually planned in advance and designed to achieve a particular objective. Pella argued that in addition to the individual liability imposed on members of such organizations, the group itself should be held criminally liable. In making this argument, Pella invoked the work of Jean-André Roux to argue that if civil liability could be imposed on corporations, criminal liability could be imposed as well.[54] Pella's list of criminal organizations included the highway gangs that terrorized France after the revolution, the Neapolitan Camorra, the Sicilian Mafia, the Spanish Mano Negra, and the Bonnot Gang.[55]

Given that Pella had already written extensively about the duties and responsibilities of states, it was only natural for him to extend the argument about criminal organizations to the international sphere. He did this, initially, in a February 1920 lecture at the University of Paris Faculty of Law, but the theory he developed was not published

the sect. Gabriel Tarde, *La Philosophie Pénale* (Lyon: Stork, 1890); *L'Opinion et la Foule* (Paris: Alean, 1901). But the republican gloss was Pella's own. Tarde placed nowhere near as much emphasis on the competing authority of the church and subscribed to a negative image of the lower classes.

[52] Pella, *L'esprit de Corps*, 33–34.

[53] See for example, Vespasian V. Pella, "Un Nouveau Délit: La propagande pour la guerre d'aggression," *Revue de Droit International* 3:1 (1929), 174–179.

[54] Pella, *L'esprit de Corps*, at 71. Pella cited Jean-André Roux, *Cours de Droit Pénal et de Procédure Pénale* (Paris: Sirey, 1920), 102.

[55] Criminal organization: Pella, *L'esprit de Corps*, at 55. The idea of criminal organizations anticipated the classification of the SS as a criminal organization at Nuremberg.

until 1925 when it appeared as part of *La Criminalité Collective des États et le Droit Pénal de l'avenir*, the treatise for which Pella is best known.[56] In the intervening years, Pella taught criminal law at the University of Iaşi, helped draft a new penal code for Romania, assisted the League of Nations as an expert on counterfeiting, participated as a deputy in the Romanian parliament, and began to construct the international associations that he hoped would unify domestic and international criminal law as well as mobilize the political support necessary to put his projects into practice.

La Criminalité Collective des États opened with the affirmation that "War of aggression is a crime!"[57] This was humanity's verdict after the war. Pella argued that support for criminal sanctions could also be found in the League of Nations Treaty, the treaty of Versailles, the draft treaty on mutual assistance, and the Geneva Protocol for the Pacific Settlement of International Disputes. Nongovernmental organizations such as the Inter-Parliamentary Union and the Association internationale de droit pénal had also expressed their support for such sanctions. Armed with this mandate from jurists, parliamentarians, and humanity, Pella set out to examine the causes of aggressive war and the means to prevent it. The entire enterprise, he explicitly noted, was premised on the notion that law was inextricably linked to the social and political phenomena it attempted to regulate.[58]

Pella argued that the immediate cause of such wars was a form of collective criminality akin to the one he had sketched out in *L'esprit de Corps*. At the origin of every war of aggression was a small, disciplined, and ideologically rigid cadre of men who used the power of the state, especially schools and the army, to instill conformism, militarism, and fanaticism with the goal of eventually inciting the public into war.[59] According to Pella, this process was facilitated by deeper conditions such as national culture, atavism, racism, a sense of exceptionalism, isolationism, sovereigntism, "the cult of violence," material interests,

---

[56] Pella, *La Criminalité Collective des États et le Droit Pénal de l'avenir*, at 9.

[57] Ibid. at 3.

[58] Ibid. at 12 ("*le Droit Pénal international ne saurait avoir ce caractère autonome de science purement juridique que voudraient lui attribuer certains jurisconsultes*").

[59] Ibid. at 24–27. An earlier version of this argument can be found in Pella, *Delicte Îngăduite*, 491. The immediate inspiration for this theory is unclear but it is worth reiterating that during this period paramilitary movements emerged throughout Europe, took over certain states, and led them into war. Pella's description was both timely and prescient.

political ambitions, and the power of military, financial, and industrial elites.

To combat these causes, Pella recommended measures designed to promote political, economic, and intellectual solidarity among nations. The long list of policies he advocated included military and moral disarmament and the employment of peacekeeping forces. Pella also called for curricular changes in the teaching of history and the democratization of foreign policy. More striking was his emphasis on social justice. Having included economic precarity on the list of reasons individuals and states turned to aggression, Pella advocated a raft of measures designed to mitigate the social dislocation that induced people to wage war.[60]

He also called for "international economic solidarity" built on the principles of "equity, liberty, and assistance."[61] The widespread recognition that ordinary crime was, in large part, the result of poverty had led to the recognition within domestic law of "an individual's right to exist," as well as measures designed to provide individuals with "the opportunity to work and live honorably." Pella argued that same logic could be extended to international society. Preventing state collective crimes required "a guarantee of economic conditions absolutely necessary for the life and peaceful development of nations."[62] This entailed equal access to primary resources, freedom of movement for workers and goods, and assistance for nations suffering from "economic and financial difficulties."[63] For instance, Pella argued that financially stable states should provide states that were financially unstable with access to credit, not in the pursuit of profit, but out of commitment to the principle of assistance.[64] With respect to domestic policy, Pella argued that problems which threatened the stability of the international order should be addressed with policies analogous to the ones he advocated at an international level: measures designed to provide "the opportunity to work and live honorably." In his speeches before the Romanian parliament, he was more explicit. Pella repeatedly invoked the country's 1921 agrarian reform as the model for social justice.

---

[60] See Pella, *L'esprit de Corps*, at 42.
[61] Ibid. at 95.
[62] Ibid.
[63] Ibid. at 99.
[64] Ibid. Pella appears to have been influenced by the monetary crisis. He advocated the creation of "an international currency, or at least, a European one." Ibid.

The causes of war were also to be addressed through international institutions. Pella advocated recourse to international dispute settlement mechanisms, the standardization and universalization of legal norms, the drafting of an international constitution, and the concentration of international executive and judicial power, respectively, in the League of Nations and the Permanent Court of International Justice. The treatise set out the relationship between the two institutions. The court would adjudicate and the League of Nations, with its monopoly on the legitimate use of force, would impose the necessary sanctions to ensure compliance with judgments.[65]

Pella rejected the notion of absolute sovereignty. In certain "exceptional cases" where states violated "the most basic principles of humanity," international repression became a legitimate means of "restoring the moral order."[66] Pella illustrated the point by invoking the "massacre of races," such as "the Armenian massacres."[67] The case was paradigmatic, so much so that it later featured on the very first page of Pella's proposal for an international criminal court.[68] Such massacres, Pella argued, justified international repression, provided that the sanction complied with traditional requirements for the use of force, such as the exhaustion of remedies.[69] Following this principle, Pella emphasized the "subsidiary character" of international repression.[70] International institutions served an interstitial function, taking up a problem only after the domestic criminal system had failed to enforce the relevant international norm. In line with this approach, Pella continued to advocate for the unification of domestic criminal law.[71]

---

[65] Ibid. at 118–120. Beginning in the 1920s, Pella also championed European federation.

[66] Ibid. at 145.

[67] Ibid. at 146.

[68] See AIDP, *Projet de Statut d'une Cour de Justice Criminelle Internationale* (Paris: Librairie des Juris-Clausseurs—Éditions Godde, 1928), 7. Pella noted that the treaty of Sèvres established the principle of criminal responsibility for those who perpetrated the massacres. The claim that the AIDP had not learned from these massacres is absolutely false.

[69] Pella, *La Criminalité Collective des États et le Droit Pénal de l'avenir*, 146. See Andrei Mamolea, 'The Myth of Legalism in U.S. Foreign Relations' (PhD diss., IHEID, 2018), chapter 3. It is a sedulously cultivated myth that prior to Nuremberg there was no legal means for the international community to intervene either diplomatically or militarily to stop crimes against humanity. Invariably, the scholars and activists who make this claim portray intervention as the ultimate solution to all matters of international justice, while ignoring the ways in which this longstanding practice has exacerbated violence and served as a cover for imperialism.

[70] Pella, *La Criminalité Collective des États et le Droit Pénal de l'avenir*, 145.

[71] Ibid. at 159–160.

Pella ended the treatise with a lengthy and very detailed overview of his proposed "international criminal law of the future." The most interesting sections categorized crimes for which individuals and states could be held liable and the relevant sanctions that could be imposed on these two different types of offenders.[72] Pella argued, first and foremost, that states should be held liable for the crime of aggression and presented a means of determining and attributing such acts. Other international criminal acts included the use of threats; the preparation and mobilization for a war of aggression; indirect intervention in the domestic politics of another state; support for armed groups intervening in another state; the violation of demilitarized zones; the refusal to comply with the decision of a competent international authority; counterfeiting; and the violation of diplomatic immunity. Acts for which individuals could be held criminally liable included declaring wars of aggression, abusing diplomatic immunity, circulating false news capable of endangering international peace, falsifying diplomatic documents, and acts that were particularly damaging to international order such as terrorism. Over subsequent years, the crimes that Pella included in this last category extended to piracy, the trafficking of drugs, women, and children, as well the crimes of barbarism and vandalism, precursors of the crime of genocide.

Pella continued to criticize the "formidable incoherence" of the laws of war, which tried "to humanize the perpetration of a crime."[73] But he recognized that even after the prohibition of aggression, international criminal justice would still have to address war crimes. Pella argued that individuals should be held criminally liable for the unjustified interment, deportation, or transfer of civilians; creating famine; denationalization of the inhabitants of occupied territories; confiscation or exorbitant requisitioning; and the counterfeiting of the local currency. Pella also included offenses he had previously listed in his doctoral dissertation, such as the killing of hostages; the bombing of undefended cities; the destruction of hospitals, educational, religious, and historic buildings; the sinking of ships without warning and without taking the necessary precautions to save the passengers and crew; the use of poisonous gas, biological weapons, and expanding bullets; the denial of quarter; the mistreatment of prisoners; the poisoning of wells; and the use of airplanes in biological warfare. The method used to derive this list is unclear. Pella likely considered these acts violations of customary international law, but he

[72] Ibid. at 183.
[73] Ibid. at 56.

never demonstrated anywhere in the text when each of these norms had crystalized.

Pella rejected the use of reprisals as a form of punishment. Atrocity could not be answered with more atrocity. Instead, he provided a list of measures that could be used to punish states. These included diplomatic, legal, and economic sanctions. The first category included the rupture of diplomatic relations and the expulsion of diplomatic staff. The second entailed the seizure and sequestration of state-owned assets as well as the suspension of rights to intellectual property and access to courts for nationals from the offending state. The final category of measures included the blockade, the boycott, the embargo, the denial of access to financial markets, and the interruption of the means of communication. Pella also supported the use of economic fines, admonitions, the removal of colonial mandates, and even temporary military occupation by League of Nations peacekeepers in cases of "exceptionally serious international violations."[74] He argued against the exclusion of states from the League of Nations, however, because this undermined the authority of the organization and stripped the offending state of obligations. Equally problematic, in his view, was the permanent withdrawal of recognition from a state or its reduction through partial or total annexation.

Pella dedicated much less attention to the punishment of individuals, arguing that punishments imposed in domestic criminal law could be adopted for international criminal law. He argued in favor of warnings, admonitions, fines, the exclusion from foreign diplomatic office, sanctions on travel, exile, and imprisonment. Pella concluded with a detailed sketch of international criminal procedure. Bulky and brimming with lists, the treatise amounted to a detailed blueprint for a new body of international law.

3.4 Forging International Consensus

La Criminalité Collective des États et le Droit Pénal de l'avenir was highly influential and even led to Pella's nomination for the Nobel Peace Prize, but the political conditions necessary for the success of such a bold project simply did not exist at the time.[75] After the end of World War I, Britain and the United States refused to honor promises to

---

[74] Ibid. at 220.

[75] Pella solicited comments and feedback on his work. Much of this correspondence was eventually published separately as *Enquête International sur Les Conceptions Developpées par M. Vespasian V. Pella* (Bucharest: Imprimerie de l'État, 1926) and as the preface to

68 ANDREI MAMOLEA

of a security guarantee they had made to France during the peace negotiations and, instead, opted for policies of imperial retrenchment. Worse still, the enormous influence these two powers continued to exercise over the fate of the continent was instead directed to dismantling existing safeguards and undermining efforts to strengthen international institutions.[76]

The Anglo-American sabotage of the 1924 Geneva Protocol was only the most prominent example of this posture. The treaty, drafted by Nikolaos Politis of Greece and Edvard Beneš of Czechoslovakia, would have explicitly criminalized aggression, required states to peacefully resolve their disputes, and created sanctions to be used against states that violated these norms. These sorts of projects were largely the work of small and medium sized powers. During this period, most of the great powers abandoned multilateralism in favor of policies modeled on the Monroe Doctrine. They asserted exclusive authority over large swaths of the globe, where they claimed international law did not apply and their fiat was law. By the time Prime Minister Austen Chamberlain declared a British Monroe Doctrine during the debates over the Briand-Kellogg Pact, similar ideas had already become popular in Germany and Japan. France, alone among the great powers, remained deeply committed to international law, multilateralism, and collaboration with the smaller powers of Europe and Latin America, the real driving force behind the defense and development of international law during this period.

Pella and his allies had no illusions about the obstacles they had to overcome in order to bring about the international criminal law of the future. Writing to congratulate him on the success of his treatise, the Greek jurist Megalos Caloyanni reminded Pella that despite the "new difficulties" that had emerged in the face of international justice, the cause for which they were both fighting was "inscribed in the conscience of humanity." "This desire," Caloyanni added, "had to be translated into will" which then had to be "imposed by

---

the second edition of his treatise. The original copies of the correspondence can be found in Mapa 1, Fondul Vespasian V. Pella.

[76] The Anglo-American appeasement of Germany was motivated by economic interests and by racial sympathy against "the Latins" and "the Slavs." The consequences of anti–Eastern European racism on international relations during this period have been woefully neglected by historians. But see the pioneering work in Robert Boyce, *The Great Interwar Crisis and the Collapse of Globalization* (Basingstoke: Palgrave Macmillan, 2009).

the people on their governments."[77] It was to this end that Pella launched himself in international associational life.

Over the course of two decades, Pella delivered many keynote speeches before organizations, such as the Inter-Parliamentary Union and the International Studies Association, to popularize his arguments and mobilize the political support needed turn them into reality.[78] These speeches were designed to inspire rather than pressure or shame. Pella understood enough about the nature of public opinion in the United States and Britain to know that flattery and encouragement would be much more effective. Through public advocacy, he worked to change international political conditions, especially in the Anglophone world. In the interim, Pella helped establish the Association internationale de droit pénal (AIDP) in 1924, an organization whose objective was to unify domestic criminal law and to sketch the blueprints for an ambitious system of international criminal justice that could be quickly put into place once the political support for it materialized.

The AIDP's commitment to the unification of domestic criminal law has led scholars to argue that it was the natural successor of the Internationale Kriminalistische Vereinigung (IKV). In fact, there were profound differences between the two organizations. The AIDP was fundamentally a product of the new consciousness that emerged during World War I. Its members were motivated by a desire to prevent the recurrence of the kind of violations of international law that had been perpetrated by Germany. The IKV, on the other hand, lacked this consciousness. The organization's most prominent leader, Franz von Liszt, signed the notorious Manifesto of Ninety-Three and spent the war denying and diminishing the seriousness of Germany's crimes.[79] The AIDP was committed to a universal multilateral rule-based system that protected the rights of states big and small. Liszt, on the other hand, embraced the notion of regional understandings of international law akin to the hegemony asserted by the United States over the western hemisphere.[80] The development of international criminal law was an

---

[77] Megalos Caloyanni to Vespasian V. Pella, Apr. 30, 1926, Mapa 1, Fondul Vespasian V. Pella.

[78] Pella's numerous speeches before the Inter-Parliamentary Union have been collected in Gheorghe Sbârnă, *Vespasian V. Pella: în slujba științei dreptului și cauzei păcii* (Ploiești: Karta-Graphic, 2011), 97–213, 293–329, 355–498.

[79] See generally Florian Herrmann, *Das Standardwerk: Franz von Liszt und das Völkerrecht* (Baden-Baden: Nomos, 2001), 114–129, 226–241.

[80] For more on this subject see Andrei Mamolea, "American International Law, Rightly Understood" (forthcoming).

70 ANDREI MAMOLEA

explicit objective of the AIDP and the main focus of its most active members, Henri Donnedieu de Vabres and Vespasian V. Pella.[81] The IKV, meanwhile, never even touched on the question of international law. When at the inaugural meeting of the AIDP, Emil Rappaport famously declared, "La vielle Union internationale de Droit pénal est morte, Vive la nouvelle Association!" he was not ushering in a succession. He was heralding a sea change.[82]

But the AIDP was not a monolith. Its members represented different generations, traditions, and schools of criminology. The Italian positivists Enrico Ferri and Raffaele Garofalo, for instance, were considerably older and more conservative than the other members. Twenty-seven years old at the founding of the organization, Pella was both younger and more progressive in his politics than most other members. He repeatedly distanced himself from Italian positivism and drew from but never belonged to the French sociological school. He engaged with the members of the Third School, the penitentiary school, the unification school, and the neo-classical school of criminology. But if we insist on categorizing Pella's views, the closest fit is undoubtedly the "conciliatory" approach associated with his French mentors, René Garraud, Émile Garçon, Alfred Le Poittevin, and Jean-André Roux. Their influence is visible in Pella's work, in a surviving outline of his course on criminal law, and from a strange but particularly candid letter of recommendation written by Constantin Dissescu, a professor of law at the University of Bucharest, in which he declared that Pella "owed nothing, or close to nothing, to the Italian positivist school."[83] In other words, despite its clear break from the IKV, the AIDP still contained multitudes. Outside the association, the diversity of opinion was even greater.

To accommodate and attenuate this diversity of opinion, the founders of the AIDP created a separate sister organization in 1928 called the Bureau international pour l'unification du droit pénal. The Bureau was designed to function as a more inclusive, neutral, umbrella organization that would coordinate and assimilate the different associations working

---

[81] On Donnedieu de Vabres see Frédéric Mégret, Chapter 6.
[82] "Assemblée Générale Constitutive," *Revue Internationale de Droit Pénal* 1: 1 (1924), 3, 11. The point is underscored by the fact that the IKV was not actually dead, but continued to exist until 1937 as a purely German organization. On Rappaport see Patrycja Grzebyk, Chapter 4.
[83] The letter is in Sbârnă, *Vesapsian V. Pella*, at 233–260. The course outline in "Raspunsul Profesorului Vespasian V. Pella la adresa Rectoratului Nr. 174 din 15/1/1928," Mapa 20, Fondul Vespasian V. Pella.

in the area criminal law, such as the International Penal and Penitentiary Commission, the International Commission of Criminal Police, the Howard League for Penal Reform, the International Law Association, the AIDP and what remained of the IKV. In 1932 the Bureau became formally affiliated with the League of Nations.

Jurists pursued two objectives within the Bureau international pour l'unification du droit pénal and the AIDP. The first was compiling and comparing domestic criminal legislation in order to distill the best practices. This was particularly useful to the many states in East Central Europe that were revising their criminal codes. Unification also allowed a great deal of reform. Pella used this opportunity to promote due process, basic standards in the treatment for prisoners, and the abolition of the death penalty.[84] The second objective of these organizations was creating consensus within the profession on subjects as basic as the guarantees provided to the accused and as contentious as corporate criminal responsibility and universal jurisdiction.[85] It is in this domain that Pella made his greatest impact. In a matter of years, ideas that were once controversial became commonplace. Specifically, Pella was able to mobilize the AIDP in favor of projects for an international criminal court and an international criminal code that were almost identical to the ambitious "international criminal law of the future" he had proposed in 1925.[86] This consensus ensured that, whatever immediate political opposition they encountered, his ideas about international criminal justice would persist.

3.5 Pella's Projects

Toward the end of his life, Pella noted that, in the immediate aftermath of World War I, a perfect "psychological moment when far-reaching and

---

[84] Pella promoted abolition in the Inter-Parliamentary Union and the AIDP. He also celebrated the mid-nineteenth-century abolition of the death penalty in Romania. See Vespasian V. Pella, *Pedeapsa cu Moartea în legătură cu Proiectul Constituției* (Bucharest: Curierul Judiciar, 1923).

[85] On corporate criminal responsibility see for example, AIDP, *Deuxième Congrès International De Droit Pénal, Actes du Congrès* (Paris: Librairie des Juris-Clausseurs—Éditions Godde, 1930), 654–669. On universal jurisdiction see for example, AIDP, *Troisième Congrès International De Droit Pénal, Actes du Congrès* (Paris: Librairie des Juris-Clausseurs—Éditions Godde, 1935), 916–920.

[86] AIDP, *Projet de Statut d'une Cour de Justice Criminelle Internationale* (Paris: Librairie des Juris-Clausseurs—Éditions Godde, 1928); Vespasian V. Pella, "Plan d'un Code Repressif Mondial," *Revue Internationale de Droit Pénal* 12:1 (1935), 348–369.

rapid action could have been taken" was allowed to slip away.[87] By the mid-twenties the political support for reform had vanished. In 1926 and 1927, the League of Nations rebuffed calls, first, for a convention providing universal jurisdiction over acts of terrorism and later for a convention against piracy. In 1928, it refused to consider the AIDP's proposal for an international criminal court.[88] The following year, Pella finally achieved a small triumph within the League of Nations when he successfully steered into existence a convention against counterfeiting. The convention provided for international police and judicial cooperation, as well as measures to facilitate extradition. Creating domestic and international enforcement mechanisms for such initiatives, however, proved more difficult.

In 1931 Pella secured appointment as League of Nations rapporteur on penal administration. He then used this position to win a mandate for the unification and reform of domestic criminal law. The following year, the League of Nations formally recognized the Bureau international pour l'unification du droit pénal as its official clearinghouse on these subjects. The full extent of Pella's plans can be gleaned from a memorandum he produced for the 1932 World Disarmament Conference. He argued that states had a duty to incorporate international obligations as far as possible into domestic constitutional and criminal law. He examined numerous international agreements that recognized a duty to respect the territorial integrity and political independence of other states, and argued that to fulfill this obligation states had to curtail their power to declare war and to criminalize acts that seriously endangered respect for international treaties. Such acts included the circulation of false news and propaganda designed to incite a war, the preparation and execution of acts against the security of another state, and the provision of aid to armed groups perpetrating such acts.

The collapse of the conference in 1934 meant that these proposals were never adopted. If the conference had not collapsed, the proposal would have likely met with opposition from Britain, which had already blocked multiple attempts to reform domestic criminal law in the League's First Committee and the Committee of Experts on Progressive Codification of International Law. It was only after the assassination of King Aleksandar

---

[87] Vespasian V. Pella, "Memorandum Concerning the Establishment of an International Criminal Court" (July 17, 1951), A/AC/48/3, 3. See also Vespasian V. Pella "Toward an International Criminal Court," *American Journal of International Law* 44:1 (1950), 37–68.

[88] See Juan Antonio Buero to Carton de Wiart, Oct. 2, 1928, R/1983/3C/C7374/7374, League of Nations Archives, Geneva.

of Yugoslavia and French Foreign Minister Louis Barthou on October 9, 1934, that Pella was able to enjoy a momentary respite from British obstructionism.

Faced with calls for an international investigation into the support provided by Italy and Hungary to the assassins, British diplomats were forced to choose between admitting that the League of Nations was powerless before such problems, agreeing to an investigation that would undermine its policy of appeasement, or supporting an anti-terrorism convention designed to prevent such attacks in the future. British policymakers disliked this last option because they believed it would constrain them from fomenting civil war in other countries and it required that British law conform to international norms. In the event, it proved to be the least unpalatable of the three choices. The promise of an anti-terrorism convention allowed British diplomats to pressure Yugoslavia and its allies into dropping demands for a full and rigorous investigation. Once these demands were dropped, British officials quietly undermined the treaty negotiations, restrained from a more full-throated opposition only by the need to "save face."[89]

Working within these constraints Pella proposed a convention that punished attacks on public officials and private persons, as well as against public buildings, infrastructure, and means of communication. The treaty also targeted those who possessed arms, incited violence, or belonged to groups organized for the purpose of carrying out such attacks. States had an obligation to suppress terrorism, facilitate police and judicial cooperation, and assist in the extradition of suspects. They were also enjoined to prevent the falsification of passports. Prosecutions would take place in domestic courts but an international criminal court would be created for cases of self-referral. This international court would determine the relevant law, the sentence, and where it should be served. Pella argued that the convention would prevent impunity for crimes that violated universal conscience, injured the interests of all states, and resulted in the loss of thousands of lives.[90]

After three years of protracted negotiations, two conventions were signed in 1937, one providing for an international criminal court and

---

[89] See generally Michael D. Callahan, *The League of Nations, International Terrorism, and British Foreign Policy, 1934–1938* (New York: Palgrave Macmillan, 2018), esp. 150, 159–162, 211–213. Studies have focused on Britain's sovereigntist opposition rather than the motives and ideas of those who championed the convention.

[90] See League of Nations, Replies from Governments, Romania, Apr. 9, 1935, Committee for the International Repression of Terrorism.

74 ANDREI MAMOLEA

another providing for measures against terrorism. The two treaties did not markedly differ from what had initially been proposal. Much of what was added during the drafting process was later stripped away. The convention against terrorism included a definition for acts of terrorism and carefully listed the standards of criminal liability, the terms for extradition, and the extraterritorial effects of criminal convictions.

The two conventions were unquestionably the result of Pella's advocacy but they do not by themselves explain why preventing terrorism and mass violence was so important to Pella's political thought. For that insight we must turn to a set of earlier parliamentary speeches in which Pella linked the prevention of terrorism to preservation peace and, further still, to the defense of human rights.

3.6 Peace as the Safeguard of Human Rights

Pella did not pursue peace for the sake of peace, or security for the sake of security. These were merely the necessary conditions for vindicating the rights of humanity. It was these rights that Pella ultimately considered the highest good. His campaign against terrorism and war cannot be understood in isolation. They must be appreciated as part of a broader commitment to protecting individual rights from the tyranny and injustice of war, terror, and mass violence.

Pella never devoted a single comprehensive work to the subject of rights but his commitment is visible in most of his writings, speeches, and legislative projects, usually in the form of a reference to rights created by the French Revolution.[91] We find such references in an early parliamentary speech in which Pella rejected arguments in favor of a *numerus clausus*—an affirmative action policy that would have apportioned university seats to reflect the ethnic and religious makeup of society—on account that such a measure would have violated the principle of equal protection before the law found in domestic and international legislation.[92] For our purposes here, however, Pella's most interesting

[91] For the period after World War II see Vespasian V. Pella, "Droits de l'homme et genocide: considerations sur la situation présente," Mar. 24, 1949, E4001C#1000/784#8*, Swiss Federal Archives, Bern.

[92] *Dezbaterile Adunarii Nationale Constituante a Deputatilor*, Dec. 8, 1923, 240–241. On individual rights as the product of the French Revolution: Ibid. at 241. Pella rightly argued that the minority treaty only protected these types of rights. I will examine in a separate work the widespread misconception that it protected collective rights. For now, suffice it to say, that the treaty states successfully lobbied for the exclusion of collective rights and that the head of the Minorities Section, Erik Colban, even went so far as to monitor the

examination of rights occurred in a speech delivered before the Romanian parliament in 1924 in which he examined the relationship between revolutionary communism and terrorism.

In 1920, Soviet-backed terrorists assassinated the Romanian Minister of Justice and, in a separate attack, bombed the Romanian Senate. Later, in 1924, after the collapse of negotiations between the USSR and Romania, Soviet-sponsored armed groups crossed into Romania, attacked the police station at Tatar Bunar, in southern Basarabia, and unsuccessfully attempted to incite an uprising against the government in preparation for the Soviet annexation of the province.[93] These events must have been on the minds of parliamentarians when Pella introduced legislation barring Romanian individuals and organizations from collaborating with foreign groups to prepare a communist revolution. The focus of Pella's speech, however, was the role of violence and atrocity more generally.[94]

Pella argued that terrorism was integral to revolutionary communism and a threat to society's most fundamental values.[95] These values included respect for life, human liberty, order, and social harmony. Pella explicitly identified society, not the state, as the victim of terrorism and his argument was cast, overwhelmingly, in the idiom of human rights. International society mattered as well, but Pella used only a fraction of his speech to address international questions, such as when he noted that, in attacking the peace settlement and the League of Nations, revolutionary communism was "the most serious threat to public international order."[96] That revolutionary communism spread through terrorism and the incitement to violence was perhaps too

work of his subordinates to ensure against the careless use of language that might imply anything other than individual rights. The assumption among certain scholars that minority nationalists should have been granted international representation betrays a tendency to write history exclusively from their vantage as well as a failure to acknowledge the harms caused within the Ottoman Empire and the successor states by the imperialist form of minority protection in place before 1919.

[93] Ludmila Rotari, *Mişcarea subversivă din Basarabia în anii 1918–1924* (Bucharest: Editura Enciclopedică, 2004), 233–278.

[94] *Dezbaterile Adunarii Nationale Constituante a Deputatilor*, Dec. 16, 1924, 1075.

[95] Pella invoked the writings of Lev Kamenev, Yuri Steklov, Vatslav Vorovsky, Grigory Zinoviev, Leonid Krassin, Leon Trotsky, Vladimir Lenin, Nikolai Bukharin, and Clara Zetkin as evidence. See Ibid. at 1106. He also relied heavily on both Karl Krautsky's *Communism and Terrorism* and Trotsky's reply bearing the same title. Pella argued that Bolshevism was the result of a mix of "Sorelian anarchism" and "Marxist doctrine." He once again denounced Sorel's "cult of violence." Ibid.

[96] Ibid. at 1107.

obvious to require further elaboration. Pella focused overwhelmingly, instead, on its internal effects.

Pella argued that "justice was a farce" under revolutionary communism. Victims were stripped of their rights. Judicial autonomy was subordinated to political power. And restraints on judicial abuse were entirely absent. Pella, who campaigned for the international abolition of the death penalty, lamented the execution of over a quarter of a million people in the Soviet Union and carefully documented the atrocities and human rights violations perpetrated by the country's criminal justice system.[97] Pella was particularly interested in the Soviet Union's "militarized system of forced labor" which, he argued, constituted "the most serious harm to individual freedom." It represented a reactionary return to slavery, serfdom, and feudal corporatism.[98] He invited the members of parliament to compare the superior principles and individual rights inscribed in the 1789 Declaration of the Rights of Man with the terrorist dogmas of the Soviet Union. Revolutionary communists had violated "the natural and unalienable rights of man" and the principle of "equality of all citizens, regardless of class." They had brutally suppressed "the freedom of conscience" and "the freedom of the press."

Returning to the immediate objective of the legislation, which was to prevent violent foreign intervention, Pella observed that revolutionary communists relied on terrorism to establish communist regimes in foreign states.[99] If the economic and social conditions for a communist revolution existed in Romania, one would have spontaneously taken place without the intervention of foreign elements. Yet these conditions did not exist. Pella pointed to the agrarian reform as one of the many reasons the country had rejected communism.[100]

In arguing against communist terrorism, Pella drew extensively on the writings of the Austrian socialist Karl Kautsky. Against revolutionary communism, more generally, he invoked the positions taken by socialist and labor politicians such as Emile Vandervelde, Albert Thomas, Ramsay Macdonald, Filippo Turati, and Philipp Scheidemann.[101] Having throttled democracy and disregarded the liberty and equality of other nations, revolutionary communism had removed itself from the ranks of

[97] Ibid. at 1108.

[98] Ibid. at 1109. In contrast, Pella chose not to elaborate on the Soviet Union's actions against property rights. His hierarchy of values is unmistakable.

[99] Ibid. at 1110.

[100] Ibid.

[101] Ibid. at 1110–1111.

the socialist movement. That was why, according to Pella, the proposed legislation specifically targeted revolutionary communism. Provided they used legal means, socialists were free to campaign to transform society, achieve a more just distribution of wealth, and even socialize the means of production.[102] The law, Pella insisted, was designed to prevent assistance to a communist revolution.

Pella was equally concerned by the threat to democracy posed by fascism. As early as 1923, he denounced the emergence of fascist movements in Romania and worked to pass legislation against incitement and hate speech.[103] This legislation was later used to shut down far-right newspapers, including in the wake of the assassination of Prime Minister Ion Duca.[104] In short, the threat posed by mass violence to individual rights, solidarity, and equal justice before the law was central to Pella's legal thought. That is why he later argued that "the international protection of the fundamental rights of man and the protection of international peace are one and indivisible." For Pella criminal law was an "instrument for the protection of human liberty."[105] If this aspect of Pella's thought has been overlooked by scholars, it is in no small part the result of the deeply mistaken notion, especially widespread during the past thirty years among English-language historians, that the peace settlement Pella struggled to defend was without higher principles or values.

3.7 The Collapse of Collective Security

Pella was able to separate his criticism of revolutionary communism from his diplomatic approach to the Soviet Union. When, for a very brief moment during the early 1930s, the USSR appeared to reconcile itself to the existing order and abandon its imperialist designs against its neighbors, Pella and his closest political mentor, the liberal Romanian Foreign Minister, Nicolae Titulescu, rushed to embrace the country as a natural

---

[102] Ibid. at 1111.

[103] *Dezbaterile Adunarii Nationale Constituante a Deputatilor*, Dec. 8, 1923, 238. Vespasian V. Pella, *Legea Presei* (Bucharest: Independenţa, 1927). Much more research remains to be done on this subject.

[104] See for example, Nicolae Iorga, *Memorii* Vol. 7, Jan. 11, 1934 (Bucharest, 1939), 131. The legislation was enforced by an Army Major also named Pella. I have not yet been able to work out the identity of this individual or his relationship to Vespasian. Major Pella was part of the Romanian delegation at meetings of the AIDP and the surname is uncommon.

[105] *Proceedings of the American Society of International Law* 43 (1949), 73. Pella, "Droits de l'homme," 6.

ANDREI MAMOLEA

ally. Romania and the USSR even signed a nonaggression treaty in 1933. Yet despite briefly joining the small states of East-Central Europe in calling for a prohibition on wars of aggression, the Soviet Union was never willing to recognize and guarantee the eastern borders of Poland and Romania, the necessary precondition for integrating itself into the collective security system comprised of France and its eastern allies.

Unwilling to abandon its territorial ambitions, the Soviet Union slowly receded from the international sphere in which it had been so eagerly welcomed. In the legal and diplomatic world, this shift was marked by Maxim Litvinov's fall from grace and the simultaneous rise of Aron Trainin, a jurist whose work embodied the belligerence, parochialism, and paranoia with which the Soviet Union of this period is more commonly associated.[106] Trainin later claimed that the object of Pella's international conferences was "to organize a peculiar kind of united criminal front against the Soviet Union," overlooking that the USSR had participated in these meetings as late as 1935.[107] As part of this drift into isolation, Stalin infamously turned on his military officers and diplomats, beginning first and foremost with those who had worked to improve relations with France and its eastern allies.

The support of Britain, the United States, or the Soviet Union would have been sufficient to preserve the system of collective security and meet the challenge posed by Nazi Germany. Denied the support of all three, the system collapsed. Each one of these three great powers signed the death warrant of the international order Pella and other champions of international law from the small states of Europe had done so much to protect. Deprived of the necessary security guarantees, small states like Romania gradually drifted into isolation and neutrality. In such circumstances, Germany quickly reestablished its traditional economic domination over

---

[106] Trainin rose to prominence during this period with the help of his supervisor, Andrey Vyshinsky, the legal architect of the Moscow Trials and the Great Terror. On Trainin see Gleb Bogush, Chapter 10 and Michelle Penn, "The Extermination of Peaceful Soviet Citizens: Aron Trainin and International Law" (PhD diss., University of Colorado, 2017).

[107] Aron Trainin, *Hitlerite Responsibility under Criminal Law*, ed. Andrew Rothstein (London: Hutchinson, 1945), 11. Trainin was obsessed with Pella. See Aron Trainin, *Ugolovnaia Interventsiia: Dvizhenie po Unifikatsii Ugolovnogo Zakonodatel'stva Kapitalisticheskikh Stran* (Moscow: Gos. izd-vo Sovetskoe zakonodatel'stvo, 1935) and *Zashchita mira i ugolovnyi zakon* (Moscow: Juridiceskoe Izdatel'stvo NKju Sojuza SSSR, 1937). Pella responded to the 1945 claim in *La guerre-crime et les criminels de guerre: réflexions sur la justice pénale internationale ce qu'elle est et ce qu'elle devrait être* (Paris: Pedone, 1946), 119–120.

East Central Europe. It then used its economic lever to interfere in domestic politics, bringing into government reactionary factions that lacked popular support.[108]

In the face of growing collaboration with Germany, Vespasian Pella continued to serve the Romanian government. He represented the country at the League of Nations until 1938 and served as Minister to Holland from 1936 to 1939. Considering that the protests of far more prominent diplomats, such as Nicolae Titulescu, were unable to stem the domestic and foreign policy realignment, it is unlikely that Pella's resignation would have had any effect on policy.[109] For his part, Pella continued to use his diplomatic position to defend the same ideals as before. Despite the country's gradual drift into neutrality, the telegrams from The Hague demonstrate his continuing support for sovereign equality and opposition to aggression in Manchuria and Ethiopia and the annexation of Austria and the Sudetenland.[110] During this period, Pella also reported on Germany's growing belligerence and the Gestapo's links to separatist groups in Eastern Europe, such as Andriy Melnyk's Organization of Ukrainian Nationalists.[111] He continued to oppose wars of aggression and the use of armed groups to incite war.

In September 1939, Pella was recalled from his post as Minister to Holland and appointed as Romania's representative to the European Commission for the Danube. Unhappy with the decision, Pella tried to reverse it.[112] Thereafter, with the outbreak of war Pella buried himself in questions of peace. What should the postwar order look like and what values should be preserved? For Pella, the answer remained unchanged. In a wide-ranging policy memorandum, he considered how the principles of collective security, the equality of states, and the guarantee of territorial integrity could be achieved. He also continued to champion the peaceful settlement of disputes, the creation of an international peace-keeping force, and arms reduction. International criminal justice,

---

[108] For instance, after the 1937 elections, the National Christian Party was placed in power despite earning less than ten percent of the vote.

[109] The nature of the question also reveals a telling double standard. Scholars seldom stop to examine the complicity of US and British jurists in undermining the international order and creating the conditions that allowed Germany to launch an aggressive war.

[110] Pella to Foreign Ministry, May 7, Aug. 27, 1936, Mar. 27, 1937, Mar. 17, July 26, Oct. 13, 1938 all in Fond 71, Olanda, 1936–1940, Vol. 2, Arhiva Ministerului Afacerilor Externe. I am grateful to the archivists for their generous help.

[111] On the OUN see Pella to Foreign Ministry, Dec. 8, 1938, Mapa 1, Fondul Vespasian V. Pella.

[112] Pella to Gafencu, Sept. 20, 1939, Fond 71, Olanda, 1936–1940, Vol. 4, AMAE.

meanwhile, continued to play an important role. The tribunal provided for by the 1937 convention against terrorism and the Permanent Court of International Justice remained obvious venues for this kind of international criminal justice.[113] Pella also continued to advocate the creation of a European federation, a project he had supported through his work at various Balkan conferences and in a number of articles on the proposals made in 1930 by the former French Foreign Minister Aristide Briand.

Pella's first major appointment during the war was to the European Commission for the Danube, where he sparred with German and Italian delegates and obstructed their attempts to dismantle the commission. This policy won him praise from liberals such as Grigore Gafencu, an exiled former Foreign Minister of Romania who resided in Switzerland.[114] Switzerland emerged during this period as a hub of activity for official and unofficial diplomats who wanted to negotiate Romania's exit from the war. The Romanian Foreign Ministry encouraged these contacts but always kept them secret from Germany. In the summer of 1943, Germany discovered that the Romanian Minister to Switzerland was in contact with intermediaries. Romania was forced to replace him. Pella was a natural choice given his outstanding reputation and extensive contacts in the country, including with Gafencu.[115] His brief tenure as Minister to Switzerland was characterized by improving contacts with the Allies. Pella also assisted Jewish refugees, protested against the deportations of Jews from Hungarian-occupied northern Transylvania, and called for the repeal of anti-Semitic legislation.[116]

Pella emerged from the war unsullied, so much so that Gafencu predicted as early as September 18, 1944 that the new government would use him as the "honorable face" with which to defend Romania's interests after the war.[117] The prediction proved correct. In 1946,

[113] Vespasian V. Pella, "Comisiunea de Studii a Ministerului Afacerilor Straine," Mar. 15, 1940, at 15, Fond 71, Romania, 1940, Vol. 8, AMAE.

[114] The activity is documented in Grigore Gafencu, *Jurnal*, Vol. 2 (Bucharest: Pro-Historia, 2007), 201–206.

[115] On Pella's meetings with Gafencu prior to his appointment see Gafencu, *Jurnal*, 70, 89–90.

[116] Eugen Filotti to Foreign Ministry, Jan. 15, 1944; Gheorghe Davidescu to Foreign Ministry, June 3, 7, 1944 in Fond 71 Elveția Vol. 13, AMAE; Vespasian V. Pella to Foreign Ministry, Aug. 7, 22, and Sept. 21, 1944, Fond 71 Elveția Vol. 14, AMAE.

[117] Claudia Chinezu, *Provocarea Europei: Exilul Elvețian a lui Grigore Gafencu, 1941–1957* (Bucharest: Pro-Historia, 2004), 263. I have carefully examined the archives of the Romanian Foreign Ministry, the published minutes of the Council of Ministers, and the published transcripts from the trials of Ion and Mihai Antonescu and have found no evidence to suggest that Pella ever betrayed the ideals he promoted as a jurist.

Romania's pro-Soviet government sent Pella to the Paris Peace Conference, alongside his old friend and high school classmate Mihai Ralea. Shortly after the conference, Ralea was appointed minister to Washington and it was with his help that Pella got transferred to the United States to act as an observer at the United Nations. Subsequent telegrams from Washington provide no information about Pella's activities, confirming reports from other observers that he acted in a purely private capacity during the drafting of the Genocide Convention.[118] In May 1948, he was recalled by the Romanian government. With Ralea's help and letters from his doctor, Pella deferred his return for several months until November 1948, when he was fired by the government. It is unclear why he was recalled and dismissed. At some point, Pella was also stripped of his nationality and rendered stateless. He never returned to Romania.[119]

There is no evidence to suggest that Pella's activity in the United States was monitored by Romania's embassy. With a single exception, Pella's name disappeared from its telegrams. The one exception was a report from April 1949 noting that Adolfo Costa du Rels, a Bolivian delegate at the United Nations, delivered an address condemning the human rights abuses in Romania, including the suppression of the press, attacks on religious freedom, and the mistreatment of Iuliu Maniu, the jailed leader of the National Peasant Party. The telegram ended by observing that Pella was in attendance, "probably monitoring the presentation of material supplied by the resistance."[120]

3.8 Postwar Years

It was only in 1947 that Pella's reputation first came under assault. The source was Raphael Lemkin, a Jewish Polish jurist who Pella had

---

[118] See also Ion Calafeteanu, *Scrisori către tovarăşa Ana* (Bucharest: Univers Enciclopedic, 2005), 302, reporting that Pella was not working, nor providing useful information.

[119] It is unclear when Pella was made stateless. He referred to this situation in his correspondence with European jurists and listed being stateless on a copy of his curriculum vitae from around late 1951. Earlier, Pella identified statelessness as a major human rights problem and declared that "the right to a nationality was fundamental to human existence." See Mapa 20, Fondul Vespasian V. Pella and Pella, "Droits de l'homme," 6.

[120] Washington, Vlad Mărdărescu to Foreign Ministry, Apr. 20, 1949. In 1952, Romania's secret police opened a file on Pella that described him as a traitor who had sought asylum in Switzerland in 1946. The document is replete with similar allegations, most of which can be easily refuted with documents from the archives of the Ministry of Foreign Affairs. See Vespasian V. Pella's file, Consiliul Naţional pentru Studierea Arhivelor Securităţii.

82   ANDREI MAMOLEA

mentored before the war and who is known today for having coined the word genocide during World War II.[121] The idea of genocide drew heavily on Pella's arguments for a universally punishable crime of barbarism. Before the war, Lemkin fully acknowledged his debt to Pella.[122] After the war, Lemkin claimed sole authorship for the idea of a crime of barbarism and actively derided the work of his former colleagues in order to exaggerate the novelty and importance of his own contributions.[123] This campaign had two dimensions, one that was sanitized and public and another that was mostly private and defamatory. We will examine these in turn.

In his public media campaign, Lemkin mischaracterized the international criminal law movement as stuffy, apolitical, and indifferent to human suffering. Against this grotesquely inaccurate image, Lemkin presented himself as a tireless maverick pursuing "one of the longest and most dramatic one-man crusades in history."[124] Lemkin claimed that before the war, "international lawyers were politely bored," with his proposals. "The old arguments arose about interfering with somebody else's business."[125] Even after the war, he complained that delegates at one conference "told him he was trying to push international law into a field where it didn't belong."[126] The same contrived narrative was recycled for the Paris Peace Conference: "heartsick and weary, Lemkin hurried from delegate to delegate. The story was always the same: Everybody was against genocide, but—."[127]

Lemkin's self-serving claims have been uncritically recycled in numerous works. They have also deeply shaped how Western scholars approach and understand Pella and the movement that he led. Over the course of

---

[121] On Lemkin see Vesselin Popovski, Chapter 11.

[122] The notion of a crime of barbarism perpetrated against a population was already in circulation before Lemkin submitted his report on the subject to the Bureau's 1933 conference in Madrid.

[123] Raphael Lemkin, *Totally Unofficial: The Autobiography of Raphael Lemkin* (New Haven: Yale University Press, 2013), 23 ("the time was ripe for me to put before the conference *my* idea . . . I formulated two crimes: the crime of barbarity and the crime of vandalism") (emphasis added). The autobiography is notoriously unreliable on questions of fact.

[124] Herbert Yahraes, "He Gave a Name to the World's Most Horrible Crime," *Collier's* (Mar. 3, 1951), 28.

[125] Yahraes, "He Gave a Name," 29. Lemkin claimed to have predicted the Holocaust in 1933 and accused "the world" of "behaving as if it was ready to acquiesce in [Hitler's] plans." Lemkin, *Totally Unofficial*, 22.

[126] Yahraes, "He Gave a Name," 56.

[127] Ibid. Pella campaigned for the creation of an international tribunal with universal jurisdiction for the crime of genocide. Pella, "Droits de l'homme," 16–17.

this chapter we have discovered that Pella's approach to international criminal law was deeply normative, politically engaged, and informed by a commitment to human rights as well as republican, liberal, and socialist values. Little of this can be found in the relevant English and German-language scholarship. Instead, the image of Pella that scholars present is almost identical to the one conjured by Lemkin sixty years earlier. It is with this in mind that we turn to the campaign of calumny launched by Lemkin against Pella in 1947.

3.9   The Misrepresentation of Vespasian V. Pella

The events that triggered this campaign were innocent enough. In May 1946, Pella won the support of key delegates at Nuremberg in favor of "a general codification of offenses against the peace and security of mankind." The following summer, in 1947, he was invited by Henri Donnedieu de Vabres to participate in a separate project devoted to drafting a convention against genocide that he and Lemkin were already working on at the United Nations. Pella and Donnedieu de Vabres suggested that the genocide convention should be expanded to include enforcement mechanisms, including an international criminal court, and that genocide should be studied alongside the Nuremberg principles. From the outset, Lemkin was hostile to his former colleagues and their proposals. Two months later, he was already disseminating vicious conspiracy theories about them.

William Jackson, the son of Robert H. Jackson, reported to his father Lemkin's "personal vendetta" against Donnedieu de Vabres. Lemkin characterized the French jurist as "a reactionary, German-minded theorist, a sort of intellectual sympathizer with the Nazis." He claimed that Donnedieu de Vabres was "only a narrow-gauge professor" who had secured his appointment on the Nuremberg tribunal through personal connections. "This is rather invidious stuff," Jackson remarked. Lemkin characterized Pella as "a shrewd, ambitious opportunist" who was now in the service of a vast communist conspiracy that was determined to stop the convention against genocide and replace it with a convention against aggression. Lemkin claimed that Pella had Donnedieu de Vabres "around his little finger" and "hitched unwittingly to the Communist wagon." This stream of falsehoods continued for many months. In June 1948, one observer wrote of

84   ANDREI MAMOLEA

Lemkin's "intense hatred" of Pella and Donnedieu de Vabres, adding that it was motivated primarily by jealousy.[128]

In April 1948, the campaign reached a new level when Lemkin was able to get Drew Pearson, one of the most widely syndicated columnists in the United States, to publish a sensationalist column. In prose dripping with orientalism, Pella was described as a "mysterious" "Rumanian wire-puller" who kept "two footmen" in his service and had arrived to the United States "on the Queen Elizabeth with his own car and chauffeur." Visitors to his home were "never without champagne and shashlik." But behind this opulence lurked a dark past. Pella had served as Minister to Switzerland for the fascist government which had slaughtered Jews and "sent many of their bodies to the I.G. Farben Soap Factories." The column added that despite being "close to Anna Pauker, Red boss of Rumania," Pella was "consulted by State Department officials" and had "engineered" a "sudden U.S. shift of policy regarding genocide." "If Congress investigated," the column added in a final McCarthyite note, "it might find some interesting backstage factors behind the operations of Rumania's Dr. Vespasian Pella."[129] When the column appeared Pella immediately asked the State Department to issue a statement refuting these falsehoods. He also provided evidence demonstrating that he was sent to Switzerland to prepare for Romania's exit from the war and that he had saved Jewish lives. As for the genocide convention, not only was he not responsible for the course of US policy, but he consistently supported a broad definition of genocide that included acts committed both by state and by non-state actors.[130]

The adoption of the Genocide Convention later that year produced no respite in Lemkin's attacks on Pella. In late 1949, Lemkin continued to place Pella at "the center" of a conspiracy that stretched from the

[128] See, respectively, "Supplementary Report," June 19, 1947, William Jackson to Robert H. Jackson, Aug. 11, 1947, and John Maktos, "Confidential Report," June 24, 1948, all in *Documents on the Genocide Convention from the American, British, and Russian Archives*, ed. Anton Weiss-Wendt (New York: Bloomsbury Academic, 2018), 53–54, 219–221, and 138, 144. See also Memorandum of Conversation, John Matkos and Raphael Lemkin, July 16, 1948, Box 2186 File 501.BD/Genocide 1945–49, RG 59, National Archives, College Park.

[129] Drew Pearson, "The Washington Merry-Go-Round," Apr. 20, 1948, Special Collections, American University Digital Research Archive. Pearson repeated these accusations on Oct. 22, 1949.

[130] For Pella's detailed response see Memorandum of Conversation: Vespasian Pella and John Maktos, Apr. 21, 1948, Box 2186 File 501.BD/Genocide 1945–49, RG 59, National Archives.

3 VESPASIAN V. PELLA

conservative American Bar Association to the liberal International League for the Rights of Man.[131] The targets of Lemkin's attacks grew to include the Czechoslovakian jurist Ivan S. Kerno and the exiled Spanish Republican Minister of Foreign Affairs Julio Álvarez del Vayo.[132] Even his allies in the World Jewish Congress (WJC) began to consider some of Lemkin's allegations "so remote from reality as to be startling."[133]

Pella first confronted Lemkin in a long conversation in January 1950. When the attacks continued, Pella sent a lengthy "cease and desist" that carefully refuted Lemkin's allegations.[134] The aim of the letter, he wrote, was "to end, once and for all, the misunderstandings that exist between us and to make you understand that I intend to use in the future all means provided by the laws and customs of this noble country ... to put an end to the profoundly unjust campaign that has targeted me for some time." Pella began by reminding Lemkin of his years of mentorship and the cordial relations the two had previously enjoyed. He had always recognized Lemkin's "paternity" over the expression "genocide" and had helped showcase his ideas at the 1947 meeting of the Bureau international pour l'unification du droit pénal in Brussels. Pella had helped draft the Genocide Convention and afterwards campaigned for its ratification, through the work of the AIDP as well as at the annual meeting of the American Society of International Law. Pella provided detailed references for each of these actions.

He then moved to Pearson's column. There was no shadow of doubt regarding the source, Pella noted, before proceeding to carefully dismantle its arguments. He mentioned again that his appointment as Minister

---

[131] Raphael Lemkin to Edward A. Conway, Dec. 19, 1949, Box 2, Raphael Lemkin Papers, American Jewish Historical Society. Lemkin continued to distribute copies of Pearson's column. A letter sent by Eugene Rostow to Drew Pearson on June 15, 1949 claimed that Pella remained "active among legal groups" that were "smothering genocide with human rights." Eugene Rostow to Drew Pearson, June 15, 1949, Box 2, Raphael Lemkin Papers, AJHS. Later that year Pearson published a third piece on Pella for a journal edited by Conway. Rostow later became a founder of the neoconservative Committee on Present Danger and a notorious nuclear holocaust apologist.

[132] Memorandum of Conversation, Raphael Lemkin and Dean Acheson, Jan. 29, 1952, Box 1342 340.I/AJ Genocide 1952–54, RG 59. For an additional attack on Pella see Paul Ginsberg to James E. Webb, Nov. 13, 1951, Box 1341, 340.I/AJ Genocide 1950–51, RG 59.

[133] Maurice Perlzweig to David Petegorsky, Apr. 18, 1951, World Jewish Congress Collection, Box B7, American Jewish Archives. I thank the archivists at the AJA for their assistance.

[134] Vespasian V. Pella to Raphael Lemkin, Nov. 2, 1950, Box 2, Raphael Lemkin Papers, AJA.

to Switzerland was designed to facilitate Romania's exit from the war. During this period he served the cause of the Allies and saved numerous Jewish lives and had the documents to prove it. The claims about his links to a communist conspiracy were equally untrue. "You knew very well that after what happened in Romania in 1948 I have not had any relationship with the regime of that country, and that I have been entirely associated with the fight against that regime," Pella wrote, reprising a point he had made during the long conversation in January. That summer Lemkin had asked Pella to lobby certain European governments for the ratification of the Genocide Convention, which he did, saving copies of all the correspondence. Pella had also recognized the autonomy of the Genocide Convention in his Memorandum to the United Nations on a Code of Offenses against the Peace and Security of Mankind.

Despite these steps, Pella continued to be the target of rumors claiming that he opposed the ratification of the Genocide Convention. Pella intended to prove by every means of publicity what he had already written: that genocide can be committed, not only by a state, but also by individuals; that he had no desire to co-opt the crime of genocide and would not include it in the project on crimes against the peace and security of mankind; that the jurisdiction of the Genocide Convention should be maintained; that the reservations made to the Genocide Convention by the Soviet Union and its satellites were harmful and should not be followed. Pella concluded with the same point he had started. He hoped the letter would make the misunderstanding disappear. In any case, Pella intended to use all of the documents in his possession to ensure the triumph of truth and to obtain satisfaction and reparation.

When Pella passed away on August 24, 1952, the attacks had not ceased. Sixty years later, the campaign against him continues, this time at the hands of scholars who uncritically recycle Lemkin's self-serving narrative. One recent article attempts to dignify his conspiracy theories and attacks on former colleagues by recasting them as part of a mere "rivalry" regarding the appropriate norms and the best means with which to implement them.[135] Lemkin is said to have "anticipated" the growing importance of lobbying governments and mobilizing public opinion in ways that the "legalists" did not.[136] Even if this statement were true, it would still not explain Lemkin's campaign against Pella. We know that it

---

[135] Mira L. Siegelberg, "Unofficial Men, Efficient Civil Servants: Raphael Lemkin in the History of International Law," *Journal of Genocide Research* 15:3 (2013), 297–316.
[136] Ibid. at 300, 306, 312.

3 VESPASIAN V. PELLA 87

is false because engaging governments and the public was central to the AIDP's work. This is why Lemkin turned to Pella when he needed help promoting the ratification of the Genocide Convention in Europe. In short, scholars must avoid taking Lemkin's rhetorical cudgels at face value. His claims to methodological novelty do not stand up to scrutiny nor do they account for his malicious attacks. An alternative explanation, suggested but never fully developed in the course of the article, is that Lemkin hated Pella and Donnedieu de Vabres for opposing collective rights.[137] The problem with this hypothesis is that almost every statesman and jurist at the time shared the same exact position. The explanation is insufficient. Perhaps instead of straining to read a deeper meaning in Lemkin's horrible behavior, scholars should pause to consider the harms he perpetrated against his victims. We should also contemplate the readiness of contemporary scholars to pile on.

The most sustained attack has come from a deeply orientalist history of international criminal justice that not only reproduces Lemkin's narrative but also casts Pella as the archetypal Balkan "other."[138] Mark Lewis strains to portray the Romanian jurist as the leader of a movement committed to preserving "conservative order," "state security," and "the existing political and social order."[139] Nothing is said about Pella's writings on the social responsibility of government, his promotion of international economic solidarity, or support for social justice and agrarian reform. Instead, the book focuses narrowly on his criticism of trade unions and twice repeats the inaccurate claim that Pella considered them to be "just as dangerous" as the mafia.[140] Pella's social thought deserves a more careful and more generous approach.

In the area of foreign policy, Pella is reduced to a caricature of a Balkan nationalist with no higher commitment than the preservation of the territorial status quo.[141] "International order" is reduced to meaning

---

[137] Ibid. at 302. Siegelberg claims "Pella and Lemkin clashed outright over the question of genocide" at the 1949 American Society of International Law conference but there is no evidence of a clash in the *Proceedings*, the only source cited in the relevant endnote. Ibid. at 308.

[138] See Mark A. Lewis, *The Birth of the New Justice: The Internationalization of Crime and Punishment, 1919–1950* (Oxford: Oxford University Press, 2014). This work contains dozens of errors about Vespasian Pella, some big, some small. I have tried to correct them whenever possible throughout this chapter.

[139] Lewis, *The Birth of the New Justice*, at 78n, 105, 132.

[140] Ibid. at 105, 123.

[141] Lewis also incorrectly claims that Pella was a primordialist. Ibid. at 104. In fact, Pella clearly believed that nations were constructed in an endless process of formation and

88   ANDREI MAMOLEA

the "post-Versailles borders."[142] Pella's engagement with counterfeiting and terrorism, meanwhile, is portrayed as a result of immediate national interests supposedly unrelated to the more important issues he had initially set forth in his work.[143] In fact, we know that Pella identified both counterfeiting and terrorism as significant threats to the international order as early as 1919. He also repeatedly emphasized the danger that terrorism posed to the rights of private individuals. Despite this, Lewis claims that the convention against terrorism was designed only to "protect state officials" and to "serve" and "strengthen states."[144] He also insinuates that this same convention was designed to facilitate the repression of minorities and political opponents.[145] Its proponents, meanwhile, are uniformly cast as supporters of "strong statism."

What part of the convention has prompted such a harsh assessment? Evidently, the source of this invective is the convention's prohibition on the incitement to violence and support for the extradition of political criminals, positions that Pella held since the early twenties and which are in no sense obviously illiberal. Most liberal systems of justice contain a "carve out" for incitement to violence and allow for the extradition of political criminals according to a carefully tailored policy of nonrefoulement. The real work behind the insinuations is done not by the by the contents of the convention against terrorism but by Lewis' characterization of its supporters and opponents. Much emphasis is placed on the opposition of "liberal Britain," with no mention made of its sovereigntist opposition to international criminal justice throughout this period.[146] The illiberalism of the convention's Eastern European backers, meanwhile, is taken for granted. When confronted with evidence that states

---

reformation driven by changes in social organization. Pella, *Cercetări asupra Sentimentului*, 8, 13, 18. He noted that cultural traditions and practices, including racism and militarism, were sometimes passed from one generation to the next but he never claimed this process was rooted in race. Pella, *La Criminalité Collective*, 36–37, 47–49. Pella's legal projects were premised on the notion that institutions shaped culture.

[142] Lewis, *The Birth of the New Justice*, 122.

[143] Ibid. at 117. See also Mark A. Lewis, "The History of the International Association of Penal Law, 1924–1950: Liberal, Conservative, or Neither?" *Historical Origins of International Criminal Law* Vol. 4 (Brussels: Torkel Opsahl, 2015), 599, 629 ("The AIDP's involvement in these problems was a reaction to revisionism in Europe").

[144] Lewis, *The Birth of the New Justice*, at 123–124.

[145] Ibid. at 143. Lewis also criticizes the jurists for failing to implement "checks on nationalism, remedies for economic disparities, or concrete methods of changing political culture." Ibid. at 144. He has unrealistic expectations regarding the power and influence of Pella and his colleagues.

[146] Ibid. at 124.

"generally viewed as liberal," such as France, Belgium, and the Netherlands, also supported the treaty, Lewis does not reconsider his characterization of the convention. Instead he searches for hidden motives.[147]

The work constantly reads illiberal motives into the actions of east European jurists and diplomats and liberal motives in actions their western counterparts. If Pella had embraced political violence, he would undoubtedly have been labeled illiberal. The fact that he rejected political violence, however, is used to establish the exact same conclusion.[148] Whatever the facts, the judgment remains the same. Pella is made to fit the Procrustean bed that renders him according to the prevailing orientalist preconception.[149]

To make up for the lack of evidence, Lewis draws vast inferences from scraps of information about Pella's inactions. Consider, for instance, the case of Germany's membership in the Bureau international pour l'unification du droit pénal. The failure to expel Germany from the organization after Kristallnacht is said to reflect "a complete lack of judgment on the part of the AIDP jurists involved in the Bureau" as well as their "conservative, pro-state security ideology."[150] These inferences are unwarranted. We know nothing about the procedures under which Germany could be expelled or the obstacles to such a decision. The lack of action is nonetheless exploited to draw all sorts of uncharitable conclusions about Pella and his colleagues. The argument shifts from innuendo to outright mischaracterization, however, Lewis claims that Pella "increased contacts" with "the Nazi legal bureaucracy" and made "overtures to Nazi jurists."[151] In fact, it was the German jurists who wrote to Pella in order to join the Bureau international pour l'unification du droit pénal.[152] Lewis also

---

[147] Ibid. at 146.

[148] Ibid. at 84.

[149] Jewish émigrés from Eastern Europe have been largely exempted from this phenomenon, their identities and narratives seamlessly assimilated into the prevailing Western orientalist gaze.

[150] Lewis, "The History," 640.

[151] Ibid. at 637, 639.

[152] See the correspondence from Leopold Schäfer in Mapa 7, Fondul Vespasian V. Pella. See also Emile Giraud, "Compte Rendu: Reunion du Bureau Inernational pour L'Unification du Droit Penal à Paris les 27 et 28 Decembre 1938," in R/3754/3A/5218/36272 League of Nations Archive, Geneva. Lewis makes much of the fact that, three years earlier, at the 1935 annual meeting of the International Penal and Penitentiary Commission in Berlin, Pella suggested to German jurists that they join the organization. That is the sum total of what Lewis labels as "overtures" and "contacts" and what may have amounted to nothing more than a brief chat.

misleadingly argues that that the AIDP "had not drawn from the lessons of the Armenian massacres" when in fact this event is mentioned on the first page of its 1928 report for an international criminal tribunal.[153]

These baseless insinuations are used to construct a moral hierarchy that places Lemkin above Pella and the WJC above the AIDP. Recycling Lemkin's narrative, the book portrays Jewish jurists and Jewish organizations as more democratic, more moral, and, especially, more "victim-centered" in their approach.[154] Such an approach, according to Lewis, included the supposedly novel idea of using international criminal prosecution "to replace a domestic legal system that had failed,"[155] a solution that Pella had advocated since 1919. Other supposedly unprecedented elements of "victim-centered" justice, such as the creation a "historical record," and demands for "restitution" also have a distinctly post–World War I vintage. Indeed, the work of the WJC resembled nothing so much as the claims for international justice made by various Balkan activists in the wake of that war . In his brief survey of those earlier campaigns for justice, Lewis readily notes that they were "mixed with nationalist politics." Yet when writing about the WJC, Lewis never identifies it a nationalist organization involved in a nation-building project.[156] Such orientalist double standards run throughout the entirety of the work and obscure the deep continuities between the Serbian, Bulgarian, and Greek nationalist claims for justice after World War I and those of Jewish nationalists after World War II. They also obscure important differences between the objectives pursued by nationalist organizations and those of the AIDP. If the latter did not invest as much of its resources in creating and disseminating a particular historical record this was in no small part because it placed more emphasis on using the moment to build an international system of criminal justice.

This commitment does not receive much attention from Lewis who, instead, misrepresents Pella's positions. The Romanian jurist is said to have opposed "laws against repressing languages," when in fact he merely argued that cultural genocide was the wrong framework to defend what

---

[153] Lewis, "The History," 641. For other insinuations along these lines see Lewis, *The Birth of the New Justice*, 79, 105. Lewis appears to strongly believe that international criminal law should have invaded the remit of the Minority Section.

[154] Lewis, *The Birth of the New Justice*, 113, 151. See the description of Henri Donnedieu de Vabres and Vespasian V. Pella's decision to continue to serve their governments. Ibid. at 191–192.

[155] Ibid. at 151.

[156] Ibid. at 68.

he considered an individual right.[157] In a final obfuscating coup de grace, Lewis tries to shift responsibility for the attacks on Pella away from Lemkin and to the Polish and Lithuanian-American groups that employed him after the war by focusing on a single episode from late 1951, over four years into Lemkin's campaign against Pella.[158] It is clear that these associations attacked Pella at Lemkin's direction and not the other way around. In sum, Lewis' account of Pella's life and work is deeply problematic. Unfortunately, this problematic characterization has proven influential.[159] Sixty years later, Lemkin's attacks have been granted an academic imprimatur. Meanwhile, his own political advocacy has largely escaped scrutiny.

The cause to which Lemkin devoted himself most energetically after the war, aside from attacking Pella and other human rights activists, was instrumentalizing the concept of genocide to legitimate military intervention, especially against the Soviet Union.[160] The early twenty-first-century warmongers routinely accused of having illegitimately conscripted Lemkin's image and ideas to legitimate US military intervention are therefore his true heirs. Their wars are Lemkin's legacy. As the world recoils from the destruction these interventions have wrought over the past thirty years, it is worth reconsidering our collective focus on Lemkin and shifting our attention to the jurist whose work Lemkin worked so hard to distort and discredit.

3.10 Conclusion

Pella worked to build a system of international criminal justice that could prevent aggression, punish atrocity, and vindicate fundamental human rights. Yet these efforts were largely unsuccessful because of the unfavorable political conditions during his life. In this respect, the postwar era was no more propitious than the twenties for building a permanent international criminal justice system. The United States and the USSR had stood aloof from earlier efforts and their postwar commitment did

---

[157] Ibid. at 198. Pella supported the right of individuals and associations to petition the United Nations or a future international court of human rights. Pella, "Droits de l'homme," 3, 7, 13.

[158] Ibid. at 281.

[159] See Douglas Irvin-Erickson, *Raphael Lemkin and the Concept of Genocide* (Philadelphia: University of Pennsylvania Press, 2016), 41, 46.

[160] Anton Weiss-Wendt, *The Soviet Union and the Gutting of the UN Genocide Convention* (Madison: Wisconsin University Press, 2017), 173, 194–198.

not extend beyond the prosecutions at Nuremberg, Tokyo, and various domestic trials. This limited form of criminal justice was a far cry from the one Pella and his colleagues had advocated. Pella's system would have required domestic legislation and international sanction to prevent war and ensure compliance with international law. Criminal trials occupied only a small part in his system of international criminal justice.

The unification of penal law never occurred, the sanctioning mechanisms Pella envisioned were never created, and, in the years since World War II, international criminal law has focused much more on the prosecution of atrocity than on the prevention of aggression.[161] In other words, the system of international criminal justice that emerged after the end of the Cold War was a mere shadow of the one that had been imagined by Pella seventy years earlier. In place of institutions capable of peacefully resolving conflict and imposing deterrents on those who choose war, the post–Cold War era witnessed the emergence of a transitional victor's justice used to cement the legitimacy of new governments. Efforts to create international legal norms and incorporate them into domestic law, meanwhile, have been largely confined to the field of human rights law, but even in this domain the expectations have been greatly reduced. Where Pella had envisioned policies of international economic solidarity and social justice, today's human rights advocacy continues to be narrowly focused on civil and political rights.

Some might argue that Pella's vision of international criminal justice was doomed from the outset for presupposing a universal convergence in values that could not and will not materialize, least of all among the great powers.[162] Yet such cynicism ignores the remarkable popularity and endurance of certain ideas that he promoted, from universal jurisdiction to the principle of subsidiarity, and even the notion of corporate criminal liability. Contemporary international criminal law testifies to the legacy of Pella's work. Pella's project, meanwhile, represents aspirations that champions of international justice have yet to achieve.

---

[161] See Frédéric Mégret, "International Criminal Justice as a Peace Project," *European Journal of International Law* 29:3 (2018), 835–858.

[162] Pella, *Delicte Îngăduite*, 449. Pella's ideas on regional and world federation require greater attention.

4

Emil Stanisław Rappaport

His Road from Abolition to Prosecution of Nations

PATRYCJA GRZEBYK

Figure 4.1 Portrait of Emil Stanisław Rappaport, 1919.

Emil Stanisław Rappaport lived in many different epochs.[1] He left his mark on the law of each of them. He lived through the time of the partition of Poland and its regained independence, as well as two World Wars. He had to face the challenges of the Cold War era, at the same time reconciling the Nazi crimes and dealing with the Soviet Union – the former liberator turning into an oppressor. These events shaped Rappaport's vision of what the law should be and taught him to negotiate a relationship with whoever was in power at the time. Having

---

[1] I would like to thank Leszek Kubicki, Stefan Lelental and Adam Redzik for their help in understanding the circumstances in which Rappaport lived and worked and for their comments concerning early drafts of this chapter.

94 PATRYCJA GRZEBYK

experienced the emergence and collapse of independent Poland not once but repeatedly, he treated the twists and turns of history as transient.

His energy was too abundant for just one role. Thus, he was not just a scholar, a lawmaker, a founder and active member of Polish and international lawyers' associations, but also a defence attorney, a judge and a mentor. In this chapter, I would like to sketch a portrait of Rappaport in each of these roles, by outlining his experiences against the background of the historical events which he lived through and which often forced him to re-examine his beliefs.

In the first part of the chapter, I focus on the early years of Rappaport's academic and scholarly career, including his mentors. I also describe his time working as a defence attorney, which had an impact on his further work on criminal enforcement law and his view on the death penalty. In the second part, I review Rappaport's contribution to the development of a legal system and court system in the newly independent Republic of Poland, focusing on his role in the Codification Committee of the Republic of Poland. He presented the insights gained during his work there among others at the forum of the Association internationale de droit pénal (AIDP). He believed that the Codification Committee was a laboratory of modern legislation, a belief shared by the AIDP.[2] In the third part of the chapter, I present Rappaport's work in various international associations of criminal lawyers, and his contributions to the unification of criminal law worldwide and the establishment of the foundations of international criminal law. In the final part, I discuss the period during and after World War II, during which Rappaport was faced with the challenges of bringing Nazi criminals to justice while dealing with the spread of Soviet influence across the Polish judiciary and academia.

4.1 A Protégé of Advocate Stanisław Patek, a Faithful Student of Franz von Liszt

Emil Stanisław Rappaport was born on 8 July 1877 in Warsaw. At the time, the city was under Russian governance.[3] Rappaport experienced first-hand the brutal methods that Russian officials used to destroy any traces of

---

[2] Emil Stanisław Rappaport, 'Le problème de l'unification internationale du droit pénal' (1929) 12 Revue Pénitentiaire de Pologne 1, 10.

[3] Austria, Prussia and Russia partitioned the territory of Poland three times – in the years 1772, 1793 and 1795. As a result, 462,000 km^2 of the former territory of the Republic of Poland came under Russian rule. In 1807, the territories seized by Russia were declared to constitute the Duchy of Warsaw (Księstwo Warszawskie). In 1815, it was transformed into

Polish culture and tradition. The experience left him sensitive to all aspects of cultural eradication of national groups. Rappaport considered himself Polish without a doubt and the topic of the independence of Poland was emotionally charged for him. He envisaged many possible scenarios for independence but was sceptical about their realization.[4]

In 1897 he enrolled at the Department of Law at the University of Warsaw, from which he graduated in 1901. The university was not as good as those in Saint Petersburg, Moscow, Qazan, Odessa, Kiev or Dorpat. However, the University of Warsaw was the only institution in Congress Poland where it was possible to study law.[5]

As a Pole, Rappaport had few chances of having an academic career in Congress Poland.[6] He was also prevented by the Russian authorities from completing his court apprenticeship on the territory of Congress Poland. This was an oppressive measure often directed against Polish lawyers. Instead, he completed his apprenticeship in Riga, at the same time teaching in private schools during the period 1902–1903. He passed his bar exam in 1904,[7] but – given the practically non-existent chances that he would be offered a position to actually work as a judge – he decided to pursue a career as a defence attorney. He practiced during the years 1906–1917, but by his own admission was really devoted to this career only in the years 1907–1908.[8]

Rappaport did not become a defence attorney for his private gain.[9] He was a member of the Circle of Political Defenders (Koło Obrońców Politycznych) under the leadership of the legendary Stanisław Patek[10] and his partner Stefania Sempołowska.[11] The Circle comprised lawyers

---

a non-sovereign state called the Kingdom of Poland, also known as Congress Poland, tied to Russia by means of a personal union.

[4] Emil Stanisław Rappaport, *Międzynarodowa przyszłość Polski* (Wydawnictwo M. Arcta, Warsaw 1916).

[5] Michał Przeperski, *Prawnik trzech epok*, 15.10.2015, https://nawokandzie.ms.gov.pl/26/opinie-2-26/prawnik-trzech-epok.html (all links were accessed on 6.11.2018).

[6] 'Jubileusz profesora dra Emila Stanisława Rappaporta' (1962) 7 *Palestra* 65.

[7] Emil Stanisław Rappaport, *Ustawa o przebaczeniu w świetle projektów francuskich (1885–1907)* (Kasa im. Józefa Mianowskiego, Warsaw 1916b) 9.

[8] Emil Stanisław Rappaport, 'Moje czasy adwokackie (1906–1917): (fragmenty wspomnień): I. Warszawskie Koło Obrońców Politycznych (1905–1910)' (1958) 2 (6) *Palestra* 12 ff.

[9] 'We didn't think, we had no time to think, of paid private practice. It was an exception arising out of professional necessity, but the rule was the Circle and its work in the Citadel.' Ibid. 14.

[10] Krzysztof Pol, *Poczet prawników polskich. Wyd. 2* (C. H. Beck, Warsaw 2011) 704.

[11] Rappaport, 'Moje czasy adwokackie (1906–1917)', 15.

96 PATRYCJA GRZEBYK

who defended political prisoners on trial in Russian courts. Rappaport said later that the work in the Circle was 'nervous and fast, with no time to think, strictly to the deadlines. Notice of the trial came just before the date it was set, and meetings with the accused were brief and difficult to arrange. After the hearing, only 24 hours to ask for pardon ... and immediately there was another defendant'.[12]

Patek and Rappaport saved numerous activists from capital punishment. The experience of working at the Circle had an immense impact on Rappaport's beliefs. He was able to see first-hand how easy it was to sentence a defendant to death, regardless of who he was or how much of a threat to the Russian authorities he presented. He also saw the inhumane conditions in which the accused were kept.[13]

It is hardly surprising that Rappaport became an ardent opponent of the death penalty. He considered it to be *l'anachronisme indiscutable*.[14] He opposed its introduction to the new Polish criminal code after Poland regained independence, but lost the vote 6:5 and the new code allowed for the death penalty.[15] Rappaport also argued that it was necessary to provide very detailed regulations as to how the penalty of imprisonment is to be implemented. At worst, he described it as 'a slow execution taking place in a dungeon, plagued by hunger and cold, with no fresh air and no light, among dirt and vermin, damp, handcuffed and chained'.[16]

While working as a defence attorney, Rappaport continued his education abroad. This had a great impact on his development as a scholar. He completed supplementary courses of studies in Paris (1903–1904, 1909–1910), Berlin (1904–1905) and London (1909).[17] He earned

[12] Ibid. 15.

[13] 'The legend of the Tenth Pavilion of the Warsaw Citadel, where political prisoners were kept, seems somewhat overdone, as if it exaggerated what the human beast is capable of when the conditions, incentives, and atmosphere are conductive to acting on every evil instinct. Yet, for decades the shadow of the Tenth Pavilion has hung heavily over Warsaw and the whole country, with the endless personal and collective tragedies that played out within those grey walls.' Rappaport, 'Moje czasy adwokackie (1906–1917)', 19.

[14] Rappaport, 'Le problème de l'unification internationale du droit pénal', 29.

[15] According to Mikołaj Korenfeld, Rappaport was of the opinion that 'the death penalty is in contravention to the most fundamental requirements of punishment', see Stefan Lelental, 'Emil Stanisław Rappaport (1877–1965) (wspomnienie ostatniego z uczniów)' in Cesare Beccaria, *O przestępstwach i karach* (University of Lodz Press, Lodz 2014) VII. See also Adam Lityński, *Wydział karny komisji kodyfikacyjnej II Rzeczypospolitej* (University of Silesia, Katowice 1991) 68.

[16] Emil Stanisław Rappaport, *Nowy System Kodyfikacji Ustawodawstwa Kryminalnego. Kodeks Karny Wykonawczy* (Wydawnictwo Biblioteka Prawnicza, Warsaw 1930) 10.

[17] Adam Redzik, Wydział Prawa in Adam Redzik (ed.), *Academia Militans Uniwersytet Jana Kazimierza we Lwowie* (Wydawnictwo Wysoki Zamek, Cracow 2015) 491.

a doctorate in law at the University of Neuchâtel in Switzerland and had it recognized in Lviv in 1920.[18]

In his dissertation, Rappaport did not disguise his approval of the French regulation (*Les lois Bérenger du 14 août 1885 et du 26 mars 1891*) that implemented suspended penalties, which in effect allowed criminal sanctions to gain an individualized dimension.[19] Rappaport argued that criminals fall into different categories. Some of them are unlikely to improve their behaviour and as such they should be isolated from society. Yet, others should be pardoned and their sentences should only serve as a caution. He believed this approach was 'a measure of extreme individualization in the field of contemporary criminal policy' and an embodiment of the ideas of mercy.[20] In addition, he recognized that it was sensible in terms of using the limited resource of the penitentiary system. Naturally, under the influence of the French and Swiss regulations, Rappaport argued as a member of the Codification Committee of the Republic of Poland that a similar mechanism should be implemented in Polish criminal law.[21] In fact, he was so convinced by the idea of individualized punishment (particularly in situations where the crime is committed in a highly emotional state of mind and long-term isolation seems disproportional to the crime, considering the character of the perpetrator) that he authored a theatrical play and published it under a pseudonym to make the public see the need for the institution of a legal pardon.[22]

There were several reasons why Rappaport believed that the issue of individualized punishment carries such immense weight. First, he had listened to lectures by leading French scholars[23] thus he was well versed in the newest trends in French and Swiss criminal law.[24] Second, and perhaps more importantly, he had participated in a seminar offered in

[18] The title of his doctoral dissertation was *La loi de pardon: étude analytique des projets français* (Recueil Sirey, Paris, Attinger Fréres, Neuchâtel 1911). See also Lelental, 'Emil Stanisław Rappaport (1877–1965)', iv.

[19] See also Emil Stanisław Rappaport, *Teoria i Praktyka Skazania Warunkowego w Polsce (1917–1939) Referat na IV Zjazd Prawników Polskich w Gdyni* (Kasa im. Józefa Mianowskiego, Warsaw 1939).

[20] Rappaport, *Ustawa o przebaczeniu w świetle projektów francuskich (1885–1907)*, 60.

[21] Lityński, *Wydział karny komisji kodyfikacyjnej II Rzeczypospolitej*, 92.

[22] Stanisław Barycz, *Strzał. Sceny z życia współczesnego w 5 aktach (7 odsłonach)* (Księgarnia F. Hoesicka, Warsaw 1934).

[23] Among others: Emile Auguste Garçon, Paul Cuche, René Garraud, Alfred Le Poittevin, Raymond Saleilles, Georges Vidal and Gabriel Tarde. See Rappaport, *Ustawa o przebaczeniu w świetle projektów francuskich (1885–1907)*, 10–12; *Wybrane zagadnienia nowoczesnej polityki kryminalnej (XX wieku)* (University of Lodz, Lodz 1960) 51.

[24] Rappaport, *Ustawa o przebaczeniu w świetle projektów francuskich (1885–1907)*, 16, 20–21.

98 PATRYCJA GRZEBYK

Berlin by Franz von Liszt[25] – a leader of the sociological school of thought in criminal law. He believed in the importance of ensuring that the punishment targets the crime and not the criminal, which was a principle often invoked by Rappaport in his writings.[26]

For his habilitation, that is, the post-doctoral academic qualification, Rappaport chose the Jan Kazimierz University in Lviv.[27] Lviv was at the time one of the leading centres for criminal and international law thanks to, for example, Juliusz Makarewicz – a former student of von Liszt.[28] When Makarewicz became the president of the Codification Committee, he involved Rappaport in its works.

Despite his habilitation, no professorship was available for Rappaport in Poland for many years. Finally, in 1937, he was awarded a professorship in criminal law at the Free Polish University in Warsaw[29] established with Rappaport's significant contribution.[30]

---

[25] Emil Stanisław Rappaport, *Walka o reformę prawa karnego w Niemczech* (Kasa im. J. Mianowskiego, Gebethner i Wolff, Warsaw 1909); *Nowe horyzonty prawa międzynarodowego w świetle publicystyki niemieckiej, Zagadnienia Polityczne* (Wydawnictwo M. Arcta, Warsaw 1916a) 5; Jerzy Sawicki, Z okazji jubileuszu 60 lat pracy naukowej prof. dr Emila Stanisława Rappaporta (1962) 7 *Państwo i Prawo* 142; Marek Olszewski, 'Jubileusz prof. dr Emila Stanisława Rappaporta' (1957) 10 *Państwo i Prawo* 657; Lelental, 'Emil Stanisław Rappaport (1877–1965)', iv–v; Stanisław Milewski, Adam Redzik, *Themis i Pheme: czasopiśmiennictwo prawnicze w Polsce do 1939 roku* (Iskry, Warsaw 2011) 206–207.

[26] See Janusz Jamontt, Emil Stanisław Rappaport (in cooperation with Rafał Lemkin), *Kodeks karny r. 1932 z dostosowanemi do kodeksu tezami z orzeczeń sądu najwyższego, odpowiedniemi ustępami uzasadnienia projektu komisji kodyfikacyjnej oraz ze skorowidzem* (Wydawnictwo Bibljoteka Prawnicza, Warsaw 1932) xxii–xxiv.

[27] Adam Redzik stresses that in his application to the Senate of the University of Lwów for *veniam legendi* on criminal law, Rappaport presented three works: 1. *Bankructwo w ustawodawstwie nowoczesnym na tle porównawczym* (1916) (published later in French as: *La baquerote dans la legislation moderne comparée* [Tenin, Paris 1927]); 2. *Rys zasad prawa karnego międzynarodowego. w świetle ustaw karnych obowiązujących w Królestwie ma tle porównawczym* (1918); *Kodeks karny dla ziem polskich część ogólna* (1916). Rappaport received *veniam legendi* from the Faculty of Law and Political Skills of the University of Lviv in 1920. The habilitation was linked with the appointment as a *docent* of the subject area (in the case of Rappaport – criminal law) limited to a specific faculty and university. In consequence, during the period 1920–1933, Rappaport travelled from Warsaw to Lviv to deliver the following classes: 'The Criminal Statute and its Scope: Comments *de lege lata* and *de lege ferenda*'; 'The Role of the Prison System in Combating Crime'; 'The Prison System'; 'Criminal Enforcement Code'. See Redzik, 'Wydział Prawa', 492; Lelental, 'Emil Stanisław Rappaport (1877–1965)', VI.

[28] Pol, *Poczet prawników polskich*, 845.

[29] Jarosław Kita, Stefan Pytlas, *W służbie nauki. Profesorowi Uniwersytetu Łódzkiego w latach 1945–2004, Pro memoria* (University of Lodz Press, Lodz 2005) 346.

[30] Under a resolution of the Polish Sejm, from 1929 onwards the Free Polish University was formally recognized as a university, and the titles and degrees it awarded were considered

4 EMIL STANISŁAW RAPPAPORT 99

It is worth remembering that long-term relationships with Lviv resulted in putting Rafał Lemkin (a long-term participant in Makarewicz's seminar) on Rappaport's radar. Rappaport supported Lemkin's career; it was probably with his help that Lemkin became a clerk at the Court of Appeals in Warsaw.[31] Then (approximately in 1929 or 1930), after winning a nomination as an assistant prosecutor in the Regional Court in Brzeżany (Tarnopol province), Lemkin was posted to work in the same position in Warsaw. Lemkin was also a clerk at the Secretariat General of the Codification Committee and helped Rappaport draft the statute on petty offences[32] as well as the first guidance notes and comments on the Polish Criminal Code of 1932.[33] Likely, Lemkin's teaching job at the Free Polish University and his position in the Bureau for the Unification of Criminal Law were also, at least in part, results of Rappaport's efforts.[34] It is beyond doubt that Rappaport and Lemkin enjoyed good relations and worked together in several international organizations.[35]

4.2 Towards a Polish Judiciary and Polish Criminal Law

In 1915, when the Russians were forced by the German and Austrian-Hungarian army to leave Warsaw, Polish people believed that freedom was closer than ever. Rappaport argued that a Polish judiciary should be established immediately in the form of civic courts (*sądy obywatelskie*) (1915). He clearly articulated the need for observing the Hague Convention (IV) respecting the Laws and Customs of War on Land, that is, including the rights and

to be equivalent to those awarded by other universities. See 'Jubileusz profesora dra Emila Stanisława Rappaporta' (1962) 7 *Palestra* 65.

[31] Ryszard Szawłowski, 'Rafał Lemkin (1900–1959) – polski prawnik twórcą pojęcia "ludobójstwo"' in Radosław Ignatiew, Antoni Kura (eds.), *Zbrodnie przeszłości. Opracowania i materiały prokuratorów IPN. Tom 2 Ludobójstwo* (Institute of National Remembrance, Warsaw 2008) 8.

[32] Emil Stanisław Rappaport, *Projekt wstępny ustawy o wykroczeniach administracyjnych wraz z sumarycznym uzasadnienieniem* (in: Komisja Kodyfikacyjna Sekcja Prawa Karnego, Tom V, Z. 7, Warsaw 1931) 4 (on this page Rappaport expresses his 'genuine thanks for reliable and most of all prompt assistance' to Lemkin).

[33] Jamontt, Rappaport, *Kodeks karny r. 1932.*

[34] Marek Kornat, 'Rafał Lemkin's Formative Years' in Agnieszka Bieńczyk-Missala, Sławomir Dębski (eds.), *Rafał Lemkin: A Hero of Humankind* (PISM, Warsaw 2010) 63.

[35] It is believed that Rappaport called Lemkin to explain to him that the Polish Ministry of Justice objects to his participation in the Madrid conference in 1933 where his paper on crime of barbarism and vandalism was presented but not discussed, see Jean-Louis Panné, 'Rafał Lemkin czyli potęga bezsilności' (2008) 3 (43) *Polski Przegląd Dyplomatyczny* 19, 37.

obligations of the occupying power.[36] In Rappaport's opinion, civic courts would be complementary to the Civic Committee (Komitet Obywatelski) and Civic Guard (Straż Obywatelska), two organizations of Polish quasi-authorities in the partitioned country.

The civic courts existed for a very brief time. They were abolished by the German authorities soon after they were founded, but the attempt itself was symbolically important, given that no Polish judiciary had existed since 1872.[37]

In 1917, Rappaport was included in the work of the Justice Department of the Provisional State Council, which was a Polish authority established in 1916 by the governments of Germany and Austria. Soon after, he was appointed as a judge at the Court of Appeals in Warsaw and posted to the Supreme Court. It was in this capacity that he participated in the first sitting of the Criminal Chamber of the Supreme Court in December 1917. In 1919, he was officially appointed to the Supreme Court and served as a Supreme Court justice – with a break during World War II – until 1951.[38] Accepting the appointment as a judge meant that he had to lay to rest whatever political ambitions he had been harbouring.[39]

In 1918, an independent Poland emerged again. It consisted of parts that had belonged to the territories of the three powers – Austria, Prussia and Russia – that had previously partitioned the country. In consequence, the unification of the law was a pressing issue. Polish authorities established the Codification Committee of the Republic of Poland[40] which had to decide whether the different legal orders should continue to coexist, whether one of them should be selected and applied across the new state, or whether a new criminal code should be enacted. The Committee decided very quickly in favour of the latter solution, a new

---

[36] Emil Stanisław Rappaport, *Sądy obywatelskie w Warszawie (Karta z dziejów przełomu sierpniowego r. 1915* (Skład główny Gebethnera i Wolffa, Warsaw 1915a) 5.

[37] Mieczysław Siewierski, 'Emil Stanisław Rappaport' (1965) 10 *Państwo i Prawo* 542, 543.

[38] Ibid.; see also Olszewski, 'Jubileusz prof. dr Emila Stanisława Rappaporta', 657.

[39] Rappaport was a founder of the Polish Progressive Party (Polska Partia Postępowa) in 1906. In his opinion, the party – along with another political party, Progressive Democracy (Postępowa Demokracja) – was a 'predecessor in spirit' of yet another political party, the Democratic Alliance (Stronnictwo Demokratyczne), which after World War II became closely tied to the communist Polish United Workers' Party and the United People's Party (Zjednoczone Stronnictwo Ludowe). Rappaport held several positions in the Democratic Alliance's Board of Lawyers, see Kita, Pytlas, *W służbie nauki*, 346–347; Olszewski, 'Jubileusz prof. dr Emila Stanisława Rappaporta', 657.

[40] *Polish Official Journal* of 1919, no. 44, item 315. The Commission started its work on 10 November 1919. See more on the Commission in Lityński, *Wydział karny komisji kodyfikacyjnej II Rzeczypospolitej*, 11 ff.

criminal code: first, because of the emergence of new trends in criminal policy, and second, as a symbolic gesture emphasizing the clean break from the policies of the partitioning powers.

Rappaport acted as the Secretary General of the Codification Committee in the period 1924–1932, after having served as the secretary of its Criminal Division since 1920. He made a valuable contribution to the work of the Committee if only because of his excellent knowledge of the legal systems of other states. A vast majority of Polish legal scholars at the time had been educated abroad and, thus, familiarity with foreign legal systems was not unusual in itself. Yet, Rappaport was not only well versed in the French and Swiss systems but was familiar with the trends in the German and Italian legal systems as well. He had co-authored a selection of Russian criminal laws with notes and explanations with Aleksander Mogilnicki, a publication which until the early 1930s was immensely helpful in the everyday work of the courts. Moreover, Rappaport was able to draw on the debates held among experts on the international level, for example, in the AIDP and at international criminal law unification conferences, in which he actively participated.

Rappaport and Mogilnicki together presented the first draft of the criminal code (based on the Russian code of 1903).[41] By taking into account various categories of crime, Rappaport managed to convey the idea in the draft that the purpose of punishment is more than revenge, namely the protection of society.[42] In this way, he provided support for the representatives of the sociological school of thought in the debate within the Codification Committee. Rappaport argued that aspects of many different approaches can be combined into a 'third way', that is, the sociological approach, and he tended to stay away from doctrinal disputes. In the 'nature or nurture' question with regard to criminal tendencies, Makowski argued that these tendencies are acquired from the environment and Makarewicz took the hereditary view. Rappaport sidestepped the issue by focusing on the necessity to implement measures that protect society regardless of what lies at the root of the crime.[43]

---

[41] Aleksander Mogilnicki, Emil Stanisław Rappaport, *Projekt kodeksu karnego dla ziem polskich* (Skład główny w księgarni E. Wende i S-Ka, Warsaw 1916).

[42] Ibid. 5–6.

[43] Elżbieta Janiszewska-Talago, *Szkoła antropologiczna prawa karnego w Polsce* (Wydawnictwo Prawnicze, Warsaw 1965) 64–66. Makowski and Makarewicz were also proponents of application of the security measures but they were willing to use this institution even before the commission of a crime whereas Rappaport was of the opinion that the commission of the crime is *conditio sine qua non* of any use of security measures.

The code entered into force on 1 September 1932 and stayed in force in Poland until 31 December 1969. Rappaport was responsible for drafting the papers to support the solutions implemented in the general part of the code,[44] that is, those pertaining to jurisdiction, including universal jurisdiction. These issues were hotly debated at the criminal law unification conference in Warsaw in 1927. Rappaport argued that a worldwide (universal) mechanism of criminal response is needed because the internal legal order of each state and international solidarity of all civilized states must be based on the obligation to punish crimes that are a danger to the entire global community (*delicta iuris gentium*).[45]

Rappaport believed that a criminal code is an instrument that protects not only the national but also the international legal order. Consequently, he worked to ensure that the Polish Criminal Code contained a regulation that penalizes inciting the public to a war of aggression (referred to as *lex Rappaport*). This regulation, contained in Article 113, read: '§ 1. Whoever incites the public to a war of aggression is punishable by imprisonment for up to 5 years. § 2. Prosecution follows only if the conduct specified in § 1 is punishable under the law of the state against which the incitement is directed.'

Rappaport believed that war could be prevented by a ban on war propaganda.[46] He argued that Article 113 of the Polish Criminal Code is an expression of the desire to 'protect the notion of peaceful coexistence of the nations', and that the enemies of this approach 'create an atmosphere of hatred, in particular by inciting a war of aggression'. Rappaport saw war as a treason against universal culture,[47] which – given the technical abilities of humankind – could jeopardize all the achievements of civilization.[48]

Importantly, Rappaport was convinced that under the Covenant of the League of Nations and the Briand-Kellogg Pact, the declarations

---

[44] Komisja kodyfikacyjna Rzeczypospolitej Polskiej, Sekcja Prawa Karnego, Tom V, Z. 3, Projekt Kodeksu Karnego w redakcji przyjętej w drugiem czytaniu przez Sekcję Prawa Karnego Komisji Kodyfikacyjnej R.P., Uzasadnienie Część Ogólnej (Warsaw 1930).

[45] Ibid. 12–13. Compare to Rappaport, 'Le problème de l'unification internationale du droit pénal', 29.

[46] See his publications: Emil Stanisław Rappaport, 'Propaganda wojny zaczepnej jako delictum iuris gentium' (1927) 44 *Gazeta Sądowa Warszawska*; 'Propagande de la guerre d'agression comme délit du droit des gens' (Warsaw 1929) 13 *Revue Penitantiaire de Pologne*.

[47] See Emil Stanisław Rappaport, *Naród Zbrodniarz. Przestępstwa hitleryzmu a naród niemiecki. Szkic analityczny, przestępczości i odpowiedzialności osobowo-zespołowej* (Wydawnictwo i Nakład Spółdzielnia Dziennikarska "Prasa", Lodz, 1945) 38.

[48] Rappaport, *Naród Zbrodniarz*, 51.

condemning wars of aggression, etc., aggressive warfare was already considered a crime, and the criminalization of war propaganda was just a consequence thereof.[49]

In his capacity as member of the Codification Committee, Rappaport was also co-responsible for presenting the statute on juvenile courts (he consulted among others with Emile Auguste Garçon on it)[50] and the statute on petty offence.[51] Yet his pet project, almost his *idée fixe*, was a draft of a comprehensive regulation of criminal enforcement. However, the draft was rejected.

Rappaport was convinced that the manner in which the punishment was carried out should be regulated in great detail, and that a criminal code is not the statute in which such regulations should be contained. He pointed out that this aspect of criminal law had already been regulated in a separate statute in several states, most notably those in South and Central America, and that Poland should follow in these progressive footsteps. For him, drafting a separate, comprehensive law on the enforcement of criminal punishments was a consequence of the individualized approach to punishment. Since there are many various categories of offenders (incidental, 'professional', etc.), there should also be many corresponding approaches to punishment. For some of the offenders, imprisonment should serve as an opportunity for resocialization, while for others it should primarily serve to isolate them from society.[52] Rappaport also believed that providing a form of supervision for former inmates was crucial to ensure that they were in fact reformed.[53] Sadly, Rappaport did not live to see his ideas in this respect materialize, even though he devoted nearly all of his scholarly efforts after World War II to his specific issue.

4.3 Between Universal and International Criminal Law

Rappaport was a co-founder and a member of several associations.[54] He was active in the Polish lawyers' associations: Towarzystwo Prawnicze

---

[49] Jamontt, Rappaport, *Kodeks karny r. 1932*, 52.
[50] Lityński, *Wydział karny komisji kodyfikacyjnej II Rzeczypospolitej*, 108.
[51] See Komisja Kodyfikacyjne Rzeczypospolitej Polskiej, Sekcja Prawa Karnego, Tom IV, Zeszyt 4: Projekt wstępny ustawy o wykroczeniach (Warsaw 1929).
[52] Rappaport, *Nowy System Kodyfikacji Ustawodawstwa Kryminalnego*, 12, 16.
[53] Ibid. 22–23.
[54] Marek Kornat, 'Barbarzyństwo- wandalizm-terroryzm-ludobójstwo. O Rafale Lemkinie i idei zdefiniowania „zbrodni w obliczu prawa narodów' (2008) 3 (43) *Polski Przegląd Dyplomatyczny* 79, 86.

104 PATRYCJA GRZEBYK

(1907–1916) and Koło Prawników Polskich.[55] He was the initiator and secretary general of another similar organization, Stała Delegacja Zrzeszeń Prawniczych, and the president of the Polish Committee for International Legal Cooperation (1927–1939). He was the *spiritus movens* behind the establishment of the Polish Criminal Law Association (Polskie Towarzystwo Ustawodawstwa Kryminalnego).[56]

Even before World War I, several Polish criminal lawyers made an attempt to establish a Polish group within the International Union of Penal Law (IUPL/UIDP), founded by Franz von Liszt, Gérard van Hamel and Adolphe Prins in Vienna in 1889. The Polish application had been rejected for political reasons mostly by German votes. The official explanation was that a nation without a state could not have its own national group within the organization. Yet, the same approach had not been followed when the Croatian group had (successfully) applied for that status earlier.[57] Wary of these experiences with German and Austrian lawyers, as well as with their Russian counterparts, Rappaport put no effort into maintaining relations with them. Instead, he focused on developing relations with his French colleagues who had supported the Polish application in the UIDP.

Rappaport's breakthrough on the international stage was a result of his contacts with Emile Auguste Garçon (French criminal lawyer, professor at the Faculty of Law of the University of Paris), who invited him to become a member of La Société Générale des Prisons – an association fighting for amelioration of prison conditions.[58] Rappaport was then able to extend the invitation to other Polish lawyers. Rappaport's activeness on the international level resulted in the subsequent creation of the Association internationale de droit pénal (AIDP) on 14 March 1924 in cooperation with Henri Carton de Wiart (Belgium), Louis Hugueney (France) and Quintiliano Saldaña (Spain).[59] The AIDP succeeded the

---

[55] Stanisław Mikke, Adam Redzik, *Adwokaci polscy ojczyźnie. Polish Advocates in the Service of their Homeland* (Naczelna Rada Adwokacka, Warsaw 2008) 184; Siewierski, *Emil Stanisław Rappaport*, 542. See also Emil Stanisław Rappaport, *Ruch Stowarzyszeniowy w Królestwie Polskim (1815–1915)* (Skład Główny w Księgarni E. Wende i S-ka, Warsaw 1915) 3,12.

[56] Kita, Pytlas, *W służbie nauki*, 348.

[57] Janiszewska-Talago, *Szkoła antropologiczna*, 41; see also Marek Wąsowicz, *Nurt Socjologiczny w polskiej myśli prawnokarnej*, (WUW, Warsaw 1989) 64.

[58] Martine Kaluszynski. 'Construire la loi. La Société générale des prisons (1877–1900)' in Pierre Muller (ed.), *L'Etat contre la politique? Les expressions historiques de l'etatisation* (l'Harmattan, 1998) 205 ff.

[59] Rappaport, 'Le problème de l'unification internationale du Droit Pénal', 11.

UIDP, which had dissolved as a result of World War I.[60] The founders of the AIDP stressed that in contrast to the UIDP, the AIDP was designed to be neutral, not take the side of any of the schools of thought within criminal law, providing a forum for criminal lawyers of all schools of thought.[61] Rappaport was a co-founder of the AIDP, its long-time Vice President (1924–1961) and then an honorary member.[62]

In the newly (re)created states, such as Poland and Czechoslovakia, as well as those where the borders had shifted dramatically (Greece, Yugoslavia, Romania), there was a pressing issue of unification of criminal law. As a consequence, according to Rappaport, the lawyers coming from those jurisdictions should be the most active.[63] It was therefore natural for Vespasian Pella from Romania to suggest that Rappaport (with the support of the Polish Commission for International Juridical Cooperation) should be in charge of organizing the first criminal law unification conference in Warsaw in 1927.[64] Pella served as the conference's secretary while Rappaport presided.

Later in 1928 at a conference in Rome, the International Bureau for the Unification of Criminal Law was founded in order to coordinate the progress of work between conferences. Rappaport was the Bureau's Vice President in the period 1928–1939. In this capacity, he worked together with Mariano d'Amelio (Italy), Megalos Caloyani (Greece), Carton de Wiart and Simon Sasserath (Belgium), Donnedieu de Vabres and Jean-André Roux (France), as well as Thomas Givanovitch (Živanović) (Yugoslavia), André Mercier (Switzerland), Auguste Miricka (Czechoslovakia) and Cuello Calon (Spain). Yet, Rappaport admitted himself that he and Pella were the driving force behind most of the organization's work.[65]

Initially, the focus of the AIDP was on the unification of the principal tenets of criminal law. At the conference in Warsaw in 1927, it was stated explicitly that the time when many states are redrafting their criminal

---

[60] Emil Stanisław Rappaport. *Konferencja Międzynarodowej Unifikacji Prawa Karnego a jej poprzedniczki* (Lodz 1934).

[61] Mark Lewis, 'The History of the International Association of Penal Law 1924–1950: Liberal, Conservative, or Neither?' in Morten Bergsmo, Cheah Wui Ling, Song Tianying, Yi Ping (eds.), *Historical Origins of International Criminal Law, Volume 4* (Torkehl Opsahl Academic EPublisher, Brussels 2015) 604 ff.

[62] Lelental, 'Emil Stanisław Rappaport (1877–1965)', xi.

[63] Rappaport, 'Le problème de l'unification internationale du Droit Pénal', 9 ff.

[64] Daniel Marc Segesser, Myrian Gessler, 'Raphael Lemkin and the International Debate on the Punishment of War Crimes (1919–1948)' (2005) 7(4) *Journal of Genocide Research* 453, 456.

[65] Rappaport, 'Le problème de l'unification internationale du Droit Pénal', 4–5.

laws is ideal for the development of core principles which could become the shared basis of these new national criminal codes. Yet, the primary focus of the conference was to set out principles regarding the criminal jurisdiction of states, including universal jurisdiction, a notion promoted by Rappaport. He believed that the development of criminal law should be headed towards the recognition of crimes under the law of nations (*delicta iuris gentium*) and the obligation to prosecute these crimes by all states (the universality principle). Rappaport argued that the mechanism of extradition, while generally recognized and practiced by states, was insufficient in combating the crimes against the law of nations.[66]

In the context of universal jurisdiction, the delegates in Warsaw agreed and confirmed that the following crimes should be considered *delicta iuris gentium*: piracy, counterfeiting of coins and securities, trade in slaves, trade in women and children, intentional use of instruments capable of producing public danger, traffic in narcotics and traffic in obscene publications, and crimes punishable anywhere under the principle of universal jurisdiction.[67]

During the conference in Warsaw, Rappaport was also able to secure support for his idea of penalizing war propaganda ('*Quiconque dans un discours ou conférence publics ou par voie de propagation ou exposition publique d'une oeuvre ou image aura tenté d'exciter l'opinion publique à la guerre d'aggression, sera puni d'emprisonnement jusqu'à cinq ans*').[68]

Rappaport believed that war propaganda facilitates the commission of the crime of war, that is, a crime against the safety and security of universal culture and civilization. In view of the Briand-Kellogg Pact of 1928, at the next criminal law unification conference, held in Brussels in 1930, the final wording of the regulation was agreed. (It included the reservation that propaganda in favour of aggressive war should be punishable under the condition that a similar penalty exists in the law of the country against which the propaganda is directed.[69])

At the subsequent conference in Paris in 1931, a resolution was adopted asking the Secretary General of the League of Nations to convene

---

[66] Rappaport, *Naród Zbrodniarz*, 31.

[67] Ibid.

[68] 'Whoever attempts to incite public opinion to war of aggression in the public discourse, public lecture, propagation or public exposition of an oeuvre or a picture, shall be subject to penalty of deprivation of liberty for up to five years' (translation by P.G.), A/CN.4/39 (1950) 2 YB ILC 341, para. 124. See more in: Michael G. Kearney, *The Prohibition of Propaganda for War in International Law* (Oxford University Press, Oxford 2007) 25.

[69] A/CN.4/39, para 124.

a conference where universal criminalization of war propaganda could be enacted. This provided backing for the initiative of the Polish foreign minister August Zaleski of 17 September 1931 regarding the adoption of a memorandum on moral disarmament. Despite the fact, often stressed by Rappaport, that interwar Europe was essentially a barrel of gunpowder, only Poland and Romania ended up adopting relevant regulations in their criminal codes: Poland in the form of Article 113 of the Criminal Code of 1932, a first formal regulation of this kind in the world. Romania criminalized war propaganda in Article 229 of its criminal code. Introduction of the mentioned provisions to Polish and Romanian legal order apparently 'exhausted the entire energy devoted to prevention in this respect in Europe'.[70] A similar regulation was also adopted in Brazil as Article 508. Notably, the authorities of Romania and Brazil explicitly declared that the regulations forbidding propaganda for war had been inspired by Rappaport's work.[71]

At the subsequent (pre–World War II) AIDP criminal law unification conferences, Rappaport's focus was on prevention and punishment. These issues also dominated his presentations at the Third International Congress of Penal Law in Palermo in April 1933, where – on his initiative – the discussion focused on the codification of legal norms regarding the implementation of the punishment. The debate proved ineffective due to the huge differences of opinion among the delegates.[72] In Europe the focus was on the unification of procedural laws rather than on enforcement regulations.

In the interwar period, Rappaport did not stop at the efforts to create a universal (unified) criminal law. Together with Pella, de Vabres, Carton de Wiart, Caloyanni, Roux, Givanovitch and other experts, he was also involved in creating the foundations of international criminal law.[73] Specifically, he participated in the work on an international criminal code.[74] Rappaport, in opposition to for example Caloyani, was convinced

---

[70] Rappaport, *Naród Zbrodniarz*, 31.
[71] Rappaport, 'Le problème de l'unification internationale du Droit Pénal', 48–49.
[72] Jerzy Śliwowski, 'Narodziny Prawa Penitencjarnego' (1934) 45 *Gazeta Sądowa Warszawska* 663.
[73] Rappaport, *Naród Zbrodniarz*, 32. See also *Zagadnienie prawa karnego międzynarodowego* (Biblioteka Prawnicza, Warsaw 1930a); Tendencje rozwojowe prawa karnego międzynarodowego (1934a) 1 *Ruch Prawniczy, Socjologiczny i Ekonomiczny* 1.
[74] Segesser, Gessler, 'Raphael Lemkin and the International Debate', 458; Lewis, 'The History of the International Association of Penal Law', 621.

that the focus should be on criminal repression of states as individual criminal responsibility was already governed by domestic law.[75]

From 1925 onwards, Rappaport was a delegate of the Polish government on the International Penal and Penitentiary Commission, which – as he himself stressed – was dominated by delegates from English-speaking countries and Switzerland.[76] Moreover, from 1933 onwards he served as the correspondent of the French Minister of Justice and was in close touch with French scholars. As a result, he published a French translation of the Polish Criminal Code of 1932 together with Roux.[77]

Rappaport's international recognition is evidenced by the fact that he was awarded the French Ordre National de la Legion d'Honneur twice (in 1924 and in 1947). His other awards included the Order of the Star of Romania (1926) and the Yugoslavian Order of St Sava (1930). He was an honorary member of the Royal Academy in Madrid (from 1928) and the Institute of Criminology in Buenos Aires (from 1950).[78] The decorations he received also reflected the friendship he maintained with scholars including Roux, de Vabres, Pella and Saldaña.

4.4 A Time of Trial: World War II and Its Aftermath

World War II put an end to the thriving international cooperation. Initially, Rappaport tried to continue his work despite the war: he still delivered lectures, even if in private, and sat on the bench as a Supreme Court judge. His work as a judge provided a pretext for the German Secret State police Gestapo to arrest him, on the allegation that he issued biased judgments against German nationals.

Rappaport spent a year in prison from June 1940 until July 1941.[79] He survived solely because of the intervention of Edmund Mezger with whom he had worked together at the AIDP and who had a good relationship with Hans Frank (together, they had published *Nationalsozialistischem Handbuch* and *Der strafrechtliche Schutz von Staat, Partei und Volk*) who

---

[75] Lewis, 'The History of the International Association of Penal Law', 625.

[76] Rappaport, *Wybrane zagadnienia nowoczesnej polityki kryminalnej*, 98.

[77] Emil Stanisław Rappaport, *Code pénal polonais du 11 Juillet 1932 et loi sur les contraventions* (Paris 1932).

[78] Kita, Pytlas, *W służbie nauki*, 348. He also received also other Polish distinctions including Krzyż Komandorski z Gwiazdą Orderu Polonia Restitutia 1923, 1946; Złoty Krzyż Zasługi 1937.

[79] Siewierski, 'Emil Stanisław Rappaport', 543.

was at that time Governor-General of the General Government of Poland (occupied territories of Poland which were not formally annexed).

After getting out of prison, Rappaport did not resume his work as a judge until February 1945. He focused on writing his memoir, the draft of which went up in flames during the Warsaw Uprising.

He survived the Uprising, but his mentor Stanisław Patek did not.[80] Rappaport and his wife Justyna (they had no children) were forcibly resettled on 2 September 1944 to an area near Końskie (Petrykozy, Gowarczów).[81] When Warsaw was freed, Rappaport decided not to return. He moved to Lodz, where the key Polish authorities were located due to the destruction of Warsaw. He reported to the Supreme Court as its former judge and also started working at the University of Lodz.[82]

Rappaport could not forget the atrocities of World War II. He contemplated the responsibility of Germany for a war of aggression and a number of war crimes and crimes against humanity as a scholar and as a judge. Between April and June 1945, prior to the end of World War II, he wrote a book entitled *Naród Zbrodniarz. Przestępstwa hitleryzmu a naród niemiecki. Szkic analityczny, przestępczości i odpowiedzialności osobowo-zespołowej* (*A Nation that is a Criminal: Hitlerite Crimes and the German Nation. Analytical Comments on Criminality and Individual-Collective Responsibility*). In it, he endeavoured to apply the principles of individual criminal responsibility to the responsibility of a nation as a whole. The starting point for Rappaport's discussion was that a nation can be a criminal just like an individual. He argued that it was not Hitler that made a Hitlerite German possible, but rather a Hitlerite Germany created Hitler (*in potentia*).[83] Rappaport invoked facts from German history as evidence of Germany's criminal nature, for example, the wars fought by the Teutonic Knights.[84] He openly admitted that his conclusions could be considered complementary to Lombroso's theory, which he found fascinating.[85]

Since Rappaport believed that the German nation was criminal by nature, he supported the (in)famous opinion of Wincenty Rzymowski (the foreign minister in the Provisional Government of National Unity,

---

[80] Rappaport, 'Moje czasy adwokackie (1906–1917)', 15.
[81] Rappaport, *Naród Zbrodniarz*, 27.
[82] The University of Lodz started its work in March 1945 but was formally established with a decree only on 24 May 1945.
[83] Rappaport, *Naród Zbrodniarz*, 19.
[84] Ibid. 14, 16.
[85] Ibid. 7.

who signed the Charter of the United Nations on behalf of Poland), who said that 'the contemporary Carthage of Hitlerite imperialism should be razed to the ground'. Rappaport suggested that Germany should come under international quarantine.[86] He believed that it was necessary to eradicate the German megalomania, which could be achieved by a long-term occupation of Germany by the allies – not in isolation, but under a type of a protectorate. He also recommended that a new German press should be established along with new art and literature. With respect to specific individuals, he argued in favour of individually payable compensatory fees or forfeiture of assets, either in whole or in part, to cover the costs of the occupation.[87] Rappaport feared another world war, in particular a nuclear one. He wanted the spirit of peace to prevail over the matter, which he believed was the only 'relatively strong guarantee that the worldwide bloodbath of World War II never happens again in the history of humanity'.[88]

In *A Nation That is a Criminal*, Rappaport argued that already in the interwar period, the issue of collective criminal responsibility had been discussed at the Third International Congress of Penal Law in Bucharest in 1929. In his opinion that was the necessary step from national laws towards an international law.[89] He also argued that with regard to a war of aggression, the collective responsibility extended to all German nationals, whether their participation was intentional or not.[90] In making this suggestion, Rappaport articulated the essence of the notion of criminal responsibility for participating in a joint criminal enterprise in the broadest form. Criminal responsibility is attributed to all members of the criminal enterprise regardless of their level of involvement in the commission of the crime. Rappaport argued that the conduct of the Germans who remained passive was comparable to that of a passenger who sits in a car with a drunk driver. The passenger understands the danger caused by the situation but is in a hurry and so, instead of stopping the driver, actually spurs him on to drive faster. This person is thus an aider and abettor, an accessory to the crime, and consequently must also be punished.[91] Moreover, Rappaport argued that an aggressive war creates

---

[86] Ibid. 9.

[87] Ibid. 41–45.

[88] Ibid. 51.

[89] Ibid. 32–33.

[90] Ibid. 33.

[91] Ibid. 37. Rappaport was referring to a discussion within the Bureau of International Unification of Criminal Law of December 1938.

an extremely dangerous situation, and the issue of responsibility for the intentional use of instruments capable of producing public danger was debated at numerous criminal law unification conferences (in Warsaw in 1927, in Brussels in 1930 and in Paris in 1931). He believed that every person who participates in a war of aggression should be considered *hostis generis humani.*[92]

From the perspective of international criminal law and individual responsibility, the comments concerning the guilt of individual members of the German nation were the most important element of Rappaport's conclusions. Despite considering the entire German nation responsible for the war of aggression (which he believed stemmed from the disappearance of international morality), he stressed that each offender should be punished in proportion to their guilt.[93] Thus, in each individual case it would be necessary to demonstrate guilt (that person's 'own, individual guilt, because by supporting – whether intentionally or recklessly, or just by passive negligence, turning a blind eye, putting a hindrance in the way of those who are fighting against the blight – I am committing a crime that that is significantly detrimental to the physical wellbeing of the general population').[94] Rappaport was thoroughly convinced that the atrocities committed by Germany should have finally pushed the world to create an international criminal code and an international criminal court.[95]

As a judge sitting on the Supreme National Tribunal (SNT) – Najwyższy Trybunał Narodowy, Rappaport had a platform where he could, to an extent, voice his opinions regarding the collective guilt of German citizens.

The SNT was established in 1946.[96] Its jurisdiction covered cases regarding crimes of persons who, under the Moscow Declaration of

---

[92] Ibid. 12.

[93] Ibid. 3.

[94] Ibid. 9.

[95] Ibid. 98.

[96] *Journal of Law of the Republic of Poland,* 1946, no. 5, item 45; with amendments introduced in *Journal of Law of the Republic of Poland,* 1946, no. 59, item 325. Unified version of the decree, see *Journal of Law of the Republic of Poland,* 1946, no. 59, item 327. More on Polish laws concerning the prosecution of Nazi criminals, see The United Nations War Crimes Commission, *Law Reports of Trials of War Criminals, vol. VII* (His Majesty's Stationery Office, London 1948) Annex; on Supreme National Tribunal see Patrycja Grzebyk, 'The Role of the Polish Supreme National Tribunal in the Development of Principles of International Criminal Law' in Morten Bergsmo, Cheah Wui Ling, Yi Ping (eds.), *Historical Origins of International Criminal Law: Volume 2* (Torkel Opsahl Academic EPublisher, Brussels 2014) 603 ff.

1 November 1943, were to be surrendered to the prosecuting authorities of the Republic of Poland. The cases regarded crimes covered by the Decree of 22 January 1946 concerning the responsibility for the defeat of Poland in September 1939, and for the fascistization of public life.[97]

The tribunal's *ratione materiae* jurisdiction was based on the Decree of the Polish Committee of National Liberation (Polski Komitet Wyzwolenia Narodowego) of 31 August 1944, concerning the punishment of fascist-Hitlerite criminals guilty of murder and ill-treatment of the civilian population and of prisoners of war, and the punishment of traitors of the Polish nation.[98] In October 1946, the Decree was amended to include the crime of participating in a criminal organization.[99]

The first trial organized before the Supreme National Tribunal took place in Poznań. It lasted from 21 June to 7 July 1946. The defendant was Arthur Greiser, the Reich Governor and Gauleiter of the NSDAP of the Wartheland (Warthegau).[100] The trial was supposed to shed light on the scale of persecutions of the population of the Wielkopolska region and on the ways in which the Reich had subdued the occupied territories. Rappaport sat on the judges' bench next to two professional judges: Witold Kutzner and Kazimierz Bzowski (who served as the presiding judge because he was also at the time the President of the Polish Supreme Court) as well as four lay judges. Rappaport's presence was very important for the Polish authorities: a lawyer of his recognition certainly lent legitimacy to the proceedings.

The judgment against Arthur Greiser was passed on 9 July 1946, before the Nuremberg judgment was issued. While Rappaport was not the presiding judge, it is generally believed that he was the author of the

---

[97] *Journal of Law of the Republic of Poland*, 1946, no 5, item 46. See also Jerzy Sawicki, Bogusław Walawski, *Zbiór przepisów specjalnych przeciwko zbrodniarzom hitlerowskim i zdrajcom narodu z komentarzem* (Spółdzielnia Wydawnicza Czytelnik, Cracow 1945).

[98] *Journal of Law of the Republic of Poland*, 1944, no. 7, item 29.

[99] See more in Leszek Kubicki, *Zbrodnie wojenne w świetle prawa polskiego* (Państwowe Wydawnictwo Naukowe, Warsaw 1963) 139.

[100] SNT, *Artur Greiser Judgment*, 9 July 1946, p. 27 ff (judgment published in: Tadeusz Cyprian, Jerzy Sawicki, *Siedem wyroków Najwyższego Trybunału Narodowego* (Instytut Zachodni, Poznań, 1962) 1 ff, and also at: www.legal-tools.org/uploads/tx_ltpdb/Greiser_PolandSupremeNationalTribunal_Judgment_report__07-07-1946__E__04.pdf, last accessed at 6.11.2018). On Greiser's case, see Mark A. Drumbl, '"Germans are the Lords and Poles are the Servants": The Trial of Arthur Greiser in Poland, 1946' in Kevin J. Heller, Gerry Simpson (eds.), *The Hidden Histories of War Crimes Trials* (Oxford University Press, Oxford 2013); Catherine Epstein, *Model Nazi: Arthur Greiser and the Occupation of Western Poland* (Oxford University Press, Oxford 2010); Czesław Łuczak, *Arthur Greiser* (PSO, Poznań 1997).

statement of grounds that accompanied the judgment.[101] Therefore it is not surprising that certain elements of that statement reflect the views that Rappaport held already in the interwar period.

The statement emphasized that the responsibility for participating in an aggressive war transcends the interests of the Polish state and nation.[102] Unfortunately, the definition of an aggressive war was not contemplated in the judgment,[103] but it is evident that – in line with Rappaport's published views from the interwar period – an aggressive war was treated as directed against the entire human culture and civilization.

The Supreme National Tribunal used not only the notion of a war of aggression, but also that of 'biological and cultural extermination (genocide) of neighbouring nations'.[104] This makes the judgment in Greiser's case not just the first judgment ever to address the responsibility for a crime against peace, but also the first one to address genocide ('a new crime against the interests of humanity and against the demands of national and international conscience'[105]). Genocide was defined as a path towards the physical and spiritual extermination of both Poles and Jews.[106]

Rappaport was familiar with Lemkin's work and he had the opportunity to meet Lemkin after World War II and lobby in favour of the adoption of the Convention on the Prevention and Punishment of the Crime of Genocide.[107] Despite his assistance in the matter, Rappaport himself did not believe that genocide constituted a separate crime. Rather, he perceived it to be a drastic form of mass-scale killing.[108]

---

[101] Siewierski, 'Emil Stanisław Rappaport', 543.

[102] Rappaport, Naród Zbrodniarz, 10.

[103] However, the issue of the legality of the German invasion was largely discussed by the court's expert/court expert, Ludwik Ehrlich; see Ludwik Ehrlich, 'Agresja III Rzeszy Niemieckiej na Polskę – pogwałcenie norm prawa międzynarodowego'; Ludwik Ehrlich, 'Zagadnienie wojny we współczesnym prawie międzynarodowym' in Ekspertyzy i orzeczenia przed Najwyższym Trybunałem Narodowym. Część I Agresja III Rzeszy Niemieckiej na Polskę i okupacja hitlerowska w Polsce w świetle prawa międzynarodowego (Ministerstwo Sprawiedliwości, Główna Komisja Badania Zbrodni Hitlerowskich w Polsce, Warsaw 1979) 11 ff.

[104] Cyprian, Sawicki, Siedem wyroków Najwyższego Trybunału Narodowego, 10–11.

[105] Ibid. 13

[106] Ibid. 14.

[107] Emil Stanisław Rappaport, 'Z międzynarodowej komisji karnej i penitencjarnej. Sesja Zwyczajna (Zebranie Ogólne) w Bernie, Lipiec – Sierpień 1948' (1948) 9/10 Państwo i Prawo 122.

[108] Stefan Lelental, 'Profesor Emil Stanisław Rappaport – uczony, kodyfikator, organizator i uczestnik międzynarodowego ruchu naukowego, inicjator uchwalenia Kodeksu

The judgment in Greiser's case also addressed the issue of responsibility for issuing an order and carrying out an unlawful order issued by a superior. The responsibility was attributed to both the person who issued the order and the person who carried it out (*delictum sui generis*). The judgment also acknowledged that inciting others to commit a crime (being a 'perpetrator in an intellectual sense') incurred responsibility. This was interpreted as participation in a criminal enterprise, a group of criminals, in which different persons play different roles of various natures and engage in various forms of direct participation. In this aspect, the judgment reflected a perspective similar to that articulated in *A Nation That is a Criminal*.

Greiser was sentenced to death. The sentence bears Rappaport's signature along those of the other judges; no information is available as to whether he opposed this decision, which was definitely in conflict with his earlier views.[109] The execution was public. It drew a crowd so massive (approximately 100,000 spectators showed up to watch)[110] that the communist authorities never made any execution public again. This was the only case before the Supreme National Tribunal in which Rappaport was a judge. This might have been a result of his views, which were being considered dissident by the communist regime. His notion of biological (endogenous) and psycho-social (exogenous) sources of crime was incompatible with the official doctrine. Moreover, his attitude to the death penalty was inconvenient, as was the existence of *A Nation That is a Criminal*.

It is surprising that Rappaport, involved as he was in the process of the development of international criminal law in the interwar era, published very little about the responsibility of Nazi criminals after World War II.[111] This is likely due to two circumstances. First, he was by this time quite old. Second, the Nuremberg law interpretation had been

---

karnego wykonawczego, nauczyciel akademicki, kierownik pierwszego w Polsce Zakładu Prawa Karnego Wykonawczego' (2015) 89 *Przegląd Więziennictwa Polskiego* 5,11.

[109] Before World War II, Rappaport argued that the right to impose the capital penalty should be reserved only for those judges who are ready to carry it out themselves. Przeperski, *Prawnik trzech epok*.

[110] Marek Przybylski, 'Publiczna egzekucja Arthura Greisera w poznańskiej prasie' in Kamila Kwasik, Jan Jaroszyński, Grzegorz Łęcicki (eds.), *Media wobec śmierci. Tom 1* (Elipsa, Warsaw 2012) 131 ff.

[111] See, for example, Emil Stanisław Rappaport, 'Przynależność do Waffen SS (formacji wojskowych Sztafet Ochronnych). Art. 4§3 dekretu z dnia 31 sierpnia 1944' (1948a) 5–6 *Państwo i Prawo* 200; 'Ludobójstwo jako delictum iuris gentium w kodeksach karnych krajowych' (1948b) 9–10 *Państwo i Prawo* 55.

monopolized in Poland by the duo of Jerzy Sawicki and Tadeusz Cyprian.

In the period 1947–1951, Rappaport served as the President of the Criminal Chamber of the Polish Supreme Court. In this capacity he must have been aware of how the new communist regime was using the justice system to persecute the opposition and how the communists were pursuing a complete takeover of the justice administration.[112] He must have witnessed how justice was perverted and courts were used as instruments of murder of the Polish national heroes: Witold Pilecki and August Emil Fieldorf (Nil), to name just two.[113]

As for the university where he worked, it is also certain that he must have witnessed blatantly biased hiring decisions.[114] It is therefore fair to ponder Rappaport's attitude towards the new Polish authorities and towards the Soviet Union. Rappaport viewed the Soviets as liberators most definitely in 1945.[115] He wrote in one of his publications that he believed the Soviet Union to be 'a democratic friend of Poland and an ally in the fight against the common enemy, Hitler's Third Reich'. Yet, declarations along these exact lines were included at the time in everything that went to print, no matter what the topic: they were simply the price of publication.

An example of Rappaport clearly making a concession to the new regime was his declaration that his chair at the university carried out its research using the Marxist method. This proved insufficient; accusations were made against him to the effect that what he called a 'dynamic school' or a 'bio-psychosocial school' was in fact a continuation of his pre-war theories and Rappaport failed to properly take class struggle into account.[116] Indeed, Rappaport's last publications suggest that with time he abandoned his radical views expressed in *A Nation That is a Criminal* and returned to the sociological school of thought and to his admiration

---

[112] On the sovietization of the judicial system of Poland, see Andrzej Rzepliński, *Sądownictwo w PRL* (Polonia, London 1990) 26 ff.

[113] Rappaport did not sit on the bench during these political trials, but critics of Rappaport stressed that Rappaport was involved in the political trials of 1930s when the Polish Supreme Court was used to establish authoritarian system in Poland. See Aleksander Mogilnicki, *Wspomnienia adwokata i sędziego* (Wolters Kluwer, Warsaw 2016) 346–347; Stefan Glaser, *Urywki wspomnień* (Odnowa, London 1974) 71–72.

[114] Bohdan Baranowski, Krzysztof Baranowski, *Trudne lata Uniwersytetu Łódzkiego (1949–1956)* (University of Lodz Press, Lodz 1990) 70–71.

[115] Rappaport, *Naród Zbrodniarz*, 27–28.

[116] Janiszewska-Talago, *Szkoła antropologiczna*, 138.

for von Liszt.[117] Rappaport was useful for the authorities when they wanted to legitimize institutions such as the Supreme National Tribunal, but not trustworthy enough to be offered any positions of power. Regarding the latter, his age also become an obstacle.

Rappaport's chief focus after World War II was his academic work at the University of Lodz, where he remained employed until 1960. He devoted his time to the study of criminal enforcement law.[118] He managed to establish a separate unit within the university dedicated to this issue. However, on 1 October 1960 the unit was dissolved, just one day after Rappaport officially retired on 30 September 1960 aged 83.[119]

After World War II, in line with his general focus on enforcement law, Rappaport became active in the Societé International de Défence Sociale/Centro Internazionale di Studi di Difesa Sociale (SIDS). It was founded on 1 January 1947 by Filippo Gramatica and published its own journal, *Rivista di Difesa Sociale*. Rappaport became a member-correspondent of the journal and a member of the Board of Directors of SIDS (from 1954), and considered the association to be as important as the AIDP.[120]

As for the AIDP itself, it was only Rappaport's persistence that ensured the survival of its Polish section throughout the Stalinist period. Rappaport convened 'conferences by correspondence' and produced formal documents that appointed new AIDP officials, even though the section was essentially non-existent in practice. Thanks to Rappaport's efforts, when the communist regime finally allowed Polish lawyers to become genuinely involved in the AIDP again, the Polish section simply resumed its active work instead of having to be formally re-established. Naturally, Rappaport became the head of the Polish section within the AIDP and was also the head of the delegations to the AIDP congresses in Athens in 1957.[121]

4.5 Conclusions

Emil Stanisław Rappaport died in August 1965 at the age of 88. Throughout his life, he steered clear of conflict. In theoretical debates, he preferred the 'third way', combining the elements of the two opposing

---

[117] Ibid. 127–129.
[118] Olszewski, 'Jubileusz prof. dr Emila Stanisława Rappaporta', 658.
[119] Lelental, 'Profesor Emil Stanisław Rappaport', 7.
[120] Lelental, 'Emil Stanisław Rappaport (1877–1965)', xiii.
[121] Kita, Pytlas, *W służbie nauki*, 347.

mainstream trends. He was hyperactive, which both annoyed and astonished those around him. Leszek Kubicki, a respected Polish lawyer in the interwar era, coined the expression 'Rappaportas' to warn others that Rappaport is around and they should take care not to stumble into him and risk getting roped into his projects for the day.

Yet Rappaport's active work between World War I and II generated tangible results. The ban on propaganda for war was included in the interwar-era criminal codes in Poland, Romania and Brazil. After World War II, it was also codified in the International Covenant on Civil and Political Rights Article 20 which reads: '1. Any propaganda for war shall be prohibited by law.' The principle of universal prosecution and the notion of a crime under the law of nations have become ingrained in the debate on the topic. Many norms of criminal law have been unified. Finally, there has been lively debate on issues of criminal enforcement and the death penalty. Moreover, Rappaport provided opportunities for numerous Polish lawyers, including Rafał Lemkin, to take the stage and exert their influence at international events. Rappaport drafted the statement of grounds that accompanied the judgment addressing responsibility for the crime against peace, the first one ever issued in legal history. He advanced the notion of criminal responsibility for participating in a joint criminal enterprise. It is important to remember that observers at Greiser's trial included inter alia Telford Taylor, who served as the prosecutor in the subsequent Nuremberg trials. Last but not least, Rappaport was a founder of the AIDP, an organization that was open to criminal lawyers of all schools of thought and that provided a forum where the contributions of lawyers from Central Europe were met with appreciation. Despite all these achievements, Rappaport is remembered in Poland mostly because of his translation of Cesare Beccaria's *Dei delitti e delle pene* (1764) into Polish.

5

International Criminal Justice as Universal Social Defence

Quintiliano Saldaña (1878–1938)

IGNACIO DE LA RASILLA DEL MORAL

> *y muy antiguo y muy moderno;*
> *audaz, cosmopolita* ...
>
> Rubén Darío, Cantos de vida y esperanza *(1905)*

Figure 5.1 Portrait of Quintiliano Saldaña (1878–1938).

5.1 Introduction

Quintiliano Saldaña García-Rubio (1878–1938) was the leading authority on international criminal law at the dawn of the discipline in Spain and the first legal scholar to teach a course on international criminal justice at The

Hague Academy of International Law, in 1925. One of the founders and vice-president of the Association internationale de droit pénale, a member of several European academies and international learned societies, a visiting professor in many European universities, and the Spanish representative at numerous international conferences, Saldaña published his academic work in several languages and was translated into others, including his own. He was also a remarkable public intellectual who wrote numerous social works on university education international affairs and a series of intellectual biographies of figures in the literature and the social and legal sciences. Quintiliano Saldaña's very prolific work in criminal law and criminology with sociological and anthropological features went on to influence the development of criminal law and criminology in Spain, and established him as one of the leading proponents of legal pragmatism in European criminal law circles in the interwar period. Saldaña understood the theory of legal pragmatism as a reaction against "religious prejudices and ethical conventionality" in the Spanish criminal law system, defining it as "anti-rationalism, anti-dogmatism, anti-traditionalism. Pragmatism is, thus, more than scepticism, positivism and empiricism; it is scientific transcendental utilitarianism."[1] Saldaña transposed his theoretical work and practical specialization in domestic criminal law and criminology into highly influential international criminal law constructs and ideas during the early formative stage of international criminal law.

An analysis and reconstruction of Saldaña's opus at the intersection of the domestic and international criminal law spheres of his theoretical and practical work is justified because the history of international criminal law cannot be grasped solely as the history of a specialized branch of law following in the wake of the progressive specialization of public international law. Instead, the historical development of international criminal law should also be examined with an attentive eye to the theoretical and practical legislative development of criminal legal trends of thought in domestic settings. Moreover, this double approach contributes to the 'historical memory' of international law in Europe and, more specifically, to the historical memory of international law in Spain.[2] The life and international legal work of Saldaña, one of the most cosmopolitan

---

[1] Quintiliano Saldaña, *Teoría pragmática del Derecho penal* (Buenos Aires: Talleres Gráficos de la Penitenciaría Nacional, 1925), pp. 5–6. All translations from Spanish and other languages are the work of the author unless otherwise indicated.

[2] Ignacio de la Rasilla, 'Playing Hide and Seek with "a Past that Will Not Pass" in the History of International Law' in Ineta Ziemele and George Ulfstein (eds.) *How International Law Works in Times of Crisis* (Oxford: Oxford University Press, 2019), pp. 223–239.

Spanish legal scholars of the first third of the twentieth century, still remains understudied, along with much of the Spanish international legal scholarship of the 'Silver Age of Spanish Culture' (1898–1936).[3]

This chapter proceeds in three parts. The first part surveys Saldaña's formative years and his early academic professional development, examining the influence of Franz von Liszt's Marburg School of Criminal Law on his academic interests and professional career until the end of World War I. The second part examines Saldaña's seminal theory of 'universal social defence' and his 1925 Hague Academy course La justice pénale internationale, which included one of the first proposals ever devised for an international criminal code. It also studies Saldaña's legislative contribution to the 1928 Spanish Criminal Code project, which is considered an example of a proto-fascist criminal code. The third part follows Saldaña's career during the Second Spanish Republic, surveying his criminal law and criminology work in the development of his theory of legal pragmatism. It also revisits his engagement with the mid-1930s international legal debates on terrorism in his contribution to the work of the International Bureau for the Unification of Criminal Law. Each of these three parts broadly corresponds to the main stages in Saldaña's polyhedral intellectual life. What is distinctive about Saldaña's singular contribution to the dawn of international criminal justice was his acute perception of the possibilities that this early phase in international criminal justice and the parallel project for the unification of criminal law offered for the development and programmatic internationalization of the theoretical cornerstones of his criminal legal theories. The chapter's conclusion revisits the mysterious circumstances of Saldaña's death during the Spanish Civil War and the dark legacy of his legal thought in the criminal law system of General Franco's regime in Spain.

5.2 The Influence of the Marburg School on Saldaña's Early Professional Development

Quintiliano Saldaña García-Rubio was born into a well-off family in the homonymous village of Saldaña in the province of Palencia in the north of Castille and León in 1878. Apart from the fact that as a child he

---

[3] The 'Silver Age of Spanish Culture' was known as such because it paralleled the intellectual and artistic achievements of the 'Spanish Golden Age,' which was a period of flourishing of the arts, literature and science that was brought to a dramatic halt by the Spanish Civil War (1936–1939). See Ignacio de la Rasilla, *In the Shadow of Vitoria: A History of International Law in Spain, 1770–1953* (Leiden: Brill-Nijhoff, 2017).

5 QUINTILIANO SALDAÑA

suffered from a severe congenital eye condition and that he attended high school in León, little is known of his childhood and adolescence.[4] This was against the backdrop of the early stages of the Spanish Restoration period (1876–1923), in which there was a negotiated 'peaceful rotation' (*turno pacífico*) between the conservative and liberal parties. This rigged electoral system served as an "efficient replacement of the mechanisms of military rebellion"[5] that had unravelled the consolidation of the Spanish constitutional liberal state since the independence of most of its overseas colonies in the 1820s.

After graduating precociously in law from the University of Valladolid in 1898, Saldaña went on to study at the Central University of Madrid, the only one of the ten universities then existing in Spain that was accredited with the provision of doctoral degrees. In Madrid, Saldaña combined his doctoral studies with research at the Institute of Criminology in 1901 and with work at Madrid's Laboratory of Experimental Psychology from 1902 to 1904. After defending his doctoral thesis *¿Qué es la pena?*[6] (*What is Penalty?*) in 1905, he prepared for the official exams for vacant criminal law chairs in Spain and obtained the chair of criminal law at the University of Santiago de Compostela in 1908, and soon afterwards the one at the University of Seville in 1909.

Immediately after taking up his chair at Seville University, Saldaña wrote La Enseñanza: lo que es, lo que debe ser (What university teaching is and what it should become).[7] After the Spanish-American War of 1898, a reform of university studies had become a very topical intellectual preoccupation in Spain. The war had resulted in an extended perception that the causes of the military humiliation and the loss of the remnants of the Spanish overseas empire lay in Spanish educational backwardness and international isolation. This had prompted a widespread intellectual debate on the 'Spanish problem,' to which the solution – as José Ortega y Gasset would famously pronounce – was Europe.[8] The goal of reforming all levels of the education system was paramount in the Regenerationism agenda. This social and intellectual programme of

---

[4] Jaime Masaveu, 'El profesor Saldaña, figura de la ciencia penal' (1967) 1–2 *Anuario de Derecho penal y ciencias penales* 401–418, at 406–407.

[5] Raymond Carr, *España 1808–1936* (Barcelona: Ed. Ariel, 1970), p. 344.

[6] Quintiliano Saldaña, *¿Qué es la pena?* (Madrid: Impr. Arias, 1908).

[7] Quintiliano Saldaña, *La Enseñanza: lo que es, lo que debe ser* (Seville: Ed. El Correo de Andalucía, 1909).

[8] The literature on José Ortega y Gasset and Spain is extremely extensive, see, for example, Juan Pablo Fusi, 'Ortega y España,' in Antonio Morales Moya et al. (eds.) *Historia de la nación y del nacionalismo español* (Barcelona: Galaxia Gutenberg, 2013), pp. 638–650.

national revitalization had initially been proposed by Joaquín Costa (1846–1911) with a democratic reformist agenda for the 'live forces' of society to take over the Spanish system of local and provincial institutionalized electoral corruption, known as *caciquismo* (from *cacique*, or local boss). A lasting influence of the Regenerationist movement was its ruthless postulation of education as the bedrock of Spanish modernization at a time when education reforms were badly needed. Illiteracy, having barely decreased from 70 per cent in 1860,[9] remained at a staggering 64 per cent at the turn of the century. This agenda was prompted by the Institución libre de enseñanza, which was established in 1876 by a group of scholars among whom were several prominent international law scholars such as Rafael Altamira, later judge at the Permanent Court of International Justice (PCIJ). During the first third of the twentieth century, the 'institutionists' played important roles in government education administration, including in a reform of university legal studies.

In La Enseñanza: lo que es, lo que debe ser, which was imbued with Regenerationism, Saldaña highlighted that "Spanish official university teaching is completely discredited,"[10] before characterizing the state of the art of legal education itself as "scientific misery."[11] Against the traditional *ex cathedra* and *magister-dixit* attitudes, Saldaña proposed reforming both the university administrative system and the law curriculum by advocating new research-oriented teaching methods and the introduction of practice-oriented learning systems in law. University reform, and the social role of education remained areas of interest in Saldaña's subsequent works. In the 1910s, he published *La Enseñanza en España*[12] (*Teaching in Spain*) and *La Educación ciudadana*[13] (*Citizenship Education*), advocating the reformist and Europeanist educational agenda of Regenerationism.

Soon after occupying his chair at Seville University in 1909, Saldaña became one of the first *pensionados* (fellows) of the Junta de ampliación de estudios e investigación científica (Board of Extension of Studies and Scientific Research). This board was established in 1907 under the presidency of the first Spanish Nobel Prize in Medicine with the mission of

---

[9] Alfredo Liebana Collado, *La educación en España en el primer tercio del siglo XX: la situación del analfabetismo y la escolarización* (Madrid: Universidad de Mayores de Experiencia Recíproca, 2009), p. 5.

[10] Saldaña, *La Enseñanza*, p. 10.

[11] Ibid., p. 9.

[12] Quintiliano Saldaña, *La Enseñanza en España* (Madrid: Impr. Torres, 1915).

[13] Quintiliano Saldaña, *La Educación ciudadana* (Madrid: Impr. Torres, 1916).

fostering the Europeanization of Spanish universities and science. It was one of several similar institutional enterprises established in European countries to encourage the internationalization of science as a remedy to the "scientific, cultural and educational stagnation that ensues from a lack of scientific exchanges and contacts."[14] As a fellow of this board, Saldaña went to study at the University of Berlin under Franz von Liszt (1851–1919), the founder of the Marburg School of criminal law. This was a key encounter for Saldaña's academic work and career, and also indirectly for the study of international criminal justice, both in Spain and internationally, in at least two main senses.

First, this was because Saldaña imported the Marburg programme to Spain, together with its postulation of a total science of criminal law – including criminal anthropology, criminal psychology and criminal statistics – and F. von Liszt's doctrinal teachings, especially in the realms of 'social defence' and the theory of preventive criminal law.[15] According to Enrique Cury, the innovation that this school of criminal legal thought brought with respect to late nineteenth century conceptions was that it "introduce[d] the consideration of the specific man in the legal appreciation of the punishable fact" in order to "evidence the sterility of a criminal law founded on abstract idealizations, and reclaim instead the instrumentalization of the punitive sanction for social purposes."[16] The doctrine of social defence, also known by its advocates as 'humanist criminal policy,'[17] developed into different schools of thought. What they had in common was an effort to integrate the theory of crime and the social science of criminality into an effective criminal law policy based on tailoring the penalty to the personal characteristics of the criminal so as to facilitate his reintegration and to better protect society. However, over time some of the practical corollaries of the different variants of the theory, such as the 'state of dangerousness' in the positivist school or the preventive imposition of security measures against 'anti-social' categories of individuals, were criticized on the basis of their underlying determinism and the risks of de-juridification of the penal sanction

---

[14] Carlos Espaliu Berdud, 'La Junta de Ampliación de Estudios e Investigaciones Científicas y el Derecho internacional' in Ignacio de la Rasilla and Yolanda Gamarra (eds.) *Historia del pensamiento internacionalista español del siglo XX* (Pamplona: Thompson Reuters Aranzadi, 2012), pp. 153–184, 160.

[15] See Enrique Cury Urzua, 'La prevención especial como límite de la pena' (1988) 41 *Anuario de Derecho penal y ciencias penales* 685–702, at 686.

[16] Ibid.

[17] Marc Ancel, *La defense sociale nouvelle: un mouvement de politique criminelle humaniste* (Paris: Editions Cujas, 1954).

they entailed. As we shall see below, in the early 1920s Saldaña transposed and extended the general conceptual category of social defence into a progressive internationalist theory of international criminal justice.

Second, and of particular relevance to Saldaña's subsequent projection in the field of international criminal justice was the fact that F. von Listz, who himself was the author of a widely disseminated and re-edited international law textbook,[18] had been one of the three founders, along with Gerald van Hamel and Adolphe Prins, of the International Union of Penal Law (IUPL, Internationale Kriminalistische Vereinigung) in 1889. The IUPL was founded in Vienna with a programmatic goal aligned with von Liszt's doctrines of "consecrating in the science of criminal law and criminal legislation" the principle that "criminality and its repression must be analysed from both a social and a juridical perspective."[19] The IUPL was dissolved with the outbreak of World War I but it was the associational antecedent of the Association internationale de droit pénal (AIDP), which was established in Paris in 1924 on the initiative of Saldaña in association with Henri Donnedieu de Vabres.[20] The AIDP defined itself as an apolitical organization whose chief purposes were to serve as a platform for academic exchanges regarding the theoretical study and practical application of criminal law and *inter alia* "to contribute to the theoretical and practical development of international penal law to achieve a universal penal law."[21] As is apparent elsewhere in this book, during the interwar period it would become one of the most authoritative fora for the development of international criminal legal studies, preparing a series of drafts for an international criminal code and a draft statute for the establishment of a criminal chamber within the PCIJ.[22] Along with the International Bureau for the Unification of Criminal Law (IBUCL), which was established in the late 1920s by some of its members, it also participated in academic debates about the drafting of two anti-terrorist conventions by a special committee set up within the League of Nations in 1934.

---

[18] Frank von Liszt, *Das Völkerrecht: systematisch Dargestellt* (Berlin: J. Springer, 1898).

[19] Ignacio Berdugo Gómez de la Torre, *La evolución del derecho penal contemporáneo y la Unión Internacional de Derecho Penal* (Salamanca: Universidad Pontificia de Salamanca, 1982), p. 14.

[20] See 'Association international de droit pénal. Assemblée constitutive tenue le 28 mars 1924 à la faculté de droit de Paris' (1924) 1 *Révue internationale de droit pénal* 3.

[21] Ibid.

[22] John A. E. Vervaele, 'The UIDP/AIDP: 125 Years Serving Criminal Justice, Human Rights and Humanity' (2015) 86 *International Review of Penal Law* 759–780.

5 QUINTILIANO SALDAÑA

Saldaña's stay with von Listz in Berlin in 1909 and 1910 was complemented by his attending courses at the Institut Solvay in Brussels (1910) and visits to the University of Leuven's Laboratory of Psychology (1910). In 1911, he also visited the Social Museum of Paris and audited courses at the Universities of Geneva and Oxford.[23] These early foreign research experiences served Saldaña very well in professional terms. In 1911, he left the University of Seville to take up the chair of criminal anthropology and advanced criminal studies in the doctoral programme at the University of Madrid. In 1913, he was also appointed professor at the Spanish Criminological Institute and he became professor of the School of Criminology and an honorary fellow of the Spanish Academy of Jurisprudence and Legislation in 1918.[24] His foreign experiences also meant a turning point in his academic production. His doctrinal work during this decade included voluminous publications on the origins of criminology,[25] criminal anthropology, criminal justice,[26] social defence and social perfection.[27] During the 1910s Saldaña also translated the eighteenth edition of F. von Listz's leading criminal law treatise *Lehrbuch des deutschen Strafrechts* (Textbook of German Criminal Law) into Spanish, appending it with historical Spanish criminal law materials.[28]

Beyond his doctrinal criminal law work and his already mentioned attention to the reform of the Spanish university system, Saldaña's production as a public intellectual developed in two main directions in the 1910s. First, he became the celebrated author of a series of intellectual bibliographies of great figures in letters and the social and legal sciences, producing a series called *Mentalidades españolas* (*Spanish Mentalities*) with works on Miguel de Cervantes,[29] José Ortega y Gasset, Pío Baroja,[30]

---

[23] Masaveu, 'El profesor Saldaña,' 407.

[24] Ibid., p. 408.

[25] Quintiliano Saldaña, *Los orígenes de la Criminología* (Madrid: Ed. Suárez, 1914).

[26] Quintiliano Saldaña, *La Antropología criminal y la justicia penal* (Madrid: Ed. Reus, 1915).

[27] Quintiliano Saldaña, *Defensa social y perfección social* (Madrid: Impr. Universidad de Madrid, 1916).

[28] Franz von Liszt, *Tratado de Derecho penal* (Traducido de la 18ª edición alemana y adicionado con la historia del derecho en España por Quintiliano Saldaña) (Madrid: Editorial Reus, 1917).

[29] Quintiliano Saldaña, 'Cervantes y su mundo' (1917) I *Revista quincenal Barcelona* 492–502. Quintiliano Saldaña, *La Criminología de "El Quijote": notas para un estudio* (Madrid, Ed. Tours, 1926).

[30] Masaveu, 'El profesor Saldaña,' 412 referring to Quintiliano Saldaña, José Ortega y Gasset (1917), Quintiliano Saldaña, Pío Baroja (1918).

Miguel de Unamuno[31] and Dorado Montero.[32] This line of intellectual bibliographical work continued in the 1920s with new works on Angel Ganivet[33] and Jeremy Bentham.[34] It also extended to the criminal law area with works on Concepción Arenal (a pioneer feminist and criminal law expert who in 1879 became the first woman to publish a book-length work on international law),[35] Enrico Ferri, the founder of the Italian School of Criminology[36] and the Marquis of Beccaria,[37] whose 1764 book *Dei delitti e delle pene* became a landmark in the reform of the tenebrous criminal law system of the *ancien régime* in Europe.

Second, Saldaña was also an attentive observer and commentator on contemporary political events in the 1910s. In 1918 he released a detailed contextual commentary on the Russian Soviet Constitution which contained its first integral translation into Spanish. He stated that he wrote this constitutional law work because "the results of a lasting tomorrow" are contained in constitutions, understood as the "normative seed of laws – the juridical lines of social crystallographied systems."[38] Furthermore, he participated in intellectual political initiatives related to international events.[39] In this sense, his active positioning regarding World War I and the hotly debated matter of Spain's neutrality in it is notable. In early 1918, he founded and became the director of *Renovación Española*, a weekly illustrated magazine, forty issues of which were published between January and November 1918. This publication served as a platform for Germanophile intellectuals and contained articles on politics, history, literature, the arts, pedagogy, the theatre and war issues.[40]

---

[31] Quintiliano Saldaña, *Miguel de Unamuno* (Madrid, Ed. Rubiños, 1919).

[32] Quintiliano Saldaña, *Dorado Montero* (Madrid: Ed. Reus, 1920).

[33] Quintiliano Saldaña, *Ángel Ganivet* (Madrid: Ed. Hernando, 1930).

[34] Quintiliano Saldaña and Juan Sánchez Rivera de la Lastra, *El Utilitarismo: estudio de las doctrinas de Jeremias Bentham su expositor en España* (Madrid: Ed. Reus, 1922).

[35] Concepcion Arenal, *Ensayo sobre el Derecho de Gentes* (Madrid: Imprenta de la Revista de legislación, 1879).

[36] Masaveu, 'El profesor Saldaña,' 412.

[37] Quintiliano Saldaña, 'Estudio Preliminar' in M. de Beccaria (ed.) *El Derecho penal: de los delitos y de las penas* (Madrid: Editorial Hernando, 1930).

[38] Quintiliano Saldaña, *La revolución rusa: la Constitución rusa de 10 de Julio de 1918* (Madrid: Ed. Reus, 1919).

[39] Ibid., p. 6.

[40] Proyecto de Filosofía en Español, 'Renovación Española' available at http://filosofia.org /hem/med/m037.htm.

5.3 The Theory of Universal Social Defence and the International Criminal Code

References to a unification of international penal law can be found scattered throughout Saldaña's works during the 1910s.[41] However, the international criminal law aspects of his legal thought mainly developed in the early 1920s. These took two main orientations. First, his previous domestic engagement with the notion of 'social defence' was transposed and extended into a detailed supranational theory of 'universal social defence' of which international criminal justice was an essential component. A second element from the domestic sphere of Saldaña's legal thought that was transposed to the international criminal legal realm was his interest in the codification and reform of the Spanish criminal law code along the lines of a preventive theory of criminal law. This area of interest is apparent in his appending of an Avant-Projet de Code Pénal International to his course La justice pénale internationale at The Hague Academy of International Law in 1925.

5.3.1 International Criminal Justice as Universal Social Defence

Saldaña's international criminal law ideas evolved in parallel with international criminal law discussions during the initial phase of the League of Nations. These ideas had entered the postwar legal-diplomatic scene as a result of the provision in the Treaty of Versailles on the international trial and individual international criminal responsibility of the former Kaiser. The cultivation of international criminal law was further nurtured by discussions on the recommendations by the advisory committee of jurists charged with drafting the statute of the PCIJ and the establishment of a parallel High Court of International Justice "competent to try crimes constituting a breach of international public order or against the universal law of nations." However, this proposal was considered premature in the light of the "non-existence of any generally recognized international criminal law at the time"[42] and prompted the Third Committee to invite the "most authoritative institutions which are devoted to the study of international law" to explore the subject further. Several international scientific associations, notably the International Law Association, the

---

[41] Masaveu, 'El profesor Saldaña,' p. 10.
[42] Historical survey of the question of international criminal jurisdiction, memorandum submitted by the Secretary-General, United Nations – General Assembly. International Law Commission, A/CN.4/7/Rev. 1, 1949, 12–14.

Inter-Parliamentary Union and, as mentioned before, the AIDP, set to work preparing a series of drafts for an international criminal code, and a draft statute for the establishment of a criminal chamber within the Permanent Court of International Justice. Encouraged by these early debates, in 1922 Saldaña published "La justicia penal internacional" in Spanish.[43] In this early work, which he continued developing in 1923,[44] he advocated, among other things, that the PCIJ should aspire to have universal compulsory jurisdiction and supreme criminal competence. These early works in Spanish became the matrix for Saldaña's Hague Academy course on La Justice pénale internationale in 1925. They were also integrated into Saldaña's own theory of universal social defence, which was originally published in French in 1924,[45] with consecutive editions and translations into other languages, including Spanish, in the following years.[46]

The point of departure for Saldaña's theory of 'universal social defence' was the application of a 'legal pragmatic' benchmark – a theory of effective law in the light of social experience. The international 'social experience' that served as a reference for Saldaña was the failure of The Hague's Permanent Court of Arbitration (PCA), to which no party made recourse at the outbreak of World War I. According to Saldaña, the failure of the PCA cast serious doubt on the potential effectiveness of the recently established PCIJ, the nucleus of which had emerged from the PCA and which had inherited the defects of its predecessor as an institution able to effectively avoid future wars.[47] This reflection prompted Saldaña to wonder whether the time was ripe to "establish a new system of legal and social defence – in the broadest sense – with the concepts of this new order being erected on social facts alone."[48]

Saldaña considered that the aftermath of the war provided the "opportunity to transform international life into universal social life."[49] By 'universal social life' he meant the antithesis of nationalism, with which different peoples wrongly attribute to themselves the "right to break the bonds that unite them."[50] For Saldaña, the new universal social life was

[43] Quintiliano Saldaña, 'La justicia penal internacional' (1922) 32 *Nuestro Tiempo*.
[44] Quintiliano Saldaña, *La justicia penal internacional* (Madrid: Impr. Alrededor del Mundo, 1923).
[45] Quintiliano Saldaña, *La defense sociale universelle* (Paris: Impr. Coueslant, 1924).
[46] Quintiliano Saldaña, *La defensa social universal. Conferencias de París, Roma y La Haya* (Madrid: Editorial Góngora, 1926).
[47] Ibid., 11–16.
[48] Ibid., 16.
[49] Saldaña, *La defensa social universal*, p. 16.
[50] Ibid., 18.

5 QUINTILIANO SALDAÑA

inspired by the emergence of a new "universal man,"[51] the embodiment of a humanism whose roots lay in the French Revolution. The emergence of a universal social life and universal man "suppose[d] the idea and require[d] the immediate reality of a legal entity placed above states."[52] Saldaña traced the roots of the upcoming 'state of universal law' by applying Auguste Comte's three-stage theory to the historical evolution of the Western intellectual internationalist tradition. In his *Cours de philosophie positive*,[53] Comte had theorized that societies, in the image of the individual mind in its search for knowledge, traverse three different theoretical stages of progress, which in turn determine their social dynamics. The 'theological or fictitious stage' is defined by a search for the essential nature of things and a related belief in supernatural forces. In the transitional 'metaphysical or abstract stage,' by contrast, supernatural forces are replaced by abstract entities, which are inherent to the diversity of beings and conceived as able to generate all phenomena by themselves. Finally, in the 'scientific or positive stage,' the human spirit admits the impossibility of apprehending absolute notions and instead focuses on discovering effective laws through reason, observation and experimentation. Similarly, for Saldaña the Western intellectual tradition had progressed from manifestations of the *Respublica Christiana* (the 'theological stage') in the Middle Ages, to intellectually influential works produced in the sixteenth, seventeenth, eighteenth and nineteenth centuries by humanist philosophers, international law scholars and federalist statesmen[54] (the 'metaphysical stage'), to the most recent works by international lawyers that have crystallized in the League of Nations (a 'positive stage').[55]

The next stage in this theory of international social progress was, according to Saldaña, a "pragmatic state of universal social life."[56] However, in order to be socially "effective," Saldaña considered that the new universal social life needed to be set "beyond the reach of particular states, and its formula, rather than being political and diplomatic, should be a juridical one."[57] For this to happen, the League of Nations,

---

[51] Ibid., 19–21.

[52] Ibid., 21.

[53] Auguste Comte, *Cours de philosophie positive* (Paris: Ed. Rouen Freres, 1830–1842 (6 volumes)).

[54] Saldaña, *La defensa social universal*, 24.

[55] Ibid., 21 to 25.

[56] Ibid., 25.

[57] Ibid., 25.

understood as "an international state" made up of particular states, should be transcended in accordance with the same historical pattern that first led to the juxtaposition of the nation-state along with feudal states, and eventually to the gradual disappearance of the latter within the nation-state. Only by first becoming "extra-national" and then "super-national"[58] (or supranational), could the League of Nations aspire to one day becoming a "league of free men." Only then, according to Saldaña's theory of universal social defence, would it be possible to bring about "a true state of universal law."[59]

Thus, for the universal state to emerge, it should not adopt as its cornerstone "sovereignty – the original sin of states – which had ruined pre-war international juridical life."[60] This was because, according to Saldaña, the "law of states [. . .] has deprived us of our natural freedom, giving us in exchange an anti-natural equality, that is, a fictional one."[61] For Saldaña, "men will not be equal before the law until the day when the law becomes unique, universal" and this achievement "depends on the extent to which men will be removed from their national armours."[62] For this purpose, Saldaña advocated a deepening and expansion of processes of on-going denationalization in the most diverse areas, including invention, trade, transport and means of communication.[63] However, not even this "progressive universal denationalization" would be enough to ensure the "triumph of universal reason over particularistic instincts." To preserve universal life and universal society it would be necessary to "protect and to defend it."[64] This is the ultimate assumption that brought Saldaña to his original theory of universal social defence.

For Saldaña, universal social defence required a scientific transformation of "sovereignty in light of its social function,"[65] or in other words that "sovereignty should be subjected to limitations born out of a social universal function."[66] A scientific approach to universal social defence also required a gradual development of an international scientific conscience that was favourable to it. Saldaña considered that this process had already begun under the League of Nations, where universal social

[58] Ibid., 26.
[59] Ibid., 26.
[60] Ibid., 27.
[61] Ibid., 33.
[62] Ibid., 33.
[63] Saldaña, *La defensa social*, 34–40.
[64] Ibid., 41.
[65] Ibid., 43.
[66] Ibid., 44.

defence was developing in a series of areas that had already started to receive protection by means of the creation of commissions and technical organizations. These different proto-dimensions of universal social defence included the military and the naval, the diplomatic, the political, the medical and sanitary, the economic and the intellectual spheres.

The next stage that Saldaña focused on was the criminal dimension of universal social defence.[67] He considered that this dimension, as the only one "devoid of particular organs in the League of Nations,"[68] should be re-organized in order for it to confront the threats that the emerging "universal solidarity society" faced. According to Saldaña, universal society was threatened by three categories of international criminality. The first of these was "essential or international criminality, or *proprio sensu*." This included four main types of international criminality: first, what he termed 'extra-national crimes,' crimes "committed outside the geographical limits of the state in the sea or the air [...] and by stateless criminals (*heitmatios*)"[69]; second, "international crime *proprio sensu*," that is crimes "prepared, continued or committed over the territory of different states or jurisdictions [...] or by criminals, who under the cloak of a nationality usually devote themselves to preparing, aiding or covering these [...] international crimes."[70] Third, there were "crimes against international law," a category he reserved for crimes "committed against a foreign state, against a head of state or government or diplomatic agents [...]" and by "international *sicarios*" at the service of a country who commit these crimes.[71] Finally, Saldaña added 'war of aggression,' defined as a "true category of war crime" (according to art. 16 of the Covenant) or international crime (according to art. 1.1 of the Treaty of Mutual Guarantee). This covered the leaders (heads of state and politicians) who caused the aggression.[72]

The other two categories in Saldaña's tripartite classification of international criminality were 'accidental international criminality' and 'eventual international criminality.' The first of these, according to Saldaña, included, inter alia, crimes committed during peacetime but in the context of military occupation or armed intervention in a foreign

[67] Ibid., 41.
[68] Ibid., 42.
[69] Saldaña, *La defensa social*, 49.
[70] Ibid., 49.
[71] Ibid., 49.
[72] Ibid., 50.

territory, while the second included situations involving "national criminals who fly abroad and are the subject of a request for extradition."[73]

For Saldaña, the inefficacy of the system of national repression for each of these categories required a complementary system of "international repression" for each category in the name of "international legal pragmatism": first, "international direct repression" against essential international criminality; and second, "international indirect repression" against accidental international criminality, both under the League of Nations; and third, "delegated international repression" by the state by delegation of the League for eventual international criminality. To exercise international repression of the first two types, the PCIJ should have both universal compulsory jurisdiction and also supreme criminal competence. According to Saldaña, this competence should be informed with a "power of appreciation" that can reach the "maximum level of judicial discretion"[74] in its application to a long list of crimes.[75]

Against this background, and because Saldaña was nonetheless aware that "universal criminal denationalization [was] nowadays a dream," he advocated paving the ground towards universal social defence by aiming for the "achievable goal" of an "international unification of criminal and penitentiary institutions."[76] He suggested establishing a Universal Penal Union[77] by international convention as a transitional formula to advance towards a future "denationalization of penalties." This would first require "unifying and codifying the dispositions of international criminal law" in order "to draft the future International Criminal Code."[78] This code, which Saldaña termed the "universal criminal code," should be appended to all national criminal codes.[79]

Finally, as a corollary to his reflections on universal social defence, Saldaña also occupied himself with what he termed "universal individual defence," which he considered to be the "counterpart and complement of universal social defence."[80] This universal individual defence required a "list of the rights of men (above the rights of citizens)." Anticipating debates that would be held at the United Nations Commission on

---

[73] Ibid., 49–51.
[74] Saldaña, *La defensa social*, 58.
[75] Ibid., 55–57.
[76] Ibid., 59.
[77] Ibid., 59–60
[78] Ibid., 62–63.
[79] Ibid.
[80] Ibid., 65.

5 QUINTILIANO SALDAÑA

Human Rights in the aftermath of World War II,[81] Saldaña advocated that the list of the rights of men should be drafted by the League of Nations and imposed, as an addition to the Covenant,[82] on all its members states.

5.3.2 The International Criminal Code

By the time his theory of universal social defence was published in 1924, Saldaña's theoretical methodological orientation in domestic criminal law had already shown a marked interest in codification and practical legal reform. He had devoted considerable doctrinal attention to a reform of the Spanish criminal code, publishing both his *Comentarios científico-prácticos al Código penal* (*Scientific-Practical Commentaries on the Criminal Code*) and *La reforma del Código penal* (*The Reform of the Criminal Code*) in 1920. In 1920 he also became a member of the Spanish Comisión permanente de Codification (Permanent Commission of Codification). This interest in reforming the Spanish criminal code continued in his book *El futuro Código penal* (*The Future Criminal Code*) in 1923. It therefore comes as no surprise that when he was appointed as the first author invited to teach a course on international criminal law at The Hague Academy of International Law he presented his own *avant-projet* for an International Criminal Code which he had begun outlining in his earlier works. This topic was of particular interest to other scholars and affiliates of the AIDP, such as Vespasian Pella, a champion of international criminal jurisdiction for international crimes, who would bring the topic up for collective discussion by the AIDP in 1926.[83]

In his 1925 course La justice pénale internationale, Saldaña approached international criminal justice as a historical institution resulting from the convergence of three distinct processes: the "evolution of facts," "the evolution of ideas" and the "evolution of institutions."[84] Each of these evolutions had, according to Saldaña, resulted in a great contemporary transformation. First, the evolution of the factual plane,

---

[81] Hersch Lauterpacht, *An International Bill of the Rights of Man* (New York: Columbia University Press, 1945).

[82] Ibid., 65.

[83] Mark Lewis, *The Birth of the New Justice. The Internationalization of Crime and Punishment, 1919–1950* (Oxford: University Press, Oxford 2014) 106.

[84] Quintiliano Saldaña, *La Justice Pénale Internationale, XX Collected Courses of the Hague Academy of International Law* (The Hague: Martinus Nijhoff, 1925) 227.

which had marked the evolution "from international legal assistance to supra-national legal existence" involved a "transformation of international legal life as a whole." Saldaña compared the traditional domain of international legal assistance – which included but was not limited to the domains of, for example, extradition and the execution of sentences, and was a complex of international public functions directly derived from the law of sovereignty, the most obvious feature of which was that it was "by definition discretionary and freely exercised"[85] – with what he termed the "post-war supra-national legal existence." Because of its continual development, its centralized structure and its necessary character,[86] the latter, while still "*in fieri*" was what "the future belongs to entirely."[87]

The second evolution was ideological. According to Saldaña, this was in turn responsible for the ongoing transformation "from international law to international justice."[88] Saldaña saw himself as contributing on the international ideological plane to the ever-evolving "domain where science and social life meet each other, that is, to the domain where ideas fight fiercely against facts in order to engender institutions."[89] In this context, after considering that "reforms in the international order are insufficient and what is needed is a true revolution,"[90] Saldaña championed the philosophy of legal pragmatism as the means to provide the science of international law[91] reconceived as 'international justice' with a different dynamic legal basis. This was defined as "active and necessary justice, provided with sanctions" which should be "applied to the life of nations in the same manner that judges apply it to individuals."[92] Saldaña saw the crystallization of this "transformation from international law to international justice" in the institutions of the League of Nations as providers of "international guarantees"[93] by sanctioning regimes.

Finally, the third process related to evolution on the institutional plane, was marked, according to Saldaña, by a third great transformation: the "passage from international arbitration to the permanent court of international justice." After examining several historical international dispute settlement mechanisms (good offices, mediation, international

---

[85] Ibid., 229.
[86] Ibid., 242.
[87] Ibid., 237.
[88] Ibid., 243.
[89] Ibid., 243.
[90] Ibid., 253.
[91] Ibid., 254.
[92] Saldaña, *La Justice Pénale*, 254.
[93] Ibid., 258.

congresses and arbitration) as examples of "half-justice," Saldaña considered the PCIJ to be the "first historical realization of an ordinary international justice"[94] in the long historical process of transition from the domain of "international injustice" to that of "international justice."[95]

Saldaña completed his analysis of these three great transformations with an *avant-project* for an International Criminal Code with the subtitle "The New International Criminal Codified Law," which was composed of 23 articles. He suggested that the project should be appended to the criminal codes of the member states of the League of Nations.[96] The code, which he described as being "at the service of international society (today, the League of Nations) in its fight against international criminality,"[97] should be presented for ratification to the national parliaments of the members of the League or authorized directly by the member states. In the case of non-compliance with this obligation within the requested deadline, the Council of the League of Nations would be empowered to take measures and the Assembly would be informed.[98] Moreover, all international criminals would be subject to the "compulsory jurisdiction and supreme criminal competence of the Permanent Court of International Justice."[99]

The draft international criminal code was divided into three parts. The first was a preliminary section in which Saldaña made the scope of the code's application in relation to other laws and its temporal, territorial and personal scopes of application explicit. The second was a general part devoted to criminal infractions and the repression thereof, and the third was a special part dedicated to individual infractions and their repression. In its turn, the special part contained two headings: one dealing with crimes against the international community or against its members, or committed in their domains; the second one dealing with crimes against directly protected individuals or nationals of the League of Nations. The code, which included aggression and breach of international obligations as types of state criminality,[100] was permeated with applications of the doctrine of social defence. Examples of Saldaña's transposition of the

---

[94] Ibid., 275.

[95] Ibid., 281.

[96] Art. 8 Avant-projet de code pénal international (le nouveau droit pénal international codifié) in Saldaña, *La Justice pénale*, pp. 379–422.

[97] Art. 1.

[98] Art. 7.

[99] Art. 23.

[100] Arts. 43 and 44.

tenets of the doctrine to the international criminal law domain included references to a "state of dangerousness,"[101] the consideration of "imprisonment" as a punishment that "in its application was but the medical-pedagogical development of a correctional treatment" and which, therefore, could "not be modified by arbitrary measures" (such as the "right to grant pardons" or "amnesty").[102] Similar logical requirements derived from the application of the doctrine required the abolition of the "death penalty, of corporal punishment or imprisonment for a pre-fixed period of time."[103] Two of the cornerstones of the doctrine captured in the catchphrases "not crimes, but criminals" (*pas de crimes, mais des criminels*)[104] and "not criminals, but men" (*pas de criminels, mais des hommes*)[105] were expressly mentioned in the code as justifications for judges being obliged to proceed to the "individualization of the sanction"[106] in accordance with a "scientific classification of criminals" and the criminal's "general human features."[107]

5.3.3 Social Defence and Domestic Legal Reform

The same interest in codification which led Saldaña to an early draft of an international criminal code and later, from 1927 onwards, to his participation in the AIDP's drafting commission for *Le Projet de Statut d'une Cour de Justice Criminelle Internationale*,[108] also led him to play a prominent role in the controversial 1928 project to reform the Spanish Criminal Code. This code was drafted during the dictatorship of General Miguel Primo de Rivera, whose uprising had brought to an end the relative stability of almost fifty years of peaceful rotation of liberal and conservative monarchical parties in the Spanish restoration system. Primo de Rivera's military coup d'état, which counted on the support of King Alphonse XIII, was a consequence of the pressures of the chronic instability and party fragmentation of Spanish politics after the end of World War I. This period had included a succession of numerous cabinets between 1918 and 1923 against the background of the

---

[101] Art. 85.
[102] Art. 85.
[103] Art. 76.
[104] Art. 52.
[105] Art. 53.
[106] Art. 52.
[107] Art. 53.
[108] Lewis, *The Birth of the New*, 109.

international post-war economic crisis, a social class struggle punctuated by numerous anarchist attacks and a protracted military struggle in Spanish Morocco against Abd el-Krim, the leader of a nationalist uprising in Rif province. Over the next seven years, General Primo de Rivera ruled first over a military administration (1923–1925) and then over a civil one (1925–1930).

In 1927, during the second phase of Primo de Rivera's regime, Quintiliano Saldaña was appointed to the National Consultative Assembly. This "first corporatist chamber in interwar Europe,"[109] the function of which was to represent the various economic, cultural, social and professional sectors, the state and provinces of Spain, was presided over by José Yanguas Messia (1890–1974), an international law professor who had previously served as Minister of Foreign Affairs (1925–1927)[110] under Primo de Rivera. Saldaña, a member of the general commission for codification since 1920, was automatically appointed to the National Consultative Assembly, whose section III had been charged with reforming the criminal law in 1926. In this position, Saldaña, who had published extensively on the Spanish criminal code and the need for a reform and was the leading sponsor in Spain of the notion of social defence, contributed prominently to the design of the Spanish Criminal Code of 1928.

Following the parameters of the doctrine of social defence, this criminal law project was the first which introduced security measures and corrective measures to the menu of penalties under Spanish criminal law. It also extended the death penalty to a new series of crimes and is considered one of the proto-fascist criminal codes in Europe. With its "systematic interpretation of social defence as political or class-based defence,"[111] it anticipated the uses to which the doctrine of social defence, with its underlying pragmatism and its stress on efficacy, was later put by authoritarian fascist regimes. In the following years, fascist criminal codes shielded themselves behind the theoretical constructions and underlying criminal law conceptions of social defence to commit all types of abuses and atrocities.

---

[109] Antonio Costa Pinto 'Corporatism and Organic Representation in European Dictatorship' in Antonio Costa Pinto (ed.) *Corporatism and Fascism: The Corporatist Wave in Europe* (London: Routledge, 2017).

[110] Years later, Yanguas Messia would become one of the staunchest international legal supporters of the legitimacy of General Franco's coup d'etat against the second Spanish republic. See de la Rasilla, *In the Shadow of Vitoria* (2017).

[111] Gabriela Cobo del Rosal, 'El proceso de elaboración del Código penal de 1928' (2012) 82 *Anuario de Historia del Derecho Español* 561–602, 565.

5.4 Saldaña and the Second Spanish Republic

With the arrival of the Second Spanish Republic in 1931, Saldaña, who as a member of the National Consultative Assembly had collaborated with General Primo de Rivera's dictatorship, lost his political ascendancy. The 1928 criminal law code was quickly abrogated and the position of the greatest Spanish criminal law figure of the period was occupied by the criminal law chairholder of the law school of the Central University of Madrid, Luis Jimenez de Asúa. De Asúa, who had been a former assistant to Saldaña's chair of criminal anthropology in the 1910s, was a socialist who had suffered repression for his vocal political dissent during the regime of General Primo de Rivera. He became the president of the Commission of the Cortes, which drafted the 1931 Spanish Constitution and contributed to the drafting of the progressive criminal code of 1932. Despite his fall from political pre-eminence, Saldaña soon came back to the front line of national and international activities during the 'conservative turn' of the Second Republic. In 1933, he founded and became director of the Laboratory of Criminology of the University of Madrid and in 1935 he became director of the School of Criminology. His role as the Spanish representative at international criminal law congresses, which had ceased in the early days of the Second Spanish Republic, regained importance after 1935.[112] Both during his term in office and afterwards, Saldaña remained an extremely prolific author. In 1928, he published a series of pioneer works in Spanish on social sexology.[113] These were followed in 1930 by what is considered the first treatise in which sexology is systematically structured as a discipline in a cohesive manner and with a doctrinal corpus in Spanish.[114]

The 1930s saw a marked decrease in attention to international criminal justice in Saldaña's academic production. During this period, his academic work was mostly focused on criminal law and criminology. His production included several books in Spanish, including *Nueva penología (penas y medidas de seguridad)* (*New Penology: Penalties and Security*

---

[112] Saldaña became the official Spanish delegate at the XI International Penal and Penitentiary Congress (Berlin, 16–24 October 1935) and the official Spanish delegate at the VI Conference internationale pour l'Unification du Droit penal (Copenhagen, 31 October to 4 November 1935). For a list of the congresses that Saldaña attended, see Masaveu, 'El professor Saldaña,' 410.

[113] Quintiliano Saldaña, *Siete ensayos sobre Sociología sexual* (Madrid: Mundo Latino, 1928).

[114] Quintiliano Saldaña, *La Sexología* (Madrid: Mundo Latino, 1930).

5 QUINTILIANO SALDAÑA

Measures)[115] in 1931, *La evolución del delito (The Evolution of Crime)* in 1934, *La Ley del Jurado comentada (A Commentary to the Law of the Jury)*[116] in 1935, and his *La biotipología criminal (The Criminal Bio-Typology)*[117] in 1935. His last work in Spanish was *La nueva criminología (The New Criminology)*,[118] published in 1936. During the 1930s, he also devoted extensive attention to intellectual refinement and the internationalization of his theory of legal pragmatism, which he understood as a "new correctionalism" in which the "penal correction was not the end of the penalty [...] but a simple means for the achievement of social defence and social perfection,"[119] with works published in French,[120] English[121] and German.[122]

Although during the 1930s the specific focus on international criminal law almost disappeared from Saldaña's academic production, he continued working on and participating in the area of the international unification of criminal law. It is in this context that he engaged in the study of terrorism, one of the areas of development of international criminal law in the late interwar period. This development, as Mark Lewis stresses, "was not exclusively on a purely liberal path" but the turn to "the categories of international crime and terrorism" was "a reaction against political and social instability"[123] in interwar Europe. The assassination of King Alexander of Yugoslavia in Marseilles in 1934 in a terrorist plot orchestrated by the Croat paramilitary fascist group Ustasa[124] was the trigger for the Council of the League of Nations to appoint an International Committee for the Repression of Terrorism in December 1934. Its mission was to draw up "a preliminary draft of an

---

[115] Quintiliano Saldaña, *Nueva penología (penas y medidas de seguridad)* (Madrid: Editorial Hernando, 1931).

[116] Quintiliano Saldaña, *La ley del jurado comentada* (Madrid: Ed. Gráfica Universal, 1935).

[117] Quintiliano Saldaña, 'Biotipología criminal: Última fórmula de la antropología criminal' (1935), *18 Revista de ciencias jurídicas y sociales* 227–315.

[118] Quintiliano Saldaña, *Nueva criminología* (Madrid: M. Aguilar, 1936).

[119] Saldaña, *Teoría pragmática*, 14–15.

[120] See Masaveu, 'El profesor Saldaña,' 413 referring to Quintiliano Saldaña, 'Le Pragmatisme pénal' (1929), Quintiliano Saldaña, *Les limites du pragmatisme penal* (1932), Quintiliano Saldaña, *La criminologie pragmatique* (1935).

[121] Quintiliano Saldaña, 'The New Criminal Anthropology' (1933) 24 *Journal of Criminal Law and Criminology* 333–350.

[122] Quintiliano Saldaña, *Die pragmatische Gerechtigkeit* (Berlin: Grunewald, 1935); Quintiliano Saldaña, 'Die Pragmatische Schule in Rechtsphilosophie und Strafrecht' (1935) XXVI *Monastsschrift für Kriminal psychologie und Strafrechtsreform* 434.

[123] Lewis, *The Birth of the New*, 144.

[124] Peter Kovacs, 'La Societe des Nations et son action apres l'attentat contre Alexandre, roi de Yougoslavie' (2004) 6 *Journal of the History of International Law* 65.

international convention to ensure the repression of conspiracies or crimes committed with a political and terrorist purpose."[125]

Saldaña, who had long been interested in the phenomenon of terrorism and had in 1927 published *El atentado social (The Social Attack)*,[126] commented on these developments writing in 1936 for the *Revue internationale de droit pénal*, the flagship of the AIDP. His contribution replicated the report he had presented in 1935 as representative of the Spanish Government to the sixth Conference of the Bureau for the Unification of Criminal Law (BUCL) held in Copenhagen.[127] According to Lewis, the BUCL was designed to achieve a unification of criminal law codes as a default or "second strategy" when "it was clear that states and the League were not ready to establish an international criminal court."[128] Since its third conference held in Brussels in 1930,[129] the BUCL had been systematically considering terrorism and recommending the adoption of a convention "to ensure the universal repression of terrorist attempts."

In his contribution to the Copenhagen conference, Saldaña defined "terrorism as a method for mastering the masses and paralysing the action of their leaders, by means of the psychological constraint of criminal intimidation." Its outcome, he continued, is "a state of violence provoked by a succession of acts of violence, executed with the aim of inspiring terror in a milieu, city or country, and by its international generalisation."[130] He then distinguished political crimes from terrorism because "the philosophy of values brought to bear on criminal law, that is to say 'legal pragmatism,' cannot be indifferent to the moral"[131] difference that lies between them, even when political crimes have been committed using the 'terrorism method'. For Saldaña, while the nature of political crime changes from country to country, the "crime of terrorism presents universal features."[132] These universal features, its "weak or almost inexistent domestic repression"[133] and the fact that terrorism was

---

[125] League of Nations, Official Journal, 15th year, No. II (Part I), pp. 1839–1840.

[126] Quintiliano Saldaña, *El atentado social: (doctrina y legislación)* (Madrid: Ed. Góngora, 1927).

[127] Quintiliano Saldaña, 'Le terrorisme' (1936) 13 *Révue internationale de droit pénal*, 26–37.

[128] Lewis, *The Birth of the New*, 113.

[129] Ben Saul, 'Attempts to Define "Terrorism" in International Law' (2005) LII *Netherlands International Law Review* 57–83, 58–61.

[130] Saldaña, 'Le terrorisme,' 28.

[131] Ibid., at 29.

[132] Saldaña, 'Le terrorisme,' 33.

[133] Ibid., 34.

5 QUINTILIANO SALDAÑA   141

"spreading" led Saldaña to conclude that an "international repression of the crime of terrorism must be instituted through agreement by all civilized states by means of an international convention"[134] and that "a permanent court of international justice" should have jurisdiction over it.

In their guiding principles, Saldaña's intervention and, more broadly, the work of the sixth Conference in Copenhagen were similar and aligned to the parallel work of the international committee of experts appointed in Geneva.[135] Eventually, concerns that the use of the stigmatizing term 'terrorism' could be manipulated to foster repressive policies targeting political opponents, including those involved in industrial disputes at a time of rising authoritarianism across Europe, prevented the inclusion of references to political or social motives underlying terrorist acts in the definition of terrorism in the Convention on the Punishment and Prevention of Terrorism of 1937. Instead, the convention contained a 'thin' definition whereby terrorism was defined in strictly criminal terms as "criminal acts directed against a State and intended or calculated to create a state of terror in the minds of particular persons, or a group of persons or the general public."[136]

After almost three years of drafts and negotiations, the Convention on the Punishment and Prevention of Terrorism and the Convention for the Creation of an International Criminal Court were open for signature at the conclusion of a diplomatic conference held in Geneva.[137] Although it was signed by twenty-four states, the 1937 terrorism convention[138] was only ratified by British India and therefore fell short of attaining the meagre three ratifications or accessions required for it to enter into force. In its turn, the Terrorism Court Convention, which was subject to the entry into force of the Terrorism Convention and the deposit of seven instruments of ratification or accession, was signed by thirteen states and ratified by none. This failed "experiment in international adjudication"[139] was taking place against the backdrop of a volatile

---

[134] Ibid., 36.

[135] Saul, 'Attempts to Define,' 61.

[136] Convention on the Punishment and Prevention of Terrorism, Art. 1.2.

[137] For the European background of "politics of appeasement and political theatre" regarding the preparatory work on the conventions, see Lewis, *The Birth of the New*, 127–130.

[138] For a more detailed analysis, see Ignacio de la Rasilla, 'An International Terrorism Court in nuce in the Age of International Adjudication' (2017) 1 *Asian Yearbook of Human Rights and Humanitarian Law* 76–108.

[139] For more, see Ignacio de la Rasilla and Jorge Viñuales (eds.) *Experiments in International Adjudication: Historical Accounts* (Cambridge: Cambridge University Press, 2019).

142   IGNACIO DE LA RASILLA DEL MORAL

pre-war European political stage.[140] In the case of Spain, one of the
signatories of both anti-terrorist conventions, it took place amidst what
was already a devastating internationalized civil conflict[141] that was the
backdrop to the dramatic fate of Quintiliano Saldaña's last years.

5.5   Shattered Dreams of Cosmopolitism in the Spanish Civil War

In early 1937, the government of the Second Spanish Republic removed
Quintiliano Saldaña García-Rubio from active service in the chair of
Criminal Anthropology and Advanced Criminal Studies that he had
occupied at the Central University of Madrid since 1911. At the outbreak
of the Spanish Civil War in July 1936, he had sought political refuge in the
Cuban embassy in Madrid, fearing for his life in a besieged capital with
internecine struggles between socialist, anarchist and communist factions. His house was looted and his library, one of the most specialized
criminal law libraries in Spain, was destroyed. Despite the many diplomatic efforts made on his behalf over the next two years, the government
of the Second Republic repeatedly denied him safe conduct to leave
beleaguered Spain or, alternatively, to cross over into the rebel General
Franco's camp.

The puzzling reluctance of the Republican government to assist on
humanitarian grounds one of Spain's most erudite cosmopolitan legal
scholars and the official representative of the Spanish government at
multiple international conferences, may be explained by Saldaña's conservative domestic political biography[142] in the radically polarized Spain
of the Spanish Civil War. However, two other interrelated factors may go
some way to accounting for the cruel fate suffered by the greatest Spanish
pioneer of international criminal justice during the Spanish Civil War.

First, several leading Spanish international law scholars had been
actively involved on the legal and diplomatic front as legal advisers and
propagandists against the Spanish Republic since the beginning of

---

[140] On the background historical causes of the "weakness of the final product," see Lewis,
The Birth of the New, 136–140.

[141] See, for example, Ignacio de la Rasilla, 'In the General Interest of Peace? British
International Lawyers and the Spanish Civil War' (2016) 17 *The Journal of the History
of International Law* 197.

[142] The ruler of Spain between 1923 and 1930, General Miguel Primo de Rivera (1923–
1930), was the father of Jose Antonio Primo de Rivera, who had founded the Spanish
Phalanx in 1933.

5 QUINTILIANO SALDAÑA

Franco's military uprising. In particular, all the Spanish legal scholars who delivered courses at The Hague Academy of International Law ended up supporting Franco's cause during the Spanish war.[143] The Association Francisco de Vitoria and the Institute Francisco de Vitoria in Salamanca, the unofficial capital of the rebels, immediately became an "essential pole of legitimizers of the 1936 rebellion, using Thomism and the theories of the Spanish Theologians from Salamanca in the sixteenth century to generate a discourse [...] against tyranny, a holy war, a crusade, a fight against believers and those without God to save the motherland from communism."[144] Unlike Saldaña, who had taught the first ever international law course on international criminal justice at the Hague Academy in 1925, these Spanish legal scholars and international lawyers went on to re-integrate the Spanish universities, where some would continue developing remarkable international careers.[145]

The second factor behind the Second Republic's attitude to Saldaña may be related to the influence of his criminal law theories on some of his own intellectual disciples. These would subsequently thrive as intellectual representatives of the 'criminal law of authorship' in the repressive criminal law architecture of Franco's early ultranationalist regime in the 1940s. The foundations of this repressive criminal law architecture were built on notions of social defence and preventive criminal law. They were indirectly laid by Antonio de Luna (1901–1967), the public international law chairholder at the Central University of Madrid, who some years later in 1948 became the co-founder and director of the *Revista española de Derecho international* (1948–1963) and in the early 1960s the first Spanish member of the International Law Commission. From 1937 to 1939, De Luna served as the first leader of the National Delegation of Justice and Law of the unified Phalangist Party[146] under the supreme

---

[143] See de la Rasilla, *In the Shadow of Vitoria* (2017).

[144] Ignacio Forcada Barona 'La influencia de la religión católica en la doctrina internacionalista española del período de entreguerras (1918–1939)' in Ignacio de la Rasilla and Yolanda Gamarra (eds.) *Historia del pensamiento iusinternacionalista español del siglo XX* (Pamplona: Thompson Reuters Aranzadi, 2012) 231–287.

[145] For instance, José Yanguas Messia, who some months into the Spanish Civil War drafted "the Junta's decree of 29 September 1936 that proclaimed Franco Head of Government of the Spanish State," became the first Spanish President of the Institut de droit international in 1956. See furthermore, de la Rasilla, *In the Shadow of Vitoria* (2017).

[146] Abel Téllez Aguilera, 'La proyectada Ley de Prisiones de 1938 y la figura de D. Federico Castejón. Historia de un conato legislativo' (2014) 257 *Revista de Estudios Penitenciarios* 9–31.

command of General Franco. The programme of the National Delegation under the leadership of De Luna was to bring about a 'judicial revolution' as part of the 'national revolution' defended by the Spanish Phalange. This became embodied in a series of legislative projects affecting realms of juridical life (from the criminal code to the penitentiary code to civil and penal procedural law) which would mark a radical change of vision from the Republican legislation. The ultimate goal of these projects was to bring about an "extremely hierarchized judicial personalist structure, independent from the executive and greatly influenced by the Phalanx."[147] With Saldaña living as a refugee in the Cuban Embassy, the drafting of the projects was entrusted to Federico Castejón, one of his disciples and later Judge at the Spanish Supreme Court, who continued working on international criminal law into the early 1950s.[148]

Quintiliano Saldaña today stands as an erudite, polyhedral and extremely gifted representative of the interwar generation of Spanish legal scholars and, regarding his international legal production, also of the second professional generation of Spanish international lawyers. Like most of the Spanish international legal scholars of the 'silver age of Spanish culture,' he began the interwar period as a passionate liberal internationalist legal reformer. His visionary juridical blueprint for universal social life, which was built on the notion of social defence (but also transcended it in its international conceptualization), was a logically structured expression of what M. Koskenniemi has called the "oceanic feeling" that continues to inspire "debates about the institutional form of a world community."[149] However, Saldaña's domestic political allegiances, like those of most of his generation of fellow Spanish international lawyers, also epitomize the feeble nature of the internationalism of the Spanish cultural and socio-economic cosmopolitan elite during an epoch of turmoil in both Spain and Europe, which was, furthermore, characterized by abyssal social inequalities and staggering gaps in the level of education across the different layers of Spanish society. On 12 October 1938, Quintiliano Saldaña García-Rubio died of malnutrition

---

[147] Ibid.

[148] See Federico Castejón, 'Proyecto de Código Penal Internacional' (1953) 2 *Anuario de Derecho Penal y Ciencias Penales* 231–251.

[149] Martti Koskenniemi, 'Projects of World Community' in Antonio Cassese (ed.) *Realizing Utopia: The Future of International Law* (Oxford: Oxford University Press, 2012), 3–13, 4.

and related afflictions as a political refugee in the Cuban embassy in Madrid. Some months later, the official end of the Spanish Civil War on 1 April 1939 marked the establishment in Spain of what turned out to be the longest personal dictatorship in the Western world in the twentieth century.

6

Henri Donnedieu de Vabres
Penal Liberal, Moderate Internationalist and Nuremberg Judge

FRÉDÉRIC MÉGRET

Figure 6.1 Portrait of French judge Henri Donnedieu de Vabres. Credit: Chris Ware/Stringer/Getty Images.

For the entire interwar period, Donnedieu de Vabres was one of the most conspicuous figures on the international criminal law scene. Indeed, he is a rare instance of a traveling companion of the interwar movement for international criminal justice who then, towards the very end of his career, had an opportunity to engage in the concrete development of international criminal law. He would promptly thereafter be asked to participate in the drafting committee to the Genocide convention and elevated to the International Law Commission. Today, he is perhaps best remembered as having been the French judge at Nuremberg and a striking figure at that ("aging, [...] spare hair, dark horn rimmed glasses, and a heavy walrus mustache")[1] but at the time he was mostly known for a long line of scholarship.

In fact, his position at Nuremberg, as we will see, was possibly an incongruous or at least a complex one for him, in tension with his known positions as a scholar. It is in this tension between a life of scholarship and the brief culmination as a judge that lie some of the most revealing paradoxes of his intellectual career. It is also what makes him a unique character in that generation-and-a-half of men[2] who sprang up in the 1920s to imagine what would become the discipline of international criminal law. Vespasian Pella may well have had more visibility but he never had the opportunity to become a judge in the sort of tribunal he had adamantly spoken for. Other judges after World War II either had intellectual ambition (Pal) or would actually go on to make significant inputs to the discipline (Bert Röling) but none came to their judicial functions with the scientific experience of a lifetime.

Donnedieu de Vabres was said to be a reserved man by all accounts. His nephew, Yves Beigbeder, who worked for him as a rapporteur at Nuremberg claims that he rarely knew the man's thoughts. Yet for all his apparent shyness, Donnedieu de Vabres was not a man scared of picking arguments with his contemporaries, something which he did with equal courtesy, erudition and regularity: with Vespasian Pella he disagreed on the very idea of having an international criminal court to try states; with Saldaña on his proposal to try individuals internationally for *atteintes à l'humanité*; with Politis on his emphasis on the individual as a subject of international law; with his fellow judges at Nuremberg on almost everything; and with Lemkin on his wrongheaded push for a crime of genocide separated from crimes against peace.

Donnedieu de Vabres hailed from a Protestant and bourgeois family from the South of France. Although his faith was discreet as befits

---

[1] Joe J. Heydecker, Johannes Leeb and Downie (eds), *The Nuremberg Trial: A History of Nazi Germany as Revealed through the Testimony at Nuremberg* (World Publishing 1962), p. 95.

[2] On the intensely masculine character of the movement, see Immi Talgren, Chapter 15.

a *notable* of the République, it nonetheless informed his outlook, and the distinguished international lawyer was not beyond broader reflections informed by his religious upbringing.[3] He would condemn the penal systems of authoritarian states, for example, on the basis that they offended both the principles of 1789 and *"la tradition chrétienne."*[4] Born in Nîmes in 1880, he had studied literature at the Université de Montpellier but eventually moved to the Université de Paris to study law, and defended his doctorate there in 1905. He began his career as a professor at the Université d'Aix followed promptly by the Université de Montpellier after obtaining the *agrégation* in 1909. He served during World War I from 1915 to 1918. In 1922, he was invited by the Faculty of Law of the University of Paris to occupy the *"chaire de droit criminel"* of the faculty, something which he did for 30 years.

Perhaps the dominant intellectual guiding thread in his career was the tension between his core commitment to criminal law and studies, and his increasing engagement with international law themes. Donnedieu de Vabres was foremost a *criminal law* professor. The mélanges in his honor refer to *"la politique criminelle moderne"*[5] and Donnedieu de Vabres was undoubtedly what might be described as a penal modernist. He taught criminal law for decades at the Université de Paris, was interested in prison reform and the study of delinquency and a pioneer of interdisciplinary collaboration with other sciences, notably criminology and forensic medicine. He collaborated with Etudes criminologiques, was vice-president of the Société générale des prisons, president of the Société de médecine légale, president of La société de patronage des prisonniers libérés protestants, and Président du Patronnage des jeunes garçons en danger moral. Moreover, Donnedieu de Vabres was an early penal comparativist, active in various interwar congresses on the unification of penal law and involved with the *Revue de science criminelle et de droit pénal comparé*. His main treatise on criminal law was entitled *Traité de droit criminel et de législation pénale comparée*.[6]

---

[3] Henri Donnedieu de Vabres, 'L'esprit Protestant et les Relations Internationales' (1935) *Revue du christianisme social*.

[4] Henri Donnedieu de Vabres, *La Politique Criminelle des États Autoritaires: La Crise Moderne du Droit Pénal* (Dalloz, 2009) 200 www.lgdj.fr/la-politique-criminelle-des-etats-autoritaires-9782247085521.html accessed December 2, 2016.

[5] Centre français de droit comparé, *Les Principaux Aspects de La Politique Criminelle Moderne, Mélanges Donnedieu de Vabres* (Editions Cujas 1960).

[6] Henri Donnedieu de Vabres, *Traité de Droit Criminel et de Législation Pénale Comparée* (Recueil Sirey 1947).

However, Donnedieu was also a keen internationalist, intent on *solidarité internationale* and the promotion of *l'esprit universel*. Like many of his contemporaries he shared a fascination with mobility, roaring automobiles and even the beginnings of the jet age.[7] For the penalist, this created untold opportunites for crime: "*Les facilités croissantes des communications, les progrès de l'automobilisme, de l'aviation même, ont mis à la disposition des malfaiteurs bien des moyens de franchir les frontières et de se soustraire aux recherches des polices nationales.*" This lead naturally to a vision in which "*A l'internationalisme du crime, il faut opposer l'internationalisme de la répression*"[8] – although as we will see Donnedieu de Vabres did not identify very strictly with that famous quote of his.

At any rate, this internationalism made him a conspicuous participant in almost all of the central international criminal law initiatives of the times, from advocating for Interpol as early as 1914, to the first projects for an international criminal court, to the Nuremberg tribunal and the Genocide Convention. Donnedieu de Vabres was very active in the creation of the Association international de droit pénal (AIDP) in 1916 of which he became the vice president. Later, his international associations would become even more explicit with his membership of the Institut de droit international in 1932, and finally, his membership of the Commission du droit international after the war. All along he had taught at the Paris Institut des Hautes Etudes internationales, and would give two courses in international law at The Hague Academy, an unusual honor for someone who did not first and foremost identify as an international lawyer.

Donnedieu de Vabres' early interest in international matters led him to be tempted by a synthesis of both criminal and international law. He can therefore be seen to have occupied the entire arc of expertise and prestige

---

[7] See for example Henri Donnedieu de Vabres, *La Répression Internationale des Délits de Droit des Gens* (Les Editions internationales 1935) 18–19.

> Il n'est pas loin, le temps où, exploitant le télégraphe, le téléphone, l'automobilisme, le malfaiteur distançait, à chaque frontière, le policier ralenti par les formes imposées de l'intermédiaire diplomatique. Aujourd'hui ... grâce au réseau de radiotélégraphie policière, se communiquent chaque jour, avec la rapidité de la foudre, d'une police nationale à l'autre, signalement anthropométriques ou dactyloscopiques, antécédents judiciaires, fréquentations habituelles de tous les grands criminels ....

[8] Henri Donnedieu de Vabres, *Les Principes Modernes du Droit Pénal International* (Librairie du Recueil Sirey 1928).

that connects criminal and international law. The conjunction of his competency as a criminalist and an internationalist was once presented as a "tour de force."[9] Interestingly, however, whereas most international criminal lawyers either migrated towards the defense and instrumentalization of public international law (Pella), or were public international lawyers interested in the potential of penal repression (Politis, Lauterpacht), Donnedieu de Vabres' own international debt was more to private international law. In that, he was very much a man of his era, an era in which, as has begun to be rediscovered recently, distinctions between private and public – and for that matter civil and criminal – law were rather more fluid than they would become.

It is to exploring the specificity of that now largely forgotten trajectory and to thinking about what it might yield for the present that this chapter is devoted. Donnedieu could alternate between realism and the occasional flight of rhetorical idealism mixed in with an attachment to legal formalism. His position could vary depending on his audience and indeed evolved over time. Yet he was also remarkably constant in his pet peeves, adherence to principle and singularity. Through them one can witness the slow unravelling of a view that was strangely at odds with its times, yet no less interesting for it.

6.1 *Droit pénal international* rather than *droit international pénal*: Donnedieu's Concept of International Criminal Law

Donnedieu de Vabres produced what may well have been one of the most original visions of international criminal law in the interwar period. Although often lumped together with fellow AIDP luminaries, his was an uncompromising and largely idiosyncratic outlook, one quite removed from what the discipline would become. Initially, though, it should be said the discipline did not amount to much, and as such was quite open to being defined on an ongoing and largely speculative basis by whomever had the ambition and the wherewithal to do so. Donnedieu de Vabres was clearly one of those and along with Vespasian Pella (in a quite different vein, as we will see) he staked the terrain early with his two 1920s monographs on international criminal law. Where Pella's work was from the outset based on a particular panoramic vision of the

---

[9] 'Henri Donnedieu de Vabres' (1952) 4 *Revue de science criminelle et de droit pénal comparé* 351.

centrality of the prohibition of criminal war, Donnedieu de Vabres' approach was much more bottom up, contemplative, and rooted in historical experience. Donnedieu de Vabres did not set out, as did his Romanian colleague, with a particular vision of what international criminal law should do, but of what its fundamental limitations were. As such Donnedieu de Vabres, no doubt, was an international lawyer of his times: before the Lotus judgment, the core of his work was already fundamentally about disputes of criminal competencies.

Donnedieu de Vabres' much-noted doctoral thesis in 1905 had been on the "Evolution de la jurisprudence française en matière de conflits de loi" and this original interest in private international law never entirely left him.[10] Even though he would soon specialize in criminal law, his passion for private international law significantly influenced his entire approach to the topic. This was both the secret to his originality albeit, at times, acted as a form of intellectual blinder. For the Sorbonne professor writing in 1922, international penal law was first and foremost the law that determined the competence of domestic criminal jurisdiction in relation to foreign jurisdictions. He gave of international criminal law the following definition: "*Le droit pénal international est la science qui détermine la compétence des juridictions pénales de l'Etat vis-à-vis des juridictions étrangères, l'application de ses lois criminelles par rapport aux lieux et aux personnes qu'elles régissent, l'autorité, sur son territoire, des jugements répressifs étrangers.*"[11] International criminal law would thus serve in relation to penal matters a role that was characteristic of private international law when it came to private law matters. This is most evident in his 1922 "Introduction à l'étude du droit pénal international" whose subtitle is, characteristically, "essai d'histoire et de critique sur *la compétence criminelle.*"[12] The analogy to private international law is clearly made, and the relationship with international criminal law would be further amplified later in his 1929 Hague Academy course.[13]

---

[10] Henri Donnedieu de Vabres, 'De La Copropriété des Navires' (1907) 21 *Annales de Droit Commercial et Industriel Francais, Etranger et International* 356; Henri Donnedieu de Vabres, 'De l'Impossibilité d'Arriver à une Solution Rationnelle et Définitive des Conflits de Lois' (1905) 32 *Journal du Droit International Privé et de la Jurisprudence Comparée* 1231.

[11] Henri Donnedieu de Vabres, *Introduction à l'étude du droit pénal international* (L Tenin 1922) 6.

[12] My emphasis.

[13] Henri Donnedieu de Vabres, 'L'action Publique et L'action Civile Dans Les Rapports de Droit Pénal International' (1929) 26 *Recueil des Cours de l'Académie de Droit International* 211–308.

His contribution to the early genesis of the discipline was to stress the extent to which inventing new forms of international penality involved not so much a transcending of the discipline as a rediscovery of its roots. In order to challenge the vision of an anchored, immobile criminal law Donnedieu de Vabres' scholarly corpus drew significant inspiration from earlier European times when the lack of clearly defined states had stimulated much thinking on transnational crimes. Indeed, Donnedieu's discourse at times exhibited a sort of nostalgia for both Antiquity and Europe in the Middle Ages, as well as a particular interest in twelfth- to sixteenth-century Italy. There were of course differences in the "new" international criminal law. Donnedieu emphasized the radically transnational character of crime in the twentieth century, as well as the increasingly outsize role of the state. New private international law rules were needed to make sense of increasingly complex and frequent conflicts of jurisdiction. The problem was that there were as many *droit pénaux internationaux* as there were states, each proposing to deal with conflicts of jurisdiction and law differently.[14] Donnedieu de Vabres, in this context, sought to develop a sort of meta-private international criminal law, or at least an international public law of private international law, normalizing certain solutions but excluding others to resolve conflicts between different national systems of *droit pénal international*.[15]

Despite his obvious acknowledgment of the specificity of international criminal law and its rootedness, in practice, in state interests, Donnedieu was deeply wary of imperialism.[16] Contra Roman nationalism, French monarchism or Prussian imperialism, he emphasized Helenic cosmopolitanism, Catholic ecumenism and Grotian humanitarianism. In the Middle Ages, "*l'Eglise est la seule puissance dont l'action . . . s'étend avec efficacité sur des hommes de races différentes, soumis à des dominations temporelles variées.*"[17] Indeed Donnedieu de Vabres went as far as to consider that the state's criminal competencies were part of a "*mission qui lui est confiée pour le bien de la société humaine.*"[18]

His views were therefore an interesting mix of particularism and universalism: particularism because his focus lay mostly in defining and

[14] Ibid. 493.
[15] Henri Donnedieu de Vabres, 'La Communauté Internationale en Droit Pénal et les Limites que lui Impose le Particularisme des Etats' (1924) 19 *Revue internationale de droit privé* 481.
[16] Ibid. (n 11) 3.
[17] Ibid. 81.
[18] Ibid. 4.

expanding the bounds of domestic jurisdiction; universalism because he tended to assume that these domestic prerogatives were determined by international law rather than exhausted by each sovereign's attempt at defining them. Throughout his academic career, Donnedieu de Vabres remained more interested in transnationalism than supranationalism. His moderate, horizontal internationalism made him a natural candidate for socialization among the small group of criminal lawyers in the inter-war whose name became associated with the AIDP. Indeed, Donnedieu de Vabres was one of its founders in 1924. But it also made him an intellectual adversary of someone like Vespasian Pella, and in general a scholar who was quite wary of *"le vertige universaliste où nous entraînent des conceptions nouvelles."*[19] If anything one might say that Donnedieu was a penalist with relatively modest ambitions for criminal law, envisaged as an extension of the interstate system seen in its best light rather than a direct challenge to it. In that model, it was almost always "criminals" who were the problem, not the state.

To the extent that Donnedieu de Vabres was interested in suprana-tional repression of international crimes, therefore, his focus was very much on the state whether as (A) a competitor in a game of asserting jurisdiction, (B) a dysfunctional cog in the machine of international criminal repression, or (C) the author of international crimes as such. Interestingly, the internationalist in him thus did violence to the crim-inalist, even though he acknowledged that it was easier to *"metre la main sur un criminel en chair et en os, de le conduire à la Haye sous bonne escorte et de l'y garder en cellule, que d'infliger ce traitement à un Etat."*

6.1.1 An International Law and Court of Coordination of Criminal Jurisdiction

The man who would become a judge at the first and historical interna-tional criminal tribunal shuddered at the possibility of international jurisdiction, considering *"avec effroi l'excès de complications et de fraîs qu'entraînerait le jugement de semblables affaires."*[20] Even with the adop-tion of the 1937 treaty on an International Criminal Court in relation to terrorism he saw a tension between the existence of that as an offence *de droit commun*, and the creation of a *"juridiction d'exception."* His posi-tion on universal jurisdiction was more ambiguous. On the one hand, he

[19] Donnedieu de Vabres, *Les Principes Modernes du Droit Pénal International* (n 8) 425.
[20] Ibid. 413.

dismissed Enrico Ferri's view that every crime that revolted "*un senti-ment universel, naturel, humain*" could be prosecuted anywhere on the basis that the universality of criminal sentiments was not the same thing as the universality of competence.[21] His universal jurisdiction was that of the "*droit universel de punir*" of states who were threatened by the mere presence of criminals in their midst, not one implemented directly in the name of the international community.

But, perhaps bizarrely after having opened the doors so widely for universal jurisdiction, he feared its invocation in the context of talk about "*délits de droits des gens.*" He disliked the excessively large remit of universal jurisdiction as presented by some and the fact that, for the sake of systematicity, it involved entrusting repression to third states based on the arbitrariness of the locus of arrest. He foresaw considerable "*difficultés diplomatiques, . . . complications matérielles, . . . frais énormes*" which made him insist that universal jurisdiction should only ever be the least favoured option. In other words, the future judge at Nuremberg thought international and universal jurisdiction to be impractical, inauthentic and leading straight to judicial error. Extradition or at least an expanded understanding of the *judex delicti*, not some theory creating a special regime for *délits de droit des gens*, was the solution to the development of international criminal law.

Instead, Donnedieu de Vabres imagined a sort of international law of the coordination of criminal law systems rather than what would today be described as international criminal law proper. The fundamental inspiration behind such a court, it could be said, was not the gravity or even international character of the crimes *ratione materiae*, but the fact that for some reason their prosecution might lead to complex and sensitive political situations between states.[22] If an international court was to have a role at all, it would therefore be that of coordinating the conflicts of jurisdiction that would inevitably arise as a result of the exercise of the unilateral domestic criminal jurisdictions of states, even if no *délits de droit des gens* existed.[23] The overriding concern was one with peace and security and the dangers and instability that might arise from multiple, competing assertions of jurisdiction.[24] He thus empha-sized the second paragraph of the 1926 Brussels declaration suggesting

---

[21] Ibid. 410–411.

[22] Donnedieu de Vabres, *La Répression Internationale des Délits de Droit des Gens* (n 7) 17.

[23] Henri Donnedieu de Vabres, 'La Cour Permanente de Justice et sa Vocation en Matière Criminelle' (1924) 1 *Revue internationale de droit pénal* 179.

[24] Ibid.

that the court be *"consultée sur le règlement des conflits de competence, judiciaire ou legislative, qui peuvent surgir entre les différents Etats."* The court would be *"quelque chose d'analogue à celui d'une Cour de Cassation qui dominerait les Etats,"*[25] in the tradition of arbitration and resolution of horizontal inter-state disputes that were much favored in the interwar period and geared towards limiting anarchy.[26]

Donnedieu's emphasis in the late 1920s was therefore characteristically modest, almost vanishingly so. The idea of the international court adjudicating disputes over criminal matters was of course hardly new and the Lotus judgment which had been rendered in 1927, marked the exact intersection of international and criminal law.[27] At best the international court should have a competence of revision of final domestic judgments on sensitive interstate criminal matters (currency falsification, murder of a foreign head of state), neither as an appeal or cassation court, but more as a jurisdiction of renvoi.

With the adoption of the 1937 Terrorism Convention, Donnedieu had the satisfaction of seeing emerge a court whose statute sought to smooth out in advance the complexities that might arise from the transnational character of terrorist offenses, reinforced the extradition regime and took due note of the need to grant repressive judgments extra-territorial effects.[28] To the extent that the court was to have jurisdiction at all, it was because a state party referred a case to it, which Donnedieu de Vabres understood could only result from a manoeuvre to avoid a conflict of jurisdiction or other nefarious inter-state consequence (such as international responsibility for a wrongful judgment) if it were to refer the case to its own courts.[29] In other words, even in that most centralized capacity, an international criminal tribunal would indirectly be contributing to the prevention of disputes between states and could therefore be described as fundamentally part of a *"réaliste et transactionnelle"* inspiration.[30] The

---

[25] Donnedieu de Vabres, *La Répression Internationale des Délits de Droit des Gens* (n 7) 17.

[26] Donnedieu de Vabres, 'La Cour Permanente de Justice et sa Vocation En Matière Criminelle' (n 23) 179.

[27] Donnedieu de Vabres was enthusiastic about that Permanent Court of International Justice's foray into matters of delimiting criminal jurisdiction. Henri Donnedieu de Vabres, 'L'affaire du Lotus et le droit pénal' (1929) II *Revue du droit international* 135–165.

[28] Henri Donnedieu de Vabres, 'La Répression Internationale Du Terrorisme. Les Conventions de Genève (16 Novembre 1937)' (1938) 19 *Revue de Droit International et de Législation Comparée* 37, 52–54.

[29] Ibid. 60–61.

[30] Ibid. 61.

court found grace with Donnedieu de Vabres because of its very discreetness. Donnedieu de Vabres did not know it then, but the 1937 Convention would never enter into force and with it may have vanished the last chance of his moderate interwar blueprint for an international criminal court becoming reality.

6.1.2 Procedural, not Substantive Vision of International Crime

One of the reasons for Donnedieu de Vabres' characteristically modest jurisdictional proposal was his difficulty in taking seriously the idea of international crimes. Indeed, for most of his interwar career Donnedieu de Vabres remained a sceptic of the idea that there even existed *délit de droit des gens* or, to be more precise, that such a notion could descriptively refer to something sufficiently specific to be worthy of that label. Like most AIDP members he believed that "international jurisdiction" should be confined to "international crimes," but what were international crimes? Donnedieu de Vabres struggled with the notion as other international criminal lawyers had before and would after him. The merely transnational character of crimes did not particularly militate for supranational jurisdiction since it actually meant that several states might have jurisdiction. Even for crimes committed in international spaces or whose location was unknown, Donnedieu de Vabres thought that principles of private international law were perfectly appropriate response to the problem of jurisdiction.

The problem was that most so-called international crimes were for him merely common crimes that happened to have a transnational, cross-border character. He listed piracy, false currency, slavery, trafficking in children, trafficking in narcotics or obscene publications. Donnedieu de Vabres conceded that all of the above might be considered to offend universal interests, "*mais ce caractère leur est-il propre? Ne peut-on pas en dire autant de la généralité des infractions à la loi pénale?*"[31] As late as 1935 and even as the criminalization of terrorism was being actively discussed and would lead to the first convention for an international criminal court, he failed to see what was specific about terrorism that would warrant making it a crime under international law given that "*l'activité des terroristes se traduit par des actes que toutes les législations positives incriminent et punissent comme délits de droit commun.*" It might be true that terrorists created a "collective danger" of spreading

---

[31] Ibid. 10.

terror, but ordinary criminal gangs or prison escapees had long done so as well, without anyone hinting that they should be repressed internationally.[32]

Donnedieu de Vabres, who would a few years later join a judgment elaborating precisely such a *loi commune*, thus struggled to imagine crimes of international magnitude that would require international judgment because of the way, for example, they might be said to "shock the conscience of mankind." He did note the existence of this "psychological" approach to defining international criminality but found that criterium to be too controversial.[33] For international jurisdiction to be justified at all, it was not so much the inherent gravity of the crime that mattered (domestic courts could surely try the gravest crimes), let alone their cross-border or ultra-border character, as much as the fact that something in their circumstances might lead one to not trust national judges to try them fairly. What Donnedieu de Vabres had in mind here were crimes committed as a result of war in a context where the impartiality and independence of national judges might be doubted.[34] In other words, there was nothing in the nature of the crimes that made them "intrinsically" international, only the "practical" problem that states might not be relied upon, in this or that case, to prosecute them diligently and fairly. This view naturally foregrounded international crimes associated with states and is reminiscent of the complementarity regime. It was broadly consonant with Donnedieu de Vabres' equally firm view that the *judex delicti* should have priority, on the horizontal level, over the *judex deprehensionis*, the latter's jurisdiction being dependent on a failure of the former.

6.1.3 Preference for the State as the Main Subject of International Criminal Law

A consequence of skepticism about the very existence of international crimes (as distinct from common crimes committed internationally) was a strong reservation about the possibility of the "individual" being the direct subject of international law. Donnedieu de Vabres was aware that already at the time he was not necessarily uttering the most popular view, but the idea of international jurisdiction over individuals did not sit well

---

[32] Donnedieu de Vabres, *La Répression Internationale des Délits de Droit des Gens* (n 7).
[33] Ibid.
[34] Donnedieu de Vabres, *Les Principes Modernes du Droit Pénal International* (n 8) 412.

with him. For one, he was wary of punishing individuals under an international criminal law which did not exist. His feeling was that talk of an international criminal jurisdiction was precocious given the absence of a substantive international criminal law and the attendant risk of violating the *nullum crimen, nulla poena* principle.

In fact, although many of his colleagues, first among which Politis, would have made an exception, following the Kaiser precedent at Versailles, for the head of state, Donnedieu de Vabres was not even convinced that the latter ought to be prosecuted internationally. First, legally speaking, the act of going to war could only be imputed to the state. The prosecution of Kaiser Wilhelm had been a failure not just because he had fled to the Netherlands, but perhaps also because at a deeper level the Kaiser's contribution to the war was not absolutely decisive. Second, psychologically and morally *"dans l'état présent de nos sociétés démocratiques, la guerre n'est possible que si, au moment où elle éclate, elle est conforme au sentiment public."*[35] He thus anticipated subsequent critiques of international criminal justice's radical focus on the head of state as a form of scapegoating.[36] Third, Donnedieu was simply incredulous that any state might one day surrender their head of state to an international court.[37]

If an international criminal court were to prosecute anyone, then a focus on "crimes of states" was essential. Such a focus would better distinguish common crimes, which might ruffle *"le sentiment 'universel' de justice ou de charité,"*[38] from crimes of a specifically sovereign character, crimes which it would be virtually "impossible" for ordinary individuals to commit. It is startling that at least as far as him and a few criminal (rather, it should be said, than international) lawyers, the issue of the criminal responsibility of the state was a non-problem.[39] Along with Pella and Saldaña, also jurists coming from a continental tradition,

---

[35] Donnedieu de Vabres, *Les Principes Modernes du Droit Pénal International* (n 8) 415.

[36] Larry Cata Backer, 'The Fuhrer Principle of International Law: Individual Responsibility and Collective Punishment' (2003) 21 *Penn State International Law Review* 509.

[37] Donnedieu de Vabres, 'La Cour Permanente de Justice et Sa Vocation En Matière Criminelle' (n 23) 186.

[38] Donnedieu de Vabres, *Les Principes Modernes du Droit Pénal International* (n 8) 418.

[39] In his very first report, Roberto Ago, the International Law Commission Rapporteur on state responsibility and a great advocate of the notion of "crime of state" acknowledged his debt to Donnedieu de Vabres and the few others around him (Pella, Saldaña) who had early on advocated on behalf of the notion. See Roberto Ago, 'First Report on State Responsibility,' UN Doc A/CN.4/217/Add.2 (1969-II), para. 141.

he displayed no unease with the idea that non-natural persons might commit penal infractions.

He clashed strongly, therefore, with Politis, who would have willingly consigned state responsibility to the dustbins of legal history. Curiously, it was Politis the international lawyer who wanted to ignore the state for the benefit of the individual, exposing himself to a retort from Donnedieu de Vabres the criminal lawyer who stood up for state criminal responsibility as such. Against Politis's radical individual methodologism and denial of the fiction of collective personality (already anticipating Nuremberg's dismissiveness of "abstract entities"), Donnedieu de Vabres retorted that the existence of group personality was "*un fait incontestable, dont l'affirmation n'a rien de métaphysique,*" especially if one resisted the German tendency to assimilate "*l'organisme social à un organisme humain.*"[40]

The focus on the state in the work of Donnedieu de Vabres (or of Vespasian Pella) can be partly explained by their equally unrelenting focus on crimes against peace. Donnedieu de Vabres liked to point out that the Geneva Protocol explicitly prohibited states from resorting to war, and that this in itself made it clear that states were the prime and probably only intended subjects of that particular injunction. However, many years later in the preparatory commission to the Genocide Convention Donnedieu de Vabres would take up this notion again insisting that genocide was first and foremost a crime of state and that only state leaders could therefore be prosecuted for it.[41]

In this context, Donnedieu de Vabres was also adamant that ordinary international responsibility would not suffice. Anticipating what would be the lengthy debates of the International Law Commission between 1970 and 2001 he noted that reparations of the consequences of aggression would frustrate efforts at justice because they would not and could not encompass "*l'éventualité de mesures de précaution et de garanties spéciales contre de nouvelles tentatives de l'Etat déjà coupable.*"[42] This was precisely the role devolved to the penal responsibility of states, one that made it all the more necessary for civil responsibility to be directed towards the past (reparations) whereas criminal responsibility would cater to the need "*par des mesures de précaution, (de) prévenir la commission, dans l'avenir, d'un préjudice nouveau.*"[43]

---

[40] Donnedieu de Vabres, *Les Principes Modernes du Droit Pénal International* (n 8) 421.

[41] Hirad Abtahi and Philipppa Webb, *The Genocide Convention: The Travaux Préparatoires* (Martinus Nijhoff Publishers 2008) 181.

[42] Donnedieu de Vabres, *Les Principes Modernes du Droit Pénal International* (n 8) 427.

[43] Ibid. 429.

He also anticipated, in a particularly prescient way, that the emergence of any system of international criminal justice, particularly one targeting states, would have to confront *"l'égoïsme sacré"* of that state when its vital interests were at stake. The only solution would be to *"mettre au service de la Société des Nations une puissance matérielle suffisante pour s'imposer cet Etat ."*[44] He continued: *"comme il n'y a pas de puissance politique réelle sans une armée, il n'y a pas de juridiction, ni de législation efficace sans une police."* In some extreme cases, the penalty might require *"le démembrement de l'Etat ou son annexion."*[45] Donnedieu de Vabres certainly could not imagine that Germany and Japan's *de bellatio* would provide – albeit in a circumscribed and isolated way – the ideal soil for the first major experiment in international criminal justice.

6.2 From *Droit Pénal International* to *Droit Pénal Interétatique*: Donnedieu in Nuremberg

The experience of being a judge at Nuremberg no doubt had considerable influence on the final years of Donnedieu de Vabres' life and career. It elevated his profile even further, but also threatened to bring his own long-held views to clash with the emerging reality of international criminal law.

6.2.1 *Participant*

As a leading French expert in international criminal law who had managed not to be compromised with collaboration with the Germans or Vichy, Donnedieu was a fairly obvious pick to be the French judge at Nuremberg. French participation was important to the new French authorities, who were eager to solidify France's precarious postwar role, after taking second seat in the preparations for the International Military Tribunal.[46] Donnedieu did not entirely escape controversy, having been acquainted with one of the defendants, Hans Frank, who as a leading Nazi lawyer had invited him in the 1930s to speak in Berlin at the Akademie für Deutsches Recht, and according to Philip Sands, even

---

[44] Ibid. 199.

[45] Ibid. 197.

[46] Ann-Sophie Schöpfel, 'La voix des juges français dans les procès de Nuremberg et de Tokyo: défense d'une idée de justice universelle' (2013) *Guerres mondiales et conflits contemporains* 101.

6 HENRI DONNEDIEU DE VABRES

having met Julius Streicher.[47] He had also, one presumes painfully, served in a university commission on Jewish students' applications which was part of a rigid quota system.[48]

Yet Donnedieu de Vabres emerged from the war his reputation intact and untainted by collaboration. A fact rarely remarked upon is that before the war he had become an expert in "authoritarian penal systems" which would surely have been useful to his fellow judges. His knowledge of National Socialism, in particular, was deep and wide, and extended through readings of the writings of key ideologues, including Rosenberg who he would end up judging and sending to the gallows. Donnedieu de Vabres, whilst displaying a certain understanding for the historical necessity of authoritarian systems in periods of turmoil, ultimately condemned them in no uncertain terms (although not, as we will see, to the point of glorifying liberal criminal justice systems). In the conclusion to his 1937 *La politique pénale des Etats autoritaires*, he criticized National Socialism for subordinating the interests of individuals to those of the state, enforcing the inequality of human races, and being based on "hate."[49]

During the war he had published mostly on the reform of juvenile criminal justice. His mention of the regime applicable to Jews in his war *traité* was typical of a strategy pursued by law professors at the time: it merely described it literally without commenting on it.[50] Not only that but Donnedieu had actually managed to be critical of the Vichy regime under German occupation. His preface to his "Le droit pénal de la guerre et de la révolution nationale" has been described as *"un des écrits les plus lucides et les plus courageux qui aient paru sous l'occupation ennemie."*[51] His son, Jean Donnedieu de Vabres, had joined de Gaulle early, and served as *chargé de mission* in his cabinet from 1944 to 1946.

Donnedieu's presence at Nuremberg was nonetheless doubly exceptional. First, Donnedieu was the only AIDP member to become closely

---

[47] Philippe Sands, *East West Street: On the Origins of 'Genocide' and 'Crimes Against Humanity'* (Knopf Doubleday 2016) chapter 129.

[48] Silvia Falconieri, 'Le "droit de la race": apprendre l'antisémitisme à la faculté de droit de Paris (1940–1944)' (2014) *Clio Themis* www.cliothemis.com/Le-droit-de-la-race-Apprendre-l accessed December 2, 2016.

[49] Donnedieu de Vabres, *La Politique Criminelle des États Autoritaires: La Crise Moderne du Droit Pénal* (n 4) 200.

[50] Dominique Gros, 'Le "statut des juifs" et les manuels en usage dans les facultés de Droit (Partie 2)' (1993) *Cultures & Conflits* https://conflits.revues.org/643?lang=en accessed November 23, 2016.

[51] 'Henri Donnedieu de Vabres' (n 9) 5.

162   FRÉDÉRIC MÉGRET

associated with the tribunal, a true representative after the war of those earlier efforts, in the twilight of his life. It is not the least of ironies that he served in an international tribunal which was the furthest from what he had advocated, although perhaps wisely Donnedieu de Vabres had insisted in 1928 that he did not wish to *"exclure à jamais la mise en oeuvre des responsabilités individuelles devant un juge international."*[52] Second, Donnedieu was the only Allied judge who was not a professional judge. Yves Beigbeder has noted that there may have been a specifically French reason for this (despite France's tradition of nominating senior civil servants rather than legal academics to senior international judge-ships). Whilst Vichy judges would have had to swear allegiance to the regime, Donnedieu de Vabres as a professor escaped that fate.[53]

The fact that, as an academic, Donnedieu had amply written on international criminal justice meant that, ironically, he had previously commented on the international judicial function that he was now occupying. The Donnedieu of 1928 had not envied what would become the position of the Donnedieu of 1945. As he put it:

> *Quand on songe à la diverges des témoignages qui se manifestent au lendemain d'un fait de guerre et dans son voisinage immédiate, on n'envisage pas sans appréhension la tâche d'un juge chargé de statuer sur les mêmes événements, dont il est éloigné et dans le temps et dans l'espace. Si l'on ajoute que les auteurs de ce fait étaient assujettis à la discipline militaire, qu'ils ont agi dans un moment de crise, dans une atmosphère de passions collectives, on plaint les magistrats chargés d'évaluer, dans de telles conditions, des responsabilités individuelles.*[54]

Yet at the same time, as the title of his 1947 course at The Hague Academy indicated – Le procès de Nuremberg devant les principes modernes du droit pénal international – he was clearly by then willing to scrutinize his experience as a judge through the light of his earlier and ongoing, broader contribution to international legal scholarship.

6.2.2 Supporter

Donnedieu obviously had gone along with the thrust of the verdict. In particular, whatever reservations he may have had about individual responsibility directly under international criminal law before the war

---

[52] Donnedieu de Vabres, *Les Principes Modernes du Droit Pénal International* (n 8) 417.

[53] Yves Beigbeder, *Judging War Crimes and Torture: French Justice and International Criminal Tribunals and Commissions (1940–2005)* (Brill 2006) 246, n 13.

[54] Donnedieu de Vabres, *Les Principes Modernes du Droit Pénal International* (n 8) 413–414.

must surely have been muted given the verdict's famous dictum that "crimes against international law are committed by men, not abstract entities." In his 1952 Hague Academy Course, he manages to concede that much, even citing Politis's "classic book" approvingly.[55] Donnedieu was very supportive of the notion that former officials did not have immunity because "*quand sont en jeu les valeurs dont la communauté universelle a la garde, non seulement la courtoisie est reléguée à l'arrière-plan, mais l'ordre public caractérisé par le respect de l'indépendance récriproque des Etats cède la préséance à la notion d'un ordre public supérieur.*"[56]

Indeed, he even went further than surely he would have imagined possible before the war. In denying the defense of superior orders or even duress, the tribunal had rendered not only to "*la suprématie de la conscience*" but to the "*souveraineté du droit international.*"[57] The repression of crimes against humanity, a reaction to the "excesses of racism," went beyond "*le cadre des interest étatiques*" and applied to "*la sauvegarde de valeures humaines.*" In striking recognition of this newfound cosmopolitanism of international criminal law, Donnedieu de Vabres stressed that repression "*d'internationale (est devenue) universelle.*"[58]

The substantive consequences of these moves were largely unavoidable. He clearly realized that Pella's vision of international criminal law, through the cataclysm of World War II, had become more significant, and this was reflected in his adoption of the expression "*droit pénal inter-étatique*," to better distinguish what had emerged at Nuremberg from his own construction of *droit pénal international.*[59] The *droit pénal inter-étatique* was, this time round, clearly born from the synthesis of criminal and public international law, rather than being a criminal law merely framed by and resorting to international law. In fact, the jurisdictional rhetorical reference to doing together what could have been done separately

> *n'exprime assurément pas toute la pensée du Tribunal. Celui-ci ne se présente pas comme le simple mandataire des quatre Etats signataires,*

---

[55] Henri Donnedieu de Vabres, 'Le Procès de Nuremberg devant les Principes Modernes du Droit Pénal International' (1947) 70 *Recueil des Cours de l'Académie de Droit International* 563.

[56] Ibid. 565.

[57] Ibid. 573.

[58] Ibid. 518.

[59] Of course, his definition of *droit pénal international* did not stick and ended up being absorbed by what was his *droit pénal inter-étatique*.

> *ni même des dix-neuf Etats adhérents à l'acte du 8 août 1945. Il se reconnaît une vocation universelle à l'effet de juger les grands criminels de guerre qui ont violé certains droits fondamentaux de l'homme. Il prend ouvertement parti pour le droit international public nouveau qui a pour sujet, non seulement l'Etat, mais l'individu.*[60]

Yet even then, Donnedieu de Vabres manage to provide a certain retrospective spin to the judgment and to interpret it in a narrower way than it has typically been understood since. He insisted, for example, on the fact that "*la carence de l'Etat allemand, consécutive à la capitulation sans conditions du 5 juin 1945, la suspension de la souveraineté allemande, ont mis les puissances occupantes en contact nécessaire et direct avec les individus à qui devait être imputé l'initiative des actes criminels.*" It was, in other words, these peculiar circumstances alone that led to individuals being prosecuted directly under international law, putting into doubt the truly precedential value of Nuremberg outside situations of occupation. Moreover, Donnedieu de Vabres was adamant in his conservative international legal belief that "*dans la société politique internationale, la qualité de sujet de droit est liée à la souveraineté, qui est le propre des Etats. Les personnes physiques ne sont nullement, quels que soient les intérêts et les responsabilités en cause, parties aux relations de droit international public.*"[61] He in fact would have held Germany culpable first, and Hitler only second,[62] and felt that the only reason Germany had not been prosecuted as such was its situation of *debelatio*. State criminal responsibility would continue to coexist with individual responsibility, even if the latter was now there to stay.

Similarly, his take on the legality and legitimacy of the tribunal was quite personal. Donnedieu de Vabres inclined to think that "*l'innovation de 1945 répondît à une notion commune de la justice, à une exigence même de la conscience universelle.*"[63] Nonetheless, far from seeing it as an absolute confirmation of the rise of international jurisdiction for its own sake, he emphasized instead the extent to which it responded to a concrete problem of penal jurisdiction. Indeed, whereas ordinary war criminals could always have been deferred to the state whose interests they had violated, the leaders (statesmen, but also propagandists or industrialists) tended to fall under no particular state's jurisdiction.

---

[60] Donnedieu de Vabres, 'Le Procès de Nuremberg Devant Les Principes Modernes du Droit Pénal International' (n 55) 576. Emphasis in the original.

[61] Ibid. 486.

[62] Ibid. 560.

[63] Ibid. 482.

Moreover, the conjoined exercise of jurisdiction by the Allies – "*Ils ont fait ensemble ce que chacun d'eux pouvait faire séparément*" – ensured that Nuremberg could be grounded quite matter-of-factly into existing concepts of sovereignty. A few years later in the context of debates on the Genocide Convention, he would advocate anew with Vespasian Pella for a criminal chamber within the International Court of Justice.

Donnedieu was not even particularly convinced by the notion that the foundation for including war crimes in the Nuremberg Charter flowed from international law directly. Rather, going back to French theories first touted during World War I and particularly when it came to "*les criminels de guerre vulgaires, c'est à dire les exécutants,*" he insisted that it was the incrimination of war crimes in broadly comparable terms in a multiplicity of domestic legal systems that made them punishable, without having to go through international law. Denouncing monist theories as unconnected to reality, he argued that the Nuremberg judges were not exercising a jurisdiction delegated by the international community, but one emanating from the depths of sovereignty, that of "*le droit pénal lui-même, le droit pénal positif,*"[64] what he elsewhere described as the "*droit pénal commun.*"[65]

That as late as 1947 he should hold views that were already and would become even more at odds with the widespread reading of the law applicable following Nuremberg shows how unrepentant he was about his life's work, even after the concrete experience of trial.[66] To an orthodox international lawyer, the invocation of a criminal *jus commune* as opposed to public international law's increasingly criminal provisions might seem totally inapposite, but it was fundamentally consistent with Donnedieu de Vabres' life work, even if it meant twisting his evaluation of Nuremberg to fit his theory *de toujours*.

6.2.3   Critique

Donnedieu was hardlly oblivious to the criticisms that were already emerging of the trial. He knew that the victors had tried the vanquished,

---

[64] Ibid. 509.

[65] Henri Donnedieu de Vabres, 'La Commission de Droit International et ses fonctions en matière pénale' (1954) *Tulane Law Review* 189, 195.

[66] It is true that the Nuremberg tribunal had sought to ground its legitimacy in the existence of war crimes in various domestic laws including those of Germany, but this was only for the purposes of establishing the existence of international law in those matters and as a luxury of precaution.

and went further hinting that the Allies may have favored the commission of crimes *"par leur incurie, sinon par leur lâcheté."*[67] A witness to Nuremberg's destruction, he could not fail to also mention the use of the atomic bomb and warned against the risk of "making martyrs." However, as a good lawyer, he left aside these "historical, philosophical and moral . . . objections." After all the *"infirmité de la justice humaine"* was a truism, especially when it appeared as a form of political justice. But Donnedieu had this to retort to the critiques: was it not true that *"il n'y a pas de justice pénale qui ne soit conditionnée par l'exercice préalable de la force . . . il n'y a pas de justice pénale qui ne soit administrée par des hommes sans reproche. Il n'y a pas de justice pénale qui n'ait à son origine la vengeance, individuelle ou collective . . ."* ?[68] And he faulted the detractors of this imperfect international criminal justice for not opening *"d'autre perspective, à défaut d'une répression humaine, donc faillible et imparfaite, que la carence de la répression."*[69]

His reservations, in fact, had less to do with this broader political critique than with what he saw as some still perplexing features of the synthesis between criminal and international law. Specifically, Donnedieu displayed a triple reluctance towards the work of the Nuremberg Tribunal which was much in evidence in a memorandum he circulated to his fellow judges. First, as a criminalist, he was the one who was most insistent on the possibility that Nuremberg resulted in a violation of the *nullum crimen* and, perhaps even more so, the *nulla poena* principle.[70] Because of the *"imprévoyange des fondateurs de la Société des Nations"* the authors of August 8, 1945 were *"constraint(s) . . . à un travail de creation."* In this context, there was no avoiding the fact that the military tribunal was *"une jurisdiction ad hoc, dont l'institution est postérieure aux infractions qu'il reçoit la mission de réprimer."* What is more, *"les incriminations sont vagues, les peines presque entièrement laissées à l'appréciation discrétionnaire des juges."*[71] Although he sided with the tribunal in finding that crimes against peace were prohibited by

---

[67] Donnedieu de Vabres, 'Le Procès de Nuremberg Devant Les Principes Modernes du Droit Pénal International' (n 55) 483.

[68] Ibid.

[69] Ibid. 484.

[70] Henri Donnedieu de Vabres, 'Le jugement de Nuremberg et le principe de légalité des délits et des peines' (1946–1947) *Revue de droit pénal et de criminologie*, 813.

[71] 'Le Procès de Nuremberg Devant Les Principes Modernes du Droit Pénal International ' (n 55) 485–486.

international law – he had said as much as early as 1928 – he was less understanding of other aspects of the indictment.

Second, and in close connection with his concern about retroactivity, Donnedieu de Vabres was wary of the notion of conspiracy which he considered to at best give "a pleasing intellectual coherence to successive episodes."[72] In fact, he had made his reservations known to his fellow judges, much to Telford Taylor's apparent irritation.[73] The memo appears to have taken his fellow judges by surprise and, as we know, Donnedieu's views did not sway the others and many of the accused were convicted of conspiracy. He would nonetheless go on to expand his views at length in his soon-to-be Hague international law course on the Nuremberg trial. His fear was not only that conspiracy was largely a common law concept, but that in portraying the sequence that led to World War II as a "cloak and dagger" intrigue between a bunch of criminals, it risked being reductionist, giving a sort of "romantic prestige" to the whole "Hitlerian enterprise."[74] Historically, however, Donnedieu de Vabres felt that simply no conspiracy had occurred because Hitler had so centralized power in his own hands that no one could be a member of a conspiracy with him on anything approaching equal terms. This was true of both aggression and war crimes. In saying this, Donnedieu de Vabres went against what had been one of the planks of the Allied effort to draft the Nuremberg Charter.

In fact, Donnedieu de Vabres felt that the focus on conspiracy served to obscure rather than shed light on the origins and nature of the war. It was important to scrutinize what had led to World War II beyond what the notion of conspiracy seemed to suggest, namely "*l'idée d'un fait isolé, accidentel et qui donne la clef des méfaits suivants.*"[75] If nothing else, World War II had been the third in less than a century between Germany and France and this pointed to structural causes. His call to examine the totality of historical circumstances having led to the war, however, was less understanding of the defendants' own similar arguments and he was aware of the need to backstop historical and contextual explanation in order to avoid them becoming mere excuses. For example, rejecting

---

[72] Cited in Kim Christian Priemel, *The Betrayal: The Nuremberg Trials and German Divergence* (Oxford University Press 2016) 144.

[73] Telford Taylor, *The Anatomy of the Nuremberg Trials: A Personal Memoir* (Knopf Doubleday 2012).

[74] Donnedieu de Vabres, 'Le Procès de Nuremberg Devant Les Principes Modernes Du Droit Pénal International' (n 55) 530.

[75] Ibid. 560.

broadly the "necessity" defense presented by the accused based on the injustice of Versailles, he insisted "*Si grand que fût le libéralisme du Tribunal, il est clair que l'évocation de précédents historiques éloignés aurait ouvert une discussion sans issue, et qu'une limite devait être imposée à l'objet du débat.*"[76]

Donnedieu de Vabres drew the ire of his fellow judges, particularly the Soviet one who argued that they were "practical people, not a discussion club." But he effectively obtained the grudging narrowing of the conspiracy charge to aggressive war, backdating it to the Hossbach Conference of 1937. Although he is said to have "thought of the judgement's take on conspiracy as his personal triumph," Kim Christian Priemel has argued that his "victory was pyrrhic when it came to the judgement's didactic function" since the narrowing down of the conspiracy by the tribunal ended up "boost(ing) the very image of a criminal clique against which Donnedieu had warned, while the temporal limitation implied that personal and mid-range explanations took precedence over structural and long-term approaches."[77]

Third, Donnedieu de Vabres would remain intensely wary of the notion of crimes against humanity and any expansion thereof. Asked to join the ad hoc committee on the Genocide Convention he would, again, be an awkward participant. On the one hand, both his status as interwar key player and now Nuremberg judge set him in a category apart, especially from the luminous but marginal Lemkin. It was almost foretold that he would be involved. On the other hand, he had already expressed significant reservations vis-à-vis any expansion of the notion of crimes against humanity, of which genocide was clearly a manifestation. Always the guardian of the established law and having been recently won over to the notion of crimes against humanity, he had almost immediately set out to reduce the scope of that precedent to make sure that the notion remained tied to crimes against peace. In this, he was merely defending the Nuremberg legacy, which insisted that crimes against humanity needed to bear a nexus to aggressive war, a nexus that was not found to exist in the case of persecutions committed before 1939. In fact, after the trial Donnedieu de Vabres seemed to draw satisfaction from the fact that "*Nulle part [le jugement de Nuremberg] n'encourt le reproche d'avoir imputé aux accusés des actes inhumains indépendants des circonstances de la guerre.*"[78]

[76] Ibid. 567.
[77] Priemel, *The Betrayal* (n 72) 145.
[78] Donnedieu de Vabres, 'Le Procès de Nuremberg devant les Principes Modernes du Droit Pénal International' (n 55) 527.

But the ink had hardly dried on the judgment that two *"criminalistes distingués,"* Aroenanu and Lemkin, were already busy, apparently oblivious to this recently settled law, trying to partly undo the tribunal's work – or at least open it up – by insisting that crimes against humanity could be committed irrespective of war, and that war crimes were merely a modality of crimes against humanity. This opening up of the notion essentially connected crimes against humanity to the emerging international human rights movement rather than the *jus in bello*. Donnedieu de Vabres described their *"conceptions nouvelles"* as *"fumeuses"*[79] and was particularly peaked by the *"phenomène curieux"* by which the UN's legislative bodies were now *"allègrement"* taking responsibility for an innovation that the Nuremberg judges had wisely resisted.[80] One can see his gripe: in leaving *"le domaine des relations extérieures pour s'immiscer dans la politique intérieure des Etats,"*[81] the repression of crimes against humanity threatened to take his favoured *droit pénal international* away from even the *droit pénal inter-étatique* or a hypothetical *droit pénal mondial*, to a much feared *droit pénal universel*.

Donnedieu de Vabres had once cautioned of elaborating a theory of the *"délits de droits des gens"* asking rhetorically: *"A quoi bon édifier une construction, si élégante ou colossale qu'elle soit, sur du sable mouvant, sur de l'argile?"* Whether he thought that the new *droit pénal interétatique* whose existence he had grudgingly hailed was on a firmer footing as a result of his own work at Nuremberg a decade later is unclear. As a delegate at the International Law Commission he implicitly deplored the focus on the new crime of genocide at the expense of codifying Nuremberg and, even more, at the expense of understanding the "old" international criminal law as central to the new postwar project. *"Le droit pénal inter-étatique est, dans une large mesure, le successeur, l'héritier du droit pénal international, dont il ne saurait, sans atteindre à l'utilité générale et à la justice, ignorer les notions fondamentales."*[82]

But for all his reservations, Donnedieu de Vabres in the final years of his life remained a steadfast supporter of the record of the Allied tribunal from which he never desolidarized himself, even though he at times kept a guarded distance from some of its aspects. However, he did make it clear that the Nuremberg experiment would be all the more legitimate

---

[79] Ibid. 521.
[80] Donnedieu de Vabres, 'La Commission de Droit International et ses Fonctions En Matière Pénale' (n 65) 197.
[81] Ibid.
[82] Ibid. 191.

that it would be retrospectively rationalized by the advancement of international criminal justice. The latter's formalization and institutionalization would make its initial coming into being through an act of power more palatable: *"L'affirmation des principes de Nuremberg est illusoire, s'il n'existe pas d'organe préconstitué et permanent, digne de les sanctionner."*[83] This was of course a statement that would become quite classical and Donnedieu de Vabres articulated the fundamental unease of the discipline with ad hocism.

6.3 Conclusion

For Donnedieu de Vabres, it might be said that the age-old problem was that of crime, not specifically of international crimes. He invoked Grotius approvingly to emphasize that the real enemy of mankind was crime itself.[84] If the gaps in the international system of repression could be remedied for ordinary domestic crimes then they would also be remedied for the graver political crimes. In fact, there was nothing special about the latter and if the well-worn tools of extradition, better police work and cooperation were the solution for the former, then so would they be for that particular subset. Donnedieu de Vabres would probably have gladly traded the prospect of a permanent international criminal court for that of a *traité universel d'extradition*. The possibility of mass criminality of the state was barely contemplated, even as Donnedieu de Vabres became a specialist in the criminal justice systems of authoritarian states. This may explain the relative neglect into which his work fell after World War II, as if his interwar work had been preoccupied with dealing with yesterday's problems rather than foreseeing those to come. It may be true that as an expert in international criminal law Donnedieu de Vabres was a "natural" choice for the French judgeship at Nuremberg,[85] but for anyone more intimately versed in his constant and firmly held views, he was also a somewhat incongruous choice.

A man of World War I and the failed experiences of Versailles, Donnedieu de Vabres was wary of the idea of individual responsibility in international criminal law, preferring a largely interstate court with competence over criminal matters. As one who had then experienced World War II and was nominated at Nuremberg, he had little choice as

---

[83] Donnedieu de Vabres, 'Le Procès de Nuremberg devant les Principes Modernes du Droit Pénal International' (n 55) 101.

[84] Donnedieu de Vabres, *La Répression Internationale des Délits de Droit des Gens* (n 7) 21.

[85] 'Henri Donnedieu de Vabres' (n 9) 2.

a judge to accept that tribunal's major premise, namely that crimes were committed by individuals. An academic who had been extremely wary of the very existence of *délits de droit des gens* and consistently incredulous about the prospect and even rationality of individual subjectivity in international criminal law thus ended up largely concurring in a historical judgment that sent eighteen accused of such crimes to the gallows, and participating in the drafting of a convention on the foremost of such crimes.

By Nuremberg it was clear that the academic in him had come to the conclusion that individual responsibility was inevitable, and that World War II had precipitated the rise of forms of international responsibility which he had clearly not thought he would witness in his lifetime. Notwithstanding, his commitment to the centrality of the state as subject of international law and source of domestic law would reemerge in less evident ways: it is what led him, for example, to a certain understanding of the position of a defendant such as Jodl as a military man largely content to execute the state's orders; and to suggesting as late as the drafting of the Nuremberg principles or the Genocide Convention that the crime should be adjudicated as a crime of state by the International Court of Justice.[86] Most importantly and to the very end, Donnedieu de Vabres persisted in his by then increasingly iconoclastic (but of course also quite enlightening) claim that "*Le droit pénal international est frère jumeau du droit international privé*," noting that the discipline's connection to public international law was a comparatively late development.[87] Donnedieu de Vabres was therefore nothing short of extremely persistent in his views, views that had been disrupted but not truly modified by his experience at Nuremberg.

Contra the cosmopolitanism of Pella or Politis, the French professor was quite insistent on the reality, resilience and desirability of taking seriously the international legal system as it was and seeking to improve it, rather than transcend it. His efforts were always efforts to pull the system up by its own bootstraps, "*par le haut*" or at least "*par le côté*" rather than by challenging its very self-definition "*par le bas*." This is what made him wary of Politis's radical deconstruction of the state. It also meant that even though he might be broadly in concurrence with his

---

[86] Laurent Barcelo, 'Aux origines de la cour pénale internationale: le projet français de chambre criminelle internationale' (2008) *Guerres mondiales et conflits contemporains* 103.

[87] Donnedieu de Vabres, 'La Commission de Droit International et Ses Fonctions En Matière Pénale' (n 65) 191.

colleague Vespasian Pella on the need to focus on the state, he also berated his Romanian colleague for his anthropomorphism and tendency to engage in an *"application, en quelque sorte photographique de certaines théories classiques du droit pénal humain"* to the international realm.[88]

If anything, a true international criminal law might arise from the painstaking convergence of domestic law systems towards a sort of *jus commune* which had never entirely departed the international legal scene,[89] itself rendering conflicts of jurisdiction and law either obsolete or at least of little incidence in practice. This would mean not only that criminal laws would converge, but also that various systems of national *droit penal international* would do so as well. This would then mean, for example, that *"le progrès de la civilisation [. . .] du resserrement de la communauté internationale"*[90] the role of the *exception d'ordre public* would be reduced. Until then, he noted *"l'impossibilité d'arriver à la solution rationnelle et definitive des conflits de competence."* In fact, *"la solution parfaite des conflits de lois pénales suppose une resemblance, parfait aussi, de ces lois. C'est dire qu'elle sera obtenue le jour meme où elle aura perdu sa raison d'être."*[91]

Strikingly, Donnedieu insisted that *"ce qu'il est urgent de reformer, si l'on veut qu'un résultat positif soit obtenu, c'est le particularisme des peuples. Le dogme de la souveraineté absolue des Etats, dogme combattu, périmé, mais toujours renaissant de ses cendres, s'oppose à ce qu'à l'internationalisme du crime réponde, victorieusement, l'internationalisme de la répression."* Rather than "universalization," he therefore chose the long road of "unification,"[92] one that finds echoes for example in the work of Delmas Marty and other authors working on the contemporary convergence of criminal law, notably in the European context. This convergence would essentially do away with the very problem that international conflict of laws and international criminal jurisdiction sought to address.

---

[88] Donnedieu de Vabres, *Les Principes Modernes du Droit Pénal International* (n 8) 428.

[89] Donnedieu de Vabres, 'La Commission de Droit International et Ses Fonctions En Matière Pénale' (n 65) 191.

[90] Donnedieu de Vabres, 'La Communauté Internationale en Droit Pénal et les Limites que lui Impose le Particularisme des Etat' (n 15) 492.

[91] Ibid. 504.

[92] Nicolae T. Buzea, 'La Règle de droit pénal et ses applications extra-territoriales (contribution à l'éclaircissement de la notion du droit international pénal' (1931) 8 *Revue internationale de droit pénal* http://gallica.bnf.fr/ark:/12148/bpt6k1254719s accessed November 29, 2016.

Aside from suggesting that we need to work to awaken "*une conscience universelle,*"[93] however, Donnedieu de Vabres left us largely in the dark about how one might embark on such a program. He suggested, for example, that "*le progrès se realise de lui-même, parce que la communauté des besoins économiques et sociaux, la propagation toujours plus large des idées, le rapprochement des civilisations determinant, entre les legislations nouvelles, une resemblance croissante*"[94] but the notion of simply waiting convergence out, perhaps with the help of a few worthy "*congrès internationaux,*" may have seemed unappealing to some of his more hurried colleagues who at any rate saw the problem as much bigger. Moreover, although seemingly wary of imperialism in the interstate context, he was also at times strangely oblivious to the darker tonalities of a world criminal law, as if convergence might not be merely the consequence of successful imperialism.

[93] Donnedieu de Vabres, *La Répression Internationale des Délits de Droit des Gens* (n 7) 20.
[94] Donnedieu de Vabres, 'La Communauté Internationale en Droit Pénal et les Limites que lui Impose le Particularisme des Etats' (n 15) 505.

7

Not Just Pure Theory

Hans Kelsen (1881–1973) and International Criminal Law

MÓNICA GARCÍA-SALMONES ROVIRA

Figure 7.1 Hans Kelsen. Photograph 1926. Photo by Imagno/Getty Images.

7 HANS KELSEN

7.1 Introduction

It is unsurprising, given his background, that Hans Kelsen should have become particularly interested in the development of international criminal law at the time of World War II. He was an Austrian legal theorist who, as a Jew, had been removed from his chair at the University of Cologne, had left Germany and by 1940 was resident in the United States of America.[1] During this period the criminal policies of the Nazi government in Germany were being put into practice, and the theory and development of international criminal law was one of Kelsen's particular interests and the subject of much of his academic work.

As early as 1920 Kelsen had expressed his views about the role of the state in the punishment of war criminals in a short review of a book by Alfred Verdross (1890–1980), a student of his.[2] With characteristically keen insight Kelsen noted that queries about the punishment of war criminals by the state – about which 'there was no doubt' – revolved around only the questions of 'who is obliged, or indeed, who has the right to punish and in what measure'.[3] Adhering to Verdross's argument against 'victors' justice', Kelsen wrote that on the one hand, the treaty of Saint Germain had left untouched Austria's right to punish war criminals from the Allied countries – as well as the right 'to prosecute those persons' – but attributed no right of extradition for Austria. He commented on the novelty of article 173, paragraph 1 and 2, under which the Allied and Associated Powers had the right to bring before military tribunals violators of the laws and customs of war, and extradition was only possible in favour of the Allies.[4]

---

[1] I am grateful to Professor Clemens Jabloner, Klaus Zeleny and Professor Thomas Olechowsky from the Hans Kelsen Institute at Vienna for their help with the research undertaken for this chapter. Kelsen's papers, most of which date from after his emigration to the US, are located at that institute. Unless otherwise stated all translations from the German are mine. Arguably, Kelsen's Jewishness played a secondary role in his activities and writings of the Nuremberg period. This is not to say that it did not play a role in his theoretical work. On this issue, see, for instance, Reut Yael Paz, *A Gateway Between a Distant God and a Cruel World: The Contribution of Jewish German-Speaking Scholars to International Law* (Leiden: Brill Nijhoff, 2013).

[2] Alfred Verdross, *Die Völkerrechtswidrige Kriegshandlung und der Strafanspruch der Staaten* (Berlin: Hans Robert Engelmann, 1920); Hans Kelsen, 'Der Völkerrechtliche Strafanspruch Wegen Völkerrechtswidriger Kriegshandlungen', Neue Freie Presse, 9 August 1920, 3.

[3] Kelsen, 'Der Völkerrechtliche Strafanspruch'.

[4] Kelsen, 'Der Völkerrechtliche Strafanspruch'; Treaty of St Germain, 10.9.1919, Parliamentary Paper. Treaty Series No11 (1919) [Cmd.400], Parliamentary Archives: GB-061.

176   MÓNICA GARCÍA-SALMONES ROVIRA

These ideas about due regard for legality and rejection of victors' justice expressed in his one-page review were intriguingly echoed in Kelsen's later involvement in the dawn of the discipline of international criminal law. The fact that, as a generalist, he could move with ease within the discipline of international law and a series of biographical facts contributed to his particular view of international criminal law, which may be summarised by reference to the following six principles.

The first of these is the repudiation of victors' justice mentioned above, which appeared as a critique in his Nuremberg writings.[5] The second is his affirmation of the unity of the legal system.[6] His first major work on international law, *The Problem of Sovereignty and the Theory of International Law*, dealt with the profoundly theoretical problems involved in reconciling the concept of state sovereignty with the concept of an international law, and sought to connect both legal orders within a unitary system.[7] Applied to international criminal law, this meant in his own words that '[t]he application of national law to the war criminal is at the same time an execution of international law'.[8] The unity of international and national legal orders leads to the key question of what constitutes the source of jurisdiction for the prosecution of crimes. Article 145 of the Austrian Constitution of 1920 contains the declaration that the Constitutional Tribunal is a 'special criminal tribunal' (*Sonderstrafgericht*) for violations of international law.[9] It is not known to what extent Kelsen was involved in

---

[5] Hans Kelsen, 'Will the Judgment in the Nuremberg Trial Constitute a Precedent in International Law?' (1947) 1 *The International Law Quarterly*, 153–71.

[6] On this issue, see, in particular, Jochen von Bernstorff, *The Public International Law Theory of Hans Kelsen: Believing in Universal Law* (Cambridge: Cambridge University Press, 2010), 78–118.

[7] Hans Kelsen, *Das Problem der Souveränität und die Theorie des Völkerrechts* (Tübingen: Verlag von J. C. B. Mohr (Paul Siebeck), 1920). For the influence that *Das Problem der Souveränität* had in the work of the Japanese Yokota Kisaburō, see the chapter by Urs Matthias Zachmann, 'Yokota Kisaburō: Defending International Criminal Justice in Interwar and early Postwar Japan'.

[8] Hans Kelsen, 'Collective and Individual Responsibility in International Law with Particular Regard to the Punishment of War Criminals' (1943) 31 *California Law Review*, 530–71, at 555.

[9] For the term 'special criminal tribunal' and its current common interpretation, see Karl Korinek, Michael Holoubek and Andrea Martin, *Österreichisches Bundesverfassungsrecht* (Wien, New York: Springer, 1999), vol. II. article 145, at 8; see also the comment on article 145 by Kelsen, Froehlich and Merkl that 'certain violations of international law that deserve criminal sanction', would be 'removed from common criminal tribunals' and ascribed 'to the constitutional tribunal'. They related article 145 to article 9. Article 9 stated that the 'the generally recognised rules of international law are part of the law of the country'. See Hans Kelsen, Georg Froehlich and Adolf Merkl, *Die*

the drafting of this particular article, but his fame in Austria largely rests on his co-authorship of this 1920 constitution. Moreover, his theory of the rationale of the unity of the legal order is clearly in play in article 145. The principle that both orders had always to be considered in international criminal adjudication also led Kelsen to develop noteworthy discussions on legal theory in the case of the legal status of Germany and Austria after World War II, as discussed below.

Third, Kelsen's realist standpoint was that (international) law is 'a specific order or organization of power'.[10] In international law the means of power were retaliation and war.[11] The seemingly opposing principles of the effectiveness of the legal order and his sharp political and methodological division between 'is' and 'ought' were reflected in his realist ideas about power.[12] But as he considered it self-evident that the international order was a primitive legal order, Kelsen conceived of sovereignty as the core element for the purposes of collective security.[13] Through the analogy of the domestic order he envisaged a progressive evolution of international criminal law. The implementation of international adjudication with individuals at the centre of international law was the last stage of a slow process. First a state must renounce war and states create together a centralised power to punish through war, that is to say, through a system of collective security. Only later would states submit to compulsory adjudication, which would eventually also apply to individuals. Kelsen, however, always wrote about this process in terms of the desirable future, never as the realised present.[14] Fourth, Kelsen did not transpose notions drawn from domestic criminal law to the international sphere. Instead, he consistently addressed issues by combining

---

Bundesverfassung Vom 1. Oktober 1920 (Wien and Leipzig: Deuticke, 1922); see also Ignaz Seidl-Hohenveldern, 'Transformation or Adoption of International Law into Municipal Law' (1963) 12 *International and Comparative Law Quarterly*, 88–124, at 100.

[10] Hans Kelsen, *General Theory of Law and State*, tr. Anders Wedberg (New Jersey: The Lawbook Exchange, 2009), 121.

[11] Which explains why Kelsen defended a theory of *bellum justum*. See Gregory M. Reichberg, Henrik Syse and Endre Begby, *The Ethics of War: Classic and Contemporary Readings* (Malden, Oxford Carlton: Blackwell Publishing, 2006), 605–13.

[12] For an analysis of this principle, see Mónica García-Salmones Rovira, *The Project of Positivism in International Law* (Oxford: Oxford University Press, 2013).

[13] Hans Kelsen, *Peace Through Law* (Chapel Hill: The University of North Carolina Press, 1944), 12.

[14] 'It is only the simple-minded enthusiast who can imagine such a far-reaching abdication of the State authority vis-à-vis its subjects before the highest grade of inter-State judicial process has been reached.' Hans Kelsen, *The Legal Process and International Order* (London: Constable, 1935), 28.

international and military law, violations of warfare law, analysis of acts of state and the qualification of war, whether war was just or legal, or neither. This principle stems from his personal history. As a young man, Kelsen was involved during World War I as a specialist in military law for the Austrian Ministry of War.[15] This gave him an insight into the political, legal and administrative machinery put in motion by large-scale conflict and the changes in power and constitutional status that the results of such conflict might involve. This four-year experience forged not only Kelsen's competence in constitutional legal theory, but also his approach to international criminal law. Moreover, it is worth noting that Kelsen was never a criminal lawyer. This differentiated him from the most acclaimed among the previous generation of German-speaking international lawyers, such as Carl Ludwig von Bar (1836–1913), Franz von Liszt (1851–1919) and Heinrich Lammasch (1853–1920). Even Lassa Oppenheim (1858–1919), who studied with the eminent criminal lawyer Karl Binding, started his academic career in Germany as a criminal lawyer. Kelsen's later activities in Washington at the War Department and the War Crimes Office related to his military knowledge and experience. Fifth, Kelsen took the view that perpetrators ought to be punished for committing crimes even if they were not classified as such under international law at the point at which they were committed, and that this should only be done in terms of justice and other natural law principles.[16] The shortcomings encountered in the application of legal positivist techniques when dealing with international criminal law led Kelsen to stress the principle of justice. Notably, the positivist legal theoretician of the twentieth century made justice one of the prominent features of his published writings on the Nuremberg trials.[17] Finally, and in accordance with the legalism and subsequent objectivity of the Vienna School, there

---

[15] For a helpful biographical account of this period, see Jürgen Busch, 'Hans Kelsen Im Ersten Weltkrieg Achsenzeit Einer Weltkarriere', in Robert Walter, Werner Ogris and Thomas Olechowski (eds.), *Hans Kelsen: Leben – Werk – Wirksamkeit* (Wien: Manz, 2009), 57–80.

[16] Robert Jackson put this idea as follows in his Report to the President: '[w]e propose to punish acts which have been regarded as criminal since the time of Cain and have been so written in every civilized code'. Robert H. Jackson , 'Report to the President by Mr. Justice Jackson, June 6, 1945', in *Report of Robert H. Jackson United States Representative to the International Conference on Military Trials* (London: Office of Public Affairs, 1945), 42–54, at 50.

[17] Kelsen, 'Will the Judgment in the Nuremberg Trial Constitute a Precedent in International Law?', 155. The same evolution happened with Kisaburō, see Zachmann, 'Yokota Kisaburō'.

was no room in Kelsen's thinking for political considerations of the type of the German doctrine of 'military necessity'. Independent of their nationality, war criminals ought to be punished.

This chapter introduces the man, his ideas and activities in relation to the early development of international criminal law. A comprehensive examination of all the issues Kelsen tackled in preparation for Nuremberg and a historical study of his personal involvement is beyond the scope of one chapter, which can only indicate topics that may be worthy of future research. Instead, my aim is to give an overview of the questions surrounding Kelsen's work on international criminal law. The chapter begins with a brief biography to help to understand the complexity of Kelsen's contributions to the development of international criminal law. Consideration of his involvement with the military in World War I sheds light on his knowledge of military law and his skills as legal adviser. Discussion of Kelsen's pure theory as it relates to the principle of individual criminal responsibility shows the connections between Kelsen's lifelong theoretical project and international criminal law. Finally, a tentative chronology of his personal participation in the preparations for Nuremberg precedes a presentation of three aspects of Kelsen's activities as a legal adviser to the US War Crimes Office: his contribution to the inclusion of individual criminal responsibility in the London Agreement, his view of the problematic jurisdiction of the Nuremberg International Military Tribunal and his conviction that new law had been created with the Charter of the International Military Tribunal (IMT) annexed to the London Agreement.[18]

7.2 Biographical Note

The copious biographical details on Kelsen now available, together with his own two autobiographies, provide abundant information on one referred to by Dean Roscoe Pound in the 1930s as 'unquestionably the leading jurist of the time'.[19] He was born in 1891 in Prague, which was then part of the

[18] Kelsen refers usually to the 'London Agreement' as a whole. Agreement for the Prosecution and Punishment of the Major War Criminals of the European Axis, and Charter of the International Military Tribunal. London, 8 August 1945. Dietrich Schindler and Jiři Toman (eds.), *The Laws of Armed Conflict: A Collection of Conventions, Resolutions and Other Documents* (Dordrecht: Martinus Nijhoff Publishers, 1988), 912–19.

[19] Matthias Jestaedt (ed.), *Hans Kelsen Im Selbstbezeugnis. Sonderpublikation Anlässlich Des 125. Geburtstages von Hans Kelsen Am 11. Oktober 2006* (Tübingen: Mohr Siebeck, 2006); Rudolg Aládar Métall, *Hans Kelsen: Leben und Werk* (Vienna: Deuticke, 1968);

Austrian Empire, but soon after his birth the family moved to Vienna. In 1912 he married Marguerite Blond by whom he was to have two daughters.

Kelsen devoted himself to his academic work from his early university days and focused his energies and ambitions on developing and disseminating a very personal general theory of law. Starting with his first publication in 1905, which was a dissertation entitled *The State Theory of Dante Alighieri* that dealt with the universal monarchy, and passing, via his Habilitation on *Problems of the State Legal Theory* in 1911, to his *General Theory of Law* in 1925, a clear thread can be traced from the very beginning of his academic career. The depth and complexity of his work steadily grew, but its breadth and novelty were present from the beginning.[20]

It is, again, impossible in the confines of this chapter to do justice to an *œuvre* comprising more than 400 texts, and to a particularly eventful life covering nearly a century, with three changes of religious faith (first to Catholicism, then to Lutheranism and finally, probably a return to his initial Judaism),[21] and three changes of citizenship. Initially Austrian, he also acquired German citizenship on accepting a professorial chair at Cologne University in 1930, and then lost them both in favour of Czech citizenship when he was called to the German University in Prague. Kelsen took refuge in the United States in 1940. He retained his Czech citizenship until 1945 and renounced it to become an American citizen. He held the Chair of Public Law in Vienna (*Staats und Verwaltungsrecht*) from 1920 until he went to Cologne in 1930. During this period, he contributed to the drafting of the Constitution of Austria and became a member of the newly created Constitutional Court of Austria. His contribution to legal theory, with the introduction of a judicial review in that tribunal, was probably the aspect of his work that he regarded most highly.[22] Due to the political turmoil in the country, Kelsen's activities in the tribunal were exceptionally controversial and were the

---

Thomas Olechowski, 'Biographische Untersuchungen zu Hans Kelsen', in Barna Mezey (ed.), *Rechtsgeschichtliche Vorträge* 64 (2011), 1–22. The quotation from Pound can be found in Roscoe Pound, 'Law and the Science of Law in Recent Theories', *Yale Law Journal*, 43 (1933), 525–36, at 532.

[20] Hans Kelsen, *Die Staatslehre des Dante Alighieri* (Vienna and Leipzig: Franz Deuticke, 1905).

[21] See Max Knight quoted by Clemens Jabloner, 'Kelsenand His Circle: The Viennese Years' (1988) 9 *European Journal of International Law*, 368–85, at 370.

[22] Stanley L. Paulson, 'On Hans Kelsen's Role in the Formation of the Austrian Constitution and his Defense of Constitutional Review', in *Rechtstheorie. Festschrift für Aulis Aarnio. The Reasonable as Rational? On Legal Argumentation and Justification* (Berlin: Duncker & Humblot, 2000), 385–95, at 389.

7 HANS KELSEN 181

reason for his moving to Germany.[23] He held the Chair of International Law at Cologne University from 1930 to 1933. Following the enactment of a 1933 law that established an Aryan-only clause for civil servants, he was removed from his position as dean and from his chair and became a refugee in Switzerland. However, few refugees can have employed exile as successfully as Kelsen did, as he used it to foster his internationalist political project. On many occasions Kelsen showed himself adept at making a virtue of necessity. For the next ten or more years until he eventually settled in Berkeley in the United States, Kelsen moved from one place to another, lecturing in international law first at the Graduate Institute of International Studies in Geneva – a post he desired due to its proximity to the League of Nations[24] – then at the German University of Prague (1936–1938), where he stayed although the political conditions were dangerous,[25] and later at Harvard University. After a period of hesitation, uncertainty and disappointment – he was not granted a professorship at Harvard despite the Rockefeller foundation's promise to cover a third of his salary if he was accepted[26] – in 1942 Berkeley University offered him a lectureship and in 1945 a position as full professor in International Law, Jurisprudence and Origin of Legal Institutions.[27]

The range of his contacts seemed limitless also because many of his students were, like him, Jewish refugees living all over the world. Kelsen's life in the United States from June 1940 onwards was an odd combination of financial insecurity – evidenced by the dozens of applications for funding and jobs in the United States to be found among his personal papers[28] – a certain general public ignorance about his theoretical work, and tremendous respect for his legal advice. His appointment to the War

---

[23] Christian Neschwara, 'Kelsen als Verfassungsrichter. Seine Rolle in Der Dispensehen-Kontroverse', in Stanley L. Paulson and Michael Stolleis (eds.), *Hans Kelsen, Staatsrechtslehrer Und Rechtstheoretiker Des 20. Jahrhunderts* (Tübingen: Mohr Siebeck, 2005), 353–84; Jestaedt, *Hans Kelsen Im Selbstbezeugnis*, 70–81.

[24] Nicoletta Bersier Ladavac, *Hans Kelsen a Genéve (1933–1940)* (Geneva: Thémis 1996).

[25] Jestaedt, *Hans Kelsen Im Selbstbezeugnis*, 88.

[26] See letter of 6 June 1941 from Joseph H. Willits from the Rockefeller Foundation to Dean James M. Landis, Law School of Harvard University, 'Hans Kelsen State in Hans Kelsen Institute (University of Vienna)' (15o.58).

[27] Jestaedt, *Hans Kelsen Im Selbstbezeugnis*, 103. The Rockefeller Foundation still contributed to Kelsen's salary for some years, as is apparent from his correspondence.

[28] For instance, see the letter from Hans Kelsen to the Bolingen Foundation (11.10.1954) thanking the Foundation for a three-year scholarship together with a report of his scientific activities during that period and asking whether there was a possibility of renewal, 'Hans Kelsen State in Hans Kelsen Institute (University of Vienna)' (15u.58).

Crimes Office was only one of the more prominent among the many occasions on which his legal advice was sought.[29] It was in fact impossible for American academia to slight one of the most important European legal theorists, however much misunderstood his approach to legal theory may have been.[30] Thus, rather than being ostracised, Kelsen participated in American academic life and was at the same time and to a striking degree given his age – fifty-eight when he arrived in the United States – and the means of communication available during that period, was also active in international academia. The unavoidable relative poverty imposed, as a result of forced emigration, on someone who had no personal fortune did not prevent him soon becoming one of the 'core émigré jurists'.[31]

Although, as we shall see, Kelsen's appointment to Berkeley came too late to enable him to participate in the Nuremberg trials, it was, nevertheless, a blessing. However, the appointment did not permanently solve his financial difficulties since he was notified that he would receive a minimal pension at the time of retirement in 1952.[32] And so the struggle continued. It is touching to find among Kelsen's papers a letter of recommendation for funding that Roscoe Pound wrote for him. Kelsen was then sixty-nine years old.[33] Perhaps this is why he seriously considered moving to Israel where one of his daughters lived and where he was offered a position as a legal adviser to the government.[34] However,

[29] Among other appointments Kelsen was legal adviser to the state of Texas against the government of the United States in several subsoil cases. 'Hans Kelsen State in Hans Kelsen Institute (University of Vienna)' (15t.58).

[30] On the reception and misunderstanding of Kelsen's theory in the United States, see D. A. Jeremy Telman, 'Introduction: Hans Kelsen for Americans' in D. A. Jeremy Telman (ed.), *Hans Kelsen in America: Selective Affinities and the Mysteries of Academic Influence* (Cham: Springer, 2016), 1–17; Brian H. Bix, 'Kelsen in the United States: Still Misunderstood', in *Hans Kelsen in America*, pp. 17–29.

[31] Mira L. Siegelberg, 'Unofficial Men, Efficient Civil Servants: Raphael Lemkin in the History of International Law' (2013) 15 *Journal of Genocide Research*, 297–316, at 305.

[32] 'I have been informed that my pension will not be more than hundred dollars a month'. Letter from Hans Kelsen to Charles E. Odegaard, 3 May 1951, in which he asked about the possibility of obtaining funding from the American Council of Learned Societies, 'Hans Kelsen State in Hans Kelsen Institute (University of Vienna)' (15j.57).

[33] 'I am very glad indeed to recommend Professor Kelsen's application to your Foundation without reservation. Professor Kelsen is by universal consent one of the outstanding leaders among the jurists of the world. Anything that he undertakes will be done in the grand manner and admirably.' Roscoe Pound, letter to the Bollingen Foundation, June 19, 1951, 'Hans Kelsen State in Hans Kelsen Institute (University of Vienna)' (16c9.61).

[34] The negotiations lasted several years and several letters were exchanged between Kelsen and Jacob Robinson and a letter of invitation (22 September 1953) was sent by the Minister of Justice, P.F. Rosen, 'to come to Israel for the purpose of settling in this country' and become 'Adviser to all Government Departments in matters of International

7 HANS KELSEN   183

Kelsen did not speak Hebrew and at over 70 years of age another move abroad, for him and his wife must have seemed overwhelming.[35] He was to remain in the United States, but made numerous trips to Europe and South America. Nine honorary doctorates were bestowed upon him during his lifetime.[36] His fame was to grow considerably after his death in Berkeley in April 1973 at the age of ninety-one, three months after the death of Marguerite, his wife and collaborator for over sixty years.

Kelsen's papers at the Hans Kelsen Institute also include the corrected proofs of an interview that took place in Mexico in 1960. His personal papers (those that survived are mainly from his American period) contain many copies of his professional letters, but copies of his personal letters are scarce. Therefore, the text of the interview sent to him for his approval shows a rare instance of Kelsen opening up, in particular about his Jewishness. Treated with all the caution due to a text not completely approved by the author, this interview excerpt serves to conclude this biographical section with a taste of Kelsen's sense of humour and spirit:

> Interviewer: 'I think we must all thank you very much for such a lively talk on what I must confess that I for one had imagine was a rather dull subject. [But you seem to have such vivacity, such enthusiasm . . . '
>
> Kelsen: 'And do you know that in private I tend to be rather pessimistic and sad? One wouldn't believe it . . . I often wonder which of my two natures is the real one . . .'
>
> I: 'Perhaps both? Many Jewish people I know have this surface of fun and wit and an undercurrent of melancholy. Perhaps it's a Jewish characteristic.'
>
> K: 'You may be right. If I were a metaphysician, I would say that it belonged to Jewish history. But as I am not a metaphysician, I say all that is nonsense. And yet, you may be right . . . '
>
> I: 'You see! You can be humorous discussing the metaphysics of Jewish melancholy.]'[37]

Public Law', 'Hans Kelsen State in Hans Kelsen Institute (University of Vienna)' (15k.58). On Jacob Robinson and International Criminal Law, see Jonathan A. Bush, 'Nuremberg and Beyond: Jacob Robinson, International Lawyer' (2017) 39 *Loyola of Los Angeles International and Comparative Law Review*, 259–86.

[35] That Kelsen did not speak Hebrew appears from his correspondence with Jacob Robinson.

[36] The complete list can be found in Jestaedt, *Hans Kelsen Im Selbstbezeugnis*, 97–105.

[37] This section within square brackets is crossed out, presumably by Kelsen. Still, he kept the text. 'Hans Kelsen State in Hans Kelsen Institute (University of Vienna)' (15r.58). Mention of a meeting with journalists in his trip to México in 1960 that seems to be the occasion of the interview can be found in Imer B. Florés, 'Una Visita a Hans Kelsen: En México' (2014) 8 *Anuario de Filosofía y Teoría Del Derecho*, 53–94, at 64.

7.3 Setting the Stage: Military Law and Pure Theory

In 1902, having completed his one-year voluntary military service, Kelsen became a Lieutenant Reservist.[38] After some initial hesitation about his fitness for active service, Kelsen took part in World War I as a military lawyer at the Ministry of War.[39] This involved a variety of duties: military advocate, reporter for petitions of mercy in cases of the death penalty for deserters and as specialist in international contracts. Of crucial importance for his future career was his interest in the constitutional aspects of the conflict that existed between the Hungarian and the Austrian military.[40] As early as 1915 he had produced a draft proposal for a Commander in Chief (*Oberkommando*) centralising all the political military decisions of the Emperor and his corps, and two separate administrations in two separate ministries. He published his ideas in 1917 in the *Journal for Military Law*.[41] The publication attracted the attention of the Minister and henceforth Kelsen became counsel to the last Minister of War of the Austrian-Hungarian Empire.[42] It is difficult to understand certain proto-military utterances to be found in that piece as being more than an attractive way of conveying some of the key points of Kelsen's constitutional and administrative theory.[43] However, it is plausible that he entertained a degree of admiration for military virtues, as is discernible in statements such as 'it would be advisable to include in the schools a type of military preliminary training'.[44]

Against critiques, Busch argues that Kelsen's work with military law during World War I rather than 'a passion' or his rendering a 'leading role in the system of the military justice', was mainly an instrument to boost his career in the right direction; that is, towards participating in the

---

[38] Busch, 'Hans Kelsen im Ersten Weltkrieg', 59.

[39] Busch, 'Hans Kelsen im Ersten Weltkrieg', 63–64.

[40] See also Kelsen's own account, which differs slightly from Busch's, in Jestaedt, *Hans Kelsen Im Selbstbezeugnis*, 47–57.

[41] First published in Hans Kelsen, 'Zur Reform der Verfassungsrechtlichen Grundlagen der Wehrmacht Österreich-Ungarn' (1918) 1 *Zeitschrift für Militärrecht*, 8–23. Republished in Matthias Jestaedt (ed.), *Hans Kelsen Werke (1911–1917)* (Tübingen: Mohr Siebeck, 2010), III, 615–29, at 615–16.

[42] Jestaedt, *Hans Kelsen im Selbstbezeugnis*, 64. The War Minister was Colonel General Rudolf Freiherr Stöger-Steiner von Steinstätten (1861–1921), Busch, 'Hans Kelsen Im Ersten Weltkrieg', 75.

[43] Kelsen, 'Zur Reform der Verfassungsrechtlichen Grundlagen der Wehrmacht Österreich-Ungarn', 615–16.

[44] Kelsen, 'Zur Reform der Verfassungsrechtlichen Grundlagen der Wehrmacht Österreich-Ungarn', 615–16.

draft of the future constitution and acquiring a professorship.[45] However, the relevance of the issues dealt with in the five memoranda that are the fruit of his two years of collaboration with Minister Stöger-Steiner (1917–1918), cannot be denied. In this regard, Schmetterer states in his edition of the two memoranda on constitutional issues that 'Kelsen dealt mainly with political questions', leaving aside 'legal technical questions'.[46] He refers, in particular, to his proposal to transform the monarchy – the Austrian part – into a federal state composed of different nationalities. In turn, Busch recognised a certain pragmatic pattern in Kelsen's activities as legal adviser both in military and constitutional law, one of 'standing on the ground of the real and political conditions, with which he is entrusted to deal legally'.[47] Put differently, Kelsen was an extraordinary lawyer, knowledgeable about the political issues at stake and with a political vision of his own. Arguably, much of his work revolving around Nuremberg at the War Crimes Office of the United States related to these skills. And yet, at the same time, Kelsen was also defending fundamental positions of his own theory. I will illustrate this idea with the help of his conception of individual criminal responsibility.

Kelsen came to write about the specific question of individual international criminal responsibility at a late stage. It was only after the Moscow Declaration of 1 November 1943, in which the 'United States, Great Britain, and Soviet Russia made the punishment of war criminals one of their war aims'.[48] But the issue of individual criminal responsibility appears in Kelsen's *œuvre* very early on, with what was initially a highly abstract standpoint against the criminal responsibility of the state gradually becoming concrete over the years and culminating in his well-known article in the *California Law Review*. His main argument against punishing the 'unreality' of the state was developed in a piece published thirty years earlier in 1914, 'On the Wrong Done by the State'. The text is hardcore 'pure theory' and, for those unfamiliar with that doctrine, difficult to read due to its level of abstraction. Kelsen's argument is about the impossibility, from a legal point of view, of the state committing a wrong. The conciseness of the German language helped him to articulate his argument that the

---

[45] Busch, 'Hans Kelsen im Ersten Weltkrieg', 59.

[46] On the memoranda, see Christoph Schmetterer, 'Hans Kelsens Überlegungen zur Reform der Österreichisch-Ungarischen Monarchie', in Clemens Jablober, Thomas Olechowski and Klaus Zeleny (eds.), *Das internationale Wirken Hans Kelsens* (Vienna: Manz, 2016), 1–10, at 1, 7.

[47] Busch, 'Hans Kelsen im Ersten Weltkrieg', 75.

[48] Kelsen, 'Collective and Individual Responsibility in International Law', 530.

186 MÓNICA GARCÍA-SALMONES ROVIRA

state was but a manifestation of law and therefore logically incapable of violating law: 'state law [*Staatsrecht*] and a wrong done by the State [*Staatsunrecht*] are mutually exclusive'.[49] Kelsen's famous critique of the syncretism of methods, that is to say the mixing of the formal juridical method of cognition with any other political, metaphysical or causal method helped him to make his case.[50] A legal person did not 'exist' in reality. Thus one could never reach an entity defined as 'state' by investigating a causal connection with events typical of criminal law.[51] The absurdity, in terms of pure theory, of claiming that the state had committed a tort or a crime was thus exposed.

In 1932 Kelsen approached the issue of individual responsibility more directly, but still from a predominantly theoretical point of view. In the lengthy chapter entitled 'Wrong and the Consequences of Wrong in International Law',[52] he explained that a 'more refined legal feeling' demanded 'the physical-natural *identification between the subject of the offence committed and the object of the consequences of the wrong*, that is to say, it dismisses so-called collective responsibility and recognizes only *individual responsibility*'. This was, he continued, a 'demand of international policy that in international law is not realised or only to a very limited extent'.[53] But theoretical work and good wishes apart, Kelsen did not view any of this as real international law until the drafters of the Nuremberg Charter created by treaty the possibility of incriminating persons for the wrongs done in the name of the state and, in his view, only for the signatories that had given their consent.

Kelsen's published and unpublished work of the early 1940s and 1950s comprises a series of historical and anthropological studies in which he analysed the principle of retribution that merits study from an international criminal law perspective.[54]

---

[49] Hans Kelsen, 'Über Staatsunrecht. Zugleich ein Beitrag zur Frage der Deliktsfähigkeit Juristischer Personen und zur Lehre vom Fehlerhaften Staatsakt', in Matthias Jestaedt (ed.), *Hans Kelsen Werke (1911–1917)* (Tübingen: Mohr Siebeck, 2010), III, 441–532, at 531.

[50] Kelsen, 'Über Staatsunrecht', 456.

[51] Kelsen, 'Über Staatsunrecht', 449, 465. See also the comments by Jestaedt Matthias, 'Editorischer Bericht "Über Staatsunrecht"', in *Hans Kelsen Werke* (Tübingen: Mohr Siebeck, 2010), III, 734–46. For the way in which Kelsen dealt later with the problem of 'law contrary to law', see Christopher Kletzer, 'Kelsen's Development of the Fehlerkalkül-Theory' (2005) 18 *Ratio Juris*, 46–63.

[52] Hans Kelsen, *Unrecht und Unrechtsfolge im Völkerrecht* (Aalen: Scientia, 1971).

[53] Kelsen, *Unrecht und Unrechtsfolge im Völkerrecht*, 105 (emphasis by Kelsen).

[54] Hans Kelsen, 'Causality and Retribution' (1941) 8 *Philosophy of Science*, 533–56; Hans Kelsen, *Society and Nature: A Sociological Inquiry* (London: Kegan Paul, Trench,

7.4 The War Crimes Office

The Austrian legal theorist was consultant for the War Department and the War Crimes Office, working directly for the Judge Advocate General (JAG), the legal arm of the War Department and the United States Army.[55] The War Crimes Office had been established in October 1944 in the Office of the JAG of the Army, which became the central agency for the State, War and Navy Departments in handling war crimes.[56] It was Major General Myron C. Cramer, the Judge Advocate General in person, and not the civilian Robert H. Jackson, who urged Kelsen to come to Washington in the crucial moments of June 1945.[57] And at least one year before that date Brigadier General John M. Weir, Assistant Advocate General and Director of the United States War Crimes Office, was Kelsen's immediate superior.

During his time at the War Crimes Office, particularly while working for the JAG, Kelsen strictly followed military, criminal and international law, without grand moral narratives, and put forward a set of emotionally detached suggestions as to the new law that ought to be created. This description fits well with Bradley F. Smith's narrative of a power struggle division within the US government, between a retributive Secretary of Treasury and a matter of fact Secretary of War. The former, Henry Morgenthau, was in favour of the imposition of rigid terms on Germany and the summary execution of major criminals. The latter, Henry L. Stimson, advocated 'judicial procedures that dealt with all the culprits from top to bottom'.[58] Roosevelt supported Morgenthau's

---

Trubner, 1946); Hans Kelsen, *Vergeltung und Kausalität. Eine soziologische Untersuchung* (The Hague/Chicago: Van Stockum & Zoon/The University of Chicago Press, 1941). Among Kelsen's papers at the Hans Kelsen Institute are also several (lengthy) unpublished studies on the topic of retribution in the history of law that evidence Kelsen's interest in this issue. For a brief speculation on a possible retributive attitude in Kelsen in some of his Nuremberg writings, see Andrea Gattini, 'Kelsen's Contribution to International Criminal Law' (2004) 2 *Journal of International Criminal Justice*, 795–809, at 800–2.

[55] On the Department of the Judge Advocate General, see 'Congratulatory Messages Received as the Department Entered its 171st Year' (1945) 2 *The Judge Advocate Journal*, 31.

[56] See Telford Taylor, *Final Report to the Secretary of the Army on the Nuernberg [sic] War Crimes Trials Under Control Council Law, No. 10* (Washington D.C.: JAG School, 1949), 2.

[57] Cramer JAG, "Telegram", 4 June 1945, War Crimes Office file, Kelsen's State, Hans Kelsen Institute (on file with the author).

[58] Bradley F. Smith, *The Road to Nuremberg* (London: Andre Deutsch, 1981), 3–74, quote at 33.

188 MÓNICA GARCÍA-SALMONES ROVIRA

suggestion until September 1944, but it fell out of favour through a combination of factors, apparently accelerated by a leak to the press.

7.4.1 Tentative Chronicle of Kelsen's Collaboration

From at least 1942 Kelsen worked as a legal adviser to the US government,[59] although little is known of his activities until May 1944.[60] Before Thomas Olechowski's recent published work on Kelsen in the United States, his activities after the summer of 1944 were only vaguely known.[61] In comparison with Hersch Lauterpacht or Raphael Lemkin, Kelsen's contribution has remained largely confidential.[62] This may have something to do with Kelsen's personality. Probably there was also a requirement 'explicit or not' of confidentiality, or it may relate to other complications arising from his position within the War Department, which are discussed below. The émigré jurist was, in any event, much employed by the War Crimes Office, to the extent that at the beginning of December 1946 the War Department asked him to submit a report on 'your knowledge of the origin and functioning' of the War Crimes Office. This formed part of a data-gathering exercise as preparation for writing of the history of that office.[63]

The files of the War Crimes Office also contain a non-exhaustive list of eight memoranda that he prepared. These deal with topics focusing on the laws on war and in particular on international criminal law. The titles are as follows: (1) 'On the Agreement for the Prosecution of European Axis War Criminals'; (2) 'On the Rule of *Ex Post Facto* Law'; (3) 'On the Definition of Aggression'; (4) 'On the Draft Executive Agreement

---

[59] Kelsen introduced himself as 'Special assistant in the United States Department of State 1942–1945' in a 1945 article: Hans Kelsen, 'Sanctions in International Law Under the Charter of the United Nations' (1945) 31 *Iowa Law Review*, 499.

[60] Olechowski considers Kelsen's first activity to be that which thus far appears to be the first one documented: a meeting of the Bureau of Areas in Washington, on 5 May 1944, to which Kelsen was invited, Thomas Olechowski, 'Hans Kelsen, The Second World War and the U.S. Government', in *Hans Kelsen in America*, 101–14, at 104.

[61] Only in Kirsten Sellars, *Crimes Against Peace and International Law* (Cambridge: Cambridge University Press, 2013), 85–7; and Mónica García-Salmones Rovira, *The Project of Positivism in International Law*, 359–69.

[62] To name only one recent study dealing with both authors, see the contributions of Lauterpacht and Lemkin in Phillippe Sands, *East West Street: On the Origins of Genocide and Crimes Against Humanity* (London: Weidenfeld and Nicolson, 2016).

[63] Letter from Colonel David Marcus (5 December 1946), Chief, War Crimes Branch to Hans Kelsen, 'Hans Kelsen State in Hans Kelsen Institute (University of Vienna)' (16c8.60).

relating to the prosecution of European Axis War Criminals'; (5) 'On the Instrument of Surrender signed by the Japanese Government'; (6) 'On Codification of the Law of War'; (7) 'On the Punishment of War Criminals and the Charter of the United Nations'; (8) 'On War Crimes as related to the preparation, launching, and opening of hostilities without warning'.[64] As a scholar Kelsen later published certain parts of the memoranda but not the substance of all of them.[65]

From the beginning of November 1944 Kelsen was based in Washington, assigned to the Foreign Economic Administration. He returned to Berkeley at the end of January 1945.[66] After that period, Captain Alwin Freeman of the War Crimes Office informed Kelsen, in an undated letter, of a meeting that would happen overseas and be attended by 'military representatives and military aides of the various United Nations'.[67] Freeman was then head of the International Law division of the JAG. He had written a dissertation in Geneva on the *International Responsibility of States for Denial of Justice*, presumably with Kelsen.[68] Freeman is also described by Bradley F. Smith as a 'one of the department's [JAG] top legal brains' and as the author, in the autumn of 1944, of an important paper entitled 'Is the Preparation and Launching of the Present War a Crime?' which effectively 'demolished the contention that aggressive war could be prosecuted on the basis of prevailing

---

[64] 'War Crimes Office; Judge Advocate General's Office (103-1-BK3)'. For instance, the memoranda on individual criminal responsibility, on the legal status of Germany (among Jackson's papers) and on the legal status of Austria are not listed there.

[65] For instance, in Hans Kelsen, 'The Rule against Ex Post Facto Laws and the Prosecution of the Axis War Criminals' (1945) 2 *The Judge Advocate Journal*, 8–12.

[66] In a letter (dated 27 December 1944) written in Washington and addressed to his superior at the University of Berkeley, Frank. M. Russell, Kelsen refers to a sixty-day appointment at that department that would finish in the 'first week of January', although he planned to stay in the capital until the end of January. 'Hans Kelsen State in Hans Kelsen Institute (University of Vienna)' (15n.58).

[67] In the same letter Alwyn V. Freeman asked Kelsen for help with his own search for a teaching position. He signs his letters 'your good friend', 'Hans Kelsen State in Hans Kelsen Institute (University of Vienna)' (16c3.60).

[68] Alwyn V. Freeman, *International Responsibility of States for Denial of Justice* (Reprint 1970) (London, New York, Toronto: Longmans, Green and Co, 1938). The book, which was the outcome of Freeman's doctorate from Geneva, is dedicated to 'Hans Kelsen', and in the 1938 'Preface' Kelsen is the first to be thanked 'for his valuable suggestions and penetrating criticism', but Freeman does not mention a supervisor. On Freeman, see Albert S. Golbert, 'Alwyn Vernon Freeman' (1983) 17 *The International Lawyer*, 701–3. Freeman's work is commented on in Zachary Douglas, 'International Responsibility for Domestic Adjudication: Denial of Justice Deconstructed' (2014) 63 *The International & Comparative Law Quarterly*, 867–900.

international law'.[69] There is no point in denying Freeman's capabilities, evidenced in his later achievements, but the fact that the paper bears a very similar title to that of a memorandum written by Kelsen,[70] that it set out in essence exactly what Kelsen had argued since 1943,[71] and that Smith mention Kelsen's name only once in passing in his *The Road to Nuremberg*, gives some idea of Kelsen's anonymity in the preparations for Nuremberg.[72] Some spectacular interventions by JAG Major General Cramer in November 1944 on questions of jurisdiction of courts that are reminiscent of the Vienna School of Law also make one wonder.[73]

In his letter Freeman asked Kelsen about several items on the request of General Weir, who 'was extremely anxious' to have in his possession the outcome of Kelsen's work: 'the proposed military agreement between the United Nations regarding principles of prosecution' and 'the program of topics that you believe should be taken up at San Francisco'. It is not clear from their exchange whether the meeting in San Francisco they both referred to was that of foreign ministers preparing the trial of major war criminals that took place in that city during 2–10 May 1945[74] or whether what was meant was the broader framework of the San Francisco Conference, which resulted in the creation of the United Nations.[75] The 'overseas' event appears to be a trip to Europe in April/May 1945, where General Weir as Director of the United States War Crimes Office met in London with Lord Simon, the British Chancellor, Rene Cassin, head of the French National War Crimes Office, Minister of Justice Mènthon, of France, Lord Wright, Chairman of the United Nations War Crimes Commission and members of the military.[76] Thus Freeman's letter

---

[69] Smith, *The Road to Nuremberg*, 103.

[70] The two-page memorandum with Kelsen's name on it is: Hans Kelsen, 'Is "Launching a War of Aggression" A Crime?' RG 0238 World War II War Crimes Records; Office of the U.S. Chief of Counsel for the Prosecution of Axis Criminality, Entry # PI-21 52: Personal Files (Lindenstrasse Files); 1945–1946.

[71] Kelsen, 'Collective and Individual Responsibility in International Law', 509.

[72] Smith, *The Road to Nuremberg*, 105.

[73] Smith, *The Road to Nuremberg*, 82.

[74] On the memorandum dated 30 April and the meeting in San Francisco, see 'American Draft of Definitive Proposal, Presented to Foreign Ministers at San Francisco, April 1945', in *Report of Robert H. Jackson*, 22–38.

[75] This is not implausible since Kelsen would later publish a study of close to 1,000 pages. Hans Kelsen, *The Law of the United Nations: A Critical Analysis of Its Fundamental Problems* (London, New York: Frederick A. Praeger, The London Institute of World Affairs, 1950).

[76] The meeting took place in London in April/May 1945, 'General Weir Confers with War Crimes Prosecutors in England and France' (1945) 2 *The Judge Advocate Journal*, 6. On the United Nations War Crimes Commission, see Dan Plesch and Shanti Sattler, 'Before

could be broadly dated between February and March 1945. Freeman asked Kelsen to send at least a draft if he had not yet completed what he had in mind.

A draft reply written in Kelsen's hand is on the back of the letter: 'I shall send the memorandum on the topics which should be taken up at San Francisco to General Weir in two or three days.' Furthermore, Kelsen stated his need to go to Washington in order to finish the rest of the work because it was indispensable for him to have '(1) the results of the negotiation of the War Crimes Commission in London, (2) Information about actual committed crimes to be prosecuted, and (3) Rules of procedure of the military courts of the states concerned'. Another piece of information that Kelsen provides in that draft answer was the following question to Freeman: 'I am wondering, why I had no news about General Weir's action with respect to my personal promotion.'[77] He could have been referring to his chair at Berkeley. Olechowsky links both Kelsen's American citizenship and his appointment to full professorship in June 1945 in Berkeley, to his collaboration with the government.[78] One must add that his work for the US government also facilitated Kelsen's search for his mother and sister from whom he had heard nothing since March 1945.[79]

Another letter from Freeman, also undated, but which seems to follow Kelsen's answer gives grounds for the contention that Kelsen's letter referred to his appointment as a legal adviser to the War Crimes Office. Freeman confided in him that the reason he had 'not heard from the War Crimes Office' was that General Weir was in London. Freeman continued 'all this confirms the attitude that I impressed on you about securing your own teaching position first'.[80] In fact, Cramer's telegram of 4 June 1945 requesting Kelsen's services in Washington 'urgently' contains the following words: 'Arrangements for emplyment [sic] on permanent basis to

---

Nuremberg: Considering the Work of the United NationsWar Crimes Commission of 1943–1948', in Morten Bergsmo, Cheah Wui Ling and Yi Ping (eds.), *Historical Origins of International Criminal Law* (Brussels: Torkel Opsahl, 2014), I, 437–72, at 448.

[77] In Alwyn V. Freeman, letter to Hans Kelsen, undated, 'Hans Kelsen State in Hans Kelsen Institute (University of Vienna)' (16c3.60).

[78] Olechowski, 'Hans Kelsen, The Second World War and the U.S. Government', 110.

[79] See letter from Kelsen (24 August 1945) to Coronel Erwin Schindler hoping for help with his inquiries about his mother and sister, and mentioning Weir's reference 'Hans Kelsen State in Hans Kelsen Institute (University of Vienna)' (16c11.61).

[80] Letter from Al Freeman, undated. 'Hans Kelsen State in Hans Kelsen Institute (University of Vienna)' (16c3.60).

be made while here on per diem basis.'[81] All this indicates that in the spring of 1945 Kelsen was working for General Weir without an official appointment. Perhaps also without receiving remuneration? With this in mind, and taking into account his precarious financial situation, his hopes for larger involvement in the War Crimes Office can be attributed to a combination of factors, professional, personal and material.

It is certain that Weir counted on Kelsen participating in the negotiations of what would be the Nuremberg Charter. On 19 June 1945 Weir wrote to the Judge Advocate's Office in San Francisco to speed up Kelsen's process of obtaining American citizenship. That letter confirms that Kelsen's citizenship was needed in the light of Weir's plan to send him to Europe – rather than as a mere reward for his collaboration.

> I understand from Dr. Kelsen that he is to take the examination for citizenship on 26 June at San Francisco. He will complete the statutory requirements of residence on 21 June. I expect to send Dr. Kelsen upon his return to Washington to Europe as a special consultant to Mr. Justice Jackson, who, as you know, is the Chief of Counsel for the United States in the prosecution of the major German war criminals. I rather expect Dr. Kelsen will remain abroad for several weeks. It is more desirable of course that he travel as an American citizen with an American passport rather than as an alien.[82]

However, Weir calculated that the process would be finished by the end of June: 'I would greatly appreciate anything that you can do to expedite his naturalization in order that it may be completed before his departure for Europe shortly after the first of July.'[83] By a twist of fate, the hearing of the petitions of Kelsen and his wife was scheduled for 28 July.[84] This delay appears to have been the true impediment preventing Kelsen from being personally present in London for the drafting of the London Agreement.

---

[81] Telegram 'Hans Kelsen State in Hans Kelsen Institute (University of Vienna)' (16c1.361).

[82] General Weir, letter (19 June 1945) to Major Herbert E. Wenig, of the Judge Advocate, Presidio of San Francisco, 'Hans Kelsen State in Hans Kelsen Institute (University of Vienna)' (16c1.361).

[83] General Weir, letter (19 June 1945) to Major Herbert E. Wenig, of the Judge Advocate, Presidio of San Francisco 'Hans Kelsen State in Hans Kelsen Institute (University of Vienna)' (16c.1.361).

[84] Letter from Major Wenig of JAG (18 July 1945) sharing with Kelsen the information received from the Immigration and Naturalization Service in San Francisco that all the depositions of the Kelsens' case had been received and approved, and announcing that the hearing for their petition was scheduled for 28 July 1945, Herbert E. Wenig, 'Letter to Hans Kelsen' (16c13.61).

7 HANS KELSEN

Following the signing of the London Agreement on 8 August 1945 Kelsen was still working for the War Crimes Office in Washington. In September there were others in Europe who thought that 'possibly' Kelsen would be needed there in his capacity of adviser to the War Crimes Office.[85] However, on 5 October 1945, Kelsen laconically wrote to Freeman that he had just received 'the notification concerning Termination of my Appointment as Consultant to the department of War'. Characteristically, he made no further comment beyond asking what to do with the extra transport tickets that he had and to whom he could send his article on the legal status of Germany.[86]

The letter of 19 November 1945 informing him that 'General Weir suffered a severe heart attack' with the fateful words '[i]t is doubtful that he will return to the office' probably signalled the end of a phase in Kelsen's life.[87] Two days later Robert H. Jackson delivered his opening speech in Nuremberg, a task the American deemed 'probably the most important' of his life.[88]

Kirsten Sellers quotes Robert Jackson answering on 7 August 1945 to the question of 'whether he would like Kelsen to join his team' in the following terms: 'I don't think so ... Most of the things that he was helpful about, we have settled, and settled the other way from what he advised.'[89] However, that answer did not do justice to Kelsen's work and real contribution to Nuremberg. We know from Jackson's own written record that he had, a few weeks before he made that comment, adopted Kelsen's solution on the key question of individual criminal responsibility, which was to become the substance of the decisive article 6 of the Charter of the IMT in the London Agreement. It may be that Jackson and Kelsen were figures too big to work together and too big as legal theorists at that.[90] Both had a vision of a momentous trial designed to lay the

---

[85] Letter from William Rappard (20 September 1945) hoping for a visit to Switzerland in that case, 'Hans Kelsen State in Hans Kelsen Institute (University of Vienna)' (16c.10.61).

[86] On 18 November 1945 General Edward C. Betts (Judge Advocate European Theatre of Operations) thanked Kelsen for sending it to him. 'Hans Kelsen State in Hans Kelsen Institute (University of Vienna)' (16c3.60).

[87] Letter from Clarence L. Yancey, War Crimes Office 'Hans Kelsen State in Hans Kelsen Institute (University of Vienna)' (16c13.61).

[88] 'Robert H. Jackson's Notes in The Reminiscences of Robert H. Jackson Columbia Univ. Oral History Research Office', 1955 www.roberthjackson.org/nuremberg-event/justice-robert-h-jacksons-opening-statement.

[89] Mr Jackson in conference with Mr Shea, from documents in the National Archives, quoted in Sellars, *Crimes Against Peace and International Law*, 109.

[90] Although Jackson never completed a law degree, he had practised law his entire life and had a legal vision for the impact of Nuremberg, see 'Robert H. Jackson U.S. Prosecutor of

groundwork for an international order of peace, both thought that the greatest crime had been the illegal war and both wanted to reach deep into the social layers that had made Nazi Germany possible.[91] Perhaps the main difference in their views was that Kelsen aimed by all means to avoid 'victors' justice'. In Kelsen's view, 'no state is subject to the jurisdiction of another state',[92] while Jackson was more worried about avoiding the appearance of it.[93] It could be argued that the distinction had little practical effect when both aimed at securing the punishment of the war criminals, if necessary by creating new law. And yet Kelsen was adamant about the need for Germany to consent to the new law and this would have presented an obstacle for the jurisdiction of the tribunal, raising the question of the status of Germany, and even of the status of Austria, as discussed below. The legal wisdom of his principled standpoint should not be underestimated, for *tu quoque* arguments would thrive among the defendants from the German *Wehrmacht*, for example 'the Allies' strategic bombing of Lübeck, Hamburg, Dresden and many other cities'.[94]

By and large the activity of 'Kelsen the legal adviser' crafting the new law is visible in his known work within the War Department and its spillover in several of his publications of the period. The following sections discuss three of his substantial contributions to his work of the War Crimes Commission: the inclusion in the London Agreement of a provision that secured individual criminal responsibility in the Charter of the IMT, his ideas about the tribunal's lack of jurisdiction, and a final note on his conviction that the London Agreement had created new law.

7.4.2 Individual Criminal Responsibility

On 5 July 1945, Justice Robert H. Jackson presented a memorandum to members of the Office of the US Chief of Counsel for the Prosecution of

---

Major War Criminals' (1945) 2 *The Judge Advocate Journal* 5; John Q. Barrett, 'Robert H. Jackson Biography', www.roberthjackson.org/article/robert-h-jackson-biography.

[91] 'Then we come to the question of organizations, by which we intend to reach a great many people, in fact, with a very few people before the court', 'Minutes of Conference, Session of June 26, Jackson, *Report of Robert H. Jackson*, 83.

[92] Kelsen, 'Collective and Individual Responsibility in International Law', 540, 543.

[93] About Jackson's caution with regard to public opinion see, for instance, Jackson, *Report of Robert H. Jackson*, 100–2.

[94] The point of *tu quoque* arguments in Priemel, and see generally chapter 8 in Kim Christian Priemel, *The Betrayal: The Nuremberg Trials and German Divergence* (Oxford: Oxford University Press, 2016), 310–50, at 311.

Axis Criminality; they were Mr Alderman, Mr Shea, and Colonel Bernays. In that text he communicated the following:

> Hans Kelsen is worried over the absence of any international law on the subject of individual responsibility. He thinks a definite declaration is essential. I think it may be desirable. The language he suggests is as follows:
>
> 'Persons who, acting in the service of any state (of one of the Axis powers) or on their own initiative, have performed acts by which any rule of general or particular international law forbidding the use of force, or any rule concerning warfare, or the generally accepted rules of humanity have been violated, as well as persons who have been members of voluntary organizations whose criminal character has been established by the court may be held individually responsible for these acts or for membership in such organizations and brought to trial and punishment before the court.'

After quoting Kelsen, Jackson concluded his memorandum by stating: 'I think it may be worth including, to stop the argument whether the law does so provide.'[95] Sellars also notes that 'Kelsen's point was taken' and that after the memo was handed to him in London, Jackson insisted on the notion that the accused were 'answerable personally'.[96] Hans Kelsen's advice caused individual criminal responsibility to become part of international law in the London Agreement and, therefore, it is thanks to him that international law could be efficiently employed during the Nuremberg Trials. Probably this was Kelsen's most important gift to the discipline of international criminal law, albeit given *in absentia* and without disclosure of the professional secret of his authorship.

The substance of Kelsen's advice was given in a memo written between 5 June and 5 July 1945, in which he provided comments on Jackson's report to the President dated 6 June 1945.[97] Kelsen remarked that Justice Jackson aimed at individual criminal responsibility. But after stating that there was 'no basis for such procedure in international law', Kelsen offered his description of the several avenues available for the creation of this 'new law' and his concrete solution. One of the available avenues was, in his opinion, customary law created through the practice of the courts. That would not be a problem, or so Kelsen thought, if the war

---

[95] For a comment see, García-Salmones Rovira, *The Project of Positivism in International Law*, 359–69.

[96] Sellars, *Crimes Against Peace and International Law*, 87.

[97] Hans Kelsen, 'Report', Library of Congress, Manuscript Division, Washington D.C., Robert Houghwout Jackson Papers.

crimes tribunal were to be under the exclusive jurisdiction of the American military courts. Ultimately the principles informing Justice Jackson's report 'expressed the feeling of the American people'. However, in the case of an international tribunal composed of judges of different nationalities, Kelsen understood that 'it will be necessary to establish certain guarantees for the application of the principles suggested in Justice Jackson's report'. In his conclusion Kelsen recommended the 'insertion' of the principles laid down in Jackson's report, that is to say the new law, 'in the international agreement', which 'anyway' would need to be concluded for the tribunals, and suggested the wording on individual criminal responsibility that Justice Jackson copied *verbatim* later to other members of the team.[98]

7.4.3 Kelsen's Memorandum on the London Agreement[99]

The extent to which Kelsen was required to comment on the Charter of the IMT and more generally on the London Agreement is unclear.[100] Once it was signed, his remarks referring to faulty drafting technique simply came too late.[101] However, his mode of expression indicates that he was asked to comment on the legality of the agreement. Timing notwithstanding, Kelsen gave a substantive opinion on the issue of the tribunal's jurisdiction.

The individuals to be prosecuted were nationals of the European Axis Powers of 'German, Italian, Hungarian, Bulgarian, Romanian and Finnish nationalities'. The states to which these persons belonged were enemy states and therefore not contracting parties. Consequently, they were 'excluded from adherence' to the Agreement. Bearing this in mind, Kelsen took the view that the main question to be addressed was that of

---

[98] Kelsen, 'Report', 4.

[99] Hans Kelsen, 'Rough Draft. Memorandum to General Weir; Subject: The Agreement for the Prosecution and Punishment of the Major War Criminals of the European Axis Signed on August 8, in the Light of Existing International Law', Judge Advocate General's Office, US National Archives (103-1-BK 3).

[100] 'Agreement and Charter for the Prosecution and Punishment of the Major War Criminals of the European Axis, August 8, 1945', Jackson, *Report of Robert H. Jackson*, 420–8.

[101] For instance, he notes that it was superfluous to include the term 'war of aggression' ('Great Britain and France resorted in 1939 to such a legal aggressive war against Germany') and reference had only to be made to an 'illegal war'. Hans Kelsen, 'Rough Draft. Memorandum to General Weir; Subject: The Agreement for the Prosecution and Punishment of the Major War Criminals of the European Axis Signed on August 8, in the Light of Existing International Law', 2.

determining the jurisdiction of the contracting parties over the 'nationals of enemy states who are being held as prisoners of war within their power'. He regarded the problem as being not the signatories' transfer of jurisdiction to the tribunal, but the fact that they could transfer only what they had: that is to say, only the jurisdiction of each state (the signatories') not that of the defendants' states. Kelsen's memorandum indicated that this issue was of essential importance. If the jurisdiction bestowed upon the tribunal by the contracting parties exceeded that which general international law conferred upon them, Germany and the other Axis Powers whose nationals would be on trial ought to give their consent. The trial could progress 'only by a treaty to which the state whose nationals are to be prosecuted is a contracting party'.[102] Hence he went on to test, in no uncertain terms, whether the agreement overreached itself in terms of the jurisdiction it bestowed upon the tribunal: '[t]he jurisdiction over captured enemy nationals for crimes committed before capture has been very much disputed'. It comprised 'violations of the rules of warfare' or 'crimes against the captor's army or people, committed prior to their capture'.[103] Moreover, according to general international law 'as soon as the status of war is terminated the prisoners must be released', and therefore 'no trial must begin or be continued'. The formulae 'all wars of aggression and illegal wars' and 'crimes against humanity' were 'certainly too wide'.[104]

In his view, one way to go about it was to obtain the adherence to the agreement of all the other member states of the United Nations, thereby transforming it into general international law. However, that path was already barred because such adherence had been left to the free discretion of the states. Kelsen considered that that had been a mistake.[105] Furthermore, the problem of excess of jurisdiction tainted both the possibility of a law creating a new crime with retroactive force and the application of individual criminal responsibility.[106] Article 7 of the Charter sought to lift the protection that general international law attributed to organs of the state. Kelsen was of the view that there was no impediment to that arrangement being made by treaty: 'this treaty however, has the desired effect only if it is concluded with the state whose

---

[102] Kelsen, 'Rough Draft. Memorandum to General Weir', 5.
[103] Kelsen, 'Rough Draft. Memorandum to General Weir', 5.
[104] Kelsen, 'Rough Draft. Memorandum to General Weir', 6.
[105] Kelsen, 'Rough Draft. Memorandum to General Weir', 6.
[106] Kelsen, 'Rough Draft. Memorandum to General Weir', 7.

organs are to be prosecuted.'[107] Without the consent of the enemy states the agreement could not 'restrict the rule of general international law protecting the interests of these states'.[108]

In summary, Kelsen thought that the legality of the London Agreement depended on the procurement of the consent of the enemy states to articles 6 and 7 of the Charter. Accordingly, he advised that consent through treaty be obtained before the trial begun.

In respect of Germany, which had no national government at that point, Kelsen suggested, as he had urged in previous occasions, the possibility of a 'condominium over the German territory and its population' of the four occupant powers. In that case 'their signature under the Agreement may be interpreted as the consent of the legitimate successor of Germany for the prosecution of German nationals'. If that were not viewed as an acceptable interpretation of the Treaty of Berlin of 5 June 1945, Kelsen recommended that 'the future German government' should conclude a treaty by which it would consent to the excess of jurisdiction represented by articles 6 and 7.

As is apparent, Kelsen moved steadily, and fundamentally on the legal plane, in opposition to any form of 'victors' justice'. In the aftermath of World War II, the political negotiations, as discussed below, seemed to him altogether barren. Furthermore, he adopted a consistent and extremely positivist position on this issue. His stance also indicated his view that international law works through the consent of states. Nevertheless, and understandably, his argument that after unconditional surrender Germany 'by virtue of *debellatio* ceased to exist as a sovereign state and as a subject of international law' while 'the term Germany' had 'for the time being only a geographical significance',[109] was increasingly met with 'bitter opposition' from Germans.[110] Apart from the memoranda, Kelsen published his ideas on the legal status of Germany in the *American Journal of International Law*, as mentioned above, and in the *New York*

---

[107] Kelsen, 'Rough Draft. Memorandum to General Weir', 8.
[108] Kelsen, 'Rough Draft. Memorandum to General Weir', 8.
[109] Kelsen, 'Rough Draft. Memorandum to General Weir', 5.
[110] For instance, Wolfgang Abendroth and Hans Nawiasky supported it, the latter on the grounds that 'when the power of the state has ceased also the state ceases'. The majority opposed it. For a detailed analysis of these positions, see Thomas Olechowski, 'Kelsens Debellatio-These: Rechtshistorische und Rechtstheoretische Überlegungen zur Kontinuität von Staaten', in Clemens Jabloner, Dieter Kolonovits, Gabriele Kucsko-Stadlmayer, Hans René Laurer, Heinz Mayer and Rudolf Thienel (eds.), *Gedenkschrift Robert Walter* (Vienna: Manz, 2013), 531–52, at 549.

Times and he seems to have considered the issue to be key to the future world order.[111]

In order to understand what political vision motivated Kelsen in his view that the status of Germany was a 'condominium' over 'belligerent occupation', it is worth quoting at length from another of his memoranda to the US government, dated 1 June 1944 and written in Berkeley, on the legal status of Austria:[112]

> Immediately after her unconditional surrender, Germany certainly will not be in the political condition of an acceptable partner to an international treaty to be concluded with the victorious States. One of the lessons which should be drawn from the experiences of the First World War is that it is useless, nay, dangerous to settle national and international problems aroused by a conflict of the dimension of a World War, by a peace treaty imposed upon the defeated State. If a peace treaty is not the result of true negotiations – which after this war is practically impossible; if the peace treaty is the dictate of a victor as any peace treaty concluded with Germany after unconditional surrender must be, then the treaty, although legally valid, is politically a farce and cannot have the specific value of a treaty which consists of the voluntary consent of the parties to the obligations conferred upon them by the treaty. The Second World War must not and cannot be terminated by the political system to be established after this war. It must not and cannot be based upon a peace treaty concluded with an enemy which has unconditionally surrendered.[113]

Would a condominium of the United States, Great Britain and the Soviet Russia over a conquered country be more palatable for the Germans than the Treaty of Versailles? Kelsen appeared to think that it would at least not be a pretence and would provide a safer foundation on which to rebuild the international order anew.

The Allies, however, had decided in the Potsdam Protocol (1 August 1945) in favour of the solution of 'supreme authority short of

---

[111] Hans Kelsen, 'The International Legal Status of Germany to be Established Immediately upon Termination of the War' (1944), 38 *American Journal of International Law*, 689–94; Hans Kelsen, 'The Legal Status of Germany According to the Declaration of Berlin' (1945) 39 *The American Journal of International Law*, 518–26; Letter to the Editors, Hans Kelsen, 'German Peace Terms; Imposing of Conditions Through New State Held Advantageous', *New York Times*, 7 September 1947, 10.

[112] Edition and Comment of this Memorandum by Thomas Olechowski, 'Hans Kelsens Gutachten zur Neugestaltung Österreichs und Deutschlands nach dem Zweiten Weltkrieg', in *Das internationale Wirken Hans Kelsens*, 121–9.

[113] Hans Kelsen, 'Austria: Her Actual Legal Status and Re-Establishing as an Independent State', in *Das internationale Wirken Hans Kelsens*, 130–40, at 136–7.

sovereignty'.[114] This constituted a *de facto debellatio* that concurred with Allies' statement to the effect that they were not annexing Germany.[115] Kelsen, who, as we saw, kept sending his article on the legal status of Germany to the upper echelons of the War Department in November 1945, found it difficult to accept this formula. He probably found it confusing, illogical and novel, since it proposed neither sovereignty for Germany nor annexation by the Allies. In his view '[t]he existence of an independent government', which was lacking, 'is an essential element of a state in the eyes of international law'.[116] Analogously, he was also convinced that Austria had disappeared as a country when Nazi Germany annexed it.[117] Moreover, as he wrote, it also affected the jurisdiction and the law of Nuremberg. Given Kelsen's stance on the dynamics of legal logic of the supremacy of international law and the unity of the legal order-the leopard could not change its spots – the pure theory would have been here at stake.

At the end of the day it seems that only a great legal theoretician could be totally serious about the legal basis of the jurisdiction of the IMTs while the generality of the agents staging Nuremberg, including Jackson, did not seem even to have suspected the existence of this problem.[118]

7.4.4 New Law

The way in which Jackson also disregarded (positivist) international legal theory, which had had its heyday just before World War II, was another

---

[114] 'Protocol of Proceedings of the Potsdam Conference' (Berlin, 1 August 1945) in Charles Bevans (comp.), *Treaties and Other International Agreements of the United States of America (1776–1949), 1931–1945* (Department of State, Washington, 1969), III, 1207–23.

[115] On this issue and for a comment on Kelsen's position, see Ryszard W. Piotrowicz, 'The Status of Germany in International Law: Deutschland Über Deutschland?' (1989) 38 *International and Comparative Law Quarterly*, 609–35, at 609–14, 612. A defence of Kelsen's position can be found in Josef L. Kunz, 'The Status of Occupied Germany Under International Law: A Legal Dilemma' (1950) 3 *Western Political Quarterly*, 538–65.

[116] Kelsen, 'The Legal Status of Germany According to the Declaration of Berlin', 519.

[117] Kelsen, 'Austria: Her Actual Legal Status and Re-Establishing as an Independent State'.

[118] Jackson opted for expediency and not for the reign of positivist legal theory as he intriguingly declared in his Nuremberg Opening Speech. 'This Tribunal, while it is novel and experimental, is not the product of abstract speculations nor is it created to vindicate legalistic theories. This inquest represents the practical effort of four of the most mighty of nations, with the support of 17 more, to utilize international law to meet the greatest menace of our times-aggressive war.' Robert H. Jackson, 'Opening Statement before the International Military Tribunal', 21 November 1945. www.roberthjackson.org /speech-and-writing/opening-statement-before-the-international-military-tribunal.

reason for Kelsen's disappointment. In order to fully understand the famous article by Kelsen, 'Will the Judgment in the Nuremberg Trial Constitute a Precedent in International Law?' one must take into account the previous counsel he gave to the War Crimes Commission and to Justice Jackson in particular.[119] The tone of the article is fascinating in that Kelsen showed that he knew the law of Nuremberg inside out and did not hesitate to amend either Justice Jackson's statements or the judgment itself.[120] He made it clear that the Kellogg Briand Pact could never have been interpreted by the Nuremberg Tribunal in such a manner that allowed specific individuals to be punished. Furthermore, the older rules governing illegal warfare under which individuals could be tried in military tribunals that applied the Hague conventions were of no relevance here.[121] As to Justice Jackson's reference to principles of criminal law being the foundation of the judgment of the criminals Kelsen retorted: 'Nobody is "subject to judgment by usually accepted principles of the law of crime", as Mr. Justice Jackson says. One is subject only to a judgment rendered by a competent court on the basis of positive criminal law.'[122] That individual criminal responsibility would exist, only if a rule of international or national law had existed, because to identify 'the international illegality of an act with its 'criminality' contradicted 'positive law and generally accepted principles of international jurisprudence'.[123] Hence Kelsen's study showed that the rule had been only created in the London Agreement[124]: 'In creating the law to be applied by the tribunal, in providing for individual criminal responsibility not only for waging war in violation of existing treaties but also for planning, preparation or initiation of such war and

---

[119] Kelsen, 'Will the Judgment in the Nuremberg Trial Constitute a Precedent in International Law?'

[120] Kelsen, 'Will the Judgment in the Nuremberg Trial Constitute a Precedent in International Law?' 153, 156–7.

[121] The conventions reproduced in Dietrich Schindler and Jiři Toman (eds.), *The Laws of Armed Conflict: A Collection of Conventions, Resolutions and Other Documents* (Dordrecht: Martinus Nijhoff Publishers, 1988).

[122] Kelsen here quotes Justice Jackson's opening address in Nuremberg, Kelsen, 'Will the Judgment in the Nuremberg Trial Constitute a Precedent in International Law?' 157.

[123] Kelsen, 'Will the Judgment in the Nuremberg Trial Constitute a Precedent in International Law?' 156.

[124] 'The International Military Tribunal was authorised to apply, and did apply, only the rules of law laid down in the Agreement of London'. Kelsen, 'Will the Judgment in the Nuremberg Trial Constitute a Precedent in International Law?' 162.

participation in a conspiracy for accomplishment of these actions, the London Agreement has certainly created new law.'[125]

Interestingly, Jackson too had strong opinions about the fact that in London he had been creating new law.[126] To explain that to the public at large or to develop an impressive speech with these dry legal principles was perhaps another matter.

7.5 Conclusions

Hans Kelsen, the most significant legal theorist of the twentieth century, contributed to key aspects of the international criminal law created for the IMT in Nuremberg. The fact that he was both a skilled legal adviser and drafter and had strong legal theoretical capabilities – a rare combination – allowed him to play a role. But this marriage of practice and theory was not always an asset. It was difficult for Kelsen to admit defeat and yield to theoretically poorer solutions when an issue concerning the development of positivist international law was at stake. This may have contributed to jeopardising his position in the War Crimes Office. However, the mere fact that Kelsen was such an influential legal theorist of international law might have been detrimental when Justice Robert Jackson was chosen as US Prosecutor. Kelsen was famously the theoretician of the pure theory. Jackson, who was both a neophyte in international law and the holder of a clear standpoint on international legal issues, did not recruit Kelsen to be part of his team. All these factors notwithstanding, and despite the fact that he was ultimately unable to be present in Europe in the summer of 1945, Kelsen had a lasting influence on the international criminal law that was applied at Nuremberg and beyond.

Kelsen's life experiences, his familiarity with the world of the military, his knowledge of military law, and probably also his conviction that military law was a law that worked, put him in a privileged position within the US military circle entrusted with the punishment of war criminals – a biographical continuation, rather than a fracture, is evident. Furthermore, the fact that Kelsen had witnessed the aftermath of World

---

[125] Kelsen, 'Will the Judgment in the Nuremberg Trial Constitute a Precedent in International Law?' 157.

[126] In face of the shock of André Gros, the French delegate in London, at the idea that they should be trying to contract the notion of 'international crime' as if they 'were a codification commission', Jackson answered: 'But we are a codification commission for the purposes of this trial as I see it. That is my commission as I understand it.' Jackson, *Report of Robert H. Jackson*, 335.

War I from the camp of the vanquished and that he was later obliged to emigrate to the United States due to his Jewish origins provided him with the ability to grasp the problems involved in the Nuremberg trials better than many of his peers. Therefore, his personal experiences endowed Kelsen's universalist idea of international criminal law with a perspective that could hardly be more objective. His collaboration with the US War Department – the aim of which was mainly efficiency – placed him in a social context in which he would have had to refrain from giving vent to emotional and passionate reactions. In any case, such restraint was an innate part of his character and personality. There is not a single hint in his writings or in his personal papers of a desire for personal retribution or even the slightest expression of contempt for the war criminals.

Kelsen was a complex man who lived in a very complex world and recurrent attempts to portray him as a naïve universalist figure disconnected from the politics of the international world around him only diminish his stature as a politician, a thinker and a scientist. He clearly appears to have become involved in the innovative creation of the laws of Nuremberg partly by coincidence and partly through his own efforts. Moreover, it is not certain that he was happy with all the law and legal theories that emerged from the trials. He regarded some of the principles as imprecise and as failing to respect the principle of sovereign jurisdiction. The last stage of his progressive pure theory envisaged a universal state with jurisdiction over individuals. However, he was also of the view that in order for this to happen, international politics must respect the rhythm of time and states must consent freely to the process taking place. This would involve states first surrendering their jurisdiction and then participating in the creation of centralised international organs including international criminal courts created with every state's consent. Kelsen's involvement in the dawn of the discipline of international criminal law makes it clear that he was an extraordinary individual. At the same time, he held an extremely positivist view of law. In other words, he was a combination of two extremes – the idealist and the individualist – in his approach to law. In important respects his individualism was attuned to the purpose of punishing war criminals. But not everyone felt comfortable with the extremely legalistic approach he took to the laws to be used in respect of this task.[127]

---

[127] This refers to the matters of jurisdiction discussed here. However, he famously had recourse to natural law principles in order to explain the retroactivity of the 'new law' of individual criminal responsibility. Hans Kelsen, 'Will the Judgment in the Nuremberg Trial Constitute a Precedent in International Law?' 165.

Ironically, however, it was the precariousness of his own legal and professional status, given that in early June 1945 he held neither US citizenship nor a permanent academic position, that prevented him from becoming one of the stars of the Nuremberg trials. But that did not prevent his being one of its many architects.

8

Principled Pragmatist?

Bert Röling and the Emergence of International Criminal Law

JAN KLABBERS[1]

Figure 8.1 Bernard Victor Aloysius Röling (1972). Credit: Joost Evers/Anefo/ Nationaal Archief, CC0.

---

[1] I am much indebted to Nico Schrijver (formerly Röling's assistant) for his willingness to share memories and impressions, though I cannot guarantee that he would subscribe to everything that follows.

8.1 Introduction

There is considerable irony in the widely held view that Bert Röling should be seen as one of the founders of international criminal law – in fact, a dual irony. First, Röling wrote relatively little on international criminal law. His academic interests were elsewhere: with the Dutch criminal law and criminology to which he devoted his early career; with the establishment of a discipline of war studies (*polemology*) for which he became well-known in the Netherlands and abroad, and with his early recognition of the influence of colonialism on the history and substance of international law.[2] In that respect, Röling is like some other figures in this book, a more or less accidental figure in the pantheon of early international criminal lawyers.[3]

Second, the little he did write on international criminal law was not all that much devoted to international criminal law in any strict sense. In writing a lot about aggression, Röling occupied himself mostly tangentially with international criminal law, as his role as dissenter at the Tokyo Tribunal also suggests. He is best-known for his dissenting opinion rendered as judge in the Tokyo Tribunal, and this opinion is mostly devoted to crimes against peace.[4] The category of crimes against peace is not a central category of today's international criminal law and, it has been argued, is unlikely to become one: despite all the fuzz surrounding the adoption of a putative definition of aggression and the inclusion of such a category in the Statute of the International Criminal Court (ICC), there are simply too many parties that will be implicated both on the side of the aggressor and the victim to apply the notion with great seriousness.[5] What is more, definitions of aggression, including the 2010 Kampala amendment to the ICC's Rome Statute, are inevitably open-ended: article 8*bis* ICC lists a number of activities that may qualify

---

[2] See B. V. A. Röling, *International Law in an Expanded World* (Amsterdam: Djambatan, 1960), which remains a classic in the field of international legal studies as one of the first studies acknowledging the influence of colonialism on international law.

[3] I take international criminal law, for present purposes, to refer to the body of law addressing conduct relating to armed conflict, rather than the law relating to extradition or mutual assistance in the prosecution of common criminals, which is nowadays more usually referred to as transnational criminal law. See in particular Neil Boister, *An Introduction to Transnational Criminal Law* (Oxford: Oxford University Press, 2012).

[4] The dissent is reproduced in B. V. A. Röling and C. F. Rüter (eds.), *The Tokyo Judgment: The International Military Tribunal for the Far East, Volume 2* (Amsterdam: Amsterdam University Press, 1977), 1043–1148. Hereafter 'Röling's dissent'.

[5] The point is made, with markedly greater subtlety, by Martti Koskenniemi, 'Between Impunity and Show Trials' (2002) 6 *Max Planck Yearbook of United Nations Law*, 1–35.

as aggression, but also specifies that determinations need to take all circumstances into account, including the gravity and the consequences of the maligned act – and that carries a great potential for emptying the prohibition of much of its contents.[6]

Nonetheless, as we will see, the concept of the 'crime against peace' was central to Röling's thought – he suffered a serious ethical dilemma revolving around this very notion.[7] What is more, Röling's dissenting opinion oozes a humanist (for want of a better term[8]) spirit that is interesting in order to understand some of the early dilemmas of international criminal justice: he was keen to understand the motives and context of Japanese aggression during World War II, and not afraid to let this context influence his decision-making. The law (such as it was) is constantly applied, by Röling, with a keen view to understanding why people behaved as they did, and herewith imbued by a sense of empathy with the perpetrator not usually immediately associated with international criminal tribunals, and even less with those that can be classified as representing some degree of 'victor's justice'.[9]

And yet, it is precisely for this reason that Röling thoroughly deserves his place in the pantheon of international criminal law. His Tokyo dissent is a constant reminder to the discipline that international criminal law is not just about rules, further rules, and yet further elements of rules – although it is that too. It is also a reminder that things may never be what they seem to be at first sight, that people taking part in nasty regimes may actually try to prevent those regimes from being nastier. His dissent suggests that the ethics of international criminal law should be handled

[6] The definition was adopted by consensus at the 2010 Review Conference held in Kampala, Uganda, and recorded as RC/Res.6, 11 June 2010.

[7] His wrestling with the concept of crimes against peace in Tokyo is not always fully appreciated by later commentators aiming to understand the black letter of international criminal law: see, for example, Harmen van der Wilt, 'A Valiant Champion of Equity and Humaneness: The Legacy of Bert Röling for International Criminal Law' (2010) 8 *Journal of International Criminal Justice*, 1127–1140. It is nicely captured though in Kees van Beijnum's excellent novel *De offers* (Amsterdam: Bezige Bij, 2016), which tells the story of a fictitious Dutch judge taking part in the Tokyo trial.

[8] Kelk refers to Röling as a 'rational humanist', and the term seems apt enough. See Constantijn Kelk, 'Bert Rölingas a Criminal Law Scholar' (2010) 8 *Journal of International Criminal Justice*, 1093–1108, at 1101.

[9] For a thoughtful discussion of victor's justice and show trials (and the distinction between them), see Neil Boister, 'The Tokyo Military Tribunal: A Show Trial?', in Morten Bergsmo, Cheah Wui Ling and Yi Ping (eds.), *Historical Origins of International Criminal Law: Volume 2* (Brussels: TOAEP, 2014), 3–29. See generally also Gerry Simpson, *Law, War and Crime: War Crimes Trials and the Reinvention of International Law* (Cambridge: Polity, 2007).

with care: good and evil may be far more difficult to distinguish than is commonly assumed.[10]

Indeed, in an important sense, Röling embodies the very ambivalence of international criminal law. International criminal law is international in name, but departs from most international law by focusing on the individual rather than the state. It is also criminal in name, but departs from most criminal law by focusing not on common crimes, but on the exceptional, politically inspired crime. It does its work operating in various grey areas: between international law and criminal law; between political crime and common crime; between institutionalized evil and individual nastiness. It oscillates between the monstrosity of evil and, in Arendt's often misunderstood phrase, the banality of evil.[11]

In much the same way as international criminal law is neither purely criminal law nor purely international law, so too many of Röling's positions are characterized by ambivalence. He was, by any standard, a peace activist, but one who opposed unilateral disarmament and upheld the mutual *détente* emanating from nuclear weapons.[12] He has been characterized as a proponent of a socially responsive and responsible law who, nonetheless, also remained a 'somewhat technical legal craftsman'.[13] He was committed to detention and punitive theories about deterrence, but also advocated fair and humane treatment of suspects. Much as he advocated humane treatment, he was not against the death penalty, and agreed that for some of the Japanese war criminals at Tokyo this was the most appropriate sentence. It is remarkable how

[10] It is surely no coincidence that his views are represented with considerable sympathy by as deep a political thinker as Shklar: see Judith Shklar, *Legalism: Law, Morals, and Political Trials* (Cambridge, MA: Harvard University Press, 1986 [1964]).

[11] See Jan Klabbers, 'Just Revenge: The Deterrence Argument in International Criminal Law' (2001) 12 *Finnish Yearbook of International Law*, 249–267. The reference is, of course, to Hannah Arendt, *Eichmann in Jerusalem: A Report on the Banality of Evil* (New York: Penguin, 1994 [1963]).

[12] Admittedly though, the older Röling became more critical of the wisdom of nuclear détente, fearing that the possession of nuclear weapons would inevitably lead to their use. The point is noted by his successor in Groningen: see Wil D. Verwey, 'Bert V. A. Röling (1906–1985)', in T. M. C. Asser Institute (ed.), *The Moulding of International Law: Ten Dutch Proponents* (The Hague: T.M.C. Asser Institute, 1995), 27–68. Röling himself would later say that sometimes peaceful relations must be sacrificed when other values are at stake. See B. V. A. Röling and Antonio Cassese, *The Tokyo Trial and Beyond* (Cambridge: Polity, 1993), 97.

[13] See Nico Schrijver, 'B. V. A. Röling: A Pioneer in the Pursuit of Justice and Peace in an Expanded World' (2010) 8 *Journal of International Criminal Justice*, 1071–1091, at 1077. Schrijver characterizes Röling as a 'reluctant dissident' (ibid., at 1091); one can understand why, but it may not be entirely compelling, as I will suggest below.

even his physical appearance is often described in ambivalent terms: he was tall and dignified and nursed strong opinions, but was said to have a soft voice.[14]

8.2 Young Röling

Bert Röling grew up in the southern, Catholic part of the Netherlands. In a sense, this version of Catholicism itself embodies a curious compromise: it is a Catholicism that is strongly influenced by the type of Calvinism that used to prevail in most of Holland – and still does in a few 'bluestocking' pockets. Hence, Dutch Catholicism is an austere version of Catholicism, without the *joie de vivre* that characterizes the Catholicism of southern Europe and Latin America, or even neighbouring Belgium. The Dutch brand of Catholicism is one where rituals have become dissociated from their original meaning; where the cathedrals are considerably less lavish than their counterparts in Italy or Spain, and where the churchgoing folk are more serious and inward-looking than elsewhere in the Catholic world.

Röling grew up in 's Hertogenbosch, a mid-sized city in the south with Holland's best-known cathedral, the St. Jan, and the seat of possibly the leading Dutch diocese. His social class was, it seems, *petit bourgeois*: his father was a businessman (running a small garment factory) who fell on hard times and tried to hide it by continuing to drive a fine car in a bid to 'keep up with the Joneses' as it were. Eventually, he failed, and crashed his car into a tree, not entirely by accident.

Röling went on to study law at what was, at the time, the Catholic University of Nijmegen. This was the place where in 'pillarized' Holland[15] the Catholic intelligentsia would send their offspring, and where Catholic politicians were trained and nurtured until well in the 1970s and 1980s.[16] Already at law school, he proved to be something of

---

[14] See Antonio Cassese, 'B. V. A. Röling – A Personal Recollection and Appraisal' (2010) 8 *Journal of International Criminal Justice*, 1141–1152. Schrijver, in an unpublished presentation, puts it even sharper: Röling spoke with a soft voice but in such a manner that everyone would listen to him. See Nico Schrijver, 'Röling-Symposium: Inleiding' (undated and unpublished, on file with the author).

[15] The classic study is Arend Lijphart, *Verzuiling, pacificatie en kentering in de Nederlandse politiek* (Haarlem: Becht, 1968).

[16] Dutch Prime Minister Andries van Agt, for example, prominent in the 1970s and 1980s, represented the Catholic political party (which merged at some point into a Christian-democrat party) and had taught criminal law at Nijmegen.

210   JAN KLABBERS

a dissenter: he was suspected of anti-Catholic agitation, and as a result came close to being expelled.[17]

Nonetheless, he managed to graduate, and moved along with his mentor Willem Pompe to the University of Utrecht, where he wrote a PhD thesis on the intersection of criminal law and criminology. Pompe had just set up a Criminological Institute at Utrecht University, and Röling worked as his assistant.[18]

Upon completion of his doctoral work, he was appointed to the bench, as a starting young judge. This too ended up involving some dissent: during the Nazi occupation of Holland, he cunningly circumvented a piece of new legislation, much to the Germans' chagrin.[19] He left his position in central Utrecht for one in peripheral Zeeland, on Holland's south western coast and far away from the centres of commerce and industry. Here he sat out the remainder of the war in relative tranquillity, and wrote a book on Shakespeare and criminal law – showing himself to be quite the visionary.[20]

In between, he spent some time studying in Germany, in Marburg in particular. Relatively little is known about his German days and the influence this may have had on his thinking. This is especially intriguing as Marburg, in the late 1920s and early 1930s, was the place to be for those with a philosophical interest. Heidegger had been teaching in Marburg, and was widely rumoured to be re-inventing western philosophy from the ground up, to make thinking 'come to life' again.[21] Notable philosophers and political theorists took their first steps in those days in

[17] His son suggests (while acknowledging that he cannot be certain) that as a teenager Röling may have been abused, or at least approached, by Catholic priests. See Hugo Röling, *De rechter die geen ontzag had* (Amsterdam: Wereldbibliotheek, 2014), at 15–16.

[18] The Pompe Institute housed what became known as the 'Utrecht School' of criminology, and still exists, although it now encompasses not just criminology but criminal law in general.

[19] The Germans had abolished the idea that individuals could be convicted conditionally. Confronted with a case of someone accused of having insulted a member of the Dutch NSB (the Nazi-like party of Holland), Röling decided not immediately to sentence the accused (apparently a decent person with unblemished record), but to postpone sentencing by three months. This technically did not qualify as a 'conditional conviction' but amounted to much the same in practice. The episode is recorded (including a newspaper clipping from 1941) in H. Röling, *De rechter*, at 28.

[20] Shakespeare briefly became a popular object of study with the emergence of international criminal tribunals half a century later: see, for example, Theodor Meron, 'Shakespeare's Henry the Fifth and the Law of War' (1992) 86 *American Journal of International Law*, 1–46.

[21] See Elisabeth Young-Bruehl, *Hannah Arendt: For Love of the World*, 2nd ed. (New Haven, CT: Yale University Press, 2004), at 49 (citing Arendt).

Marburg, including Hannah Arendt, Hans Jonas, Hans-Georg Gadamer and Leo Strauss. There is not much evidence of any clear and direct influence of this type of thinking to be found in Röling's work and it is possible that he never even realized the lofty company he was keeping, and that as a law student he would not have come into contact with the exalted work going on in Marburg's philosophy department at any rate. On the other hand, however, Röling never was a black letter lawyer; much of his work testifies to a broader interest, so nor can it be categorically excluded that he was aware of the intellectual developments taking place around him – and possibly influenced by them.

Having moved back to Utrecht after the war, he came to be appointed to a so-called extraordinary chair (in the Dutch system, these are part-time chairs sponsored by some external benefactor) at Utrecht University, a chair of Indonesian[22] criminal law and procedure. This was set up, it seems, to provide a counterweight to the traditional chair of Indonesian law that existed in Leiden.[23] What Röling was probably not very aware of was that his new chair in Utrecht was meant to serve the interests of the oil industry – Indonesia was, and remains, a big oil-producing nation and the faculty concerned has been called the 'Oil Faculty'; the Leiden chair, by contrast, was deemed too progressive.[24] It was against this background, and before he could actually start his academic work,[25] that he was selected to become one of the judges in the Tokyo Tribunal.

What captures the imagination when thinking about the relatively youthful pre-Tokyo Röling is that already as a young man he displayed a marked tendency towards brinkmanship. He dissented both as a student in Nijmegen and as young judge in Utrecht; in both cases, he dissented strongly and cleverly; and yet in both cases, he stopped just

---

[22] Indonesia as a name only came in vogue after the country achieved its independence; it used to be referred to as Dutch Indies. I will nonetheless consistently speak of Indonesia, if only because the term Dutch Indies is difficult to turn into an adjective.

[23] The Leiden chair will forever be associated with Cornelis van Vollenhoven, who occupied it during the early part of the twentieth century and was also an international lawyer of repute, best known for his *De drie treden van het volkenrecht* (The Hague: Martinus Nijhoff, 1918). On Van Vollenhoven, see the biography by Henriette de Beaufort, *Cornelis van Vollenhoven 1874–1933* (Haarlem: Tjeenk Willink, 1954).

[24] See Röling, *De rechter*, at 174.

[25] See C. G. Roelofsen, 'Röling, Bernardus Victor Aloysius (1906–1985)', in *Biografisch Woordenboek van Nederland*, available at http://resources.huygens.knaw.nl (last visited 7 January 2015).

short of personal disaster.[26] He did not go as far as to get himself expelled from the Catholic University; he did not go as far as to be incarcerated or worse under the German occupation, and he even (something he later deeply regretted) signed a declaration that he was of Aryan blood.[27] He typically managed to craft careful compromises between the demands of his own conscience and the demands of the powers around him – he would do the same in Tokyo, and thereafter as well.[28]

8.3 Tokyo Calling

Röling was not, it seems, the first choice, or even the second choice to join the Tokyo Tribunal as the Dutch judge. The Netherlands, being the parent country of one of the countries invaded by Japan, was entitled to send both a judge and a prosecutor, and both positions proved difficult to fill. The Dutch government had a well-defined interest in participating in full: it felt that the 'Japanization' of Indonesia had to be part of the indictment, something less obviously a priority for the other participating states. But while it had a serious interest, it found it difficult to find properly qualified people. Some candidates were excellent lawyers but uncomfortable working in English; some were politically not considered acceptable as representatives of the kingdom; some were unavailable or reluctant to leave their families behind.

Eventually the choice fell on the relatively young and inexperienced Röling for the judicial position, and W.G.F. Borgerhoff Mulder as the Dutch prosecutor.[29] An assistant prosecutor was appointed precisely to handle the Japanization charge: this was J. S. Sinninghe Damsté, who had been working in Indonesia as a lawyer for many years.[30] And whatever the Dutch interest may have been, the government was not rewarding its representatives royally: especially at first, the financial compensation was

---

[26] His son drily remarks that Röling was no hero, and well aware of it. See H. Röling, *De rechter*, at 29.

[27] Ibid., at 75.

[28] Cassese suggests that the 'most notable facet' of Röling was his nuisance value: Röling would never bow to the orders of superiors but also refrained from performing his disobedience centre stage. See Röling and Cassese, *The Tokyo Trial*, at 9.

[29] On the selection, see L. van Poelgeest, *Nederland en het Tribunaal van Tokio* (Arnhem: Gouda Quint, 1989), 27–35.

[30] In the part of his memoires addressing the Tokyo Tribunal, he concentrates first and foremost on the Japanization charge. See J. S. Sinninghe Damsté, *Advocaat – Soldaat* (Amsterdam: Van Soeren, 1999).

decidedly meagre, such that Röling's wife complained.[31] On the other hand, the judges were placed in the most luxurious hotel in Tokyo, the Imperial Hotel designed by Frank Lloyd Wright, and Röling ended up living in a suite in the hotel during his time in Japan. Luxurious as the hotel was, it was far from sound-proofed: Röling complained about noise produced by his lusty and apparently somewhat sadistically inclined next door neighbor.[32]

These appointments of Röling as judge and Borgerhoff Mulder as prosecutor would prove problematic, in that Borgerhoff Mulder was far more 'senior' than Röling – who was the youngest judge on the tribunal by a considerable margin – and felt that he himself would have made a far superior judge.[33] Hence, in relations between the two, a certain *jalousie de métier* was never far away, and Borgerhoff Mulder did little, it seems, to support Röling.[34]

The Tokyo Tribunal consisted of nine judges and nine prosecutors drawn from the states that signed the Instrument of Surrender concerning Japan (i.e. Australia, Canada, China, France, the Netherlands, New Zealand, the USSR, the United Kingdom and the United States of America), plus two additional ones. The United Kingdom insisted that India be separately represented, upon which the US countered by proposing a separate seat for the Philippines – neither of these were independent at the moment the tribunal was created. The chief prosecutor was an American (Joseph Keenan), as this was America's project, Japan having surrendered in effect to General Douglas MacArthur. The chief justice was Australia's Sir William Webb, but his influence was never great and was considered to be waning towards the end of the proceedings. In the end, twenty-eight high-ranking Japanese military and political officials were prosecuted for crimes against peace, war crimes and crimes against humanity, on the basis of a charter promulgated by

---

[31] See Röling, *De rechter*, at 98.

[32] Ibid., at 59–61.

[33] Röling himself told people that he and Borgerhoff Mulder got along just fine, but nonetheless depicted him as lazy and pompous, in no uncertain terms. See ibid., at 207.

[34] It cannot be ruled out (but has never been investigated as far as I am aware), that class jealousy may have also been a factor. Many of the members of the Dutch legal establishment, like Borgerhoff Mulder and Sinninghe Damsté, had double-barrelled last names, indicating if not nobility then at least considerable privilege. Röling, by contrast, hailed from more common origins, his father having been a small-time businessman. It cannot be excluded that the legal establishment viewed Röling as a clever upstart. Röling himself, on the other hand, is said to have had a lifelong fascination with nobility, and was 'a bit of a snob'. See ibid., at 288.

MacArthur, one modelled on the London Charter that gave rise to the Nuremberg Tribunal.

8.4 Crimes against Peace

Röling proved critical of the Tokyo Tribunal on several points, and it has been suggested that here he discovered the disregard of international law for viewpoints other than that of the West.[35] His most fundamental criticism of the tribunal related to its very jurisdiction. In essence, his problem was this. According to him, the tribunal should only be operating if the tribunal itself was in harmony with, or at least not in contravention of, international law. To some extent, this was never problematic: it was clear, to Röling as well as to his fellow judges, that prosecuting individuals for war crimes would itself be in harmony with international law. Where he did have an issue though was in the prosecution of individuals for committing crimes against peace. This, he felt, was a new category, which as a crime leading to individual responsibility did not yet have a basis in international law.[36] Hence, to the extent that the Tokyo Tribunal was engaged with prosecuting individuals for crimes against peace, it would be in tension with international law as it existed prior to World War II.

What complicates matters was that Röling's position came with a degree of sophistry and, no less awkward, that he would eventually change his mind – not by much, but just enough to appease himself, and to estrange him from most of his fellow judges.[37] The sophist elements were, as they became apparent in his correspondence with Dutch international law professor J. H. W. Verzijl,[38] as follows. Röling never contested that victorious powers would have the power to make new law after a conflict. Likewise, he never doubted that they would have the power – and the right – to act against their erstwhile enemies. Moreover, in every legal order it was possible to take protective measures against those who

---

[35] See Verwey, *Bert V. A. Röling*, at 34–35.

[36] While war had been, at least in some ways, outlawed in the 1928 Briand-Kellogg Pact, this treaty did not envisage anything even approximating individual responsibility – if anything, it was still firmly based on statist assumptions.

[37] The degree of ostracization is perhaps best symbolized by the awkward circumstance that the lead prosecutor, Joseph Keenan, co-authored a monograph on the tribunal just after it had finished its work, and never once mentioned Röling – or Pal, for that matter. See Joseph B. Keenan and Brendan F. Brown, *Crimes Against International Law* (Washington, DC: Public Affairs Press, 1950).

[38] As reported in van Poelgeest, *Nederland en het Tribunaal*, at 73–74.

were not of sound mind, or otherwise a menace to society. Hence, it would not be much of a problem, legally speaking, if victorious powers were to send enemy leaders into exile (he was fond of recalling Napoleon's fate as a precedent) or to lock them up and throw away the key. But, so he suggested, this owed nothing to considerations of crime and punishment – this had nothing to do with criminal law. Instead, this type of action was engaged in not so as to punish a criminal, but so as to render an enemy harmless.[39]

By contrast, in making new law, the lawmaker does not have unlimited powers: new law must be made (so we may surmise) following the existing rules on law-making and, preferably, not run counter to existing law. Either way, the lawmaker does not have '*plein pouvoirs*'.[40] In the end, Röling himself put it well in a concept judgment presented to his fellow judges: 'Using war crime trials for the purpose of eliminating undesirable elements would mean the mixing up of justice and expediency, and would frustrate both.'[41]

It was this insistence on the need to demonstrate the prior legality of the crime against peace that landed him in hot water with his fellow judges in Tokyo as well as with the Dutch government. These univocally suggested that the jurisdiction of the tribunal stemmed from its charter, and that by accepting the assignment (i.e. a seat on the bench) Röling had accepted as much. Whether the charter itself was in conformity with international law was neither here nor there; this was not a matter for the tribunal to express itself on.

This official position was, quite obviously, a pragmatic position, but not without problems even on its own grounds. After all, the Tokyo Charter rested not on the consent of all states concerned, not even only those on the winning side, but was in essence contained in a decree issued by General MacArthur, following Japan's surrender.[42] It would have been fine, so Röling may be understood, to view this as the exercise of powers by a victorious power, but it was far more problematic to regard this as

---

[39] One cannot help but wonder what Röling would have made of the incarceration without trial of terrorism suspects in Guantanamo; his analysis seems rather Schmittian. On the notion of the enemy in international legal thought, see Walter Rech, *Enemies of Mankind: Vattel's Theory of Collective Security* (The Hague: Martinus Nijhoff, 2013).

[40] See van Poelgeest, *Nederland en het Tribunaal*, at 74.

[41] Quoted in ibid., at 77.

[42] MacArthur's promulgation, in turn, gave effect to paragraph 10 of the Potsdam declaration of 26 July 1945 (initially declared by the USA, the UK and China, later also adhered to by the USSR), which offered Japan the chance to surrender and promised that 'stern justice shall be meted out to all war criminals'.

the starting point of new law – and if it was indeed new law, it by definition violated the *nullum crimen sine lege* principle.

Complicating the picture further was the awkward circumstance that on one reading of the facts, the Dutch were never the victim of Japanese crimes against peace. Quite the opposite: the Dutch declared war on Japan after the latter had attacked Pearl Harbour, at a time when the war had not yet reached Indonesia. Hence, from this perspective, Japan could not be viewed as having initiated aggression against the Netherlands. This made Röling's position all the more difficult, for how can one apply the notion of crime against peace when no such action has taken place against your own state even as it is supposed to be the very justifying factor for your own presence on the tribunal?

There are counterarguments, of course. Perhaps Japanese imperialism in Asia generally could be seen as paving the way for aggressive war, rendering any particular attack less relevant for legal purposes. Or perhaps it could be argued that the decisive moment took place a week before Pearl Harbour, when the Japanese government decided to start war against the US, the United Kingdom and the Netherlands, but felt it strategically wiser not to issue formal declarations of war.[43] Be that as it may, it would have been easier for Röling, no doubt, had there been an initial act of aggression by Japan against the Netherlands.[44]

Still, Röling managed to reach a position that eased his conscience without completely giving up on it. At some point, he decided that the creation of a new category of crime against peace was actually inherent in being victorious after a just war. In a letter to the Dutch government written in the summer of 1948, not too long before the judgment was arrived at, he reached the conclusion that since the victorious powers are responsible for keeping the peace after conflict, they actually can lawfully use criminal trials as political instruments. Where his earlier position had juxtaposed politics versus law, he now brought politics and law together: dealing with the enemy by judicial means was among the tools in the toolkit of the powerful, even if done more in order to render harmless any opponent than in order to achieve judicial retribution.

---

[43] See van Poelgeest, *Nederland en het tribunaal*, at 44.

[44] The tribunal eventually treated the Dutch behaviour as self-defence against an imminent attack, although in the literature it is sometimes suggested that the Netherlands resorted to collective self-defence, as discussed in Neil Boister and Robert Cryer, *The Tokyo International Military Tribunal: A Reappraisal* (Oxford: Oxford University Press, 2008), at 123.

It followed, however (and this was crucial for Röling) that enemies thus identified should never be executed. It would be perfectly okay to incarcerate them, even after what would essentially be a show trial. But this would have to occur on the basis of a paradigm shift: the individual was seen as an enemy, no longer (or not at all) as suspect of a crime. And thinking in terms of the enemy-as-enemy would not justify the imposition and execution of the death penalty – this was bolstered under reference to the Nuremberg trial, where none of the suspects had been sentenced to death for crimes against peace only.[45] In his letter to the government, Röling referred to the importance of just war (*bellum justum*), and it seems accurate to regard this as an important condition – surely any aggressive victors would be less justified in rendering enemies harmless.

Inventive as Röling's position appears, he reached it only after considerable soul-searching. One of the intriguing elements of his position is that he was constantly aware of representing his country, and not just any country but, as he repeatedly confirmed, the country of Grotius. He described himself in this way in his correspondence with Verzijl, referred to above, as well as his correspondence with Leiden's professor Van Eysinga[46] in 1946. This suggests that the link between war crimes trials and the concept of just war may have been germinating for a considerable period of time.

Röling would maintain his position consistently and to the end. His dissenting opinion finishes with how he would sentence the various suspects, and it comes as no surprise that he would sentence none of those suspected and found guilty of crimes against peace to the death

---

[45] Quoted in ibid., at 88. Cryer suggests that Röling may have missed a beat here: while it is true that no one at Nuremberg was sentenced to death for crimes against peace alone, it is not clear that the judges at Nuremberg were sentencing on this basis. See Robert Cryer, 'Röling in Tokyo: A Dignified Dissenter' (2010) 8 *Journal of International Criminal Justice*, 1109–1126, at 1116.

[46] There is some confusion on the identity of this person. Van Poelgeest refers in the text of his book (*Nederland en het Tribunaal*, at 74) to W. J. M. V. van Eysinga, but gives him a different fourth initial (W. J. M. W.) in the index. Hugo Röling's biography of his father (*De rechter*) echoes van Poelgeest's index, referring to W. J. M. W. van Eysinga. Most likely however is that the person concerned was W. J. M. van Eysinga, a former Dutch judge in the Permanent Court of International Justice. At the relevant time, Van Eysinga was emeritus professor at Leiden, and without doubt a highly influential member of the Dutch foreign policy establishment – he enjoyed the confidence of Queen Juliana, who had been his student, as had several Ministers of Foreign Affairs. The repertory of law professors at Leiden only mentions this Van Eysinga: available at http://hoogleraren .leidenuniv.nl/search?f1-faculteit=Rechtsgeleerdheid;docsPerPage=1;startDoc=119.

penalty: 'From the law as it now stands, it follows that no one should be sentenced to death for having committed a crime against peace.'[47] Instead, he would either advocate acquittal or incarceration. Indeed, even much later in the mid-1950s, when discussions ensued about pardoning those who had been incarcerated, he felt that those found guilty of crimes against peace alone should be pardoned: they were no longer in a position to do any damage.[48] Since Röling viewed incarceration for crimes against peace not as punishment but as the temporary neutralization of a threat, it followed that there was no obstacle, to his mind, to granting pardons once the threat had disappeared.[49]

8.5 Individual Responsibility

Röling's dissent was not limited to the concept of crimes against peace: on two other issues he made his mark, both related to individual responsibility. On both topics, his humaneness shone through: his remarks on command responsibility and on the defence of superior orders both demonstrate an empathy with the position of the individual whom circumstances force to make a decision in difficult circumstances that is often absent from international criminal law writings. In quasi-Aristotelian terms, his dissent displayed considerable empathy or compassion for the plight of individuals in a difficult situation, and appreciated that such individuals need to possess the virtue of practical wisdom (*phronesis*) in considerable measure.[50]

It is not unlikely that Röling's thinking on command responsibility was coloured by the then recent example of the *Yamashita* case – indeed, Röling discussed it at some length.[51] As is well-known, Japanese General Yamashita was found guilty by an American military tribunal after World War II of war crimes, due to the simple fact that armed forces

---

[47] See 'Röling's dissent', at 1116.

[48] The Dutch government thought otherwise and used the power to pardon as a bargaining chip in getting Japan to pay reparations. See, very critical, van Poelgeest, *Nederland en het Tribunaal*, especially at 143.

[49] See ibid., at 131, citing a letter from Röling to the Dutch Ministry for Foreign Affairs dated July 1955.

[50] Aristotle, in his *Ethics*, never referred to empathy as a virtue, and it seems that both the word and the concept are of relatively recent origin. That said, it appears to be a great virtue for a judge (or a court) to possess: see Jan Klabbers, 'Doing Justice? Bureaucracy, the Rule of Law and Virtue Ethics' (2017) 6 *Rivisto de Filosofia del Diritto*, 27–50. For Aristotle, I have used the 1976 Penguin edition, translated by Thomson.

[51] See 'Röling's dissent', at 1063.

under his command engaged in such crimes. The fact that he was cut off from his troops and had no chance of influencing them on the spot was all but ignored, both by the military tribunal and, later, the US Supreme Court (which affirmed the ruling of the military tribunal). While Yamashita had nominally been in charge, he was practically speaking not in a position to do anything of relevance or even to be made aware, and this must have touched a nerve with Röling – even though his description of the US Supreme Court decision is remarkably arid.[52]

When discussing the command responsibility of Japanese suspects in Tokyo, Röling underlined that command responsibility rested on three pillars: knowledge, power and duty. An individual in a position of authority can only meaningfully be held to account if he or she has knowledge of what goes on, has the power (and is in a position) to intervene, and has an obligation to do so. Still, the separation between the pillars need not be taken too far: 'the duty may imply the duty to know'.[53] And while Röling acknowledged that the scope of command responsibility may be extensive, he felt one could not simply assume the responsibility of every government member for any atrocity committed in the field or against prisoners of war or civilians.[54] Cabinet liability, as Cryer has called it, would be too broad a concept for Röling.[55]

Röling devoted a section of his dissent specifically to command responsibility. By contrast, his treatment of superior orders was less systematic and overt: it mostly came out when he discussed the punishments he thought appropriate to various accused.[56] Thus, when discussing the fate of defendant Hata, whom he characterized as a 'professional soldier', he approvingly noted that the prosecution seemed well aware of military manners and the need for loyalty and obedience. 'Soldiers nor sailors, generals nor admirals should be charged with the crime of initiating or waging an aggressive war, in case they merely performed their military duty of fighting in a war waged by their government.'[57]

---

[52] He later explained that Yamashita 'could not have known what happened'. See Röling and Cassese, *The Tokyo Trial*, at 71.

[53] See 'Röling's dissent', at 1063.

[54] See 'Röling's dissent', at 1064.

[55] See Cryer, *Röling in Tokyo*, at 1120.

[56] Röling's thoughts on this point are admirably systematized by Van der Wilt, *The Legacy*.

[57] See 'Röling's dissent', at 1117. Strikingly, he almost repeats himself a few pages later: 'Soldiers and sailors should never be considered to wage an aggressive war in the sense of the Charter, even if they be Generals or Admirals, as long as they do not, in that capacity, decide government policy.' Ibid., at 1120.

Ironically perhaps, in light of Röling's sensitivity to non-Western cultures, behind this sentiment lay a rather traditional and possibly quite Western idea on the respective roles of government and military. The dominant Western tradition, after all, separates the military and political spheres, and places civilian authority firmly in charge – a model that may not command universal support.[58] The military, so Röling stated over and over again, was merely supposed to be a tool of the government; it should not interfere in politics, and should possibly even be protected against having to 'meddle in politics'.[59] On the other hand, in wartime Japan, it would seem the military occupied an independent position; so much so that it could often ignore commands from the civilian authorities.[60]

If Röling's treatment of command responsibility is largely compelling, therefore, his 'superior order' treatment is more problematic. Partly, this is because he sometimes conflated the defence of the superior order with command responsibility. Partly it is because he limited the discussion of superior orders mostly to relations between the government and the military and in the context of crimes against peace – he said little of note about superior orders instructing soldiers to commit war crimes.

8.6 An Ethical Dilemma

It seems that Röling, initially not hindered by too much knowledge of international law and justice, upon his appointment slowly started to realize that he had become embroiled in an undertaking of questionable moral status. As time progressed, he increasingly realized that the Tokyo Tribunal was largely about victor's justice and was, in fact, less about doing justice than it was about punishing Japan. It took him a while to get there.[61] For all his misgivings, he felt quite strongly, early on, that the court's decision should be unanimous – in fact, it was he who had

---

[58] Chayes suggests that the model no longer accurately describes reality – if it ever did. See Antonia Chayes, *Borderless Wars: Civil Military Disorder and Legal Uncertainty* (Cambridge: Cambridge University Press, 2015).

[59] Röling himself places the term in inverted commas, and under reference to the Nuremberg judgment refers to the army as 'the honorable profession of arms'. See 'Röling's dissent', at 1117–1118.

[60] See, for example, his discussion of the limited role played by Foreign Minister Hirota: 'Röling's dissent', at 1126.

[61] But once he arrived at his conclusion, he stayed faithful to it. If anything, the passage of time made him more critical still of the Tokyo Trial: see B. V. A. Röling, 'The Nuremberg and Tokyo Trials in Retrospect', in Cheriff Bassiouni and Ved P. Nanda (eds.), *A Treatise*

enthusiastically drafted an early memo of the tribunal on precisely this point.

He would, however, slowly come to change his mind. While it remains speculative at best to indicate why he did so, several factors are likely to have influenced his thought. First, he proved to be a hard-working student, and it is by no means eccentric to suppose that if on arrival he did not quite know what he was doing in international law, after a while he started to understand the system better; and the better he got to know it, the more outrageous must have seemed the attempt to create a new regime on crimes against peace and apply it retro-actively – at least to the trained criminal lawyer.

Second, it also seems plausible that the arrival of the Indian judge, Judge Pal, exercised some influence. Pal made it clear, right from the start, that he was going to write a dissent – therewith breaking through the unanimity of the tribunal. Since Pal would go it alone, Röling might have felt more comfortable in also going it alone and, as a result, may have felt more comfortable in further developing his own thoughts and positions. In a sense, Pal took the chestnuts out of the fire, allowing Röling to follow.

And maybe, just maybe, there was a third factor at play. Röling was having difficult relations with pretty much everyone involved. He did not get along with the Dutch prosecutor. After it became clear that he might be interested in writing a dissent, most of his fellow judges by and large excommunicated him, forcing him to dine alone or with Pal. His opposition to the crimes against peace concept meant that he had a difficult relationship with the Dutch ambassador and the government at large. He even managed to distance himself from his nominal colleagues of the international law establishment in the Netherlands. And in the meantime, the trial went on and on, lasting far longer than originally scheduled which, in turn, also meant that he was separated from his wife and family for much longer than initially anticipated. He did, to be sure, find ways to entertain himself, engaging in sports and music (he was an enthusiastic violinist) and, rumour has it, fraternizing with a Japanese woman.[62] Be

---

on *International Criminal Law. Volume I: Crimes and Punishment* (Springfield, IL: Charles C. Thomas, 1973), 590–619.

[62] The rumour is fairly strong and seems to have been acknowledged even by his son. See Röling, *De rechter*. Note also that novelist Van Beijnum has his life in Tokyo revolve around an extra-marital affair, and that a second novelist (who actually knew him) pictured him as something of a ladies' man: see W. F. Hermans, *Onder Professoren* (Amsterdam: Bezige Bij, 1975).

that as it may, Röling could easily have gotten away with throwing in the towel and resigning – as he was close to doing once or twice. The big question then is why he did not resign but, instead, kept going in the face of so much opposition.

The most plausible answer, it seems, is that he relished the opposition. He was an iconoclast by vocation, who thrived on ambivalences and going against the grain. He had done so before Tokyo, as a student in Nijmegen and as a young judge under the German occupation of the Netherlands. He would do so several times in his professional life after Tokyo as well. On one occasion in the late 1950s, he published a pamphlet endorsing the independence of New Guinea, the last remaining part of Indonesia under Dutch control. This earned him the anger of then Foreign Minister Joseph Luns, and may have cost him the prestigious chair at Leiden.[63]

There are, of course, (at least) two ways to interpret such behaviour. On one interpretation, it simply suggests he was a man of principle, who would not compromise on his strongly felt beliefs and would do whatever the situation demanded of him morally, while disregarding the consequences. This, however, while not untrue, would be a bit too glib. Röling had quite a few narrow escapes, where his principled stand ultimately did not cost him much. He turned away from Catholicism, but could nonetheless graduate in Nijmegen and move to Utrecht with his mentor Pompe. As a young judge in occupied Holland he annoyed the Germans, but could sit out the war in relative peace and quiet in Zeeland while continuing to work. His stance on New Guinea may have upset the foreign policy establishment a little, but his chair in Groningen was never under threat, and he was free to develop his plea for recognition of the plight of the Global South in all quietude.

Much the same applies to his affection for *polemology*: it is not immediately obvious that close to the government, in Leiden, he would have been able to do what he achieved in far-away Groningen – and he was smart enough to have made that calculation.[64] And while he did not

---

[63] Apparently, the Law Faculty at Leiden had expressed a strong preference that Röling be appointed; hence, Röling himself was convinced that not being appointed in Leiden had been due to political opposition, and was reportedly very angry when news reached him that he would not be appointed there. See Röling, *De rechter*, at 362. One commentator expresses some doubts, however, but without further explanation. See Roelofsen, *Röling*.

[64] Reportedly, when the Polemological Institute was set up in 1962 on Röling's initiative, the leadership of the University of Groningen felt the need to ask him, in confidence, whether he was a communist. As reported in ibid.

make many friends in Tokyo, it turns out his dissent has survived the passage of time far better than the majority opinion. It does not seem all that far-fetched that with all these episodes, he was quite aware of what he could and could not afford to do. Hence, a portrayal of Röling as a proto-Kantian *Prinzipienreiter* does not seem very accurate – it does not seem to do him a great deal of justice.

Perhaps then a second interpretation might be more accurate. It is not so much that principles played no role for him (they did), but that instead of applying them and seeing them through to the end, he rather enjoyed playing the martyr or at least having a certain nuisance value. Many of his main professional episodes suggest that he took some comfort from seeing how far the envelope could be pushed, whether the pushing was against the Catholicism of the university, the German occupier, the Dutch government's colonial policies and the Dutch international law establishment or, indeed, the majority at the Tokyo Tribunal. In all cases, he pushed from a rather secure position, and in all cases, he made sure never to go too far. He upset the Germans, but did not get arrested (or worse); he may have upset the university patrons, but never quite got expelled; he upset the Dutch government, but was never stripped of his chair; and he upset his brethren at the tribunal, but all it cost him was social ostracism.

If the above sounds perhaps a little negative, it is not meant to be. There is much to be said for what might be called a principled pragmatism in politics, and against supporting principles with great absolutism.[65] Principles will need to be applied in constantly differing contexts and situations, and principles never apply themselves. In other words, it takes practical wisdom to assess when the situation calls for the application of a particular principle. In addition, decision-makers rarely (if ever) have the luxury of being able deeply to contemplate the proper solution: they typically work under great time pressure, and with incomplete information. Hence, to merely insist on rigid application of principles usually misses the mark – even the clearest principle needs to be accompanied by a sense of practical wisdom.[66]

Some ethical dilemmas merely lead to tragic choices: Röling could have quit the tribunal, but that would perhaps (most likely, even) merely

---

[65] And note that he was ready to put his money where his mouth was: having sentenced individuals to death, he asked to be present at the execution because he thought that was the proper thing to do. The request was denied. See Röling and Cassese, *The Tokyo Trial*, at 65.

[66] See generally Friedrich V. Kratochwil, *The Status of Law in World Society: Meditations on the Role and Rule of Law* (Cambridge: Cambridge University Press, 2014).

have resulted in the appointment of a less conscientious individual, and would have meant that he had to remain silent. In such circumstances, it may be better to bite the bullet and write a powerful dissent than to give up altogether. The problem though is that this usually only becomes clear with hindsight: the *problematique* of the 'burgomaster in wartime' (to stay on under foreign occupation in order to prevent worse things from happening) can appear opportunist as well as idealist.[67]

Be that as it may, it seems clear that Röling's own dilemma made him sensitive and receptive to the dilemmas some of those accused in Tokyo may have faced.[68] Struggling with his own conscience on how to participate in what was – at least to some extent – a show trial, he may have been more open to the plight of those who joined the Japanese government during the war in an attempt to prevent it from further aggression and atrocities. In other words, building on his own experience he may have come to appreciate the experiences of others. Even if the situations were not identical (joining an aggressive government is, after all, different from joining an international tribunal), nonetheless they were comparable enough, creative of dilemmas of similar structure. And in being open and receptive to the plight of some of the suspects on trial, Röling demonstrated to have internalized Aristotle's ethical lessons. Ethics, so Aristotle teaches us, is a matter of character, and reflective individuals continuously aim to improve and become more virtuous. Ethics is not a matter of finding a rule and sticking to it, no matter the consequences; nor is ethics a matter of calculating what the best thing to do is given the circumstances. Instead, ethics is first and foremost a matter of the character of the individual facing a dilemma, with the individual concerned having to draw on character traits such as courage, honesty, magnanimity, temperance and, perhaps most of all, practical wisdom and their sense of justice.[69]

8.7 Röling's Charisma

It seems undeniable that Röling had considerable charisma. He managed, for instance, to make a huge impression on Antonio Cassese, who not

---

[67] For a fine treatment, see Avishai Margalit, *On Compromise and Rotten Compromise* (Princeton, NJ: Princeton University Press, 2010).

[68] His son Hugo suggests that there may have been something of a Japanese conspiracy going on to 'soften Röling up' by inviting him into society, by seeking contact through music and even by introducing him to pretty women. See Röling, *De rechter*, at 84–86.

[69] See Aristotle, *Ethics*. The list is not exhaustive.

only dedicated a book to Röling[70] and interviewed him at length for another book,[71] but also never tired of introducing Röling to others.[72] Röling must also be one of the very, very few law professors who end up being immortalized in novels.[73] If in W. F. Hermans' classic 1975 *Onder Professoren* he merely occupies a cameo, and the portrait of him there is mostly caricature, he is the central character in a more recent novel, Kees van Beijnum's *De Offers* as well as a recently released film.[74]

Novelist Hermans was working as a lecturer at Groningen University, felt under-appreciated and wrote a vengeful portrait of vanity, self-indulgence and arrogance at a provincial university. Röling is by no means central to the story but is cast as a seriously obese professor with two passions: the pursuit of female students, and his newly invented science of war studies under the heading 'polemology'. Like most caricatures, there is some basis in reality for this casting: Röling may not have been a serial womanizer but is generally reported to have had an eye for female beauty and had by then turned polemology into the centre of his academic work.

What attracts novelists to Röling is, one may presume, the complexity of his character, riddled as it is with seeming contradictions. People are generally expected to behave with some consistency, and outcries emerge when people are seen to be acting 'out of character' – a recent example is that of the world famous moral philosopher who has made a career out of speaking out against extreme poverty, but allegedly engaged in exploitative sexual relationships with female students from the Global South. Part of the outcry relates – and rightly so – to him exercising power in improper manner; but part of it also has to do with consistency or coherence in human action: someone who stands up for certain values should not be seen to transgress those values himself.

In a more subtle and interesting manner, something similar may apply to Röling, constantly struggling with his conscience and constantly engaged in an inner struggle to guarantee the unity of his virtues. The man held opinions that seem difficult to reconcile with one another: in

---

[70] See Antonio Cassese, *International Law in a Divided World* (Oxford: Oxford University Press, 1986).

[71] See Röling and Cassese, *The Tokyo Trial*.

[72] See Antonio Cassese, *Five Masters of International Law* (Oxford: Hart, 2011).

[73] The only other candidate who immediately comes to mind is F.F. Martens, immortalized in Jaan Kross, *Professor Martens' Departure* (New York: New Press, 1995, Hollo trans.).

[74] The film *Tokyo Trial*, directed by Pieter Verhoeff and Rob King, opened worldwide on 25 September 2017.

favour of peace, but also for nuclear deterrence; empathic with the suspects in the dock in Tokyo and insisting on a fair trial, but by no means shying away from imposing the death penalty. This extended to his private life: with wife and children far away in Holland, he was attracted to Japanese women, and his son surmises there may have been several lovers during the Tokyo years, but insists on denying that any of them may have been prostitutes: 'My father was not monogamous, but he was never a john, even though this is unprovable.'[75]

It is this complexity that Van Beijnum captures in his excellent novel *De Offers*, in which the Dutch judge at the Tokyo Tribunal (Judge Brink, in the novel) ends up cheating on his wife back home in the Netherlands, deserting his Japanese lover and their baby and leaving her war-invalid brother in the dark, while simultaneously aiming to do justice to the defendants before the tribunal and, arguably, being much more success-ful in doing justice professionally than privately. If there is a doctrine of the unity of the virtues, as Aristotle posited, then Judge Brink has a hard time keeping this unity together – and perhaps the same applied to Judge Röling.[76]

8.8   Röling's Legacy

If it is fair to say that Röling's place in the pantheon of international criminal law rests on several ironies, it is nonetheless also true that a compelling case can be made that he ought to be included in the pantheon precisely because of these ironies or ambivalences. Put differently, it is precisely his focus on the surroundings of international criminal law (as opposed to international criminal law *simpliciter*) that earns him his rightful place as one of the founding fathers. His legacy, it would seem, can be seen in threefold manner.

First, there is the overarching disciplinary level. Röling's early interest was not just in Dutch criminal law, but also in criminology – witness the topic of his doctoral thesis, witness also his involvement with his mentor

---

[75] '*Mijn vader was niet monogaam, een hoerenloper was hij niet, al kun je dat nooit bewijzen.*' Words attributed to Hugo Röling in Tom Vennink, 'Roman versus biografie', at www .nrcreader.nl/artikel/6964/roman-versus-biografie, visited 7 January 2015. Incidentally, the paper publishing it is generally considered the most serious Dutch quality newspaper. Elsewhere, Hugo Röling acknowledged that his father was not monogamous but would never get carried away and was never really chasing skirts. See Röling, *De rechter*, at 176.

[76] Many hold the doctrine of the unity to be unworkable, if only because we can rarely see what goes on in someone's private life. See, for example, C. A. J. Coady, *Messy Morality: The Challenge of Politics* (Oxford: Clarendon Press, 2008).

Pompe and the criminological work of the Pompe Institute. One of the things coming out strongly in his 'regular' criminal law work is a belief in the idea that many criminals can better their lives, and that punishment should remain humane and proportional. Moreover, for some, psychiatric treatment might be more appropriate than a prison sentence, and law should not lose track of such circumstances. Likewise, he was keen on eradicating root causes of economic injustice, rather than incarcerating economic criminals for long periods of time.[77] His Tokyo dissent clearly oozes much the same spirit: a desire to understand the human impulses and recognition of the old biblical maxim about 'throwing the first stone'. It cannot be a coincidence that his later interest in international law came to be accompanied by an interest in polemology. Polemology, for Röling, is to international law what criminology is to criminal law: the social science indispensable for the proper understanding of the law. Polemology helps to explain the contents of international law; it helps to explain why states and people act the way they act.[78]

What remains obscure is why he felt that precisely the science of war and peace might help to understand international law – others might have opted for a different social science perspective, perhaps thinking that international law could better be explained by means of an intellectual alliance with, say, international political economy or, as is not uncommon, with the academic discipline of international relations. But perhaps this was a generational matter: many who lived through the war must have felt that peace was an essential condition for other aspects of life, whereas economic structuralism of any kind would have carried Marxist overtones that, for this generation and in the midst of the Cold War, may have been difficult to embrace. Moreover, the emphasis on power employed by many of his contemporaries active in the discipline of international relations failed to capture some of the salient aspects of international law in general, and international criminal law in particular.

Intriguingly though, and in marked contrast to many of today's international criminal lawyers, for Röling the 'peace versus justice' question generally had to be answered by emphasizing peace. His international

---

[77] For a brief overview in English of Röling's thoughts on criminal law generally, see Kelk, *Criminal Law Scholar.*

[78] Röling's Institute brought together scholars from fields as different as sociology and physics, or economics and biology, who would all shine their light on the different causes and consequences of aggression. See, for example, B. V. A. Röling (ed.), *De oorlog in het licht der wetenschappen* (Assen: Van Gorcum, 1963). If the term *polemology* is not commonly used, similar ideas inform 'peace studies' or 'conflict studies'.

criminal law was never about fighting 'the culture of impunity'; his approach to the *ius in bello* was, and remained, about securing or restoring the peace.[79] Indeed, he recognized that sometimes attempts to legislate justice might end up disturbing peace; the bloodshed often associated with claims for self-determination may be considered illustrative.[80]

The second part of his legacy can be found on the level of the detailed application of international criminal law. For him, it was clear that if trials were to take place, then those accused of even the gravest violations nonetheless merited a fair trial, and while representing the Netherlands in various United Nations organs during the 1950s he proved to be a fierce (but thoughtful) proponent of the creation of a permanent international criminal court.[81] He was not against harsh sentencing, including the death penalty, but he would not dream of throwing out the rule-book in order to secure a conviction, and would have applauded, for example, recent decisions by the ICC to stop prosecutions in cases of weak evidence.[82] The law, to him, was not merely a pragmatic instrument, although he recognized that it could be this for others. But for Röling, the law had a moral quality of its own.[83] Notwithstanding his interest in the social sciences, whether criminology or polemology, he remained lawyer enough to appreciate the virtues of a proper prosecution and defence, presided over by properly trained judges applying the law in an open and honest manner.[84]

The third part of his legacy is less clear-cut and less obvious, but can nonetheless be discerned. Already throughout his dissent, he displayed a remarkable willingness to take different, non-western cultures seriously, and his lengthy stay in Japan opened up a new culture to which he was quite receptive. While admittedly his remarks on superior orders

---

[79] Verwey makes a similar observation, and drily notes that in doing so, Röling approached the *ius in bello* '(r)ather unconventionally'. See Verwey, *Bert V. A. Röling*, at 42.

[80] See further Jan Klabbers, 'The Right to be Taken Seriously: Self-determination in International Law' (2006) 28 *Human Rights Quarterly*, 186–206.

[81] For very useful discussion, see Lisette Schouten, 'From Tokyo to the United Nations: B. V. A. Röling, International Criminal Jurisdiction and the Debate on Establishing an International Criminal Court, 1949–1957', in Bergsmo et al. (eds.), *Historical Origins*, 177–212.

[82] See ICC-01/09–01/11, *Prosecutor v. William Samoei Ruto and Joshua Arap Sang*, decision of 5 April 2016.

[83] Röling noted in his diary, with some disdain, that others treated the law as purely instrumental. This now was a sentiment he could not share, and his son imagines that his father would have deemed the instrumentalist view to constitute 'jesuit trickery' (*paaps gesjoemel*). See Röling, *De rechter*, at 226.

[84] He also advocated shooting those who received the death penalty, rather than hanging them, unless they had been exceptionally cruel themselves. See ibid., at 163.

may have owed much to a western distinction concerning the proper roles of government and the military, nonetheless his dissent is sensitive to different cultural notions and perspectives – without bowing to them. His stay in Japan planted the seeds for his growing conviction that international law ought not to be complicit in the suppression and exploitation of non-Western peoples and their cultures, but should rather involve the 'annulment of the former law of domination', be of general application rather than based on a distinction between civilized nations and others, and should expand so as to come to include a social justice component.[85]

8.9 To Conclude

Röling stands as one of the intellectual forefathers of international criminal law, and while his place there is somewhat ironic, it is nonetheless well-deserved. Perhaps less obviously though, he should be remembered for his ethical stance. The principled pragmatist that Röling was clearly struggled with a large ethical dilemma (whether to participate in what was to a considerable extent a show trial) and a few smaller ones as well, relating to command responsibility and the superior order defence. In all of these, he eventually let himself be guided by a sense of empathy or compassion with the accused, trying to look at the world through their eyes, and from the vantage point of their cultural traditions.

In doing so, he provides a nice exemplar of the virtuous judge,[86] the sort of judge who realizes that law is never a matter of algorithms and dictionary definitions, but also involves courage, carefulness, temperance and perhaps most of all the practical wisdom – Aristotle spoke of *phronesis* – to apply one's technical skills properly.[87] Röling is by no means the only judge in recorded history to display this set of judicial virtues,[88] but the example he offered in Tokyo still shines.

---

[85] See Röling, *Expanded World*, at 121.

[86] For philosophical underpinnings, see Amalia Amaya, 'Exemplarism and Judicial Virtue' (2013) 25 *Law & Literature*, 428–445.

[87] See, for example, Colin Farrelly and Lawrence B. Solum (eds.), *Virtue Jurisprudence* (New York: Palgrave Macmillan, 2008); Amalia Amaya and Ho Hock Lai (eds.), *Law, Virtue and Justice* (Oxford: Hart, 2013) and Iris van Domselaar, 'Moral Quality in Adjudication: On Judicial Virtues and Civic Friendship' (2015) 44 *Netherlands Journal of Legal Philosophy*, 24–46.

[88] Without using the vocabulary of Aristotelian ethics, the examples offered by Hutchinson are instructive. See Allen Hutchinson, *Laughing at the Gods: Great Judges and How They Made the Common Law* (Cambridge: Cambridge University Press, 2012).

9

Retelling Radha Binod Pal

The Outsider and The Native

ROHINI SEN AND RASHMI RAMAN

Figure 9.1 Doctor Pal Memorial, Yushukan Museum, Tokyo. Credit: Richard Cummins/Lonely Planet Images/Getty Images Plus.

> When time shall have softened passion and prejudice, when Reason shall have stripped the mask from misrepresentation, then justice, holding her scales, will require much of past censure and praise to change places.[1]

---

[1] Radha Binod Pal, Dissenting Opinion at the IMTFE, pp. 700–701 (hereinafter referred to as "Dissent"). See Pal, Radhabinod. *International Military Tribunal for the Far East: Dissentient Judgment of Justice R.B. Pal*, Sanyal, 1953.

9 RADHA BINOD PAL

231

9.1 Why Revisit Radha Binod Pal Now?

Radha Binod Pal, the Indian judge at the International Military Tribunal of the Far East[2] has been marginalized since his famous dissent for political and intellectual reasons. He has previously been discussed almost exclusively in mainstream academia in the context of the dissent[3] and has never been allowed to escape the penumbra of this dissentient identity. Recently, he has found his way back into the Indian critical legal imagination.[4] In the course of this chapter on Pal and his work, we hope to show that the dissent is part of an embedded identity, a complex legal journey and a deep consciousness of the inner morality of law. While the dissent gave Pal a foothold in the international legal community, he has been deprived of an intellectual biography as an international lawyer, an identity he is believed to have fostered during and after his time at the IMTFE.

---

[2] Hereinafter referred to as the IMTFE.

[3] See, among others, Minear, Richard. *Victors' Justice: The Tokyo War Crimes Trial*, Princeton University Press, 1971; Piccigallo, Philip R. *The Japanese on Trial: Allied War Crimes Operations in the East, 1945-1951*, University of Texas Press, 1979; Kopelman, Elizabeth S. "Ideology and International Law: The Dissent of the Indian Justice at the Tokyo War Crimes Trial." *New York University Journal of International Law and Politics* 23 (1990): 373-444; Nandy, Ashis. "The Other Within: The Strange Case of Radhabinod's Judgment on Culpability." *New Literary History* 23 (1992): 45-67; Kei, Ushimura. *Beyond the "Judgment of Civilization": The Intellectual Legacy of the Japanese War Crimes Trials, 1946-1949*, The International House of Japan, 2003; Kei, Ushimura. "Pal's 'Dissentient Judgment' Reconsidered: Some Notes on Postwar Japan's Responses to the Opinion." *Japan Review* 9 (2007): 215-224; Futamura, Madoka. *War Crimes Tribunals and Transitional Justice: The Tokyo Trial and the Nuremberg Legacy*, Routledge, 2008; Boister, Neil and Cryer, Robert. *The Tokyo International Military Tribunal: A Reappraisal*, Oxford University Press, 2008; Totani, Yuma. *The Tokyo War Crimes Trial: The Pursuit of Justice in the Wake of World War II*, Harvard University Press, 2009, pp. 218-245; Takeshi, Nakajima. "Justice Pal (India)," in Tanaka, Yuki, McCormack, Tim and Simpson, Gerry (eds.). *Beyond Victor's Justice?: The Tokyo War Crimes Trial Revisited*. Martinus Nijhoff, 2011, pp. 127-146; Nandy, Ashis. "Justice Radhabinod Pal and India–Japan Relationship: The Voices of Asian Intellectuals," India-Japan Dialogue, Japan Foundation Lecture, 2012-2013; Sellars, Kirsten. *"Crimes against Peace" and International Law*, Cambridge University Press, 2013.

[4] Banerjee, Milinda. *Decolonization and Subaltern Sovereignty: India and the Tokyo Trial*, Palgrave Macmillan, 2016; Banerjee, Milinda."Does International Criminal Justice Require a Sovereign? Historicizing Radhabinod Pal's Tokyo Judgment in Light of His 'Indian' Legal Philosophy." *Historical Origins of International Criminal Law* 2 (2014): 67-117; Banerjee, Milinda. "Sovereignty as a Motor of Global Conceptual Travel: Sanskritic Equivalents of 'Law' in Bengali Discursive Production." *Modern Intellectual History* (2018) https://doi.org/10.1017/S1479244318000227; Singh, Prabhakar. "A Lawyer's Account of the 'Death of Sanskrit' Thesis." *Economic & Political Weekly* 52 (2017).

To Pal, the IMTFE in Tokyo was an imperialist instrument to crush anti-imperial revolts[5] and a site for imperial law making and 'authorization'.[6] A proponent of legal pluralism, Pal was deeply suspicious of this 'utopian state of order beyond conflict'.[7] Today's international community traces its origins to the imperial past of Western hegemonic states,[8] and the view of modern day international law, especially from the colony, is one of hesitation and acceptance.[9] The contemporary relevance of Pal lies in acknowledging this imperialist shadow, which is administered through institutions that promote the "common goal" and "common method" theory of international law.[10] The IMTFE and Pal's dissent thus force us to revisit some yet unresolved questions in the practices of international courts and tribunals up to this day. In this chapter, we therefore locate Pal as an 'ancestral' voice in the struggle of the third world to articulate its stance in international law through the prism of international criminal justice. Pal's dissent, written among the ruins of Empire, becomes foundational in understanding the tragedy of the 'other' in international law.

The democratic deficit that has characterized institutions of international criminal law injected into the global community since the 1990s – the International Criminal Tribunal for the former Yugoslavia (ICTY) and International Criminal Tribunal for Rwanda (ICTR), and notably, the International Criminal Court (ICC) – has not been free from 'neo-imperial' asseveration.[11] Permanent, ad hoc or hybrid, these institutions

---

[5] Lingen, Kerstin Von. *War Crimes Trials in the Wake of Decolonization and Cold War in Asia, 1945-1956: Justice in Time of Turmoil.* Springer International Publishing, 2016.

[6] Khan, Adil Hasan. "International Lawyers in the Aftermath of Disasters: Inheriting from Radhabinod Pal and Upendra Baxi." *Third World Quarterly* 37, no. 11 (2016): 2061–2079; Khan, Adil Hasan. "Inheriting a Tragic Ethos: Learning from Radhabinod Pal." *AJIL Unbound* 110 (2016): 25–30; Varadarajan, Latha. "The Trials of Imperialism: Radhabinod Pal's Dissent at the TokyoTribunal." *European Journal of International Relations* 21, no. 4 (2015): 793–815.

[7] Khan, "International Lawyers in the Aftermath of Disasters," 2066.

[8] Singh, Prabhakar. "Reading RP Anand in the Postcolony: Between Resistance and Appropriation," in Jochen von Bernstorff and Philipp Dann (eds.). *The Battle for International Law in the Decolonization Era.* Oxford University Press, 2019, pp. 297–318.

[9] Alexandrowicz, Charles H. "New and Original States: The Issue of Reversion to Sovereignty." *International Affairs (Royal Institute of International Affairs 1944-)* 45, no. 3 (1969): 465–480.

[10] Khan, "Inheriting a Tragic Ethos," 26–27; Varadarajan, "The Trials of Imperialism," 800–802.

[11] Graubart, Jonathan, and Varadarajan, Latha. "Taking Milosevic Seriously: Imperialism, Law, and the Politics of Global Justice." *International Relations* 27, no. 4 (2013):

have been marked by formal success coupled with a failure to reimagine justice and free it from the charge of foundational imperialism. Pal, a supporter of a truly collaborative[12] ICC has long cautioned us against formalizing the status quo.[13] The moorings of the alternative morality he proposed are in his formulation of an inclusive, international community through struggle and change where 'past censure and praise' is finally being displaced. "We must not be complacent or believe so readily in the inevitability of success"[14] cautions Pal against the stagist conception[15] of international law, history and the international legal community. Pal's fears may well have proven to be true.

Pal is an outsider to international criminal law, and his visceral critique of the institutionalization of this system reveals the deep roots of third-world resistance and Hindu legal philosophy that can only be fully comprehended when one engages with his work beyond the dissent.[16] Through our retelling, we hope to give form to Pal's imagination of international law – one that speaks from colony to hegemony – as a truly universal project. In doing so, we wish to understand Pal as a 'native' and an archetypal international lawyer instead of an outsider who challenged an imperial system. Our resurrection of Pal is therefore threefold – to locate him as one of the early exponents of international criminal law, to identify him as a proto-ideologue of third-world resistance to international law, and to critically engage with his legal philosophy that ably predicted the limits of institutionalized 'imperial' justice.

The second section looks at Radha Binod Pal's early years and his encounter with international law before and after the dissent. We study Pal's international legal career after the Tokyo Trials and assess his work during his fourteen years as a member of the International Law Commission. The third section locates Pal in the historical-social context of colonial India. His crucial years in undivided Bengal, the seat of many anti-colonial revolts in India, helps us better understand the motivation and formulation for his dissent. In the fourth section, we look at the

---

439–460; Bharadwaj, Atul. "International Criminal Court and the Question of Sovereignty." *Strategic Analysis* 27, no. 1 (2003): 5–20.

[12] Pal, Radhabinod. *Crimes in International Relations.* University of Calcutta, 1955, Preface.

[13] Ibid.

[14] Pal, Radhabinod. *International Law in a Changing World.* New York, 1963, pp. 92–93.

[15] Chakrabarty, Dipesh. "Postcoloniality and the Artifice of History: Who Speaks for 'Indian' Pasts?" *Representations* 37 (1992): 1–26; Spivak, Gayatri Chakravorty. *A Critique of Postcolonial Reason.* Harvard University Press, 1999.

[16] Hill, Barry. "Reason and Lovelessness: Tagore, War Crimes, and Justice Pal." *Postcolonial Studies* 18, no. 2 (2015): 145–160.

dissenting judgment, particularly, his use of law as a technique despite the absence of any formal Western training in international law. This part also tries to respond to some of the critiques of the dissent. We conclude by offering a sketch of Pal as an ancestral voice in the critique of international criminal justice and as a proto-ideologue of Third World Approaches to International Law.

9.2 Radha Binod Pal before and after the IMTFE

Radha Binod Pal has been given many identities through incomplete interpretation and subsequent co-option both in the East and the West: accidental international lawyer, sympathizer of the Japanese cause, Indian nationalist, anti-colonial, and politically motivated representative of the third world on the bench.[17] Two of these identities endure and require unpacking – the 'only international lawyer at IMTFE' and the 'reluctant nationalist'.[18] Pal has been described by Minear and Brook as the only judge on the bench of IMTFE who was trained in international law. Ashis Nandy[19] and subsequent authors have since questioned the accuracy of this pronouncement and credited this impression to Pal's exceptional ability to learn the law on the job. As a 'reluctant nationalist', Pal emerges as something of a loose cannon that shook the very foundation of the trial efforts through his scathing dissent. His appointment, primarily to facilitate an additional concurring vote from the Commonwealth of Britain,[20] showed that the British and Indian governments could not have possibly known that his would be the strongest anti-establishment voice on that bench. Through an excavation of his place of birth, formative years and lived experiences, we situate Pal and his dissent in the international legal plane.

[17] Jayasimha, Shreyas. "Victor's Justice, Crime of Silence and the Burden of Listening: Judgement of the Tokyo Tribunal 1948, Women's International War Crimes Tribunal 2000 and Beyond." *Law, Social Justice and Global Development* (2001) https://warwick.ac.uk/fac/soc/law/elj/lgd/2001_1/jayasimha/; Yasuaki, Onuma. "The Tokyo Trial: Between Law and Politics." In C. Hosoya, N. Ando, Y. Onuma and R. Minear (eds.). *The Tokyo War Crimes Trial: An International Symposium.* Kodansha International, 1986, pp. 45–52.

[18] Bose, Sugata, and Jalal, Ayesha. *Nationalism, Democracy and Development: State and Politics in India.* Oxford University Press, 1999.

[19] Nandy, Ashis. "The Other Within: The Strange Case of Radhabinod Pal's Judgment on Culpability." *New Literary History* 23, no. 1 (1992): 45–67.

[20] Documentary, www.youtube.com/watch?v=tAAck_82jVo&t=1191s.

9 RADHA BINOD PAL

Radha Binod Pal was born in January 1886 in the village of Selimpur (today in the Kushtia district of Bangladesh) in undivided, occupied British India. Nandy writes that the Pals were a poor family and belonged to a low caste; they were *kumbha-karas* (potters by vocation). Radha Binod was the only son of his parents and grew up in abject rural poverty along with his two sisters. The family was always economically unstable, and Nandy notes that their fears increased when Pal's father renounced the world and deserted his wife and young children in 1889. Pal seems to recall with ambivalence the itinerant mendicancy and confused asceticism of his *boiragi* (renunciate) father. In subsequent works he was to go on to author on Hindu law – he believes in the sanctity of the traditional Hindu family structure in which parents provide for and protect the children.

Poverty forced his mother to work as a domestic help in the home of a rich relation in an effort to sustain her children. This powerful single parenting strongly impacted Pal as a child and he moved through life with his mother as the centre of his universe and his moral compass. The intensity of the maternal influence also shaped the young Pal's world-view. He used the word *chirodukhini* (ever tragic) to capture his vision of the beleaguered, forsaken motherland. Nandy has poignantly traced this image to his early association with his own forsaken, tragic hero of a mother who soldiered on against all adversity, to provide for her children. Acutely aware of his mother's ambitions for himself,[21] Pal braved childhood adversity and emerged with a long list of competitive scholarships supplementing the reluctant patronage of strangers to put himself through school and earn a Master's degree in mathematics with distinction from Presidency College, Calcutta in 1908.[22] A second powerful woman emerged at this point, in the person of his wife Nalini Bala, who encouraged and supported Pal much as his mother had once done.[23] Pal worked for a few years before suddenly shifting gears and studying law. He earned his Master's and then his Doctorate in Law with the highest distinction from Calcutta University in 1924 and wrote his dissertation on the archaic canon of Hindu law – this subsequently became

---

[21] Ibid.; Nandy, "The Other Within," p. 60 (his mother, herself uneducated, wants her son to become like Sir Gurudas Bannerji, an eminent jurist and judge of the Calcutta High Court).

[22] Nandi, Kiruna K. "Dr. Radhabinode Pal: A Tribute." *The Modern Review* for March 1967.

[23] Chakravarty, Radha. *Novelist Tagore: Gender and Modernity in Selected Texts.* Routledge India, 2016; Inden, Ronald B. and Ralph W. Nicholas. *Kinship in Bengali Culture.* Orient Blackswan, 2005.

his now authoritative work that deals extensively with the philosophy of Hindu law and its history.[24]

From 1923 when he started teaching law at Calcutta University until 1941 when he was appointed judge at the Calcutta High Court, Pal was primarily a lawyer and scholar. This period coincided with India's gradual transition out of British colonial rule. Largely perceived as an innocuous ally of Great Britain, India became the only colony to participate in the war crimes commission for the IMTFE. When Pal began his career as a law professor in Calcutta, he was forty years old. He is described as "one of the ablest practitioners of his time, a distinguished educationist and a prolific and widely read author of legal treatises" as well as possessing "an independence of spirit and judgment that defied frowns just as firmly as it cased nothing forever."[25] Pal also served as a legal advisor to the government of British India in 1927, because of his invaluable contribution to the British Indian Income Tax Act of 1922.[26] Pal's steady past performance at the bar notwithstanding, India's legal pool contained bigger names trained in international law and this made his appointment to the tribunal a surprise and a non-event.

Despite suggestions to the contrary,[27] Pal had no formal training in international law. However, his mindset was quite international and his pronouncements were closer to the purported 'universalism' of international law. By the time he was appointed in Tokyo, Pal had published two primary works on philosophy of law and history of law,[28] and after the judgment, he incorporated the substantive parts of his dissent into two books on international relations.[29] His learning of international law on the job, infused with his own understanding of

---

[24] Pal, Radhabinod, *The Hindu Philosophy of Law in the Vedic and Post-Vedic Times Prior to the Institutes of Manu*, Biswabhandar Press, Calcutta; Pal, Radhabinod, *The History of Hindu Law in the Vedic Age and in Post-Vedic Times Down to the Institutes of Manu*, University of Calcutta, Calcutta, 1958. Milinda Banerjee approximates the dates of publication of the two books to 1927 and 1929 respectively. The University of Calcutta enlarged edition is dated 1958. See, Banerjee, "Does International Criminal Justice Require a Sovereign?" at 73. Tagore Law Lectures, Radha Binod Pal 1925 (*Law of Primogeniture with Special Reference to India, Ancient and Modern*. Oriental Press, 1923).

[25] Advocate Amal Kumar Sen, reflecting on Pal in an anecdotal publication celebrating 150 years of the Calcutta High Court.

[26] Alexandrowicz, C. H. "International Law in India." *The International and Comparative Law Quarterly* 1 no. 3 (1952): 289–292.

[27] Minear, *Victor's Justice*.

[28] Pal, Radhabinod. *The History of the Law of Primogeniture: With Special Reference to India, Ancient and Modern*. University of Calcutta, 1929.

[29] Pal, *Crimes in International Relations*; Pal, *International Law in a Changing World*.

Hindu legal philosophy, was testimony to this scholarship and intellect. On the one hand, Pal was not entirely unorthodox as an exponent of international criminal law. For example, his writing shows an openness to principles of international humanitarian and criminal law, when he quoted Lauterpacht on the relevance of individuals as subjects of international law.[30] On the other hand, Pal openly questions racism and imperialism in Tokyo at a moment that ought to have been a celebration of international law's accomplishments. He was wary of the tendency to assume a common cosmopolitan horizon in a world riddled by polarities. As Pal put it:

> I should only add that the international community has not as yet developed into "the world commonwealth" and perhaps as yet no particular group of nations can claim to be the custodian of "the common good". International life is not yet organized into a community under the rule of law. A community life has not even been agreed upon as yet. Such an agreement is essential before the so-called natural law may be allowed to function in the manner suggested. It is only when such group living is agreed upon, the conditions required for successful group life may supply some external criteria that would furnish some standard against which the rightness or otherwise of any particular decision can be measured.[31]

Scholars have privileged the judge as an individual, drawing upon both biography and intellectual history in order to chart how a particular decision was reached.[32] Those scholars who have sought to study the colonial judiciary as an institution rather than an assortment of individuals, by contrast, have argued against judicial autonomy and have portrayed tribunals as an instrument of power/authority/hegemony for dominant classes.[33] A "rule of colonial difference" was marked in the courts[34] where the everyday operation of the law in the colonial state was

---

[30] Dissent, p. 145.
[31] Dissent, p. 151.
[32] Segal, Jeffrey A. and Harold J. Spaeth. *The Supreme Court and the Attitudinal Model Revisited.* Cambridge University Press, 2002; Keith, Arthur Berriedale. *The Sovereignty of the British Dominions.* Macmillan, 1929; Alexandrowicz, Charles H. "The Juridical Expression of the Sacred Trust of Civilization." *American Journal of International Law* 65, no. 1 (1971): 149–159.
[33] Baxi, Upendra. "Taking Suffering Seriously: Social Action Litigation in the Supreme Court of India." *Third World Legal Studies* 4 (1985): 107; Bingham, Tom. *The Business of Judging: Selected Essays and Speeches: 1985–1999.* Oxford University Press, 2011.
[34] Chatterjee, Partha. *The Nation and its Fragments: Colonial and Postcolonial Histories.* Vol. 11. Princeton University Press, 1993.

"structured through the politics of race, often privileging Europeans over Indians as participants in the legal system."[35]

It is amidst these tensions that Pal's scholarly and professional identity was formed. On the one hand, Pal's training in the rigorous common law system imparted to him the discipline he demonstrated as a judge. On the other hand, it was also this system that troubled him and motivated him to fight from within. In the nineteenth century, Europeans domiciled in India had widely protested the move to permit Indian lawyers to try Europeans in cases before them.[36] However, by the twentieth century, the legal profession allowed merit to overcome race – Indian lawyers dominated the bar and several Indians were appointed to the judiciary.[37] By 1944, the majority of High Court judges in India were Indian, although there were limits to this judicial cosmopolitanism.[38] While Indian judges were allowed to rub shoulders with their British counterparts, they were often barred from entering certain premises and looked upon as second-class participants.[39] Pal was a product of this climate. It is in this environment that he learned to both conform to the system and challenge it for all that it represented and oppressed.

Pal, the 'reluctant nationalist' is equally interesting and perhaps more apposite to a discussion on the ideological sites of the intellectual history of international criminal law. After the IMTFE, Pal inhabited a milieu of silence both in Western scholarship and among the Indian political/legal diaspora. Despite his many appointments and roles (as the chairman of the ILC and three-time member, national professor of jurisprudence, etc.) one cannot help but note the forced marginalization (both within and outside) of Pal and his legacy. Pal, perhaps like the IMTFE, was for a long time deliberately

---

[35] Kolsky, Elizabeth. *Colonial Justice in British India: White Violence and the Rule of Law.* Cambridge University Press, 2010; Bailkin, Jordanna. "The Boot and the Spleen: When Was Murder Possible in British India?" *Comparative Studies in Society and History* 48 (2006): 462–493. De, Rohit. "'A Peripatetic World Court' Cosmopolitan Courts, Nationalist Judges and the Indian Appeal to the Privy Council." *Law and History Review* 32, no. 4 (2014): 821–851.

[36] Hirschman, Edwin. *"White Munity": The Ilbert Bill Crisis in India and the Genesis of the Indian National Congress.* Heritage, 1980.

[37] De, Rohit. "Emasculating the Executive: The Federal Court and Civil Liberties in Late Colonial India: 1942–1944." In Terence C. Halliday and Lucien Karpik (eds.). *Fates of Political Liberalism in the British Post-Colony: The Politics of the Legal Complex,* Cambridge University Press (2012): 59–90.

[38] De, "A Peripatetic World Court."

[39] Ibid.

ignored and left uninvestigated.[40] Pal lost international visibility not simply because of the absence of contemporary recognition, but also because of his gradual ideological rift with the newly formed Indian government. This was even though the government did not look kindly on the work of the IMTFE. While it made sense for a new sovereign state to adopt a position of moderation, the rejection of Pal's dissent also seemed to have come from a place akin to rejection of another sub-continental voice, that of the politician Subhash Chandra Bose.[41] Pal's support of armed struggle and resistance against imperialism, his admiration of Bose and Japan's historical ties with Bengal[42] are keys to decoding both his personality, and the response to his judgment. Pal's statements are in parts echoes of Bose's aggressive stance against imperialism, and it is this inheritance that Nehru rejected in his dissociation from Pal's judgment. Prime Minister Jawaharlal Nehru's confidential cable to the Governor of West Bengal on 29 November 1948, reflected his views on Pal's performance candidly:

> We are unanimously of opinion that you should not send any telegram to General MacArthur. He is mere mouthpiece of other Governments and has no discretion. Apart from this any such move on our part would associate us with Justice Pal's dissenting judgment in Tokyo trials. *In this judgment wild and sweeping statements have been made with many of which we do not agree at all, we have had to inform Governments concerned informally that we are in no way responsible for it.* Any statement sent by you might well create great difficulties for us without doing much good to anyone else.[43]

This has led many scholars to contend in retrospect that Pal's selection may have also been a bureaucratic blunder by British colonial

---

[40] Brackman, Arnold C. *The Other Nuremberg: The Untold Story of the Tokyo War Crimes Trials.* Morrow, 1987; Chang, Maria Hsia and Robert P. Barker. "Victor's Justice and Japan's Amnesia: The Tokyo War Crimes Trial Reconsidered." *East Asia* 19, no. 4 (2001): 55–84; Boister, Neil. "War Crimes Tribunals and Transitional Justice: The Tokyo Trial and the Nuremberg Legacy [Book Review]." *New Zealand Yearbook of International Law* 5 (2007): 375.

[41] Subhash Chandra Bose was a Bengali-Indian freedom-fighter and founder of the Indian National Army (INA). The INA was conceptualized by Japanese Major Iwaichi Fujiwara during Bose's escape to Japan. Bose intended for the INA to be an army that would fight alongside the Japanese against British occupied India.

[42] Bose, Sugata. "Instruments and Idioms of Colonial and National Development." *International Development and the Social Sciences* (1997): 45–63.

[43] Emphasis added. Gopal, S. (ed.). *Selected Works of Jawaharlal Nehru,* vol. 8. Jawaharlal Nehru Memorial Fund, 1989, p. 415.

authorities[44] and that Pal's appointment was an act of overstepping by the war department (subsequently chastised).[45] It was argued that Pal, with his qualifications, nationalist leanings and intellectual investment in India's independence movement could not have been the intended choice[46] of the Indian Governor General's secretariat.[47] However, subsequent research and interwar correspondence has revealed this not to be true.[48] It simply highlights how little was known about Pal at the time, and the amount of incorrect information that circulates even today.[49] Pal's legacy has often been misinterpreted by the pernicious cycles of Chinese whispers that only archival research may someday hope to lay to rest.[50]

Pal's public image underwent a metamorphosis after his return from the Tokyo Tribunal.[51] The photographs we see of him show the 'brown sahib' in Western dress and trope. But in writings by friends of the family and others who remember him, Radha Binod Pal was the quintessential 'Bengali babu' who dressed as was the style for older Bengali men – in *dhoti* and *Panjabi* with the occasional relaxation of the accompanying barefoot code to allow for Western socks and shoes.[52] Unlike Nagendra Singh and B. N. Rau,

---

[44] Ryall, Julian. "Revealed: Blunder That Allowed Dissenting Judge to Sit on Japanese War Crimes Tribunal." *South China Morning Post.* October 14, 2009, www.scmp.com/article/695342/revealed-blunder-allowed-dissenting-judge-sit-japanese-war-crimes-tribunal; See Varadarajan, "The Trials of Imperialism."

[45] Ibid.

[46] Ibid.

[47] Ibid.

[48] Nandy, "The Other Within."

[49] See Dissent.

[50] Interestingly, Netflix has created new interest in the lives of Pal and Röling by making the popular docu-drama *Tokyo Trial* which has generated wide interest in and a new surge of studies in the trials. See, Tallgren, Immi. "Watching 'Tokyo Trial'." *London Review of International Law* 5 (2017): 291–316.

[51] "Radha Binod Pal," *The Hindu*, January 11, 1967.

[52] Nandy; *dhoti* is the hand-woven, unstitched cloth used by an older generation of Bengali men as a formal dress. *Panjabi* is a long upper garment, stitched from natural fabrics that accompanied this traditional dress. A Bengali "*babu*" was the colonial co-option of "*babu-dom*" or the manners and dress of British Indian bureaucracy adopted by the general population in order to appear genteel. Just as Gandhi, originally a British trained barrister, exclusively appearing in photographs from his early days in a Western three-piece suit and trousers, returned to the Indian independence movement and shunned all forms of Western influence, adopting the humble folded and tucked version of the *dhoti* and a handwoven shawl as his iconic dress of later years, so too did many Indians educated abroad or working in high-profile public positions deliberately opt exclusively for Indian dress as a symbol of their Indianness and in rejection of the inequitable trade practices of the British in exporting cloth from India and dumping British garments back in Indian markets. The public burning of British-made goods was a significant episode in the Swadeshi movement which came towards the end of the independence struggle and was characterized by the call to produce in

contemporary Indians who were actively engaged in international law, Pal was also not an upper-caste Hindu.[53] He stayed rooted in his humble beginnings, despite his professional ascent. In some ways, public opinion on Pal was born only in the context of the trial and his dissent – and on this, Calcutta was divided. On the one hand were those who admired Pal because they over-simplified his judgment and thought him a sympathizer of Japan[54] and by extension, a supporter of Subhash Chandra Bose and his fiery Indian National Army.[55] And then there were others who were on the fence because they had serious misgivings about fascism albeit in the Japanese form during the interwar years. In fact, it is questionable whether Pal himself bought into the Japanese narrative, aside from expressing his vague admiration for the spirit of nation that dared to rival the ambitions of the colonial West.[56]

Pal's time at the IMTFE is marked by a looming sense of ostracization and silence. The publication of the dissent was banned in Japan, and the ban was not lifted till the departure of McArthur and the American forces.[57] Despite the impact of his critique, the judgment served to alienate the newly independent government of India.[58] Pal was forced

India. It is no surprise that the direct political event that set off the Swadeshi movement was the Partition of Bengal by Curzon that we discuss later in this chapter.

[53] Perhaps this is of questionable value, but it is surely interesting that these two eminent and successful international lawyers (both educated at Cambridge) who were Pal's contemporaries in many ways were born into privilege. Rau was born in a wealthy family of intellectuals and had ample opportunity to study at the best universities; Singh was born in the royal family of Dungarpurkar and into enviable fortune and privilege.

[54] Varma, Lalima. "Japan's Policy Towards South Asia: Shifting Paradigms." International Symposium paper 2009, available at https://nichibun.repo.nii.ac.jp/?action=repository_action_common_download&item_id=1249&item_no=1&attribute_id=20&file_no=1;
Borah, Rupakjyoti. "Japan and India: Natural but Wary Allies." *New Zealand International Review* 36, no. 4 (2011): 23; Panda, Rajaram. "India-Japan Relations: Dawn of a New Relationship?" *Indian Foreign Affairs Journal* 9, no. 2 (2014): 182.

[55] Bose, "Instruments and Idioms of Colonial and National Development"; Subhash Chandra Bose's war against the British was celebrated in Bengal by those who were disillusioned with Gandhi's vision of the path to Indian independence and his moderation of the Indian National Congress.

[56] Pal is almost scheduled to lead this committee looking into Netaji Subhas Chandra Bose's (NSB)'s death. Pal discussed it publicly more than once. Writing to Japan-based freedom fighter A. M. Nair in 1953, he had rooted for a proper inquiry. See Dhar, Anuj. "Why 1955 Japanese Report about Netaji's Death Is Bogus." DailyO – Opinion News & Analysis on Latest Breaking News India. September 5, 2016. www.dailyo.in/politics/netaji-files-subhas-chandra-bose-death-russia-japan-nehru-ashis-ray-congress/story/1/12775.html.

[57] Pal, *The Hindu Philosophy of Law in the Vedic and Post-Vedic Times*; *The History of Hindu Law in the Vedic Age*.

[58] Nehru's cable in November 1948 to Kailash Nath Katju, the Governor of West Bengal stating that Pal's sweeping comments in the dissent may not be seen as the Government of

to return to Bengal and publish his own copy of the dissent as the first printed version. Pal's time at the IMTFE coincides with the transition of colonized India into an independent sovereign state (1946–1948) and his own professional trajectory and politics mirror the anti-colonial movement itself. The eclipsing of Pal is perhaps comparable to Zafrullah Khan's time at the ICJ.[59] As a contemporary of Khan, a Pakistani judge (formerly from undivided India) who presided over the South West Africa Cases in the ICJ,[60] Pal was also subjected to marginalization and racism at the IMTFE.[61] It is relevant to note that despite Pal's dissent, in 1954 he was backed by Britain as India's nomination to the ICJ. What is interesting, however, is that he lost this election to none other than Zafrullah Khan, Britain's original nominee who was soon becoming another anti-colonial voice to reckon with in the international political/legal domain. This nomination can perhaps be explained by Gerald Fitzmaurice's (senior legal advisor to Great Britain) confidential cable to the United Kingdom delegation in the UN where he says that Dr Pal:

> [h]as been a colleague of Professor Lauterpacht's on the International Law Commission and, except perhaps on directly colonial issues, might well be influenced by him or by some of the other better Judges, such as Judges Basdevant of France, Klaestad of Norway and Read of Canada. [...] If there is to be an indifferent Judge on the Court, it is perhaps better, within limits, to have someone who will at least pay some regard to what his betters may think, than someone who will obstinately adhere to his own view in all circumstances.[62]

India' official position on all issues; Gopal, S. (ed.), Selected Works of Jawaharlal Nehru, vol. 8, Jawaharlal Nehru Memorial Fund, Teen Murti House, New Delhi, 1989, p. 415. Nehru's views on the Pal judgment have been discussed by A. G. Noorani, "The Yasukuni 'Hero'," in *Frontline*, 2007, p. 24.

[59] Kattan, Victor. "Decolonizing the International Court of Justice: The Experience of Judge Sir Muhammad Zafrulla Khan in the South West Africa Cases." *Asian Journal of International Law* 5 no. 2 (2015): 310–355; Murti, B. S. "India's Complaint to the World Court on Judge Zafrulla Khan's Political Speeches on Kashmir." *Indian Journal of International Law* 8 (1968): 547.

[60] Ibid.

[61] Khan was forced to withdraw from the second phase of the South West Africa cases by Sir Percy Spender in order to ensure that his vote does not alter the judgment. Kattan, "Decolonizing the International Court of Justice," 34–38; Similarly, open displeasure was expressed against Pal by Lord Patrick, the British judge from the IMFTE, particularly after Pal expressed his intention to dissent. Lord Patrick was adamant that Pal be sent back to India and wrote to authorities back home to facilitate this process.

[62] See the confidential telegram sent from the Foreign Office in London to the United Kingdom Delegation to the United Nations in New York dated 19 November 1954 signed

This assessment is surprising given Pal's history less than a decade before. Pal was very vocal at the IMTFE but was considered less of an anti-colonial concern by the British during the election for the ICJ.[63] This is probably because unlike Khan (who dabbled in politics at the United Nations General Assembly (UNGA) and wielded tremendous influence there, for example on the vote on partition of Palestine)[64] Pal remained a quintessential judge all his life. His form of resistance was structured and expressed within the framework of judicial critique and pronouncements. This limited his sphere of influence but also made him and his critique a prime, unadulterated intellectual source of international law-making within the framework while clearly articulating the imperial politics of international law itself.

Pal remained an active legal participant in international law in the 1950s and 1960s as well. He consolidated his dissent into a complete volume of work known as *Crimes in International Relations*[65] to continue advocating for a truly universal common society in order to establish criminality by consensus. Pal remained suspicious of any efforts to treat international criminal justice as an institutionalized project. In 1954, he abstained from voting on a draft code of international criminal law (Draft Code of Offences against the Peace and Security of Mankind), which was debated at the sixth session of the United Nations International Law Commission, held in Paris. His argument for the abstention, as outlined in that session, was that given the nature of international relations at that period, a mere code of international criminal law would be unable to bring about real justice. It might indeed have the opposite effect of giving dominant powers an excuse to commit injustices.

His experience at the IMTFE was a constant reminder of the limits and horrors of institutionalized justice, and in some ways, as an outsider to international law, he had the foresight to demand a more comprehensive transformation in international relations than the needs of the hour suggested. Pal's prescient advice was that "in the name of building for justice we must not unwittingly build a suffocating structure for injustice."[66] His suspicion was grounded in his anxieties about the re-imposition of colonial

---

by Kelvin White on behalf of P. E. Ramsbotham in "Election of the Successor to the Late Sir Benegal Rau as Judge at the ICJ," 14 December 1954, DO 35/7123. TNA.

[63] Gopal, *Selected Works of Jawaharlal Nehru*, pp. 7–9.

[64] Kattan, "Decolonizing the International Court of Justice," 59.

[65] Graubart and Varadarajan, "Taking Milosevic Seriously"; Pal, *Crimes in International Relations*.

[66] Graubart and Varadarajan, "Taking Milosevic Seriously"; Pal, *Crimes in International Relations*, pp. iii–ix (quotes from pp. viii and ix).

structures through seemingly neutral instruments of law. Pal's last writings in the 1960s revisited issues of global justice – a concern that haunted him throughout his career at and beyond the IMTFE. Noteworthy was a United Nations Law Commission Report from 1962, which Pal authored in his capacity as Observer for the Commission at the fifth session of the Asian-African Legal Consultative Committee held in Rangoon, Burma. This report is perhaps one of Pal's final meditations on the path to global justice in a deeply unequal world. For Pal, global justice could only be attained when a truly inclusive, diverse and hierarchy free global community was able to come together to decide upon notions of justice and crimes. He stated, "It would emerge through tension and conversation between normative-transcendental ideals and ground-level struggles against oppression, linking the universalism of justice with the concreteness of ever-changing historical realities."[67]

After his work at the ILC, he returned to practice in Calcutta and was greeted by strained financial circumstances on account of his prolonged absence, dependents and incumbents.[68] For the most part, he was largely ignored by the Indian government and was appointed the National Professor of Jurisprudence shortly before his death. In a conversation with Karuna Nandi around the time of this appointment, Pal discussed his desire to work on the concept of law as the foundation for a democratic society. He was hoping to present rule of law (based on fundamental ethics of social living and not as an administrative tool) as the bedrock of a democratic polity in its appropriate historical, social and ethical context. This may very well have been his intellectual *magnum opus*. Pal's quest for global justice is perhaps a focused culmination of his years of excavating Hindu legal philosophy, his time at the IMTFE and his synergy with an early sense of pan-Asianism. Somewhere along his journey, Pal started embodying and being subsumed within the very movements he mirrored. In his last twenty years in independent India, his services to this new sovereign nation were gradually overshadowed by other events.[69] Both in India and Japan, Pal's judgment and Pal were interpreted, co-opted and used/misused in many ways.

[67] Report on the Fifth Session of the Asian–African Legal Consultative Committee (Rangoon, January 1962) by Mr Radhabinod Pal, Observer for the Commission, pp. 153–154.

[68] He needed to support thirteen children. See family tree created by Dr Modhumita Roy (nee Pal), granddaughter of Justice Radhabinod Pal – "Radhabinod Pal." *Wikipedia*, 2018, https://en.wikipedia.org/wiki/Radhabinod_Pal. Accessed 8 December 2018.

[69] Nandy, "The Other Within," at 46.

Even though Pal is also to be understood by how others understood his work, not all understood him as he was. Röling, for example, one of Pal's fellow judge at the IMTFE, surmised that Pal's dissent was motivated by a pan-Asian sentiment. To him, "it was a more or less belated reaction against the [Western] aggressive wars by which the [Western] colonial system was established centuries ago ... I think Pal's judgment is understandable if we look at the past, but not when we look at the future."[70] This stance, however, suggests that Röling failed to perceive how deep the roots of imperialism went for Pal (and what he represented) and how his apprehensions were not limited to the past alone. It is, in fact, only by grasping his larger Bengali/Indian anti-colonial discourses that one can step past the limits of his dissentient identity and see his overarching concern about the "ineradicable relation between nation-state sovereignty, racist-nationalist imperialism and political idolatry"[71] that persisted beyond the colonial moment.

9.3 History, Anger and Colonialism

The leaves of a tree delight us more than the roots.[72]

That history alone is the true context to fully understand political and social events is an interpretation of Tolstoy's view of history. To him, history does not reveal causes; it presents only a "blank succession of unexplained events."[73] The idea that we are part of a larger scheme of things than we can comprehend is the driving force behind ascribing to the identities of women and men, the burden of greatness that is the cost of hindsight – a hasty attempt to fill in the blanks with figures and dates that may explain the inexplicable. In rejecting the opposing view that history is made by real people of flesh and blood, who through their lived experiences, go on to influence the course of events that we then call

---

[70] Hans Röling, Question-and-Answer Period, International Symposium 2009, available at https://nichibun.repo.nii.ac.jp/?action=repository_action_common_download&item_id=1249&item_no=1&attribute_id=20&file_no=1, at 152–53.

[71] Tagore, Rabindranath. *Nationalism*. Book Club of California, 1917, and in general his Bengali and English writings, especially from the 1910s onwards; Ghose, Aurobindo. "The Ideal of Human Unity," in *The Complete Works of Sri Aurobindo*, vol. 25, Sri Aurobindo Ashram Publication Department, 1997, pp. 293–299, 372–382, 443–450.

[72] Tolstoy, Leo N. *Complete Works*. Moscow/Leningrad, 1928–1964, vol. 1, p. 222 (18–26 March 1847).

[73] Berlin, Isaiah. *The Hedgehog and the Fox: An Essay on Tolstoy's View of History*. Princeton University Press, 2013.

history is to attribute to these accidental heroes a symbolism of being more than they perhaps knew they were to be.[74]

The deliberation required to be a hero and to occupy a historically significant position in the course of events was not known to Radha Binod Pal.[75] His "heroism" was closer to the Tolstoyan view of history – his early education in British India and his intellectual mooring in the tradition of non-violent ideological resistance[76] while serving in his official capacity, speak to the tragedy of his times. Pal, like many of his contemporaries[77] embodied, without revealing his hand prior to his appointment as judge at IMTFE, the deep sense of loss and bewilderment that characterized the colonial encounter and the bitterness and anger of post-colonial India – of fatigue and disenchantment with the experience of Empire. The essence of his heroism was an anti-heroic stance.[78]

Bengal, the place of Pal's birth, is also the seat of anti-colonial, anti-imperial self-determination in India[79] where the Swadeshi movement rears its powerful head for the first time in 1900s.[80] When Pal was nineteen years old and studying mathematics in college, a political event took place in Bengal that moved him to deeply interrogate the motives of the British, and awakened his political understanding about the harsh realities of colonialism. This was the Partition of Bengal in 1905

---

[74] Bronowski, Jacob. *The Ascent of Man.* Random House, 2011 ("history is not events, it is people").

[75] Brook, Timothy. "The Tokyo Judgment and the Rape of Nanking." *The Journal of Asian Studies* 60, no. 3 (2001): 673–700; Wakabayashi, Bob Tadashi, ed. *The Nanking Atrocity, 1937–1938: Complicating the Picture.* Berghahn Books, 2017 ("Nothing would be achieved by seeking any premature escape from the guilt of history," p. 49).

[76] *The Collected Works of Mahatma Gandhi* (Electronic Book), New Delhi, Publications Division Government of India, 1999, 98 volumes., vol. 5, pp. 216–218; Pyarelal, *The Last Phase.* Navajivan Press, 1956, vol. 1, pp. 112–114 ("Let the allies set up their trial of war crimes," Gandhi had pronounced, "they could achieve nothing." "Those who have their hands dyed deep in blood cannot build a non-violent order for the world," Gandhi wrote. "If they, the victors, are so arrogant as to think they can have lasting peace while the exploitation of the colored and the so called backward races goes on, they are living in a fool's paradise."); Sinha, Gayatri. "The Afterlives of Images: The Contested Legacies of Gandhi in Art and Popular Culture." *South Asian Studies* 29 no. 1 (2013): 111–129.

[77] Rabindranath Tagore, Rash Behari Bose, Surendranath Banerjee, Surya Sen, Barindra Kumar Ghosh, Saratchandra Chattopadhyay. See Hill, "Reason and Lovelessness." See also Sen, Amartya. "Tagore and His India." *New York Review of Books.* June 26, 1997, p. 44; Hotta, Eri. "Rash Behari Bose and His Japanese Supporters: An Insight into Anti-Colonial Nationalism and Pan-Asianism." *Interventions* 8, no. 1 (2006): 116–132.

[78] Campbell, Joseph. *The Hero with a Thousand Faces.* Vol. 17. New World Library, 2008.

[79] Banerjee, "Does International Criminal Justice Require a Sovereign?"

[80] Bengal's awakening and the roots of Pal's anti-colonialism through Tagore, Bose etc., see Banerjee, "Does International Criminal Justice Require a Sovereign?"

by Lord Curzon, the British Viceroy of India (1899–1905). The event reverberated through India and started a firestorm of political protests. Bengal was partitioned because the British saw "a great political advantage in severing the eastern districts, which [were] deemed to be 'a hotbed of the purely Bengali movement, unfriendly if not seditious in character.' It was thought that partition would also weaken the tyrannical character of the press and the leaders of Calcutta." The ostensible reason given to Indians by Lord Curzon was that partition was effected to give Bengalis a much better administration and to collect revenue. However, historical studies of the era by scholars show that the main purpose for partition was to split up and thereby weaken a solid body of opponents to British rule. Opposition to the partition of Bengal was formidable and organized on a vast scale, which sent the British reeling and ultimately trying to undo their folly, but the damage was done and lasting.[81]

In 1945–1946, Delhi saw the Red Fort trials of the Indian National Army (INA). Members of the INA were tried for high treason against the British Empire in response to an active Asian effort to join resistance forces across India, Burma and Malaya which Japan had supported.[82] Nowhere in India was the effect felt as strongly as it was in Calcutta – the eastern front where the fulcrum of the intellectual nationalist movement traces its origins to. Varadarajan[83] speculates that Bengal's affiliation with the INA, its support of armed struggle, alliance with axis powers and powerful anti-colonial history are keys to decoding both Pal and his judgment. Pal's critics are virulent, but anti-colonial and anti-imperial isn't synonymous with uncritical sympathy for the defendants, and Pal's dissent strongly condemned the Japanese mirroring the imperial inheritance as well. Pal was arguably just another product of these times – his thinking and his personal politics could not have escaped the scarring influence of the violent and defensive end of colonial rule and impoverished, post-colonial India, struggling to realize her sovereignty after 400 years of being denied a voice.

Pal was alleged to be an Asian nationalist and as such not immune to being impressed by growing Japanese might.[84] Sumit Sarkar, a historian,

---

[81] Pinto, Vivek. "Justice Radhabinod Pal and the Tokyo War Crimes Tribunal: A Political Retrospective of His Historic Dissent." *International Christian University Publications, 3-A, Asian Cultural Studies* 35 (2009): 179–196.

[82] Sellars, Kirsten. "Meanings of Treason in a Colonial Context: Indian Challenges to the Charges of 'Waging War against the King' and 'Crimes against Peace'." *Leiden Journal of International Law* 30, no. 4 (2017): 825–845.

[83] Varadarajan, "The Trials of Imperialism."

[84] Khan, "International Lawyers in the Aftermath of Disasters."

writes that the Japanese victory "was ecstatically hailed by the Bengal press, even children were given nicknames like Togo [Heihachiro, a Fleet Admiral in the Imperial Japanese Navy] or Nogi [Count Maresuke, a prominent figure in the Russo Japanese War] after Japanese military leaders."[85] Here may lie the early origins of Pal's Pan-Asian ideology.[86] The view in Asia was often one marked by gratitude to and suspicion of imperialist Japan at the same time. "It is true Russia's defeat was welcomed by the other Asian peoples," O'Dwyer says. "Even Gandhi was moved. It showed they were not destined to be forever under Western domination. But India's admiration for Japan may be also due to the fact that they didn't experience Japanese occupation."[87] For Pal, by contrast "the return of the just war as the basis of American ideology led to two pernicious events: the bombing and the trials were two branches from the same ideological stalk, two expressions of the same worldview."[88] An anti-colonial, whether in *dhoti* or Western dress, is not necessarily an ultra-nationalist one – we must be cautious before ascribing to Pal such political identities.

Pal, an absolute pacifist, was in that respect true to his Hindu, Vaishnavite abhorrence for violence in all forms. He was thoroughly repelled by both Japanese and American violence in the Pacific theatre.[89] He condemned the Japanese occupation of Manchuria and expressed his disgust with the Japanese construct of colonial "Manchukuo." Pal wrote that the Japanese atrocities committed in China, South and Southeast Asia imitated Western colonial habits and were a tragic erosion of Eastern sensibilities. Pal also strongly condemned the philosophy behind the movement of the Japanese Imperial Army in the Pacific theatre. The horror and violence of the Bataan Death March of April 1942 stand out in Pal's dissent. So too, in commenting on the conduct of the Japanese Army in the Nanking massacre, did Pal use the strongest of terms insisting that "The devilish and fiendish character of the atrocities cannot be denied." More controversially for his colleagues at the tribunal, Pal also castigated the use of the atomic bomb, comparing it to the atrocities committed by the Nazis. Echoing the principle of

---

[85] Sarkar, Sumit. *Modern India 1885–1947.* Springer, 1989, p. 109.

[86] Pinto, Vivek. "Justice Radhabinod Pal and the Tokyo War Crimes Tribunal," 188.

[87] Simone, Gianni. "A Trip around the Yushukan, Japan's Font of Discord." *Japan Times,* 28 July 2014.

[88] Kopelman, "Ideology and International Law," at 409.

[89] Pal, Radha Binod, "Renunciation of Force in Inter-State Relations." *India Quarterly* 16, no. 4 (1960): 349–357.

distinction from the Geneva Conventions, Pal wrote in eerie similarity to the ICJ's Nuclear Weapons Advisory Opinion 1996 half a century later, when he noted that the indiscriminate destruction of lives and property was "still" illegitimate in warfare.[90] He compared the United States' decision to use the atomic bomb as the only "near approach" to the directives by the German Emperor during the World War I and the Nazi leaders of World War II.

9.4 The Dissent: Legal Philosophy and Contributions to International Criminal Law

The last two decades have seen a gradual reinvigoration in scholarship on the IMTFE.[91] However, it is worth questioning this belated excavation – why did the IMTFE and its jurisprudence remain ignored, despite the fanfare for its inauguration, heralding it as one of the "greatest trials in history"?[92] Could one of the reasons possibly be Pal's scathing dissent?

Unlike Nuremberg, the IMTFE did not exhibit any manner of consensus about process, goal and outcome.[93] It was marked by tension and dissonance, and this very dissent and absence of consensus was noted as a failure of the brand of criminal justice that Nuremberg wished to uphold.[94] Subsequent readings have, however, relocated Pal and his dissent as one of the most important critiques of the criminal justice system – one that was both ahead of its time as well as transcending the context within which it was produced. Timothy Brook, accentuates the impact of Pal's judgment on international criminal jurisprudence, writing,

---

[90] See, Stephens, Dale. "Human Rights and Armed Conflict: The Advisory Opinion of the International Court of Justice in the Nuclear Weapons Case." *Yale Human Rights and Development Law Journal* 4 (2001): 1. See also, Anghie, Antony. *Imperialism, Sovereignty and the Making of International Law.* Vol. 37. Cambridge University Press, 2007.

[91] See, generally, Boister and Cryer, *The Tokyo International Military Tribunal*; Sellars, *"Crimes against Peace"*; Kopelman, "Ideology and International Law"; McCormack and Simpson, *Beyond Victor's Justice?*

[92] Varadarajan, "The Trials of Imperialism"; see generally Anghie, *Imperialism, Sovereignty and the Making of International Law.*

[93] The IMTFE judgment comprises of three dissents and the bench had witnessed two significant change in its composition since its inception, including the belated addition of three judges post the commencement of the trial.

[94] Brackman, *The Other Nuremberg*; Boister and Cryer, *The Tokyo International Military Tribunal.*

> In the course of revisiting the Tokyo Judgment, I [Brook] have found my most perceptive guide to be Radhabinod Pal. Pal's was the most devastating [judgment] in rejecting the core charge at Tokyo, that Japan had waged an aggressive and therefore illegal war, [...] Pal's dissent illustrates that the fundamental problem with the Tokyo trial was America's attempt to make a moral and legal virtue out of a political necessity.[95]

A two-fold engagement with the dissent and its legal philosophy will perhaps allow us to better acquaint ourselves with the intellectual underpinnings of Pal's postulates and verdicts both within and outside the tribunal. Pal critiqued the political context in which institutionalized justice has emerged post Nuremberg. He notes that early imperialism took the form of conflict-laden acquisition of colony[96] but the real value of his dissent lies in elucidating how none of the ostensibly new features of the post–World War II era shed the shackles of imperialism.[97] It makes us reflect on the dominant narrative of progressive change in global politics, as embodied in international legal institutions.[98] Thus, Pal's omission may not be an oversight and instead betrays a desire to gloss over what, more than half a century later, remains one of the most sizzling critiques of the institutional and political foundations of international criminal justice and international law itself.

9.4.1 Revisiting the Dissent

The IMFTE was marked by the dominating presence of the United States of America, ably supported by the British Commonwealth.[99] Not only was the court convened by General Douglas MacArthur, the Supreme Commander for the Allied Powers, but he also ensured that the legal team on either side was dominated with American presence. The decision to not indict the Japanese Emperor Hirohito to ensure that Japan retains a nominal figurehead was also openly insisted on by the General. Reeking of American paternalism, the trial was almost an afterthought reluctantly agreed on so that it sat easy on the American conscience.[100]

---

[95] Timothy Brook, "The Tokyo Judgment and the Rape of Nanking." *The Journal of Asian Studies* 60 no. 3 (2001), 677; Kopelman, "Ideology and International Law."

[96] Dissent, 135; Varadarajan, "The Trials of Imperialism."

[97] Ibid.

[98] Varadarajan, "The Trials of Imperialism," at 795.

[99] Ibid.; Yuki Takatori, "America's' War Crimes Trial? Commonwealth Leadership at the International Military Tribunal for the Far East." *Journal of Imperial and Commonwealth History* 35 no. 4 (1946–48), 549–568.

[100] Nandy, "Justice Radhabinod Pal and India–Japan Relationship."

Jackson, as Chief of Council for the United States wrote to Truman – "we could execute or otherwise punish them without a hearing. But indiscriminate execution or punishments without definite findings of guilt fairly arrived at would violate pledges repeatedly given and would not sit easily on the American conscience or be remembered by our children with pride."[101] In his dissent, Pal responded to this communiqué with characteristic outrage, stating

> it is indeed surprising that no lesser a person than Mr. Justice Jackson in his considered report to a no lesser authority than the President of United States could insert these lines in the 20th century. On what authority, one feels inclined to ask, could a victor execute enemy prisoners, because they were all prisoners ... the war criminals, without a hearing. I do not think that during the recent centuries any victor has enjoyed any such right as is declared by Mr. Justice Jackson in his report.[102]

Nothing sets the tone and texture of Pal's dissent better than this response to Jackson's conduct and it is from here one marks Pal's characteristic assertion of the trial as victor's justice and complete rejection of its legality and legitimacy.

The structure of Pal's dissent is intriguing. He questions the legality of the court as well as its pronouncements using the same legal grammar. The force of his argument lies in categorizing the tribunal as nothing but victor's justice, the trial having been clouded by the predisposition towards a guilty verdict. In his words, while a victor *"can dispense to the vanquished everything from mercy to vindictiveness ... the one thing [they] cannot give the vanquished is justice."*[103] Pal premised his argument on the visible exclusion of the bombing of Hiroshima and Nagasaki from the indictments,[104] the disregard of the colonial trajectory and use of expansive force historically, the composition of the tribunal and absence of neutrality.[105] For Pal, the act that came closest to the Nazi regime's barbarity was not Japan's expansion but, in fact, the bombing of Hiroshima and Nagasaki by the USA. The absence of any indictment to that effect was a resounding failure of the tribunal and its purpose. In his words, *"It would be sufficient for my present purpose to say that if any discriminate destruction of civilian life and property is still illegitimate in warfare, then, in the Pacific war, this decision to use the atom bomb is the*

---

[101] Minear, *Victors' Justice*; Nandy, "Justice Radhabinod Pal and India–Japan Relationship."
[102] Dissent; Nandy, "Justice Radhabinod Pal and India–Japan Relationship."
[103] Dissent, p. 18, paras 1–5.
[104] Dissent, p. 66.
[105] Dissent, p. 591.

only near approach to the directives of the German Emperor during the first world war and of the Nazi leaders during the Second World war. Nothing like this could be traced to the credit of the present accused."[106]

Having rejected the legality of the tribunal itself and advocated for the acquittal of all those indicted on that basis, he then went on to pronounce on the contents of the indictment and their validity and applicability. Here too, Pal used the inconsistency of the charges to question the premise of the tribunal and its absences. One of his biggest concerns regarding the framing of charges was around the retroactive application of law and creation of criminality through acts that were hitherto legally permissible. He questioned the notion of crimes against peace and the strategic criminalization of waging aggressive war.[107] As far as Pal was concerned, all Japanese atrocities should come under class B and C as war crimes and crimes against humanity, rather than class A crimes, which dealt with crimes against peace. These were sufficient to establish criminality in the given context. On that score, his position was clear – Japan did stand in violation of existing laws. But the culpability of those indicted should only be tested against laws that are applicable. Attempting to introduce notions such as illegality of aggressive war retroactively only served to highlight the colonial double standards of the victors and their selective politics. Waging aggressive war, argued Pal, had been understood to be the right of the sovereign state, and this practice derived a sense of legitimacy from colonial expansion itself. To hold Japan to differential standards did nothing but unearth the dubious discriminatory practices of the allies.[108]

In his understanding of the Japanese war of aggression, Pal repeatedly insists on the relevance of historical contexts and classifying Japanese acts of expansion as inspired by, enabled by and a product of two centuries of the Western colonial project.[109] However, his characterization of Japan's war as a war of self-defence is a strange departure from his otherwise precise deployment of legal analysis. Pal is correct in enunciating that the traditional use of the right of self-defense allows a state to assert it against its estimation of a potential threat. However, it seems a bit of a stretch to extend it to the threat emanating from an ideology, in this case communism, in order to construct Japan's expansionist war as a claim of self-

---

[106] Dissent, p. 621, para. 1, emphasis added.

[107] The right to wage aggressive war is not prohibited in 1937 and even the subsequent enactment of the Paris pact has not acquired binding legality under international law at the time of this trial.

[108] Dissent, p. 107.

[109] Dissent, pp. 107–109.

defence.[110] This highlights Pal's own deep-rooted suspicion of communist practices and he seems to almost justify Japan's expansionism as a necessity to survive communist overtures.[111] Despite its strong context, Pal's justification of Japan's aggressive war from 1946 sometimes almost reads like a *tu quoque* argument. He reprimands the allies for their own violent, colonial past in targeting Japan's war of self-defence.[112] While the censure stands on its own merits, it cannot legally preclude a condemnation of similar conduct, even if it is by the former colonies themselves. Where Pal is most resonant in this is perhaps at his larger observation on the international community as a work in progress

> I believe no one will seriously contend that domination of one nation by another became a crime in international life ... it must be held that the object itself was not yet illegal or criminal in international life. In any other view, the entire international community would be a community of criminal races. At least many of the powerful nations are living this sort of life and if these acts are criminal then the entire international community is living that criminal life, some actually committing the crime and others becoming accessories after the fact in these crimes.[113]

Another substantive concern Pal has with the tribunal is its appalling standard of evidence. The tribunal had set aside issues like rules of evidence, allowing for second- and even third-hand testimony that could not be corroborated.[114] Pal argued that there was simply not enough substance to establish the charges against the defendants. The particular individuals who were being tried could hardly be accused of committing the "crimes against peace" with which they were charged and the most conclusive charge that could be framed against them was their inability or failure to prevent certain atrocities from being

[110] Dissent, p. 118, para. 2.

[111] Dissent, p. 307, para. 2; Pal on communism,

> We might have to take into our consideration THE WORLD TERROR of these factors, the growth of Communism in China, its connection with the Soviet Russia and its probable effect on Japanese interest in China. We might have to consider whether the circumstances would indicate the bona fides of the measures taken by Japan to forestall the danger, if any, involved in such developments. The so-called threat of Communism being a new development in international life and in lives of the states, the question would require a very serious and careful consideration ...

[112] Boister and Cryer, *The Tokyo International Military Tribunal*; Sellars, *"Crimes against Peace."*

[113] Dissent, p. 107, para 2.

[114] Sellars, *"Crimes against Peace"*; Boister and Cryer, *The Tokyo International Military Tribunal*; Nakajima, "Justice Pal (India)"; Dissent, p. 661.

committed.[115] This was not a recognized form of criminality and in the absence of evidence to the contrary (and this despite questioning the standard of evidence employed itself) the only logical outcome was a declaration of innocence.

Maybe it is not going too far to think of the judgment as a secular *Upanishad*, a wild sutra for the anxious, nuclear age, and one written by the 'core of his secret self',[116] to use Nandy's phrase. Pal was always holding to the belief that because we are part and parcel of each other, 'culpability is seldom entirely divisible'.[117] Law, for Pal, was a combination of legal principles and a social order. He marked Vedic law as the advent of law itself.[118] And in some ways, Pal himself appears to be a strange link between modern international law and ancient India's doctrinal jurisprudence. Perhaps a closer look at his legal philosophy will help locate Pal in a broader schema of jurisprudence.

9.4.2 Pal's Legal Philosophy and Reasoning

The hallmark of Pal's dissent is his misgiving about uniform and universal international law.[119] Pal was deeply suspicious of "universal" international law in a deeply unequal society. His narrative was one in which there could be no version of "shared norms" in the absence of a truly homogenous community.[120] He critiqued the political context in which institutionalized justice had emerged post Nuremberg and may have simultaneously believed in a system which would be truly inclusive and equal.[121] However, he understood this path to be uncertain and fraught with struggle. His anti-colonial dispositions meant that he was sensitive to early imperialism and its investment in colonial acquisition.[122] Pal's condemnation of imperial and legal violence[123] finds favour in the Buddhist Dhammapada position which virtually

---

[115] Dissent, p. 523.

[116] Nandy, "Justice Radhabinod Pal and India–Japan Relationship," at 60.

[117] Ibid., pp. 58–59.

[118] Pal, *The Hindu Philosophy of Law in the Vedic and Post-Vedic Times*, at Preface.

[119] Khan, "International Lawyers in the Aftermath of Disasters"; Varadarajan, "The Trials of Imperialism," at 798–802.

[120] Ibid., p. 27.

[121] A position not very dissimilar from TWAIL I scholars such as R. P. Anand but predating him by several decades.

[122] Varadarajan, "The Trials of Imperialism."

[123] Dissent.

sees law as a substitute of violence.[124] This is possibly why, for Pal, the imperialist nature of the tribunal was in itself a manifestation of violence, leading to its outright rejection by him. Most of Pal's understanding of justice is rooted in Hindu Vedic philosophy, however, in rejecting such violence, he is seen moving away from Hinduism, identifying Buddhism as the true egalitarian principle. This rejection of violence is distinct from Gandhi's use of *ahimsa* as a political tool[125] because for Pal, essentialization of violence can be necessary to achieve rule of law and an equal society, and this marks a good segue to Pal's views on just war and sovereignty.

The interpretation of Pal's legal philosophy has often been limited by temporal and geographical thresholds. Those who study Pal through the IMTFE (predominantly Western scholars) have positioned him along the positivist graph, etching out his quasi-naturalist leanings while acknowledging that Pal inhabited a complex politico-legal plane.[126] But Pal remains a study in progress unless one goes beyond the dissent, into his scholarship, and the theological and moral terrains it occupies. Nandy, the first to seek to give Pal his Bengali-Hindu roots back, makes him less abstruse and no longer a strict constructionist who was fixated on exonerating the Japanese of all charges but those of war crimes through the illegality of retroactive application of law. This bequeathal helps us go beyond such limited constructs and helps us locate his conception of culpability in Hindu legal philosophy.[127] What is often perceived as an idiosyncratic betrayal of Pal's positivist leanings[128] and manifestations of nationalist rhetoric and radicalism in the dissent[129] can be better understood as a form of naturalism that is not rooted in the Western, monotheistic[130] legal order.

For Pal, the legal order flows from social order, and, at the same time, is governed by a sense of cosmic reason.[131] Law in ancient India goes beyond the Hobbesian, Austinian notions of social order and contract and is a form of 'divine reason' that derives sanction from a moral-

---

[124] *The History of Hindu Law in the Vedic Age and in Post-Vedic Times*, p. 335.

[125] Gandhi, *Collected Works*, vol. 5, pp. 216–218; Pyarelal, *The Last Phase*, pp. 112–114.

[126] Koppelman, "Ideology and International Law"; Boister and Cryer, The Tokyo International Military Tribunal.

[127] Nandy, "The Other Within."

[128] Kopelman, "Ideology and International Law."

[129] Ibid.

[130] Banerjee, "Does International Criminal Justice Require a Sovereign?"

[131] Pal, *The History of Hindu Law in the Vedic Age and in Post-Vedic Times*; Banerjee, "Does International Criminal Justice Require a Sovereign?"

juridical praxis.[132] Pal's quest for an impartial, equal global justice lay in "a philosophical genealogy rooted in his excavation of ancient Indian concepts and especially that of an overarching cosmic-moral order described in Vedic texts as *rta*."[133] The two components of this order are – 'a transcendental, inflexible moral core or divine reason (*rta*) and the immanent world of law, dynamic, flexible and specific in relation to shifting historical legality (*vrata*, conceptualized as the positivist element of flexible legality)'.[134] The cultural texture of the justice he believed in could not have singular culpability divorced from social context. He emphasized again and again that legal order flows from social order.[135] For Pal, cultural diversity represented a higher form of social evolution, one in which society would become "transformed by passing from the condition of relatively indefinite and disconnected uniformity into that of determinate and connected diversity, the constituent elements of the community becoming more and more decidedly individualized."[136]

This is of course a significant departure from the overarching idea of natural law invoked by Joseph Keenan (the prosecutor at the IMTFE and the then Assistant Attorney General of the United States) and Webb (Australian judge and president of the IMTFE),[137] where they envision a 'superior' moral order as the basis of sanction for a legal order directly derived from it. It was this continuity of the empire through the vision of a superior moral order based on Christian ethos that Pal protested against. In particular, all forms of Western jurisprudence tend to revolve around the notion of the state and statehood[138] and attempting to locate Pal along those lines does great disservice to his rejection and suspicion of sovereignty itself. Pal rejected all forms of hierarchy (race, caste, class, gender) as the very basis of the imperial order of states, one that was incapable of rendering true justice. In doing so, Pal was led to the confusing duality in his arguments: on the one hand, rejection of imperial sovereignty and of the law and justice emanating from such a sovereign (as the only form of sovereignty prevalent in international law) and on the other hand, the embracing of sovereignty (including, for example,

---

[132] Banerjee, "Does International Criminal Justice Require a Sovereign?" pp. 67–117.

[133] Banerjee, "Does International Criminal Justice Require a Sovereign?" at 69.

[134] Pal, *The Hindu Philosophy of Law in the Vedic and Post-Vedic Times*, pp. 6–10, 55–60; *The History of Hindu Law in the Vedic Age and in Post-Vedic Times*, pp. 146–148.

[135] Ibid., pp. 55–56.

[136] Ibid., pp. 173–174.

[137] Kopelman, "Ideology and International Law."

[138] Anghie, *Imperialism, Sovereignty and the Making of International Law*, pp. 744–746.

Japanese sovereignty) as the necessary evil to be adopted in order to effectively counter colonial institutions and practices.[139]

The IMTFE's rejection of the possibility of diversity was also at the heart of Pal's dissent, borrowing heavily from this notion of Hindu law. Milinda Banerjee frees Pal from the linear narrative that has grown around him on account of what he claims is "a focus limited to his Tokyo Judgment, to the almost total exclusion of his other juridical writings as well as the broader Indian discursive context, has obscured Pal's remarkably nuanced vision of global justice."[140] Pal's view on governance is actually a product of a very critical perspective on the "dependence of sovereignty on social stratification and hierarchical command."[141] Pal's quest for an impartial, global justice thus stems from a philosophical lineage rooted in his deep excavation of ancient Indian concepts. His work on Hindu legal philosophy responded to all racial assertions about India's lack of 'real law' and accurately countered the charges of 'oriental despotism'.[142]

9.5   Conclusion: Proto-Ideologue of TWAIL

Pal as a proto-ideologue to, and ancestral voice in, the third world approach to international law is perhaps the best explanation for his judgment, to Western scholars.[143] Pal's TWAIL sensibilities (and anti-colonial roots in Bengal)[144] led him to locate despotism and the sanction for it in Hebraic-Christian monotheism.[145] Contemporary TWAIL scholars often begin their critique with the assertion that international law is predominantly the law of Christian Europe, and embodies the value system of Occidental culture and often, Catholic values (an opinion expressed and confirmed by every account of the history of the law of

---

[139] Banerjee, "Does International Criminal Justice Require a Sovereign?"

[140] Ibid.

[141] Ibid., pp. 68, 69.

[142] Metcalf, Thomas R. *Ideologies of the Raj.* Cambridge University Press, 1995; Trautmann, Thomas R. *Aryans and British India.* University of California Press, 1997; Jayaswal, K. P. *Hindu Polity: A Constitutional History of India in Hindu Times* (2 volumes in 1), Butterworth, 1924.

[143] See generally Vivekananda (F. Snyder and S. Sathirathai eds.). *Third World Attitudes Toward International Law: An Introduction.* Advaita Ashrama, 1987.

[144] See, for example, Vivekananda. "The Soul and God," in *The Complete Works of Swami Vivekananda*, vol. 1, Advaita Ashrama, 1972, pp. 489–502; "Maya and the Evolution of the Conception of God," in *The Complete Works of Swami Vivekananda*, vol. 2, Advaita Ashrama, 1976, pp. 105–117.

[145] Pal, *The Hindu Philosophy of Law in the Vedic and Post-Vedic Times*, at 246.

nations).[146] Pal's call for pluralism and the rejection of Austinian sovereignty is truly the precursor to TWAIL, if not the alternate, more far-reaching TWAIL inherited by the likes of Baxi, Guha Ray and Hidayatullah.[147] Pal's ideology (now beyond his dissent) is a realization of Kunz' notion of the anti-colonial movement as a 'challenge to Europe and the occidental world of white man'.[148]

The idea of Pal as a proto-ideologue to TWAIL is context appropriate, since ideas of TWAIL were not understood and assimilated until later. From the perspective of the TWAIL vision, his dissent is not just an example of courage in extreme circumstances, but it is also an impassioned plea to posterity[149] to radically overhaul international law and make room for a great variety of frames of reference. In a broad sense, the IMTFE can be regarded as an exercise in Orientalism, the term as used by Edward Said.[150] It enacted "a Western style for dominating, restructuring, and having authority over" Japan and many people accepted its version of events and attributions of responsibility as meting out of justice.[151] It was not until Pal's dissent that a structural critique of Western imperial, institutionalized justice emerged, recasting Japan's actions in a completely different light from that of the official judgment.

Pal's analysis was focused on the past actions of the Western powers and their colonial history, before it turned its gaze onto Japan. It was distinct both in its form and content, and was unmistakably the view of a non-Westerner.[152] Pal could be seen as making "a courageous shout of the colored races against the white race."[153] This questioning of the one-sidedness of the trial was not, however, synonymous with pro-Japan sentiments or nationalism. Rather, it reflected a concern that

---

[146] See Kunz, Josef L. "Pluralism of Legal and Value Systems and International Law." *American Journal of International Law* 49 no. 3 (1955): 370–376; Anand, Ram Prakash. *New States and International Law*. Pinnacle Technology, 2008; Shklar, Judith N. *Legalism: Law, Morals, and Political Trials*. Harvard University Press, 1964.

[147] Singh, Prabhakar. "India Before and After the Right of Passage Case." *Asian Journal of International Law* 5 no. 1 (2015): 176–208.

[148] Kunz, "Pluralism of Legal and Value Systems," at 11; Anand, New States and International Law.

[149] Guha Roy, S. N. "Is the Law of Responsibility of States for Injuries to Aliens a Part of Universal International Law?" *American Journal of International Law* 55 (1961): 863.

[150] Said, Edward. *Orientalism: Western Representations of the Orient*. Pantheon, 1978, p. 3.

[151] Ushimura, *Beyond the "Judgment of Civilization."*

[152] Ibid.

[153] Ushimura, *Beyond the "Judgment of Civilization"*; Fuji Nobuo 冨士信夫. Watashi no mita Tōkyō saiban (II) 私の見た東京裁判（下）. Kōdansha Gakujutsu Bunko, 1987, p. 349.

"Formalized vengeance can bring only an ephemeral satisfaction, with every probability of ultimate regret."[154] Here, the scholar of legal philosophy and Hindu jurisprudence overshadowed the singular narrative of the 'non-Western' judge indicting imperial powers.

In rejecting the legality of the IMTFE, Pal identified imperialism and colonialism as crimes far bigger than aggression. His anti-colonial sentiments are strong and clear as he looks to decimate the imperial status quo. Pal's questioning of the status quo is reproduced in the radical form of TWAIL that has inherited Pals suspicions of colonial institutions and mandates. He recalled the prosecuting powers' history of violence in Asia, and warned that they might deploy the charge for their own self-interests, such as maintaining 'the very status quo which might have been organized and hitherto maintained only by force by pure opportunist "Have and Holders"'.[155] For Pal, restraint in the anti-colonial struggle was simply unacceptable, for the colonized 'cannot be made to submit to eternal domination only in the name of peace'.[156] Pal insisted that anti-colonial justice should take precedence over peace rather than peace taking precedence over justice (the latter being in his opinion the premise for the concept of crimes against peace).

That the essentially imperial framework of international law could offer any space for prior sovereign consent in a deeply unequal reckoning between the vanquished and the victor seemed absurd to him. He emphasized the need to acknowledge uncertainty, plurality and removing the 'crime of imperialism' for a truly universal international community to emerge.[157] The new international legal order could only aspire to reflect this diversity by emancipation of the hitherto oppressed. Pal envisaged a fundamental change in the relationship between the colonized and the colonisers for this possible community to emerge. Pal can easily be seen as one of the original architects of the TWAIL mission, and his critique as an inspiration in the following decade for TWAIL efforts in the UN to dismantle colonialism and to recognize self-determination as a right.[158]

---

[154] Dissent, p. 112; Sellars, Kirsten. "Imperfect Justice at Nuremberg and Tokyo." *European Journal of International Law* 21 no. 4 (2010): 1085–1102.

[155] Dissent, p. 115.

[156] Dissent, p. 114.

[157] This is a position often actively taken by R. P. Anand in his work on the International Courts and Tribunals.

[158] Simpson, Gerry. *Law, War & Crime: War Crimes Trials and the Reinvention of International Law.* Polity Press, 2007; Khan, Adil Hasan. "Inheriting a Tragic Ethos: Learning from Radhabinod Pal." *AJIL Unbound* 110 (2016): 25–30.

10

Aron Trainin

The Legal Mind Behind A Soviet International Criminal Law Project

GLEB BOGUSH

Figure 10.1 Aron Trainin. Courtesy of Evgeny Altshuler, Aron Trainin's grandson, family photo album.

International scholarship on the history of international criminal law (ICL) is dominated by a critical approach to Soviet legal science and its

10 ARON TRAININ

contribution to the 'birth' and development of the discipline. International scholars tend to reduce all Soviet influence to the political organization of the trials in Nuremberg and Tokyo. Furthermore, Soviet scholars are exposed simply as diligent servants of the political leaders. Their concepts and influence on the development of both ICL in general and, as a consequence, a specifically 'Soviet' version of ICL have not received sufficient attention.[1]

It is true that the Soviet ICL project was fundamentally tainted by its total dependency upon political context of the totalitarian state and the violations of the norms of ICL by the Soviet state itself, which was involved in aggression, war crimes, and crimes against humanity.[2] Nevertheless, it would be erroneous to fully disregard the role of Soviet lawyers and their contributions to ICL.[3] Aron Trainin, whose life and academic achievements are the subject-matter of this chapter, is notable in this regard. He is the only Soviet legal scholar, whose legacy is occasionally addressed in the ICL scholarship.[4] Trainin owes his rather limited recognition for developing some of the crucial concepts of ICL before and during the Nuremberg trials.[5] Among all the Soviet 'leaders' of the ICL project, Aron Trainin is in fact unique since he never assumed any governmental or judicial positions. He was called by the government to assist as a renowned academic in the 'legal front' during World War II, but his Nuremberg mission was a clear exception in his academic career.

Writing about Trainin is rather difficult as much in his biography is hidden. Most publications about Trainin circumvent both the early

---

[1] Unsurprisingly, in Soviet and to an extent in modern Russian legal literature the role of Soviet scholars is presented as important and even crucial for the development of ICL in a complimentary and non-critical discourse. The writings of the former Russian Deputy Prosecutor General Alexander Zvyagintsev may serve as notable examples: A. G. Zvyagintsev, *Rudenko: General'nyy prokuror SSSR* (Moscow: OLMA Media Group, 2008); *Nyurnberg: Glavnyy protsess chelovechestva: Nyurnbergsiy nabat* (Moscow: Eksmo, 2015).

[2] L. Mälksoo, *Russian Approaches to International Law* (Oxford: Oxford University Press, 2015), pp. 136–9.

[3] As George Ginsburgs stated: "As one might expect, the record of Soviet contributions to the history of international law is neither as rosy as some have painted nor as crimson as others have claimed." G. Ginsburgs, 'The View from Without', 62 *American Society of International Law Proceedings* 196 (1968), 41.

[4] See e.g. E. van Sliedregt, *Individual Criminal Responsibility in International Law* (Oxford: Oxford University Press, 2012), pp. 21, 25.

[5] I. Schulmeister-André, *Internationale Strafgerichtsbarkeit unter sowjetischen Einfluss. Der Beitrag der UdSSR zum Nürnberger Hauptkriegsverbrecherprozess* (Berlin: Duncker & Humblot, 2017).

262   GLEB BOGUSH

period and the decline of his career.[6] Almost all his contemporaries, friends and colleagues, who could shed light on the missing pages, have passed away. Trainin's file in the archives of the Russian Academy of Sciences contains limited material and much is missing.[7] Nonetheless, it is possible to piece together a number of biographical elements to produce an intellectual portrait.

10.1   Early Years

Aron Naumovich[8] Trainin was born into a Jewish merchant family in Vitebsk, now Belarus, in 1889.[9] His home region at that time was situated within the so-called pale of settlement, an area in the Russian Empire designated for the settlement of Jews. With few exceptions, Jews could not reside permanently outside this area. Vitebsk at that time had a sizable Jewish population and became an important centre for Jewish religious and cultural life. Yiddish was likely to be Trainin's mother tongue.[10] Trainin's Jewish background played an important role throughout his entire life. Interestingly enough, his first academic papers were dedicated to the legal status of Jews in the Russian Empire.[11]

Trainin left his parents' house at the age of ten and, despite all anti-Jewish sentiments, managed to obtain a good education, perhaps the best in the country. Due to his father's early death, he had to earn a living by

---

[6] See, for instance, R. A. Rudenko (ed.) *Izbrannyye proizvedeniya: Zashchita mira i ugolovnyy zakon* (Moscow: Nauka, 1969), pp. 5–14.

[7] A recent doctoral thesis in history by Michelle Penn, however, presents a thorough insight into Trainin's biography, drawing interesting parallels between him, Raphael Lemkin and Hersh Lauterpacht: M. J. Penn, 'The Extermination of Peaceful Soviet Citizens: Aron Trainin and International Law' (2017), History Graduate Theses & Dissertations https://scholar.colorado.edu/concern/graduate_thesis_or_dissertations/df65v791t (accessed 29 February 2020).

[8] Aron Trainin should not be confused with another prominent legal scholar Ilya Pavlovich Trainin, a director of the Institute of State and Law of the Soviet Academy of Sciences and a member of the Soviet War Crimes Commission.

[9] Nowadays Belarus is also the homeland of another 'ICL co-creator', Raphael Lemkin, who was born in Bezwodne, on the other end of 'the pale of settlement'. See Vesselin Popovski, Chapter 11.

[10] Penn 'The Extermination of Peaceful Soviet Citizens: Aron Trainin and International Law', p. 68.

[11] 'Jews and Military Recruitment' (*Russkiye vedomosti* newspaper, 1909); 'Class Differentiation of the Jews in Russia' (*Pravo* journal, 1910), 'Process of Lawlessness' (*Russkiye vedomosti* newspaper 1912). See the list of his publications on the website of the Archive of the Russian Academy of Sciences: http://isaran.ru/?q=ru/person&guid=33°E395A-A761-B82E-EBA7-8829E66814AA (accessed 7 January 2019).

giving private lessons. Trainin attended a gymnasium in Kaluga (150 kilometres southwest of Moscow), which he graduated from with honours in 1903. Later in the same year, he was admitted to the law faculty of the Imperial (now State) Moscow University, his alma mater and home institution throughout his academic life.

Trainin was politically active and embraced socialist ideas as a university student (1903–1908). In the period 1905–1907 he took an active part in the social democratic student organization of the university, and was even arrested twice for participating in student demonstrations. The title of his diploma paper 'Class Struggle and Criminal Punishment in the History of Russian Law' was also quite indicative. In spite of his political activism, upon graduation from the university in 1908 Trainin was offered a position as an assistant at the Department of Criminal Law.

In 1912, following the example of a group of prominent professors, Trainin left Moscow University in protest against the restrictions placed on the university's autonomy by the Tsarist Ministry of Education.[12] Instead, he started working at the Shanyavsky People's University as an assistant professor. He was a practicing attorney and the editor of the Jewish intelligentsia weekly 'Novyy Put' (New Way). His further political engagement was also linked to Jewish themes. In 1917, Trainin was nominated by the Jewish National Election Committee and participated, unsuccessfully, in the elections for the Russian Constituent Assembly having opposed the Bolsheviks and their allied Jewish socialist 'Bund'.

After the 1917 Bolshevik revolution, Trainin completed his doctoral dissertation 'Insolvency and Bankruptcy' (a rather unusual topic for socialist criminal law), and returned in 1920 to Moscow University. He became one of the first Soviet criminal law professors who built a successful career as a prominent legal expert. The striking fact about Trainin's career is that, while being politically very active, he never joined the Communist (Bolshevik) Party. It seems likely that Trainin was a Menshevik, given his affiliation with the Social Democrats and his later silence on the October revolution.[13] Although Trainin never joined the ruling party, he still managed to rise to the heights of his profession.

---

[12] In 1911, the Tsarist government unfairly dismissed a number of university professors and instructors, thus flouting the charter. More than 130 professors protested against these dismissals by resigning from their positions at the university. As the conflict between the government and the university continued, more than 1,000 students were expelled, some of them arrested.

[13] Penn, 'The Extermination of Peaceful Soviet Citizens: Aron Trainin and International Law', p. 48.

10.2 Trainin as a Criminal Law Scholar

Unlike some founding figures of ICL, Trainin was first and foremost a national criminal law scholar. Public international law entered his research focus only at a later stage. While his writings leave little doubt about his competence in public international law, he never fully focused on international law. Trainin still remains a leading authority for students of criminal law in Russia and the post-Soviet space.[14]

As a legal scholar Trainin had very broad research interests. While his dissertation focused on what is now called Economic Criminal Law, Trainin's major criminal law works were dedicated to general theoretical problems, such as the structure of criminal law and complicity. His criminal law publications (more than 300 titles) reveal his sympathy for the positivist (sociological) school, especially in the early years. His major monographs and textbooks include sections on the causes of crime and other criminological theories.[15]

His most important contribution to Soviet criminal law was an elaboration of the concept of 'sostav prestupleniya' ('crime compound' or corpus delicti). Originally, corpus delicti was borrowed from German criminal law in the early nineteenth century (primarily from the works of Paul Johann Anselm von Feuerbach), but was ultimately elaborated in its own way by the Russian and Soviet criminal law doctrine. In Soviet criminal law scholarship and case law, corpus delicti was defined as a system of elements which are necessary (conditio sine qua non) and sufficient (quantum satis) grounds for identifying an act as a crime. Corpus delicti includes four elements – an 'object', an 'objective element', a 'subjective element' and a 'subject'. It has become a standard conceptualization in Soviet and Russian criminal law.[16]

Another important contribution of Trainin to Soviet criminal law was his study on the theory of complicity (criminal participation). Published in 1941, his Ucheniye o souchastii (Study on Complicity),[17] was the first

---

[14] Most recently, Trainin's 'selected works' on criminal law, including ICL, have been published in Saint-Petersburg in 2004: A. N. Trainin (ed. N. F. Kuznetsova), Izbrannyye Trudy (St. Petersburg: Yuridicheskiy Tsentr Press, 2004).

[15] A. N. Trainin, Obshcheye ucheniye o sostave prestuplyeniya (Moscow: Gosyurizdat, 1957).

[16] For instance, the Russian Criminal Code uses the term 'sostav prestupleniya', stating that "The commission of a deed containing all the elements of a crime [sostav prestupleniya], provided for by this Code, shall be the grounds for criminal responsibility" (article 8), www.legal-tools.org/en/browse/record/0656c9/ (accessed 19 March 2019).

[17] A. N. Trainin, Ucheniye o Souchastii (Moscow: Yuridicheskoe Izdatel'stvo NKYu SSSR, 1941).

monograph on the subject in the Soviet Union and the result of several years of studies. Trainin defined complicity as "a joint participation of several persons in the commission of the same crime, participation in which each of the actors must be causally linked to and guilty of the criminal outcome."[18] Trainin's theory required a knowledge element, that is, the accomplices' awareness of the perpetrator's actions. This understanding of complicity precluded a purely 'objective' imputation as well as the reduction of complicity merely to a prior agreement between the accomplices. Trainin's complicity concept was largely used in Soviet and Russian criminal law. It is worth mentioning that the publication of the monograph followed the peak of the Stalinist regime's political repressions, when complicity charges were routinely and notoriously used during political trials. While Trainin occasionally referred to the fight against the 'enemies of the people', it is hard to see how his own balanced concept related to this practice. Trainin's complicity concept has been seen by some scholars as a precursor to the Nuremberg Trial's broad conspiracy charges.[19] However, there is little in Trainin's scholarship that supports the thesis of his significant impact on the Nuremberg conspiracy concept.[20]

Trainin's criminal law writings were rich in references to German, French and English sources, as well as the Russian pre-revolutionary scholarship, while politically necessary references to Marxist classics and statements of Politburo members were surprisingly rare.

In 1938, Trainin's academic career progressed when he joined the Academy of Sciences of the USSR Institute of Soviet State and Law. He served as the head of the criminal law unit and taught simultaneously at Moscow State University, where he served as the head of the Department of Criminal Law from 1942 until 1954.

Of particular importance for Trainin was his long-term collaboration with Andrei Vyshinsky, a prominent Soviet lawyer and diplomat, and one of Stalin's major executioners during the repressions. At several stages of Vyshinsky's spectacular career, he was an immediate superior

---

[18] Ibid., p. 53.

[19] See e.g., F. Hirsch, 'The Soviets at Nuremberg: International Law, Propaganda, and the Making of the Postwar Order', *American Historical Review* 2 (2008), 707; K. Sellars, 'Treasonable Conspiracies at Paris, Moscow and Delhi The Legal Hinterland of the Tokyo Tribunal', in K. Sellars (ed.), *Trials for International Crimes in Asia* (Cambridge: Cambridge University Press, 2015), p. 707.

[20] It is equally difficult to agree that the book was "an apparent change of direction" in Trainin's scholarship: K. Sellars, *Crimes against Peace in International Law* (Cambridge: Cambridge University Press, 2013), p. 49.

of Trainin: as the rector of Moscow State University, the director of the Institute of State and Law, and, finally, as foreign minister (People's Commissar for Foreign Affairs). Vyshinsky himself was a legal scholar whose works, despite his sinister role in Stalinist repressions, were noticeable. In fact, Vyshinsky seemed to have a deep interest in Trainin's scholarship; he edited, at least officially, his books and wrote introductions to some of them. The very active role of Vyshinsky in Trainin's career is quite evident and acknowledged by Trainin himself.[21] The reasons remain unclear (it may have been a common Menshevik past, banal friendship or something else), however, Trainin was almost all his adult life under the mentorship of Vyshinsky. Vyshinsky's support for Trainin's work helps to explain why he survived the Stalinist terror. In 1936, Vyshinsky prevented the arrest of any of his subordinates in the Prosecutor General's office. Although the order did not directly protect Trainin, who worked under Vyshinsky in academia, it reveals Vyshinsky's desire to protect his subordinates.[22]

Despite the strong bonds between the two, there is no firm evidence to suggest that Trainin participated in the repressions or actively supported the political terror, like Nuremberg judges Nikitchenko[23] and Volchkov, Prosecutor Rudenko and many other Soviet characters.

10.3 First Steps in International Criminal Law

In 1935, Trainin published his first ICL-related book – *Ugolovnaya interventsiya (Criminal [Law] Intervention)*[24], in which Vyshinsky wrote a preface. In *Criminal Law Intervention*[25] Trainin discussed at length the popular projects of codification of international crime, focusing more on what we call now 'transnational' or 'treaty crimes', as well as

---

[21] Penn, 'The Extermination of Peaceful Soviet Citizens: Aron Trainin and International Law', p. 87, fn. 37.

[22] Ibid., p. 87.

[23] Nikitchenko, a judge of the Soviet Supreme Court, was zealous in 'judicial' terror. A Party commission found that during his mission in the Far East, he rendered 102 death sentences by telegram, without seeing the defendants and was involved in massive fabrication of criminal cases. See 'Pospelov commission' report, 09.02.1956. www.alexanderyakovlev.org/almanah/inside/almanah-doc/55752 (accessed 15 April 2019).

[24] The Russian connotation of the word интервенция (intervention) in the title of the book was a clear reference to the Allied intervention on the side of the 'white' movement in the Civil War in Russia in 1918.

[25] A. N. Trainin, *Ugolovnaya interventsiya. Dvizheniye po unifikatsii ugolovnogo zakonodatel'stva kapitalisticheskikh stran* (Moscow: Sovetskoye Zakonodatel'stvo, 1935).

the establishment of an international criminal court.[26] The focus of this book was, however, a critical assessment of the so-called unification movement, which he described as a project of "the united front of Capitalist countries"[27] against the USSR.

Trainin's sharp criticism of the unification movement was directed against the tendency of 'bourgeois' scholars to attempt the "mechanic, artificial criminalisation of complex political and legal relations," an attempt which was "of no help, but only harmed the cause of peace".[28] Addressing terrorism in particular, Trainin accused the International Bureau for the Unification of Criminal Law members of "slanderous attempts to identify terrorism and communism". He concluded that the primary goal of the bureau was not "to fight individual political terror but the struggle against mass revolutionary actions". Back in 1935, Trainin was rather sceptical of Raphael Lemkin's[29] ideas on the crimes of 'vandalism' and 'barbarity'.[30] In his view, these initiatives were just an attempt to soften the anti-communist character of the unification movement through a humanist pretext.

He believed that the unificators' activity merely diverted attention from truly international crimes, above all the crime of aggression. Trainin addressed the issue of aggression in international law, which would become his main area of interest. In 1935, he wrote that "military aggression is a huge, immeasurable consequence for the evil which threatens death and devastation to millions of workers".[31] He was further inspired by the idea of the Polish Professor Emil Rappaport[32] that the incitement to aggression should be punishable under criminal law, an idea that Trainin would share until the end of his academic career.

However, Trainin's first study on ICL did not provide a separate definition of international crimes, a positive 'alternative agenda' for the codification of international crimes nor the establishment of an international

---

[26] The draft statute of the International Criminal Tribunal, as a part of the Permanent Court of International Justice, was prepared by the International Association of Penal Law (AIDP). The statute was translated into Russian and published as the annex to Trainin's book.

[27] Trainin, *Izbrannyye Trudy*, p. 453.

[28] Trainin, *Izbrannyye Trudy*, p. 464. See also P. A. Filippov, *Ocherki zhizni I tvorchestva utschenykh-kriminalistov (iz istoriyi ugolovnogo prava XIX-XX vv)* (Moscow: Zertsalo, 2014), p. 410.

[29] Spelled as 'Lemken' in the book and Vyshinsky's preface.

[30] A. N. Trainin, *Ugolovnaya interventsiya*, pp. 42–43.

[31] Ibid., p. 19.

[32] See Patrycja Grzebyk, Chapter 4.

criminal court. In 1937, two years after *Criminal Law Intervention* Trainin published his second book *Zashchita mira i ugolovnyy zakon* (*The Defence of Peace and Criminal Law*), in which he elaborated the ideas expressed in his debut study. He did not abandon his criticism of existing international arrangements and projects, but this time focused more closely on the enforcement mechanism of the League of Nations. In particular, Trainin described the unsuccessful international efforts to criminalize aggressive war, noting that the Kellogg-Briand Pact of 1928 and the Pan-American Conference of 1928 renounced wars of aggression, but failed to provide any workable mechanisms to punish such crimes.

In his second ICL book, Trainin further elaborated his vision of what constituted an international crime. He clearly identified peace as the main value to be protected by ICL, devising the phrase 'crimes against peace' that would later find its way into the Charter of the International Military Tribunal.[33] A careful reading, however, shows that Trainin understood peace in a broad sense, so that every crime that targeted 'international communication' actually endangered peace.[34] Here, Trainin introduced for the first time the idea of 'international communication' as a main value to be protected by ICL. Though initially it was most probably another wording for 'international relations',[35] it could be seen also differently – as indicating important achievements of the modern civilization which warrant international legal protection, for instance, (in today's context) critical internet infrastructures or international civil aviation.

In 'Defence of Peace' Trainin developed his previous argument, which placed aggression at the centre of his international criminal law concept. He defined the "urgent duty of Soviet lawyers" as the exposure of "theoretically incorrect and politically harmful trends [in legal science] and at the same time [the transformation] of criminal law into a real weapon against a common enemy – war and fascism".[36] Vyshinsky again attached his name to Trainin's work as editor and wrote an introduction in which he proclaimed that "criminal law must be utilized for defending peace, must be mobilized against war and against the instigators of war".[37] It is obvious, however, that the issue of aggression in Trainin's

---

[33] K. Sellars, *'Crimes against Peace' and International Law*, pp. 55-8.

[34] Trainin, *Izbrannyye Trudy*, p. 549.

[35] As reflected in Trainin's writing, in socialist criminal law it is believed that the principal protected value of criminal law is "social relations".

[36] Trainin, *Izbrannye Trudy*, p. 551.

[37] A. N. Trainin, *Zashchita mira i ugolovnyy zakon* (Moscow: Yuridicheskoe Izdatel'stvo NKYu SSSR, 1937), p. 9.

writings was highly politicized. It was continuously stressed that the Soviet Union was the only truly peace-loving nation surrounded by capitalist aggressors. This vision had one important implication: any activity against the Soviet state could be seen as a crime against peace.

However, political developments in the wake of World War II temporarily stopped Trainin's enthusiastic efforts in ICL. In 1939, following the replacement of People's Commissar for Foreign Affairs Maxim Litvinov for Vyacheslav Molotov,[38] the Soviet Union fundamentally changed its foreign policy course, signed a 'non-aggression pact'[39] and de facto allied with Nazi Germany in the partition of Poland, and was subsequently expelled from the League of Nations for the act of aggression against Finland. Following the change of the Soviet political agenda, Trainin, rather unsurprisingly, published nothing further on ICL and his criticism of fascism and aggression was silenced for a few years.

10.4   In and Around Nuremberg

In 1941, as Germany invaded the Soviet Union and a growing consensus on the responsibility for Nazi atrocities started to emerge, Trainin resumed his work on ICL, and was later called on to assist the Soviet government in framing the future criminal prosecution of Nazi leaders. Vyshinsky also played a key role in what would turn out to be Trainin's most important venture.

In 1942–1943 Trainin published several newspaper articles and delivered lectures about the legal response to Nazi atrocities in the occupied Soviet territory. These atrocities would not be brushed away as simply acts committed in the course of war, but would be treated as criminal offenses that needed to be punished. Trainin referred to the criminal (as opposed to merely political) responsibility of the 'Hitlerites', and positioned their acts as criminal violations of international law.[40]

Trainin had personal reasons to be especially affected by the events in the occupied territories. His hometown Vitebsk was occupied in July 1941 and

---

[38] Litvinov had a reputation as a 'liberal', favoured negotiations with Britain and France and, according to popular belief, was non-negotiable for Hitler because he was a Jew. In his first two ICL books, Trainin referred to Litvinov a lot.

[39] Dominik Zimmermann, *Molotov-Ribbentrop Pact (1939)*, Max Planck Encyclopedia of Public International Law [MPEPIL], http://opil.ouplaw.com/home/EPIL (accessed 20 March 2019).

[40] 'The Criminal Responsibility of the Hitlerites', A Lecture by Doctor of Juridical Science Professor A. N. Trainin, *Pravda*, 13 September 1943, p. 4.

by the end of the year Nazis exterminated almost the entire 16,000 Jewish population of the city.[41] Though it has not been confirmed, there may have been Trainin's neighbours and relatives among the victims.

In 1944, several months after the first public Soviet trial of Nazi war criminals in Kharkiv, Trainin published his most famous work *Ugolovnaya otvetstvennost' gitlerovtsev* (*The Criminal Responsibility of the Hitlerites*), the first monograph in the Soviet Union on the legal assessment of Nazi crimes. Vyshinsky attached himself to the work as its editor, this time as Deputy Commissar of Foreign Affairs, and again wrote the introduction. In this book, Trainin, after repeating his critique of the previous ICL efforts, further elaborated his view of the nature of international crimes. Trainin reiterated his view that international crimes threaten primarily the 'connection'[42] between states and peoples, which objectively exists regardless of conflicting interests of various nations and differences in patterns of political and economic systems.[43]

Setting a legal scene for the prosecution of Nazi leaders, Trainin acknowledged the complexity of complicity in international crimes, "created by the extremely complex relationship between the individual accomplices".[44] Trainin dedicated a whole chapter to complicity, defining it as "a complex phenomenon", that "embraces various understandings among criminals" that can include "the dangerous form of participation in an organization, bands, blocs, gangs, conspiracies". In such cases, he explained, a member of an organization "may not know all the other members" of the organization "but should answer for all their criminal activities".[45]

---

[41] P. Longerich, *Holocaust: The Nazi Persecution and Murder of the Jews* (Oxford: Oxford University Press, 2010), p. 223.

[42] The Preamble of the ICC Statute speaks of the "common bonds" between peoples.

[43] "[I]nternational crime – and in this precisely lies its profound peculiarity, is an infringement of this most important achievement of human society, an infringement of the connection between States and peoples, a connection which constitutes the basis of relations between nations and countries". A. N. Trainin, *The Criminal Responsibility of the Hitlerites* (English translation, Moscow: Legal Pub. House NKU, 1944), p. 40.

[44] Ibid., pp. 109–110.

[45] Ibid., p. 110. Such extensive forms of liability were again discussed later in the 1990s in the ICTY's exploration of what would become a Joint Criminal Enterprise (JCE) as a somewhat amorphous mode of tying individuals to complex organizations and the crimes they committed. Another relevant ICL concept, employed by the ICC in the *Katanga and Chui* case (*The Prosecutor* v. *Germain Katanga and Mathieu Ngudjolo Chui*, ICC-01/04-01/07-716-Conf, Decision on the Confirmation of the Charges, 26 September 2008), is "perpetration through an organization", see T. Weigend; 'Perpetration through an Organization: The Unexpected Career of a German Legal Concept', 9 *Journal of International Criminal Justice* 1 (2011), 91–111.

Trainin distinguished between different kinds of liability: merely political, moral and material liability could be attributed to the state, whereas only physical persons were to bear legal responsibility. This was in contradistinction to much interwar writing that had often focused on states as the primary targets of ICL. He claimed that "none of the fundamental principles of criminal justice is adapted to bring before a criminal court anything so complicated and unique as a modern state".[46] However, this rejection of the Crime of State doctrine was not unanimous among Soviet scholars. In many Soviet writings, it was stated that international crimes may be committed by states and the state's guilt is thus a prerequisite for individual responsibility.[47]

Trainin's central argument was that the 'Hitlerites' should be tried for the waging of war and, in the process, committing a fundamental crime against peace. Arguing that peace is the greatest social value, Trainin claimed that aggression was the gravest of all international crimes. He further suggested that crimes against peace should become part of "a new convention on international crime", which would be part of a "general system of treaties defining the new regime of international relations after the defeat of Hitlerism".[48] This was consonant with his writings prior to the war in which he advocated for the idea that aggression encompasses all other international crimes committed during the war, an idea that was famously echoed in Nuremberg judgement on crimes against peace: "[I]ts consequences are not confined to the belligerent states alone, but affect the whole world. To initiate a *war of aggression*, therefore, is not only an international crime; it is the *supreme international crime* differing only from other war crimes in that it contains within itself the accumulated evil of the whole."[49]

The Criminal Responsibility of the Hitlerites was translated into several languages, most importantly into English,[50] and circulated among the Allies during the preparations for the Nuremberg Tribunal. Representatives of the four powers at the London Conference in 1945 actively discussed Trainin's

---

[46] Ibid., 102.

[47] These doctrinal views may be deemed to have implications far beyond the academic discussion. The failure to distinguish state and individual responsibility could be traced also in the Russian legal position on landmark cases before the ECtHR: G. Bogush, 'Russia and International Criminal Law', 15 *Baltic Yearbook of International Law* (2015), 178.

[48] Trainin, *The Criminal Responsibility of the Hitlerites*, p. 53.

[49] Trial of the Major War Criminals before the International Military Tribunal, Official Documents in the English Language (Nuremberg, 1947), p. 186.

[50] The book was also published in 1946 in London under a slightly different title: A. N. Trainin, *Hitlerite Responsibility under Criminal Law* (London: Hutchinson, 1946).

book.[51] Robert Jackson in his report repeatedly referred to Trainin's opinion that a war of aggression or initiating war in violation of treaties is an international crime. Furthermore, he seemed to acknowledge Trainin's view on the nature of that international crime stating that:"the American representatives conceive of this case as more than the trial of many particular offenses and offenders. It involves our whole attitude towards the waging of aggressive war, which, we think, as Professor Trainin has pointed out in his book, is an international crime".[52]

Trainin, together with the future tribunal's judge Iona Nikitchenko, participated in the London conference and signed the London Charter.[53] During the negotiations, he was active, made statements mostly on procedural matters, and even went as far as pointing to similarities between Soviet and American law.[54] Nonetheless, there were at least two things Trainin was intransigent about: he insisted that Berlin should be the permanent trial venue, the archival location and the place of detention. In this case, Trainin was without a doubt trying to fulfil Stalin's wishes since the placement of the tribunal in the Soviet occupation zone of Berlin would have made it easier for the Soviet state to influence the tribunal. Another item on Trainin's political instructions from Moscow was to ensure that the charter of the future tribunal would refer only to Nazi war crimes to avoid the possibility of Soviet war crimes being discussed in the courtroom.[55]

Apart from his official responsibilities as an advisor, Trainin was included by the Politburo in the Moscow-based Commission under the leadership of Vyshinsky, who directly 'supervised' the course of the Nuremberg trials and advised the Soviet prosecution team. Recently published documents of that supervisory body[56] reveal the extent of the

---

[51] According to Priemel, "Trainin's booklet made an immediate impression. Abstracts of the book were circulated among those already working on the conceptualization of war crimes, and English and French translations soon made the tract available to a wider public where it was kindly received." C. Priemel, *The Betrayal: The Nuremberg Trials and German Divergence* (Oxford: Oxford University Press, 2016), p. 63.

[52] Report of Robert H. Jackson, United States Representative to the International Conference on Military Trials (London, 1945), www.loc.gov/rr/frd/Military_Law/Jackson-report.html, p. 126.

[53] A curious fact is that only the Soviet side was represented by two signatories.

[54] On Trainin's participation in the London Conference and the influence of his ideas on the legal framework of the Nuremberg Trial, see F. Hirsch, 'The Soviets at Nuremberg: International Law, Propaganda, and the Making of the Postwar Order', 2 *American Historical Review* (2008), 701–730.

[55] Ibid.

[56] N. S. Lebedeva (ed.), *SSSR I Nyurmbergskiy protsess. Neizvestnyye i maloizvestnyye stranitsy istoriyi* (Moscow: MFD, 2012).

Kremlin's and Vyshinsky's control over every single step of the Soviet judges and prosecutors, and other members of the Soviet delegation. The Commission even imposed sanctions for some misdeeds, criticizing Nikitchenko and Rudenko for allowing some undesirable witnesses to testify. It actually directed the positions of the Soviet judges during the deliberations and the content of Nikitchenko's dissenting opinion. During the consideration of the Katyn massacre, Trainin was included in the special Commission supervising the presentation of the Katyn evidence by the Soviet prosecution team, though there is no information about his role and the level of his awareness of the details. One can only guess whether Trainin was aware of what really had happened in Katyn while sitting at a table together with major perpetrators of the massacre.[57]

Despite Trainin's significant contribution to 'the Soviet part' of the trial, he received no distinction for his mission. His name was not even included in the draft decree awarding state decorations to the judges, prosecutors and other members of the Soviet delegation to the Nuremberg trials, which was at any rate rejected by Stalin. In fact, Trainin's only domestic reward for the work in Nuremberg was an associate membership in the Academy of Sciences. There could be two explanations: first, it may have been a sign of Stalin's dissatisfaction with some results of the trial.[58] Second, with regard to Trainin, it could also be a sign of the first dark clouds hanging over his head. There is no information about Trainin's involvement in the Tokyo proceedings or any other war crime trials after Nuremberg.

10.5 Post-Nuremberg Trajectory

Upon completion of the trial in Nuremberg, Trainin published several papers and brochures dedicated to various aspects of the trial, mostly on the substantive law of the tribunal. He also published a short memoir *At the Nuremberg Trial*,[59] where he expressed his appreciation for the historical record of the tribunal and its judgments. He dedicated a lengthy section praising the contribution of the Soviet representatives

---

[57] Two members of the commission, NKVD representatives Bogdan Kobulov and Vselovod Merkulov, were members of the 'troika', an extra-judicial body that officially rendered pre-determined judgments, and directly supervised the executions of the Polish prisoners.

[58] Stalin's dissatisfaction was largely reflected in Judge Nikitchenko's dissenting opinion, written based on Stalin's instructions: *SSSR i Nyurmbergskiy protsess*, p. 505.

[59] A. N. Trainin, *Nyunrbergskiy protsess* (Moscow: RIO VYuA, 1946).

to the trial, and Judge Nikitchenko's dissenting opinion, calling the acquittals of Schacht, von Papen and Fritsche a major setback of the trial. Trainin wrote: "when there is a need in support of democracy and peace, then the voice of the Soviet representative is heard".[60]

The most important monograph written by Trainin in the postwar period, and his last work on international criminal law was published under the title *Zashchita mira i bor'ba s prestupleniyami protiv chelovechestva* (*Defence of Peace and the Fight against Crimes against Mankind*) in 1956.[61] In this voluminous monograph Trainin summarized previous writings, elaborating the notion of *'prestupleniya protiv chelovechestva'* (crimes against mankind), which has been used by the United Nation (UN) International Law Commission and was an overarching name for what we would today understand as 'international crimes'. In that respect, he showed a clear awareness that something like a broader system of international criminal law was emerging that went far beyond the particulars of Nuremberg.

For Trainin, 'crimes against mankind' covered "the whole range of criminal acts which threaten the peace and security of nations".[62] He differentiated between *'prestupleniya protiv chelovechestva'* ('crimes against mankind') and *'prestupleniya protiv chelovechnosti'* ('crimes against humanity'). Trainin's approach to crimes against humanity was rather ambiguous. In his last book on ICL, he mentioned this category only when describing the IMT Charter, but then omitted the notion in his classification of international crimes by equating crimes against humanity with genocide. The misleading character of that equation should have been obvious to Trainin, who himself was involved in drafting the IMT Charter. Trainin's writings therefore tend to show that the disappearance of 'uncomfortable' notion of crimes against humanity in Soviet criminal law has not been accidental.[63]

Classifying crimes against mankind, Trainin distinguished between three categories: 'Crimes against the foundations of peaceful coexistence of nations', 'Crimes against the laws and customs of war' and 'Crimes against the foundations of the physical existence of nations – genocide'.

---

[60] Trainin, *Izbrannyye Trudy*, p. 687.

[61] A. N. Trainin, *Zashchita mira i borba s prestulpyeniyami protiv chelovechestva* (Moscow: Izdatel'stvo AN SSSR, 1956).

[62] Ibid., p. 113.

[63] A different interpretation is presented by V. Tochilovsky, 'Crimes Against "Humaneness"?: The Russian Interpretation of Crimes Against Humanity', 16 *Journal of International Criminal Justice* 5 (2018).

The first category of crimes against mankind closely resembles the Nuremberg concept of crimes against peace that Trainin elaborated before and during World War II. He introduced some changes to the concept and suggested differentiating between two forms: direct military aggression and indirect aggression – economic and ideological. Indeed, ideological aggression was an especially important political concept for the Soviet state during the nuclear arms race period and the attempt by the Soviet Union to lead the peace movement. It included not only the incitement to war but also the propagation of weapons of mass destruction, as well as the promotion of fascist or Nazi views, racial and national exclusiveness, hatred and contempt for other nations.[64] In line with the official Soviet position that the Soviet Union was the only country in the world genuinely interested in establishing world peace, Trainin stressed the necessity of prohibiting weapons of mass destruction, accusing again 'new imperialists' such as the United States of using chemical and biological warfare in Korea. At the same time, Trainin moved away from a more pacifist concept of aggression that criminalized all kinds of wars: he distinguished between illegal aggressive wars and just wars of liberation.

The second category of crimes against humankind essentially encompassed war crimes as they have been defined by the IMT Charter and 'grave breaches' of the Geneva Conventions of 1949.

The third and last crime in Trainin's classification of crimes against mankind was genocide. In 1948, he first addressed genocide in the article "The Fight against Genocide as an International Crime" published in the *Soviet State and Law Journal*, in which Trainin radically changed his approach to Lemkin's invention. Trainin distinguished three forms of genocide: physical genocide – 'direct physical extermination of people belonging to a certain race or nation', biological genocide – 'prevention of childbirth, sterilization, prohibition of marriage, complete separation of the sexes, forced abortions' and the third special form – 'a national and cultural genocide aimed at destroying the national culture of persecuted peoples, its achievements and heritage'. The inclusion of cultural genocide was in line with the Soviet position at the time of the drafting of the convention.[65] Just as with the conceptualization of aggression, the United States with its racial segregation was given as an example of a country in which genocide was

---

[64] Trainin, *Zashchita mira I bor'ba s prestulpyeniyami protiv chelovechestva*, p. 128.
[65] W. A. Schabas, *Genocide in International Law: Crime of Crimes. Second Edition* (Cambridge: Cambridge University Press, 2009), p. 90.

taking place, reinforcing the official Soviet narrative.[66] More generally, Trainin reiterated his previously well-known opinion that the "state and other legal entities can and should bear political and financial responsibility for crimes against mankind, but the subjects of criminal liability may only be individuals".[67] Trainin was of the opinion that a crime against mankind represented not just an episodic but systematic actions such as the preparation of aggression, a policy of terror, the persecution of civilians, which require "extensive and cohesive work of many units and individuals". The complexity of the efforts needed for the implementation of criminal activities directed "against the interests of all mankind" led to the conclusion that the most typical form of complicity in the commission of this kind of crime was complicity *sui generis* and "involve[d] lasting and cohesive activities in the form of participation in a criminal association".[68] According to Trainin, the term 'criminal clique', an association of political, military and financial leaders, best described this sort of criminal association.[69]

10.6 Trainin's Fall

At the beginning of the 1950s, shortly after the completion of the Nuremberg trials, Trainin was caught in the midst of the campaign against 'cosmopolitans', Soviet academics mostly of Jewish origin, and became the main object of ideological attacks at Moscow State University and the Academy of Sciences of the USSR. The campaign was anti-Semitic, not only because of the ethnic affiliation of the victims, but also due to labelling victims as 'Zionists'.

'Charges' against Trainin included not only covert Zionism, but, as in the cases of the other 'rootless cosmopolitans', such 'political mistakes' as insufficient references to the works of Stalin and other Soviet leaders and, instead, 'unnecessary' reliance on 'bourgeois' authors.[70] Trainin's rather innocent and apolitical monograph on the structure of the Soviet criminal law was heavily criticized for 'theoretical weakness' and met negatively by engaged reviewers in 1952.[71] The same year, an

---

[66] A. N. Trainin, 'Bor'ba s genotsidom kak mezhdunarodnym prestupleniem', 5 *Sovetskoye gosudarstvo i pravo* (1948), 3.

[67] Trainin, *Zashchita mira I borba s prestulpyeniyami protiv chelovechestva*, p. 124.

[68] Ibid., p. 173.

[69] Ibid., p. 220.

[70] Penn, 'The Extermination of Peaceful Soviet Citizens: Aron Trainin and International Law', p. 216.

[71] Ibid., p. 217.

anonymous article 'Overcoming Lags in Jurisprudence' was published in *Izvestiya* (ironically, the newspaper where Trainin had regularly published), claimed that Trainin monopolized his sphere of research and enjoyed an unjustified privileged position in Soviet legal academia. The writer proclaimed that Trainin's work "did not reach the high level of scientific work". These failures stood in sharp contrast with "the duty of Soviet scholar lawyers [to] respond with attention and care to the party" and create work "worthy of the great era of the building of communism".[72]

As a result of the bullying campaign, Trainin had to resign from his position as head of the department at Moscow State University, where he nevertheless remained professor. While Trainin was able to publish widely and even travel abroad in the late 1940s, by the early 1950s Trainin appeared less frequently.[73] Stalin's death and, very probably, Vyshinsky's protection, saved Trainin and other lawyers from the worst-case scenario.[74]

However, as evidenced by Trainin's colleagues, the campaign and treacherous behaviour of many friends and colleagues worsened his health and he died of a heart attack[75] on 7 February 1957.[76] *Izvestiya*, the same newspaper that had four years earlier published the infamous anonymous pamphlet about Trainin issued an obituary for him. The newspaper described Trainin as "one of the first Soviet legal professors" who was active for many years as a professor at Moscow State University and worked on the "struggle against aggression". His role in the Nuremberg Tribunal was noted and the obituary writer declared that everyone who knew Trainin appreciated his "deep humanity, sensitivity, and tenderness".[77] Unlike some of his colleagues, Trainin was honoured post-mortem, and his books continued to be published.

---

[72] 'Preodolet' otstavanie pravovoi nauki', *Izvestiya*, 23 January 1953, pp. 2–3.

[73] Penn, 'The Extermination of Peaceful Soviet Citizens: Aron Trainin and International Law', p. 210.

[74] The fate of the leaders of Jewish Anti-Fascist Committee is quite indicative. In 1952 most prominent members of the committee were arrested on trumped-up spying charges, tortured, tried in secret proceedings and executed in the basement of Lubyanka Prison: J. Rubenstein and V. P. Naumov, *Stalin's Secret Pogrom: The Postwar Inquisition of the Jewish Anti-Fascist Committee (Annals of Communism)* (New Haven, CT: Yale University Press, 2001).

[75] Another interesting parallel between Trainin, Lemkin and Lauterpacht is the same cause of death – a heart attack.

[76] N. F. Kuznetsova, 'Vvedeniye' (Introduction) in Trainin, *Izbrannye Trudy*, p. 7.

[77] 'A. N. Trainin', *Izvestiya*, 10 February 1957.

10.7 Conclusions

Despite the specific Soviet understanding of international law, ranging from a complete rejection to the extremely pragmatic view of it as a tool for securing the geo-political and ideological goals of the state, Soviet scholars contributed to the framing of the Nuremberg and Tokyo trials and thus objectively helped to shape international criminal law. Among them, Aron Trainin deserves a special distinction.

As a leading Soviet legal academic and legal advisor of the Soviet delegation in Nuremberg, Trainin significantly influenced the formulation of the idea of prosecuting Nazi leaders for a conspiracy against peace. Aggression as the supreme evil, 'mother of all crimes'[78] was in the centre of Trainin's ICL concept. His passionate dedication to the criminalization of aggression could be indeed compared to Lemkin's obsession with genocide.

It is true that Trainin was not the first jurist during the war to advocate for the criminalization of aggression – Hersch Lauterpacht had addressed the issue in greater detail a year before him, as did Rappoport and Pella before the war.[79] Nonetheless, as Kirsten Sellars rightly states, it was important that the idea of the crime of aggression developed "not as any single national monologue, but as an intermittent international dialogue involving jurists in the Soviet Union, Britain and the United States, as well as those attached to the European governments-in-exile".[80] Trainin, as a Soviet academic, was one of the esteemed voices in that dialogue.[81]

To be honest, there was no proper academic communication between Trainin and his western colleagues, as Trainin's participation in

---

[78] On today's relevance: F. Mégret, 'What is the Specific Evil of Aggression?' in Kreß. Bariga (ed.), *The Crime of Aggression: A Commentary*, Vol. 2 (Cambridge: Cambridge University Press, 2017), pp. 1416–1420.

[79] H. Lauterpacht, 'The Law of Nations and the Punishment of War Crimes', *British Yearbook of International Law*, 1944, 81.

[80] Sellars, *Crimes against Peace and International Law*, p. 50.

[81] William Schabas noted: "Soviet enthusiasm for the prosecution of aggression had never really been in doubt, and the international law arguments in support had been developed by its leading specialist Professor A.N. Trainin." He noted that the British representative to the London Conference pointed out that Trainin had treated aggression as a "crime against peace" and not as a "crime of war" and a compromise in the terminology was agreed to by all." See W. Schabas, 'Origins of the Criminalization of Aggression: How Crimes Against Peace Became the "Supreme International Crime"', in Mauro Politi and Giuseppe Nesi (eds.), *The International Criminal Court and the Crime of Aggression* (Aldershot and Burlington, VT: Ashgate/Dartmouth, 2004), p. 28.

international dialogue was somewhat limited. The dialogue worked mostly in the form Trainin's heavily politicized critique of the 'bourgeoisie' scholarship. With the exception of his Nuremberg monograph on the responsibility of the Hitlerites, all Trainin's writings have been published in Russian and have not been translated to English or French. He could comfortably criticize Lemkin, Pella, de Vabres and others, but did not have to respond to them.

It is difficult if not impossible to try to evaluate what Trainin's trajectory would have been, had he worked in a freer country. It is quite possible that Trainin's contribution to ICL and international criminal justice would be much more meaningful and noticeable, and would not be limited to being the 'human face' of an abominable totalitarian system. Trainin's case may serve as a good example of the limitations imposed on legal scholars in a totalitarian state system and the dangers arising from the collaboration with such a system. His fate in the postwar Soviet Union is quite revealing. Though he shortly survived the last of Stalin's purges, instead of being rewarded for his role in the Nuremberg trial he received a harsh blow from the totalitarian system.

The scientific value of Trainin's works is beyond doubt. Everyone who is familiar with the propaganda tomes of Soviet scholars citing 'comrade Stalin' on every page would notice a difference between these works and Trainin's books and articles. Moreover, talking about victims of Nazi war criminals, he often mentioned Jews and did not opt for the euphemism 'peaceful Soviet citizens'. Despite unavoidable controversy, Aron Trainin deserves credit for promoting ideas of justice for international crimes and world peace.

11

The Complex Life of Rafal Lemkin

VESSELIN POPOVSKI

Figure 11.1 Raphael Lemkin. Credit: Bettmann/Contributor/Getty Images.

Rafal Lemkin's personal life – described once as 'one of the most remarkable in the 20th century'[1] – was dynamic, complex and full of uncertainties. He grew up in an educated, polyglot and tolerant family. His mother, Bella née Pomeranz, owned a large library of books and taught Rafal to read a lot, to speak many languages and to respect all cultures. At the age of twelve, it is said, that he had read *Quo Vadis* by Henryk Sienkiewicz, and learned how

---

[1] Adam Jones, *Genocide: A Comprehensive Introduction* (2nd ed., New York: Routledge, 2011), p. 123.

the Roman Emperor Nero threw Christians to the lions as entertainment for the crowd. Asking his mother why some people were killed simply because of who they were, and why police did not stand up in their defence,[2] his mother responded that once a state wanted to eliminate a group from its lands, its citizens became 'accomplices and not the guardians of human life'.[3]

This chapter inquires how the biographical in Lemkin influenced the intellectual, how certain formative experiences – as a Jew born on the 'blood lands'[4] and raised in an anti-Semitic environment – shaped Lemkin's education and career. The historical context had brought Lemkin to the definition of 'genocide' long before he came up with the term intellectually. Indeed Lemkin had been led to first define the crimes of barbarity and vandalism during the conferences on the unification of criminal law in the early 1930s. Much later, when collecting and analyzing the Nazi decrees issued to rule the occupied territories and writing his book *Axis Rule in Occupied Europe*[5] during World War II, he came up with the term 'genocide'. Lemkin was instrumental in the adoption of the UN General Assembly Resolution 96(I) 'The Crime of Genocide' in 1946, and together with Pella and Donnedieu de Vabres drafted the UN Convention for the Prevention and Punishment of Genocide, adopted on 9 December 1948. Lemkin spent the rest of his life devoting all his energy and passion for urging UN member-states to ratify the convention.

Lemkin's role at the dawn of international criminal law (ICL) needs to be critically contextualized. His voice was an important warning against the Holocaust, but he was also a romantic believer in the power of international law, an idealist sometimes inconsistent and contradicting his previous statements – for example, his oscillation between the narrow and the broad ethnonational-religious definition of groups. On one hand, Lemkin raised a strong voice of advocacy for individual rights when criticizing the Soviet and the Italian penal codes in the late 1920s; on the other, he became obsessed almost atavistically with the collective rights and the intent to destroy ethnic, religious and national groups. In his emphasis on groups as victims of atrocities, he departed from

---

[2] Phillipe Sands, *East West Street: On the Origins of 'Genocide' and 'Crimes Against Humanity'* (London: Weidenfeld and Nicholson, 2016), p. 142.

[3] 'Raphael Lemkin', Holocaust Memorial Day Trust, available at www.hmd.org.uk /resource/raphael-lemkin/.

[4] The term belongs to Timothy Snyder, *Bloodlands: Europe Between Hitler and Stalin* (New York: Basic Books, 2010).

[5] Raphael Lemkin, *Axis Rule in Occupied Europe: Laws of Occupation, Analysis of Government, Proposals for Redress* (Washington, DC: Carnegie Endowment for International Peace, 1944).

humanitarian law and human rights, both focusing on the individual. Some questioned Lemkin's liberal views, in the words of Stephen Holmes 'The idea that killing a culture is irreversible in a way that killing an individual is not, reveals the strangeness of Lemkin's conception from a liberal-individualistic point of view.'[6]

Lemkin's life, private and public, was uneven. He never fell in love and never had a family, he moved from one place to another, frequently changed jobs and never had a home. He neglected a full-time professorship at Yale to remain in New York and to lobby states to ratify the Genocide Convention. With no wife and children, with no career and with fewer and fewer friends, Lemkin simply could not find purpose in anything else, apart from the codification of genocide. Although his invention, Lemkin died alone, with just seven people attending his funeral in 1959. The only writer who referred to Lemkin in the decades after his death was Herbert Maza, French legal scholar, who once stressed the importance of individual initiatives of jurists, like Lemkin, for the advancement of international law.[7]

Forgotten since the 1950s, Lemkin was 'resurrected' in the 1990s when the crime of genocide entered into the jurisdictions of the statutes of the two ad hoc international criminal tribunals for Yugoslavia (ICTY) and Rwanda (ICTR). In 1998 – 50 years after the adoption of the Genocide Convention – the ICTR issued the first-ever conviction in an international tribunal for genocide (Akayesu[8]). In the same year, Lemkin's crime became part (Art. 6) of the jurisdiction of the Rome Statute of the International Criminal Court (ICC),[9] signed by 139 states, as of now. In 2010 Omar al-Bashir, president of Sudan, was charged by the prosecutor of the ICC with three counts of genocide among other crimes. The Special Court for Sierra Leone and the Extraordinary Chambers in the Courts of Cambodia also have jurisdiction over the crime of genocide. In 2004 Kofi Annan, then UN Secretary-General, launched the Action Plan to Prevent Genocide and appointed the first Special Adviser on the Prevention of Genocide with the mandate to monitor violations of ethnic and racial origin, act as a mechanism of early warning and make recommendations to the Security Council.

---

[6] Stephen Holmes quoted by Jones in *Genocide*, p. 12.

[7] Herbert Maza, *Neuf Meneurs internationaux: de l'initiative individuelle dans l'institution des organisations internationales pendant le XIXe et le XX siècle* (Paris: Sirey, 1965), pp. 342–355.

[8] *The Prosecutor v. Jean-Paul Akayesu*, Case No. ICTR-96-4-T, 2 September 1998.

[9] Rome Statute, Art. 6, available at http://legal.un.org/icc/statute/99_corr/cstatute.htm.

The crime of genocide has been widely accepted and recognized. The International Court of Justice (ICJ) regards the prohibition of genocide as *jus cogens* norm and admits that principles, underlying the Genocide Convention, are recognized by civilized nations and are binding on states *erga omnes*, even without conventional obligation.[10] Prosecutors, instead of taking the easier road to file charges of crimes against humanity, meticulously look for evidence to identify intent to destroy groups as such and to file charges of genocide. It seems that few prosecutors will pass the opportunity to prosecute genocide every time there has been even a chance of making the case.[11]

Lemkin's invention is also part of the developing 'universal jurisdiction'.[12] Genocide is not only legally non-derogatory but also morally magnetic. So much so that during the massacre of Tutsis in Rwanda in April–June 1994, the US administration refused to call it a genocide, under the – perhaps mistaken – belief that this would have forced it to commit militarily. Advocates for action enthusiastically draw on the strong stigmatizing effect of the word genocide, even at the risk of diluting its meaning. The 'conceptual proliferation'[13] with gendercide, politicide, classicide, urbicide and, more recently, democide, ecocide, eliticide, fratricide, linguicide, memoricide, cybercide, etc.[14] additionally demonstrates the attraction of Lemkin's word.

Yet the term genocide is not without ambiguities. Whilst the discipline has been prompt to lionize Lemkin as its *visionnaire* and his intellectual production has been profoundly studied, the term 'genocide' itself has continued to build a mixed legacy, and the disciplinary competition between lawyers, historians and anthropologists as to the understanding

---

[10] See *Reservations to the Convention on Genocide*, [1951] ICJ Rep. 15, p. 23; See also *Case Concerning Barcelona Traction, Light and Power Co. (Belgium v. Spain)*, [1970] ICJ Rep. 3, p. 32.

[11] Radislav Krstić (Case No. ICTY-98–33) was sentenced to thirty-five years in prison for aiding and abetting genocide. Judges for the first time officially confirmed Srebrenica as a legally proven case of genocide, as it had been planned by the Bosnian Serb army. Vidoje Blagojević (Case No. ICTY-02-60) was sentenced to eighteen years, he commanded a local Bosnian Serb brigade at the time, and was not among the principal perpetrators in Srebrenica, but the judges accepted the prosecutor's argument that the practical assistance Blagojević rendered had a substantial effect on the commission of the crime of genocide.

[12] Michelle Knorr, 'The International Crime of Genocide: Obligations Jus Cogens and Erga Omnes, and their Impact on Universal Jurisdiction', *Essex Human Rights Review*, Vol. 7, Issue 2, 2011, available at http://projects.essex.ac.uk/ehrr/V7N2/Knorr.pdf.

[13] Martin Shaw, *What Is Genocide?* (Cambridge: Polity Press, 2007), p. 63.

[14] Jones, *Genocide*, pp. 26–29.

of the term continues. The persistent focus of *competition mémorielle* between different groups remains controversial. One of the central dilemmas is what importance the crime has with other crimes. Genocide is often seen as the 'crime of all crimes' in judgments of international tribunals.[15] This created expectations that almost all atrocities could be labeled as genocide. In 2005 the International Commission of Inquiry on Darfur[16]concluded that the situation does not amount to genocide, but only to crimes against humanity. Immediately human rights groups protested the commission's finding as if crimes against humanity were not as grave as genocide.[17] Why should impede the conditions of life of a group be seen as intrinsically graver than less specifically targeted but larger-scale atrocities, or prolonged violations such as slavery and colonialism? Cannot crimes against humanity be just as, if not more, murderous in their scope? Do we risk paying less attention to other crimes because we over-focus on genocide?

Lemkin's work and the crime of genocide need to be separated. The Genocide Convention has undoubtedly taken a life of its own since 1948 and there may be something slightly quaint about continuing to attribute that dynamic to Lemkin. At the same time, understanding the distinctiveness of his approach compared to what became the dominant one in ICL might help in dealing with some of the ambiguities in the prosecution of genocide. As Martin Shaw wrote: 'It is to the Convention, rather than Lemkin himself, that most refer in defining genocide. This tendency is unfortunate because, although Lemkin's was far from the last word, he offered a more adequate understanding.'[18] Naming a major crime is one thing, but assessing the complex life and legacy of Lemkin in his numerous enterprises requires an in-depth examination and a nuanced approach.

Aside from his most significant contribution, Lemkin was initially a relatively minor figure in the eclectic pantheon of those who are the object of this book. It is interesting to chart the gradual lionization of Lemkin that typically foregrounds the importance of the lone individual

---

[15] *Prosecutor* v. *Kambanda,* Judgment and Sentence, Case No. ICTR-97–23-S, 4 September 1998, at para. 16; *Prosecutor v. Serashugo*, Sentence, Case No. ICTR-98–39-S, 2 February 1999 at para. 15.

[16] Report of the International Commission of Inquiry on Darfur to the United Nations Secretary-General, Geneva, 25 January 2005, available at www.un.org/news/dh/sudan/com_inq_darfur.pdf.

[17] Noelle Quenivet, 'The Report of The International Commission of Inquiry on Darfur: The Question of Genocide' in *Human Rights Review*, Vol. 7, Issue 4, 2006, pp. 38–68.

[18] Martin Shaw, *What Is Genocide?* p. 17.

in promoting a cause. By contrast with all other figures, Lemkin has been the object, probably as a result of his close and unique association with the crime of genocide, of considerable scholarly interest. In that respect, Lemkin is comparable to a figure such as René Cassin, one of the fathers of the Universal Declaration of Human Rights, adopted one day after the Genocide Convention on 10 December 1948.[19] What does that interest say about the need to ground the discipline of ICL in some heroic figures? What does it mean that this figure was once so isolated and neglected?

11.1 Books on Lemkin

The first full-length book entirely on Lemkin, written by James Joseph Martin, was published as late as in 1984.[20] It is mostly biographical and only descriptively elaborates on the invention of genocide as a major development in ICL. The often-mentioned Pulitzer prize-winning book *A Problem from Hell*[21] by Samantha Power devotes only sixty pages to Lemkin and focuses mainly on his unsuccessful struggle to persuade the US Congress to ratify the convention.

John Cooper in 2008 published the fullest biography so far.[22] Dominik Schaller and Jurgen Zimmerer, the editors of the *Journal of Genocide Research*, in 2008 published 'Origins of Genocide: Raphael Lemkin as a Historian of Mass Violence',[23] a critical assessment of Lemkin's influence on international law and his historical analysis of mass murders, showing the connection between the two. In 2010, Stephen Leonard Jacobs edited a collection of Lemkin's articles on genocide[24] and in 2014 he also published Lemkin's unfinished *History of Genocide*,[25] collating a large scholarly work, elucidating obscure references and adding a critical introduction. In 2011, William Korey *An Epitaph for Raphael*

---

[19] Jay Winter and Antoine Prost, *René Cassin and Human Rights* (Cambridge: Cambridge University Press, 2013).

[20] James Joseph Martin, *The Man Who Invented Genocide: The Public Career and Consequence of Raphael Lemkin* (Torrance, CA: Institute for Historical Review, 1984).

[21] Samantha Power, *A Problem from Hell: America and the Age of Genocide* (New York: Harper, 2002).

[22] John Cooper, *Raphael Lemkin and the Struggle for the Genocide Convention* (Basingstoke: Palgrave Macmillan, 2008).

[23] Dominik J. Schaller and Jurgen Zimmerer (eds.), *Origins of Genocide: Raphael Lemkin as a Historian of Mass Violence* (Abingdon: Routledge, 2013, a reprint from 2008 *Journal of Genocide Research*).

[24] Stephen Leonard Jacobs, *Lemkin's Thoughts on Nazi Genocide* (New York: Bloch, 2010).

[25] Stephen Leonard Jacobs, *Lemkin on Genocide* (Lanham, MD: Lexington Books, 2014).

Lemkin.[26] Lemkin's autobiography, titled *Totally Unofficial,*[27] was published in 2013, after an Australian scholar Donna-Lee Frieze undertook a profound collection and classification of all existing Lemkin's writings about his life. This is not a typical autobiography; one can regard it as an attempt by Lemkin to understand his obsession with the crime of genocide. Like most autobiographies, it needs to be read with caution, as it alternates between the emotional,[28] the biased, the self-imposing, the narcissistic and the frivolous. Polish authors also wrote on Lemkin – Ryszard Szawlowski,[29] Marek Kornat,[30] Agnieszka Bieńczyk-Missala,[31] Adam Reznik[32] and others undertook in-depth research in archives and produced some excellent historical assessments.

More recently Douglas Irvin-Erickson published a comprehensive biography[33] shedding light on the origins of genocide and contextualizing these within Lemkin's intellectual career. The book is the first to explore the in-depth connection between Lemkin's philosophical writings, his juridical works, the politics at the time and examines how the meaning of genocide changed over previous decades.

Philippe Sands wrote *East West Street*, a detective legal thriller and a family history combined, covering both Lemkin's journey to define genocide and Hersch Lauterpacht's journey to define crimes against humanity.[34] Extraordinarily the two lawyers started their journeys from

[26] William Korey, *Epitaph for Raphael Lemkin* (New York, 2001).

[27] Donna-Lee Frieze (ed.), *Totally Unofficial: The Autobiography of Raphael Lemkin* (New Haven, CT: Yale University Press, 2013).

[28] Some suggested that the publisher asked Lemkin to write his autobiography with more emotion. See Tanya Elder, 'What You See Before Your Eyes: Documenting Raphael Lemkin's Life by Exploring his Archival Papers, 1900–1959' in *Journal of Genocide Research* Vol. 7, Issue 4, 2005, pp. 469–499.

[29] Ryszard Szawlowski, 'Lemkin (1900–1958): The Polish Lawyer Who Created the Concept of Genocide' in *The Polish Quarterly of International Affairs*, Issue 2, 2005, pp. 98–133.

[30] Marek Kornat 'Barbarity-Vandalism-Terrorism-Genocide. On Raphael Lemkin and the Idea of Defining "the Crime under the Law of Nations"' in *The Polish Quarterly of International Affairs*, Issue 2, 2008, pp. 79–98.

[31] Agnieszka Bieńczyk-Missala and Sławomir Dębski (eds.), *Rafal Lemkin: A Hero of Humankind* (Warsaw: The Polish Institute of International Affairs, 2010); Agnieszka Bieńczyk-Missala (ed.), *Civilians in Contemporary Armed Conflicts* (Warsaw: Warsaw University Press, 2017).

[32] Adam Redzik and Ihor Zeman, 'Masters of Rafal Lemkin: Lwow School of Law' in Bienczyk-Missala, Civilians in Contemporary Armed Conflicts, pp. 237–242. Adam Redzik also provided me his draft article (not yet published at the time of writing) 'Rafal Lemkin: Co-author of the Modern International Criminal Law'.

[33] Douglas Irvin-Erickson, *Raphael Lemkin and the Concept of Genocide* (Philadelphia, PA: University of Pennsylvania Press, 2016).

[34] Sands, East West Street.

the same place, Lviv University, at about the same time, without particularly knowing each other.

Seyla Benhabib compares the life and academic writings of Lemkin with those of Hanna Arendt and presents the disagreements between them in the scope of crimes and the role of universal jurisdiction.[35] Legal scholars, writing textbooks on genocide, devoted large parts to Lemkin's role.[36]

James Fussell, an expert on Lemkin and webmaster of the 'Prevent Genocide' organization, did extensive research in archives and libraries in the USA and Europe, interviewing tens of Lemkin's former associates, colleagues, family members, their children and published the data on www.preventgenocide.org.

Lemkin has been an object of fascination, but although the literature on him surged in the last twenty years, some parts of his life remain mysterious, incomplete, leaving gaps in years, facts and names. Some authors uncritically present Lemkin as an unsung hero,[37] and heavily rely on Lemkin's writings, producing a one-sided heroic image of him. Some copy questionable or incorrect data from each other. One can see confusion in his year of birth (1900 or 1901[38]), in which universities did he study,[39] and unbelievable references to Lemkin as a 'French jurist',[40] or as 'a Polish émigré to London'.[41] Even serious scholars continue to repeat misrepresentations, such as that Lemkin served in the Polish Army, that he fought against the Soviets in 1919–1920 and against the Nazis in 1939, or that he was wounded.[42] Lemkin never served in the army, nor was he

---

[35] Seyla Behnabib, 'International Law and Human Plurality in the Shadow of Totalitarianism', in Goldoni and McCorkindale (eds.) *Hanna Arendt and the Law*, pp. 191–214.

[36] Shaw, What Is Genocide?; Jones, *Genocide*, pp. 8–14 and 456–459.

[37] Michael Ignatieff, 'The Unsung Hero who Coined the Term "Genocide"', in *The New Republic*, 21 September 2013.

[38] Lemkin himself should have corrected his year of birth from 1901 to 1900 when checking his biographical entries, but he let it be repeated. The mistake was originally made by the *New York Post* article on 17 June 1948, see Szawlowski, 'Lemkin (1900–1958)', p. 101.

[39] Tanya Elder writes that he went to study linguistics at Lviv University in 1919, then to Heidelberg in Germany to study philosophy, both wrong, see Elder, 'What You See Before Your Eyes', p. 475.

[40] Guglielmo Verdirame, 'The Genocide Definition in the Jurisprudence of Ad Hoc Tribunals', *International and Comparative Law Quarterly*, Vol. 49, July 2000, p. 281.

[41] Isidor Walliman, Michael Dobkowski (eds.), *Genocide and the Modern Age: Etiology and Case Studies of Mass Death* (New York: Praeger, 1987), p. 100.

[42] 'When in September 1939 the German forces attacked Poland Raphael Lemkin was drafted into the Polish Armed Forces and wounded' p. 458 of Daniel Marc Segesser and Myriam Gessler, 'Raphael Lemkin and the International Debate on the Punishment

288 VESSELIN POPOVSKI

ever wounded – in September 1939 the engine of the train, on which he was hiding to escape, was hit by a bomb but Lemkin was not injured.

Some of the lies came from Lemkin himself. When applying to Jagiellonian University in Krakow in 1920 he forged a document saying that he had served in the army[43] to gain admission, but a year later he was expelled from the university exactly because his forgery was discovered.[44] Al Kennedy in the article 'My Hero: Rafael Lemkin' claiming that Lemkin 'changed the world with a word',[45] repeated several lies, for example, that Lemkin was wounded in 1939 defending Warsaw. He was not defending Warsaw, he was running away from the city. Kennedy also wrote that Lemkin lost his job as a Public Prosecutor because of the paper on the 'crime of barbarity' that he presented at the League of Nations' Legal Committee meeting in Madrid. Lemkin did not present a paper in Madrid, and he was not fired for writing it, he volunteered to quit the Public Prosecution Service and joined the Bar of the District Chambers to earn more money. Nor was he ever 'jobless and chastened' because of anti-Semitism or because he was too anti-German at a time when Poland wanted to be on good terms with Hitler, as Samantha Power wrote.[46]

Polish writers present a more balanced and truthful picture of Lemkin, instead of making him an exaggerated hero or a constant victim. Lemkin himself presented his life as multiple victimhood. The first victimhood is geographical: Lemkin was born on the borderline between two aggressive Empires – Germany and Russia. The second victimhood is religious: Jews were discriminated against by both the Russians and the Nazis. The third victimhood is historical: in his short lifetime, Lemkin witnessed two world wars, the Armenian genocide, the anti-Semitic pogroms, the Polish-Soviet War, the Holodomor (mass starvation in Ukraine), the Holocaust and the Cold War.

Lemkin explains the first two victimhoods in his autobiography:

> I was born in a part of the world history known as Lithuania or White Russia, where Poles, Russians and Jews had lived together for many centuries. They disliked each other and even fought, but despite this, they shared a deep love for their towns, hills, rivers. It was a feeling of

of War Crimes (1919–1948)' in *Journal of Genocide Research*, Vol. 7, Issue 4, 2005, pp. 453–468.

[43] At the time, service in the army was a requirement to enroll in university.

[44] Redzik and Zeman, 'Masters of Rafal Lemkin', p. 239.

[45] *Guardian*, 9 March 2012, available at www.theguardian.com/books/2012/mar/09/my-hero-al-kennedy-raphael-lemkin.

[46] Power, *A Problem from Hell*, p. 22.

common destiny that prevented them from destroying one another completely. This area was between ethnographic Poland to the west, East Prussia to the north, Ukraine to the south, and Great Russia to the east.[47]

The peoples of this region were well acquainted with the consequences of living on the edge of empires, they saw bloodshed and upheaval, they knew about purges and persecution. As John Cooper wrote: 'Growing up in a contested borderland over which different armies clashed ... made Lemkin acutely sensitive to the concerns of the diverse nationalities living there and their anxieties about self-preservation.'[48] The next section of Lemkin's autobiography titled 'Buying the Right to Live' explains the religious victimhood – Jews in the Russian Empire were prohibited from owning land, and Lemkin recalls how his father had to pay a prohibitive tenure to the farm owner, as well as bribes to a local police official, whom the children learned to fear 'as a symbol of our bondage'.[49] In 1906 dozens of Jews were killed in Byalistok in a climate of pogroms and anti-Semitism and Lemkin developed a deep resentment of injustice, discrimination and violence. Later he lost forty-nine members of his family in the Holocaust and the visceral experience of anti-Semitism firmed up his commitment to define and punish such crimes.

Lemkin was a close witness to historical tragedies. His village became an area of combat between Russian and German troops in World War I. Lemkin's family buried their books and valuables and evacuated into the forest. German artillery destroyed their home, troops seized crops, horses and livestock. Rafal witnessed his malnourished brother Samuel, dying from the flu pandemic, becoming the first of many victims in his family. Witnessing anti-Semitism, discrimination of national and religious groups, and impunity for massacres, pogroms and deliberate starvation gradually encouraged Lemkin to devote his life to the development of a legal system to address international crimes, including the extermination of national, ethnic and religious groups as such.[50]

11.2 Legal Studies

Lemkin's studies were constantly interrupted because of the war, but he managed to pass the graduate exams and obtain a diploma from the

---

[47] Frieze, *Totally Unofficial*, p. 3.
[48] Cooper, *Raphael Lemkin and the Struggle for the Genocide Convention*, p. 24.
[49] Frieze, *Totally Unofficial*, p. 12.
[50] Sands, *East West Street*, p. 156.

Byalistok gymnasium in June 1919 and in the summer he enrolled to study at Jagiellonian University in Krakow. In 1921, however, he was expelled from Krakow when it was found that his certificate of service in the Polish Army was forged.[51] Lemkin moved to Lviv and enrolled in Jan Kazimierz University. The development of his legal thinking, interest and devotion to criminal law was deeply influenced by several Polish law professors, although noticeably Lemkin does not acknowledge them in his biography.[52]

One of the most influential academics to shape Lemkin's education was his tutor both in Krakow and in Lviv, Juliusz Makarewicz.[53] Lemkin was also significantly indebted to Emil S. Rappaport,[54] who helped him considerably in finding jobs and engaging in international activities. Thanks to Rappaport Lemkin became a lecturer at the Free Polish University in Warsaw and engaged in the work of the Association internationale de droit pénal (AIDP). The young Lemkin was also helped by Waclaw Makowski,[55] the main author of the Polish Penal Code of 1932. Others to whom Lemkin should have shown gratitude include the constitutional lawyer Stanislaw Starzynski[56] and the energetic professor of public international law Ludwik Ehrlich.[57]

---

[51] Adam Redzik provides the most detailed account on this episode. See also Sands, *East West Street*, p. 145. It is unclear in what capacity Lemkin served in the Polish Army. Marek Konrat writes he was a volunteer assistant to a military judge. Lemkin himself wrote he was a volunteer in a martial court, but Adam Redzik found a document, kept in the archives of Lviv University, that Lemkin served in an ancillary sanitary unit. See Redzik and Zeman, 'Masters of Rafal Lemkin', p. 238.

[52] It seems his relationship with his professors froze after he escaped to the USA in 1941. Most of them remained in Poland and survived Lemkin, but they hardly mentioned him and he did not mention them in his writings. See Sands, *East West Street*, pp. 150–156, Szawlowski, 'Lemkin (1900–1958)', pp. 103–105.

[53] Juliusz Makarewicz (1872–1955) – one of the best representatives of the sociological schools of criminal law in Poland. Professor in Jagiellonian University, Krakow and in Lvov. Member of the Polish Codification Committee and co-author of the 1932 Penal Code.

[54] Emil Stanisław Rappaport (1877–1965) – one of the creators of the doctrine of international criminal law. Co-founder, member of the Senate and professor of criminal policy of the Free Polish University in Warsaw. After 1948 full professor in Łódź University. Supreme Court Judge (1919–1951) and later Judge in the Supreme National Tribunal till his retirement in 1960. A member of the Polish Codification Committee. One of the founders of the AIDP, its vice-chairman between 1924 and 1939. He proposed that not only aggressive war, but also the propaganda of aggressive war should be considered an international crime.

[55] Wacław Makowski (1880–1942) – representative of the naturalistic direction in criminal law. Seven-term Minister of Justice. Member of Parliament, Speaker of the Sejm. Co-author of the 1932 Polish penal code and the 1935 constitution.

[56] Redzik and Zeman, 'Masters of Rafal Lemkin', p. 239.

[57] Ludwik Ehrlich (1889–1968) – educated in Germany, England and Poland. He created the first, in this part of Europe, Diplomatic School in Warsaw, where many future

11 RAFAL LEMKIN

Lemkin's legal studies were impacted by two murders and the follow-up trials. In 1921, Soghomon Tehlirian, an Armenian who had lost all his family in 1915, killed Mehmed Talaat Pasha, the Ottoman ex-Minister of Interior and architect of the Armenian genocide.[58] The news brought Lemkin back to his earlier curiosity about mass crimes and he decided to take more courses in criminal law. Even though the Ottoman authorities deported and systematically exterminated 1.5 million Armenians, they later enjoyed immunity. Lemkin inquired about the Armenian massacres in dialogues with Makarewicz and discovered that the scope of war crimes defined at the Hague Conferences was not detailed enough to include the type of atrocities committed against a particular ethnic group. Not only was international law missing, but there was no political will to prosecute the Ottoman perpetrators of atrocities against the Armenians. Lemkin found out that even though a Turkish court sentenced Talaat Pasha and other leaders, most of them were allowed to flee Turkey. These criminals received lifetime protection from the German government and enjoyed respectable and comfortable lives equal to retired officers.[59]

The second murder was in 1926, when the Ukrainian ex-leader Symon Petlura, notorious for his anti-Jewish pogroms in Ukraine, was shot dead by the Jewish émigré Shwartzwald as an act of revenge. In the same way as with Tehlirian earlier, the jury declared Shwartzwald not guilty. Lemkin, at the time working as a clerk in the Warsaw Appeal Court, regarded this as another signal that something was missing in the international legal order and that a new judicial system needed to be established to prevent and prosecute such crimes, in particular, so that individual victims would not need to undertake revenge assassinations.[60]

Witnessing these two trials, Lemkin started questioning absolute sovereignty, and in particular its tendency to act as a shield for leaders to persecute their people. The idea of sovereignty was based in a long

---

international lawyers studied (Louis Sohn among them). Professor of the Jagiellonian, Krakow, and of Lviv University. Ad hoc judge of the Permanent Court of International Justice in The Hague.

[58] Eric Bogosian, *Operation Nemesis: The Assassination Plot that Avenged the Armenian Genocide* (Boston, MA: Little, Brown, 2015).

[59] Dan Eshet, *Totally Unofficial: Raphael Lemkin and the Genocide Convention* (Chicago, IL: Midpoint Trade Books, 2007), p. 3.

[60] Lemkin described the revenge killing of Talaat Pasha and Simon Petlura as 'beautiful crimes'. Such acts of revenge might be crimes in the eyes of law, but in the eyes of morality, they are 'beautiful'. See Szawlowski, 'Lemkin (1900–1958)', p. 103.

evolution in European legal thought, but one of its implications was traditionally thought to be that kings and princes had unlimited prerogatives and authority over the territory of the state under their control and that whatever atrocities they might commit fell within the domestic affairs of their state. At a time when this was hardly fashionable, Lemkin was one of the first to argue in international law, foreshadowing the much later language of the Responsibility to Protect (R2P)[61] that sovereignty should be connected with the responsibility to people, that sovereigns should act only in the interest and benefit of their citizens. Most notably, he argued, sovereignty could not be conceived as a right to kill millions of innocents.[62] The solution was to develop a comprehensive system uniting the criminal laws of all nations and to establish a permanent international criminal court to exercise jurisdiction over such crimes.

Lemkin enthusiastically joined Rappaport and Vespasian Pella who urged the League of Nations to deliberate and develop international criminal jurisdiction to prosecute international crimes either through an international criminal court or through domestic criminal courts applying universal jurisdiction. Pella at the first general meeting of the AIDP proposed the establishment of an International Bureau for the Unification of Criminal Law (IBUCL) to undertake concrete work towards the unification of the criminal law of the European states. The unification of criminal law was seen at that time as a major step towards a more ambitious agenda to create a legal system to prevent and punish various international crimes – not historical ones such as piracy and slavery, rather contemporary crimes such as aggression, the propaganda of war, war crimes, terrorism, etc.[63]

Lemkin could build on his experience as a translator and scholar in domestic and comparative criminal law. Together with Kochanowicz, he translated the 1927 Soviet penal code and the 1932 Polish penal code into English with the collaboration of Malcolm McDermott, a law professor from Duke University. As part of a seminar lead by Makarewicz and Makowski in Lviv University, Lemkin also undertook a comparative study of a large number of other criminal codes – in addition to the

---

[61] World Summit Outcome, General Assembly Document A/60/L.1/2005, para 138–139, available at: www.un.org/en/development/desa/population/migration/generalassembly/docs/globalcompact/A_RES_60_1.pdf.

[62] Steven L. Jacobs and Samuel Totten (eds.), *Pioneers of Genocide Studies* (New Brunswick, NJ: Transaction Books, 2002), p. 371. See also, Sands, *East West Street*, p. 148.

[63] *Gradual Unification of Criminal Law and Co-operation of States in the Prevention and Suppression of Crime* (Geneva: League of Nations, 1933).

Soviet and the Italian, also those of Latvia, Yugoslavia, Denmark, China, Turkey, Argentina and others.[64]

Presided over by Makowski, the first IBUCL conference was convened in Warsaw in 1927. The conference accepted Rappaport's proposals that not only aggressive war but also the propaganda for aggressive war should be considered an international crime. It also discussed a list of *delicta juris gentium* – such as piracy, counterfeiting of coins, trade in slaves, trade in women and children, intentional use of instruments capable of producing public danger, trade in narcotics and traffic in obscene publications – and declared those crimes to be punishable anywhere by any criminal court under the principle of universal jurisdiction.[65] Lemkin attended the first conferences on the unification of criminal law and soon after was elected as secretary-general of the Polish branch of the AIDP, the Polish Society of Criminal Legislation. The next conferences in Brussels in 1930 and Paris in 1931 took up the issue of intentional use of instruments capable of producing public danger and were the opportunity for Lemkin's first 'great moment'[66] in an international forum. Some delegates from Eastern Europe proposed to subsume acts of terrorism under this heading, but others, amongst them Rappaport and Lemkin, opposed this.

The 1931 conference in Paris decided to create a commission to continue the debate on the intentional use of instruments capable of producing public danger and to present reports at the fifth IBUCL conference in Madrid in 1933. One report was written by the secretary-general of the AIDP Jean-Andre Roux, who proposed to concentrate on terrorism and to try to fix minimal penalties in national criminal law for this offence.[67] Lemkin disagreed with Roux, pointing out that terrorism was only one of the crimes capable of producing public danger, and that other crimes had to be dealt with by employing the principle of universal jurisdiction. Lemkin referred to decisions taken by the IBUCL conferences in Warsaw, Brussels and Paris and argued that terrorism did not yet constitute a legal concept, but rather embraced a variety of different criminal acts. Later Lemkin

---

[64] Szawlowski, 'Lemkin (1900–1958)', p. 110.

[65] For the whole documentation from the first conference, see Michel Potulicki (ed.), *Actes de la 1-ere Conference d'Unification du Droit Penal* (Paris: Librairie du Recueil Sirey, 1929).

[66] An expression from Szawlowski, 'Lemkin (1900–1958)', p. 112.

[67] Jean-Andre Roux, 'Terrorisme', in Manual Lopez-Rey (ed.), *Actes de la V-eme Conference Internationale d'Unification du Droit Penal* (Paris: Pedone, 1935), pp. 42–47.

contributed a report on 'Terrorisme'[68] to the sixth conference of the IBUCL in Copenhagen in 1935 in which he argued that not only internal terrorism – political acts of terrorism – but also international terrorism should be included in discussions.[69] His relative wariness with the offence and his insistence that it be subsumed in a much larger category nonetheless set him apart from the others and suggested a certain ability to see beyond 'the crime of the moment'.

11.3 Crimes against Collectivities: 'Barbarity' and 'Vandalism'

For the Madrid conference of the IBUCL in 1933 Lemkin wrote a report on crimes against collectivities, such as barbarity and vandalism. This was timely because the same year in Simele, Iraq, Assyrians were massacred. Lemkin argued for a return to the original concept of the intentional use of instruments capable of producing public danger, and the inclusion of acts of barbarity, vandalism, provocation of catastrophes, interruption of international communications as well as the propagation of human, animal or vegetable contagions. Further, Lemkin pointed to acts of extermination and destruction of culture and works of art as violations, which had to be punished everywhere independently of the location of such acts. He ended up proposing an international convention to ensure the repression of such offences.[70]

Sadly, however, Lemkin could not go to Madrid to present his paper. The Polish Minister of Justice Czeslaw Michalowski told Rappaport days before the conference that Lemkin was unwanted in Madrid and he would not issue him an exit visa. The reason was that Lemkin – writing on barbarity and vandalism – was seen as too anti-Nazi at a time when the European states were trying to accommodate Hitler. Rappaport could not oppose Michalowski's decision and he told Lemkin not to go to Madrid. More disturbingly, Rappaport did not interfere with the dropping of Lemkin's paper from the agenda for discussion.

Lemkin did not take up the issues of barbarity and vandalism further in the following conferences because terrorism became the dominant topic within the AIDP and the League of Nations after the murder of Yugoslav King Alexander and French Foreign Minister Louis Barthou in Marseilles on 9 October 1934. Not surprisingly the sixth IBUCL conference in

---

[68] Raphael Lemkin, *Terrorisme* (Paris: Pedone, 1938).
[69] Kornat, 'Barbarity-Vandalism-Terrorism-Genocide', p. 134.
[70] Lemkin, *Les Actes*, p. 56.

Copenhagen in 1935 dealt heavily with the issue of terrorism, but Rappaport and Lemkin showed reluctance to push for a draft convention and create an international criminal court to prosecute terrorism.

Lemkin's paper for the Madrid conference remains academically significant as it presented a list of five international crimes subjected to universal jurisdiction, adding two newly defined crimes – barbarity and vandalism – to terrorism, interruption of international communications and causing catastrophes through intentional chemical contamination. Lemkin argued that these five acts can be added to piracy and slavery and be considered as crimes by all nations. Accordingly, the universal jurisdiction should apply and a person who commits such acts should be arrested and brought to trial in any country, no matter where the crime was committed and no matter what is the nationality of perpetrators and victims. Lemkin's paper was visionary, timely and forward-looking – Nazi acts of barbarity and vandalism against Jews were on the cusp of happening. Lemkin, but also others, whose families had experienced anti-Semitism personally or who had read *Mein Kampf* carefully, knew it. Writing on the crime of barbarity and vandalism Lemkin predicted like no one else at the time what would happen a decade later in the Nazi concentration camps.

11.4   From 'Barbarity' to 'Genocide'

When Poland was invaded by Nazi Germany in September 1939, Lemkin ran away from Warsaw but did not get far as the engine of his train was hit by a bomb. He escaped by hiding from the Nazis and making the Soviet patrols think he was a poor worker instead of a senior lawyer. Lemkin reached his home and there met his parents, who in a life-costing mistake chose instead of running as refugees to stay. Lemkin left for Vilna, Lithuania and from then he would have neither a home nor a family. He wrote to Karol Schlyter, Minister of Justice of Sweden, whom he knew from the IBUCL conferences, with a plea for refugee passage. Being granted such, in February 1940 Lemkin arrived in Stockholm. He learned Swedish and began lecturing at Stockholm University. But even in neutral Sweden Lemkin did not feel safe and with the help of Professor McDermott, with whom he had translated the 1932 Polish Penal Code, Lemkin received an offer to teach at Duke University in the USA. He embarked on a miraculous winter journey through all of Russia, across the Pacific, to finally reach Seattle where he felt safe for the first time in his life.

In June 1941 he received a letter from his parents who were soon after deported to a concentration camp where they met their death.[71] Lemkin moved to work for the War Department in Washington from where he lobbied US politicians to take action against the Nazis. One day listening on the radio to Churchill speaking about emerging reports of entire districts being exterminated, and calling these a 'crime without a name', Lemkin became inspired to invent the crime of genocide.

This happened at the time when Lemkin was writing a book based on his analysis of the Nazi decrees in occupied Europe. Lemkin persuaded the Carnegie Endowment to expand the initial plan for a 200-word monograph on the Military Government in Europe into a 670-page book to include all 330 decrees and name it *Axis Rule in Occupied Europe: Laws of Occupation, Analysis of Government, Proposals for Redress* (hereafter *Axis Rule*). This expansion allowed more analytical chapters on German police practices, on the laws against Jews and a ninth and last chapter of the book titled 'Genocide'. The Carnegie Endowment wanted the book to show the difference between the occupation policy of the Allies and the Axis Powers to give the troops, liberating Europe from the Nazi occupation, a list of modes and agencies to redress the damage done to persons and property under occupation. Lemkin agreed but also used the book to pursue his agenda – to convince the readers that the anti-human occupation of large parts of Europe had been marked with outrages against human rights, morality and religion.

Axis Rule was an ambitious and sophisticated legal work that went far beyond the framing of genocide. Lemkin's documentation of decrees passed by Germany and other Axis states to rule on thirty-five countries and occupied territories was the first of its kind. Although genocide was only discussed in the final chapter and not even mentioned in the foreword, *Axis Rule* became famous for its conceptualization and popularization of genocide. Lemkin linked the Axis occupation with the goal to annihilate the Jews and the Poles and showed that Hitler was aiming not only to win the war but to ethnically cleanse the territory of Europe and achieve Germanization through the disintegration of other cultures, languages and nationalities. Lemkin wrote:

---

[71] Lemkin lost about fifty members of his family in the Holocaust. The only ones who survived were his brother Elias with his wife and two sons. They were sent to a Soviet labour camp, from where Lemkin successfully helped them to emigrate to Montreal in 1948.

New conceptions require new terms. By genocide, we mean the destruction of a nation or an ethnic group. This new word is made from the ancient Greek word *genos* (race, tribe) and the Latin *cide* (killing), thus corresponding in its formation to such words as tyrannicide, homicide, infanticide, etc. Generally speaking, genocide does not necessarily mean the immediate destruction of a nation, except when accomplished by mass killings of all members of a nation. It is intended rather signify a coordinated plan of different actions aiming at the destruction of essential foundations of the life of national groups, to annihilate the groups themselves. The objectives of such a plan would be disintegration of the political and social institutions, of culture, language, national feelings, religion, and the economic existence of national groups, and the destruction of the personal security, liberty, health, dignity, and even the lives of the individuals belonging to such groups. Genocide is directed against the national group as an entity, and the actions involved are directed against individuals, not in their capacity, but as members of the national group.[72]

Studying in detail the Nazi decrees, Lemkin understood earlier than anybody else that genocide was Hitler's hidden purpose, a new technique through which the occupation of territory led to ethnically changing the population. Lemkin, correctly, did not claim that he was introducing a new concept entirely; rather his aim was to re-formulate afresh and unify in one word what had been described previously in his writing on 'barbarity' and 'vandalism'.[73]

Lemkin further developed the concept of genocide in several journal articles, explaining why it is necessary to introduce the concept of genocide in ICL and to set up a convention for the prevention and punishment of genocide.[74] He renewed his cooperation with the AIDP and published two articles in the *Revue International de Droit Penal* (1946, No. 3–4) in its special issue devoted to the future of the ICL after World War II. The first article developed his concept of genocide and the links between genocide and crimes against humanity[75] and the second was *mot-a-mot* translation of his final chapter, 'Genocide', in *Axis Rule*.[76] In another publication, he added a memorandum proposing the inclusion of anti-genocide clauses to the peace treaties prepared at

---

[72] Lemkin, *Axis Rule in Occupied Europe*, p. 79.
[73] Lemkin, *Axis Rule in Occupied Europe*, pp. 48–56.
[74] Raphael Lemkin, 'Genocide' in *The American Scholar*, Volume 15, Issue 2, 1946, p. 229.
[75] Raphael Lemkin, 'Genocide: A New International Crime. Punishment and Prevention' in *Revue International de Droit Penal*, Vol. 17, Issue 3–4, 1946, pp. 360–370.
[76] Raphael Lemkin, 'Le Genocide' *in Revue International de Droit Penal*, Volume 17, Issue 3–4, 1946, pp. 371–386.

the time with the Allies of the Third Reich.[77] The evolution and systematization of his views on genocide as a crime under international law were published in the *American Journal of International Law.*[78]

11.5   Dichotomy Individual-Collective

Several major elements surface in Lemkin's gradual theorization of genocide. His work shows the complex dynamic between the individual and the collective. As a comparative criminal law scholar, Lemkin had left little doubt as to where he fell between the prerogatives of collectivities and the rights of individuals. He emphasized the unique character of totalitarian codes, concluding that they played more of a societal role, serving and protecting the totalitarian state, rather than remedying the needs of individual victims. Lemkin exhibited strong liberal tendencies when emphasizing guarantees of the rights of individuals. For example, in critiquing the Soviet penal code, he advocated for a ban on the use of analogy, and the need for strict compliance with the principle of *nullum crimen sine lege.*[79]

Lemkin's commitment to human rights did not prevent him from putting considerable early emphasis on crimes against collectivities. He defined the crime of barbarity as premeditated destruction of national, racial, religious and social collectivities. The goal of the crime of barbarity, he argued, was not only to harm an individual but also to damage the collectivity to which the individual belongs. 'Offenses of this type bring harm not only to human rights, but also and most especially they undermine the fundamental basis of the social order.'[80] Lemkin illustrated the crime of barbarity with the deportation of Armenians in 1915 and insisted that this 'new crime' must be declared illegal in international law. He theorized that acts of barbarity were persecutions on religious grounds, against minority groups and include an embargo on food and medicines. He included cultural vandalism and cultural devastation as a common thread in the intent to destroy a particular group that shared

---

[77] Raphael Lemkin, 'Le Crime de Genocide', *Revue de Droit international, des sciences, diplomatiques, et politiques,* Volume 15, Issue 4, 1946, pp. 213–223.

[78] Raphael Lemkin, 'Genocide as Crime under International Law' in *The American Journal of International Law,* Volume 41, Issue 1, January 1947, pp. 145–151.

[79] Szawlowski, 'Lemkin (1900–1958)', p. 112.

[80] Raphael Lemkin's 1933 proposal to make extermination of groups an international crime – Prevent Genocide International, www.preventgenocide.org/lemkin/madrid1933-english.htm (last visited 2 December 2016).

ethnicity, religion or social identity.[81] 'These crimes undermined the culture that we share as human beings' wrote Lemkin.[82]

It is worth pointing out how Lemkin in his paper for the Madrid conference articulated 'barbarity' and 'vandalism' as acts both against individuals and against collectivities. He started with a list of crimes under the law of nations that could derive from humanitarian postulates – trade in women and slaves for example – that concerned the protection of individual freedoms and dignity and that prevented treatment of human beings as a commodity.[83] Then he listed other crimes under the law of nations – aggressive war and propaganda – that served to protect normal relations between groups. Some crimes were, therefore, attacks on individual rights, whereas others affect relations between an individual and a group, or between groups. But there could also be crimes that combined the two elements, these are: "in particular attempts against an individual as a member of a group. In such cases, a perpetrator aims not only at harming an individual but at inflicting damage on the group to which the individual belongs. Such violations are aimed not only against human rights but also, and above all, against public order."[84] Lemkin logically concluded: "The consequences of such acts usually go beyond relations among individuals, they shake the very basis of harmony in mutual relations between particular groups. Such acts directed against individuals constitute a general interstate danger."[85]

Lemkin in an article in 1946 firmed up the understanding of genocide as both exterminations of national groups and as persecution of individuals because of their belonging to those groups, regardless of their national characteristics.[86] He emphasized that individuals are subject to extermination as members of such groups and for that reason only. This academically narrow understanding of genocide is important to remember, even if in some public statements Lemkin may have used the word also for crimes broader than that, for example for Stalin's starvation of a population (Holodomor).[87] Because of the stigmatizing effect that the

---

[81] Szawlowski, 'Lemkin (1900–1958)', pp. 114–116; Kornat, 'Barbarity-Vandalism-Terrorism-Genocide', pp. 85–87.

[82] Quoted by Dan Eshet, *Totally Unofficial*, p. 11.

[83] Lemkin, *Les Actes*, p. 4.

[84] Lemkin, *Les Actes*, p. 5.

[85] Raphael Lemkin, *La protection de la paix par le droit penal, Rapport presente au IVe Congres International de Droit Penal* (Paris, 26–31 Juillet 1937).

[86] Raphael Lemkin, 'Genocide' in *The American Scholar*, Volume 15, Issue 2, 1946, pp. 227–230.

[87] Redzik and Zeman, 'Masters of Rafal Lemkin', p. 16.

word genocide immediately produces, it has been used to advocate prevention and punishment of other crimes, not falling into what has been narrowly defined by Lemkin.

Lemkin was willing to envisage the destruction of groups as resulting from a variety of techniques. In terms of *mens rea* the focus might be narrowly on the intention to destroy groups as such, but the methods of how to achieve the destruction of the groups could be broad. According to Lemkin, genocide is more of a process than a single act and as such, it starts with the destruction of the national pattern of the oppressed group, national, social or religious. A broader understanding of the methods of the genocide made it possible to include such criminal acts as forced sterilization and abortions in concentration camps. Genocide was a modern crime, according to Lemkin, a crime committed with the use of modern technology and organization.[88] More specifically, as he showed in *Axis Rule*, it was a crime that had its roots in a variety of legal practices. One of his main theses concerned the uses of the law in implementing a policy of systematic discrimination and extermination. Not only were the Nazi occupiers not prevented from committing their crimes by the law, Lemkin argued, but they introduced acts and rules to 'legalize' their misdeed. In so doing they invoked a unilaterally utilitarian conception of law – the law is what is useful to the German nation. Lemkin aimed to present the Axis rule of occupation as, in fact, anti-rule, as quasi-law derived from the 'law of necessity'.[89] In the process, Lemkin also forged a strong connection between the protection of individuals and the international legal order, a connection that would, of course, become central to the adoption of the post-war legal edifice.

Lemkin's work at the dawn of the discipline is notable for disentangling genocide from war crimes and even war altogether. He foresaw the extermination of Jews not simply as another war crime but as something entirely detachable from the 'fog of war'. Barbarity and vandalism were irreducible criminal enterprises to the tradition of war crimes inaugurated at the Hague Conferences and could occur both in time of war and in time of peace. Few at the time even conceived of crimes against

---

[88] Raphael Lemkin, 'Genocide: A Modern Crime', in *Free World*, Volume 4, April 1945, pp. 39–43.

[89] Such attempts were also made during World War I – Theobald von Bethmann-Holweg who is known for his willingness to voluntarily appear and respond to accusations of crimes instead of Kaiser Wilhelm II, attempted to 'justify' the German occupation of Belgium as follows: 'Necessity knows no law. Anyone who is struggling for a supreme aim must think only of how he can hack his way through.' See Lemkin, *Axis Rule*, p. 78.

humanity, and even fewer would have been ready to detach them from their strong nexus with armed conflict. Lemkin, by contrast, emphasized that genocide was not solely a problem of wartime, but can occur at any time.

11.6 Codification of Genocide

At the end of World War II, a debate emerged around how to punish the Nazi war criminals, with some – Stalin, Churchill, Morgenthau – supporting summary execution, and others – F. D. Roosevelt, Henry Stimson – preferring an international military court. Most of the legal scholars supported the idea of a trial, not summary execution. Lemkin himself did not particularly advocate for a trial but was nonetheless supportive of the effort to prosecute senior Nazi leaders. He wrote that Hitler and his associates had to be regarded as common criminals and tried in Allied military courts.[90] He sent his book *Axis Rule* to Supreme Court Justice Robert H. Jackson, who became Chief Counsel at the International Military Tribunal in Nuremberg and invited Lemkin to join his team. It was in Nuremberg that Lemkin, browsing the documentation, found how his family perished in the Holocaust.

Lemkin made it to Nuremberg because of his encyclopedic knowledge, but he was seen as too passionate and emotional, therefore ill-suited to deal with the specifics of legal matters.[91] Most of the prosecutors tried to avoid him, Benjamin Ferencz wrote "We were all extremely busy. This new idea of his was not something we had time to think about ... We wanted him to leave us alone so we could convict these guys of mass murder."[92]

The Nuremberg Charter provided for three categories of crime – crimes against peace, war crimes and crimes against humanity and in the last category it included 'murder, extermination, enslavement, deportation and other inhumane acts'. The word genocide did not appear, the British delegation having opposed the word apparently because it did not exist in the Oxford Dictionary.[93] As a result, the word genocide could not make it into the verdict. Nonetheless, under Lemkin's influence, it was added in the Indictment of 6 October 1945. The twenty-four defendants

---

[90] Raphael Lemkin, 'The Legal Case Against Hitler' in *The Nation*, Volume 160, Issue 8, 1945, pp. 205–207.

[91] Sands, *East West Street*, pp. 186–188.

[92] Quote from Power, *A Problem from Hell*, p. 50.

[93] Korey, *Epitaph for Raphael Lemkin*, p. 47.

were accused of conducting 'deliberate and systematic genocide, viz., the extermination of racial and national groups, against the civilian population of certain occupied territories to destroy particular races and classes of people and national, racial, or religious groups, particularly Jews, Poles, and Gypsies'. Interestingly, the Nuremberg Indictment, specified 'class' as one of the identifiers the target group, going beyond what Lemkin expressed in *Axis Rule*, but alluding to his 1933 definition of 'crime of barbarity' in which social groups were listed. The word genocide could be found in some of the prosecutorial addresses in Nuremberg, for example in the Neurath case the British deputy prosecutor Sir David Maxwell-Fyfe, while questioning the accused, directly quoted the 'well-known book by Professor Lemkin'.[94] The word genocide was also used in some of the concluding statements by the British and French prosecutors.[95]

Lemkin wrote that the

> Nuremberg-judgment only partly relieved the world's moral tensions. Punishing the German war criminals created the feeling that in international life as in civil society crime should not be allowed to pay. But the purely juridical consequences of the trials were wholly insufficient. The quarrels and other follies of the Allies, which permitted Hitler to grow and become strong, survived these proceedings and found expression in Nuremberg's refusal to establish a precedent.[96]

In 1946 Lemkin took part in the first post-war ILA conference in Cambridge where he spoke on genocide in front of almost 300 lawyers. He sent a letter to the UN Secretary-General Trygve Lie, presenting his vision for international regulations on genocide, and Trygve Lie invited him to become a consultant on the UN Legal Committee and he moved to New York in October 1946. On 11 December 1946, the first General Assembly passed resolution 96/1 titled 'Crime of Genocide', which determined genocide as 'a crime under international law, which the civilized world condemns and for the commission of which principals and accomplices ... are punishable'.

---

[94] Trial of the Major War Criminals before the International Military Tribunal, Nuremberg 14 November 1945–1 October 1946, Nuremberg 1948, Vol. XVII, p. 61.

[95] For a comprehensive list and analysis of all texts related to genocide at Nuremberg, see Hilary Earl, 'Prosecuting Genocide Before the Genocide Convention: Raphael Lemkin and the Nuremberg Trials, 1945–1949' in *Journal of Genocide Research*, Volume 15, Issue 3, 2013, pp. 317–337.

[96] Frieze, *Totally Unofficial*, p. 122.

The resolution can be seen as a long-awaited victory for Lemkin, but its adoption was not preordained. Sir Hartley Shawcross, the British attorney general, at one point announced: 'Nuremberg is enough! A Genocide Convention cannot be adopted!' There was an ominous silence among the delegates. Lemkin wrote: 'I sat with a sunken head at a luncheon table on the terrace of a small café near the Palais de Chaillot. It was Indian summer, caressingly warm. The sun was shining, but it could not reach my frozen inner self.'[97] The next morning Lemkin was in the office of the Lebanese Prime Minister asking for support in the hope of gaining an ally on the drafting committee. Learning that the British might seek support from New Zealand to oppose the convention, Lemkin moved to the office of Prime Minister Peter Fraser winning his trust and earning the approval of his delegation. A day later, Pakistan joined the coalition alongside India. In the words of their delegate Begum Ikramullah, the Genocide Convention 'is written with the blood and tears of more than one million Muslims who perished through genocide during the partition of India in 1947'.[98]

In 1947–1948 a committee of experts (Lemkin, Pella and de Vabres) drafted the text of the Genocide Convention. It limited the range of acts proposed initially by Lemkin in *Axis Rule*, to broadly defined physical and biological destruction. Other acts, proposed by Lemkin, such as the destruction of language, culture or religion, were omitted. The victim categories were also limited to members of national, ethnic, racial and religious groups, but political and social groups were excluded from the list, in compliance with the Soviet position. The concept of 'cultural and national genocide', strongly advocated by the Soviet Union, was not taken into account either. Similarly, the Soviet demand to add in the preamble a relationship between fascism and genocide was rejected.

The Genocide Convention was the first of many human rights treaties later adopted by the United Nations. Its focus on the protection of national, racial, ethnic and religious groups from threats to their very existence fitted well with the then-emerging priorities of both the United Nations and the emerging human rights movement, aimed at the eradication of racism and xenophobia. Furthermore, it drew early emphasis on the role of criminal justice and accountability in the protection and promotion of human rights, although it would be decades before that association was acted upon.

---

[97] Frieze, *Totally Unofficial*, p. 157.
[98] Frieze, *Totally Unofficial*, p. 159.

From 1948 onwards Lemkin lectured in criminal law at Yale University and in 1955 he became Professor of Law at Rutgers, but his real mission was to pressure diplomats to find a way to achieve more ratifications of the convention. His health deteriorated, he was separated by the Cold War from his former colleagues and mentors in Poland, and became antisocial, disappearing for days from the handful of friends he had. On 28 August 1959, the year of his fifth Nobel Peace Prize nomination, Lemkin died from a heart attack in the press office of a publisher. His tireless regimen no doubt hastened his early death. He died, to use the expression of Tanya Elder, of "genociditis, exhaustion from working on genocide".[99] The US did not ratify the convention and the idea of international tribunals with jurisdiction to prosecute genocide had to wait another thirty-five years.

Lemkin's project to create an internationally recognized law to criminalize genocide was legalistic in its implicit faith in the power of law-making. However, Lemkin jealously wanted to distance the convention from those promoting the renewal of international law in a period defined by realist scepticism about interwar approaches. He rooted genocide in a religiously infected moral idiom that could distance his project from those pursuing a broader agenda of international legal codification, one more focused on preserving international peace and security, rather than combatting atrocities. Lemkin's concern to preserve the basic idea behind the minority treaties set him apart from other international jurists working towards the establishment of binding legal enforcement of the protection of individual human rights.

Some may think of Lemkin as an outsider, obsessive artisan of one word, which he wished to be inscribed everywhere, who nominated himself five times for the Nobel Peace Prize, only to leave a tenured professorship at Yale to live in misery in New York, whilst bullying diplomats to ratify an improbable convention. Lemkin was indeed an unusual and in some ways marginal character, where other early exponents of ICL had much more solid and completed careers and lives, left significant literature and died in dignity. But Lemkin had the unusual capacity to abstract from his personal experience and elevate a certain concept to universality. Genocide as a concept has established a unique stranglehold on legal imaginations.

The legacy of Lemkin and the Genocide Convention is thus ambiguous. Many critiques of the convention are reasonable. For example, the

---

[99] Elder, 'What You See Before Your Eyes', p. 492.

requirement to prove a special intent – the intent to destroy, in whole or in part, a national, ethnical, racial or religious group – can raise a difficult prosecutorial hurdle and maybe too psychologizing in complex societies where violence can result as much from anonymous social and economic forces as from individuals. Another discomfort with the convention is that it establishes an informal hierarchy – once the word genocide gains traction in political circles and public discussion as the 'crime of crimes', it elevates the protection of groups above that of individuals and creates considerable pressure to have certain events characterized as genocide, possibly at the expense of other equally grave but more specific charges.

The term genocide, with its focus on group irreducibility, may heighten a sentiment of 'them' v. 'us', burnishing feelings of group identity, and may unwittingly reinforce the very conditions that it seeks to prevent. For some, to be labelled victims of genocide can become an essential component of national identity without contributing to the resolution of historical disputes or making mass killings less frequent. If groups can be victims, moreover, then they can also be perpetrators.

A deeper problem lies with the very fluidity and constructed nature of 'racial', 'ethnic' or 'religious' groups. Lemkin's vision tended to see these groups as pre-constituted and intangible where our contemporary sensitivities tend to see them as highly constructed. A modern critic may feel that Lemkin was to a certain extent blinded by a nineteenth-century romantic view on identities, minorities and groups. Is there not a risk that in protecting 'racial groups' for example one might unwittingly reinforce a racialized vision of the world? And if genocide is a racializing process rather than one based on some pre-existing notion of race, then do we need a strong notion of racial groups to begin with?

Yet from the Yazidis in Syria to the Rohingya in Myanmar, there has unfortunately been no shortage of groups targeted as such, whether they exist in some fundamental or merely socially constructed sense. In that respect, even if he could not foresee all developments, Lemkin at least forged a concept that could evolve with the times and remains highly relevant today.

12

Stefan Glaser

Polish Lawyer, Diplomat and Scholar

KAROLINA WIERCZYŃSKA AND GRZEGORZ WIERCZYŃSKI[1]

Figure 12.1 Portrait of Stefan Glaser. Resources of the National Digital Archive, Koncern Ilustrowany Kurier Codzienny – Archiwum Ilustracji.

---

[1] We would like to thank many people who talked to or spoke with us about Glaser and shared their knowledge and materials, including Professor Leszek Kubicki who knew S. Glaser personally, Professor Wojciech Zalewski, Professor Idesbald Goddeeris, Professor Damien Scalia, Dr Raluca Grosescu, Dr Szymon Zaręba, thank you very much for your great help. We are especially grateful to the editors of this volume – Immi and Frédéric for their patience (Immi) and criticism (Frédéric).

Introduction

Stefan Antoni Glaser was neither born in Poland nor did he die there. Nonetheless, he emphasized his Polish nationality, patriotism and attachment to the country throughout his entire life. Poland did not exist as an official state at the time of his birth on 20 January 1895. In the course of three partitions in the seventeenth century,[2] the territory was divided between the Habsburg Austrian Empire, the Russian Empire and the Kingdom of Prussia. Glaser's birthplace, Tarnów, was part of the Kingdom of Galicia and Lodomeria, a subdivision of the Habsburg Austrian Empire. On 30 April 1984, Stefan Glaser died while in exile in Brussels, still not at home.

During his long and productive life he experienced life both under occupation and the restoration of the Polish state after World War I.[3] Moreover, while he witnessed the interwar period in Poland, which marked a period of recovery in Europe after the devastation of World War I, he was also present throughout the rise of Hitler, Stalin and Mussolini, the commencement of a new tragic war, and finally the Communist period in Eastern Europe, which he spent in exile. He never got a chance to return to a democratic Poland, although as a great enthusiast of European integration he must have hoped for Poland to develop into a stable, pluralistic and democratic country. Those formative experience had a great impact on Glaser as a key figure of international criminal law and his contribution to this emerging discipline.

The aim of the present chapter is to present Stefan Glaser – a witness of epochal events, a criminal lawyer and advocate in political trials, a scholar and a scientist – and above all a witness to the first international criminal trials against individuals. He drafted provisions to prosecute war criminals, and engaged in the negotiation of the UN Convention on the Non-Applicability of Statutory Limitations to War Crimes and Crimes against Humanity. The chapter will focus specifically on how his Polish experience influenced his approach to international criminal law and his writings on individual criminal responsibility for international crimes.

The first section seeks to contextualize Glaser's subsequent role as an international criminal lawyer by focusing on his bibliography, including the "Polish part" of Glaser's life (which ended when the Germans invaded

---

[2] On the history of the three partitions of Polish territory see J. Lukowski, *The Partitions of Poland 1772, 1793, 1795* (Routledge: London 1999).

[3] A. Prażmowska, *Poland: A Modern History* (I.B. Tauris: London, New York 2010) 86.

Poland in 1939). This period of his life encompasses his education, work and early academic career, as well as his political struggles and writings. Subsequently, the discussion will focus on the life of Glaser as an international criminal lawyer, from the commencement of World War II to its aftermath. This part will deal with Glaser's work for the International Commission for Penal Reconstruction and Development and the United Nations War Crimes Commission, as well as his later career as an academic at various universities. Glaser was an erudite criminal lawyer, who was extremely active during the interwar period. We attempt to present how these experiences allowed him to start his life anew several times.

Furthermore, our contribution will emphasize Glaser's scholarly activities and writings on the Nuremberg trial and his contributions to the discipline of international criminal law. We present various topics covered by Glaser throughout his career, such as the extradition principle, the principle of legality and the principles of individual criminal responsibility. We hold that in Glaser's life his Polish background along with his political struggles had a significant impact on his writings and ideas.

12.1 Glaser's Biography

12.1.1 Life, Education, Early Academic Career: The Polish Years

Although World War II was the catalyst for Glaser's international career, it is necessary to present the Polish period of his life as his starting point. This is important, because while his intellectual upbringing occurred in Poland, his beliefs, writings, political struggles and the experiences he gained early in his career are essentially "international" in nature. Moreover, his political struggles and beliefs and experiences gained during his early professional work and writings within an "international" context. Altogether, these factors had a very significant impact on him as a rising international criminal lawyer and are an essential part of his story.

Glaser studied law in Vienna (1914–1916) and in Lviv (1916–1918), where he obtained a doctorate in legal sciences (after passing three exams, the so-called *rygorozy doktorskie*)[4] under the scientific

---

[4] M. Gałązka, 'Stefan Glaser' in A. Dębiński, W. Sz. Staszewski, M. Wójcik (eds), *Profesorowie Prawa Katolickiego Uniwersytetu Lubelskiego* (Wydawnictwo KUL: Lublin 2008) 139; A. Redzik, 'Uczeni juryści w dziejach KUL. Artykuł recenzyjny' (2007) 9 *Państwo i Prawo* 112.

12 STEFAN GLASER

supervision of Professor Juliusz Makarewicz[5] and more importantly, Professor Piotr Stebelski.[6] Stebelski had a considerable influence on him and could be recognized, in a certain European tradition, as his mentor. Glaser admired him specifically for his devotion to his chosen profession as a teacher and his commitment to science.[7]

Shortly after obtaining his doctorate, in 1921 Glaser obtained his habilitation[8] at the Jagiellonian University in Cracow, in the Department of Criminal Law and Criminal Procedure chaired by Edmund Krzymuski. Krzymuski was an eminent Polish criminal lawyer, author of the first written commentary on the Polish criminal law system,[9] and at the same time the most popular representative of the classical school of criminology. He had a definite impact on Glaser's further views, notably in relation to the issue of punishment and the prevention of crime. This will be developed below but it is worth mentioning that the classical school was founded on the assumption that people have a free will in making decisions and that punishment can be a deterrent for crime, so long as it is proportional to the committed crime, and is carried out effectively. Krzymuski claimed that for the punishment to be useful, it had to be a proportional and just payment for a committed crime.[10]

It was professor Krzymuski who recommended Glaser to the rector of the university in Lublin. Glaser worked there until 1924, first as a deputy professor and later as Associate Professor of Criminal Law and Procedure. In 1924, Glaser moved to the University of Vilnius, where he chaired the Department of Law and Criminal Procedure. He started his work with an inaugural lecture on the rule of extradition towards political offenders.[11]

---

[5] See *Historia Katedry*, online at www.kul.pl/historia-wydzialu,11451.html.

[6] Redzik, 'Uczeni juryści', 112; see also A. Redzik, 'Wydział Prawa' in A. Redzik et al. (eds), *Academia Militans: Uniwersytet Jana Kazimierza we Lwowie* (Wydawnictwo Wysoki Zamek: Cracow 2015) 495.

[7] After his death, Glaser wrote: 'a man of extraordinary advantages of mind and heart, a silent and tireless worker has left the group of professors of the University of Jan Kazimierz; a man who gave all his life to his chosen profession and science, which he loved so much' (translated by the authors), see A. Redzik, 'Przegląd Prawa i Administracji' u schyłku życia Ernesta Tilla (2)' (2007) 7–8 *Palestra* 171.

[8] Habilitation is a post-doctoral qualification which formally determines whether a person is sufficiently qualified as scholar and teacher to be a university professor in a specific field. It is a degree needed to obtain full professorship in due course.

[9] E. Krzymuski, *Wykład prawa karnego ze szczególnem uwzględnieniem ustaw austriackich* (Drukarnia Uniwersytetu Jagiellońskiego: Cracow vol. 1, 1885; vol. 2, 1887).

[10] E. Krzymuski, *Szkoła pozytywna prawa karnego we Włoszech* (Published by author: Lviv 1889) 7.

[11] The position of Glaser on extradition will be presented and developed below.

Glaser was a strong supporter of extradition, which he saw as an instrument of common interest, maintaining international order. Being, however, engaged in political struggles, he thought that extradition is not admissible in the context of political offences.

12.1.2 Political Struggles

Glaser's scientific career at the University of Vilnius was interrupted by politics. The situation was complex, as Poland had only recently gained independence, and its borders were contested. In 1920 Poland was fighting with Soviet-Russia and its relations with Lithuania were normalized only before the World War II. Meanwhile in Germany, the National Socialist German Workers' Party, commonly known as the Nazi Party became the largest political party in the Reichstag, leading to the rise of Adolf Hitler.

Józef Piłsudski, the First Marshal of Poland responsible for regaining Polish independence in 1918, carried out the coup d'état in May 1926. It resulted in the seizure of power by non-democratic parties. From this moment on, Piłsudski emerged as a dictator. In 1930, after the dissolution of the parliament, members of the opposition were arrested and detained in the Twierdza Brześć fortress (Brest fortress), deprived of liberty and tortured (some of them died in unexplained circumstances). Later they were prosecuted in the so-called Brest Trial.

Polish professors from almost all academic institutions protested against this development. Glaser was one of the initiators and signatories of the Brest protest in Vilnius. In response, state authorities undertook an educational reform. The state limited the autonomy of institutions of higher education,[12] that resulted in the shutdown of fifty-three departments across various universities, and the forced retirement of several dozens of professors.[13] Glaser was one of them. He was forced to retire at the age of thirty-nine. Glaser had felt that it was his moral duty to support the protest, and his expression of academic solidarity meant that he had to leave the university and abandon his academic career in Poland.

---

[12] See for example J. Jastrzębski 'Reforma Jędrzejewicza w państwowym szkolnictwie akademickim II Rzeczypospolitej. Wzmocnienie prerogatyw władz państwowych' [Jędrzejewicz's reform and the national higher education system in the second Polish Republic. Strengthening the prerogatives of national authorities] (2011) *Zeszyty Naukowe Uniwersytetu Jagiellońskiego*, 138 *Prace Historyczne* 159.

[13] A. Paczkowski, trans. J. Cave, *The Spring Will Be Ours, Poland and the Poles from Occupation to Freedom* (The Pennsylwania State University Press: Pennsylvania 2003) 28; R. Crampton, B. Crampton, *Atlas of Eastern Europe in the Twentieth Century* (Routledge: London 1996) 103.

These events influenced his further work in many different ways. Most importantly, he moved to Warsaw and began a new job as a legal counsellor, representing defendants in political trials.[14] He represented many persecuted and prosecuted members of the political opposition, even those who had completely different political views from his own. The judgments were hardly ever satisfactory. Many faced ridiculous political charges, such as betrayal, political disobedience or offences against marshal Piłsudski. Many were imprisoned for these offences. Glaser recalled those trials in his memoirs and described the harassment he experienced, for example through the confiscation of his newly printed articles.

Together with political trials, arrests of many prominent figures, academics, politicians, journalists, followed. After Piłsudski's death, things even worsened as the National Democrat party regained most of their political power. As a result of the actions of its radical faction, the status of Jewish citizens deteriorated, with anti-Semitic actions, boycotts, demonstrations and even attacks – organized or inspired by nationalists. The peak of anti-Semitism was the introduction of ghetto benches, a form of segregation of Jewish students through seating in universities. According to J. Bardach, Glaser, who was a National Democrat, lost his sympathy for that movement once it revealed its strong totalitarian tendencies.[15] This experience had a strong imprint on his political views, in particular, his attitude towards human dignity and individual rights and freedoms. This is visible in his further political engagements, and both in his writings and his career as an international lawyer.

In 1935, Glaser, who remained active in international circles,[16] participated in the International Penal and Penitentiary Congress in Berlin, which

---

[14] These years are covered by Glaser in his memoire: S. Glaser, *Urywki Wspomnień* (Odnowa: London 1974) 28–29. It must be noted that Glaser knew and was in contact with Rafael Lemkin and Emil Rappaport, Vespasian Pella or Henri Donnedieu de Vabres. In addition, they were all members of the Association Internationale de Droit Pénal (AIDP), see R. Szawłowski 'Rafał Lemkin Warszawski Adwokat (1934–1939), Twórca Pojęcia "Genocyd" i Główny Architekt Konwencji z 9 grudnia 1948 r. ("Konwencji Lemkina"). W 55-Lecie Śmierci' [Rafał Lemkin, Warsaw lawyer (1934–1939), author of the word genocide, and main architect of the convention on genocide (Lemkin's convention), on the 55th anniversary of his death] (2014) 9 *Palestra* 306 et seq., also E. S. Rappaport, 'Le problème de l'unification internationale du Droit Pénal' (1929) 12 *Revue Pénitentiaire de Pologne* 1.

[15] J. Bardach, '"Urywki Wspomnień", Stefan Glaser, Londyn 1973: recenzja' (1976) 67/1 *Przegląd Historyczny* 155–158.

[16] It was quite a common practice at the time that academics and specialists practicing criminal law were active in international circles; see for example Rafael Lemkin or Emil Rappaport.

312   KAROLINA WIERCZYŃSKA AND GRZEGORZ WIERCZYŃSKI

dealt with the latest innovations in German criminal law and practice. During that time, Nazi Germany had decided to abandon the *nullum crimen sine lege* principle and to allow judges to make use of analogies in criminal trials in order to fill gaps in the law. Political opponents were being converted into "useful members of human society" in concentration camps.[17] Glaser was asked by Józef Lipski, the Polish ambassador to Germany, to refrain from criticising Hitler's policies. He refused and expressed his critical views of the Nazi sterilization policy and castration, both part of a policy of eugenics aimed at the creation of a "clean German race". Glaser believed that such a policy violated human dignity and defied any moral values.[18] His German host professor, Gustav Aschaffenburg, encouraged him to speak up. In his memoires, Glaser recalled that his frankness resulted in temporary suspension of his passport after returning to Poland.[19]

In March 1939, Glaser, together with many others who were alarmed at the dramatic situation in Poland, tried to alert President Ignacy Mościcki of the inevitable German attack and urged him to act promptly, in order to reconcile political parties by granting amnesty to political prisoners and pursuing more cautious policies towards Germany. However, no attention was paid to them and instead, they faced ridicule.

12.1.3   World War II

On 1 September 1939 Poland was invaded by Germany, and it turned out that all the fears of Polish intellectuals were justified. The Polish Minister of Foreign Affairs Józef Beck did not manage to deter the Germans from this aggression, even though he was willing to spend time hunting with Herman Goering just before the war.[20] The Polish policy of avoiding confrontation had not secured Poland against the German invasion, which marked the start of World War II.

After the war commenced, Glaser joined Władysław Sikorski's government[21] in France, first in the Department of Justice, and later as

---

[17] G. H. C. Bing, 'The International Penal and Penitentiary Congress, Berlin, 1935' (1935) 4 *The Howard Journal* 195–198; K. Chiedu Moghalu, *Global Justice: The Politics of War Crimes Trials* (Praeger Security International: Westport, CT, London 2006) 37–8.

[18] Glaser, *Urywki Wspomnień*, 88–9.

[19] Paraphrased by authors, see Glaser, *Urywki Wspomnień*, 88–9.

[20] Ibid. Lipski was also invited to a hunting party by Goering and welcomed by Hitler; see A. L. Patterson, *Between Hitler and Stalin: The Quick Life and Secret Death of Edward Śmigły-Rydz, Marshall of Poland* (Dog Ear Publishing: Indianapolis 2010) 108.

[21] Before the military coup in 1926 Sikorski was serving as prime minister and also as minister for military affairs. During World War II he was the prime minister of the Polish

a Minister Plenipotentiary to the governments of Belgium and Luxembourg. Meanwhile, in 1942, he initiated the establishment of the Association of University Professors and Lecturers of the Allied Countries in Great Britain, and the Polish Faculty of Law at the University of Oxford in 1944.[22] Simultaneously, Glaser was also active in international institutions preparing for future trials of war criminals. He took part in the work of the International Commission for Penal Reconstruction and Development (ICPRD). It was established in 1941 in Great Britain and consisted of eminent professors, including Hersch Lauterpacht. The ICPRD established a committee to study possibilities to punish war crimes before domestic courts.[23]

In the autumn of 1943, Glaser took part in the constituent meeting of the United Nations War Crimes Commission (UNWCC),[24] created to collect materials and documentation on the atrocities committed during World War II, and where possible, identify the perpetrators of war crimes. He chaired the Committee on Legal Questions (Committee III) of the UNWCC.[25] Due to some personal and political perturbations, he had to leave the commission before the Nuremberg trial started, as he had been asked to take over the diplomatic mission in Belgium.

12.1.4 The Postwar Period

In 1945, Glaser resigned from his diplomatic mission in Brussels because the Polish government-in-exile was derecognized (instead replaced with the communist government of the Polish People's Republic). He

---

government-in-exile and commander-in-chief of the Polish military forces. He tended to have good relations with Soviet Russia, despite the Russian invasion of Poland in 1939. The close ties were cut following Sikorski's request to the International Red Cross to investigate the Katyn massacre. Sikorski died in a mysterious plane accident in 1943.

[22] Glaser, *Urywki Wspomnień*, 93–95.

[23] M. Garrod, 'The British Influence on the Development of the Laws of War and the Punishment of War Criminals: From the Grotius Society to the United Nations War Crimes Commission' in R. McCorquodale, J.-P. Gauci (eds.), *British Influences on International Law, 1915-2015* (Brill Nijhoff: Leiden, Boston 2016) 349.

[24] Initially called the United Nations Commission for the Investigation of War Crimes, see more C. Stahn, 'Complementarity and Cooperative Justice Ahead of Their Time? The United Nations War Crimes Commission, Fact-Finding And Evidence', online at https://papers.ssrn.com/sol3/papers.cfm?abstract_id=2390765.

[25] UNWCC, Minutes of the seventh meeting, 1 February 1944, online at www.legal-tools.org/doc/a3c690/pdf/; the other members of the committee were: Dr Y. Liang (China), Dr Bohuslav Ečer (Czechoslovakia), M. C. Stavropoulos (Greece) and Dr Lawrence Preuss (United States of America).

recommenced his work as a chair of the Department of International Criminal Law at the University of Liege, resuming his academic career. Even though he had attempted to uphold good relations with the Polish People's Republic for some time in order to appease the communists and stay in Belgium as diplomat, he did not succeed. At the same time, his approach was not acceptable to Polish authorities in London, who were continuously critical of him.[26] As a result, he neither wanted to return to Poland nor could he act as a diplomat for the country. He thus took a professorship at the university in Louvain and Ghent (although never with a permanent chair). In the 1950s, he was perceived as the main representative of Polish exiles in Belgium and a representative of "free" Poland.[27] As his position in Belgium was quite stable, and as a former ambassador and scientist, he also worked as an expert in the permanent commission of the Belgian Foreign Ministry on problems of criminal law and international relations.[28] Thus, he decided to remain in Belgium, where he took an active part in the life of Polish exiles. He repeatedly critiqued the policies of the Communist bloc and specifically the Soviet Union's violations of international law.[29]

12.2 Scientific Activity

12.2.1 Glaser as a Representative of the Classical School of Criminology

Stefan Glaser was a very prolific author. It is said that he wrote seventy-seven articles published in scientific journals and fifty-seven commentaries to judgments (so-called glosses), as well as a few books between 1930 and 1939. The majority of his writings were in Polish, and referred mostly to criminal law and criminal procedure, although it was unusual at the time to link these two branches of law.[30] His books formed the basis for the modern science of criminal law and procedure in Poland, and they

---

[26] I. Goddeeris describes Glaser's attempts and the policies of the government-in-exile in the post-war decades, 'Stefan Glaser: Collaborator in European Umbrella Organizations' in M. Dumoulin, I. Goddeeris (eds.), *Integration or Representation? Polish Exiles in Belgium and the European Construction* (Academia Bruylant: Louvain-la-Neuve 2005) 81–82.

[27] Goddeeris, 'Stefan Glaser', 82–83.

[28] I. Goddeeris, 'Stefan Glaser', 83.

[29] See the wide-ranging observations of Goddeeris, 'Stefan Glaser', 85 et seq.

[30] M. Cieślak, 'Stefan Glaser (1895–1984)' (1985) 4 *Państwo i Prawo* 105; W. Zalewski, 'Glaser Stefan Antoni (1895–1984)', in B. Hołyst (ed.), *Wielka Encyklopedia Prawa*, vol. XIII, Criminal Law (Fundacja "Ubi societas, ibi ius", Warsaw 2018) 93–95.

are still widely known and cited even today. Owing to the partitions, Glaser had experienced criminal law under different criminal systems, which may have prepared him for the intellectual work of devising international criminal law institutions.[31] He laid the foundations for the development of a unified system of the modern Polish science of criminal law.[32] The works of his predecessors, including the abovementioned Krzymuski and his "System of Criminal Law", were written before Poland regained independence, hence these publications lacked references to Polish law and the practices of Polish courts. Glaser filled this gap and developed the ideas further.

Glaser had strong views concerning the essence of "a penalty" and its aims and functions. He was one of the strongest interwar proponents who had a strictly retributive view of punishment. As a result, in analysing the functions of punishment, he was broadly critical of the views of Q. Saldaña, who represented pragmatic views focused on the results of punishment.[33] He was equally critical of F. Liszt, another proponent of the sociological school,[34] who rejected the theory that punishment serves only as retribution in his Marburg Programme and preferred the special preventive punishment theory. According to this theory, the purposes of punishment are broadly understood, and include deterrence, rehabilitation and societal protection. Criminal sanctions take into account the psychological characteristics of the perpetrator. By contrast, Glaser was convinced that a penalty could not be perceived through the prism of its social utility value. He rejected the views of the sociological school not out of a fear that it might lead to harsher punishment, but because he was afraid that replacing punishment with protective measures would lead to an excessive leniency in criminal sentences.[35] He insisted that punishment should be a form of retaliation which should be proportional to the gravity of the crime. Any preventive measure included in the criminal system should only complement the genuine criminal sanction. He argued that criminal sanctions are intimately tied to the exercise of

---

[31] To mention just a few S. Glaser, *Polskie prawo karne w zarysie* (Księgarnia Powszechna: Cracow 1933); *Polski proces karny w zarysie* (Księgarnia Powszechna: Cracow 1934); *Kodeks karny komentarz* (co-author A. Mogilnicki) (Księgarnia Powszechna: Cracow 1934).

[32] Cieślak, 'Stefan Glaser '.

[33] S. Glaser, *Kara odwetowa i kara celowa. Zalety i braki teorii pragmatycznej (Peine d'utilité et la peine de représaille)* (Drukarnia państwowa: Lublin 1924) 18.

[34] See www.deutsche-biographie.de/gnd118573519.html#ndbcontent.

[35] Glaser, *Polskie prawo karne w zarysie*, 248–254.

316   KAROLINA WIERCZYŃSKA AND GRZEGORZ WIERCZYŃSKI

public power and should remain the sole prerogative of the criminal justice system.[36]

Although strongly rooted in criminal law dogmas, Glaser was also interested in other classical questions of criminal law that had some influence on developing his views on international criminal law. Exemplary therefore are the question of political offences,[37] the extradition of political offenders,[38] Beccaria and the spirit of humanitarianism,[39] the validity of criminal law in the context of time,[40] or functions of punishment and the normative science of guilt.[41] These broad interests were a result not only of his strong involvement in political trials as a legal counsellor, but also of his scientific life. He remained an active participant, often taking part in conferences and international congresses aimed at the unification of international criminal law.[42]

Among other questions, Glaser devoted a significant part of his attention to strictly international problems. He focused on the relationship between international and internal law, specifically, on issues surrounding extradition, human trafficking[43] and the development of international criminal law. His other interests concerned, for example, the necessity to publish legislative acts as a precondition for their entry into force and their subsequent validity.[44] These reflect his further interests

---

[36] Ibid., 256; Glaser, *Kara odwetowa*, 18–19.

[37] He discussed for example the sense of corporal punishment in the context of political criminals, see S. Glaser, 'Geneza przestępstwa politycznego' (1926) 8 *Palestra* 345.

[38] S. Glaser, 'Nowe kierunki w międzynarodowem prawie karnem a ekstradycja' (1929) 3–4 *Palestra*.

[39] S. Glaser, 'Beccaria a reforma ustaw karnych w duchu humanitaryzmu' (1922) 9–16 *Gazeta Sądowa Warszawska*.

[40] S. Glaser, *O mocy obowiązującej ustawy karnej pod względem czasu (La rigeur de la loi pénale par rapport au temps)* (Książnica Polska: Lublin 1921).

[41] S. Glaser, *Normatywna nauka o winie* (Drukarnia Rolnicza: Warsaw 1934).

[42] See broadly in Section 12.2.2.

[43] As the topic will not be elaborated further it must be mentioned that Glaser addressed the issues of slavery and human trafficking, regulated in a series of anti-human trafficking treaties dealing with slavery, servitude, white slave traffic and forced labour. By comparing the provisions of the Polish penal code to these treaties, Glaser drew attention to the insufficient protections in the Polish regulations. The Polish provisions did not broadly regulate these crimes, because these acts were punishable as delicts and not as crimes under the Polish code (in such cases the imprisonment had to be less than five years), compare S. Glaser, 'Międzynarodowe zwalczanie handlu żywym towarem a polski kodeks karny' (1938) 9 *Gazeta Sądowa Warszawska* 129–130.

[44] Glaser, *O mocy obowiązującej ustawy karnej*, 7.

12.2.2 From Extradition to Universal Repression

By 1924, the issue of extradition was already within the scope of Glaser's interest. His inaugural lecture in Vilnius published later that year[46] was devoted to the issue. For Glaser, the interests of the international community underlying extradition were based on the interests of states. He held that extradition was an expression of the principle of solidarity, a principle of mutual protection of governments and nations in the face of the gravest crimes.[47] He strongly believed that it was in the interests of the international community to unify laws existing between states. He believed that the more willing states were to co-operate with each other and to broadly accept the concept of universal jurisdiction, the more unified the law would be. His views coincided with the views of other representatives of international criminal law doctrine gathered in the Association Internationale de Droit Pénal (AIDP), such as S. E. Rappaport and H. D. de Vabres.

In the late 1920s, Glaser published a series of articles on the question of extradition.[48] He presented a fairly bold view in favour of the internationalization of national systems of criminal justice. These included the broad application of universal jurisdiction and the creation of an international court of criminal justice which would be able to exercise jurisdiction over both states and individuals who violated international law. He was of the opinion that states should act in solidarity when cross-border co-operation among different national criminal justice systems and states was required. He was a proponent of setting aside the principles of territoriality and nationality, with their limitations, and instead favoured universal repression concerning *delicta iuris gentium* and other crimes which could be the ground for extradition.

Universal repression in this sense meant that the perpetrator of the crime would be subjected to the jurisdiction of a particular state

---

[45] S. Glaser, 'Nullum crimen sine lege' (1942) 24 (1) *Journal of Comparative Legislation and International Law*.

[46] S. Glaser, *Zasada extradycji w odniesieniu do przestępców politycznych* (Nakład Gebethnera i Wolffa: Warsaw, Cracow, Lublin, Lodz 1924).

[47] Ibid., 10.

[48] Glaser, 'Nowe kierunki w międzynarodowem prawie karnem a ekstradycja', 134; (1929) 5 *Palestra* 215; (1929) 6–7 *Palestra* 260; (1929) 8–9 *Palestra* 354; (1929) 12 *Palestra* 542; (1930) 6–7 *Palestra* 293; (1930) 8–9 *Palestra* 373.

regardless of their citizenship and regardless of where the crime was committed. Glaser, as mentioned above, strongly believed that the general tendency was to unify domestic criminal provisions and internationalize systems of justice.[49] He, however, did not propose a full rejection of the rule of extradition although as a supporter of universal jurisdiction he made quite a strong argument for the revision of its rules. He emphasized the advantages of extraditions in the procedural context. His arguments in favour of extradition were connected with the better (direct) opportunity to collect documents, conduct forensic analyses and interrogate witnesses in the *forum delicti commissi*.

More fundamentally, in his writings concerning extradition, Glaser often referred to the common interests of justice and underlined that these could only be obtained through the "solidarity of states". He analysed the interests of justice through the prism of the interests of the whole international community. That is why he strongly advocated for the unification of criminal legislation between states. Certainly, his views were shaped by the progressive inclinations of the AIDP and its congresses, and the views of others gathered within it. Unfortunately, his was solely a European perspective based on the systems of criminal justice developed in Europe. He never discussed international solidarity or cooperation beyond the realms of the old continent. Hence, his opinions might today be considered as naïve and, indeed, provincial.

In the context of a functioning model of extradition, Glaser insisted on the unification of the principles governing extradition. He was of the opinion that states should not prohibit the extradition of their own citizens, or at least that their protection should be limited (he advocated for the equal treatment of nationals and other citizens in international relations[50]). Glaser's argument was connected to the fact that it was procedurally easier to judge a person in the *forum delicti commissi* and that to impose a penalty there would better achieve the objectives of punishment, namely, retaliation for the damage caused and prevention of further crimes.

Glaser also put forward the abandonment of the rule of strict specialization (or rule of speciality). He thought that if the requesting state obtained the offender, their prosecution should not be limited only to the criminal offences specified in the extradition request. With the exception of political offences, the requesting state should have the right to punish

---

[49] Glaser, 'Nowe kierunki w międzynarodowem prawie karnem a ekstradycja', 137.
[50] Glaser, 'Nowe kierunki w międzynarodowem prawie karnem a ekstradycja', 226.

every type of crime, even a lesser one. He also criticized the principle of reciprocity in extradition proceedings, arguing that an assessment of reciprocity was pointless when states had different legal systems and political practices. Furthermore, he held that the principle of reciprocity acts against the unification of international law. Finally, he also called for the abandonment of the rule of dual criminality, noting that a violation of the interests of one state amounted to a violation of the common interests of justice, and that all states had an interest in the punishment of criminals.

At the same time, Glaser saw limits to the institution of extradition. He noted that only grave crimes could be the grounds for an act of extradition, that is such gravity was a *conditio sine qua non* of extradition. The qualification of the crime, its gravity and the penalty that could be imposed[51] were only fundamental issues for the requesting state, but should not be for the requested state. In his opinion it was qualifiying as a serious crime made by the requesting state (where the crime was committed and whose legal order had been violated) that was sufficient reason to justify the costly and inconvenient procedure undertaken by the requested state. He did not see any reason to focus on the rule of speciality in the context of crimes qualified in the requesting state as especially grave.

Additionally, Glaser objected to the modification of penal sanctions. He considered situations in which states did not extradite but adjudicated offenders, resulting in reduced sentences or the dismissal of cases, problematic. He thought that a criminal should be genuinely prosecuted or extradited, not released or pardoned. The latter would be equal to shielding a person from criminal justice.

His position was more nuanced when it came to political crimes. It must be recalled that he was an active counsellor in political trials. He understood the reasons behind the attempts to change the form of a government. This is what led him to consider that *forum delicti commissi* was not a proper forum to adjudicate "political criminals". Citing Guizot ("*l'immoralité des délits politiques n'est ni aussi claire ni aussi immuable que celle des crimes privées*")[52] he tried to express his concerns that in political trials, the state adjudicated a case according to its own narrow interests. In his opinion, the judges in political trials were often

---

[51] In today's doctrine we might refer to the identity of conduct, or "same conduct" test – as developed by the ICC.

[52] Glaser, 'Nowe kierunki w międzynarodowem prawie karnem a ekstradycja', 271.

unjust and prejudiced. For him political criminals deserved more privileged treatment than ordinary criminals, and Glaser thus fell on the side of the prohibition of the extradition of political offenders.[53] He linked this principle to the mutual obligation of a state granting asylum to conduct criminal proceedings with respect to a given offender if, besides the political offence, they also committed an ordinary criminal offence, so that the granting of asylum would not be tantamount to immunity.

Additionally, he had rather progressive views on the procedural protection of individuals, especially an individual's right to a fair trial during the extradition procedure, which also militated for a more restrained practice of extradition. In particular, he insisted that a decision on extradition must be a decision issued by the judicial branch, and not the administrative one. As such, extradition could no longer be an act of international comity, but had to be an act of justice. Such a position was unusual at the time, especially bearing in mind that the ideas postulated by Glaser were deeply inconsistent with the practice of the Polish state. Following the military coup in 1926, Poland was constantly violating the rights of individuals while trying political opponents (this period in the history of Poland was characterized as a dictatorship[54]). In defending a strong concept of extradition yet outlining equally strong liberal protections, Glaser sought to reconcile the ideals, on the one hand, of an international criminal co-operation enthusiast and on the other hand, of a liberal figure in a dictatorial regime, keen on both the protection of Polish exiles and foreign refugees in Poland itself.

12.2.3 The Principle of Legality: Between Strict Adherence and the Need to Repress International Crimes

When reading early texts by Glaser he appears as a legalist, an advocate of strict adherence to and non-retrospectivity of law. He rejected the derogation of the *nullum crimen sine lege* principle and the admissibility of analogy as applied by judges in the Soviet Union and in Nazi Germany. Glaser criticized Donnedieu de Vabres for propagating views which permitted (although to a moderate extent) the use of analogy in criminal law. He underlined that within the framework of theories based on the individualization of criminal responsibility, the *nullum crimen* principle

---

[53] It must be noted that his postulates were for example mirrored in the 1957 European Convention on Extradition, see Art. 3 (1).

[54] Compare, M. B. B. Biskupski, *Independence Day: Myth, Symbol, and the Creation of Modern Poland* (Oxford University Press: Oxford 2012) 41.

was one that fundamentally guarantees citizens' rights and freedoms in a domestic order whereas analogy granted unlimited powers to judges.[55]

In 1942, Glaser published an article concerning the *nullum crimen sine lege* principle and its violation by Nazi Germany.[56] He was very critical of the policies of German courts and criminal judges, who were equipped with broad discretions to apply the analogy principle in national criminal cases. Taking *nullum crimen sine lege* as a fundamental principle, Glaser wrote that "the judge is thus deprived of all creative capacity in this sphere. He may never complete the penal law by introducing new crimes constituted by novel elements".[57] Glaser also criticized the use of custom in criminal law, stating that "criminal law cannot originate from custom, and as custom is never able to create new forms of an offence, consequently it cannot justify a punishment". Rather, "[i]n the case of lacuna, the criminal judge must pronounce an acquittal, even when it would be to the advantage of society that the act in question should be punished".

For Glaser, as a criminal lawyer deeply rooted in liberal criminal procedures, the principle of *nullum crimen sine lege* was an element of procedural protection designed to protect the individual against undeserved punishment and prevent arbitrary state actions.[58] Simultaneously, Glaser cited German masters – jurists who also understood this principle to be part of criminal doctrines before the Hitler era, including Liszt, Binding, Beling, Hippel, Frank and even Mezger.[59] The latter was regarded as Hans Frank's master.

After the war, however, it seemed that Glaser changed his views. Many scholars who criticized the German and Russian approach to the *nullum crimen sine lege* principle accepted the solutions applied during the Nuremberg trials, including addition of the new category of crime, namely crimes against humanity, to the jurisdiction of the tribunal. Glaser, as a liberal advocate of penal law, was in favour of a strong concept of legality, but as a member of a nation that had suffered enormously during the war, he was probably less inclined to insist on the defence of the legality principle.

---

[55] S. Glaser, 'Prawo karne na kongresach międzynarodowych (Paryż, Haga)' (1937) 10 *Palestra* 878–879.

[56] Glaser, 'Nullum crimen sine lege', 29–37.

[57] Glaser, 'Nullum crimen sine lege', 33.

[58] However, it should be noted that he allowed for analogy in international law, a topic which is developed below.

[59] Glaser, 'Nullum crimen sine lege', 34.

322   KAROLINA WIERCZYŃSKA AND GRZEGORZ WIERCZYŃSKI

Commenting on the Nuremberg trial, Glaser came back to his previous considerations concerning the *nullum crimen sine lege* principle, noting that the idea of the legality of crimes and punishment is not mandatory in public international law (from this moment on he strictly distinguished, perhaps opportunistically, between national and international law in this regard). Nonetheless, Glaser was of the opinion that the Nuremberg Charter literally rejected the principle of legality but not the idea or spirit conveyed by it.[60] For him there was no space for the principle, if understood as norms codified in conventions, and he stressed that norms (for example prohibiting the commission of war crimes) had to be traced back to other sources of international law – specifically to international customary law.[61] He was against determining the scope of culpable acts by taking into account only written sources.

This made him a proponent of the utilization of analogy in international criminal law and was met with much criticism,[62] although he clearly did not suggest that criminalization should be unregulated by law (*analogia legis*) nor did he try to justify the creation of a new class of criminal conduct. He was rather referring to the idea of crimes and offences already known and defined in the criminal codes of many states, and which as such were thus illegal. For him, it was clear that the defendants were aware of the illegality of their actions at the time of the crime.[63] He found it necessary to resort to the principles already applied in international law. Accordingly, he justified the final scope of the material jurisdiction of the Nuremberg Charter as those crimes, which were already known in international law and national codes. Thus, punishment of such crimes could not be assessed as *ex post facto* punishment.[64]

---

[60] S. Glaser, 'The Charter of the Nuremberg Tribunal and New Principles of International Law'- text presented by Glaser at the Conference held at the Faculty of law, University of Bale, 8 May 1947, published in G. Mettraux (ed.), *Perspectives on the Nuremberg Trial* (Oxford University Press: Oxford 2008) 55, 61 et seq.

[61] Ibid.

[62] J. Graven, 'Principes fondamentaux d'un code répressif des crimes contre la paix et la sécurité de l'humanité' (1950) *Extrait de la Revue de Droit International de Sciences Diplomatiques et Politiques*, 52; L. Gardocki, *Zarys prawa karnego międzynarodowego* [Sketch of the criminal international law] (Państwowe Wydawnictwo naukowe: Warsaw 1985) 108.

[63] This view was also shared by Kelsen who pointed out that the rule excluding retroactive legislation is not valid in international law at all. See H. Kelsen, 'Will the Judgment in the Nuremberg Trial Constitute a Precedent?' in G. Mettraux (ed.), *Perspectives on the Nuremberg Trial* (Oxford University Press: Oxford 2008) 283.

[64] Glaser, 'The Charter of the Nuremberg Tribunal', 66.

Glaser thus agreed with Graven, who claimed that the blind application of the *nullum crimen sine lege* principle in international law would shield the perpetrator of an international crime from justified punishment.[65] Glaser argued that not all the crimes could be foreseen by international legislators, and that it would be unacceptable for crimes to go unpunished because the international legislator had not foreseen them. He subsequently argued that because international criminal justice was in its initial stages of creation one needed to combine legal reasoning and actual sources to circumscribe the contours of prohibited conduct. But there was no room in international law for a rigid legalism, and it was necessary to resort to general principles of criminal justice (*analogia juris*) to identify the contours of conduct which was already prohibited in customary or treaty law.

For Glaser, reasoning by analogy in international criminal law was necessary in order to ensure the law's effectiveness. He referred to this necessity many times in his further writings (still opting, however, for strict adherence to the legality principle in domestic law, even at the cost of effectivity),[66] and pointed out that reasoning by analogy was already accepted by the Nuremberg and Tokyo tribunals. Additionally, he emphasized that the formulation of treaties or statutes, leaving to the discretion of the court how to interpret the notion of "other inhumane acts" or "grave breaches" created the need to apply reasoning by analogy. Clearly, Glaser was merely suggesting that one use analogy based on the *ejusdem generis* canon to precisely determine the scope of general terms contained in statutes or treaties.[67]

12.2.4 Preparing the Nuremberg Trial

The transformation of Glaser from a liberal advocate of penal law advocating for strict adherence to the legality principle into the lawyer who accepted departures from the legality principle is connected to his personal experience and to his involvement in the preparations for the Nuremberg trial.

---

[65] Ibid., 64.

[66] S. Glaser, 'La culpabilité en droit international pénal' (1960) 1 *Recueil des cours de l'Académie de La Haye*, 576 et seq.; S. Glaser, *L'Arme nucléaire à la lumière du droit international* (Pedone: Paris 1964) 39.

[67] Cassese refers to this as a popular, well-recognized and acceptable method, so the critics seem to be premature. See A. Cassese, P. Gaeta, *Cassese's International Criminal Law* (Oxford University Press: Oxford 2013) 34.

Glaser was extremely active in international institutions preparing for future trials of war criminals. As already mentioned he took part in the work of the ICPRD and participated in the constituent meetings of the UNWCC after the autumn of 1943. The actions of those two bodies were crucial for the development of international criminal law and the creation of the International Military Tribunal in Nuremberg. In the ICPRD, Glaser prepared a report on the rights to be accorded to persons suspected or accused of war crimes. The report was based on the answers to a questionnaire (consisting of thirty-three questions referring to relevant problems) given by the scholars who took part in the works of the ICPRD.[68] It was a critical analysis of the received responses, presented together with Glaser's suggestion of a Minimum Code of Rules.[69] These documents were the basis for the deliberations and evaluation in the ICPRD. As a consequence, the final report was a redrafted and a corrected version compiled, incorporating the reflections of the committee and a critical analysis by Glaser.

The report underlined the idea confirmed by all participants to the questionnaire, namely the necessity for the application of a democratic conception of criminal procedure in war crimes trials, in order to preserve the proper balance between the interests of society and those suspected or accused of war crimes. It referred to certain rights that should be granted to suspected or accused persons, specifically the right to consult with a lawyer, the presumption of innocence, and the right to be detained in a prepared facility (which was not called a prison). Wide-ranging discussions were devoted to the question of detaining persons as a preventive measure. In Glaser's opinion, detention would not be acceptable in cases of minor offences. Detention periods should be determined by the legislator and should not be longer than six weeks. Additionally, it should be up to a judge to decide about any extension of that period. The accused ought to be informed of the nature of the charges upon arrest. He should have the right to appeal to a higher court, and the decision of such a court must not increase the sentence. Glaser was of the opinion that a *reformatio in peius* is not an element of a democratic procedure. Contrary to the majority, Glaser called for the counting of the period of detention as part of a sentence. In fact, this provision was included in the

---

[68] International Commission for Penal Reconstruction and Development, Committee on the rights to be accorded to persons suspected or accused of crimes, Questionnaire, online at http://purl.flvc.org/fsu/fd/FSU_MSS_20130729_B17_F8_06_04.

[69] Draft of a Minimum Code of Rules, June 1943, see online at www.legal-tools.org/doc/b3c657/pdf/.

draft of the Minimum Code of Rules,[70] with the exception of situations where the accused caused a delay. Glaser agreed with the majority that any person detained unjustly should have the right to obtain redress.

The degree of restraint exhibited by the scholars of the ICRPD working alongside Glaser is remarkable. It is true that the lawyers involved were conducting scholarly professional work, and that the main decisions about international prosecutions – decisions that would be taken at the highest political level – had still not been taken. In due course, international prosecutions of leading war criminals would take less liberal forms than those envisioned by Glaser with the ICPRD. Nonetheless, the intellectual leadership of Glaser showed that these lawyers, intellectuals and politicians were unwilling to violate the rules, which they saw as being at the heart of their profession. Justice, not vengeance, was the goal of future war trials as far as they were concerned.

Glaser's work in the ICPRD was important not only because it actually created general criminal policy towards war criminals, but also from a more jurisdictional point of view. In the memorandum he submitted to the commission, Glaser wrote that national courts should have priority over any international tribunal, that is, that national jurisdictions should in principle conduct the prosecutions. An international tribunal should be created only as an exception, to adjudge special types of cases. Criminal cases before a national court would be more effective and allow for making reparations to the aggrieved community.[71]

The work in the UNWCC was a collective effort, which led to the prosecution of war criminals in Nuremberg. Its members took into account the concept and listing of war crimes committed by the enemy,[72] the character of national regulations (the work was not conducted in a legal vacuum, they treated national systems as a point of reference to create a model of international criminal prosecution) including the system of criminal justice established by the Axis[73] and individual

---

[70] Ibid., see Art. 9.

[71] Memorandum on the establishment of an international tribunal, by Professor S. Glaser, G.4, 10–11, cited by T. Cyprian, J. Sawicki, *Prawo norymberskie. Bilans i perspektywy* (Wydawnictwo E.Kuthana: Warsaw, Cracow 1948) 173.

[72] See UNWCC, Report of the Sub-Committee as adopted on 2 December 1943, see online at www.legal-tools.org/doc/4cb3b4/pdf/; Minutes of nineteenth meeting, 23 May 1944, online at www.legal-tools.org/doc/3b6215/pdf/.

[73] UNWCC, Minutes of the tenth meeting, 22 February 1944. See the annex with the resolution prepared by Glaser, online at www.legal-tools.org/doc/497f83/pdf/.

criminal responsibility.[74] Although it was presented as a collective effort, some of Glaser's personal input is nevertheless visible in the discussions, for example when he suggested to "treat as guilty of war crimes persons in charge of districts in which war crimes are committed, and judges applying illegal laws and regulations".[75] Such an approach was undoubtedly a consequence of his critical attitude towards judges who had colluded with legislative powers, both those in Nazi Germany (for example judges using analogy when prosecuting individuals) as well as Polish judges prosecuting the opposition[76] in the interwar period. Glaser also proposed broadening the scope of the definition of war crimes to include taking hostages among the civilian population,[77] again a consequence of his war experiences.

Although Glaser did not have an opportunity to finish his work with the UNWCC, he strongly identified himself with the results of its work and was a supporter of the Nuremberg judgment and principles. This is reflected in his writings over the following decade.

12.2.5 The Anachronism of the Doctrine of State Sovereignty

Glaser would henceforth devote much of his writings to the new discipline of international criminal law in recognition of the fact that, as he put it, *"Ce ne fut donc qu'après la seconde guerre mondiale que le droit international pénal obtint une existence effective."*[78] The creation of an international criminal jurisdiction, the Nuremberg Tribunal, and the development of international criminal law in the specific context of the international responsibility of individuals were obvious symptoms of this new trend.[79] The achievements of the Nuremberg trial were described by Glaser, who noted that the "Charter[80] recognized individuals as subjects of international law" and that it "broke with the doctrine of immunity for

---

[74] UNWCC, Minutes of the sixteenth meeting, 2 May 1944, online at www.legal-tools.org/doc/9ad0d9/pdf/.

[75] Ibid., 4.

[76] Particularly meaningful in this regard were the criminal processes against W. Korfanty and S. Cywiński, Glaser's friends, see Glaser, *Urywki Wspomnień*, 50–59, 60–73.

[77] UNWCC, Minutes of the seventeenth meeting, 9 May 1944, online at www.legal-tools.org/doc/30d564/pdf/.

[78] Glaser, 'La culpabilité en droit international pénal', 474 et seq.

[79] See for example S. Glaser, 'Vers une juridiction criminelle internationale' (1952) *Revue pénale suisse* 281–306.

[80] Charter of International Military Tribunal.

what is called an 'act of state'".[81] As to the subjectivity of the individual in international law, Glaser remarked that individuals are grouped into nations and he placed the individual as the core subject of international law. He noted that modern international law is solely interested in individuals, and thereby rejected the views of N. Politis that during the war the only responsible parties are governments. He described legal persons as a creation of jurists, adding that the law should be at the service of humankind[82] and that international criminal law generally recognizes only the criminal responsibility of individuals for breaches of international law.[83] At the same time Glaser noted that international law rejected the doctrine of collective responsibility and underlined that even an individual acting in the name of a state would be individually responsible for their own acts, not the acts of the state.[84]

Referring to the Nuremberg judgment Glaser insisted that the very notion "act of state", emanating from the doctrine of sovereignty, should be treated with scepticism. He underlined that in modern international law there is no space for the notion of absolute sovereignty understood as the absolute independence and autonomy of the state.[85] In his view, the sovereignty of a state was limited by the equal independence and autonomy of other states. For this reason, Glaser characterized the notion act of state as an anachronism.[86] Glaser rooted the individualization of guilt and penalties in criminal law and criticized any ideas referring to the responsibility of states in criminal law.[87]

[81] S. Glaser, 'The Charter of the Nuremberg Tribunal and New Principles of International Law' – text presented by Glaser at the conference held at the Faculty of Law, University of Basel, 8 May 1947, published in G. Mettraux (ed.), *Perspectives on the Nuremberg Trial* (Oxford University Press: Oxford 2008) 55; S. Glaser, 'La charte du tribunal de Nuremberg et les nouveaux principes du droit international' (1948) 13 *Schweizerische Zeitschrift fur Strafrecht*.

[82] Glaser, 'The Charter of the Nuremberg Tribunal', 57, 61.

[83] Ibid., 57; Glaser, 'La culpabilité en droit international pénal', 481 et seq.; S. Glaser, 'L'acte d'État et le problem de la responsabilité individuelle' (1950) 1 *Revue pénale suisse*, 1–17. In this context Glaser was seen as an opponent of criminal responsibility of the state, contrary to Jean Graven or Vespasian Pella. See J. Graven 'Le proces des medecins Nazis et les experiences pseudo-medicales, Esquisse d'une étude de synthèse' (1962) 8 *Extrait Des Annales De Droit International Médical*, 33; and Graven, 'Principes fondamentaux d'un code répressif', 38.

[84] Glaser, 'L'acte d'État et le problem'.

[85] Glaser, 'The Charter of the Nuremberg Tribunal', 58.

[86] Ibid., 62.

[87] S. Glaser, 'L'Etat en tant que personne morale est-il pénalement responsable?' (1949) *Revue de Droit pénal et de Criminologie*, February, 425 et seq.

He explained that only individuals could be subjected to criminal conduct.[88]

He also focused on international crimes and their constituent elements. In relation to initiating a war of aggression as a crime against peace, he recalled first the international documents treating an aggression as an international crime (referring to texts by Grotius and de Vattel who recognized illegal and legal wars [just/unjust wars] and the text of 1924 Geneva Protocol for the Pacific Settlement of International Disputes). Additionally, he referred to the labelling of aggression used by the Nuremberg Tribunal as "the supreme international crime". In relation to the notion of crimes against humanity, both in the charter and during the trial, Glaser referred to the principle that humanity would be protected by the possibility of an imposition of criminal sanctions as a result of the violation of such norms.[89] The notion of humanity was his point of reference, with universal values justifying the punishment of the most horrible crimes.

These were his first remarks concerning international crimes, and were further developed in his subsequent writings.[90] His views were not particularly novel for this time, but they show that Glaser was a strong defender of the achievements of the Nuremberg Tribunal, and his own ideas were developed on the grounds of that trial.

12.2.6 Representing Modern International Criminal Law

Glaser's reflections and concerns in relation to the Nuremberg trial and principles formed the basis for modern international criminal law, they were a part of the past – connected with the nightmare of World War II. Glaser was keen on addressing some of the challenges that were already emerging in the post-war era and that made international criminal law a potentially significant tool in international governance. In the following years, he would remain focused on the development and consolidation of international criminal law. His first ever monograph[91] on international

---

[88] Glaser, 'The Charter of the Nuremberg Tribunal', 61–62; he developed this problem in his further writings for example Glaser 'L'Etat en tant', 425.

[89] Glaser, 'The Charter of the Nuremberg Tribunal', 69.

[90] Especially interesting as Glaser's considerations concerning the intent to commit the crime were probably not developed before in the literature, see for example S. Glaser, *Infraction international: Ses éléments constitutifs et ses aspects juridiques* (Librarie générale de droit et de jurisprudence: Paris 1957).

[91] S. Glaser, *Introduction à l'étude de droit international penal* (E. Bruylant: Brussels 1954); Glaser, *Infraction international*; S. Glaser, *Droit international pénal conventionnel* (E. Bruylant: Brussels 1970 – vol. I, 1978 – vol. II).

criminal law had a great impact on the post-war solidification of the discipline and his works eventually became classics.[92] In his era, the discipline of international criminal law already had its strong supporters, and its doctrine was broadly developing.

Glaser's book *Droit international pénal conventionnel* is a systemic overview of his previous works and writings (hence in many instances repetitive), and at the same time a modern exposition of international criminal law. It may count as the *opus magnum* or the sum of Glaser's ideas, especially given that it was his last written monograph (in two volumes). Some of his ideas had by then been used in resolutions and/or international conventions so he managed to refer to them. The monograph is also unique because its second volume was published eight years after the first one, taking stock of the significant changes that had happened in the interval.

In the first volume, he described the origins and the definition of the "new" discipline. For him, these originated at the Nuremberg and Tokyo trials, which for the first time prosecuted individuals for violations of international law.[93] Glaser referred to international criminal law as a discipline *in statu nascendi*, presenting its challenges in formation, specifically its codification, jurisdiction and doctrine. His systemic approach is consequently devoted to these issues throughout the work. He was particularly keen on underlining the role of doctrine in the development of international criminal law. As "fathers" of the discipline he mentioned Emer de Vattel, Paweł Włodkowic (Paul Wlodkowic), François de Vitoria and Hugo Grotius.[94] He also stressed that the concept of international criminal law in his era was given a more precise exposition by the likes of Quintiliano Saldaña, Vespasian Pella and Jacques Dumas,[95] which was probably his way to point out those he was most intellectually indebted to.

In terms of codification, in addition to his references to conventions which directly refer to international crimes, Glaser noted the problems

---

[92] Moreover, he is extensively cited by eminent scholars of the discipline, such as J. Graven, Ch. Bassiouni, Y. Dinstein, W. Schabas, C. Kress.

[93] Glaser, *Droit international pénal conventionnel*, vol. 1, 16–17; for more on the responsibility of individuals, see also S. Glaser 'L'Acte d'Etat et le problème de la responsabilité individuelle' (1950) *Revue de droit pénal et de criminologie*, October, 1 et seq.

[94] It might not be obvious at the first but authors like de Vitoria and Włodkowic or Grotius were connected to the development of international criminal law in many aspects, especially through the concept of just war. However, we must remember that he was at the same time significantly impacted by the developments of the AIDP.

[95] Ibid., 35–9.

with codifying the crime of aggression or preparing the Statute of the International Criminal Court.[96] In the second volume, he referred to the resolution of the United Nations adopted by the General Assembly on the definition of aggression, writing that aggression was recognized as an international crime against peace and consequently the commission of such a crime gave rise to an international responsibility.[97] Glaser was very optimistic about the definition. He viewed this definition as the element of the development of a new discipline but he could not foresee that this definition would not be accepted in the final text of the Statute of the International Criminal Court in 1998, nor that it would take almost a decade to come to an international agreement on the issue.

In addition, Glaser noted the responsibility to prosecute international crimes was left to states and their national courts, as no international criminal tribunal existed at that time. Hence, he consistently called for the establishment of such a court. In his view, an international court is needed to define international atrocities and to ensure that they did not remain purely theoretical conceptions. He suggested, quite strikingly, that the creation of an international criminal jurisdiction (i.e., establishment of an international tribunal) was a necessary condition for the existence of international criminal law, and for the realization of international criminal justice.[98]

For Glaser, the creation of international criminal jurisdiction could be useful because national courts might not be impartial. In addition, he acknowledged that international crimes were in effect committed by states themselves, more precisely, individuals acting in the name of a sovereign. In his opinion cases concerning international crimes such as war crimes, crimes against humanity or crimes against peace would never be brought before national courts. Additionally, he stressed that the concept of sovereignty, as used by states, would be an insurmountable obstacle to the creation of an international criminal jurisdiction.[99] Despite being very optimistic about international co-operation before the war, he noticed that international co-operation was dependent on the will of states.

The substantive part of both volumes of *Droit international pénal conventionnel* is devoted to international atrocities, and Glaser refers to all international conventions and regulations (the second volume is

---

[96] Ibid., 27 et seq.
[97] Glaser, *Droit international pénal conventionnel*, vol. 2, 28.
[98] Glaser, *Droit international pénal conventionnel*, vol. 1, 200–202.
[99] Ibid., 237–238.

a further development of these ideas) which in his opinion address international criminal responsibility. Aside from some remarks on the differences between the grave crimes, their nature[100] and the character of criminal charges, special attention is paid to the question of statutory limitations to war crimes, crimes against humanity, and genocide.

In the early 1960s, the drafting and ratification of a convention on the non-applicability of statutory limitations to the gravest crimes was a crucial issue, as certain grave Nazi crimes could have been left unpunished if the statute of limitations had expired on all crimes committed by Nazi forces. Glaser was engaged in the AIDP's project on drafting an international convention on this issue.[101] He expressed very strong opinions[102] on statutory limitations. He opted for the convention on the non-applicability of statutory limitations, which referred to all the gravest crimes of international concern, including crimes against peace and specifically the crime of aggression.[103] He argued that the crimes should not be defined anew, but that the previously existing definitions from different international instruments should be used. Glaser expected not only a broad application of the principle of universal jurisdiction for grave crimes, but also the prosecution of grave crimes by nation state and/or international courts.

Efforts towards adoption were ultimately successful, and the Convention on the Non-Applicability of Statutory Limitations to War Crimes and Crimes against Humanity was opened for signature in 1968. Nevertheless, the majority of Glaser's proposals were not used in the final wording, including his proposal for a broad subject matter for the convention and the application of universal jurisdiction. He wanted to move the

---

[100] It is worth noting that Glaser found that the crime of genocide can affect only one member of a group if the offender had the intention to exterminate the group (Glaser, *Droit international pénal conventionnel*, vol. 1, 112), an idea promulgated by Rafał Lemkin; see R. Lemkin, *Axis Rule in Occupied Europe: Laws of Occupation – Analysis of Government – Proposals for Redress* (Carnegie Endowment for International Peace: Washington, D.C. 1944) 79–80. This idea was only confirmed in the practice of the ICTR (Judgment of the ICTR, *Prosecutor v. Ndindabahizi*, ICTR-2001–71-I, 15.07.2004, par. 471). Even though the ad hoc tribunals, both ICTY and ICTR, were generally calling for an interpretation that such a crime must concern a substantial and significant part of the group (see Judgment of the ICTY, *Prosecutor v. Radovan Karadž ić*, IT-95-5/18-AR98bis.l, 11.07.2013, par. 66 et seq. Judgment of the ICTR, *Prosecutor v. Clement Kayishema and Obed Ruzindana*, Judgment, ICTR-9S-l-T, 21.05.1999, paras. 96–97).
[101] See: 'Le projet de convention international sur l'imprescriptibilite des crimes de guerre et des crimes contre l'humanite, Enquete et avis de l'Association Internationale de Droit Pénal, O.N.G. dotée du Statut consultative des Nations Unies', (1966) 3–4 *Revue Internationale de droit penal*.
[102] Réponse de M. Stefan Glaser, ibid., 471–486.
[103] Ibid., 472.

concept of criminal justice in international matters forward, but states were not ready to broaden the scope of the convention. Nonetheless, Glaser is considered as a founding father of the convention.[104]

Prescription was a further concept discussed by Glaser in *Droit international pénal conventionnel*. He held that it cannot be applied automatically, and that a certain assessment considering the interests of justice is needed. In his view, the prescription of the punishment for crimes listed in the abovementioned convention cannot be justified.[105] In the second volume of *Droit international pénal conventionnel* Glaser specifically referred to the European Convention on the Non-Applicability of Statutory Limitation to Crimes against Humanity and War Crimes, noting that while the international convention also regulated the question of extradition, the European Convention remained silent on the issue,[106] thus making it more restrictive.

Glaser was very devoted to the new discipline of international criminal law which replaced his beloved criminal law as his core focus, although he had developed his idea of internationalization all his life. To begin with, his vision was tied to the idea of unification of national laws as developed by the AIDP; later, his views transformed upon noticing the force encapsulated in international law. He broadened his perspective. On the one hand, he was of the opinion that international law had supremacy over national laws (in justifying this supremacy, he used to refer to the Hague lectures of Verdross), and that states were obliged to adapt their legislation so as to conform to international law. Consequently, this would lead to a partial unification of national laws.[107] On the other hand, he believed that the unification of domestic laws should occur in certain limited contexts, specifically European integration.[108] This, then, is what marked his transformation from a national into an international criminal lawyer.

12.3   Conclusions

For a multitude of reasons, Glaser must be perceived as a significant scholar of international criminal law. In the 1920 she had already written

---

[104] Cieślak, 'Stefan Glaser (1895–1984)', 106.

[105] Glaser, *Droit international pénal conventionnel*, vol. 1, 119.

[106] Glaser, *Droit international pénal conventionnel*, vol. 2, 197.

[107] Ibid., 174; Glaser, 'La culpabilité en droit international pénal', 475 et seq.

[108] See his statement announced on 8 May 1948 during the European Congress in The Hague: www.cvce.eu/obj/statement_made_by_stefan_glaser_at_the_congress_of_euro pe_the_hague_8_may_1948-en-d5dc5d46-a39c-495c-8e8b-21cb67b43efa.html.

about the idea of international criminal justice and the creation of an international criminal court.[109] He would devote his main research after World War II to this emerging discipline. His main achievements consist of monographs on international criminal law. The most important are probably the two-volume introduction to international criminal law, the broad study on the elements of crimes and the study on culpability. He was the first academic who collected various forms of sources and *opinio juris* to give scholarly support for the development of a new discipline to be studied at institutions of higher education. At the same time, Glaser was a lawyer involved in some of the political and judicial contestation of his times, especially in Poland. He supported and represented the oppressed members of Poland's political opposition before Polish courts, he fought also against impunity for grave crimes through his work in the UNWCC, providing advice on the draft for the Convention on the Non-Applicability of Statutory Limitations for Grave Crimes.

The ideas he focused on – international criminal responsibility, the possibility for the criminal responsibility of states and collective responsibility – are still present and incorporated in international criminal law. Notions of his work on collective responsibility are also present in the current discussions on non-state actors. The principle of national sovereignty, perceived as an anachronism by Glaser and many other scholars, remains alive and the "mantra of sovereignty"[110] is repeatedly invoked by states which do not want to be bound by international conventions on criminal responsibility or human rights. Nevertheless, it should be noted that the banner of sovereignty does not mean that the commission of genocide or crimes against humanity, which were considered by Glaser as grave international crimes, can be immunized.

Although he strongly argued for the creation of a permanent international criminal court, he continued to perceive the importance of national jurisdictions, almost as if he was responding to a contemporary controversy over the principle of complementarity and the future of international law.[111] Therefore, his views on extradition can be perceived as very progressive for the time. Although generally the Statute of the International Criminal Court and European Arrest Warrant demand the extradition (surrender) of states-parties' own citizens, this is still seen as the exception and not a legal principle that is

---

[109] Glaser, 'Nowe kierunki w międzynarodowem prawie karnem a ekstradycja'.
[110] As described by Louis Henkin, L. Henkin, 'That "S" Word: Sovereignty, and Globalization, and Human Rights, Et Cetera' (1999) 68 (1) *Fordham Law Journal* 1–14.
[111] Stahn, 'Complementarity and Cooperative Justice'.

broadly accepted in general international law. Additionally, the argument for conducting cases in the *forum delicti commissi* is today invoked when justifying the advantages of national systems of prosecutorial justice over the prosecution of perpetrators before the International Criminal Court.

Glaser's views on individual responsibility, the protection and freedom of individuals, and the responsibilities of states towards individuals were torn between his criminal lawyer's liberal instincts and his position on efforts to punish the gravest international crimes after World War II. His rather cavalier attitude towards the principle of legality and analogy in international law – especially from someone who had been so critical of Nazi criminal lawmaking – has since been largely rejected. For example, Article 22 (2) of the Rome Statute directly refers to the prohibition of extending the definition of a crime by analogy, although *ejusdem generis* reasoning is still possible in the context of determining the notions included in the statute, such as "other inhumane acts" (Article 7 (2)(k)) or "other forms of sexual violence" (Article 8 (2)(b)(xxii)).

In his life and writings, Glaser often recalled the notions of solidarity, justice, humanity and the principle of legality – values that guided him throughout his entire life. Although he is often perceived as a French or even Belgian author and was buried in Comblain-la-Tour in Belgium,[112] he remained Polish throughout his life and never accepted any other citizenship.

---

[112] See for example C. Kress, 'Towards a Truly Universal Invisible College of International Criminal Lawyers' *FICHL Occasional Paper Series*, online at www.toaep.org/ops-pdf /4-kress, 4.

13

Yokota Kisaburō

Defending International Criminal Justice in Interwar and Early Post-War Japan

URS MATTHIAS ZACHMANN

Figure 13.1 Yokota Kisaburō. Credit: Kyodo News/Contributor/Getty Images.

As the oldest non-Western advanced industrial country, Japan has established an impressive track record in its support of multilateral organizations and particularly institutions of international adjudication, even when this might not be in its immediate national interest. Thus, despite not being a permanent member of the Security Council, it is one of the biggest financial donors to the United Nations. Although it has at times been on the receiving end of unfavourable rulings, Japan submits to the International Court of Justice and contributes to this work with one sitting judge (Owada Hisashi, until 2018). Moreover, despite legal and political hindrances (such as its constitution and its close alliance with the US) and with considerable hesitation of legal experts, Japan had ratified the Rome Statute that created the International Criminal Court by 2007 and is, again, one of the most substantial financial contributors to this central institution of international criminal law.[1]

Nor is this compliance and support of central institutions of global governance a recent thing. In fact, one might generally subscribe to Judge Owada Hisashi's observation on Japan's historical engagement with the international community that 'one is struck by the fact that Japan has by and large been practising her diplomacy in conformity with the existing international order' and that 'Japan's direction has [...] been characterized as a consistent series of attempts to integrated into full-fledged membership of the period'.[2]

The story is, of course, somewhat more complex than this, as Owada himself readily admits, recalling the Asia-Pacific Period (1937–1945) and the build-up towards it since 1931 as a period 'when Japan turned into a power to challenge the *status quo* of the prevailing international order'.[3] The challenge however did not end with the war, one could argue, but remained latent if muted. This shows particularly well in reactions to the

---

[1] On the implementation process, see Jens Meierhenrich and Keiko Ko, 'How Do States Join the International Criminal Court? The Implementation of the Rome Statute in Japan' (2009) *Journal of International Criminal Justice* 7, 233–256; see also Philipp Osten, *Der Tokioter Kriegsverbrecherprozeß und die japanische Rechtswissenschaft* (Berlin: Berliner Wissenschaftsverlag, 2003), pp. 172–183. Japanese names in the main text are given in their traditional order, that is, family names first, but for consistency in the European order throughout the footnotes.

[2] Hisashi Owada, 'Japan, International Law and the International Community', in N. Ando (ed.), *Japan and International Law Past, Present and Future: International Symposium to Mark the Centennial of the Japanese Association of International Law* (Den Haag: Kluwer Law International, 1999), p. 370. For a brief overview on modern Japan's engagement with international law, see Masaharu Yanagihara, 'Japan', in B. Fassbender and A. Peters (eds.), *The History of International Law* (Oxford: Oxford University Press, 2012), pp. 475–499; Yasuaki Ōnuma, '"Japanese International Law" in the Prewar Period: Perspectives on the Teaching and Research of International Law in Prewar Japan' (1986) *The Japanese Annual of International Law* 29, 23–47; Yasuaki Ōnuma, '"Japanese International Law" in the Postwar Period: Perspectives on the Teaching and Research of International Law in Postwar Japan' (1990) *The Japanese Annual of International Law* 33, 25–53.

[3] Owada, 'Japan, International Law', p. 370.

aftermath of the war, namely the so-called Tokyo Trial, or International Military Tribunal for the Far East, of 1946–1948 which, together with the Nuremberg Trials, constitutes one of the starting points of international criminal justice.[4] While the iconic glow of the Nuremberg Trials has even increased over time, the Tokyo IMT in comparison is viewed with considerable scepticism, particularly in Japan.[5] At the surface, this may resonate with observations on the difficulties Japan has had in coming to terms with the past in general since (although the routine comparisons with Germany in this respect are of only very limited analytic merit).[6] However, we would argue that it also points towards a deeper-seated ambivalence towards international norms and standards that, despite Japan's outward compliance with it on the whole, has formed a constant background noise in Japan's engagement with international law in modern times.[7] This ambivalence towards the standards of international community already becomes apparent in a continuation of Owada Hisashi's comment on Japan's 'period of aberration', qualifying it as follows: 'Even the period of aberration that has just been referred to could be seen as having an element of reaction against what she perceived to be the rejection of Japan from the circle in which she wanted to find her place.'[8] However, it becomes most apparent when looking at key figures in Japan's engagement with international criminal justice.

No other figure illustrates Japan's historically ambivalent attitude towards multilateralism, international adjudication and, particularly, criminal justice better than its early exponent in Japan, namely the international lawyer Yokota Kisaburō (1896–1993). This ambivalence is

---

[4] For the role of Tokyo and Nuremberg in the history of international prosecutions, see Robert Cryer, Hakan Friman, Darryl Robinson and Elizabeth Wilmhurst, *An Introduction to International Criminal Law and Procedure* (Cambridge: Cambridge University Press, 2007), pp. 91–101.

[5] For comparisons, see Bruno Simma, 'The Impact of Nuremberg and Tokyo: Attempts at a Comparison', in N. Ando (ed.), *Japan and International Law: Past, Present and Future* (The Hague: Kluwer Law International, 1999), pp. 59–84; Manfred Kittel, *Nach Nürnberg und Tokio: Vergangenheitsbewältigung in Japan und Westdeutschland 1945 bis 1968* (Munich: Oldenbourg, 2004). For Japanese responses over time, see Madoka Futamura, *War Crimes Tribunals and Transitional Justice: The Tokyo Trial and the Nuremberg Legacy* (London: Routledge, 2008).

[6] Carol Gluck, 'The "Long Postwar": Japan and Germany in Common and in Contrast', in E. Schlant and J. T. Rimer (eds.), *Legacies and Ambiguities: Postwar Fiction and Culture in West Germany and Japan* (Baltimore: Johns Hopkins University Press, 1991), pp. 63–78.

[7] Urs Matthias Zachmann, 'Does Europe Include Japan? European Normativity in Japanese Attitudes Towards International Law, 1854–1945' (2014) *Rechtsgeschichte – Legal History* 22, 228–243.

[8] Owada, 'Japan, International Law', p. 370.

already reflected in the assessment of his role in the development of international legal studies today. On the one hand, he is celebrated as one of the 'heroes' of the history of international law in Japan, notably for his role as theoretical innovator in the discipline, including introducing Hans Kelsen's 'Pure Theory of Law' to interwar Japan and using it for his own vision of a 'world state'. He was also one of the few public intellectuals at the time who criticized Japan's militarist actions on the continent in the face of severe peer pressure and censure from the public. For this, he was rewarded in the post-war period by being a close advisor to both the US occupational forces and the Japanese government, contributing to the Tokyo Trial, representing the government in international commissions and eventually, at the height of his career, being appointed as Chief Justice of Japan (1960–1966), presiding over the Supreme Court of Japan in important decisions at the time. Thus, institutionally speaking, Yokota was certainly the most influential jurist of Japan's post-war period and one of the most eminent advocates of international criminal justice of the time. On the other hand, Yokota has been criticized from early on for a certain tendency towards 'trivializing' Kelsen's theories for his own idiosyncratic vision of the international community that overemphasized analogies with the domestic state and thus ignored the political and social realities of the time.[9] Although Yokota with this may have represented the liberal, optimistic spirit of Japan's 1920s, few colleagues followed him in this idealism. Thus, academically speaking, Yokota's influence was diminishing by the decades. And finally, Yokota, again from early on, was attacked in the public for his liberal and internationalist convictions as being 'unpatriotic' or 'un-Japanese'. This is a continuous trait of his reputation until today, so much so that a search engine, based on the frequency of previous searches and occurrence of the combination on Japanese websites today, will give as the first auto-complete prediction to his name the combination 'Yokota Kisaburō, traitor (*baikokudo*)'.

Thus, the following exposition not only intends to present Yokota Kisaburō as Japan's most famous exponent of international criminal law in Japan, at the same time it also serves as an illustration of the development of international law as a discipline and the complex historical attitude of Japan towards international adjudication and criminal prosecution.

---

[9] Akira Wani, 'Yokota, Kisaburō', in Michael Stolleis (ed.), *Juristen: Ein biographisches Lexikon, Von der Antike bis zum 20. Jahrhundert* (Munich: C. H. Beck, 2001), p. 682.

13.1 The History of International Law in Japan before Yokota Kisaburō

When Yokota completed his studies of international law in the 1920s and began his rise to become one of its most eminent representatives in Japan, the discipline was already well established and had acquired some cachet as a 'practical' discipline.[10] The symbolic date for the start of the discipline can probably be set at the year 1863 when the two Japanese jurists Nishi Amane (1829–1897) and Tsuda Mamichi (1829–1903) travelled to Leiden in Holland to study, among other subjects, the so-called law of nations. Having returned to Japan in 1865, Nishi proceeded to compile his lecture notes into the first textbook written by a Japanese, published under the title *Bankoku kōhō* (*The Law of Nations*) in 1868. This was not the first publication on international law in Japan as such, as three years earlier, in 1865, a Japanese translation of the Chinese textbook *Wanguo gongfa* (*The Law of Nations*) had been published, which in turn had been a translation of Henry Wheaton's *Elements of International Law* (1836). A multitude of translations of Western textbooks, soon from the original languages, followed.

The study of international law was, from the beginning, motivated by immediate practical concerns and political necessity, most importantly to fend off Western intrusion and restore national sovereignty. As is well known, Japan until the 1850s had pursued a strict isolationist policy with very limited diplomatic and trade relations, but was forced by the mid-nineteenth century to reopen its country towards the Western powers. This resulted in diplomatic treaties concluded between 1858 and 1869 that were called 'unfair' or 'unequal' treaties by the Japanese, for the simple reason that they unilaterally granted Western residents in specially designated ports in Japan extraterritorial rights and the privilege of consular jurisdiction.[11] The abolishment of this privilege was one of the most contentious issues not only in Japan's foreign relations with the Western powers, but also in domestic politics for the rest of the nineteenth century, as it came to symbolize to the Japanese public everything that was bad and meddlesome about Western imperialism in general.

---

[10] For overviews of the history of international law in modern Japan, see Urs Matthias Zachmann, *Völkerrechtsdenken und Außenpolitik in Japan, 1919–1960* (Baden-Baden: Nomos, 2013); Douglas Howland, *International Law and Japanese Sovereignty: The Emerging Global Order in the 19th Century* (New York: Palgrave Macmillan, 2016); Kinji Akashi, 'Japan – Europe', in Bardo Fassbender and Anne Peters (eds.), *The History of International Law* (Oxford: Oxford University Press, 2012), pp. 724–743.

[11] Cf. Turan Kayaoglu, *Legal Imperialism: Sovereignty and Extraterritoriality in Japan, the Ottoman Empire, and China* (Cambridge: Cambridge University Press, 2010).

The study of Western international law in Japan then, as most of the foreign policy at the time, was aimed to get rid of these treaties and negotiate new, more equal ones. In this, Japan was remarkably successful and starting with Britain in 1894, Japan renegotiated new treaties that came into force in 1899. This came also with military success, as when Japan defeated China in 1894/95 and Russia in 1904/5. Again, the study of international law, and particularly the law of war, served to demonstrate in each instance that Japan fought a perfectly 'just' and 'lawful' war. It is therefore no coincidence that the establishment of academic chairs of international law, first at Tokyo Imperial University in 1895 and later, in 1899, at Kyoto Imperial University, happened around the same time of these successes. In the same way, Japan's biggest professional association of international lawyers, which still exists today, the Japanese Society of International Law (Kokusaihō gakkai), was founded in 1897 at the suggestion of the Japanese Foreign Ministry with the express purpose that the society should serve as a think tank for studying legal problems associated with Japan's new status as an imperial, and soon hegemonic, power in East Asia.

International law then was an immensely practical science from the beginning and associated with Japan's meteoric rise as a great power in the late nineteenth century. By the early twentieth century, most Western experts of international law saw Japan as having successfully acceded to the 'family of nations', the only non-Western one besides the ailing Ottoman Empire. Yet, despite these successes, there remained a strong scepticism among Japanese politicians, diplomats, jurists and intellectuals towards the alleged universality of Western norms and the suspicion that these might just cover up a double standard in real politics that favoured the Western great powers. This suspicion seemed to be confirmed by the so-called Tripartite Intervention of 1895, a multilateral intervention that forced Japan to retrocede part of the spoils of the Sino-Japanese War to China, and seemed to demonstrate that Japan did not have the same rights in war as Western countries. The second shock came with the decision in the so-called House Tax Case in 1905 in which the International Court of Arbitration in The Hague confirmed, against Japanese protests, the exemption of houses of foreign residents in Japan from the regular house tax.[12] Although this was probably more due to poor negotiation skills of the Japanese in the first place, it was again seen

---

[12] Douglas Howland, 'The Japan House Tax Case, 1899–1905: Leases in Perpetuity and the Myth of International Equality' (2015) *Zeitschrift für ausländisches und öffentliches Recht* 75, 413–434.

as proof on the Japanese side of the existence of a double standard.[13] Moreover, if Japanese leaders had not been wary enough already, the experience impregnated Japanese politicians, diplomats and lawyers with an almost religious fear of international adjudication, or any possibility of international interference in the future.

Thus, when World War I ended (in which Japan had only a tangential role) and the victorious powers convened in Paris in 1919, Japan sent its delegation with the express order that it try to obstruct the establishment of any multilateral institution, such as a 'league of nations', but in case this was unavoidable, to follow the general trend.[14] This policy of ostensible co-operation and covert hesitance shaped the rest of Japan's League of Nations period until 1933 and also characterized its attitude towards international adjudication. Japan was active in the League of Nations and also the Permanent Court of International Justice (it even put forward its President 1930–1933, Adachi Mineichirō), but it did so more for prestige than out of conviction, and often (like any great power would do) tried to sway decisions so as to fit its own particular political agenda in East Asia.[15] It was only in the later phases of the negotiations on the General Act on the Pacific Settlement of International Disputes (1928) that the Japanese government seemed to overcome its accustomed reserve towards adjudication and signalled a more co-operative stance. However, before this bore fruition, the Manchurian Incident of 1931 intervened.[16]

13.2 Yokota's Role and Early Advocacy of International Criminal Justice in Pre-War Japan

This was the political background against which Yokota Kisaburō rose to prominence as an international lawyer in Japan and, in the early 1930s, began to advocate for the absolute prohibition of war and international adjudication. He did so against much resistance, as we shall see.

---

[13] Owada, 'Japan, International Law', p. 356.

[14] Zachmann, *Völkerrechtsdenken*, pp. 85–119; Thomas W. Burkman, *Japan and the League of Nations: Empire and World Order, 1914–1938* (Honolulu: University of Hawaii Press, 2007).

[15] See, for example, Japan's position in the so-called Corfu Incident (1923) in which Japan voted in favour of Italy with respect to its own interests in East Asia; Zachmann, *Völkerrechtsdenken*, p. 101; Toshiya Ikō, *Kindai Nihon to sensō ihō-ka taisei* (Tokyo: Yoshikawa kōbunkan, 2002), pp. 25–29.

[16] Zachmann, *Völkerrechtsdenken*, pp. 152ff; Ikō, *Kindai Nihon*, p. 48.

Yokota had graduated from the Faculty of Law of Tokyo Imperial University in 1922 and proceeded straight to the position of assistant professor (*joshu*) at the same university. As topic for the 'assistant's thesis' that would qualify him as full professor, Yokota chose the subject of international adjudication. This triggered his interest in Hans Kelsen's 'Pure Theory of Law' and the positivist thought of the Vienna School.[17] During his researches, Yokota hit upon Hans Kelsen's treatise *Das Problem der Souveränität und die Theorie des Völkerrechts* (*The Problem of Sovereignty and the Theory of International Law*, 1920). Yokota was particularly impressed, as he recalled in his autobiography, of Kelsen's critique of the traditional concept of sovereignty as a corollary of great power imperialism and militarism that led Europe into World War I, and his advocacy of a monistic view of domestic and international law that would put limitations to this concept of unbridled sovereignty. In 1923, as one of his first scholarly publications, Yokota published a review of Kelsen's work and thus began to establish his name as an expert on continental international legal thought in Japan.[18] In 1926, as the traditional preparation for full professorship at a Japanese university, the Ministry of Education ordered Yokota to embark on a two-year long Grand Tour, which Yokota chose to spend at French and German universities and, thanks to the generosity of the Carnegie Peace Foundation, for another half-year at Harvard Law School. The German leg of his tour, Yokota spent at the Kaiser-Wilhelm-Institut für Ausländisches Öffentliches Recht in Berlin (the predecessor of the Max Planck Institute in Heidelberg). During a brief stay in Vienna in 1927, he also tried to contact Hans Kelsen who, however, was abroad at the time.

Having returned to Japan in in 1928, Yokota was appointed to the Second Chair for International Law at Tokyo Imperial University, working in tandem with his former teacher and holder of the First Chair, Tachi Sakutarō (1874–1943). Yokota remained in this position until retirement at the regular age of 61 in 1957. In time, Yokota would step into the functions of his former teacher Tachi who, until his death in 1943, had been the official advisor of the Ministry of Foreign Affairs. Yokota would

---

[17] Kisaburō Yokota, *Wataskushi no isshō* (Tokyo: Tokyo shinbun shuppankyoku, 1976), pp. 44–99, 137–146; for biographic information on Yokota, see also Hisashi Owada, et al., 'Yokota Kisaburō sensei o shinonde' (1994) *Jurisuto* 1041, 66–81.

[18] Kisaburō Yokota, 'H. Kelsen, Das Problem der Souveränität u. die Theorie des Völkerrechts, 1920' (1923) *Kokka gakkai zasshi* 37:12, 128–152 (still under the name Iwata Kisaburō).

assume this position in the post-war period, along with many other prestigious assignments.

During his pre-war academic career, Yokota devoted his attention to a number of fields: he continued his studies of Kelsen's theories and, in co-operation with other renowned scholars, published a seminal study of Kelsen's thought in 1932.[19] Moreover, when Kelsen published his summa, the treatise *Reine Rechtslehre* (*Pure Theory of Law*) in 1934, Yokota immediately set to work and translated it in three weeks, with publication of the Japanese translation under the title *Junsui hōgaku* (*Pure Theory of Law*) in 1935.[20] Inspired by Kelsen's positivism and radical monism, Yokota also proceeded to develop his own variant of a pure theory of law. This has been often criticized as a trivialized and over-determined interpretation of Kelsen's theories.[21] However, Yokota was well aware of the differences and argued that the theoretical edifice he built was inspired by the same motives and ideas, rather than based on a faithful exploration of Kelsen's theories.[22] As such, Yokota was much more outspoken and explicit in his advocacy of a liberalist vision of the international community and of the absolute primacy of international law over domestic law than Kelsen himself. This internationalist position becomes already apparent in the often-quoted introduction of his principal pre-war work, his 1934 textbook on international law:

> I would like to briefly clarify the position of this book: First, it is the position of the Pure Theory of Law, and this book describes international law from this position. [...] Secondly, it is the position of the international legal community [*kokusaihō dantai*]. International law is the legal order of the international legal community as one single legal community. It is not just the outward law of individual states. It must be grasped with the international community at the centre. It cannot be viewed with individual states at the centre.[23]

However, not only did Yokota postulate the absolute primacy of international law over domestic law. At the same time, and reversing the direction of his argument, he also assumed strong structural parallels, even a veritable isomorphism between the domestic and the international legal regime. Thus, Yokota argued that on the one hand international law

---

[19] Yokota et al., *Keruzen no junsui hōgaku.*

[20] Yokota, *Watakushi no isshō*, p. 138.

[21] Cf. Wani, 'Yokota, Kisaburō', p. 682.

[22] Kisaburō Yokota, 'Keruzen to watakushi', in Ukai Nobushige and Nagao Ryūichi (eds.), *Hansu Keruzen* (Tokyo: Tōkyō daigaku shuppankai, 1974), p. 196.

[23] Kisaburō Yokota, *Kokusaihō*, 2 vols. (Tokyo: Yūhikaku, 1933/34), vol. 1, pp. 1–2.

344 URS MATTHIAS ZACHMANN

was woefully under-developed compared to state law, and on the other that both spheres were nonetheless governed by the same basic principles, one should use domestic legal structure for norm-production in the international sphere.[24]

However, what this amounted to was an almost one-to-one projection of classical state divisions and categories onto the international community. This becomes immediately apparent in the division of Yokota's textbook itself that was structured in its main parts into three chapters titled 'international legislation' (*kokusai rippō*), 'international administration' (*kokusai gyōsei*) and 'international judiciary' (*kokusai shihō*). Thus, Yokota in effect developed the idea of a 'world government', which was very much in the liberal spirit of many internationalist-minded intellectuals of the time.[25] It was also decidedly unrealistic, considering the political and economic developments of the era. This becomes even more apparent in Yokota's idea of war as a measure of 'enforcement' (*kyōryoku shikkō*) and, depending on the circumstances, an 'international unlawful act' or tort (*kokusai fuhō kōi*) that entitled the victim to damages, or an 'international crime' (*kokusai hanzai*) that entitled the international community (represented by the League of Nations) to criminal prosecution and punishment.[26] Yokota had developed this idea from the early 1930s, starting with an article entitled 'The Absolute Prohibition of War' ('Sensō no zettai-teki kinshi', 1931) that started with the emphatic lines: 'The prohibition of war! The prohibition of war! That is the main subject of the twentieth century. It is the most important subject of the international society of the twentieth century, nay, of the whole humanity of the twentieth century.'[27] In this article, Yokota reflected on the gradually evolving process of the outlawry of war since the First Peace Conference at The Hague in 1899, particularly focusing on the three 'landmark towers' of the process, that is the League of Nations Covenant, the Kellogg-Briand Pact of 1928 and the most recent proposal for the amendment of the Covenant in harmonisation with the Kellogg-Briand Pact. Although it was doubtful, he argued, whether this proposal would be immediately accepted, there was nonetheless no doubt about the general global tendency towards the total outlawry of war and that war, even today, in certain circumstances, was

---

[24] Yokota, 'Keruzen to watakushi', p. 193.
[25] Cf. Zachmann, *Völkerrechtsdenken*, pp. 106–108, 118 with further references.
[26] Yokota, *Kokusaihō*, vol. 2, pp. 141ff; Yokota, *Watakushi no isshō*, pp. 118ff.
[27] Kisaburō Yokota, 'Sensō no zettai-teki kinshi: saikin no Renmei kiyaku kaisei-an' (1931) *Gaikō jihō* 632, 14–29 at 14.

illegal and therefore constituted an international crime. For the understanding of Yokota's strong support of the Tokyo Trial in the early postwar period, it should be emphasized already here that Yokota, right from the beginning, made only a very marginal distinction between war as an illegal act or tort, and war as an international crime, that is, a punishable act. His explanation of the difference, however, did not address the substantial differences between torts and crimes but was a purely formal, procedural one that modelled itself on procedural differences between criminal and civil law suits in domestic law: whereas in civil law suits it was the victim who acted as plaintiff and sued for damages, in criminal procedures, it was not the victim but the state or, in international crimes, the international community that brought charges. Thus, Yokota's minimal formal definition of international crime was simply: 'International crime is an unlawful act that is sanctioned by punishment.'[28] There was no explanation of what additional moment or quality of the unlawful act actually triggered the state, or the international community, to step in and start a prosecution, and what would be the formal pre-conditions for punishing the perpetrator as a criminal. This would become particularly problematic in Yokota's support of the Tokyo Trial later.

In the following years, Yokota devoted a number of scholarly studies to this idea of war as an international crime, as well as concentrating on his original academic pursuit, the essence of international adjudication.[29] From the standpoint of his idea of an 'international legal community', this was but a logical consequence. However, Yokota's theories met with fierce criticism by his colleagues from the start, and with the unfolding political crisis they became increasingly dissociated from reality. One of his sharpest critics was Taoka Ryōichi (1898–1985), an international lawyer first based at Tōhoku Imperial University in Sendai, later at Kyoto Imperial University.[30] Taoka was of the same generation as Yokota, but had a radically different approach to international law. If Yokota could be described as an idealistic positivist, Taoka was a realist whose main approach was the interpretation of international law in its

---

[28] Yokota, 'Sensō no zettai-teki kinshi', 27. For the differentiation of tort and crime, see 27f.

[29] Yokota, *Watakushi no isshō*, pp. 143–146; Yokota published his thesis in 1941 under the title 'The Essence of International Adjudication' (Kisaburō Yokota, *Kokusai saiban no honshitsu* (Tokyo: Iwanami shoten, 1941)).

[30] For a portrait of Taoka and his role in international law studies in Japan, see Urs Matthias Zachmann, 'TAOKA Ryoichi's Contribution to International Legal Studies in Pre-War Japan: With Special Reference to Questions of the Law of War' (2014) *Japanese Yearbook of International Law* 57, 134–162.

346   URS MATTHIAS ZACHMANN

relation to the political and social conditions of the time. As such, he strongly emphasized the independent nature of international law as reflective of the unique political structure of the international community, thus harshly criticizing any facile attempts at borrowing from domestic law.

Based on this understanding, Taoka also famously attacked and dissected the Kellogg-Briand Pact as a *'frommer Wunsch'* or *'bel idéal'*, that is, wishful thinking.[31] The international community – contrary to Yokota's rosy visions of a world government – did not yet provide the necessary means of peaceful conflict solution. In such a situation, prohibiting war without giving a state any other means of self-help to defend itself against inequities other than in conditions of imminent armed attack constituted a 'bad law' (*akuhō*) that risked 'the danger of being broken without any qualms of moral unjustness on the part of this state'.[32] This was the general tenor among Japanese jurists at the time,[33] and it goes without saying that it did not bode well for the reception of the idea of 'crimes against peace' that would become the core of the prosecution's case in the Tokyo Trial.

Moreover, in the face of rising popular criticism against international law and the loss of its authority among the public in late 1930s and 1940s Japan, Taoka mounted a harsh critique against those idealist representatives of 1920s and early 1930s internationalism who, through their overly optimistic visions of the effectiveness of international law had inflated public expectations and thus led to an all the bitterer disappointment and rejection when these could not be met. Thus, in a thinly veiled attack against Yokota, Taoka wrote:

> When the Treaty of Versailles was signed, there was a number of scholars who said: 'A new order [*shin-chitsujo*] has begun today,' and claimed: 'All international law from now on must take its root in this treaty,' and they tried to explain international law according to this principle. The negative influence that such a frivolous attitude has on the authority of international law today should make these scholars deeply reflect on their errors. [...] Generally speaking, when interpreting the norms of positive law, we must not read our own ideals into them, however lofty these are. We must

---

[31] Ryōichi Taoka, 'Fusen jōyaku no igi' (1932) *Hōgaku* (Tōhoku daigaku) 1:2, 1–35, at 34. Taoka uses the German and French phrases in the original.

[32] Ryōichi Taoka, 'Utagau-beki fusen jōyaku no jikkō' (1932) *Gaikō jihō* 654, 95–105 at 105.

[33] Zachmann, *Völkerrechtsdenken*, pp. 149–157; see also Masaharu Yanagihara, 'The Idea of Non-Discriminating War and Japan', in Michael Stolleis and Masaharu Yanagihara (eds.), *East Asian and European Perspectives on International Law* (Baden-Baden: Nomos, 2004), pp. 179–201.

separate the interpretation of norms from the propagation of ideals. If a scholar confuses both and under the pretence of explaining the positive law reads his own subjective idealism into it, and if it becomes evident that these ideals are unrealistic, then he gives people the impression that the norms as such cannot be realized and has greatly damaged the reputation and authority of international law.[34]

However, Yokota also suffered other attacks for his idealistic convictions that were much more acute and threatening than those coming from his colleagues.[35] Thus, in September 1931 the Manchurian Incident occurred which, in hindsight, signalled the final demise of the League of Nations period: the Japanese Kwantung Army stationed in southern Manchuria staged a minor bomb attack on the tracks of the South Manchurian Railway (operated by Japan and guarded by the Kwantung Army) near Shenyang (Mukden) and used this as a pretext to 'defend' itself, secure Japanese special interests in Manchuria and, in the process, occupy the whole territory. Although the action constituted a form of insubordination against the central government in Tokyo, the latter soon acquiesced and sanctioned the fait accompli. The public, too, was jubilant on the whole. Yokota, however, stuck to the letter of the law and published two weeks later in the *Tōkyō daigaku shinbun*, the university newspaper, an article in which he raised the rather rhetorical question whether the occupation of the whole of Manchuria as defence measure against the destruction of some several meters of train tracks (it turned out it was only some 80 cm) was not excessive. If so, since China had already called upon the League of Nations and given the latter's responsibilities, it was only natural that this would lead to an international inquiry. In a public lecture event organized on the occasion, Yokota became even more explicit, denouncing Japan's occupation of Manchuria as outright illegal. This was reported in major metropolitan newspapers, whereupon a deluge of ultranationalist attacks broke against Yokota himself and Tokyo University as his employer. Thus, the radical newspaper *Nippon* denounced him outright as a traitor whose un-Japanese opinions soiled the national honour. It called upon the university and the Ministry of Education to let him go and ended its diatribe with the ominous demand that this 'traitorous scoundrel' should be 'punished with blood and iron' (*tekketsu-teki seisai*).[36]

---

[34] Ryōichi Taoka, 'Kokusaihō hitei-ron to shōrai no kokusaihō-gaku' (January 1942) *Gaikō jihō* 890, 1–14 at 6, 11; Zachmann, 'TAOKA Ryoichi's Contribution', p. 24.

[35] Yokota, *Watakushi no isshō*, pp. 119–133.

[36] Yokota, *Watakushi no isshō*, p. 126.

348   URS MATTHIAS ZACHMANN

In fact, Yokota was bombarded with letters in a similar vein, threatening him with assassination, and signed in blood. This was not an empty threat, as Japanese extremists since 1928 had started a campaign of 'politics by assassination' which, until 1936, resulted in a series of murders of prime ministers, politicians and leaders of industry and finance and was eventually successful at cowing the civil leadership into submission to the military. When Yokota had to leave for a conference in Shanghai soon after his contentious statement, therefore, colleagues urged him to stay abroad for a while. Yokota returned, but in the following decade became much more circumspect. He still criticized Japan's actions, such as the attack on Pearl Harbour, as illegal in the classroom,[37] and continued to publish scholarly articles, but refrained from speaking in public as explicitly as before.

13.3   Yokota's Role and Advocacy of the Tokyo Trial in Post-War Japan

The Manchurian Incident of 1931 prepared the grounds for the Second Sino-Japanese War that erupted in 1937 and which, in turn, indirectly led to the decision to attack Pearl Harbour in 1941 and the expansion of the conflict into an all-out war, the Asia-Pacific War. Although Japan in the first months of the Pacific War scored remarkable successes, the tide soon turned against it, and a gradual roll back of Japan's military presence began. While the general public only knew for sure that things went badly by early 1945 when US fighter planes descended on Japanese cities, razing them to the ground by carpet bombing, Japanese politicians, diplomats and intellectuals close to political circles already prepared for defeat and post-war occupation under the United Nations starting in late summer 1944, with the Dumbarton Oaks Conference as a key turning point.

Yokota, too, was approached around this time by a think tank close to the Foreign Ministry with the task of conducting a study on the normative structure of the post-war order under the United Nations. He immediately set to work and completed his study in March 1945.[38] During the third raid on Tokyo in May 1945, Yokota's house burned down. Yokota thus received the news of Japan's capitulation in

---

[37] Yokota, *Watakushi no isshō*, pp. 166–168.

[38] Yokota, *Watakushi no isshō*, pp. 117–118. The study was published in 1947 under the title *Kokusai rengō no kenkyū* (*A Study of the United Nations*, Tokyo: Ginza shuppan-sha, 1947).

August 1945 while staying at his summer house in Karuizawa and remembered his reactions as follows:

> There had been a rumour going around for some days that the government had accepted the Potsdam Declaration and wanted to end the war. Already two days ago I had heard this as an assured fact from [the journalist] Matsumoto Shigeharu who had evacuated to Nanbara in Karuizawa. The emperor was scheduled to make an announcement on August 15th at noon, and I waited impatiently for it. When I finally heard that the war was over, I was so relieved that I almost shouted 'Banzai!' Finally we were relieved of the nightmare of war. Hopefully the military would be dissolved, and a peaceful and free Japan would be born. It was lucky that we lost the war. If we had won, the military would have expanded its power even further and would have pushed us even further into militarism.[39]

Yokota, who had been forced to lay low for the past decade, finally saw his time come and, in the following five or six years that coincided with the occupation of Japan under the Supreme Commander for the Allied Powers – but effectively under the US military forces – developed a frenetic whirl of activity. Between 1945 and 1951, he published no fewer than twenty monographs, not to mention an enormous number of articles and opinion pieces, as well as taking on a larger number of speaking assignments. He wholeheartedly welcomed the new policies of the occupying forces which, in themselves, were quite idealistic and aimed at the forging of a 'New Japan' that would be democratic in all sectors of public life, the economy and society, and peaceful, with a constitution that would prohibit military action and the means to undertake these once and for all. In fact, in December 1945, Yokota together with six colleagues from the Law Faculty founded a study group that until 1953 investigated the occupational statutes and their legal consequences for Japan and even published a journal for the purpose of disseminating their findings.[40] In this capacity, Yokota and other members of the group worked in close co-operation with the occupation authorities, and colleagues remembered that he was often called into the headquarters of the American forces on this business or in relation to the Tokyo Trial.[41]

While the bulk of Yokota's pre-war publication had been academic and was addressed to his peers, his writings in the early post-war period

---

[39] Yokota, *Watakushi no isshō*, p. 183.
[40] Yokota, *Watakushi no isshō*, pp. 184–198.
[41] Zachmann, *Völkerrechtsdenken*, p. 317.

350   URS MATTHIAS ZACHMANN

were intended to be popular and educate the people in the international democratic life of the New Japan. Among the varied subjects of his publications, particularly two stood out most prominently: the propagation of the idea of a world government and the advocacy of international criminal prosecution in the form of the Tokyo Trial.

The idea of world government was but a logical continuation of his pre-war thought, as we have seen, and was a popular topic among jurists in the heady early days of the post-war period, particularly American lawyers (but less so among Yokota's colleagues, who rather feared the construct as yet another pretext for domestic intervention).[42] Again, Yokota declared with considerable flourish:

> The establishment of a world state [*sekai kokka*] is the problem of the century. It is the fateful task of the twentieth century. The fate of humanity and civilization depends on whether the twentieth century can solve this problem or not. If it succeeds in solving it, the survival of humanity and existence of civilization may luckily be continued. But if not, the extinction of humanity and the destruction of civilization will be unavoidable. Thus, with the fate of humanity and civilization in our hand, it is our task to establish a world state.[43]

Thus, as before, but now even more forcefully, Yokota argued for the 'liquidation' (*seisan*) of state sovereignty and the establishment of 'world sovereignty' (*sekai shuken*). Yet, with his accustomed optimism, he saw this task already half accomplished, namely in the founding of the United Nations and the accession of an overwhelming majority to it.[44]

His stance on international criminal justice must be seen as linked to his overarching commitment to a world state. In line with his pre-war advocacy of international adjudication and prosecution of international crimes, but also due to his documented and well-known criticism of Japanese militarism, Yokota became the most credible spokesman and advocate of the International Military Tribunal for the Far East that convened in Tokyo in April 1946 and adjourned in November 1948. Starting on 6 November 1945, that is, before the Supreme Commander General MacArthur in January 1946 had even ordered the establishment

---

[42] Cf. Tabata Shigejirō's rather critical discussion of 'world government thought' (Shigejirō Tabata, *Sekai seifu no shisō* (Tokyo: Iwanami shoten, 1950)) that was so popular at the time.

[43] Kisaburō Yokota, 'Sekai kokka-ron' (1946) *Sekai* 9, 17–29 at 17. It should be mentioned that the rather repetitive style of this passage is representative of Yokota's popular writings of the time.

[44] Ibid., pp. 27ff.

of the International Military Tribunal for the Far East and, in fact, even before the International Military Tribunal in Nuremberg had launched, Yokota had begun to argue for criminal prosecution of Japanese war criminals in a flood of publications.[45]

In January 1946, for example, he published an article in the popular journal *Chūō kōron* entitled 'War Crimes and the Revolution of International Law' that outlined his main theses.[46] He observed that people nowadays were generally rather unclear about the nature of war crimes. This was because the concept of war crimes had undergone a complete change with the recent war. The old notion of war crimes, that is, the violation of the *ius in bello*, was not gone, but two equally, or even more important variants had been added, namely crimes against peace and crimes against humanity. While Yokota limited the latter to the Holocaust and, later, to Japanese maltreatment of prisoners of war,[47] he explained the category of crimes against peace as follows:

> Until now, war crimes had been merely the violation of particular rules or customs in the conduct of war. As such, they may be serious enough, but they may have constituted just one incident or one phenomenon in a long war. But crimes against peace comprise the instigation of the whole thing *per se*, including those acts and phenomena and much more acts and phenomena besides.[48]

Moreover, Yokota observed that there was a tendency among the Japanese to misunderstand the phrase 'war responsibility' (*sensō sekinin*) that lay at the root of war crimes as meaning to have failed at waging war and thereby bringing defeat on the Japanese nation. This was not so, in fact, and leaders who had instigated a war should be punished even if the war had been successful, provided it was an unjust (*futō*) war.[49] That the Japanese war, starting with the Manchurian Incident, had been an aggressive, rapacious war that violated international law, particularly the Kellogg-Briand Pact and was therefore unjust, was beyond doubt.

> Therefore, those who have instigated an aggressive war [*shinryaku-teki sensō*] have violated international law, have committed a crime according to international law and must therefore be punished as international

---

[45] For a (not exhaustive) list of these publications, see Yokota, *Watakushi no isshō*, pp. 202–203. The first Nuremberg Trial began 20 November 1945.

[46] Kisaburō Yokota, 'Sensō hanzai to kokusaihō no kakumei' (1946) *Chūō kōron* 61:1, 31–40.

[47] Cf. Yokota, 'Sensō hanzai', 32; *Watakushi no isshō*, p. 201.

[48] Yokota, 'Sensō hanzai', 32.

[49] Ibid., 33.

criminals. Applying this to the recent war, unfortunately, Japan's war has violated the Kellogg-Briand Pact and therefore was an aggressive war. And because this is so, those who have instigated it must be punished as war criminals.[50]

What is noteworthy here, again, is the rather simplistic conflation of 'illegality' and 'criminality' that already characterized his pre-war exposition of international crimes. It is particularly remarkable, as Yokota thereby sidestepped the most sensitive issue of international criminal prosecution of the time, namely the prohibition of retroactivity and the general principle of *nullum crimen sine lege*, the insistence on which would become the mainstay of the Japanese defence team during the trial.[51] For Yokota, there was no doubt that the mere unjustness and illegality of the war made it self-evident that its instigation would also constitute a crime.

This also became apparent in Yokota's summa on the subject, a monographic study of more than 300 pages that he published in July 1947 (i.e. while the Trial was still well under way) under the title *On War Crimes* (*Sensō hanzai-ron*). Despite considerable differentiation of argument and accumulation of material, Yokota still upheld his argument and his categorical support of the trial. He acknowledged the problem of retroactivity, or *nullum crimen*, as the most central issue and devoted a substantial portion of the book to its discussion. In the end, however, Yokota chose the simple, natural-law inspired recourse of prioritizing substance over form:

> In these debates, there are not a few who are opposed against those newly constituted war crimes by simply pointing out their newness. They argue that these had not been explicitly defined as war crimes until now and that there had been no previous convictions of such war criminals. That is, they oppose punishment for formal reasons, i.e. on the basis that there was no law, or because there is no precedent, and mainly from the perspective of legal technicalities.
>
> But the important thing is the substance [*jisshitsu*]. If in substance these actions were of a criminal nature, then there is reason to punish them. If substantially there is enough reason to do so, then we should not randomly overemphasize some small formal imperfections. And we surely should not ignore the substance over some formal inconsistencies or legal technicalities.[52]

[50] Ibid., 37.

[51] Yuma Totani, *The Tokyo War Crimes Trial: The Pursuit of Justice in the Wake of World War II* (Cambridge, MA: Harvard University Asia Center, 2008), pp. 84–85; see also Yokota's conclusion cited in the next paragraph.

[52] Kisaburō Yokota, *Sensō hanzai-ron* (Tokyo: Yūhikaku, 1947), p. 5.

About the substance, that is, the moral justness and necessity of the punishment, Yokota had no doubt, having been a critic of Japanese imperialism from the very first hour, as it were, and thus speaking with the highest moral authority. Thus, he continued, re-emphasizing the moral gravity of Japan's errors – to offset 'technical' imperfections – also stressing the political and pedagogical necessity for punishment:

> This [the priority of substance] we must keep in mind with regards to Japan. In the recent war, Japan has conducted an extremely aggressive warfare, and in this war, has perpetrated acts of astounding brutality. [...]
>
> Generally speaking, the problem of war crimes is not merely a matter of clarifying the responsibility for deeds of the past, it is at the same about lessons for the future. Especially for Japan, it is about becoming better in the future. It is a preparation and a point of departure towards a better future. Herein lies the true purpose and deep meaning of why we care about war crimes and why we must punish their perpetrators.
>
> Looking back, since the Manchurian Incident and over a long time span of fifteen years, Japan, dragged into this by its military and bureaucrats, has fought an extremely aggressive war. Time and again it has perpetrated aggressions of an inhumane imperialism. It has ignored treaties, defied justice and committed horrendous atrocities. That this was wrong is clear to everyone today. Thus, we must absolutely mend our ways. We must move towards peace and cooperation. We will work for mutual profit and progress. And only then will real happiness and improvement also be possible for Japan.[53]

It becomes quite apparent here that, despite the fact that the bulk of the study was devoted to 'legal technicalities', Yokota was not particularly concerned with these and saw the Tokyo Trial, in fact, more as a justified political and pedagogical exercise for the future. Thus, whereas in the pre-war period, Yokota tended to insist on the letter of the law and used his positivism as a weapon against what he saw as dangerous tendencies towards nationalism and militarism (such as the Manchurian Incident), in the post-war period we can observe a progressive erosion of Yokota's positivism in favour of the morally and politically just solution.

Ironically, Yokota thereby assumed a position of anti-formalism that was, in fact, the trademark of his opponents and critics during the pre-war period, as the short digression on Taoka Ryōichi's criticism of him may have shown. The reversal of positions becomes particularly poignant when comparing Yokota's pro-prosecution arguments with the arguments of the

---

[53] Ibid., p. 6.

Japanese defence during the Trial.[54] Thus, it is patently obvious that it was not 'clear to everyone' in Japan at the time that they had fought a war that was 'wrong', and even so, those indicted for having committed 'crimes against peace needed a proper defence. The Japanese government already in October 1945 had started to prepare for a possible trial and put together a defence team. Among the Japanese lawyers who took on this unenviable task was Yokota's former colleague at Tokyo Imperial University, Takayanagi Kenzō (1887–1967). Takayanagi's expertise had not really been in international law, but rather Anglo-American law and legal philosophy, and it was most likely for the former and his linguistic expertise that he was picked and, in fact, became one of the chief proponents of the Japanese defence during the trial. As such, he published in 1948 the treatise *Kyokutō saiban to kokusaihō/The Tokyo Trials and International Law* that constituted his rebuttal of the Chief Prosecutor but which could be – and has been – read at the same time as a direct response to Yokota's *Sensō hanzai-ron*.[55]

In the same way as Yokota had been critical of Japan's military expansion on the continent since the early 1930s, likewise there was continuity in Takayanagi's taking up the Japanese defence. Indeed, Takayanagi had defended Japan's policy in public lectures abroad even before and during the war. Where his sympathies stood in legal terms was also quite clear, as the following quote in Takayanagi's book of a diatribe by the jurist John Bassett Moore (1860–1947) against 'Genevan' positivism showed:

> Indeed, the latter's [i.e. the United States'] foremost international jurist, John Bassett Moore, denounced Genevan international law and the Protocol inspired by it – proceeding as they did on the facile assumption that there was a close analogy between the law within a State and the international law and the international system governing a society of sovereign nations – as a 'bedlam theory', destructive of sound international law.[56]

Thus, Takayanagi sided in principle with the pre-war anti-formalists such as Taoka Ryōichi and, obvious to all involved, against Yokota's facile equation of the international community with a world government and the resulting prosecution of war as an international crime.

[54] For a more detailed study of the Japanese defence and a fuller discussion of the following argument, see Urs Matthias Zachmann, 'Loser's Justice: The Tokyo Trial from the Perspective of the Japanese Defence Counsels and the Legal Community', in Kerstin von Lingen (ed.), *Transcultural Justice at the Tokyo Tribunal: The Allied Struggle for Justice, 1946–48* (Leiden, Boston: Brill, 2018), pp. 284–306.

[55] Totani, *Tokyo War Crimes Trial*, p. 211.

[56] Kenzō Takayanagi, *Kyokutō saiban to kokusaihō/The Tokyo Trials and International Law* (Tokyo: Yūhikaku, 1948), p. 26.

In practice, however, Takayanagi was part of the faction within the defence team that gave counsel to the civil leadership indicted as war criminals. As such, his main strategy was to demonstrate that the International Military Tribunal had no standing and the prosecution no legal grounds for their accusations, as there had been no positive law at the time of the Asia-Pacific War that explicitly criminalized the waging of an aggressive war, thus invoking the *nullum crimen* principle. Whereas the Japanese defence of military leaders tried to argue that, substantively, Japan's war had been justified, this rather formal argument was the mainstay of the Japanese civil defence and recurs throughout Takayanagi's rebuttal with an almost nauseating repetitiveness. Ironically, however, Takayanagi thereby relied on a formalist, positivistic line of argumentation that would have been consistent with Yokota's legal philosophy, but contradicted his own. Yokota, on the other hand, as we have seen, relied after the war on an anti-formalist, naturalist approach which would have been consistent with Takayanagi's (or Taoka's) pre-war legal philosophy, but generally contradicted his own. Thus, so strong was the pull of the political, that both opponents switched sides, perhaps merely for strategic gains. This may also be the reason why both statements *ex parte*, that is, Yokota's *Sensō hanzai-ron* (1947) as pro-prosecution and Takayanagi's *Kyokutō saiban to kokusaihō* (1948) as pro-defence, often seem disingenuous and fail to convince. Not surprisingly, the lacklustre quality of the Japanese defence had been already commented upon by contemporaries, as Judge Röling remembered that people described the attitude of the Japanese lawyers as 'putting flowers gracefully upon the grave of their clients', as having already given up.[57]

For the time being, however, it was Yokota who stood on the winning side of history and of public opinion. While the reactions to the Tokyo Trial were rather mixed (and rather cautious) among his lawyer colleagues, the general public in Japan during and in the first decade after the trial took surprisingly well to it, albeit for very different reasons than Yokota.[58] Thus, as the 'story line' (the 'Tokyo Trial historical narrative', *Tōkyō saiban shikan*) of the prosecution and the judgment goes, it was the military leadership and the bureaucrats that hijacked the reins of the state

---

[57] B. V. A. Röling and Antonio Cassese, *The Tokyo Trial and Beyond: Reflections of a Peacemonger* (Cambridge: Polity Press, 1993), p. 38.

[58] For early responses to the Tokyo Trial, see Totani, *Tokyo War Crimes Trial*, pp. 190–216; Futamura, *War Crimes Tribunals*, pp. 69–76; Osten, *Tokioter Kriegsverbrecherprozeß*, pp. 115–120; Yasuaki Ōnuma, *Tōkyō saiban, sensō sekinin, sengo sekinin* (Tokyo: Tōshindō, 2007), pp. 129–142.

and dragged, bullied and manipulated the deceived populace into the Asia-Pacific War. This basically let off the common people scot-free, symbolized also in the decision not to indict the emperor as the symbol of the nation. This was a popular message, and since the population in Japan (including the soldiers at the front) indeed had had their own share of suffering during the war (albeit conveniently forgetting the manifold number of Asian victims abroad), they also thought the punishment of their former leaders who had brought this suffering upon them as just. Political parties, finally, which re-constituted themselves in the post-war democratization process, also used the Tokyo Trial for their own strategic gains, trying to blacken opponents who had collaborated in the war. Thus, the dawn of international criminal justice in Japan soon gave way to the usual politicking of everyday life.

13.4 Conclusion

For Yokota, the pull of the political became even stronger in the following decades. His reputation had already suffered to some extent for his rather open taking sides and speaking *ex parte* for the occupational forces. This was not helped either when, under the impression of the Korean War (1950–1953) and the US insistence on Japan's rearmament, Yokota distanced himself somewhat from his former idealistic vision of a neutral, unarmed Japan and came to defend the highly contentious US-Japanese Security Alliance of 1951/60.[59] Thus, whereas Yokota until then had been only vilified by the ultra-right, he now also came under attack by his former liberal supporters who, particularly when he acceded to the position of Chief Justice (1960–1966) and had to preside over unpopular political judgments, accused him of 'selling out' and 'betraying' (*hensetsu*) his former opinions.

However, Yokota never recanted or betrayed his unwavering support for international criminal justice and of the Tokyo Trial. Yet, this too proved increasingly unpopular in the changing political climate of post-war Japan. Thus, whereas initially the trial was seen as positive, the onset of high economic growth between 1955 and 1972 and a return of many collaborators into the echelons of national politics led to the gradual renaissance of a revisionist nationalism in parts of the political elite and general population that soon saw the Tokyo Trial in a more negative light. This, in turn, favoured Takayanagi's line of defence (often abbreviated with the slogan 'victor's justice') over Yokota's side

---

[59] Zachmann, *Vöklerrechtsdenken*, pp. 309–316.

of the story.[60] Either side, as we have seen, could not quite convince with their arguments. However, it speaks to Yokota's character and intellectual calibre as a jurist that, while not immune to the pull of political forces altogether, he certainly, under immense pressure from peers and the public alike, remained steadfast in his conviction of the necessity of international criminal justice and thus was truly the discipline's most notable early exponent in Japan.

The pronouncement of the judgement of the Tokyo International Military Tribunal (which Yokota helped to translate into Japanese[61]) in 1948 also marked the end of Yokota's active engagement with international criminal law. Hence, Yokota's energies were devoted to matters that were more pressing for Japan, such as the security alliance with the US that dominated the legal (and public) discussion until 1960. As President of Japan's Supreme Court between 1960 and 1966 he was, likewise, more concerned with domestic matters. Internationally, Yokota undertook the representation of Japan (from 1957 as legal advisor of Japan's Foreign Ministry) in a number of international commissions and organisations, such as the International Law Commissions (from 1957) or the International Labour Organisation (from 1968).[62] Thus, Yokota's withdrawal from the field of international criminal law then was not only motivated by personal career choices but in a way symbolized Japan's withdrawal from this area in general, both on the scholarly as well as practical level. Henceforth, the attention of most international lawyers was devoted mostly to legal matters concerning international relations (and maritime law).[63] It was only the end of the Cold War and the, at first reluctant, but recently more pro-active Japanese stance towards global governance as well as the discussion around the Rome Statute that has led to a renewed interest and renaissance in the study of international criminal law in recent decades.[64]

---

[60] The attention by then, however, had shifted from Takayanagi's defence to Judge Pal's dissenting opinion. For the later post-war reception of the trial, see Totani, *Tokyo War Crimes Trial*, pp. 215–245, with a focus on Judge Pal's dissenting opinion; Futamura, *War Crimes Tribunals*, pp. 76–86; Osten, *Tokioter Kriegsverbrecherprozeß*, pp. 121–129.

[61] Yokota, *Watakushi no isshō*, pp. 201–212.

[62] See the chronology of Yokota's life in *Watakushi no isshō*, pp. 665–668.

[63] On this development, see Ōnuma, '"Japanese International Law" in the postwar period', *passim*.

[64] On this, see the references in footnote 1.

14

Jean Graven

Interdisciplinary and International Criminal Lawyer

ROMANE LAGUEL AND DAMIEN SCALIA

Figure 14.1 Jean Graven. Credit: Photothèque Université de Genève.

14 JEAN GRAVEN

14.1 Introduction

This book offers the opportunity to present a little-known jurist in international criminal law (ICL), Professor Jean Graven. Although he was present at the Nuremberg trials[1] and, following his time there, wrote some articles and books in the field, Jean Graven is not remembered amongst international criminal lawyers as a precursor or as a figure of early ICL. Yet as the author of certain developments in the notion of crimes against humanity, he deserves his place in this book. Moreover, his belief in and his contribution to ICL, notably as a partisan and broker of the discipline, are not negligible.

That being said, Jean Graven was not only an (international) criminal lawyer, he also showed an interest in short-story writing, poetry and music. His belief in the law was coupled with a humanist faith. This way of life has echoes in his approach to ICL, which is strongly tinted by the need to defend victims and a concern for humanity. He thus belongs to a certain tradition of ICL humanists and optimists who did much to move the discipline away from its interwar moorings in the search for peace, and towards a more "humanitarian" sensitivity. As he explained in the introduction to his Geneva lectures, first of all he believed into criminal law: "we should entrust criminal law with the defence of international peace and universal order, a task neither diplomacy nor the politics of the League of Nations were able to carry". Finally, he was also an interdisciplinary researcher, never hesitating to approach crimes, criminals and victims with other tools than law, an approach that remains relevant to this day.

Born in Sion (Switzerland), Graven chose to donate his books and notes to the library of this city. They are now all grouped in the *Fonds Jean Graven* which is accessible to the public on request. We have had access to these archives, and some others available online, in order not only to peruse Jean Graven's courses – which are not published – but also to his notes and correspondence with other criminal lawyers of his time. Among the small group of international criminal lawyers described in this book, Graven was first and foremost a criminal lawyer, and one who came relatively late to ICL. The considerable investment he made in the discipline after the war is nonetheless testimony to how it captivated the imaginations of some criminal lawyers, in ways that shed an interesting light on the specifically criminal origins of ICL.

---

[1] We have no certainty as to why Graven was present in Nuremberg. He seems to have been there as a correspondent for the *Journal de Genève*, but also as a representative of Switzerland. However, we found no official mission statement.

Before analysing the content of the courses and contributions of Jean Graven to ICL, the principles he defends in international criminal law and its contributions to crimes against humanity, the first section will briefly describe his life.

14.2 A Skilful Lawyer

Jean Graven died in 1987 in Marrakech (Morocco). After law studies at the University of Geneva, he was awarded his doctorate in 1927 and settled as a lawyer and notary in Sion, his birthplace. He then became clerk of the Swiss Federal Court from 1930 to 1943 and began his work as professor of criminal law and procedure in 1943. From 1956 to 1960, he was dean of the Law Faculty and, from 1962 to 1964, rector of the University of Geneva. In parallel, he was a judge at the Court of Cassation of Geneva, over which he presided on multiple occasions between 1943 and 1969.

In addition to this, Jean Graven became a member the International Association of Penal Law (IAPL), of which he would eventually become the president. In 1947, he created the *International Journal of Criminology and Forensic Police*. He was also a member and later the assistant secretary of the International Bureau for the Unification of Penal Law at the end of the 1940s. He was made Doctor Honoris Causa from the Universities of Rennes, Lyon, Liège, Fribourg-en-Brisgau, and was a Chevalier de la Légion d'honneur. Because his life, both as an academic and as a practitioner of law, was eventful, we will seek to contextualise his major contributions to ICL (14.2.1) before addressing the major intellectual movements in which Jean Graven took part (14.2.2).

14.2.1 A Man of His Times, Practitioner, and Scholar

Jean Graven's legal career took place in a fully evolving social and juridical context. Initially, his interest for both the national and the cantonal law of his *"pays valaisan"* (a region of Switzerland) led him to dedicate himself equally to practice – as a lawyer and as a notary – and as to theory, with the publication of many historico-legal articles about the specificities of the law of the Canton of Valais.[2] Beyond his work on the

---

[2] J. Graven, "L'Ecole de droit valaisanne (1807–1908)", *Annales valaisannes: bulletin tri-mestriel de la Société d'histoire du Valais romand*, 1965, 13, pp. 177–242; J. Graven, "Les

positive law in force, Jean Graven published articles about the law that touched on the societal concerns of his time. He also worked with tremendous thoroughness in collaboration with the International Committee of the Red Cross, fully engaging his lawyer's soul in their defence. Two areas have received his particular attention: the protection of non delinquent prison inmates and the redaction to the criminal provisions of Geneva Convention. In the first, he was struck that those who had not actually been prosecuted for penal offences may have been worse off than those delinquents who were the concern of normal "penitentiary science".[3] In the second area, Graven was an imminent member of the working group on the penal provisions of the Geneva Conventions.[4] As explained by Lewis, "Graven's involvement created a very brief intersection between the Red Cross project and the line pursued by the criminological jurists and their pursuit of a permanent international criminal court".[5]

That being said, a great part of his career focused on ICL. Jean Graven lived through the two world wars and most of the conflicts related to the Cold War. The apex of his legal career (in the 1960s) coincided with the emergence and institutional consolidation of many great international bodies. The increased importance of the UN's interventions following the colonial period, the noticeable dawn of an "International Criminal Court"[6] and the expansion of humanitarian actions are examples of the historical and juridical background against which Jean Graven operated. The international judicial context of the time had also undergone great changes both because of the creation of specific institutional organs and because of the redefinition of ICL's subjects. This context allowed Graven to demonstrate his ability both as a practitioner and an academic.

As a practitioner, to begin with, he was as has already been hinted, a member of significant international institutions, which played an essential part in the evolution of ICL. He participated in the eighth conference of the International Bureau for the Unification of Penal Law, in which prominent

---

dispositions pénales des franchises du Valais savoyard en particulier de Monther (1352)", *Annales valaisannes: bulletin trimestriel de la Société d'histoire du Valais romand*, 1952, 8, 1–2, pp. 57–72.

[3] J. Graven, "Minimum Rules for the Protection of Non-Delinquent Detainees", *International Review of the Red Cross*, 1968, 8, 83, pp. 59–70, p. 59. In this article, all quotations are translated by the authors.

[4] Thanks to B. van Dijk for bringing Graven's involvement to my attention.

[5] M. Lewis, *The Birth of the New Justice*, Oxford, OUP, 2014, p. 259)

[6] See J. Graven, *Les leçons à tirer des projets d'établissement d'une cour criminelle internationale*, Fonds Jean Graven, Library of Sion, Switzerland, no. 20, 22 October 1965.

professors also sat on board (such as Donnedieu de Vabres, Caloyanni, Pella, Boussarie, Chevalier, Cornil) in 1947. This institution, born from the horrors of World War I and the strong reaction to them particularly in the West, was created to codify and define the exact terms of ICL, which had been too vague or even non-existent until then.[7] Graven was also a member of the International Association of Penal Law,[8] over which he presided from 1963 to 1969, and of the Commission médico-juridique de Monaco[9] as well as an expert of the International Committee of the Red Cross.

Jean Graven's efforts to contribute to the evolution of a new world order were the expression of the will of a lawyer, determined to bring peace back to humanity by means of a new international justice. His vision of justice fell within a tradition of thinkers who sought to combine an inherent commitment to *ius naturale* with what was otherwise a quite positivist conception of law.

14.2.2 *A Classical Thinker, Idealist and Humanist*

As a scholar, Jean Graven's ambitions went far beyond ICL and, although his focus on the latter is the core of this chapter, it is worth mentioning briefly his interests in a range of other fields. He not only published numerous academic articles in national and comparative penal law publications, he also did so in other legal fields, including the history of law[10] (specifically taking an active interest in Beccaria, Montesquieu, von Liszt[11] and Ferri), medical law[12] and social insurance law.[13] However, it mainly is his professional path as a penal law expert, and his ability to implement interdisciplinary research that is striking. His path is that of a classical legal

---

[7] See analytical reports of the eighth International Conference for Unification of Penal Law, where Graven was assistant to the president. *Eighth International Conference for Unification of Penal Law, Brussels, 10 and 11 July 1947*, Paris, Pédone, 1949.

[8] See "Procès-verbal de la réunion de l'AIDP, siège du tribunal militaire international (Nuremberg) 18 mai 1946", *Revue internationale de droit pénal*, 73, 1, 2002, pp. 321–5.

[9] *Monaco Medico-Legal Commission* (translated by the authors).

[10] J. Graven, *Essai sur l'évolution du droit pénal valaisan jusqu'à l'invasion française de 1789 précédé d'une étude générale des sources et des institutions législatives et judiciaires*, Lausanne, Pache-Varidel & Bron, 1927.

[11] J. Graven, *Franz von Liszt et le nouveau droit pénal suisse*, Melun, Administrative, 1952.

[12] J. Graven, "Les procès des médecins nazis et les expériences pseudo-médicales esquisse d'une étude de synthèse", *Extrait des Annales de droit international médical*, Monaco, 1962.

[13] J. Graven, "Les dispositions pénales des franchises du Valais savoyard en particulier de Monthey (1352)", *Annales valaisannes: bulletin trimestriel de la Société d'histoire du Valais romand*, 1952, 8, 1–2, pp. 57–72.

expert, but also of a humanist, idealist and positivist, attached to the idea of natural justice (his ardent Catholicism clearly visible behind the legal expert's authority). This can be seen, for example, in his simultaneous commitment to the *lex scripta* and fundamental principles of penal law on the one hand, and interdisciplinarity and curiosity about a range of distinct fields on the other. For example, he published *L'argot et le tatouage des criminels: étude de criminologie sociale*[14] (*Criminals' Slang and Tattoos: A Social Criminology Essay*) in 1962, a work of pure criminology, in which he dismissed Lombroso's atavistic theories of crime in favour of understanding criminal slang and tattoos as sophisticated criminal codes. He thus placed himself in a long lineage of classical and liberal thinkers which would be a key element in his approach to ICL and his belief in the necessity of punishing international criminals.

His peculiar commitment to positivism is also something that shaped his approach to ICL, a discipline that was consumed at its beginnings by the tension between a positivist aspiration and the fundamental morality of its goals. Graven believed in the power of the law as a means to build a better society. This was quite clear in his work on the death penalty for example[15] against which he sought to argue as a jurist and not simply a moralist, through a comparison of several national and even sub-national penal laws. The positive law decline of the death penalty seemed to confirm its lack of usefulness as a punishment.

Despite this quite clear commitment to positivism, Graven also insisted in his university reopening address in the year 1962–1963 ("Think, Act, Live within the law"[16]) – as rector of the University of Geneva- that "Professors of law should teach cult and love of law more than legality." To which he added: "one can not prefer an injustice to a disorder".[17] In fact, "the law was precisely established to regulate with *humanitas*, with *equitas*, and I dare even say at the same time with Roman master's *pietas*, the relations of men between them".[18] He added that using, interpreting or practicing law should be realised with magnanimity.

---

[14] J. Graven, *L'argot et le tatouage des criminels: étude de criminologie sociale*, Neuchâtel, Ed. de la Baconnière, 1962.

[15] J. Graven, *Peut-on se passer de la peine de mort?* Faculdade de Direito, Universidade de Coimbra, Coimbra, 1967.

[16] J. Graven, *Penser, Agir, Vivre selon le droit, suivi du message de bienvenue aux étudiants*, Discours de M. le Recteur, 5 November 1962, Geneva, Georg, 1962, p. 5.

[17] Ibid., p. 15.

[18] Ibid., p. 36.

In short, Professor Graven was a positivist with a strong Christian undercurrent, a believer in criminal law as a force for human rights. This is clear, for example, in his writings on euthanasia.[19]

Moreover, his positivism was tainted with a strong universalism – this would only become clearer with his work on ICL – even when working in domestic contexts. Called upon as an expert to help draft the new Ethiopian Penal Code of 1957, for example, he attracted the praise of Pierre Bouzat, who highlighted that: "Realism, for a reformist, consists in never forgetting the primary quality of a legislation, as innovative as it may be, is to not offend the beliefs and convictions of the people it is made for." Nonetheless, the dean went on "This concern to preserve Ethiopian traditions does not, [...] prevent the reformist from boldly engaging on the path of a criminal law based on the most recent concepts of criminology."[20] As it happens, Graven used this opportunity to equip the Ethiopian criminal code with incriminations suppressing war crimes, crimes against humanity and the crime of genocide. Such legal provisions were clearly ahead of their time, leading Graven to comment that "in this sector, the Ethiopian Penal Code set a standard which is strongly placing it at the forefront of legislations".[21]

Jean Graven was thus first and foremost a criminal lawyer, but one whose intellectual career had already led him to reflect on many of the fundamental issues that would prove useful to the development of his work on ICL. It gave him a local grounding that was also a springboard for his more cosmopolitan endeavours.

How then might this intellectual outlook influence and have an impact on ICL, or at the very least contribute to its reach?

14.3   Jean Graven, a Defender and a Broker of International Criminal Law

In addition to introducing international crimes into the Ethiopian Penal Code, as an academic, Jean Graven contributed to the ICL evolutions that surrounded him by proposing the foundations of a "theoretical structure" for an international criminal court[22] and by expressing his support

---

[19] Art. 114 Swiss Criminal Code – entry into force when Graven writes his book.

[20] Le Code pénal de l'Empire d'Ethiopie du 23 juillet 1957, note bibliographique, *Revue internationale de droit comparé*, 13–3, 1961, pp. 653–654.

[21] Ibid., p. 31.

[22] See Graven, *Les leçons à tirer des projets d'établissement d'une cour criminelle internationale*, document in private archives.

for the criminalisation of individual actions, for example, in the context of crimes against peace.[23] In fact, and despite his many other interests, his most fundamental and well known contributions focused on ICL. As an emerging area of law, Jean Graven was, during his time, one of the few professors who specialised in ICL. His work, often exhaustive but referenced by few, covered the crucial birth of concrete ICL and notably the Nuremberg Trials and the trials conducted under the Control Council Law No. 10 (14.3.1). Beyond that he participated in the expansion of ICL as a scientific domain. For example, he delivered some of the earliest ICL courses in different universities, notably those of Geneva, Tehran and Cairo. He was active as a scholar in several practical proposals in different scholarly organisations, among which the IAPL[24] (14.3.2.). The lecture that Graven finally delivered at The Hague Academy of International Law about crimes against humanity is maybe his most successful and remarked doctrinal contribution, all the more since today the question of a convention on crimes against humanity is once again a current issue (14.3.3).

14.3.1   Analysis of Nuremberg and the Allied Trials

It is important to highlight that, just after Nuremberg, Graven argued that the legality principle (of crimes and penalties) was not binding at the international level. As he put it: "to apply this principle blindly to international subjects would signify, in effect, the complete reversal of the meaning of the maxim; it would no longer assure the Rule of Law and the protection of the innocent from unjust condemnation; on the contrary, it would block the law and shield the guilty justified punishment".[25]

When faced with the criticism regarding the possible violation of the principle of legality of Nuremberg, Graven argued that "[t]he Nuremberg Trial, answering these objections, places itself above purely formal considerations to reach a higher and more general conception of justice, as well as of the obligations of international law."[26] To strengthen this position, he quoted Biddle, the American judge: "the maxim *nullum crimen, nulla poena sine lege* can only reflect that a general justice and [...] the real question was not to know whether it was 'legal' from

---

[23] J. Graven, "De la Justice internationale à la paix (Les enseignements de Nuremberg)", *La Revue de Droit international de sciences diplomatiques et politiques*, 4, 1946, p. 17.

[24] Association Internationale de Droit Pénal.

[25] J. Graven, "En assistant au procès des criminels de guerre, Les enseignements de Nuremberg", *Journal de Genève*, 173, 25 July 1946.

[26] J. Graven, Le droit pénal international, I, Course, 1965–1966, p. 73.

366 ROMANE LAGUEL AND DAMIEN SCALIA

a formal point of view but to know if it was 'just' from the point of view of the right to judge the aggressors. With these terms, the question implies an obvious answer".[27]

Some years later, in 1950, however, he advocated a strict respect for the legality of crimes and penalties: "There will be no regular, equal, serene and undisputed international criminal justice, to which everyone can consent and accept to be submitted to, as long as it will not be founded on the principle of the legality of crimes and penalties."[28] In order to respect the legality principle, he advocates that all sanctions/punishments known in national law should have their place in international law – and not only imprisonment.

The whole extent of Graven's analysis of the Nuremberg Trials and their functioning, prompted him to make different proposals to define crimes in ICL (as we shall see), but also to support the establishment of an international criminal court. In his important article *De la Justice internationale à la paix (Les enseignements de Nuremberg)*[29] (From International Justice to Peace (Nuremberg's lessons)), Jean Graven claimed that Nuremberg was a "revolution" in ICL, and would encourage the creation of an international criminal court. According to Graven

> It is clear that such a "revolution", such a disruption of common knowledge by the establishment of Nuremberg's jurisdiction and procedure, could not be without raising objections and oppositions. It is somewhat comparable to the one through which – not without difficulty and struggles – the emerging State substituted itself to personal justice and enforced its law against the law of retaliation [. . .] lastly, it is also comparable to the revolution by which, in the Age of Enlightment and under the influence of philosophers and jurists who spoke "in the name of reason and humanity", the liberal State demolished the old system of inquisitorial justice, of the "*justice de cabinet*", secret and "scholarly", in order to "let the light into the courtrooms", with oral, public and contradictory debate, in conformity with the popular sentiment, and with the system of free discussion and judgement that prevailed in Nuremberg.[30]

This long quote fully illustrates the importance that Graven granted to Nuremberg for the institutional evolution of ICL and the opening of new horizons for the creation of a "universal" criminal court. To exemplify this,

[27] Ibid., p. 74.

[28] J. Graven, *Lettre adressée au Comité pour les Relations Internationales à Paris (Vème)*, 6 July 1947.

[29] J. Graven, "De la Justice internationale à la paix (Les enseignements de Nuremberg)", *La Revue de Droit Internationale de Sciences diplomatiques et politiques*, 4, 1946, p. 10.

[30] Ibid.

it is worth quoting him again: "Whatever the (undeniable) imperfections and (numerous and sometimes harsh) objections that it provoked, this first attempt at international criminal justice indeed constitutes a 'turning point' for international law and universal history."[31]

It is also worth considering Jean Graven's position regarding the possibility for an international criminal court to judge individual war criminals. Nuremberg initiated the possibility of judging individuals in the field of ICL. By saying that "international justice must not, any more than national justice, become a spider's cobweb capturing the flies and leaving the wasps free",[32] referring to Ferri's metaphor, Jean Graven condemned the traditional immunities of the laws of war, or diplomatic immunities when an "alleged offender" is a state's representative. He emphasised his point by referring, once again, to the Nuremberg experiment. He argued that if the creation of an international criminal court after World War I was a failure, it was precisely because of the impossibility of judging individuals as war criminals.[33]

Hence, Nuremberg was a paramount topic of analysis for Graven. He actively contributed to Nuremberg's extensive study and legacy by offering follow-ups through his participation in international conferences, his publications and his academic courses in different universities. It is in this way that he can be considered as an influencer, a promoter of ideas in the field of ICL. His role as a "narrator" of Nuremberg is best illustrated by his series of short (above mentioned) articles, published daily during the trial in the *Journal de Genève* newspaper. Graven described the facts and procedure with great precision, and took advantage of the opportunity to promote his ideas concerning the creation of a universal criminal court but also the further development of ICL: "A new 'catalogue of offences and penalties' must be established, in order to make sure all these 'new' crimes (in fact centuries old, alas) are struck, and that Abel's blood does not continue to scream in vain. It is of course towards the codification of ICL that these first attempts must be directed."[34]

Even more than on Nuremberg, Graven's work extended to many post-war trials and particularly on Nazi doctors' trials or on

---

[31] See Graven, *Les leçons à tirer des projets d'établissement d'une cour criminelle internationale*, p. 29.

[32] J. Graven, "En assistant au procès des criminels de guerre, Les enseignements de Nuremberg", *Journal de Genève*, 179, 1 August 1946.

[33] Graven, "De la Justice internationale à la paix", p. 17.

[34] J. Graven, "En assistant au procès des criminels de guerre, Les enseignements de Nuremberg", *Journal de Genève*, 178, 31 July 1946.

Eichmann's.[35] In *Esquisse d'une étude de synthèse* (A Draft for a Synthetic Study) about Nazi doctors' trials,[36] Graven, then a member of the *Commission médico-juridique de Monaco,* exhaustively describes the medical experiments (or "more accurately 'pseudo-medical', as they cannot enter the frame of healthcare's function"[37]) carried out by the Nazis in the camps of Auschwitz Dachau, Natzweiler, Ravensbruck and Buchenwald. In particular, he described the trial of Karl Brandt and twenty-two other indicted Nazis, judged on 20 August 1947 by the No. 1 American Military Court. Here, Graven, as often, provides us with a well-documented study, but he also seized the opportunity to make a proposal for a "legal solution in favour of the protection of health services in times of war" – and for an international instrument pertaining to doctors (legal?) duties.[38] With these observations of Nuremberg, Graven's career as a life-long promoter of the tribunal's legacy and the prospects for an ICC was launched and he would, henceforth, devote most of his energies to that task.

14.3.2 *The Defence and the Dissemination of International Criminal Law*

From his observations of Nuremberg and of other trials, Jean Graven not only drew evidence-based or descriptive studies: he first and foremost established himself as a great advocate of this nascent and promising law whilst proposing (or participating in) various legal and judicial developments. Graven became famous for his advocacy of an ICL, through the many lectures that he gave on the topic. Graven's teaching was primarily dispensed in Geneva but also in Tehran and in Cairo, which contributed to a large-scale dissemination of his legal ideas. In his lectures, he regularly paid tribute to early ICL theorists, especially Pella, whom he quoted on numerous occasions.[39] He insisted, for example, that ICL has been developed "under the relentless creative impulsion of Pella".[40]

---

[35] J. Graven, "Comment juger le jugement Eichmann ? Le bilan du procès", 16 (1), *Revue internationale de criminologie et de police technique,* 1962, pp. 19–60.

[36] J. Graven, "Les procès des médecins nazis et les expériences pseudo-médicales. Esquisse d'une étude de synthèse", *Extrait des annales de droit international médical,* June 1962.

[37] Ibid., p. 4.

[38] J. Graven, "Les procès des médecins nazis et les expériences pseudo-médicales", pp. 49–50.

[39] J. Graven, Le droit pénal international, I, Course, 1965–1966, p. 33. We would like to thank Professor C. N. Robert for providing us with the typewritten version of the course that Professor Graven taught in 1965–1966 at the Geneva University.

[40] Ibid., pp. 35–42.

Each of his lectures began with an outline of great historical and intellectual currents. For a self-professed positivist, Graven was remarkably open to the influence of philosophical ideas on the course of international criminal justice. For example, he was a great admirer of Plato's "Critias" which, according to him, constituted an essential premise of the very idea of an international codification and the first draft of an "ideal international constitution".[41] Specifically, his teachings promoted criminal law as the best means to guarantee (or restore) international peace, a path on which he followed Pella's almost Messianic idealism.[42]

Notwithstanding, his stance had initially been very harsh towards the Nuremberg Trials. In 1947, in a survey completed by the French Council on foreign relations (at the request of Donnedieu de Vabres) about the creation of an international criminal court,[43] Graven wrote that: "The Institution of the Nuremberg Trials, this poor last-resort, this second hand and makeshift international repressive jurisdiction, which nevertheless met the required needs of universal conscience."[44] His judgement seems to have rapidly evolved towards a much broader appreciation of what Nuremberg, for all its shortcomings, might actually herald, and he left little doubt about which side of that debate he fell on.

His tendency towards an apology for international criminal justice also appears in his teaching and in particular in the lectures given at the University of Geneva – access to which was given to us by one of his old students.[45] Graven was of course aware that

> in Nuremberg as in Tokyo, international repression was only made possible because the United Nations had previously been victorious. The accusation in Nuremberg did not conceal that by instituting the International Court it ran the risk of being a merely a legal decoy little short of an act of revenge ... subtly covered by a judicial procedure.[46]

But he replied to this criticism by stating: "In all truth, this force {the allies'] was at the service of Justice, of which it was the condition."[47] Graven was happy to reproduce the justification given by the Nuremberg

---

[41] J. Graven, ICL Course, without date, p. 2.

[42] J. Graven, Le droit pénal international, I, Course, 1965–1966, p. 2.

[43] J. Graven, *Réponse à l'enquête du Comité français pour les relations internationales*, July 6, 1947, Fonds Graven 274, pp. 1–7.

[44] Ibid., p. 2.

[45] This course was given to us by Professor Robert of the University of Geneva. For any access request, please contact us.

[46] J. Graven, Le droit pénal international, I, Course, 1965–1966, p. 71.

[47] Ibid.

judges. In passing, he was also keen to attribute the merit of the trial to the United Nations rather than the major Allies, thus subtly glossing over the political dimension of post-war justice in order to focus only on its universal dimension.

Jean Graven was therefore a man of his international criminal era and part of what would become a long line of apologists for international criminal justice, ready to defend Nuremberg against all criticism, justified or not, in the name of justice and universal values. Whatever deficiencies appeared at this early stage were "very understandable because, in the absence of the rules of a well-established International Criminal Law, different judicial systems and principles were used to establish the Charter and guide the judges who had the great responsibility of applying it." In this context "Any solution, in these conditions, could only be a bid and a compromise, and therefore rise to discussion, independently from the extraordinary and truly revolutionary novelty in International Law, that the accomplished trials and sentences delivered against the 'Major War Criminals'." Moreover, the deficiencies of these early beginnings would be redeemed eventually by the rise of a fully developed ICL and perhaps even an ICC: "Despite its imperfections, this first try at an international criminal justice represents a dramatic turning point [...] Starting with this first and solemn judicial and practical consecration, International Criminal Law will henceforth fully enter the paths of legislative formulation and codification, and fully access to the title of a true science."[48]

The promotion of ICL is also evident in numerous writings and proposals for the development of ICL, among which a major project stands out: a repressive *Code of Crimes Against the Peace and Security of Mankind*,[49] which was influenced by many theories developed by others that he often quoted – Glaser, Pella, Donnedieu de Vabres, etc. Graven, as a continental jurist attached to *lex scripta*, emphasised the importance of great principles of an international criminal code, as well as of the creation of an international criminal court. As discussed earlier, among those principles, Graven both promoted the principle of legality and accepted the fact that the Nuremberg Trials had been in breach of it. He nonetheless sought to make this principle the primary one, and the one which justified the importance of a code: the relevance of substantive

---

[48] Ibid., pp. 80–81.

[49] J. Graven, "Principes fondamentaux d'un Code répressif des Crimes contre la paix et la sécurité de l'Humanité", *Extrait de la Revue de droit international de sciences diplomatiques et politiques*, 1950, pp. 1–66.

law.[50] The code Graven submitted followed the structural division of national criminal codes.

First, he developed the "need for a 'general section' which establishes the fundamental principles for the implementation of repression"[51] – these principles must thus "precede and regulate *all* the punitive provisions applicable to *any* crime belonging to the international or inter-State legal sector, and naturally serve as a basis for the elaboration of the hoped for, studied and partly already long prepared *future project of an International Criminal Law Code (futur projet de Code pénal international)*." Here, he mentioned Pella's projects, hinting that his work would stand to gain from such principles.[52]

The second section of the code Graven envisaged concerned the incriminations themselves: crimes against peace, war crimes and crimes against humanity, in ways that would have been quite familiar in the post-Nuremberg era. Regarding crimes against peace, Graven had the ambition of an important extension of the preparatory acts including – as the Swiss legislation did at the time – the fact of having contacts with foreign countries or the simple fact of founding (or provoking the foundation of) an organisation aimed to accomplish a serious inimical act against the state.[53] Although he acknowledged that such acts are predominantly of internal nature, he does not exclude that they could "depending on the circumstances, result in a foreign intervention or an attack on the peace".[54] In the same vein, he wished the repression of a mere "*intellectual crime preparation* – the simple intent – to attack the peace by the creation of tensions and propaganda".[55] He also emphasised the need to incriminate the use (production, trade and supplying) of "certain means of warfare prohibited by conventions (chemical, biological, toxic or even nuclear warfare)", as Swiss law already did.[56] We return below to the more arduous question of crimes against humanity.

In order to support his proposals, Graven once again based himself on Switzerland's new law. Graven mentioned the basic requirement of a harmonisation of national laws regarding war crimes – a field in

---

[50] Ibid., p. 4.
[51] Ibid., p. 6.
[52] Ibid., p. 8.
[53] Ibid., p. 9.
[54] Ibid.
[55] Ibid.
[56] Ibid., pp. 19–20.

which Switzerland seems to be a very proficient.[57] As this harmonisation was a prerequisite for creating an international criminal code, once the necessary harmonisation would have been reached, it would be the aim of competent international law jurists to earn a large trust in order to fulfil the ambition of a code of specific war crimes.

The project Graven would like to see come into being also contained a third part on "Perpetrators and their responsibilities".[58] Strikingly in view of how focused on individual criminal responsibility ICL has become, Graven considered that international criminal responsibility could come in various forms, with an emphasis on the collective: first of the states, of criminal communities and organisations, and then only individual responsibility.

The fourth part was to be dedicated to sanctions, and, referring to Glaser, he emphasised the respect of the principle of the legality of penalties: "Every potential criminal must not only know which acts are prohibited by International Criminal Law under penalty, but also to which exact sanctions they expose themselves by committing these acts."[59] This principle being respected, the international criminal code must clearly state the sanctions corresponding to each responsibility and crime, as well as the different possible sanctions featured in examples found in national legislations, which can be other sanctions than incarceration.

Finally, Graven deemed that a fifth part of this criminal code would be dedicated to the jurisdictional competence – thus repeating the answers he already gave in 1947 to the inquiry led by the French Committee for International Relations, on Donnedieu de Vabres's initiative, in 1947, on the creation of an international criminal court.[60] Here, he referred to Pella's projects (2 June 1949 report "Towards an International Jurisdiction" communicated in the name of the United Nations International Criminal Law Association), of the commission of experts for the elaboration of the Convention on the Prevention and Punishment of the Crime of Genocide. However, in Graven's opinion, the court should only deal with the most important crimes and leave "the less important war crimes"[61] to the national jurisdictions, except when the

---

[57] Ibid., p. 17.
[58] Ibid., pp. 35 ff.
[59] Ibid., p. 52.
[60] Graven, *Réponse à l'enquête du Comité français pour les relations internationales*, pp. 1–7.
[61] Graven, "Principes fondamentaux d'un Code répressif des Crimes contre la paix et la sécurité de l'Humanité", p. 61.

states cannot judge them or when there is a risk if a national jurisdiction prosecutes them. Graven thus suggested the principle of complementarity, which has become so central to the adoption and the operation of the International Criminal Court, albeit with a broader, more eclectic sense of subsidiarity:

> When [...] national repression is *not possible*, either because the State is somehow an instigator or an accomplice of such crimes it morally supported or tacitly approved, or because its judicial institutions cannot judge them properly, or because there is reason to fear, when referring to similar judgments, divisions in the public opinion, demonstrations and civil unrest, unjustified acquittals, resentments on the part of or with foreign States due to disputable acquittals or contestable condemnations, then the *international jurisdiction* naturally must be referred to and substitute to the failing or paralysed national jurisdiction, in order to avoid the repression being in the same situation.[62]

Here, he followed the example of Switzerland and its Federal Criminal Court which deals with cases referred by the Cantons for reasons of opportunity. He did not go any further with his project, and we can wonder why Graven left it at that, remaining on a level of principles, and did not himself further write the articles of the code he wished to elaborate. Hence, although he stated what the fundamental principles of an international repressive code should be, and centralised the projects of various national legislations and existing legal propositions to chart a course, he was more often only inspired by the will to innovate rather than truly innovative, and remained a limited influence on the early practice of ICL. Indeed, already at the first international congress of criminal law with the International Criminal Law Association in 1926 (long before Graven joined this organisation as a member), discussions were under way to create an international criminal court governed by codified rules. Thus, we can read in the first report of the congress that "The congress expresses the wish: that Permanent Court in International Justice should get repressive competence." And "All offences committed by States or individuals must be foreseen and punished in accordance to specific texts."[63] Those early ideas of ICL show in some way that Graven is at his time inspired by innovative and existing questions.

---

[62] Ibid., p. 62. See also: Graven, *Réponse à l'enquête du Comité français pour les relations internationales*, pp. 1–7.

[63] "Ier Congrès international de droit pénal (Bruxelles, 26 – 29 juillet 1926)", *Revue internationale de droit pénal*, 86, 1, 2015, pp. 27–30.

Nonetheless, and in addition to this project, he repeatedly produced thought-pieces and guidelines for the future of ICL. The answer he gave to the inquiry led by the French Committee for International Relations [64] is a prime example. The same applies to his participation in the project of a convention on war crimes, crimes against the peace and crimes against humanity[65] for which, as the president of the International Association of Penal Law, but also because he had previously worked on the question of prescription,[66] he went on to write the introductory report and presented the questionnaire submitted to the association's members. In this particular case, after a presentation of historical developments regarding prescription, the report indicated a willingness to see an international convention both written and adopted on the Non-Applicability of Statutory Limitations to War Crimes, Crimes against the Peace and Crimes Against Humanity, thus joining, in modesty as he himself mentioned, the position adopted by the author of the report.[67]

14.3.3 Graven's Essential Contribution: Crimes against Humanity

Above all, Graven was committed to ensuring that crimes against humanity would be defined as broadly as possible and encompass all human rights violations contained in the Universal Declaration. At the eighth Conference of the International Bureau for the Unification of Penal Law, during which a definition of crimes against humanity was debated, Jean Graven, as he opened the sessions, declared: "One must consider the London Charter of April the 8th 1945 and work from there. It is a precedent, but it is only a beginning. [...] There is no one crime against humanity; there are only crimes (plural) against humanity."[68] Graven subsequently gave the course on crimes against humanity, at the

---

[64] Graven, *Réponse à l'enquête du Comité français pour les relations internationales*, pp. 1–7.

[65] J. Graven, "Introduction et Questionnaire", in *Projet de Convention sur les crimes de guerre, les crimes contre la paix et les crimes contre l'humanité*, Association internationale de droit pénal, without date.

[66] J. Graven, "Les crimes contre l'humanité peuvent-ils bénéficier de la prescription?" *Revue pénale suisse*, 1965, pp. 119 ss.

[67] J. Graven, "Introduction et Questionnaire", in *Projet de Convention sur les crimes de guerre, les crimes contre la paix et les crimes contre l'humanité*, Association internationale de droit pénal, without date, p. 429.

[68] See analytical reports of the eighth International Conference for Unification of Penal Law, Brussels, 10 and 11 July 1947, Paris, Pédone, 1949.

Academy of International Law, in 1950.[69] This course highlighted Graven as an early champion of the normative development of crimes against humanity, a position he continued to hold long after his 1950 course. Nowadays, as the project of a convention against crimes against humanity is resurfacing, it is important to re-read Graven in that light. Indeed, since 2013, the International Law Commission has been working on the drafting and adoption of a convention on the prevention and punishment of crimes against humanity,[70] considering that "a global convention on prevention, punishment and inter-State cooperation with respect to crimes against humanity appears to be a key missing piece in the current framework of international law and, in particular, international humanitarian law, international criminal law and international human rights law".[71]

Although we were unable to locate any related documentation, it appears that Graven, in his Geneva course in the year 1965–1966, referred to a project of an international convention on crimes against humanity, written under the auspices of the *Mouvement national judiciaire français* (National French Judicial Movement). He himself referred to this project as a "counter-project on genocide".[72] It seems that Graven would have preferred the Convention on the Prevention and Punishment of the Crime of Genocide had not been adopted, as he considered a convention on crimes against humanity a better option. He thus criticised Lemkin's definition of genocide: "Although the term genocide has become widely accepted, it distorts the exact notion of crimes against humanity by giving it too specific a meaning, by emphasizing its means (the reference to the killing of a particular ethnic or racial group), and too broad an object (racial extermination being the worst crime but not the only one)." He also pointed out that "the admissibility of persecution and extermination for political reasons (next to racial, national, religious reasons) would be more justified than the – so-called – cultural and patrimonial genocide occurring with the destruction of goods, monuments, works of art . . . ".[73] His struggle for the criminalisation of crimes

---

[69] J. Graven, "Les crimes contre l'humanité", *Extraits du recueil des Cours de l'Académie de droit international*, Paris, Sirey, 1950.

[70] ILC, *First Report on Crimes against Humanity*, A/CN.4/680, 17 February 2015.

[71] Ibid., section 12. See also ILC, *Crimes against Humanity: Texts and Titles of the Draft Preamble, the Draft Articles and the Draft Annex Provisionally Adopted by the Drafting Committee on First Reading*, A/CN.4/L.89, 26 May 2017.

[72] J. Graven, Le droit pénal international, II, Course, 1965–1966, p. 4.

[73] Ibid., p. 3.

against humanity thus brought Graven to rapidly criticise the Convention on the Prevention of the Crime of Genocide – particularly because it excluded political genocide: "We can even ask ourselves if, any sort of genocide led by a State or a Government that orders or tolerates it, will not be at the end of the day motivated by political reasons."[74]

Graven's scepticism about the adoption of the Genocide Convention had much to do with how he felt that an opportunity had been missed to more broadly codify crimes against humanity. As early as July 1947, under the aegis of Leon Cornil, the eighth Conference of the International Bureau for the Unification of Penal Law had been held, with the participation of Graven, but also of Pella, Herzog, Bouzat and many others.[75] The discussion focused on the definition of crimes against humanity and three options, summarised by Graven, appear:

> the first one wanted to guarantee the protection of all human rights or those considered as essential (including the right to have citizenship, to start a family . . .); on the opposite side, there was a narrower conception, founded on a more restrictive conception of "genocide", which wanted to grant international legal protection solely to offenses against human life; lastly, the third option aimed at penal protecting all the rights inherent to human beings as such, i.e. to apply to all acts directed against life, physical integrity and health, religious and political freedom . . . .

The conference came to the unanimous conclusion that:

> until we have a legislation which will establish as an offence against humanity all harm done to human fundamental rights, and notably the right to life . . . in order to meet the imperative vows of universal conscience, we immediately have to guarantee the repression of homicide and of all acts which nature is to suppress human life, committed against groups of individuals because of their race (their nationality, their religion or their opinions . . .).[76]

This repression was to apply in times of war and peace and had to be "organised on an international level and guaranteed by an International Criminal Law jurisdiction, whenever the perpetrators are rulers, state bodies or state *protégés* as well as when national criminal law does not permit repression."[77]

---

[74] Ibid., p. 11.

[75] Eighth International Conference for Unification of Penal Law, Brussels, 10 and 11 July 1947, Paris, Pédone, 1949.

[76] Graven, "Les crimes contre l'humanité", p. 59.

[77] J. Graven, Le droit pénal international, II, Course, 1965–1966, p. 5.

The conference hence supported the project of the convention on genocide, but Graven, even if he recognised the advances brought by that, remains very critical of it. Indeed, in 1968, he published an article in *Etudes internationales de psycho-sociologie criminelle*, in which he argued that "this unanimity was artificial because of all the reservations which surrounded its acceptance and we can ask ourselves if it didn't therefore practically lose all its strength".[78]

Graven remained sceptical towards the Genocide convention and still wished for a convention on crimes against humanity. It was, in fact, to crimes against humanity that he dedicated his famous 1950 Hague Academy lecture. Graven was mindful that the definition of crimes against humanity produced by the charter of the Nuremberg Trials and applied not only by that court but also by post-war allied trials was vulnerable to criticism: too restrictive an interpretation of "political, racial and religious" motivations[79] as well as the necessary link between crimes against humanity and other crimes that fell under the court's competence meant that the notion hardly fulfilled its moral and intellectual promise.[80]

The third part of his lecture is the key one and offers a more personal approach: *Synthèse et construction de la théorie juridique des crimes contre l'humanité*[81] (Synthesis and Judicial Theory Construction on Crimes against Humanity). As usual, Graven remained rather evasive in his proposals and only emphasised the principles to follow in order to establish a development of the repression of crimes against humanity. In this context, he perhaps predictably first underlined the need to develop an international legislation respectful of the principle of legality and "to precisely delimit, in the law, the characteristics and the scope of 'crimes against humanity' strictly speaking".[82] Most importantly, however, he suggested that "crimes against humanity as *crime sui generis* have to be detached from the war or peace conditions, in contrast to crimes against the peace and war crimes".[83] This of course anticipated what would be one of the main developments of the notion in the 1990s, a development whose need could already be perceived in the 1950s. Graven foresaw the

---

[78] J. Graven, "Sur la prévention du crime de génocide: Réflexions d'un juriste", *Etudes internationales de psycho-sociologie criminelle*, 1968, pp. 7–18, p. 12.

[79] Ibid., p. 38.

[80] Ibid.

[81] Ibid., pp. 111–165.

[82] Ibid., p. 114.

[83] Ibid., p. 115.

more philosophical dimension of the notion and emphasised that "the guiding principle is that crimes against humanity must be conceived as crimes against the person or the human condition".[84]

Hence, Graven disagreed with Donnedieu de Vabres who had argued that a special intent or motive was required for crimes against humanity. For Graven, this was too narrow:

> It is not only by its *intent* – to destroy, to weaken, or persecute a group or a community – and by its motive – racial passion or hate, or political and religious hate – that these crimes distinguish themselves and deserve to be recognised as such by International Law. It is also by the political *intent* [. . .], by their especially wide, atrocious and dangerous *means*, by the circumstances in which they are committed, often with the support or at least the tolerance of the State, and moreover by the inherent characteristics of the victims that are targeted, all elements law naturally take into consideration to erect, distinguish or qualify their incrimination.[85]

His was therefore a very broad notion of crimes against humanity, one in which neither the subjective nor the objective element dominated. That notion clearly incorporated genocide, but was also much broader.

As for the *actus reus*, Graven stood for the necessity of "all human rights recognised by a text or a 'bill of rights', either national or international"[86] has to be protected (and their violation has to be repressed) under this qualification. He then referred to the Universal Declaration of Human Rights for the appropriate list, specifying that the violation of these rights must be "serious". Wishing for an objective criterion, he focused on what he described as innate rights – contrary to the rights of "social man". Within the category of innate rights, he included "the right to life, freedom and safety", the right to honour and reputation but also the right to be married and start a family,[87] all of which are already stated in the proposal based on the 1946 International Conference for the Unification of Penal Law.[88] He excluded political and civic rights however – under the pretext that such a focus would cause "practically continuous interferences in the States' internal affairs",[89] though regretting it.

[84] Ibid., p. 117.
[85] Ibid., p. 117.
[86] Ibid., p. 120.
[87] Ibid., p. 125.
[88] See analytical reports of the eighth International Conference for Unification of Penal Law, where Graven was assistant to the president. Eighth International Conference for Unification of Penal Law, Brussels, 10 and 11 July 1947, Paris, Pédone, 1949.
[89] Graven, "Les crimes contre l'humanité", p. 128.

Graven then presented the "degrees of completion of the crime" which must be punished: "the conspiracy or the common plan to commit a - crime,[90] the incitement and the propaganda leaning towards provoking or allowing it, as well as the preparatory acts directly leaning to its commission and meant to ensure its success and implementation".[91] He also referred to the different types of liability – of the state, collectivities or individuals – outlined in his *Principes d'un Code répressif des crimes contre la paix et la sécurité de l'humanité* (Principles of a Repressive Code for Crimes against the Peace and Security of Mankind) discussed earlier. However, when it came to the criminal accountability of legal entities – which at the time steered numerous debates – Graven went back to Pella's theses. After having stated that "one must stop questioning the 'liability' of States, collectivities, communities and criminal groups founded on the classic conception of *individual responsibility* [. . .] One must come back to the *real issue* and ask [. . .] if there is not another *form* of accountability, based on other criteria"[92]: a social and legal accountability punished by "appropriate measures or sanctions of international social defence".[93]

In his characteristic style, Graven concluded his lecture on individual accountability with several generalities: "there is a simple principle from which we should once again begin, and it is that each individual criminal must be accountable for his crime, under the condition he did commit one and is indeed himself convinced he did it".[94] He thus refuted immunities but also the condemnation of individuals who had themselves committed a crime merely as a result of group membership: "it would be terribly distressing if International Criminal Law consecrated an offense of belonging to a criminal association such as created by the no. 10 Law of the Allied Control Council in Germany and the French law of September 15th 1948".[95]

14.4 Conclusion

A true jack-of-all-trades, an outstanding jurist, a forerunner and practitioner of interdisciplinarity, Jean Graven has without a doubt marked his

---

[90] According to the author, these must not be constituent elements of the offence of the crime against humanity but must, on the contrary, be punished (ibid., p. 132).

[91] Ibid., p. 131.

[92] Ibid., pp. 142–143.

[93] Ibid., p. 144.

[94] Ibid., p. 146.

[95] Ibid., p. 151.

time and territory – intellectual as well as geographic. As an idealist and humanist thinker, he has led and written important studies in a range of areas other than ICL (criminal and medical law, criminology and socio-psychology, etc.) all of which are, by the way, time and again quoted by the Swiss jurists he himself partially taught. For Graven, the Nuremberg Trial is an opportunity for innovation, one that he was happy to channel through the various learned societies dedicated to ICL of which he was a member and, increasingly, a leading figure. Nonetheless, and even if he was regularly in touch with the authors quoted in this publication, it is difficult to speak of Jean Graven as one of the true forefathers of ICL. He is better described as a promoter, partisan and even vulgarizer of that then emerging discipline. He assumed such roles first in university, where he taught ICL very early on, then in non-legal learned societies, in which he summarised studies of his time, and lastly on an international level, as in Ethiopia, where he contributed to the dissemination and incorporation of ICL. As a prominent in-house *pénaliste* in various scholarly societies with a broader remit he was listened to and quoted often by his contemporaries, such as Glaser,[96] or by several present-day jurists,[97] mainly for his lecture in The Hague, which has brought him a modest posterity in the field. His legacy may be ripe for re-assessment in the light of the current project for a Convention on the Prevention and Punishment of Crimes against Humanity, a treaty which if it were to come to fruition, would realise Graven's wish for a specific convention on the subject. But as Graven had thought, this convention was only a counter-project to the convention against genocide, maybe it is no longer necessary.

[96] S. Glaser, *Droit international pénal conventionnel*, Vol. II, Brussels, Bruylant, 1978, p. 116, note 107; S. Glaser, "Le terrorisme international et ses divers aspects", *Revue internationale de droit comparé*, 25, 4, 1973, pp. 825–850, p. 849, note 61. J. Graven is also quoted in F. Clerc, "Jean Graven(1899–1988)", *Revue de Science Criminelle et Droit Pénal Comparé* 3, 1988.

[97] G. Mettraux (ed.), *Perspectives on the Nuremberg Trial*, Oxford, Oxford University Press, 2008.

15

Absent or Invisible?

'Women' Intellectuals and Professionals at the Dawn of a Discipline

IMMI TALLGREN

Figure 15.1 Katherine Fite Lincoln and Justice Robert H. Jackson Seated at a Desk, ca. 1945. Credit: Harry S. Truman Library & Museum.

Figure 15.2 Rebecca West (1892–1983). Credit: Hulton Archive/Stringer/Getty Images.

382 IMMI TALLGREN

15.1 Awakening

The question [...] is how can we enter the professions and yet remain civilized human beings; human beings, that is, who wish to prevent war?[1]

The inspiration for this chapter came from my belated awakening as co-editor of the book.[2] The project was already well-formed when it really struck me that the table of contents contained zero chapters on *women* intellectuals or professionals. All our distinguished, multidisciplinary team of authors, men and women, had chosen to write about men. I was perplexed. How did this happen? Was it because there really were no women to 'enter the history' worth writing about in our chosen period of time (1900–1950), or was it that none were discovered? Was it our (the editors') bias, not having reached the right scholarly forums? We had contacted scholars specialising in international criminal law across the globe, either lawyers or historians. Early on, we had briefly addressed the problem and then shrugged it off as unfortunate but unresolvable. We had of course seen occasional references to women involved in the International Military Tribunal (IMT) and other post–World War II trials, where the rare women mentioned were represented as the *first and only*. The impression was that their main accomplishment was the fact of having been there, the only 'one wearing a skirt'.[3] But were there key women intellectuals and professionals we could have suggested to aspirant participants to the project? No names popped up.

Not being able to name a single intellectual or professional in our period of focus that could be treated on an equal level with the other (male) characters – and I will get back to what equal level is supposed to mean – became my first research finding. Suddenly its significance detonated. Since the late 1990s, international criminal law is lauded as one of the key successes of feminist approaches to international law.[4] But

---

[1] Virginia Woolf, *Three Guineas* (New York: Harcourt, 1938), p. 75.

[2] I would like to thank warmly Hilary Charlesworth, Karen Knop, Martti Koskenniemi, Frédéric Mégret, Tanya Monforte, Sofia Stolk, Sergey Vasiliev, all other readers, and the participants of the Helsinki workshop in December 2017 for their comments and inspiration. I am grateful to the Finnish Cultural Foundation and the Kone Foundation for supporting my research.

[3] John Q. Barrett, 'Katherine B. Fite: The Leading Female Lawyer at London & Nuremberg, 1945', in Elizabeth Andersen and David M. Crane (eds.), *Proceedings of the Third International Humanitarian Law Dialogs* (Washington, D.C.: The American Society of International Law, 2010), p. 18. See also, Susanne Schattenberg, 'Ein Diplomat im Kleid: Aleksandra Kollontaj und die sowjetische Diplomatie', in Corina Bastian et al. (eds.), *Das Geschlect der Diplomatie: Geschlechterrollen in den Aussenbeziehungen vom Spätmittelalter bis zum 20. Jahrhundert* (Cologne, Weimar, Vienna: Böhlau Verlag, 2014).

[4] See, for example, Janet Halley, et al., *Governance Feminism: An Introduction* (Minneapolis: University of Minnesota Press, 2018).

15 'WOMEN' AT THE DAWN OF A DISCIPLINE   383

strikingly, as I discovered, even the most recent histories of this discipline of law and its institutional practice, be they written by international lawyers, legal historians, or sociologists, are practically silent on women.[5] With regard to the intellectual and professional history of international criminal law, the first impression one gets is that women enter as late as in the 1990s. I felt I was staring at a puzzling discontinuity: how is it that (most) international feminist activists had 'found' and considered so promising for their objectives a legal and intellectual project that hardly any women had a previous investment in?

However, as soon as I started to talk about my discovery, colleagues and new acquaintances from conferences or shoptalk came up with an anecdote and a new name or two. I noticed that if one zooms out of the established canon of the discipline's history, exceptions become visible. Names and traces of work appear, and at times images of those 'skirts'.[6] To quote Diane Marie Amann, the pioneer scholar on this question: '[c] onventional accounts of post-World War II trials tend to relegate women at Nuremberg to the occasional cameo appearance. Yet women of many nationalities were present throughout, from the Allied lawyers' first inspection of the Nuremberg courthouse until the end of the last of twelve Nuremberg trials.'[7] The French Doctor of Law

---

[5] See, e.g., Mark Lewis, *The Birth of the New Justice: The Internationalization of Crime and Punishment, 1919–1950* (Oxford: Oxford University Press, 2014); Morten Bergsmo, Cheah Wui Ling and Yi Ping (eds.), *Historical Origins of International Criminal Law*, 4 vols. (Brussels: Torkel Opsahl Academic EPublishers, 2014–2015); Kevin Jon Heller and Gerry Simpson (eds.), *The Hidden Histories of War Crimes Trials* (Oxford: Oxford University Press, 2013); Yuki Tanaka, Tim McCormack and Gerry Simpson (eds.), *Beyond Victor's Justice? The Tokyo War Crimes Trials Revisited* (Leiden: Martinus Nijhoff Publishers, 2011).

[6] See, e.g., Susanne Schattenberg, 'Ein Diplomat im Kleid: Aleksandra Kollontaj und die sowjetische Diplomatie', in Corina Bastian et al (eds.), *Das Geschlect der Diplomatie: Geschlechterrollen in den Aussenbeziehungen vom Spätmittelalter bis zum 20. Jahrhundert* (Cologne, Weimar, Vienna: Böhlau Verlag, 2014).

[7] Diane Marie Amann, 'Cecelia Goetz, Woman at Nuremberg' (2011) 11 *International Criminal Law Review* 607–20 at 608. See also Diane Marie Amann, 'Politics and Prosecutions: From Katherine Fite to Fatou Bensouda', in Elizabeth Andersen and David M. Crane (eds.), *Proceedings of the Fifth International Humanitarian Law Dialogs* (Washington, D.C.: American Society of International Law, 2012), p. 14. Cecelia Goetz, 'Impressions of Telford Taylor at Nuremberg' (1999) 37 *Columbia Journal of Transnational Law* 669–72; Amann, 'Cecelia Goetz, Woman at Nuremberg'; Kevin Jon Heller, *The Nuremberg Military Tribunals and the Origins of International Criminal Law* (Oxford: Oxford University Press, 2011), p. 34. Other names, such as Sadie Arbuthnot, Mary Kaufman, Belle Mayer, Dorothea Minskoff, and Esther Johnson appear in, e.g., Diane Marie Amann, 'Portraits of Women at Nuremberg', in Elizabeth Andersen and David M. Crane (eds.), *Proceedings of the Third International Humanitarian Law*

Aline Chalufour worked both at the IMT and the first Ravensbrück trial in Hamburg.[8] A few women acted as defence attorneys, such as Elisabeth Gombel who was a lead defence counsel.[9] Women were also present both at the IMT and the successor Nuremberg trials as interpreters and in various clerical roles. At the IMT for the Far East in Tokyo, attorney Grace Kanode Llewellyn worked as an assistant prosecutor and other mainly US women lawyers and staffers had various tasks.[10] There were no women judges in those trials, but women judges did feature in some of the national post–World War II trials for crimes one would today label 'international' – even if at the time they applied national law. Judge Marguerite Haller, for example, took part in 215 cases in the Rastatt trials (1946–1954) held in the French occupied zone of Germany.[11] There were also women defence attorneys in Rastatt, such as German national Helga Kloninger. Hertta Kuusinen was the only woman among the fifteen judges in the Finnish trial for the responsibility for war in 1945–1946.[12]

And so on. No doubt, tens or hundreds or more names of prosecutorial staff members, defence lawyers, judges or clerks, legal secretaries, and the like could be singled out and added to the list, depending on where one draws the line for the relevant contexts. As soon as one admits that there were no clear borders between national, transnational, European, and international law, as there arguably are nowadays, academics and professionals active in their respective national law, as well as in transnational law, enter the picture.[13] Contiguous fields of law and

---

Dialogs, pp. 31–54. Amann and other scholars have also brought into view women in different roles on the IntLawGrrls blog (www.intlawgrrls.com).

[8] Telford Taylor, *The Anatomy of the Nuremberg Trials: A Personal Memoir* (Boston: Little, Brown, 1992) refers to her as a senior member of staff, 'an administrator who spoke excellent English and served as interpreter on important occasions', p. 213.

[9] See, e.g., Kim Christian Priemel, *The Betrayal: The Nuremberg Trials and German Divergence* (Oxford: Oxford University Press, 2016), p. 161.

[10] See Shana Tabak, 'Grace Kanode Llewellyn: Local Portia at the Tokyo War Crimes Tribunal' (2013) *International and Comparative Law Perspectives* 7–9; Diane Marie Amann, 'Glimpses of Women at the Tokyo Tribunal', *University of Georgia School of Law Legal Studies Research Paper* 2019–02 https://ssrn.com/abstract=3309257.

[11] See, e.g., 'Marguerite Haller, La Femme dans la magistrature', Cour d'appel de Douai, Audience solennelle de rentrée du 16 septembre 1961 (Douai: G. Lannier, 1961), p. 11.

[12] On the trial, see Immi Tallgren, 'Martyrs and Scapegoats of the Nation? The Finnish War-Responsibility Trial, 1945-1946', in Morten Bergsmo, Cheah Wui Ling, and Yi Ping (eds.), *The Historical Origins of International Criminal Law*, vol. II (Brussels: Torkel Opsahl Academic EPublisher, 2014), pp. 493–538.

[13] For examples, see Sara Kimble and Marion Röwekamp (eds.), *New Perspectives on European Women's Legal History* (New York: Routledge, 2016); Rebecca Mae Salokar

15 'WOMEN' AT THE DAWN OF A DISCIPLINE 385

social sciences adjacent to law, such as the thematic area currently known as criminology, were amongst those exhibiting early traces of women's work in international forums. By contrast, key academic associations of interest to this research project, such as the International Union of Penal Law and its successor the International Association of Penal Law (AIDP), remained male bastions, at least with regard to leading roles.[14] Likewise, the United Nations War Crimes Commission (1943–8) lacked women in visible roles.

Further, one could focus on women who were in politics (civil-society activists, parliamentarians, and other comparable roles), who had an institutional role (in national or international administration, courts or tribunals, or anything comparable), who wrote and published (academics, authors, journalists). Pacifism was a cause carried by many women activists, including Bertha von Suttner who was awarded the Nobel Peace Prize in 1906.[15] The Women's International League for Peace and Freedom and other associations played a role from early on, and notably organised the Hague Peace Conference in 1915.[16] Various international campaigns, such as the one against white slavery were driven by activists like Lady Rothschild, Mary Hyett Bunting (Lady Bunting), Bertha Pappenheim, and others from the League of Jewish Women (Jüdischer Frauenbund).[17] Following the legendary early activists of humanitarianism such as Florence Nightingale and Clara Barton,

---

and Mary L. Volcansek (eds.), *Women in Law: A Bio-Bibliographical Source Book* (Westport: Greenwood Publishing Group, 1996), Mary Jane Mossmann, *The First Women Lawyers: A Comparative Study of Gender, Law and the Legal Professions* (Oxford and Portland: Hart, 2006).

[14] In the special session of the AIDP held at the Nuremberg courthouse in 1946, the names of Aline Chalufour and Delphine Debenest appear on the participants list, see Henri Donnedieu de Vabres, 'Procès-verbal de la réunion de l'AIP siège du tribunal international (Nuremberg)' (2015) 86 *Revue Internationale de Droit Penal* 915. No women have ever been appointed president of the AIDP. The first woman secretary-general was Katalin Ligety (2008–14).

[15] Irwin Abrams, 'Betha von Suttner and the Nobel Peace Prize' (1962) 22 *Journal of Central European Affairs* 286–307.

[16] See, e.g., Laura Beers, 'Advocating for a Feminist Internationalism Between the Wars', in Glenda Sluga and Carolyn James (eds.), *Women, Diplomacy and International Politics Since 1500* (London: Routledge, 2016) 202; Freya Baetens, 'The Forgotten Peace Conference: The 1915 Congress of Women', in Rüdiger Wolfrum (ed.), *Max Planck Encyclopedia of Public International Law* (Oxford: Oxford University Press, 2010); Leila Rupp, 'Constructing Internationalism: The Case of Transnational Women's Organizations, 1888–1945' (1994) 99 *American Historical Review* 1571–1660.

[17] See Paul Knepper, *The Invention of International Crimes: A Global Issue in the Making, 1881–1914* (New York: Palgrave Macmillan, 2010), p. 192.

386   IMMI TALLGREN

Renée-Marguerite Cramer (later Frick-Cramer) was the first woman to enter the International Committee of the Red Cross (ICRC), which she did in 1918, slowly to be followed by others.[18] Several well-known journalistic commentators at international criminal trials were women, including Rebecca West, Erika Mann, Martha Gellhorn, and Victoria Ocampo.[19] Finally, Hannah Arendt and Judith Shklar feature as the only 'historical' women whom scholars of international criminal law today typically refer to.[20]

For a moment, it seemed as if the famine turned into a feast of women, from fields close or far, if not lawyers then almost, in similar tasks, also from early on in international law.[21] Somewhat daunted, I wondered what to do with those names and fragments of information, searching for an approach if not a 'method'. Most importantly, how to represent adequately my contradictory discoveries, the fragments of presence and the total absence in our research project figuring big names, Hans Kelsen, Vespasian Pella, Henri Donnedieu de Vabres, and company? My discovery of the absence of women was not unique, to put it mildly. Women are absent from the disciplinary, intellectual, and professional histories of almost any field of activity beyond household work or midwifery.[22] Even if women have recently become more visible in scholarship of international law, and a few occupy prominent positions in international legal institutions, research on women's roles in the past of international law

---

[18] As Daniel Palmieri, 'Guerre, humanité et féminité: le Comité international de la Croix-Rouge et les femmes (1863–1965)', in Jean-Marc Delaunay and Yves Denéchère (eds.), *Femmes et relations internationales au XXe siècle* (Paris: Presses Sorbonne Nouvelle, 2006), p. 192 writes, 'between 1919 and end of 1965, they were only six to enter, whereas 56 new members were men'. See also Silvia Cadei, 'Le comité de CICR: une affaire d'hommes?' 2 *Histoire & Genre Automen* (2017) 74–83 and John Hutchinson, *Champions of Charity: War and The Rise of The Red Cross* (Boulder: Westview Press, 1996) for critical observations on gender and the ICRC.

[19] See, e.g., Carl Rollyson, 'Reporting Nuremberg', in *Rebecca West and the God That Failed* (Lincoln: iUniverse, 2005), pp. 79–85.

[20] However, in addition to not being lawyers, they wrote their work relevant in this context after the timeframe of our research project. See, e.g., David Luban, 'Hannah Arendt as a Theorist in International Criminal Law' (2011) 11 *International Criminal Law Review* 621–41.

[21] To mention a prominent example, see Christine de Pizan pictured as 'mother of international law', www.ejiltalk.org/founding-fathers-of-international-law-recognizing-christine-de-pizan/.

[22] For a landmark study, see Laurel Thatcher Ulrich, *A Midwife's Tale: The Life of Martha Ballard, Based on her Diary 1785–1812* (New York: Alfred Knopf, 1990). On the changes towards new ventures and resources in the history of women, see Laurel Thatcher Ulrich, *Well-Behaved Women Seldom Make History* (New York: Vintage Books, 2007).

and its broader intellectual history remains rare. At the same time, asking the notorious 'women question' with regard to histories of international criminal law may seem too *passé* – and reductive. How could research 'on women' be conducted today – decades after the post-structuralist questioning of identity, agency, power, and knowledge – without adhering to a positivist stream of scholarship that considers the category women unproblematic, monolithic, and foundational?[23] The difficulty starts in circumscribing the meanings given to 'being a woman/man' in this field of international law, today and in 'the past'. Even a superficial reading of gender and women studies, or women's, feminist, and gender histories, suffices to convince the reader of the complexity. As critics have argued since the 1970s, efforts to shed light on women – and sex and gender – easily fall back to binary patterns, compensatory or separatist spheres, potentially re-strengthening the sexual difference or the misunderstanding that only women 'have gender' or 'suffer from gender', and may also come close to semi-universal essentialism, ignoring the intersectionality of class, sexuality, race, culture, nationality, religion, and the contexts in time and space.[24]

When I confronted the absence in 2016, its banality did not make it less puzzling. Nor could I find a reason to continue acting as if the absence were without material consequences for international criminal law and its institutional practice today. That we had a table of contents containing zero chapters on women intellectuals or professionals was potentially a consequence of too tight academic specialisation, if not segregation, leading to a fragmented understanding I set out to rectify. I soon noticed, however, that 'rectifying' the absence is far from simple, leading to broader interrogations than just the choice of an academic community or particular authors. How does the absence of women in histories of international criminal law connect, for example, to scholarship in feminist approaches to international law, on how 'the international legal system is gendered at a deep level and its mantle of rationality and

---

[23] Kathleen Canning historicises the changes in historiographical research on women and gender in 'Gender History: Meanings, Methods and Metanarratives', in *Gender History in Practice: Historical Perspectives on Bodies, Class and Citizenship* (Ithaca: Cornell University Press, 2006). See also Denise Riley, *'Am I That Name?' Feminism and the Category of Woman in History* (Houndmills: Macmillan, 1988).

[24] See, e.g., bell hooks, 'Postmodern Blackness', in *Yearning: Race, Gender and Cultural Politics* (Boston: South End Press, 1990). See also, e.g., Renate Bridenthal, Claudia Koonz and Susan Stuart, *Becoming Visible: Women in European History* (2nd edn., Boston: Houghton Mifflin, 1987).

objectivity is a chimera',[25] to quote Hilary Charlesworth and Christine Chinkin? Beyond the complex epistemological and methodological choices in historiographical terms, the absence also opens perplexing questions on how various types of agency are valued inside the discipline. How exactly should one go about the task: should one look only for exceptionally important women or 'women worthies',[26] to borrow Gerda Lerner's term for women whose achievements did not differ significantly in kind from those of men in the same context? What if there appears to be none, even of the latter kind, but only women as secretaries and assistants, for example: should one turn to quantitative research, collecting, listing, categorising, and organising the numbers and types of any women encountered? Based on what taxonomy?

I chose to make these interrogations and obstacles the core of my chapter. Aspiring to ask 'large questions in small places',[27] I am sketching two microhistories[28] starring contrasting types of individuals: the first a professional of international law, the second an intellectual with no legal background. Tentatively, I claim a prominent place for them in the intellectual history on international criminal law – even if they have so far occupied a tiny slot in its backyard. My chapter, therefore, becomes an invitation to write more comprehensive histories in which women, and indeed other underrepresented groups, are present. My chapter is also a way of interrogating the problematic aspects of representing individuals as women, in particular, deviant from a normative understanding of an 'international criminal lawyer'. I start by discussing various ways by which an absence in histories – as in this research project – can be countered, reflecting on the choices that matter in representing presence – and absence. I analyse how my two examples of individuals have been so far represented, pointing to frequent tropes in narrating the *first and only*. I discuss, first, the effect of the particular types of sources typically available for the one searching for women. I question, second, the predominant emphasis on exceptionality where the sex and gender seem to override any other characteristics of the individual in question and, third, how gendered the attention to sociological

---

[25] Hilary Charlesworth and Christine Chinkin, *The Boundaries of International Law: A Feminist Analysis* (Manchester: Manchester University Press, 2000), p. 95.

[26] Gerda Lerner, *The Majority Finds Its Past: Placing Women in History* (Oxford: Oxford University Press, 1979), pp. 145–6.

[27] C. W. Joyner, *Shared Traditions: Southern History and Folk Culture* (Urbana, University of Illinois Press, 1999), p. 1.

[28] Carlo Ginzburg, 'Microhistory, Two or Three Things That I Know about It' (1993) 20 (1) *Critical Inquiry* 28.

profiles and private life is. Fourth, I address the difficulties in concretely defining professional hierarchies or the exact outputs of the marginal(ised) subjects. Through the microhistories, I question the role their characters could be claimed to have, compared to other figures in this volume, and thus examine more broadly what it means to be in the margins of what is in many ways a dominating project. I also ponder on what attitudes the characters sketched in the microhistories may have held towards current feminist causes and typical expectations with regard to women's participation. I end with thoughts on why one asks the question on sex and gender of those who figure in our intellectual histories – on the moves or desires that figure behind the search.

15.2 On Ways of Countering an Absence

Not only in international criminal justice, but in international law more broadly the first impression is that few women were professionally active in the period 1900–1950. Only a few names of the first and only, again, are likely to be vaguely known, if at all. The first woman elected to the Institut de droit international, established in 1873, was Suzanne Bastid, as late as in 1956. She then came to be the first female member of the International Court of Justice (ICJ), designated as an ad hoc judge by Tunisia in 1982.[29] Others, such as Sarah Wambaugh (1882–1955), were active in particular fields of international law in said period even if they were not lawyers by education.[30] Their names, however, do not make part of what we today typically understand and teach our students as the past of international law that counts. Martti Koskenniemi's *The Gentle Civilizer of Nations*, for example, covering the period 1870–1960, refers only to (white) men, 'fathers and grandfathers in the profession' of international lawyers.[31] Similarly, David Armitage's *Foundations of Modern International*

---

[29] See Jacqueline Lucienne Lafon, 'Suzanne Bastid-Basdevant', in Salokar and Volcansek, *Women*. Rosalyn Higgins became a permanent judge at the ICJ in 1995.

[30] Sarah Wambaugh was 'an instructor in history and government, and an expert in international affairs', specialising in plebiscites, see *Sarah Wambaugh, 1882–1965. Collection of Documents Related to Plebiscites*, https://hollisarchives.lib.harvard.edu/repositories/5/resources/4543.

[31] Martti Koskenniemi, *The Gentle Civilizer of Nations: The Rise and Fall of International Law 1870–1960* (Cambridge: Cambridge University Press, 2001), p. 5. Koskenniemi does not 'exclude the possibility – indeed, the likelihood – that in the margins [. . .] there have been women and non-Europeans whose stories would desperately require telling so as to provide a more complete image of the profession's political heritage', p. 9.

Thought deals only with 'the landmarks of a heavily subscribed Anglo-centric canon of political thinkers, completely male'.[32]

If 'international law is what international lawyers do and think' and its histories are narratives about 'how the profession ended up being what it is today',[33] intellectual and professional histories become a powerful example of how the past is operating in present times. The hefty absence of women in histories of international criminal law and its institutional practice this chapter evokes could be addressed from various methodological premises, with different approaches: representing it, hiding it, surviving it, contesting or re-enacting it. I already evoked academic works in women's history, gender history, and gender studies above. In this chapter, those approaches could include questioning whether there really were an insignificantly small number of women intellectuals and professionals during the relevant time period and in the relevant context, or have many more been ignored, forgotten in archives, neglected in histories, biographies, and other accounts, so that they have become invisible. Answering such questions requires a critical approach towards current historiography, as well as strategies for unearthing hidden or forgotten histories and invisible actors, work currently undertaken also by post-colonial and global historians.[34] The aesthetic choices of representing the occasionally discovered presence on the canvas of absence may also evoke alternate or counterfactual histories,[35] as well as visual and performative re-enactments 'pointing at what is missing and cannot be retrieved'.[36]

A focus on the absence of women and its preconditions, consequences, and meaning implicitly presumes a group, a frame, an 'epistemic community' or otherwise described category of *international*

---

[32] Glenda Sluga, 'Turning International: Foundations of Modern International Thought and New Paradigms for Intellectual History' (2015) 41 *History of European Ideas* 103–15; see David Armitage, *Foundations of Modern International Thought* (Cambridge: Cambridge University Press, 2012).

[33] Martti Koskenniemi, *The Gentle Civilizer of Nations: The Rise and Fall of International Law 1870–1960* (Cambridge: Cambridge University Press, 2001), p. 7.

[34] See, e.g., Dipesh Charkabarty, *Provincializing Europe: Postcolonial Thought and Historical Difference* (Princeton: Princeton University Press, 2000); Arnulf Becker Lorca, *Mestizo International Law: A Global Intellectual History 1842–1933* (Cambridge: Cambridge University Press, 2014); Onuma Yasuaki, *International Law in a Transcivilizational World* (Cambridge: Cambridge University Press, 2017).

[35] See Gavriel D. Rosenfeld, *The World Hitler Never Made: Alternate History and the Memory of Nazism* (Cambridge: Cambridge University Press, 2011) pp. 11–12; Richard J. Evans, *Altered Pasts: Counterfactuals in History* (London: Little, Brown, 2014).

[36] Wouter Werner, *Representing Absence: The Use of Re-enactments in Documentary Films on Mass Atrocities* (on file with the author).

15 'WOMEN' AT THE DAWN OF A DISCIPLINE 391

criminal lawyers.[37] Whom such a group is considered to comprise and why, its inclusions and exclusions, its hierarchies, are all relevant questions, even beyond the tight methodological constraints of prosopography.[38] Research efforts to find women benefit from recent research on 'legal lives writing',[39] which seeks to understand legal actors as parts of professional communities and analyses the individual roles therein. The narrative perspective from which such 'imagined communities'[40] are represented also identifies the position of power of those drawing the borders of the community.

Further, writing on women almost by definition becomes an exercise in 'histories from below', in other words efforts to redirect attention from known actors and structures to those which have not been deemed worthy of interest because of their lower position in the hierarchy. Beyond the actors I have chosen to discuss (intellectuals and professionals in law), attention could be further broadened to include the secretaries, assistants, spouses, mothers, and daughters behind influential men. The question could be the degree to which the work of those women, often in the private or semi-private sphere, enabled that of the men with whom they were associated.[41] Such an approach would turn the attention to the delimitations of the private and the public, as well as the related political economies, also the attention economies of historiography and research work in general. Were there men who enabled women's work in international law? As Mary Ellen Waithe writes on women philophers, '[a]ll women ... had significant connections with male scholars while the obverse is not the case. The parts played – enhancing or distorting – by patrons, fathers, teachers, confessors,

---

[37] See, e.g., Claus Kress, 'Towards a Truly Universal Invisible College of International Criminal Lawyers', *FICHL Occasional Paper Series*, No. 4, available at www.legal-tools.org/doc/82bf10/; Andrea Bianchi, 'Epistemic Community', in Jean d'Aspremont and Sahib Singh (eds.), *Concepts of International Law* (Cheltenham: Edward Elgar, 2019).

[38] See, e.g., Katherine Keats-Rohan (ed.), *Prosopography Approaches and Applications: A Handbook* (Oxford: Unit for Prosopographical Research, Linacre College, University of Oxford, 2007).

[39] See Linda Mulcahy and David Sugarman (eds.), *Legal Life Writing: Marginalized Subjects and Sources* (Hoboken: Wiley Blackwell, 2015).

[40] Benedict Anderson, *Imagined Communities* (London: Verso, 1991): 'imagined because the members of even the smallest nation will never know most of their fellow-members, meet them, or eve hear of them, yet in the minds of each lives the image of their communion.' p. 6.

[41] See, e.g., Hilary Callan and Shirley Ardener (eds.), *The Incorporated Wife* (London: Croom Helm, 1984); Cynthia H. Enloe, *Bananas, Beaches and Bases: Making Feminist Sense of International Politics* (London: Pandora Press, 1989).

preachers, scribes and assistants, need to be understood for a full comprehension'.[42]

A related but separate set of research questions could explore the causes and consequences of women's absence – and invisibility – and its temporal and geographical continuities and breaks. Any analysis of these questions should, by implication, also lead one to interrogate past and current structures, mechanisms, and practices that have supported and still support the sex and gender difference in the professional field, ranging from legal education and academic research to institutions, professional networks, bar associations, benches, and publication policies to celebratory traditions. The microhistories I turn to in the following have been stirred by aspects of all the premises and approaches mentioned.

15.3 Two Microhistories

15.3.1 The 'Leading Exception'[43]: Katherine B. Fite

> Justice Jackson, with a party that included Miss Katherine Fite (a State department lawyer assigned to assist the Justice), had noticed a gleam of metal in the debris. It proved to be a medal attached to a ribbon. With great show of gallantry, Jackson hung the decoration around Miss Fite's neck. There was a chorus of demand for translation of the German legend on the medal: 'Order of Motherhood, Second Class'.[44]

Katherine Boardman Fite (1904–89) has recently surfaced as the most visible of the women lawyers working at the IMT in Nuremberg. She was a US Department of State lawyer serving at the Office of the Legal Adviser, and was seconded to the team of Justice Jackson, US Chief of Counsel, in 1945. Her role concentrated in particular on the early phases of the tribunal: the negotiations of the London Agreement and preparations for the trial. Fite periodically assisted Jackson's staff in Washington until he relocated to London, where Fite joined the team in mid-July 1945. In London, she was present at a few sessions of the Allied negotiations on the London Agreement, but she spent most of her time doing

---

[42] Joan Gibson and Mary Ellen Waithe, 'Introduction', in Mary Ellen Waithe (ed.), *A History of Women Philosophers, Volume II* (Dordrecht: Kluwer Academic Publishers, 1989) p. xxix.

[43] Barrett, 'Katherine B. Fite', pp. 14.

[44] Taylor, *The Anatomy*, describing a visit to Hitler's Reich chancellery in 1945, p. 127.

15 'WOMEN' AT THE DAWN OF A DISCIPLINE 393

preparatory work related to the drafting of the IMT Charter.[45] She made new contacts, and at least once took part in a meeting of the United Nations War Crimes Commission.[46] From London she accompanied Justice Jackson and a delegation of US, British, and French officials on a preparatory trip to Nuremberg, to see the planned courthouse and the city.[47] She also travelled with Jackson to Berlin, Cecilienhof in Potsdam – where the Potsdam agreement was negotiated – Frankfurt, Cambridge – to meet Professor Lauterpacht – and elsewhere.[48]

When she moved to Nuremberg in early September 1945, she helped to prepare the charges and the trial against the Reichskanzlei, by planning and attending interrogations of suspects. She only rarely sat in during the proceedings of the court after the opening session of 20 November, claiming a lack of time due to the heavy workload but also noting that 'the courtroom presentation is dull and tedious'.[49] Blaming bad organisation and low morale, she left Nuremberg in late December 1945, and thus did not participate in any major part of the trial. Back at the State Department in Washington, she followed the proceedings from a distance, writing an official summary of the IMT's judgment[50] and continuing to keep in touch with Jackson and other staff in Nuremberg at reunions in the USA.

Katherine B. Fite features in three recent articles, all of which rely mainly on the same source: her file in the archives of the Harry S. Truman Library.[51] The file includes Fite's correspondence with her parents, friends, and colleagues during her stay in Nuremberg and shortly

---

[45] Letter 19 August 1945 by Katherine B. Fite to her parents, 'War Crimes Trials File', Katherine Fite Lincoln Papers, Truman Presidential Museum & Library, Independence, MO (all the letters in the following notes are by Fite to her parents from this archive) and Barrett, 'Katherine B. Fite', p. 17.

[46] Letter 19 August 1945.

[47] Letter 23 July 1945. See also Barrett, 'Katherine B. Fite', p. 18. Taylor, *The Anatomy*, pp. 64–5, describes the trip but does not mention the presence of Fite.

[48] Letters 23 and 27 July, and 5 August 1945. On the visit to Cambridge, see also Philippe Sands, *East West Street: On the Origins of 'Genocide' and 'Crimes Against Humanity'*, p. 111-3.

[49] Letter 9 December 1945. See also, letter 21 October 1945; letter 20 November 1945; letter 27 November 1945.

[50] See Katherine B. Fite, 'The Nürnberg Judgment: A Summary', XVI Department of State Bulletin No. 392, 5 January 1947, at 9-19, reprinted as *U.S. Dept. of State Publication* 2727, European Series (1947) (referred to by Barrett, 'Katherine B. Fite').

[51] See Barrett, 'Katherine B. Fite'; Amann, 'Politics and Prosecutions'; and Amann, 'Portraits'. For the archives, see 'War Crimes Trials File', Katherine Fite Lincoln Papers, Truman Presidential Museum & Library, Independence, MO, an index of which is available at www.trumanlibrary.org/hstpaper/lincoln.htm.

thereafter, as well as a short biographical note and a few official documents concerning her secondment. These were the parts of the file I was able to access. This highlights an important epistemological aspect that framed my tentative effort to include Fite as an intellectual figure amongst other figures discussed in this project: Fite did not write legal journal articles or commentaries on international criminal justice (other than the summary mentioned above). She never published autobiographical accounts of her experiences in London and Nuremberg, or Washington, for that matter. She was not an academic and she is barely visible in official documents, commentaries, and memoirs – Telford Taylor's much-read memoir, for example, contains only two minor references to her.[52]

The most substantial information on Fite and her opinions on the Nuremberg IMT stems from her private correspondence, written in a casual, vivid, and intimate style. Her views on the drafting of the indictment and her accounts of confrontations with the accused and witnesses have to be extracted from her letters, in which she also shares her concerns about her hair and her diet, begging her parents for winter stockings and towels. Another reason why her letters are thin as sources on the trial might be that she may have been worried about confidentiality of mail in the 1945 conditions of occupation, refraining from adding much detail about the files on which she worked. The question of sources makes a striking difference compared to the other characters discussed in the project, who published academic, professional works and/or memoirs, and are not hard to find in legal and historiographical studies. Their notoriety and dominance, in fact, tends to cumulate, correlating closely with the number of positions they occupied and the honours that they were awarded. I highlight this difference as an example of how research on the *first and only* has to cope with 'double marginalisation', that is, an inferior position of women both in their life contexts and in the sources that remain of them.[53] A further aspect I pay attention to is the intertwinement of the public and the private lives in the rarer and often private sources one can access on women, and to which value judgements of minor legitimacy as 'diaries and letters only' are attached.

Another key aspect that emerges in particular from John Q. Barrett's warm-hearted article on Fite – who 'was, like Jackson, smart, outspoken,

---

[52] Taylor, *The Anatomy*, p. 127 and 215.

[53] See Rosemary Auchmuty, 'Recovering Lost Lives: Researching Women in Legal History' (2015) 42 (1) *Journal of Law and Society* 34–52; Mulcahy and Sugarman, *Legal Life.*

active, independent, and a very fine lawyer'[54] – is the narrative focus on her exceptionality. Barrett explains that he searched through long descriptions of how the Nuremberg trials came about, preparations both in the USA and in international encounters, and even considering the defendants at the IMT; he finds 'not one woman'.[55] Barret reminds his readers of how 'no woman was permitted to address the International Military Trial',[56] after which 'one leading exception' is introduced: Katherine Fite. Barrett underlines how Fite's 'employment by Justice Jackson was, because of her gender, a notable event'.[57] No matter that Fite may have been very similar to a large majority of the US staff involved in the post–World War II justice effort with regard to all other imaginable criteria such as social status, 'race', education, employment, religion, cultural preferences, political opinions, and worldview. These aspects do not count next to her gender that sets her apart. The dilemma is to see whether Fite would ever have been written on, to start with, had she been a man.

What was the background of this exceptional woman? The way in which it is accounted for also seems to relate to her gender. Fite was born in Boston, and she obtained a degree in law from Yale in 1930.[58] As Barrett reports, Fite's 'father chaired the political science department' of Vassar College.[59] He does not mention the professional situation of her mother, which is not specified in Fite's biographical note in the archive either. Both of the above-mentioned international lawyers, Bastid and Wambough, are also represented as daughters of their fathers, professors of law,[60] and Goetz was the daughter of a lawyer, too.[61] Barrett then turns to Katherine Fite's marital situation. She 'was single until age of fifty-two

---

[54] Barrett, 'Katherine B. Fite', p. 16.

[55] Barrett, 'Katherine B. Fite', p. 13.

[56] Barrett, 'Katherine B. Fite', p. 14 fn 6, refers to Joseph E. Persico, *Nuremberg: Infamy on Trial* (New York: Viking, 1994), p. 212 describing a radio report on this subject by CBS reporter Howard K. Smith.

[57] Barrett, 'Katherine B. Fite', p. 15, referring to *New York Times*, 'Woman Joins Staff of War Crimes Group', 11 July 1945, p. 4.

[58] See the 'Biographical Sketch' at Katherine Fite Lincoln Papers, www.trumanlibrary.org/hstpaper/lincoln.htm.

[59] Ibid; Barrett, 'Katherine B. Fite', p. 14.

[60] See, Lafon, 'Suzanne Bastid-Basdevant'; Wambaugh 'moved to the intensely academic environment of Cambridge, Massachusetts, when her father Eugene Wambaugh, a specialist in constitutional and international law, was appointed to the faculty at Harvard Law School', www.encyclopedia.com/women/encyclopedias-almanacs-transcripts-and-maps/wambaugh-sarah-1882-1955.

[61] Amann, 'Cecilia Goetz', p. 609.

(1957), when she married Francis French Lincoln and became Katherine Fite Lincoln'.[62] Portrayals of many early women professionals, authors, activists, and scholars seem to interweave their private and public lives more closely than those of men: questions of marriage, motherhood, and childcare are addressed, and the choices made by the individual appear to determine both her career and character more strongly than in the case of men.[63] Anthea Taylor argues that even today, '[b]eing partnered remains crucial to women's ability to become viable (and visible) subjects, and therefore viable citizens'.[64] Fite, an international lawyer at the age of forty in London and Nuremberg is pictured as the prodigious single woman, a devoted daughter writing letters about her adventures and successes to her parents. The reader may not be able to resist wondering whether an international lawyer and a wife and mother would have left the USA, given the uncertain conditions in Europe in 1945. The fact that husbands and fathers very often did so does not seem to require any particular attention. Parenting and career were mutually exclusive choices only for women. Women also tend to get described physically to a greater extent than men do. At the time of Fite's assignment in Nuremberg, media stories on women lawyers did not omit commentary on their looks, hair, and clothes: relief was palpable when they still looked like women, despite their professional role.[65]

The greatest challenge in including Katherine Fite in this project relates to the difficulties of defining her professional rank, role, individual professional output, and opinions. Barrett attempts to describe her hierarchical position and importance, deploring the lack of an organisational chart: she was near (below) top lawyers who 'served near the top ranks'. She thus appears to be on the third level down from Jackson, and 'both Jackson and Alderman leaned on her regularly'.[66] It is mentioned how she brought historical and professional knowledge of diplomacy, treaty drafting, and negotiation with her from the State Department's Legal Adviser's office. She contributed, for example, to the the analysis of the

---

[62] Barrett, 'Katherine B. Fite', p. 15.

[63] See, e.g., on Elisabeth Gombel, defence lawyer at Nuremberg, 'Briefe an Elisabeth', *Der Spiegel* 34/1948, 21.08.1948.

[64] Anthea Taylor, *Single Women in Popular Culture: The Limits of Postfeminism* (Palgrave Macmillan, 2012) p. 3.

[65] As Tanya Monforte discusses, this expectation has not changed in all contexts, 'Soft Power as Metaphor: The Gender of Security'. in Caroline Leprince and Cassandra Steer (eds.), *Women, Peace and Security: Feminist Perspectives to International Security Studies* (Montreal and Kingston: McGill-Queen's University Press, in press).

[66] Barrett, 'Katherine B. Fite', p. 17.

15 'WOMEN' AT THE DAWN OF A DISCIPLINE 397

Kellogg-Briand Treaty, countering the objection that it would be retroactive criminalisation to prosecute German defendants for waging aggressive war.[67] However, the 'brilliant partner, Col. Benjamin Kaplan', with whom Fite was 'working in tandem'[68] on the Reich cabinet case, is likely to be a more familiar name than Fite to today's readers.[69] Colonel Murray C. Bernays wrote in a memorandum to Jackson that Fite 'has done a great deal of work in the documentation and interrogation group under my personal direction. She has brought to our duties unusual understanding of our problems, based upon her long and intense contact with this subject while she was on duty in the Office of the Legal Adviser in Washington.'[70] By comparison, Taylor, who explains in detail the functioning and structure of Jackson's early team and the negotiation of the London Charter, does not refer to Fite at all in that part of his book.[71]

Fite's own accounts of her working days indicate a sharp and critical mind. She is enthusiastic about her new experiences and encounters, yet she remains lucid: 'You don't have a marvellous time in a ruined city, in a hostile country, at a criminal trial where you look out of the window all day and interrogate men you hope to hang.'[72] When she 'engineered an interrogation with Frick', she describes 'a ratty, shifty looking man'[73] and her mixed feelings: 'You find yourself feeling sorry for the devils [. . .] but then you stop and think of the fiendish mass exterminations.'[74] Of her encounter with von Ribbentrop, she states: 'there he was, the great Ribbentrop, on exhibit like a lion or a tiger'.[75] The interrogation of Keitel was 'one of the most dramatic scenes I have ever seen enacted'.[76] What

---

[67] Barrett, 'Katherine B. Fite', pp. 17–18.

[68] Barrett, 'Katherine B. Fite', p. 23.

[69] The index of Taylor's 'The Anatomy' contains 12 references to him. See also, e.g., David Childs, 'Benjamin Kaplan: Judge who Played a Crucial Role in Preparations for the Nuremberg trials', Independent, 9 September 2010, www.independent.co.uk/news/obituaries/benjamin-kaplan-judge-who-played-a-crucial-role-in-preparations-for-the-nuremberg-trials-2075318.html; Bruce Weber, 'Benjamin Kaplan, Crucial Figure in Nazi Trials, Dies at 99', New York Times, 24 August 2010, www.nytimes.com/2010/08/25/us/25kaplan.html.

[70] Memorandum to Mr. Justice Jackson, dated 17 August 1945, in Katherine Fite Lincoln Papers, www.trumanlibrary.org/hstpaper/lincoln.htm.

[71] Taylor, The Anatomy, chapters 3 and 4.

[72] Letter 14 October 1945.

[73] Letter 14 October 1945.

[74] Letter 14 October 1945, see also letter 19 November 1945.

[75] Undated letter, September 1945.

[76] Letter 1 October 1945.

did the other side in these interactions, in other words the accused, think of the few women professionals they encountered, such as Fite? The Nuremberg prison psychologist Gilbert's account of the IMT accused describes their attitudes towards women in general as varying from spiteful contempt to lustful sexism or chivalrous posturing.[77] This would be an interesting avenue to follow, but to my regret it is beyond the scope of this chapter.

After her first couple of months of enchantment with the personality of Justice Jackson, Fite grew critical of him: 'I think the Justice has made a mistake by giving the papers to understand that only the U.S. means business [...] the other 3 have now ganged up to put the heat on us and maybe rush us through.'[78] Jackson was 'not a strong man', and 'the indictment was rushed through'.[79] Fite was a meticulous lawyer, disappointed with 'careless work' and 'office politics': 'some time ago I found a very serious error in punctuation in the signed [London] charter which was, of all places, in the section of crimes vs. humanity – i.e. the Jews, and quite changed the sense'.[80] On the same occasion, she dismisses the US judge Francis Biddle as 'a weak appointment'.[81] She also deplores how 'our case' – that is, the one against the Reich cabinet – will be headed by 'a most incompetent man [who] has been put second in command' by Jackson.[82]

How did Katherine Fite experience her role as one of the very few women in the professional ranks at the IMT? She comes across as self-confident, if very conscious of her particular situation. The letter she wrote about her first visit to Nuremberg with Jackson in July 1945 describes an improvised working meeting with Jackson and General Betts, the judge-advocate in the European theatre of operations and his assistant, Colonel Fairman: 'We went over a bit of business and I felt as tho [sic] I were in very high quarters, but spoke up nevertheless.'[83] Fite acknowledges to her parents she is getting special treatment 'by virtue of my female and perhaps State Dept [Department] status'.[84] She explains:

[77] G. M. Gilbert, *Nuremberg Diary* (New York: Farrar, Straus and Company, 1947).
[78] Letter 8 October 1945.
[79] Ibid.
[80] Ibid. Sands, *East West Street*, tells how '*someone* noticed a minor discrepancy in the texts of Article 6(c) on crimes against humanity, the problem of a semi-colon. [...] The consequence could be significant.' p. 113.
[81] Ibid.
[82] Letter 16 December 1945.
[83] Letter 23 July 1945.
[84] Ibid.

> [T]ho [sic] being the only woman on the staff has many drawbacks, from
> the social point of view it pays. A masculine society is eager for women
> and we have the added advantage of being in civilian clothes. [...] My
> army colleagues are, I am sure, jealous of my trips, for I do go places and
> travel in high circles but they are very gallant about it.[85]

At the same time, Fite is ambivalent about her special status. She refers to
the interview with the New York *Herald Tribune* for the 'Woman's page'
as 'a horrible experience'.[86] Later in Nuremberg and describing her active
social life, she notes: 'You see the panel of eligible women for such parties
is small. So I always get there and usually get a seat of honour. It's fun, and
also an effort when you are tired – as I am today.'[87] Fite complains how
she 'lack[s] congenial feminine companionship', and is happy to make
friends with Aline Chalufour, a French lawyer.[88]

In terms of the intellectual history of international criminal justice, what
particular role could Fite be claimed to have carried out? Was she an
insider or an outsider, and did her gender matter? As I have mentioned,
she published hardly any work that could be referred to in the scholarship
or case law. She was not a member of academic or professional associations
such as the AIDP. She seems to have purposely avoided contact with some
of the activist milieu, such as Dr Ecer, 'an international trouble-maker'.[89]
Even if she is occasionally sharply critical of Jackson and the whole effort in
her correspondence, she generally confined herself to the US team and her
Department of State affiliation. In her context and time, how did she relate
to concerns that nowadays characterise feminist approaches to international (criminal) law? Was she, the daughter of a white North American
professor, flying around Europe with Justice Jackson and attending 'long
dress parties' and concerts, so far removed from the experiences of the
(women) victims that she did not feel any special concern about them?

Posing such questions today is anachronistic and perhaps also nasty.
As is known, the victimisation of women was not explicitly taken up at
the IMT. Thus far I have not come across any particular signs that issues
nowadays considered as gender-related in the prosecution of international crimes were on Fite's mind while she was working in Jackson's
team. In her letters, her reflections on being a woman relate exclusively to
her personal experiences in a masculine working environment. She

---

[85] Letter 5 August 1945.
[86] Ibid.
[87] Letter 11 November 1945.
[88] Letter 14 October 1945.
[89] Letter 3 December 1945.

400   IMMI TALLGREN

simply does not seem to identify with women's victimhood in any manner that would suggest a special interest or bias. A clumsy comparison might be made to lawyers of Jewish background who were occasionally suspected of bias when dealing with Nazi crimes. The example of Georg Schwarzenberger, later a famous critic of international criminal law who was ousted from Germany in 1934, is illustrative.[90] When asked why he did not personally participate in the intellectual efforts to bring about the Nuremberg trials, Schwarzenberger said: 'A victim should not become the judge.'[91]

Katherine Fite and other US women lawyers like her with roles in post–World War II international criminal justice did not appear to feel any particular connection to victimhood. Fite rather seemed to have felt she was in a moral position to judge, untroubled by the dilemma of victor's justice. She identified with her country's politics and assumed the special standing of the USA in the world. When the USA launched its atomic bombs on Japan, Fite commented to her parents: 'I'm torn between wishing we hadn't been the ones to launch it and being so profoundly thankful it has ended the war. I suppose it's not worse to kill civilians one way than another.'[92] Upon returning to the USA, she wrote: 'Europe is a sad worn out continent. [...] The U.S. is sitting atop the world. [...] We have to run the world – but the vast majority have no idea what the rest of the world is like. And how can equilibrium be maintained between wealth and energy on the one hand and poverty and exhaustion on the other?'[93]

15.3.2   The Woman 'With a Man's Brain'[94]: Rebecca West

> Tomorrow dinner will meet Rebecca West and will make English love if she hasn't grown too fat.[95]

---

[90] See Stephanie Steinle, *Völkerrecht und Machtpolitik – Georg Schwarzenberger (1908–1991)* (Baden-Baden: Nomos, 2002).

[91] Stephanie Steinle, 'Georg Schwarzenberger (1908–1991)', in Jack Beatson and Reinhard Zimmermann (eds.), *Jurists Uprooted: German-Speaking Emigré Lawyers in Twentieth Century Britain* (Oxford, Oxford University Press, 2004), p. 672. See also.

[92] Letter 12 August 1945.

[93] Letter 28 December 1945.

[94] Carl Rollyson; George Bernard Shaw on West (find Ref.).

[95] The U.S. Judge Francis Biddle's notes from 21 July 1946, as quoted by Taylor, *The Anatomy*, pp. 547–8.

Unlike Katherine Fite, Rebecca West (born Cicely Fairfield in 1892, died Dame Rebecca West in 1983) published a large number of books and articles. She was a famous author, literary critic and journalist, a controversial celebrity of her time, and her works are still read and studied today.[96] She was not a lawyer, she never had any official function in the institutional practice of international criminal law, and she did not specialise in international criminal justice – it was merely one of the many fields about which she wrote. However, she did publish perhaps the most astute and lively contemporary analysis of the Nuremberg IMT and of questions of war and justice beyond the trial, based on her presence as a reporter for the *New Yorker*. She went on to give a critical analysis of the Allies' post–World War II justice, occupation, and its aftermath in essays that were compiled in *A Train of Powder*.[97]

Tentatively including her as a character in an intellectual history of the discipline again means reaching beyond the core. In my experiment in this chapter, I justify it by her notoriety and the quality of her writing. Also, her background, profile, and approach to the Nuremberg trials contrast interestingly with Fite's. West's childhood was overshadowed by financial difficulties and an unstable, and later absent, father. She grew up under the influence of her mother and sisters. She had no formal university education, but was keen to learn autonomously, and started to publish, with her work attracting attention, before her twenties. Written in her fifties, West's impressions and criticisms of the Nuremberg trials were then meant to be read by people other than Mum and Dad: she addressed a broad audience with a literary style based on research. West was not a civil servant bound by the codes and customs of professional conduct, as Fite was in the State Department. Nevertheless this 'George Bernard Shaw in skirts'[98] also had to face her difference: her gender. West's biographies depict her as a 'feminist' and a somewhat troubling 'free woman', paradoxically considering that she chose not to disclose the fact that she gave birth unmarried, and despite the fact that she appears to have desired and later appreciated marriage. Her Nuremberg reports do not dwell on her personal concerns with daily life or on the experience of being in the minority sex as a court reporter. She never

---

[96] There are three biographies on West, see, Victoria Glendinning, *Rebecca West, A Life* (New York: Alfred A. Knopf, 1987); Carl Edmund Rollyson, *Rebecca West: A Life* (New York: Scribner, 1996); Lorna Gibb, *West's World: The Extraordinary Life of Dame Rebecca West* (London: Macmillan, 2013).

[97] Rebecca West, *A Train of Powder: Six Reports on the Problem of Guilt and Punishment in Our Time* (Chicago: Ivan R. Dee, 1955).

[98] Rollyson, *Rebecca West*, jacket text.

asks why there were no women amongst the judges, visible members of the prosecutorial teams or defence lawyers. Nor did she focus on the victimisation resulting from sexual or gendered violence, apart from a few passages referring to the struggles of German women during the early phases of the occupation, specifically in Berlin.[99]

Although not a lawyer, West did not shy away from analysing the trial and its actors, or the broader stakes of law, war and justice – the winners and losers, the occupiers and the occupied. She was sensitive to the irony of the Soviet judge reading out the verdict that condemned the Nazis for deportation, 'for taking men and women away from their homes and sending them to distant camps where they worked as slave labour in conditions of great discomfort'.[100] She observes the differences between the four powers co-organising the trial, pointing out 'temperamental and juristic differences among the nations'.[101] She suggests, for example, that the perception among some spectators that the 'tribunal was soft and not genuinely anti-Nazi'[102] because not all of Nazi Germany's seven organisations were condemned, was attributable in part to the 'silver voice untarnished by passion'[103] of the caricature upper-class British judge whose turn it was to read out that part of the judgment.

West's general appreciation of the IMT and of post–World War II international criminal justice more broadly is mixed. She acknowledges that the trials had to take place: 'the Nazi crimes of cruelty demanded punishment'.[104] Occasionally, she even recognises the IMT trial as 'a step farther on the road to civilization'[105] – referring to the admirals' case on submarine warfare. She reads their acquittal by the IMT as a confession by the Allies, a '*nostra culpa* of the conquerors' for 'the British and Americans had committed precisely the same offence'.[106] At the same time, she critically observes how this highly relevant sign of honesty

---

[99] At the time, the rapes and forced prostitution of women in occupied Germany were not addressed openly in public. See the belatedly well-known (and controversial) diary by Anonyma, *Eine Frau in Berlin* (Frankfurt/M., Eichborn, 2003); and Atina Grossmann, 'The "Big Rape": Sex and Sexual Violence, War, and Occupation in German Post-World War II Memory and Imagination', in Karen Hagemann and Sonya Michel (eds.), *Gender and the Long Postwar* (Baltimore: John Hopkins University Press, 2014).

[100] West, *A Train of Powder*, p. 51.

[101] Ibid, p. 47.

[102] Ibid, p. 47.

[103] Ibid, p. 48.

[104] Ibid, p. 49.

[105] Ibid.

[106] Ibid.

15 'WOMEN' AT THE DAWN OF A DISCIPLINE 403

'evoked no response at the time, and it has been forgotten'.[107] She attributes this to the character of international law, which 'as soon as it escapes from the sphere of merchandise … is a mist with the power to make solids as misty as itself'.[108] She points in particular to its apologetic and utopic facets, 'the dangers of international law', in the example of how the argument of protecting minorities (the Germanic populations) was first used by Hitler to justify his invasions of Germany's neighbours, and then used again by the Allies to justify the trial she witnessed.[109]

Her last report, published in 1954, reads like a general commentary on Allied post–World War II justice beyond the IMT. She deplores the fact that the trials' records are less than accessible to the general reader: they are too lengthy, not fully translated or available (the Soviet part), and costly. For West, this aggravated how 'these trials have set up a dozen itching abscesses of ignorance and hatred in the public mind'. Much of that situation, in her opinion, related to 'a real national difference, not to be wiped out by an improvisation such as the Nuremberg trial' in the procedural laws between the continental versus the English and American traditions.[110] For West, the unaccustomed roles and balance of power of the actors in the trial and the detention of the accused before and during the trial 'revolted' the accused and many Germans, giving them the impression of a hideous continuity with the Nazi regime's disregard of the rights of the accused.[111] The noble goal, the triumph of 'the Rule of Law in all its beauty', was not attained.[112]

One might be tempted to picture West as a forerunner in the interdisciplinary critique of international criminal justice, a sharp woman on the correct side of history, ahead of others. However, West did not, for example, question the death penalty as such. In the context of Nazi crimes and the general overwhelming presence of violence and death during the war and its aftermath, very few individuals openly objected to it for ethical or legal reasons. At the same time, she did not take the death penalties issued by the IMT lightly. West refers to 'a profound aversion' to the capital punishment that, she believed, was shared by many who had participated in the trial for a longer period, seeing 'the man in the

---

[107] Ibid.
[108] Ibid.
[109] Ibid, p. 50.
[110] Ibid, p. 240.
[111] Ibid, pp. 240–3.
[112] Ibid, p. 240.

murderer out'.[113] She expected the punishments to be rational and moderate: 'For when society has to hurt a man it must hurt him as little as possible and must preserve what it can of his pride, lest there should spread in that society those feelings which make men do the things for which they get hanged.'[114] She consistently took a clear-cut position on media practices at international criminal trials. Contrary to some journalists and historians who regretted the gap in the film record of the trial, West agreed with the court, which had decided that the defendants should not be photographed during the sentencing session: 'It might be right to hang such men. But it could not be right to photograph them when they were being told that they were going to be hanged.'[115]

West's critical approach and personal style appears as a precursor to Hannah Arendt's later (and more elaborate) report of the Eichmann trial.[116] West's work could also be compared to that of another woman author and scholar of her time, Freda Utley (1898–1978), who similarly commented on the problems with procedural law, pre-trial detention, the weak position of the defence, and the rejection of the trials by the German public. Utley, like West, was not a lawyer, having a degree in history. Unlike West, she did not attend the Nuremberg trials, but was a correspondent in Germany in 1948. Her book *The High Cost of Vengeance* (1948) is extremely critical of Allied post–World War II justice and the occupation policy in general. She specifically addresses the IMT, the American Nuremberg trials, and the Dachau trials. In comparison to West's sweetly ironic tone, Utley's work is more like an accusation or a pamphlet – aggressive and bitter. Biographical commentaries on Utley refer to her suffering in, and because of, Stalin's Soviet Union, in particular to the detention and death of her Russian husband.[117] Her association with McCarthyism had an effect on how her work was received, both at the time and in hindsight. In comparison, West's anticommunism was perhaps less programmatic, but it also tainted her work in the eyes of many leftists, in particular in the USA.[118] In *The High Cost of Vengeance*, Utley openly declares her intent to present a counter-narrative (although without using the word), 'a drop

---

[113] Ibid, pp. 42, 43.
[114] Ibid, p. 41.
[115] Ibid, pp. 40–1.
[116] In Hannah Arendt, *Eichmann in Jerusalem* (New York: Viking Press, 1964), Arendt does not refer to West's work.
[117] For a collection of excerpts, see http://fredautley.com/.
[118] Rollyson, *Rebecca West*, pp. 284–5.

15 'WOMEN' AT THE DAWN OF A DISCIPLINE 405

in the ocean compared to the continuous, and somewhat monotonous, spate of books, articles, newspaper reports, and radio commentary which have by now established an accepted legend'.[119] She stated, for example, how:

> [c]ompared with the rape and murder and looting engaged in by the Russian armies at the war's end, the terror and slavery and hunger and robbery in the Eastern zone today, and the genocide practiced by the Poles and Czechs, the war crimes and crimes against humanity committed by the Germans condemned at Nuremberg to death or lifelong imprisonment appeared as minor in extent if not in degree.[120]

Such views were provocative, and Utley was accused of revisionism. She also made a virulent and detailed attack on the torture and inhuman treatment of the accused by US officials in the Dachau trials, deploring the euphemism of 'persuasive methods' used by the US authorities to describe the conduct.[121] Her claims concerning Allied torture were extremely marginal at the time, but may strike a chord with today's reader.[122] Utley is more optimistic about international law than West – if only the law was respected. However, 'we [the Allies, the US in particular] tore up the Atlantic Charter and copied the Nazis in our repudiation of international law'.[123] Like West, she does not mention the lack of participation of women in the post–World War II trials, nor does she emphasise their victimisation, except for a passing mention of rape (committed by the Russians). However, Utley's noble and romantic portraits of 'ill-fed but neat' German women under occupation, 'who although they were driven by hunger to become prostitutes, preserved a certain innate decency, and by responding to kindness with affection and loyalty, often won the love of American boys who started out only to enjoy the pleasures which war offers to the victors',[124] differ from West's nuanced analysis of the 'fraternisation'.

What did Rebecca West contribute to the discipline of international criminal law, and what were her connections to other figures involved? Whereas her readership is likely to have been wider than that of most

---

[119] Freda Utley, *The High Cost of Vengeance* (Chicago: Henry Regnery Company, 1949) p. 302.
[120] Ibid, p. 182.
[121] Ibid, pp. 182–212, p. 187.
[122] See, e.g., Tomaz Jardim, *The Mathausen Trial: American Military Justice in Germany* (Harvard University Press, 2012).
[123] Utley, *The High Cost*, p. 14.
[124] Ibid, p. 17.

legal commentaries of the Nuremberg trials, she does not count as a specialist in the field. The traces of her connections to the intellectuals discussed in this book, or to other key figures and institutional actors, are restricted to a particular 'scandalous' context.[125] Apart from the human-interest stories, it is hard to find information about the exact sources, relations and influences on which she based her opinions about post–World War II international criminal justice. It seems clear that West was ready to follow any leads that would 'throw a bright light on Nuremberg and on the possibilities of affecting human conduct by international action'.[126] Her conception of international criminal justice oscillated between occasional hope and sheer disappointment, often disguised as irony – she remained distanced, true to her role as an observer, a journalist, and an independent author. One can recognise her soul-mates in today's scholarship in interdisciplinary approaches that do not shy away from questioning the meaning behind the legal façade and the ritual of highly mediatised international criminal trials.[127] Her observations on the importance and complexity of national differences in procedural law, rooted in varying expectations of justice in different legal cultures, remain pertinent.[128] To many expert observers, not to mention West's main concern, that is, the general public in the home states of the accused and the victims, current hybrid procedures in international criminal trials appear lengthy, costly, and incomprehensible.

15.3 What Difference Would It Make?

She was clearly not a shrinking violet, but her gender brought few new policy perspectives to the Committee.[129]

Don't you tell a soldier he does not know the cost of war![130]

---

[125] Taylor and West's biographers engage in a detailed description of a liaison between the US IMT Judge Francis Biddle and West. Further, Justice Jackson is told to have 'snubbed Rebecca', see Taylor, *The Anatomy*, pp. 547–8.

[126] West, *A Train of Powder*, p. 234.

[127] See, e.g., Christine Schwöbel (ed.), *Critical Approaches to International Criminal Law: An Introduction* (New York: Routledge, 2014); Gerry Simpson, *Law, War and Crime: War Crimes, Trials and the Reinvention of International Law* (Cambridge: Polity, 2007).

[128] For an example of the same discussion with an *état de lieux* some seventy years later, see Kirsten Campbell, 'The Making of Global Legal Culture and International Criminal Law' (2013) 26 (1) *Leiden Journal of International Law* 155–72.

[129] David P. Forsythe, *The Humanitarians: The International Committee of the Red Cross* (Cambridge: Cambridge University Press, 2005), p. 204, on Denise Bindschedler-Robert.

[130] An outcry by Lieutenant-General Frank Benson to a woman advisor opposed to a drone strike in The Eye in the Sky (UK: dir. Gavin Hood, 2015).

15 'WOMEN' AT THE DAWN OF A DISCIPLINE   407

This chapter flags not only the intriguing lack of women but also the apparently minimal – or repressed? – anxiety about it. How is it that one knows so little of women at the dawn of international criminal law and its institutional practice? Why does this absence not attract more attention in this field in which feminist activism and women's professional engagement have recently become both so striking and so vulnerable: striking in the major quantitative growth of women's participation and qualitative rise in their level of responsibility; vulnerable in how what constitutes great progress for many is also subject to claims of riding on essentialist stereotypes of victimisation of (all) women and the particular critique of white women agitating for 'saving brown women from brown men'.[131] In the same timeframe, changes towards women's inclusion have taken place in most if not all other fields of professional expertise, social activity, and academic research. In international law, human rights (the Convention on the Elimination of Discrimination against Women), the law on the use of force, and international criminal law are the key fields of the change.[132] Amongst them, the institutional practice of international criminal law is where women figure most visibly in positions of responsibility.[133] There have been firsts for everything: the chief prosecutors of the International Criminal Tribunal for the former Yugoslavia and the International Criminal Court, the president of the International Criminal Court, and a women-only bench.

These changes are typically attributed to two concomitant and interrelated transformations in international law, international relations, and civil society (mainly in the Global North). First, scholarship known today as 'feminist approaches to international law' emerged – painfully, as a contestation – in the early 1990s.[134] It was argued that women were

---

[131] Rephrasing Gayatri Spivak, 'Can the Subaltern Speak?' in Cary Nelson and Lawrence Grossburg (eds.), *Marxism; and the Interpretation of Culture* (Urbana: University of Illinois Press, 1988), pp. 271–313.

[132] For a critical analysis, see, Gina Heathcote, *Feminist Dialogues: Successes, Tensions, Futures* (Oxford: Oxford University Press, 2019).

[133] See, e.g., Daniel Terris, Cesare P.R. Romano and Leigh Swigart, *The International Judge: An Introduction to the Men and Women Who Decide the World's Cases* (Waltham, MA: Brandeis University Press, 2007); Nienke Grossman, 'Sex Representation on the Bench and the Legitimacy of International Criminal Courts' (2011) 11 *International Criminal Law Review* 643.

[134] See Hilary Charlesworth, Christine Chinkin and Shelley Wright, 'Feminist Approaches to International Law' (1991) 85 *The American Journal of International Law* 613; Dorinda G. Dallmeyer (ed.), *Reconceiving Reality: Women and International Law* (Washington, D.C.: American Society of International Law, 1993); Dianne Otto, 'Feminist Approaches to International Law', in Anne Orford and Florian Hoffmann (eds.), *The Oxford Handbook of the Theory of International Law* (Oxford: Oxford University Press, 2016).

underrepresented in academic and professional circles, and that this had major substantive consequences. Broader access by women and recognition of their agendas in international law and institutions became a subject of activism. Second, violence in the former Yugoslavia and Rwanda triggered legal and political changes; international criminal law started to attract major interest in academia, civil society, and the media, often with an emphasis on rape and other forms of sexual violence. Feminist approaches found a particular territory in which one could claim that women's experiences were indispensable and unique. International criminal law and more broadly accountability for sexual and gendered violence became a strategic entry point for women lawyers, professionals, and intellectuals in international legal institutions, academia, and policy-making. Yet the entry may not always have been simple.

John Barrett concludes his article on Katherine Fite on a positive note, no doubt meant as a compliment to her and encouragement for today's women: 'She was the kind of talent whose gender I hope today would not be noticed – I hope that she would be like the women among us in the field of international justice: high-level, accomplished persons, professionally indistinguishable from the men.'[135] This good-willed wish stands in contrast with feminist scholarship in international law. The mere presence of women as a nominal indicator of 'progress' matters little if they remain under pressure to become indistinguishable from men, the thus-far dominating normative model for professionals. Gina Heathcote refers, in the context of law on the use of force, to 'the limitations of strategies centred on adding women to existing institutions: as this does little to challenge the organization's structure or the normative outputs of the institution'.[136] Instead, 'the incorporation of women's narratives from outside the mainstream of international law to explain, analyse, and challenge the international law on the use of force is necessary'.[137] Barrett's remark may also come across as implying that some women, in the past or now, are not such 'high-level, accomplished persons' as Fite was; they were or are just quota-women, not living up to expectations built on the male model. Another kind of typical expectation lurks behind David Forsythe's remarks on Denise Bindschedler-Robert at the ICRC, quoted above: the rare woman entering a position of responsibility was failing to bring in through 'her gender [...] new policy

---

[135] Barrett, 'Katherine B. Fite', p. 29.

[136] Gina Heathcote, 'Feminist Perspectives to the Law on the Use of Force', in Marc Weller (ed.), *The Oxford Handbook of the Use of Force in International Law* (Oxford: Oxford University Press, 2015) p. 118.

[137] Ibid, 119.

perspectives'.[138] The first and only should first join in the men's game on conditions gendered masculine, exceed them, and then reform the game – preferably making it better for all.

The contradictory expectations of women needing to be both *just like men* yet somehow *different or more* may seem to muddle the sense of research efforts on identifying women's particular place(s) and role(s) in the past. What difference would it make? The interrogation can be split in two: first, what would it mean to bring to light more women in the histories of a discipline; second, what does the entry of women in a field of professional and intellectual activity change? The intuition in both cases is that having more women involved in professional roles would lead to more account being taken of women's experiences than previously. A further intuition is that women's experiences would differ from those of men. Empirical knowledge on how exactly these intuitions would play out is, however, not open to us.[139] A further complication relates to the situational position of women whose experiences would be considered relevant: there are juxtapositions of 'elite women' versus women understood more broadly.[140]

In the legal and policy instruments of current or recent international criminal courts, a particular role professional women are explicitly assigned to relates to expertise on sexual and gendered violence, as well as on counselling and supporting victims.[141] Patricia Wald suggests one motivation for this: 'Since women and children are most often the victims of war, it is especially important that women have adequate representation on these international war crimes courts.'[142] Beyond quantitative objectives, one can recognise various expectations on women, such as their capacities for empathy with the suffering and their soothing 'nature' as an intuitive extension of biological motherhood.[143] As is known, the traditionally protected key

---

[138] Forsythe, *The Humanitarians*, p. 204.

[139] For accounts by or on women professionals in international criminal justice, see Josephine Dawuni and Akua Kuenyehia (eds.), *African Women Judges on International Courts: Unveiled Narratives* (New York, Routledge, 2017); Navanethem Pillay, 'Equal Justice for Women: A Personal Journey' (2008) 50 *Arizona Law Review* 657; Patricia M. Wald, 'Women in International Courts: Some Lessons Learned' (2011) 11 *International Criminal Law Review* 401.

[140] Heathcote, 'Feminist Perspectives', fn. 132.

[141] For a detailed analysis, see Louise Chappell, *The Politics of Gender Justice at the ICC* (Oxford: Oxford University Press, 2016) pp. 51–86.

[142] Patricia Wald, 'Myths About Women's Careers in Law' (2013–14) 2 (1) *University of Baltimore Journal of International Law* 12.

[143] See, e.g., Sara Ruddick, *Maternal Thinking: Towards a Politics of Peace* (Boston: Beacon Press, 1995); Maria Drakopoulou, 'The Ethic of Care, Feminist Subjectivity and Feminist Legal Scholarship' (2000) 8 *Feminist Legal Studies* 199, 200.

subject of humanitarian law was the soldier either in combat or *hors de combat* for particular reasons, whereas later changes in law and institutional practice have brought civilians to the fore.[144] The expectation of women's special expertise has been argued to rest on the essentialist notions of women's interests and vulnerabilities – eventually victimhood – in direct opposition with the equality claims.[145] There are signs that the practice – and politics – of international criminal justice has generally become more attuned to sexual and gendered violence, beyond heteronormative conceptions.[146]

Another quest behind the expectation that women as prosecutors, judges, academics or diplomats would make a difference relates to the idea of moral leadership by women, again based on nature, culture, and/or experience of women. Pacifism, or more generally expressed moral concern for the future of humanity, are considered feminine – even Adolf Hitler scorned the 'waving of olive branches and tearful misery-mongering of pacifist old women'.[147] An alternative – presumably superior – set of values that dismisses male morality and condemns the devastations created by male-driven advances in technology, politics, law and other fields that men have traditionally dominated, as well as assumed male ideologies such as nationalism, has been and remains present in some feminist movements and ideologies.[148]

---

[144] Judith Gail Gardam, 'The Law of Armed Conflict: A Gendered Regime?' in Dorinda Dallmeyer (ed.), *Reconceiving Reality: Women and International Law* (Washington, D.C.: American Society of International Law, 1993); Helen Kinsella, *The Image Before the Weapon: A Critical History of the Distinction Between Combatant and Civilian* (Ithaca: Cornell University Press, 2011).

[145] See, e.g., Janet Halley, 'Rape in Rome: Feminist Interventions in the Criminalization of Sex-Related Violence in Positive International Criminal Law' (2008) 30(1) *Michigan Journal of International Law* 1–123; Kiran Kaur Grewal, 'International Criminal Law as a Site for Enhancing Women's Rights? Challenges, Possibilities, Strategies' (2015) 23 (2) *Feminist Legal Studies* 149; Karen Engle, 'Feminisms and Its (Dis)contents: Criminalizing Wartime Rape in Bosnia and Herzegovina' (2005) 99 (49) *The American Journal of International Law* 778; Doris Buss, 'Performing Legal Order: Some Feminist Thoughts on International Criminal Law' (2011) 11 *International Criminal Law Review* 409. Beyond international criminal law, see Iris Marion Young, 'The Logic of Masculinist Protection: Reflections on the Current Security State' (2003) 29 (1) *Signs: Journal on Women in Culture and Society* 1.

[146] See, e.g., Kimi Lynn King and Megan Greening, 'Gender Justice or Just Gender? The Role of Gender in Sexual Assault Decisions at the International Criminal Tribunal for Former Yugoslavia' (2007) 88 (5) *Social Science Quarterly* 1049; Kimi L. King, James D. Meernik and Eliza G. Kelly, 'Deborah's Voice: The Role of Women in Sexual Assault Cases at the International Criminal Tribunal for the Former Yugoslavia' (2017) 98 *Social Science Quarterly* 548; Grossman, 'Sex Representation'.

[147] Hitler, *Mein Kampf*, as referred to by Gilbert, *Nuremberg Diary*, p. 115.

[148] For discussion, see, e.g., Lynne Segal, *Is the Future Female? Troubled Thoughts on Contemporary Feminism* (London: Virago Press, 1987); Alexandra Brodsky and Rachel Kauder Nalebuff (eds.), *The Feminist Utopia Project* (New York: The Feminist Press, 2015).

An author who was active during the period of our research project, Virginia Woolf, famously underlined the senselessness of 'the male world of aggression, uniforms, and glory'.[149] In *Three Guineas*, written as she was about to witness a world war for the second time, she tried to produce a woman's (or rather, audaciously, *the women's*) reply to the question: 'how shall we prevent war?' Woolf proposed an 'Outsiders Society' based on differences in values and desires, autonomous and separate from bloody patriarchy.[150]

The dream of an alternative, less violent society, locally and/or globally, still can be identified as one of the leitmotifs of feminisms, also in international law.[151] Tempting and occasionally plausible as the alternative appears, it also may have served to perpetuate the exclusion of women, if not a self-inflicted evasion of some political and professional fields and contexts: 'The dominated can tell stories, they can fantasize, they can create Utopia, but they cannot devise the means of getting there. They cannot make use of maps, plan out the route, and calculate the odds.'[152] In the context of international criminal law, arguments positing women's moral superiority in rejecting war may have correlated with claims about the lack of women's professional experiences in the military and of their leadership in situations of crisis. Katherine Fite and Rebecca West were involved in international criminal justice just a few years after Virginia Woolf wrote: 'scarcely a human being in the course of history has fallen to a woman's rifle'.[153] Technological warfare with automated and *unmanned* systems have since done away with expectations of what is physically required for the conduct of war. Still, the claim of a lack of experience of life and the world as broad as that of men haunts women. The lack of such experience, gendered masculine, may be taken to stand for a lack of credibility in assuming positions and making decisions. In the context of international criminal justice, such decisions concern the legality of war and the criminality of a particular conduct in using force, a minefield in which neutrality may stand for ignorance and involvement

---

[149] Elaine Showalter, *A Literature of Their Own* (London: Virago, 2009), p. 241. Woolf was ambivalent about the word 'feminism', if not the movement altogether, see, e.g., Woolf, *Three Guineas*, pp. 101–2.

[150] Woolf, *Three Guineas*, e.g., pp. 109–14.

[151] For discussion, see, e.g., Hilary Charlesworth, 'Are Women Peaceful? Reflections on the Role of Women in Peace-Building' (2008) 16(3) *Feminist Legal Studies* 347; Barbara Ehrenreich, 'Feminism's Assumptions Upended' (2007) 24(1) *South Central Review* 170.

[152] Sheila Rowbotham, 'Women's Liberation and the New Politics', in Michelene Wandor (ed.), *The Body Politic: Writings from the Women's Liberation Movement in Britain 1969–1972* (London: Stage 1, 1972), p. 9.

[153] Woolf, *Three Guineas*, p. 6.

412   IMMI TALLGREN

for entanglement – as critics purport to argue. As recent scholarship underlines, however, such reductive narratives of women's involvement with decision-making on violence and use of force are a false necessity.[154]

Finally, when posed by the intellectuals and professionals of today, the question 'what difference would it make' is part of a quest for the 'origins' of women in the professional sphere, of their place and appurtenance in an imagined lineage and tradition. It becomes an interrogation of their experienced or perceived legitimacy. As this chapter suggests, going back in time women in important positions in histories soon become rare. The few that surface tend to appear small in comparison with other figures of their time. The past looks empty or hostile to orphans lacking 'mothers and grandmothers in the profession'.[155] How to canalise the desire to possess one's history, take/make portraits of early women and squeeze them into the family album of a 'college of international criminal lawyers',[156] crowded with accomplished men? Recent methodological inventions and revolts that may facilitate the discovery and visibility of women by adjusting the criteria of belonging, changing the zoom, or selecting a new frame, are tempting and creative. The challenge that remains is to walk away from mourning and melancholia towards the recognition and inclusion of women, without collapsing into essentialism, revisionism, or hagiography. Whatever the new directions taken, the first step is to problematise international law's need for its histories as a celebration of individual geniuses and their (intellectual) next of kin.[157]

Katherine Fite, as well as several other professionals, carried out tasks in institutional positions at key moments of past international criminal justice. Rebecca West and other authors and correspondents witnessed and analysed international criminal justice in contributions that merit attention, including in academic research. Even if in most cases white, educated, and from socially privileged classes, these women had heterogeneous backgrounds, beliefs, and politics. They were not necessarily particularly drawn to causes today labelled as women's own, such as

---

[154] See, e.g., Diane Otto, 'A Sign of "Weakness"? Disrupting Gender Certainties in the Implementation of Security Council Resolution 1325' (2006) 13 *Michigan Journal of Gender and Law* 113; Gina Heathcote, *The Law on the Use of Force: A Feminist Analysis* (London: Routledge, 2013).

[155] Rephrasing Koskenniemi, *The Gentle Civilizers*, p. 5.

[156] Kress, *Towards*.

[157] Compare to problematising versus rethinking versus rejecting the idea of a canon in literature, see Jan Gorak, *The Making of the Modern Canon: Genesis and Crisis of a Literary Idea* (London: Athlone, 1991).

criminal responsibility for sexual and gendered violence. Women were not absent nor were they invisible, however, as the traces and echoes presented demonstrate. Some women participated and took positions, argued and expressed themselves, even if at times using idioms different from the mainstream of the collective efforts, institutional events, and academic publications that presently structure the narrative of international criminal justice. Those forums were dominated by men who combined roles in academia, professional and intellectual associations, governments, diplomacy and international institutions. Their stories make out the core of this book – and set out the level of importance in the eyes of today's readers of histories of international criminal law. Yet, as Jean-Luc Godard put it, '*c'est la marge qui fait tenir la page*'.

The whys and wherefores of the margins are questions that haunt anyone attempting to engage in a historical inquiry based on sex and gender – or 'race', sexual orientation, class or other marker of presumed 'otherness', for that matter. A research mission to unearth forgotten or unvalued figures inevitably entails taking positions on the way agency and importance are construed – a much discussed issue in and beyond feminist, women's, and gender histories. Thus far, elsewhere-familiar questions concerning women's intellectual and professional inputs and their perceptions inside and outside the core of a social or academic context have not been addressed in international criminal law. Beyond epistemological challenges and broad sociological explanations, the politics of memory and identity are at stake. Whose experiences and accomplishments are valued, rendered authoritative in curriculums and footnotes, cherished in festschrifts and colloquiums? What images of past actors are transmitted further to students and young professionals? The moment has come both to reflect on what the meagre involvement in the past of actors other than (what appears as) white heteronormative men has meant and still means to the construction, salience, and legitimacy of international criminal justice, and to question whether our understanding of the past as just described is not merely the currently dominant historical narrative, obscuring others. More research on the imagined intellectual continuities and breaks, on lacunas of agency and over-expositions of identity could incite engagement with the prospects of renewal of the discipline, of roads not yet taken. Special rewards may follow from also paying attention to figures located outside the professional ranks of lawyers, or to legal professionals not canonised as 'key intellectuals'. Marginalised figures may have a different kind of voice that challenges the myopic arrogance of the core – if any such were left.

INDEX

Advisory Committee of Jurists, 41, 42

Aggression, 5, 8, 49, 50, 52, 55, 57, 59, 62, 63, 64, 66, 68, 78, 79, 83, 91, 92, 102, 103, 106, 109, 110, 111, 113, 159, 167, 168, 189, 196, 197, 200, 206, 207, 216, 219, 224, 227, 252, 253, 259, 261, 267, 268, 269, 271, 272, 275, 276, 277, 278, 290, 292, 293, 299, 312, 328, 330, 331, 351, 352, 353, 355, 397, 411

Arendt, Hannah, 208, 210, 211, 287, 386, 404

Aristotle, 218, 224, 226, 229

Association internationale de droit pénal (AIDP), 9, 10, 16, 17, 18, 21, 22, 44, 45, 46, 65, 69, 70, 71, 72, 77, 85, 87, 88, 89, 90, 94, 101, 104, 105, 107, 108, 116, 117, 124, 128, 133, 136, 140, 150, 153, 156, 161, 267, 290, 292, 293, 294, 297, 311, 317, 318, 329, 331, 332, 362, 365, 373, 374, 385, 399

Atrocities, 49, 67, 75, 91, 92, 219

Barbarism, 33, 66, 82, 99

Baron Edouard Descamps, 28, 41, 42

Beccaria, Cesare, 96, 117, 316, 362

Bellot, Hugh, 8, 11, 32, 36

Bluntschli, Johann Caspar, 27, 34

Briand-Kellogg Pact, 68, 102, 106, 214

British Committee of Enquiry on Breaches of Laws of War, 30, 40, 47

Brown Scott, James, 12, 28, 39

Bureau International pour l'Unification du Droit Pénal, 50, 70, 71, 85, 89

Caloyanni, Megalos, 25, 44, 46, 47, 68, 69, 105, 107, 361

Carnegie Peace Foundation, 342

Central Powers, 38, 39

Churchill, Winston, 32, 38, 296, 301

Code of Offenses against the Peace and Security of Mankind, 86

Codification, 94, 97, 98, 99, 100, 101, 103, 189, 290, 301

Collective criminality, 63

Collective security, 77, 215

Command responsibility, 218, 219, 220, 229

Commission on the Responsibility of the Authors of War and on Enforcement of Penalties, 36, 38, 42

Communism, 76, 115, 314

Counterfeiting, 54, 56, 63, 66, 72, 88, 106, 293

Crimes against peace, 147, 159, 166, 168, 206, 207, 213, 214, 216, 217, 218, 220, 221, 252, 253, 259, 268, 271, 275, 301, 330, 346, 351, 354, 364

Criminal responsibility, 59, 60, 65, 71, 108, 109, 110, 117, 158, 159, 164, 179, 185, 189, 193, 194, 195, 196, 197, 201, 264, 307, 308, 320, 326, 327, 331, 333, 372, 413

Crowd theory, 52, 61, 62

Death penalty, 71, 76, 94, 96, 114, 117, 184, 208, 217, 218, 226, 228, 363, 403

Democracy, 62, 76, 77, 274

Domestic law, 49, 55, 56, 58, 64, 92, 108, 171, 172, 323, 343, 345, 346

INDEX

Donnedieu de Vabres, 7, 25, 70, 83, 87,
90, 105, 146, 147, 148, 149, 150,
151, 152, 153, 154, 155, 156, 157,
158, 159, 160, 161, 162, 163, 164,
165, 166, 167, 168, 169, 170, 171,
172, 173, 281, 311, 320, 361, 369,
370, 372, 378, 385, 386
Duty to prosecute and punish, 56

Édouard Rolin-Jaequemyns, 28, 36
Enforcement, 72, 83, 94, 98, 103, 107,
116, 117, 268, 304, 344
Equality of states, 79
Extradition, 56, 58, 59, 88, 106,
155, 170, 175, 206, 308, 309,
310, 316, 317, 318, 319, 320,
332, 333

First Hague Peace Conference, 28
Fite, Katherine, 383, 392, 393, 395, 396,
397, 398, 400, 408, 411, 412
Frank, Hans, 108, 160, 321

General Act on the Pacific Settlement of
International Disputes, 341
Geneva Conventions, 27, 35
Geneva Protocol for the Pacific
Settlement of International
Disputes, 63, 328
Genocide, 7, 12, 81, 84, 85, 86, 87, 91,
105, 113, 147, 149, 159, 161, 165,
168, 171, 182, 188, 275, 280, 281,
282, 283, 284, 285, 286, 287, 288,
289, 291, 292, 294, 295, 296, 297,
298, 299, 300, 301, 302, 303, 304,
372, 375, 400
Convention on the Prevention and
Punishment, 113, 372, 375, 380
Germany, 30, 31, 32, 68, 69, 78, 79, 80,
89, 100, 109, 110, 111, 147, 160,
164, 165, 167, 175, 177, 178, 181,
187, 189, 193, 194, 196, 197, 198,
199, 200, 210, 269, 287, 288, 290,
295, 296, 310, 312, 320, 321, 326,
337, 379, 384, 400, 401, 402,
403, 404
Graduate Institute of International
Studies (Geneva), 181

Graven, Jean, 323, 327, 329, 358, 359,
360, 361, 362, 363, 364, 365, 366,
367, 368, 369, 370, 371, 372, 373,
374, 375, 376, 377, 378, 379, 380
Grotius Society, 11, 25, 26, 30, 31, 32,
33, 35, 37, 40, 41, 43, 47, 313

Hague Academy of International Law,
149, 151, 162, 365, 377
Hague Rules of Land Warfare, 41,
43, 47
Hitler, Adolf, 310, 410
Hostage taking, 55, 66, 326
Human rights, 74, 228, 249, 283, 284,
285, 333, 378
Humanitarianism, 152, 316, 385

I.G. Farben, 84
Imprisonment, 67, 96, 102, 103, 316,
366, 405
Institut de Droit International (IDI),
29, 30, 41, 48
International Bureau for the
Unification of Criminal Law
(IBUCL), 105, 267, 292
International Committee of the Red
Cross, 27, 313, 361, 362, 386,
406
International community, 26, 65, 154,
165, 232, 233, 237, 253, 259, 317,
318, 336, 337, 338, 343, 344, 345,
346, 354
International Court of Arbitration, 340
International criminal, 1, 2, 3, 4, 5, 6, 7,
8, 9, 10, 11, 12, 14, 15, 16, 17, 18,
19, 20, 21, 22, 23, 27, 34, 41, 42, 43,
45, 46, 47, 48, 49, 50, 54, 55, 56, 59,
63, 65, 66, 67, 68, 69, 71, 72, 80, 82,
83, 87, 88, 90, 91, 92, 94, 101, 107,
111, 114, 118, 119, 120, 123, 124,
127, 128, 132, 133, 135, 136, 138,
139, 140, 142, 143, 144, 146, 147,
150, 151, 152, 153, 154, 156, 158,
160, 162, 163, 166, 169, 170, 172,
175, 176, 177, 178, 179, 185, 186,
188, 195, 202, 203, 206, 207, 208,
210, 218, 226, 227, 228, 229, 232,
233, 234, 237, 238, 243, 249, 250,

416 INDEX

260, 267, 268, 274, 278, 279, 282, 286, 290, 292, 295, 307, 308, 314, 315, 316, 320, 322, 323, 324, 325, 326, 327, 328, 329, 330, 331, 332, 333, 336, 337, 338, 350, 352, 356, 357, 359, 360, 366, 367, 368, 369, 370, 372, 373, 375, 382, 383, 386, 387, 388, 389, 390, 394, 399, 400, 401, 402, 403, 405, 406, 407, 409, 410, 411, 412, 413

International Criminal Court (ICC), 1, 3, 5, 10, 27, 34, 35, 41, 42, 43, 44, 45, 46, 47, 48, 65, 71, 72, 83, 111, 147, 149, 153, 156, 158, 170, 206, 228, 232, 233, 267, 268, 270, 278, 282, 292, 295, 319, 330, 333, 334, 336, 361, 364, 366, 368, 369, 370, 372, 373, 407, 409

International law, 2, 4, 7, 10, 12, 13, 14, 26, 27, 28, 29, 30, 31, 32, 33, 37, 38, 39, 40, 41, 42, 43, 45, 54, 56, 66, 67, 68, 69, 70, 78, 82, 86, 98, 110, 147, 148, 149, 150, 151, 152, 153, 154, 156, 157, 163, 164, 165, 166, 167, 171, 176, 177, 178, 181, 186, 187, 190, 195, 197, 198, 200, 202, 206, 208, 214, 215, 220, 221, 223, 227, 229, 232, 233, 234, 236, 237, 241, 243, 250, 252, 254, 256, 257, 258, 259, 261, 264, 267, 269, 278, 281, 282, 285, 290, 291, 292, 298, 302, 304, 314, 317, 319, 321, 322, 323, 326, 327, 329, 332, 333, 334, 336, 337, 338, 339, 340, 342, 343, 345, 346, 347, 351, 354, 365, 366, 372, 375, 382, 384, 386, 387, 388, 389, 390, 395, 403, 405, 407, 408, 411

International Law Association (ILA), 9, 10, 11, 25, 29, 40, 41, 42, 43, 44, 45, 46, 47, 71

International Law Commission (ILC), 147, 169, 233, 242, 243, 274, 375

International League for the Rights of Man, 85

International Penal and Penitentiary Commission, 71, 89, 108

International society, 58, 64, 344

International Union of Penal Law (IUPL), 9, 104, 124, 385

Internationalism, 149, 153, 346

Jackson, Robert H., 83, 84, 178, 187, 190, 193, 194, 196, 202, 272, 301

Japan, 68, 160, 176, 212, 213, 215, 216, 218, 220, 228, 231, 239, 241, 244, 247, 248, 250, 251, 252, 253, 258, 335, 336, 337, 338, 339, 340, 341, 342, 345, 346, 347, 348, 349, 350, 352, 353, 354, 355, 356, 357, 400

Judges, 33, 39, 43, 45, 112, 114, 147, 157, 161, 162, 165, 166, 167, 168, 169, 196, 211, 213, 214, 215, 217, 221, 228, 238, 249, 266, 273, 283, 312, 319, 320, 321, 326, 369, 370, 384, 402, 410

Jurisdiction, 41, 42, 43, 44, 45, 47, 50, 54, 56, 59, 71, 72, 86, 92, 102, 106, 111, 112, 151, 152, 153, 154, 155, 156, 157, 158, 164, 165, 166, 172, 176, 179, 190, 194, 196, 197, 198, 200, 203, 214, 215, 282, 283, 287, 292, 293, 295, 304, 317, 318, 321, 322, 326, 329, 330, 331, 339, 366, 369, 372, 373, 376

Just War, 216, 217, 248, 255, 329

Kaiser Wilhelm, 38, 39, 40, 41, 158, 300, 342

Kelsen, Hans, 7, 174, 175, 176, 177, 178, 179, 180, 181, 182, 183, 184, 185, 186, 187, 188, 189, 190, 191, 192, 193, 194, 195, 196, 197, 198, 199, 200, 201, 202, 203, 322, 338, 342, 343, 386

Laws of humanity, 29, 43, 44

Laws of war, 25, 28, 29, 30, 32, 33, 34, 35, 36, 40, 41, 42, 50, 59, 66, 282, 313, 367, 375, 410

League of Nations, 4, 8, 42, 44, 59, 63, 65, 67, 71, 72, 75, 79, 89, 102, 106, 181, 268, 269, 288, 292, 294, 341, 344, 347, 359

Legalism, 178, 323

INDEX

Lemkin, Rafael, 5, 7, 8, 81, 82, 83, 84, 85, 86, 87, 90, 91, 98, 99, 105, 107, 113, 117, 147, 168, 169, 182, 188, 262, 267, 275, 277, 278, 279, 280, 281, 282, 283, 284, 285, 286, 287, 288, 289, 290, 291, 292, 293, 294, 295, 296, 297, 298, 299, 300, 301, 302, 303, 304, 305, 311, 375

Lloyd George, David, 37, 38, 39

Lusitania, 32

Manchurian Incident, 341, 347, 348, 351, 353

Marburg School of Criminal Law, 17, 120, 123, 210, 211, 315

Martens, Fjodor Fjodorovitch, 28, 29, 43, 44, 225

Marxism, 75, 115, 227, 265

Military court, 32, 37, 301

Monroe Doctrine, 68

Moynier, Gustave, 3, 25, 27, 28, 29, 34, 35, 42, 43, 59

Nazis, 78, 89, 93, 94, 111, 112, 114, 147, 160, 175, 194, 200, 210, 249, 251, 252, 269, 270, 272, 275, 278, 279, 281, 285, 287, 294, 295, 296, 297, 300, 301, 312, 320, 321, 326, 331, 334, 367, 397, 400, 402, 403

Netherlands, 89, 158, 206, 209, 212, 213, 216, 221, 222, 226, 228, 229

Non-governmental organizations (NGOs), 63

Nuremberg Tribunal, 3, 4, 7, 8, 62, 65, 83, 92, 112, 114, 117, 146, 147, 149, 154, 159, 160, 161, 162, 163, 164, 165, 166, 167, 168, 169, 170, 171, 175, 176, 178, 179, 182, 183, 185, 186, 187, 190, 191, 192, 193, 194, 195, 200, 201, 202, 203, 204, 214, 217, 220, 231, 239, 249, 250, 254, 259, 261, 265, 269, 271, 272, 273, 274, 275, 276, 277, 278, 279, 301, 302, 303, 308, 313, 321, 322, 323, 324, 325, 326, 327, 328, 329, 337, 351, 359, 362, 364, 365, 366, 367, 368, 369, 370, 371, 377, 379, 380, 382, 383, 384, 385, 386, 392, 393,

394, 395, 396, 397, 398, 399, 400, 401, 403, 404, 405, 406, 410

Occupation, 47, 67, 110, 161, 164, 199, 210, 212, 222, 224, 248, 272, 296, 297, 300, 307, 347, 348, 349, 394, 401, 404, 405

Oppenheim, Lassa, 34, 178

Paris, 9, 27, 28, 29, 34, 36, 38, 39, 40, 42, 59, 60, 62, 65, 71, 78, 81, 82, 89, 96, 97, 98, 104, 106, 108, 111, 148, 149, 161, 243, 252, 265, 282, 293, 294, 299, 323, 328, 341, 362, 366, 374, 376, 378, 386

Paris Peace Conference, 36, 38, 40, 42, 81, 82

Pearl Harbor, 216, 348

Pella, Vespasian, 7, 8, 25, 44, 45, 49, 50, 51, 52, 53, 54, 55, 56, 57, 58, 59, 60, 61, 62, 63, 64, 65, 66, 67, 68, 69, 70, 71, 72, 74, 75, 76, 77, 78, 79, 80, 81, 82, 83, 84, 85, 86, 87, 88, 89, 90, 91, 92, 105, 107, 108, 147, 150, 153, 158, 159, 163, 165, 171, 172, 278, 279, 281, 292, 303, 311, 327, 329, 361, 368, 369, 370, 371, 372, 376, 379, 386

Permanent Court of International Justice (PCIJ), 65

Piracy, 66, 72, 106, 156, 292, 293, 295

Poisonous gas, use of, 55, 66

Poland, 44, 78, 93, 94, 95, 96, 97, 98, 100, 102, 103, 105, 107, 109, 110, 111, 112, 115, 117, 269, 287, 288, 289, 290, 295, 304, 307, 308, 310, 312, 313, 314, 320, 333

Positivism, 70, 178, 198, 200, 202, 203, 255, 256, 264, 342, 345, 362, 363, 369, 387

Primacy of international law, 55, 343

Prisoners of war, 26, 33, 35, 40, 112, 197, 219

Propaganda, 30, 62, 72, 102, 103, 106, 107, 117, 279, 290, 292, 293, 299, 371, 379

Prosecution, 48, 90, 92, 111, 117, 154, 158, 176, 189, 190, 192, 198, 206,

214, 219, 228, 269, 270, 272, 273, 278, 284, 318, 325, 331, 334, 338, 344, 345, 346, 350, 351, 352, 353, 354, 355, 399
Public international law, 119, 143
Punishment, 24, 25, 32, 33, 34, 35, 37, 38, 39, 40, 48, 56, 67, 96, 97, 98, 101, 103, 105, 107, 112, 175, 185, 194, 195, 202, 215, 218, 227, 287, 297, 300, 309, 313, 315, 316, 318, 319, 321, 322, 323, 328, 332, 344, 345, 352, 353, 356, 363, 365, 366, 374, 375, 402, 403

Rape, 34, 55, 404, 405, 408
Rappaport, Emil Stanisław, 8, 70, 93, 94, 95, 96, 97, 98, 99, 100, 101, 102, 103, 104, 105, 106, 107, 108, 109, 110, 111, 112, 113, 114, 115, 116, 117, 267, 290, 292, 293, 294, 295, 311, 317
Rastatt trials, 384
Republicanism, 51, 58, 61, 62, 83
Röling, Bert, 7, 205, 206, 207, 208, 209, 210, 211, 212, 213, 214, 215, 216, 217, 218, 219, 220, 221, 222, 223, 224, 225, 226, 227, 228, 229, 355

Saldaña, Quintiliano, 7, 17, 25, 104, 108, 118, 119, 120, 121, 122, 123, 124, 125, 126, 127, 128, 129, 130, 131, 132, 133, 134, 135, 136, 137, 138, 139, 140, 141, 142, 143, 144, 147, 158, 315, 329
Sanctions, 50, 63, 65, 66, 67, 68, 97, 273, 315, 319, 328, 366, 372, 379
Slavery, 76, 156, 284, 292, 295, 316, 385, 405
Social justice, 59
Sovereignty, 28, 48, 61, 65, 165, 176, 177, 200, 245, 247, 255, 256, 257, 258, 291, 292, 327, 330, 333, 339, 342, 350
Soviet Union (USSR), 8, 58, 75, 76, 77, 78, 81, 86, 91, 93, 94, 115, 168, 185, 199, 253, 260, 261, 262, 263, 264, 265, 266, 268, 269, 270, 271, 272, 273, 274, 275, 276, 277, 278, 279,

281, 288, 292, 293, 295, 296, 298, 303, 310, 313, 314, 320, 402, 403, 404
Spanish Civil War, 120, 142, 143, 145
State Department, 392
Supreme National Tribunal (SNT), 111, 112, 113, 114, 116, 290

Taylor, Telford, 8, 117, 167, 383, 384, 394
terrorism, 56, 66, 72, 74, 75, 76, 80, 88, 153, 155, 156, 215, 267, 292, 293, 294, 295
Tokyo Tribunal (International Military Tribunal for the Far East), 3, 4, 7, 92, 160, 206, 207, 208, 211, 212, 213, 214, 215, 216, 217, 219, 220, 221, 222, 223, 224, 225, 226, 227, 228, 229, 231, 232, 233, 234, 236, 237, 239, 240, 246, 247, 248, 250, 255, 257, 259, 261, 265, 273, 278, 323, 329, 337, 338, 340, 341, 342, 343, 345, 346, 347, 348, 349, 350, 352, 353, 354, 355, 356, 357, 369, 383, 384

Unification, 47, 49, 56, 59, 65, 69, 70, 92, 94, 100, 101, 102, 105, 106, 107, 111, 148, 172, 267, 281, 292, 293, 311, 316, 318, 319, 332
United Kingdom, 47, 213, 216, 242
United Nations (UN), 25, 81, 83, 86, 110, 111, 188, 189, 190, 191, 197, 206, 228, 242, 243, 244, 284, 303, 308, 313, 330, 336, 348, 350, 369, 372, 385, 393
United States, 12, 67, 69, 78, 81, 84, 91, 175, 178, 180, 181, 182, 183, 185, 187, 188, 190, 192, 199, 200, 203, 213, 249, 250, 256, 272, 275, 278, 313, 354
University, 74, 98, 115, 161, 180, 223, 225, 263, 288, 309, 342, 347, 401

Verdict, 63, 162, 163, 251, 301, 402
Versailles Peace Treaty, 39, 40

INDEX

Victims, 75, 90, 206, 216, 288, 303, 344, 345, 400

von Liszt, Franz, 9, 69, 94, 98, 104, 116, 120, 123, 124, 125, 178, 362

War crimes, 25, 32, 33, 34, 35, 36, 38, 39, 111, 112, 162, 178, 179, 182, 185, 187, 188, 189, 190, 191, 193, 194, 201, 202, 207, 231, 232, 233, 234, 239, 240, 247, 248, 250, 259, 262, 278, 307, 308, 312, 313, 331, 332, 337, 352, 354, 355, 357, 374, 383, 384, 385, 392, 393, 395, 406

War criminals, 32, 33, 43, 48, 164, 175, 179, 185, 190, 192, 194, 202, 203, 208, 215, 251, 270, 279, 301, 302, 307, 313, 324, 325, 351, 352, 355, 366, 367

West, Rebecca, 386, 400, 401, 404, 405, 411, 412

Women's International League for Peace and Freedom, 385

World Jewish Congress, 85

World War I, 3, 9, 11, 25, 29, 32, 33, 34, 35, 36, 42, 48, 53, 59, 67, 69, 90, 104, 105, 117, 148, 165, 170, 178, 179, 184, 199, 203, 289, 300, 307, 342, 362, 367

World War II, 94, 100, 103, 108, 109, 110, 113, 114, 116, 117, 175, 177, 190, 198, 200, 207, 214, 218, 231, 297, 301, 352, 383, 384, 402

CPSIA information can be obtained
at www.ICGtesting.com
Printed in the USA
LVHW081910270721
693842LV00006B/541